OPENING THE

Bringing the Gospel of Matthew to Life
Insight and Inspiration

George Martin

the**WORD** among us® *press*

Published by The Word Among Us Press
9639 Doctor Perry Road
Ijamsville, Maryland 21754
www.wordamongus.org

12 11 10 09 08 1 2 3 4 5
ISBN: 978-1-59325-130-7

Imprimatur	Nihil Obstat
+Most Rev. Victor Galeone	The Rev. Msgr. Harold Bumpus, Dr. Theol.
Bishop of St. Augustine	Censor Librorum
April 14, 2008	Diocese of St. Petersburg
	April 8, 2008

Royalties from the sale of this book go to the Catholic Near East Welfare Association to assist the church in the Holy Land.

Excerpts are taken from the *New American Bible with Revised New Testament and Revised Psalms.*
Copyright © 1991, 1986, 1970 by the Confraternity of Christian Doctrine, Washington, D.C. Used with permission. All rights reserved. No part of the *New American Bible* may be reproduced in any form without permission in writing from the copyright owner.

Translations of material from Josephus (page 300) and Psalms of Solomon (page 354) are by Kevin Perrotta.

The maps on pp. 687 and 688 are reprinted with permission of Loyola Press.
Copyright © 2005 Loyola Press. All rights reserved.

Excerpts from the English translation of the *Catechism of the Catholic Church* for use in the United States of America, copyright © 1994, United States Catholic Conference, Inc.–Libreria Editrice Vaticana. Used with permission.

Cover by John Hamilton Design
Cover Art: St Matthew, c. 1610-14 (oil on panel) by El Greco (Domenico Theotocopuli) (1541-1614)
Indianapolis Museum of Art, USA/The Clowes Fund Collection/The Bridgeman Art Library

Made and printed in the United States of America

Library of Congress Cataloging-in-Publication Data

Martin, George, 1939-
  Bringing the Gospel of Matthew to life : insight and inspiration / George Martin.
     p. cm. -- (Opening the Scriptures)
  Includes bibliographical references and index.
  ISBN 978-1-59325-130-7 (alk. paper)
  1. Bible. N.T. Matthew--Commentaries. I. Title.
  BS2575.53.M37 2008
  226.2'07--dc22
                        2008012114

To my wife, Mary,
who taught me love

ACKNOWLEDGMENTS

I drew on the knowledge and insights of many biblical scholars in writing this exposition of Matthew's gospel. Footnotes acknowledging my debts to them would have complicated a book intended to be as simple as possible, but my debts are real nonetheless. Some of the commentaries and studies I consulted are listed in the bibliography at the end of this book. My indebtedness to these scholars does not, of course, imply their endorsement of my interpretation of Matthew.

I am also indebted to many individuals for their help and encouragement. Among them I must single out Mary Martin and Susan Manney, who read the manuscript and made many suggestions. I am grateful to The Word Among Us Press for taking on this gospel series, and to its editors, Patricia Mitchell and Bert Ghezzi, for their help and enthusiasm. Kevin Perrotta edited the manuscript for content and frequently rescued me from my ignorance; I and my readers are indebted to him. I thank Margaret Procario and Chrissy Koyala for their care in preparing the manuscript for publication.

Above all, I am grateful to my wife, Mary, to whom I dedicate this book, for gracefully accepting that my idea of a Florida retirement is spending my time studying and writing about Scripture.

CONTENTS

PREFACE

The two disciples who walked with the risen Jesus on the road to Emmaus exclaimed afterward, "Were not our hearts burning [within us] while he spoke to us on the way and opened the scriptures to us?" (Luke 24:32).

We too would like the Scriptures opened to us so that we could understand their meaning, their significance, their message. No book can duplicate what Jesus did for the two disciples on the road to Emmaus or replace the guidance of the Holy Spirit. But a book can explore what meaning the words of Scripture had for their first readers and what message an inspired author conveys by his or her words. The aim of this book is bring the Gospel of Matthew to life for its readers. This can be understood in two ways. The words of the gospel come to life for us when, as twenty-first century Christians, we gain insight into their original first-century meaning and context. Then, as followers of the risen Jesus, we can be inspired to apply that gospel message to our lives today.

While this book has some features of a commentary, it is not a scholarly commentary. Many issues and questions that are of legitimate interest to scholars are passed over. The focus of this book is on what Matthew's words meant when he wrote them, with an eye toward their meaning for readers today. This book is intended for men and women who want to read and understand Matthew's gospel as Scripture, as God's word conveyed in human words.

Reading a gospel as Scripture is like having a conversation. Conversing requires listening. Good listening means paying close attention to what the other person is saying; it can also mean noting what is implied and what may be left unsaid. This book will closely examine the text of Matthew's gospel, sometimes commenting on the meaning of the words the author uses, sometimes drawing out an implication, occasionally noting what is left unsaid.

A good conversation presumes the two parties share some common background. For example, a conversation about American politics requires that those conversing have a shared knowledge of the American system of government and American political parties. Similarly, understanding the Gospel of Matthew requires some knowledge of Jewish life and thinking in Palestine in the first third of the first century. What Jesus did and said must be understood in light of the context in which he lived. This book will try to fill in some of that background, as far as we can reconstruct it today, to help make sense of Jesus' teachings and actions.

Another factor that makes good conversations possible is the two parties' knowledge of each other. Often our conversations revolve around interests and concerns that arise from our experiences and personal situations. We converse quite easily with old friends who know us and our concerns. What was Matthew's situation, and what were his concerns? This book adopts the commonly held view that Matthew's gospel was written about A.D. 85, quite possibly in Antioch, and was addressed to a local church that was Jewish Christian in its origins but with an increasing number of Gentile converts. Matthew's church-in-transition was estranged from the emerging leadership of a Judaism-in-transition, with each group trying to chart the course for the future of God's people. I will occasionally suggest what significance Matthew's words might have had in the context of this estrangement between Matthew's church and other Jewish leaders. A short essay at the end of this book addresses the writing of Matthew's gospel. Rather than saying more in this preface about the Gospel of Matthew, we will let its character and purpose unfold in the text.

This book focuses on the gospel that is "According to Matthew," the title it bears in the oldest manuscripts. It does not try to compare or synthesize what Matthew wrote with the other gospels. It is difficult to carry on four conversations at once; it is easier to pay attention to one person at a time. After paying close attention to the Gospel According to Matthew, we can later compare what Matthew wrote with what Mark, Luke, and John wrote. For each passage of Matthew, this book indicates where similar material may be found in the other gospels.

This book deals with the text of Matthew's gospel as it has come down to us in the Bible. It does not go into matters like the sources Matthew may have drawn on, nor does it generally raise questions like, "Did this really happen exactly as Matthew presents it?" While such considerations can have validity, it is the Gospel of Matthew as we have it that is inspired Scripture for us. This book presents what I hope is a responsible interpretation of the Gospel of Matthew, laying out the meaning I find in Matthew's words. I make no claim that my interpretation is the only possible reading of Matthew: there are riches of meaning in a gospel that no single exposition can capture.

A few words about the format of this book:

The traditional chapter and verse numbers assigned to the Gospel of Matthew are printed at the top of each page to assist readers in locating passages. Some sections of Scripture are introduced by a few sentences of orientation that give the context of the reading. A list of parallel passages in the other gospels and of related Old Testament and New Testament passages are provided for each section of Scripture. The exposition follows, with the words of Scripture set in boldface type.

Interspersed throughout the book are some blocks of information about the social, economic, political, and religious background of Matthew's gospel and about scriptural terms of special interest. I also offer my comments at a few points. An index at the end of the book lists the page where each background entry and comment is located.

Interspersed throughout the text are questions for reflection. They indicate ways that a reader might ponder and apply the text. Using these reflection questions is optional; much more important are the questions that Matthew's gospel itself poses for you. If reading a gospel as Scripture is like having a conversation, then listening to the words of Scripture is only half of the conversation; the other half is our response. This book cannot supply your side of the conversation; you must do that yourself. This book can lay out Matthew's side of the conversation as I understand it and raise issues for you to reflect on and respond to. The most important issues, invitations, questions, and challenges will be those that the gospel itself puts to you.

I considered calling this book *Listening to the Gospel according to Matthew*. Matthew's original audience did not usually read his gospel but listened to it being read aloud at a gathering of Christians, perhaps for the Eucharist. Many in Matthew's first audience were illiterate; few were wealthy enough to afford their own copy of a gospel.

We, too, listen to the Gospel of Matthew being read aloud in the context of worship. In the Catholic liturgy, after a passage from Matthew is read the reader proclaims, "The Gospel of the Lord." The reader does not say, "The Gospel of Matthew." Even though we are listening to words written by Matthew, our real conversation partner is the Lord Jesus. We listen to Jesus teaching even if it is Matthew who gives expression to Jesus' words. It is Jesus who invites our response, even if it is Matthew who conveys Jesus' invitation.

One response to reading a gospel is prayer. There is a long tradition in the church of "sacred reading" (*lectio divina* in Latin). This type of reading involves paying careful attention to a passage of Scripture, verse by verse and word by word, and pausing for reflection and prayer. My fondest hope is that this book will prove useful as an aid to sacred reading. I suggest that those who wish to use this volume for prayerful reading return to the words of Scripture after having read the exposition, offer a brief prayer asking for the guidance of the Holy Spirit, and enter into conversation with the one who speaks to them through the Gospel of Matthew.

NOTES ON THE FORMAT AND TEXT

Each page contains the text of the Gospel of Matthew, printed in boldface type, accompanied by a verse-by-verse exposition. Everything else, printed in smaller or different type, is auxiliary material and consists of the following:

- *Orientations* to certain passages in Matthew's gospel, when such introductions might be helpful
- After the text of each passage of Matthew, *Gospel parallels*, indicating where similar material may be found in the other gospels, along with Old Testament (OT) and New Testament (NT) references to material that bears on the passage from Matthew
- *Old Testament quotations* that might throw light on the passage in Matthew
- Questions for the reader's *reflection*
- *Background* information pertaining to the world of Jesus or of Matthew's audience
- A few *comments* that explore implications of Matthew's gospel

Scripture citations that do not include the name of a biblical book refer to the Gospel of Matthew. For example, the citation 8:34 would be to chapter 8, verse 34, of Matthew's gospel.

Scripture citations follow the chapter and verse numbering used by the New American Bible. Other translations sometimes employ slightly different numbering—for example, in Malachi and some of the psalms.

The New American Bible requires preservation of certain of its conventions, including its paragraph breaks and square brackets around words not found in all ancient manuscripts. When poetry is set here as prose, the New American Bible requires that slashes be used to indicate line breaks.

The Catholic Church and most Orthodox Churches accept as canonical Scripture the books of Baruch, Judith, 1 and 2 Maccabees, Sirach (Ecclesiasticus), Tobit, and Wisdom (Wisdom of Solomon), along with some additional material in the books of Daniel and Esther. Protestant Churches do not accept these writings as part of the biblical canon, but some Protestant Bibles include them in a section labeled Apocryphal Works.

ABBREVIATIONS USED FOR BOOKS OF THE BIBLE

Acts . . . . Acts
Amos . . . . Amos
Baruch . . . . Baruch
1 Chron. . . . . 1 Chronicles
2 Chron. . . . . 2 Chronicles
Col. . . . . Colossians
1 Cor . . . . 1 Corinthians
2 Cor . . . . 2 Corinthians
Dan . . . . Daniel
Deut. . . . . Deuteronomy
Eccl . . . . .Ecclesiastes
Eph . . . . Ephesians
Esther . . . . .Esther
Exod . . . . Exodus
Ezek . . . . Ezekiel
Ezra . . . . Ezra
Gal. . . . . Galatians
Gen . . . . .Genesis
Hab . . . . Habakkuk
Haggai . . . . Haggai
Heb . . . . Hebrews
Hosea. . . . . .Hosea
Isaiah . . . . Isaiah
James . . . . James
Jer . . . . .Jeremiah
Job . . . . Job
Joel. . . . . .Joel
John. . . . . .John
1 John . . . . 1 John
2 John . . . . 2 John
3 John . . . . 3 John
Jonah. . . . . .Jonah
Joshua . . . . .Joshua
Jude . . . . Jude
Judges. . . . . .Judges
Judith. . . . . .Judith
1 Kings . . . . .1 Kings

2 Kings . . . . .1 Kings
Lam . . . . Lamentations
Lev. . . . . .Leviticus
Luke. . . . . .Luke
1 Macc. . . . . 1 Maccabees
2 Macc. . . . . 2 Maccabees
Mal . . . . Malachi
Mark . . . . Mark
Matt. . . . . .Matthew
Micah . . . . .Micah
Nahum . . . . .Nahum
Neh . . . . Nehemiah
Num . . . . Numbers
Obad . . . . .Obadiah
1 Pet . . . . 1 Peter
2 Pet . . . . 2 Peter
Phlm . . . . Philemon
Phil . . . . .Philippians
Prov. . . . . Proverbs
Psalm(s) . . . . Psalms
Rev . . . . Revelation
Rom. . . . . Romans
Ruth . . . . .Ruth
1 Sam . . . . 1 Samuel
2 Sam . . . . 2 Samuel
Sirach . . . . .Sirach
Song . . . . Song of Songs
1 Thess . . . . . . .1 Thessalonians
2 Thess . . . . . . .2 Thessalonians
1 Tim. . . . . 1 Timothy
2 Tim. . . . . 2 Timothy
Titus . . . . .Titus
Tobit . . . . .Tobit
Wisd . . . . Wisdom
Zech. . . . . .Zechariah
Zeph . . . . Zephaniah

CHAPTER 1

ORIENTATION: *Matthew begins his gospel by situating Jesus within God's plan of salvation for his people. The manner in which Jesus' ancestors are listed hints that Jesus' birth is the beginning of God doing something new and startling.*

The Family History of Jesus
1 The book of the genealogy of Jesus Christ, the son of David, the son of Abraham.

2 Abraham became the father of Isaac, Isaac the father of Jacob, Jacob the father of Judah and his brothers. **3** Judah became the father of Perez and Zerah, whose mother was Tamar. Perez became the father of Hezron, Hezron the father of Ram, **4** Ram the father of Amminadab. Amminadab became the father of Nahshon, Nahshon the father of Salmon, **5** Salmon the father of Boaz, whose mother was Rahab. Boaz became the father of Obed, whose mother was Ruth. Obed became the father of Jesse, **6** Jesse the father of David the king.

David became the father of Solomon, whose mother had been the wife of Uriah. **7** Solomon became the father of Rehoboam, Rehoboam the father of Abijah, Abijah the father of Asaph. **8** Asaph became the father of Jehoshaphat, Jehoshaphat the father of Joram, Joram the father of Uzziah. **9** Uzziah became the father of Jotham, Jotham the father of Ahaz, Ahaz the father of Hezekiah. **10** Hezekiah became the father of Manasseh, Manasseh the father of Amos, Amos the father of Josiah. **11** Josiah became the father of Jechoniah and his brothers at the time of the Babylonian exile.

12 After the Babylonian exile, Jechoniah became the father of Shealtiel, Shealtiel the father of Zerubbabel, **13** Zerubbabel the father of Abiud. Abiud became the father of Eliakim, Eliakim the father of Azor, **14** Azor the father of Zadok. Zadok became the father of Achim, Achim the father of Eliud, **15** Eliud the father of Eleazar. Eleazar became the father of Matthan, Matthan the father of Jacob, **16** Jacob the father of Joseph, the husband of Mary. Of her was born Jesus who is called the Messiah.

17 Thus the total number of generations from Abraham to David is fourteen generations; from David to the Babylonian exile, fourteen generations; from the Babylonian exile to the Messiah, fourteen generations.

Gospel parallels: Luke 3:23-38
OT: Gen 12:1-3; 22:18; 38; Joshua 2; 6:20-25; Ruth 1-4; 2 Sam
7:12-16; 11

1 The book of the genealogy of Jesus Christ, the son of David, the son of Abraham. Matthew begins his gospel by telling his readers who Jesus is. Jesus lived in a culture in which personal identity was based on kinship (if asked who he was, a man in Jesus' culture would tell who his parents and grandparents were). The **genealogy,** or family history, that Matthew provides for Jesus (verses 2-16) not only conveys who Jesus is but hints at where he fits into God's plans (verse 17). Matthew highlights two of the points made by the genealogy by writing that Jesus is **the son of David** and **the son of Abraham.** We will say more shortly about what it means that Jesus is descended from David and Abraham. Matthew also calls Jesus the **Christ,** or Messiah, and Matthew's gospel will proclaim and explain what it means that Jesus is the Christ.

Son of David: See page 16
Messiah, Christ: See page 349

For reflection: How has the heritage I received from my ancestors shaped who I am?

It may seem odd for Matthew's opening words to characterize what follows as **the book of the genealogy** of Jesus Christ, since the genealogy takes up only the next fifteen verses: this short passage is hardly a book! But Matthew wrote in Greek, and here as elsewhere in his gospel there are nuances that do not carry over in translation. The Greek expression translated as **the book of the genealogy** can also be translated as "the record of origins," and it occurs twice in the Greek version of the Book of Genesis. Once it refers to an account of God's creation of the universe (Gen 2:4), and the other time it refers to an account of God's creation of the human race (Gen 5:1). Some of Matthew's Greek-speaking Jewish Christian readers would have heard echoes of these Genesis passages and taken them as a hint that the Gospel of Matthew is an account of God's creative activity at work again, this time through Jesus Christ.

2 Abraham became the father of Isaac, Isaac the father of Jacob, Jacob the father of Judah and his brothers. God began doing something new for the human race when he called **Abraham** to leave behind his past and travel to a new land, where he would become the father of a great people (Gen 12:1-2). By beginning his genealogy with **Abraham** and identifying Jesus as *the son of Abraham* (verse 1), Matthew situates Jesus within the plan of salvation that God inaugurated with Abraham. Whatever Jesus will do is in continuity with what God began with Abraham. Genesis notes that God's call to Abraham would be of benefit to all the people of the earth (Gen 12:3; 22:18). What God will accomplish through Jesus will likewise be for the whole human race.

Abraham became the father of Isaac: Abraham more literally *fathered* or *begot* Isaac, who in turn fathered Jacob, and Jacob fathered Judah and his brothers. The basic structure of the genealogy is a record of human begettings, of who fathered whom.

3 **Judah became the father of Perez and Zerah, whose mother was Tamar.** Matthew's genealogy of Jesus unfolds as anyone familiar with the Old Testament might expect—until it comes to **Tamar.** Jewish genealogies were normally all-male affairs. Matthew did not mention Abraham's wife Sarah, nor the wives of Isaac and Jacob, but he includes **Tamar,** whose motherhood was strange to say the least. Tamar was by Jewish tradition an Aramean woman. She had been married to first one and then another of Judah's sons, and was left childless after her husbands died. Taking matters into her own hands to ensure an heir, she posed as a prostitute, had intercourse with her father-in-law **Judah,** and conceived **Perez and Zerah:** the story is told in Genesis 38. She was an ancestor of Jesus—but why does Matthew mention her, after passing over women with more edifying stories? We will come back to this question later, for this will not be the last puzzle in Matthew's genealogy.

Matthew continues his genealogy for Jesus: **Perez became the father of Hezron, Hezron the father of Ram.** No surprises here.

4 **Ram the father of Amminadab. Amminadab became the father of Nahshon, Nahshon the father of Salmon:** still no surprises.

5 **Salmon the father of Boaz, whose mother was Rahab.** Just when it might seem like the surprises were over, Matthew inserts a second non-Israelite with an irregular life in Jesus' ancestry. **Rahab** was a Canaanite prostitute who sheltered two Israelite spies (Joshua 2), and whose life was spared when

15

Jericho fell (Joshua 6:20-25). **Boaz became the father of Obed, whose mother was Ruth.** Another woman, another foreigner: **Ruth** was a Moabite widow whose devotion to her widowed Israelite mother-in-law led her to move to Bethlehem, where she married **Boaz** (Ruth 1–4). Her story is edifying, yet one strand of Mosaic law prohibited Israelites from marrying Moabites (see Deut 23:4; Neh 13:1-3, 23-27). Despite whatever irregularity there might have been in her marriage to Boaz, her great-grandson turned out to be one of the greatest Israelites ever. Her son **Obed became the father of Jesse, and**

6 **Jesse the father of David the king.** Matthew highlights the significance of **David** by making it explicit that he was **the king.** The establishment of kingship meant a change in the life of God's people. Autonomous tribes joined together to form a state with central rule. David was not just any king; he was the king to whom God made the promise that his descendants would rule over God's people forever (2 Sam 7:12-16). The dynasty of David came to an apparent end with the exile (verse 12), but hopes arose among God's people that a descendant of David would once again rule over them. Matthew proclaims Jesus to be the Christ and the son of David, the descendant of David who is the Messiah (verse 1).

BACKGROUND: SON OF DAVID Broadly speaking, any descendant of David could be called a son of David (as Joseph is—Matt 1:20). The Messiah was commonly expected to be a descendant of David (Matt 22:42; Mark 12:35; Luke 20:41; John 7:42) and therefore could be called the Son of David. While the Old Testament provides ample basis for such expectation, no Old Testament passage uses the title "Son of David" as a title for the Messiah. (The Messiah is, however, called the Son of David in one of the *Psalms of Solomon,* a nonbiblical writing from around 50 B.C.) It is striking that during Jesus' public ministry, others call him the Son of David only in conjunction with his healings (Matt 9:27; 12:23; 15:22; 20:30-31; Matt 21:9 may not be an exception: see Matt 21:14-15 and 19:2). There is evidence that popular Jewish tradition looked upon Solomon, a son of David, as an exorcist and a healer, and some scholars suggest that Jesus was hailed as the Son of David during his ministry because he, too, exorcised and healed. Matthew proclaims Jesus to be the Son of David who is the Messiah (Matt 1:1, 16-17). Luke's gospel makes it explicit that Jesus is the descendant of David through whom God's promise of an everlasting reign for the house of David will be fulfilled (2 Sam 7:12-16; Psalm 89:3-5, 29-38; Luke 1:32-33). *Related topics: Nonbiblical writings (page 198), Psalms of Solomon (page 354).*

David became the father of Solomon, whose mother had been the wife of Uriah. A more literal translation would be, "David fathered Solomon by the wife of Uriah." The story is told in chapter 11 of 2 Samuel. **Uriah** was a Hittite who served as an officer in David's army. While Uriah was away during a war, David had an adulterous affair with Uriah's wife Bathsheba, and she became pregnant. David arranged for Uriah's death, and then took Bathsheba as his wife. Their first child died, but their second child, Solomon, succeeded David on the throne. Matthew could simply have written that David fathered Solomon, but Matthew chose to include a fourth woman in Jesus' ancestry, a woman who was married to a foreigner if she was not a foreigner herself; a woman who, like Tamar, conceived a child not by her husband.

Why did Matthew include Tamar, Rahab, Ruth, and Bathsheba in the genealogy of Jesus? Two features shared by these women seem to be, first, that they were foreigners or were married to a foreigner. Their presence in Jesus' ancestry foreshadows salvation being extended to Gentiles as well as Jews through Jesus. Second, despite some sexual or marital irregularities, these women were part of Jesus' ancestry and God's plan of salvation. This prefigures the divinely planned irregularity of Mary becoming pregnant but not by her husband Joseph.

For reflection: What meaning do I find for myself in Matthew's inclusion of these women in Jesus' genealogy?

7 **Solomon became the father of Rehoboam, Rehoboam the father of Abijah, Abijah the father of Asaph.** Matthew's readers who were familiar with the history recounted in 1 and 2 Kings could have read the list of kings in this and the following verses as a shorthand way of describing the decline and fall of the kingdom of David. The bare listing of names cloaks a messy and often depressing history. **Solomon** enjoyed great opulence (1 Kings 10:14-29), but promoted idolatry (1 Kings 11:1-13). After his death, ten of the twelve Israelite tribes broke away from the rule of **Rehoboam** (1 Kings 12), reducing David's empire to little more than the tribal lands of Judah and Benjamin.

8 **Asaph became the father of Jehoshaphat, Jehoshaphat the father of Joram, Joram the father of Uzziah.** The kings who succeeded David and

Solomon were often undistinguished, with a sprinkling of the very good and the very bad.

9 **Uzziah became the father of Jotham, Jotham the father of Ahaz, Ahaz the father of Hezekiah.** Isaiah addressed his prophecy about the birth of Immanuel to **Ahaz** (Isaiah 7:10-16); **Hezekiah** led a religious reform (2 Kings 18:1-7).

10 **Hezekiah became the father of Manasseh, Manasseh the father of Amos, Amos the father of Josiah.** Jesus had royalty among his ancestors, but they included sinners such as Manasseh, who promoted idolatry during his fifty-five-year reign (2 Kings 21:1-18). His grandson **Josiah** introduced much-needed religious reforms (2 Kings 22:1–23:30), but they were too little and too late to ward off the exile.

11 **Josiah became the father of Jechoniah and his brothers at the time of the Babylonian exile.** The Babylonian army's destruction of Jerusalem in 587 B.C. and the deportation of its upper-class citizens marked the end of rule by the dynasty of David. Just as the establishment of kingship was a turning point for God's people, so was its loss. Those who returned from exile to the tribal lands of Judah became known as Judeans, which gives us the word "Jews." National identity was found in following God's laws; God's people were no longer a sovereign state.

12 **After the Babylonian exile, Jechoniah became the father of Shealtiel, Shealtiel the father of Zerubbabel.** The last two men, named in the Book of Ezra (Ezra 3:2), were among those who tried to restore worship in Jerusalem after the exile.

13 **Zerubbabel the father of Abiud. Abiud became the father of Eliakim, Eliakim the father of Azor.** There is no mention in the Old Testament of **Abiud** and those listed after him in Matthew's genealogy. This is best taken as an indication that they were quite ordinary people—the sort who do not leave any mark on the pages of history. Jesus had illustrious ancestors in David and Solomon; he had many more ancestors who led unnoticed lives.

14 Azor the father of Zadok. Zadok became the father of Achim, Achim the father of Eliud: more unknown ancestors.

15 Eliud the father of Eleazar. Eleazar became the father of Matthan, Matthan the father of Jacob: still more unknowns.

16 Jacob the father of Joseph, the husband of Mary. We know nothing of this Jacob; with the names of Joseph and Mary we enter familiar territory. Joseph is identified as the husband of Mary: Matthew will shortly clarify that although they were husband and wife, according to marriage customs of the time, they had not yet begun to live together (1:18).

Matthew adds concerning Mary, Of her was born Jesus who is called the Messiah. Matthew's lengthy listing of who fathered whom takes a turn, as Matthew writes that of Mary was born (literally, was begotten) Jesus. The passive Greek construction Matthew uses implies that Jesus was begotten by God; Matthew will later make this explicit (1:20). Generation upon generation of human begetting culminates in the divine begetting of Jesus, the Messiah.

Messiah, Christ: See page 349

17 Thus the total number of generations from Abraham to David is fourteen generations; from David to the Babylonian exile, fourteen generations; from the Babylonian exile to the Messiah, fourteen generations. Matthew sees a pattern in the genealogy, with turning points coming every fourteen generations. God began something new with Abraham, calling him to be the father of a people. The kingship of David was a turning point: descendants of David were to rule over God's people forever. Yet this seemed to end with the catastrophe of the Babylonian exile, another major turning point. Now, fourteen generations after the last major turning point, God sends the Messiah to his people. Jesus is a new turning point in God's unfolding plan.

If a person's genealogy tells us who the person is, then Jesus is a Jew descended from Abraham and David. Jesus' past is Israel's past; Jesus marks the next stage in God's plan for his people.

For reflection: What insight does Matthew's genealogy give me into who Jesus is?

An Annunciation to Joseph

18 Now this is how the birth of Jesus Christ came about. When his mother Mary was betrothed to Joseph, but before they lived together, she was found with child through the holy Spirit. **19** Joseph her husband, since he was a righteous man, yet unwilling to expose her to shame, decided to divorce her quietly. **20** Such was his intention when, behold, the angel of the Lord appeared to him in a dream and said, "Joseph, son of David, do not be afraid to take Mary your wife into your home. For it is through the holy Spirit that this child has been conceived in her. **21** She will bear a son and you are to name him Jesus, because he will save his people from their sins." **22** All this took place to fulfill what the Lord had said through the prophet:

> **23** "Behold, the virgin shall be with child and bear a son,
> and they shall name him Emmanuel,"

which means "God is with us." **24** When Joseph awoke, he did as the angel of the Lord had commanded him and took his wife into his home. **25** He had no relations with her until she bore a son, and he named him Jesus.

OT:Deut 22:23-27; Isaiah 7:1-16
NT:Luke 1:26-38; 2:1-7, 21

18 Matthew concluded his genealogy of Jesus by saying of Mary, "Of her was born Jesus who is called the Messiah" (1:16). Now Matthew tells his readers **how the birth of Jesus Christ came about.** Matthew does not describe the birth itself, but recounts circumstances surrounding the birth of Jesus. **When his mother Mary was betrothed to Joseph, but before they lived together:** Jewish marriage involved two stages. Shortly after puberty, a young woman **was betrothed** by her father to a young man. After betrothal the couple was considered married and were spoken of as husband and wife, even though the bride continued to live in her father's house and the couple refrained from sexual relations. For her to have sexual relations with another man was adultery. A year or longer after betrothal the husband would bring his wife to live in his house (the scene in 25:1-13), and they would begin to have sexual relations. Mary and Joseph are in the first stage of their marriage: **Mary was betrothed to Joseph,** but it was **before they lived together.**

Marriage practices: See page 479

During this time, **she was found with child through the holy Spirit.** In Matthew's Greek, the expression **was found with child** simply means that Mary was pregnant; it does not necessarily mean that her pregnancy was a matter of public knowledge. The words, **through the holy Spirit,** are Matthew's explanation to his readers of how Mary became pregnant. Matthew does not describe the circumstances of Mary's conceiving through the Holy Spirit but only conveys that it had happened. What follows indicates that Joseph learned that his wife, Mary, was pregnant and knew that he had not fathered her child, but Joseph does not yet know that her child was conceived through the Holy Spirit.

19 **Joseph her husband, since he was a righteous man, yet unwilling to expose her to shame, decided to divorce her quietly.** When Joseph learns that Mary is pregnant, he can only conclude that she has been unfaithful to him—as hard as that might have been for him to believe. The word **righteous** means that Joseph is upright and does God's will. The law of Moses called for the stoning of a betrothed woman who willingly had sexual relations with a man who was not her husband (Deut 22:23-27). It is unlikely that the death penalty was enforced at the time of Jesus, but

---

BACKGROUND: THE SPIRIT The opening verses of the Old Testament speak of a "mighty wind" (Gen 1:2) that sweeps over the waters as God begins his work of creation. The phrase translated "mighty wind" might also be translated "Spirit of God," for the same Hebrew word means "wind," "breath," or "spirit," and the Hebrew word taken here to mean "mighty" is also the word for God. It is the breath of God breathed into humans that gives life (Gen 2:7). When the Old Testament speaks of the Spirit of God, it generally refers to God's influence or power at work, as in, for example, the inspiration of prophets (Isaiah 61:1). The Spirit of God is not yet thought of as a person in the Old Testament. The New Testament bears witness to a deeper experience and understanding of the Spirit. Paul speaks of the Spirit many times in his letters but writes more about what the Spirit does than who the Spirit is. In the Gospel of John, Jesus speaks of the Spirit as the Paraclete, or Advocate, who will carry on his work (John 14:16-17, 26; 15:26; 16:7-11). The Gospel of Matthew ends with Jesus' instruction that people be baptized "in the name of the Father, and of the Son, and of the holy Spirit" (Matt 28:19). The Council of Constantinople in 381 proclaimed the Spirit to be "the holy, the lordly and life-giving one, proceeding forth from the Father, co-worshipped and co-glorified with Father and Son, the one who spoke through the prophets."

Joseph takes Mary's apparent adultery as a very serious matter. Joseph is compassionate and decides to end their marriage as **quietly** as he can, minimizing Mary's public **shame.** A Jewish writing allows a husband to divorce his wife in the presence of two witnesses, and that was perhaps what Joseph intended to do.

Matthew's account leaves gaps. How did Mary learn of and understand her pregnancy? What did she tell and not tell Joseph? Did Joseph think that divorcing her would free her to marry the father of her child? These gaps are signs that Matthew is not trying to recount all the thoughts of Mary and Joseph and all that happened. Nor will Matthew's gospel be a complete biography of Jesus. Matthew, like each gospel author, selectively presents certain things in order to convey a message to his readers. We must pay attention to what Matthew wrote rather than lament what he did not write.

20 **Such was his intention when, behold, the angel of the Lord appeared to him in a dream.** Angels were God's messengers: the Hebrew and Greek words for **angel** also mean "messenger." Dreams could be vehicles of revelation—quite notably in the life of the man after whom Joseph was named, Joseph the son of Jacob (Gen 37:5-11; 40:5-23; 41:1-43). The angel addresses **Joseph** as **son of David:** part of Joseph's role in God's plan will be to accept legal paternity of Jesus, thereby making Jesus also a **son of David** (1:1).

Angels: See page 33

The angel has two directives for Joseph. First, he is to proceed with the second stage of marriage with Mary: **do not be afraid to take Mary your wife into your home.** This would normally mean having a wedding feast (22:2; John 2:1-10), which would be a public proclamation that Joseph continued to accept Mary as his wife. Joseph is to take Mary into his home despite her pregnancy, **for it is through the holy Spirit that this child has been conceived in her.** In Matthew's account, this is the first time Joseph hears the explanation of her pregnancy. Matthew does not recount Joseph's immediate reaction—but then, neither has he recounted Mary's reaction to a child being conceived in her through the Holy Spirit. Matthew continues to leave gaps as he focuses on what is essential: Jesus was conceived **through the holy Spirit,** through the power of God; Jesus is, therefore, the Son of God (3:17; 14:33; 16:16; 17:5; 27:54).

21 The angel tells Joseph that Mary **will bear a son,** informing Joseph of the gender of the child that she is carrying. Then the angel gives a second directive to Joseph: **and you are to name him Jesus.** In ancient Jewish custom, a father's naming of a newborn infant meant accepting paternity of the child. By naming Jesus, Joseph legally confers his own descent from David upon Jesus.

Children were normally named after family members (see Luke 1:59-63), but none of the ancestors listed in Joseph's genealogy (verses 2-16) were named **Jesus.** The name **Jesus** (*Yeshua* in Aramaic, Joseph's native language) is a form of the Hebrew name *Joshua*. Joshua had been Moses' right-hand man, and many Jewish boys were named after him. But the child Mary was carrying was to be named Jesus **because he will save his people from their sins.** Hebrew personal names were often compounds formed with God's name; *Joshua* in Hebrew means "Yahweh (the Lord) helps" or, in the popular understanding of the time, "Yahweh saves." Jesus' name indicates that **he,** Jesus, **will save:** Jesus will save as God saves. Jesus will save **his people:** Jesus' people are the Jewish people, the children of Abraham (1:1-2). Matthew's gospel will conclude with Jesus' command to "make disciples of all nations" (28:19); Gentiles as well as Jews will be the people whom Jesus saves. Jesus will save his people **from their sins.** How Jesus will do this will become apparent in the course of Matthew's gospel (see especially 20:28; 26:26-28).

God's name: See page 488

For reflection: How have I experienced rescue from my sins?

22 Matthew comments on the significance of the conception and birth of Jesus: **all this took place to fulfill what the Lord had said through the prophet.** Since what God was doing through Jesus continued what God had done for his people in the past, Matthew can find meaning in past words and deeds of God in light of Jesus. Mary's pregnancy will **fulfill** a prophecy of Isaiah in the sense of revealing a fuller meaning of this prophecy.

23 **"Behold, the virgin shall be with child and bear a son, / and they shall name him Emmanuel,"** which means **"God is with us."** Isaiah delivered this prophecy in 734 B.C. to Ahaz, the king of Judah, when Ahaz feared an invasion led by the kings of two neighboring countries (Isaiah 7:1-16). Isaiah assured Ahaz that if he relied on God he had nothing to fear. When

Ahaz doubted God's protection, Isaiah told him that God would give him a reassuring sign: a young woman (Ahaz's wife?) would become pregnant and bear a son. Before her child could tell right from wrong, the threat from these neighboring countries would have vanished. The sense of the prophecy is that the child would be conceived in a normal manner. There was no expectation at the time of Jesus that the Messiah would be born of a virgin.

> The Lord himself will give you this sign: the virgin shall be with child, and bear a son, and shall name him Immanuel. . . . Before the child learns to reject the bad and choose the good, the land of those two kings whom you dread shall be deserted.
>
> Isaiah 7:14, 16

When the Book of Isaiah was translated into Greek, the translator used the Greek word for virgin to translate the Hebrew word for young woman, and Matthew quotes the prophecy in Greek. Matthew saw that the words, **the virgin shall be with child and bear a son,** applied to Mary and Jesus, for Mary was a virgin when Jesus was conceived in her through the Holy Spirit. Since the Lord spoke through Isaiah (verse 22), his prophecy can have more meaning than Isaiah may have realized.

"They shall name him Emmanuel," which means **"God is with us."** The name **Emmanuel** represents a Hebrew compound word that means just what Matthew says: **God is with us.** In Isaiah's prophecy, giving a child this name would have been an affirmation that God stands by his people and will protect them (see also Isaiah 8:9-10). Through Jesus, God continues to stand by his people. Yet there is a fuller meaning in Jesus being called **Emmanuel:** he who was conceived through the Holy Spirit is indeed God-with-us. Matthew's gospel will end with the risen Jesus telling his disciples, "I am with you always" (28:20). God becomes and remains present to us in Jesus. In Isaiah's prophecy, it is the child's mother who gives him the name "Emmanuel"; Matthew writes that **they** shall name him Emmanuel, hinting that God is made present in Jesus not only to Mary but to all who call upon Jesus to save them from sin (verse 21).

For reflection: How am I most aware of Jesus' presence? Do I have an abiding sense that God stands by me?

24 **When Joseph awoke, he did as the angel of the Lord had commanded him and took his wife into his home.** Joseph does what is asked of him and takes Mary **his wife into his home,** the second step of the marriage process.

25 Matthew adds, lest there be any doubts that Jesus was conceived through the Holy Spirit, that Joseph **had no relations with her until she bore a son.** In English, to say that "I will be home until six" implies that I will not be home after six. In Greek, however, to say that something did not happen **until** a certain time does not imply that it happened afterward. In light of ancient traditions, the Catholic Church teaches that Mary remained a virgin throughout her life. After Jesus was born, Joseph carried out the second of the angel's instructions: **he named him Jesus** (see verse 21). Jesus is the Son of God by conception through the Holy Spirit, and the Son of David through Joseph's naming him and accepting him as his son.

> *For reflection: What does it mean for me that Jesus is both the Son of David and Son of God?*

Matthew refers only in passing to the birth of Jesus. Joseph has occupied center stage, with what we would think of as the most important events—the conception and birth of Jesus—happening off in the wings. Matthew's account centers on the angel's message to Joseph and its significance (verses 20-23), preceded by a recounting of why the angel's message was necessary (verses 18-19) and followed by a recounting of Joseph doing what the angel asked of him (verses 24-25). We may wish that Matthew had included more details of how everything happened, but we should not miss the profound significance of what Matthew tells us: Jesus was conceived in Mary through the Holy Spirit so that he could be God-with-us, saving us from our sins.

> *For reflection: Am I upset by the gaps in Matthew's story? Would my faith in Jesus be different if I had only Matthew's and not Luke's account of how Jesus came to be born?*

CHAPTER 2

The Homage of the Magi

[1] When Jesus was born in Bethlehem of Judea, in the days of King Herod, behold, magi from the east arrived in Jerusalem, [2] saying, "Where is the newborn king of the Jews? We saw his star at its rising and have come to do him homage." [3] When King Herod heard this, he was greatly troubled, and all Jerusalem with him. [4] Assembling all the chief priests and the scribes of the people, he inquired of them where the Messiah was to be born. [5] They said to him, "In Bethlehem of Judea, for thus it has been written through the prophet:

[6] 'And you, Bethlehem, land of Judah,
    are by no means least among the rulers of Judah;
since from you shall come a ruler,
    who is to shepherd my people Israel.'"

[7] Then Herod called the magi secretly and ascertained from them the time of the star's appearance. [8] He sent them to Bethlehem and said, "Go and search diligently for the child. When you have found him, bring me word, that I too may go and do him homage." [9] After their audience with the king they set out. And behold, the star that they had seen at its rising preceded them, until it came and stopped over the place where the child was. [10] They were overjoyed at seeing the star, [11] and on entering the house they saw the child with Mary his mother. They prostrated themselves and did him homage. Then they opened their treasures and offered him gifts of gold, frankincense, and myrrh. [12] And having been warned in a dream not to return to Herod, they departed for their country by another way.

OT:2 Sam 5:1-2; Micah 5:1-3

1 **When Jesus was born in Bethlehem of Judea, in the days of King Herod:** Matthew again mentions the birth of Jesus (see 1:25), adding two pieces of information. First, Jesus was **born in Bethlehem of Judea.** This is the first mention in Matthew's gospel of a geographical location, for we were not told where Mary and Joseph lived during their betrothal (1:18-25). **Bethlehem,** five miles from Jerusalem, was the ancestral city of David (1 Sam

16:1-13). Matthew specifies that he is referring to Bethlehem **of Judea,** for there was another village named Bethlehem in Galilee (Joshua 19:15).

Judea: See page 397

Matthew also tells his readers that Jesus was born **in the days of King Herod**—the Herod usually referred to as Herod the Great. The Roman Senate gave **Herod** the title "king of the Jews" in 40 B.C., but he did not consolidate his rule until 37 B.C. Herod died in 4 B.C.; Jesus was born during the latter part of Herod's reign. (A calendar miscalculation in A.D. 533 results in Christ being born B.C.—before Christ.)

Herod the Great: See page 35

After Jesus had been born in Bethlehem during the rule of Herod, **magi from the east arrived in Jerusalem.** The word **magi** originally referred to a Persian priestly caste, but later was more broadly used for those who possessed esoteric knowledge. These magi come **from the east,** a region that included Persia, Babylon, Arabia, and other lands.

2 The magi come to Jerusalem **saying, "Where is the newborn king of the Jews? We saw his star at its rising and have come to do him homage."** They observe a **star at its rising**—at its first appearance in the sky. What they might have seen (a supernova? a conjunction of planets? a comet?) is a matter of conjecture, but Matthew's concern is the significance of what the magi saw, not its nature. The magi interpret the **rising** of the star as signaling the birth of a **king of the Jews.** There was an ancient belief that heavenly signs marked the birth of great men. Some Jews applied the Scripture passage, "A star shall advance from Jacob" (Num 24:17), to the coming of

---

BACKGROUND: BETHLEHEM lies about five miles south of Jerusalem. Its name means "house of bread," perhaps because grain crops were grown in adjacent fields (see Ruth 1:22–2:23). King David's family lived in Bethlehem (1 Sam 16:1-13), giving it its chief claim to fame in the Old Testament. It was otherwise not an impressive village. The prophet Micah called it "too small to be among the clans of Judah," but nonetheless prophesied, "From you shall come forth for me / one who is to be ruler in Israel" (Micah 5:1). Micah's prophecy was the basis for an expectation that the Messiah would not only be a descendant of David but would also come from Bethlehem (John 7:42), but this expectation of a Bethlehem origin was not shared by all at the time of Jesus (see John 7:27). Bethlehem was still a rather modest village at the time of Jesus' birth.

27

the Messiah, and the magi may have known of this. The magi come to Jerusalem and ask about **the newborn king of the Jews** so that they may **do him homage.** The star alerted them to his birth, but Matthew does not portray it guiding them on their journey. The magi simply come to the Jewish capital city—Jerusalem—looking for its newborn king.

3 **When King Herod heard this, he was greatly troubled.** Herod was paranoid about preserving his power and had several of his own sons killed to remove them as potential threats to his rule. When Herod **heard** that magi had arrived in Jerusalem asking about a newborn "king of the Jews," Herod was **greatly troubled,** for his title was king of the Jews, and he didn't want any other claimants to it. Matthew adds that **all Jerusalem** was greatly troubled **with him.** This is hard to understand, for Herod was not popular with the people, and they should have welcomed the prospect of his replacement.

4 **Assembling all the chief priests and the scribes of the people, he inquired of them where the Messiah was to be born.** Herod assembles the chief religious authorities subservient to him (the high priest served at Herod's pleasure), along with **scribes** (scholars in religious matters), and asks them where **the Messiah** is to be born. The magi are looking for the newborn "king of the Jews" (verse 2); Herod understands that the one they are searching for is **the Messiah.** Many Jews expected that the Messiah would restore Jewish independence, ending domination by Rome and its agents—agents such as Herod. Herod wants to know **where the Messiah was to be born** so that he can remove this threat to his rule.

High priest, chief priests: See page 566

Scribes: See page 138

Messiah, Christ: See page 349

5 **They said to him, "In Bethlehem of Judea, for thus it has been written through the prophet":** Herod would not have needed to consult experts, for many Jews interpreted a prophecy of Micah to mean that the Messiah would come from Bethlehem (Micah 5:1; see John 7:42).

6 **And you, Bethlehem, land of Judah, / are by no means least among the rulers of Judah; / since from you shall come a ruler, / who is to shepherd my people Israel.** Matthew quotes Micah a little freely and incorporates

the phrase, "shepherd my people Israel," from 2 Samuel 5:2. The sense of the prophecy is clear: someone special will be born in Bethlehem who will rule over God's people and shepherd them. Many Jews identified this ruler with the Messiah. Jesus fulfills this prophecy: he was born in Bethlehem (verse 1), and he will care for men and women as a shepherd cares for a flock (see 9:36; 26:31).

> But you, Bethlehem-Ephrathah,
>> too small to be among the clans of Judah,
> From you shall come forth for me
>> one who is to be ruler in Israel;
> Whose origin is from of old,
>> from ancient times. . . .
> He shall stand firm and shepherd his flock
>> by the strength of the LORD,
>> in the majestic name of the LORD, his God.
>> *Micah 5:1, 3*

> You shall shepherd my people Israel and shall be commander of Israel.
>> *2 Samuel 5:2*

7 Then Herod called the magi secretly and ascertained from them the time of the star's appearance. The magi do not seek out Herod; Herod summons them after having learned of their interest in a newborn king of the Jews (verses 2-3). He does so **secretly,** indicating that his motives are not aboveboard. Herod wants to know **the time of the star's appearance,** for that will tell him the age of the child whose birth it marks. Herod's interest in knowing this will become evident later (2:16).

8 Herod tells the magi that the child would have been born in Bethlehem. **He sent them to Bethlehem and said, "Go and search diligently for the child. When you have found him, bring me word, that I too may go and do him homage."** Herod has anything but **homage** in mind for Jesus.

9 After their audience with the king they set out. The magi begin their quest for Jesus because of a star, a revelation through nature. (Paul writes that God reveals himself through his creation: Rom 1:19-20.) Natural revelation goes only so far: it leads the magi to Jerusalem, but not yet to Jesus. God's revelation through nature must be completed by God's revelation to his people and through their writings, the Scriptures. The prophet Micah provided the link that leads the magi on their next step toward Jesus.

For reflection: What insights into the mystery of God have I learned from creation?

God also provides individualized guidance, helping us apply the message of Scripture. For the magi, God's guidance takes the form of the reappearance of the star that had alerted them to the birth of Jesus: **And behold, the star that they had seen at its rising preceded them, until it came and stopped over the place where the child was.** Bethlehem lay south of Jerusalem, and stars normally travel east to west, not north to south. What it meant for a star to stop over a house is difficult to visualize. Matthew is less interested in the mechanics of what happened than in the result: the magi are led to the **place where the child was.**

For reflection: How have I experienced God's guidance?

10 **They were overjoyed at seeing the star:** literally, they rejoiced exceedingly with great joy. Their overflowing joy makes sense if they have not seen the star since its rising but it has now reappeared. The heavenly sign that led the magi to begin their quest helps them finish it.

For reflection: What has God done that has given me the greatest joy?

11 **and on entering the house they saw the child with Mary his mother.** Jesus looks like any other child of his age; only the star marking the house signals that this **child** is the object of the magi's quest. Matthew speaks of Jesus and Mary being in **the house;** from what Matthew has earlier written (1:20, 24), this would seem to be Joseph's house in Bethlehem. We will shortly learn that Jesus may be almost two years old when the magi arrive (2:16). Matthew's gospel reads as if Joseph and Mary live in Bethlehem and are not just making a short visit there when Jesus is born. (See the Comment "Matthew and Luke on the birth of Jesus" on page 40.)
 They prostrated themselves and did him homage. To prostrate oneself on the ground before another person is an act of profound **homage,**

homage appropriate for a king (1 Sam 24:9; 1 Kings 1:16, 23, 31). The magi have made their journey to do homage to the newborn king of the Jews (verse 2). The image of their giving Jesus **homage** has a second level of significance. Bowing down in homage is also an act of worship of God (Gen 24:26, 48; Exod 4:31). Matthew will recount Jesus' disciples bowing in homage before him as the Son of God (14:33; see also 28:9). In Matthew's account, the first people to give Jesus the homage due him are magi—Gentiles—foreshadowing the admission of Gentiles into the church.

For reflection: What postures of worship do I use to give homage to Jesus?

Then they opened their treasures—literally, their treasure boxes—**and offered him gifts of gold, frankincense, and myrrh.** These are gifts fit for royalty (Psalms 45:9; 72:15). Gold, frankincense, and myrrh were products of regions that the magi may have come from or traveled through on their quest for Jesus (see Isaiah 60:6). **Frankincense,** made from a tree rosin, was burned for its pleasant smell (Exod 30:34-35); **myrrh,** also made from a tree rosin, was used as a perfume (Song 3:6, which also mentions frankincense). Later interpreters found symbolic significance in each of these gifts, but Matthew probably understands them simply as expensive presents.

For reflection: What gifts am I able to give Jesus?

Nowhere in Matthew's account are we told how many magi there were. Popular tradition settled on three, based on their having brought three presents. Popular tradition also made them kings by applying the words of Psalm 72:10 to them.

12 **And having been warned in a dream not to return to Herod, they departed for their country by another way.** Just as God guided Joseph at a critical point through a dream (1:20-21), so the magi are **warned in a dream** to steer clear of Herod, and they comply. Nothing further is heard of them, or of their star.

Different people reacted differently to the birth of Jesus. Herod is "greatly troubled" when he hears about it (verse 3) and schemes to eliminate this threat to his rule (verses 7-8). Chief priests and scribes understand the meaning of Scripture (verses 4-6), but make no effort to go to Bethlehem to see its fulfillment; by walking five miles, they could have shared in what the magi traveled perhaps hundreds of miles to experience. It is left to magi—Gentiles—to offer Jesus homage. The response Jesus receives at his birth foreshadows the response he will receive during his public ministry. Many will be indifferent to him and his message. Some will be hostile and seek his death, and Jesus will be executed as "the king of the Jews" (verse 2; see also 27:11, 29, 37). Some will be drawn to him; some will become his disciples. The church he will leave behind will welcome Gentiles as well as Jews.

For reflection: Have I been hostile to Jesus? Indifferent? How far am I willing to journey to find him and do him homage?

Out of Egypt
¹³ When they had departed, behold, the angel of the Lord appeared to Joseph in a dream and said, "Rise, take the child and his mother, flee to Egypt, and stay there until I tell you. Herod is going to search for the child to destroy him." ¹⁴ Joseph rose and took the child and his mother by night and departed for Egypt. ¹⁵ He stayed there until the death of Herod, that what the Lord had said through the prophet might be fulfilled, "Out of Egypt I called my son."

¹⁶ When Herod realized that he had been deceived by the magi, he became furious. He ordered the massacre of all the boys in Bethlehem and its vicinity two years old and under, in accordance with the time he had ascertained from the magi. ¹⁷ Then was fulfilled what had been said through Jeremiah the prophet:

¹⁸ "A voice was heard in Ramah,
     sobbing and loud lamentation;
Rachel weeping for her children,
     and she would not be consoled,
     since they were no more."
OT:Jer 31:15; Hosea 11:1

13 **When they had departed, behold, the angel of the Lord appeared to Joseph in a dream.** This is the second time that an **angel** tells Joseph what God wants him to do (see 1:20-21).

The angel told Joseph, **Rise, take the child and his mother, flee to Egypt.** The beginning of the habitable part of **Egypt** lay about two hundred miles west-southwest of Bethlehem. Egypt was a traditional place of refuge for Israelites fleeing danger (1 Kings 11:40; 2 Kings 25:26; Jer 26:21). Colonies of Jews lived in various place in Egypt (2 Macc 1:1, 10), and Joseph could have found refuge for his family with them. The angel told Joseph, **stay there until I tell you.** Joseph is not told how long he is to remain in Egypt; he is to await further orders. The angel asks for open-ended but not blind obedience: the angel explains to Joseph why it is necessary for him to **flee to Egypt** with his family. **Herod is going to search for the child to destroy him.** Egypt, like Palestine, was under Roman rule, but it was outside the range of Herod's authority. The expression translated **is going to search** suggests an imminent search. Herod wants to **destroy** Jesus, foreshadowing others who will later also want to destroy him (27:20).

For reflection: Has God asked open-ended obedience of me, telling me only the next step I am to take?

BACKGROUND: ANGELS The Hebrew and Greek words translated as "angel" also mean "messenger," and angels appear in early Old Testament writings as messengers of God. These messengers are not always clearly distinguished from manifestations of God himself (Gen 16:7-13; Exod 3:2-6). Some Scripture passages speak of members of God's heavenly court, sometimes calling them "the sons of God," meaning "heavenly beings" (Job 1:6), or calling them the "host (army) of heaven" (1 Kings 22:19-22), an expression that can also refer to stars (Deut 4:19). Cherubim are heavenly beings, too (Ezek 10:18-20; see also Gen 3:24). Thus, the Old Testament speaks of a variety of heavenly beings without relating them to one another, without calling all of them angels, and without defining their nature. Individual angels are not named until late Old Testament writings; Raphael (Tobit 5:4; 12:15), Gabriel (Dan 8:16), and Michael (Dan 10:13) are the only three angels named in the Old Testament. Michael, the prince (or guardian angel) of God's people (Dan 12:1), contends with other heavenly beings who are the guardians of other nations (Dan 10:13, 20-21). Speculations about angels multiplied late in the Old Testament era and are reflected in Jewish writings that did not become part of Scripture. The perplexing account in Genesis of "the sons of heaven" (literally, "sons of God"; see Job 1:6) who had intercourse with women (Gen 6:1-4) developed into a story of the fall of some angels who led humans into sin. The chief of the fallen angels was given various names, including "Satan." At the time of Jesus, angels were generally thought of as human in form (2 Macc 3:26; Dan 8:15-16) but with heavenly rather than earthly bodies, not needing to eat or drink (Tobit 12:19). *Related topics: Nonbiblical writings (page 198), Satan (page 55).*

---

14 Joseph rose and took the child and his mother by night and departed for Egypt. Joseph obeys God's instructions, and does so promptly: departing **by night** can be interpreted to mean that Joseph woke from the dream, gathered his family, and immediately **departed for Egypt,** not even waiting for daylight.

Joseph and his family can be looked upon as patron saints for today's political refugees. Yet Matthew does not dwell on the hardships they might have experienced. Matthew portrays Joseph as a man living an upright life that periodically takes sudden turns. Joseph is betrothed to Mary—but discovers she is pregnant, and learns from an angel that it is through the Holy Spirit. In due course her child is born—then magi arrive, quickly followed by angelic instructions to flee to Egypt. We might think of Joseph as a patron saint for those whose lives take unexpected turns as they try to remain faithful to God.

For reflection: What unexpected turns has my life taken? What can I learn from the example of Joseph?

15 He stayed there until the death of Herod: Matthew looks ahead to Herod's death in 4 B.C. Matthew does not tell us the length of Joseph's sojourn with his family in Egypt. It is not their time in Egypt that is significant for Matthew but their departure from Egypt, which Matthew sees foreshadowed in Scripture: **that what the Lord had said through the prophet might be fulfilled, "Out of Egypt I called my son."** Hosea's prophecy (Hosea 11:1) originally referred to Israel's exodus from Egypt at the time of Moses. In the prophecy, God speaks of the people of Israel as his son. Matthew finds greater meaning in these words when they are applied to Jesus, for Jesus is indeed the Son of God, conceived through the Holy Spirit (1:18, 20; see also 3:17; 17:5). The genealogy of Jesus (1:2-16) shows that Jesus' past is Israel's past; Jesus' departure from Egypt after the death of Herod brings to mind the Israelites' exodus from Egypt at the time of Moses—the foundational event in Israel's history.

Son of God: See page 52

When Israel was a child I loved him,
out of Egypt I called my son.
Hosea 11:1

16 Matthew returns to his account of what happens after the magi return home. **When Herod realized that he had been deceived by the magi, he became furious.** Herod has counted on the magi identifying the "new-born king of the Jews" for him, so that he can eliminate this potential threat to his rule. Herod has learned the date of the child's birth (2:7) and knows that the child was born in or near Bethlehem (2:4-5), and that is enough for Herod to act on. **He ordered the massacre of all the boys in Bethlehem and its vicinity two years old and under, in accordance with the time he had ascertained from the magi.** The Herod who had several of his own sons killed when he thought they threatened his rule would certainly have had no scruples about killing the sons of others. Herod takes no chances: he orders the death of **all** boys in and near Bethlehem aged two and younger, in order to be sure of killing the one he is interested in. The number killed may have been, by one estimate, around twenty, if Bethlehem had a population of one thousand. Scripture scholars

---

BACKGROUND: HEROD THE GREAT   Two individuals are called Herod in the gospels: Herod the Great, who ruled when Jesus was born, and his son Herod Antipas, who ruled Galilee during Jesus' public ministry. Herod the Great's father was an Idumean, a people of Edomite ancestry who had been forcibly converted to Judaism in 129 B.C. Herod the Great's mother was an Arabian princess, making Herod and his sons half-Jewish at best in the eyes of many. Herod the Great's father was an administrator employed by Rome to oversee Judea. After his father was poisoned by Jewish opponents, Rome made Herod king of Judea, Samaria, Galilee, and some territories to the east and south. Herod the Great was ambitious, shrewd, and ruthless in eliminating any who stood in his way. He undertook projects in a manner that bordered on megalomania, dotting his kingdom with palaces, massively redoing the Temple complex in Jerusalem, and building temples to the Roman emperor in other cities. He had ten wives and many children, some of whom he murdered on suspicion that they were plotting against him. Herod the Great ruled from 37 to 4 B.C. At his death, Rome divided up his kingdom among three of his sons. Archelaus was made ethnarch (ruler of a people) of Judea, Samaria, and Idumea, but ruled so incompetently that Rome removed him in A.D. 6 and appointed Roman governors to rule his territory. Philip was made a tetrarch, a title that originally meant the ruler of a fourth of a kingdom but later was used for rulers of lesser rank than kings. Philip was given rule over a territory that lay north and east of the Sea of Galilee and included Bethsaida and Caesarea Philippi. He ruled well until his death in A.D. 33 or 34. A third son, Herod Antipas, was made tetrarch of Galilee and of a region east of the Jordan River. *Related topic: Herod Antipas (page 298).*

---

see a parallel between Jesus' escaping Herod's massacre and Moses' escaping the slaughter of Hebrew infant boys ordered by the pharaoh (Exod 1:15-2:10). Jesus will not be another Moses—Jesus will be much more—but there will be similarities between Jesus and Moses.

Herod probably includes a margin for error when he orders the massacre of boys **two years and under,** but this still indicates that the magi arrived some time after Jesus' birth—presumably more than a year later. Matthew's account reads as if Joseph, Mary, and Jesus have been living in Bethlehem during this time.

17 **Then was fulfilled what had been said through Jeremiah the prophet.** Matthew again finds that what happens in the life of Jesus brings out a new meaning in a passage of Scripture. **Jeremiah** prophesied during the time when Babylon conquered Jerusalem and exiled its leading citizens. Jeremiah poetically describes the heartbreak of exile by invoking the image of Rachel, one of the wives of Jacob, weeping for her descendants as they are being led past her grave into exile:

18 **A voice was heard in Ramah, / sobbing and loud lamentation; / Rachel weeping for her children, / and she would not be consoled, / since they were no more.** Rachel was buried at Ramah, a site about six miles north of Jerusalem (Gen 35:16-20; 1 Sam 10:2). In the time of Jeremiah, **Ramah** served as a gathering point for those being forcibly exiled (Jer 40:1). Jewish tradition later associated the location of Rachel's grave with Bethlehem, to the south of Jerusalem (Gen 35:19; 48:7); a tomb of Rachel is venerated on the outskirts of Bethlehem to this day. Matthew follows this later tradition, and interprets Rachel weeping for her children as Rachel weeping for the boys killed by Herod.

> *In Ramah is heard the sound of moaning,*
>   *of bitter weeping!*
> *Rachel mourns her children,*
>   *she refuses to be consoled*
>   *because her children are no more.*
>   *Jeremiah 31:15*

It is chilling that the birth of Jesus should be followed by the coldly calculated execution of innocent children. It foreshadows the execution of an innocent Jesus (26:3-5; 27:1-2).

Settling in Nazareth

19 When Herod had died, behold, the angel of the Lord appeared in a dream to Joseph in Egypt **20** and said, "Rise, take the child and his mother and go to the land of Israel, for those who sought the child's life are dead." **21** He rose, took the child and his mother, and went to the land of Israel. **22** But when he heard that Archelaus was ruling over Judea in place of his father Herod, he was afraid to go back there. And because he had been warned in a dream, he departed for the region of Galilee. **23** He went and dwelt in a town called Nazareth, so that what had been spoken through the prophets might be fulfilled, "He shall be called a Nazorean."

19 **When Herod had died**—in 4 B.C.—**behold, the angel of the Lord appeared in a dream to Joseph in Egypt.** The angel has previously instructed Joseph to take his family to Egypt and "stay there until I tell you" (2:13). Joseph is now told what to do next.

20 The angel says, **Rise, take the child and his mother and go to the land of Israel.** There is no longer need for Joseph and his family to live in exile, **for those who sought the child's life are dead.** Matthew refers to **those** who sought to kill Jesus, as if Herod was not alone in wanting Jesus dead, but Matthew has not told his readers who else joined in Herod's actions. Matthew might have been less concerned about their identities than in bringing out another parallel between Jesus and Moses. Moses fled to Midian out of fear for his life, but was later told by God that it was safe for him to return to Egypt, "for all the men who sought your life are dead" (Exod 4:19). Likewise, any who sought to kill Jesus are now dead.

21 **He rose, took the child and his mother, and went to the land of Israel.** Joseph, as always, does exactly what God's messenger instructs him to do.

22 **But when he heard that Archelaus was ruling over Judea in place of his father Herod, he was afraid to go back there.** After Herod's death, his kingdom was divided among three of his sons. **Archelaus** became the ruler

of Judea, which included Bethlehem. Joseph **was afraid to go back there**—
back to Bethlehem where he had been living—because **he heard** that
Archelaus now ruled over it. Archelaus was as ruthless as his father Herod
but lacked Herod's talents. To quell a potential revolt after Herod's death,
Archelaus's troops killed three thousand Jews in the Temple precincts at
Passover. Rome deposed and exiled Archelaus in A.D. 6.

Joseph returns to Judea, but is afraid to return to his home in Bethlehem because the murderous Herod has been succeeded by a murderous
son. Joseph does not have to decide on his own what to do next, for he
again receives divine guidance. **And because he had been warned in a
dream, he departed for the region of Galilee.** Herod Antipas, another
son of Herod, had been appointed by Rome to rule over **Galilee**, a **region**
roughly fifty-five miles north of Bethlehem. Herod Antipas was a more
tolerant ruler than Archelaus, and posed less threat to Joseph's family.

Galilee: See page 68

For reflection: How has God guided me when I did not know what to do?

23 **He went and dwelt in a town called Nazareth:** Joseph and his family settle in **Nazareth.** Matthew calls it a **town,** but it was a farming village with
a population of only several hundred. If Joseph wanted a safe, anonymous place to raise Jesus, Nazareth fit the bill. Nazareth was so little
known that there was apparently no established way of transliterating its
Hebrew/Aramaic name into Greek. Matthew mentions Nazareth three
times in his gospel (2:23; 4:13; 21:11) and spells it differently (in Greek)
each time, perhaps reflecting the spellings used by different sources Matthew drew on in writing his gospel.

BACKGROUND: NAZARETH was an insignificant farming village located on a sad-
dle in a hill overlooking the Jezreel Valley in southern Galilee. Archaeologists tell us
that it was no more than ten acres in size at the time of Jesus and had less than four
hundred inhabitants—likely only around two hundred. The scanty remains from the
first century suggest that its houses were rather insubstantial, with fieldstone walls
and thatched roofs. No luxury items of any kind have been found on the site. Nazareth is not mentioned in the Old Testament; its unimportance is reflected in Na-
thanael's question "Can anything good come from Nazareth?" (John 1:46). There was
nothing to distinguish Nazareth from other small farming villages in Galilee during the
years Jesus called it home.

Matthew sees significance in Jesus' being raised in Nazareth: it was **so that what had been spoken through the prophets might be fulfilled, "He shall be called a Nazorean."** Being **called a Nazorean** means being known as someone from Nazareth. Jesus will be identified as "Jesus the Nazorean" (26:71) to distinguish him from other men named Jesus. Matthew sees additional meaning in Jesus' being called a **Nazorean,** for Matthew understands it as a fulfillment of **what had been spoken through the prophets.** This has long puzzled interpreters, for there is no mention whatsoever of Nazareth in the Old Testament. Matthew may have been aware of this, for he writes in terms of what has been spoken through **the prophets** in general rather than by a specific prophet. The most common explanation is that Matthew invokes several Old Testament passages by means of wordplay. Isaiah prophesied regarding a "shoot that shall sprout from the stump of Jesse, / and from his roots a bud shall blossom" (Isaiah 11:1), referring to a descendant of David's father, Jesse. The Hebrew word for bud is *netser,* which is similar to "Nazareth/Nazorean." In Judges, a man specially consecrated to the service of God is called a *nazir* in Hebrew (Judges 13:5, 7; 16:17), which also is similar to "Nazareth/Nazorean." Such associations can convey that Jesus the Nazorean is a descendant of David specially consecrated to the service of God.

When we look back at how Matthew has recounted events that took place after the birth of Jesus, we are struck by the prominence given to Joseph. Jesus has been named but once (2:1), and thereafter referred to only as "the child" (2:8, 9, 11, 13, 14, 20, 21). Mary has likewise been named but once, as "Mary his mother" (2:11), and is thereafter only referred to as "his mother" (2:13, 14, 20, 21). Joseph has been named three times (2:13, 14, 19), and the spotlight has been on his protecting his family by following angelic guidance. Joseph hears and obeys God's word to him (1:20-24; 2:13-15, 19-23); he is a model for doing the will of God (7:21; 21:28-32). Matthew's portrayal of Joseph also evokes the memory of the first Joseph, who understood dreams and cared for his family as refugees in Egypt (Gen 37; 40–41; 45–46).

It is also striking that, while Joseph has been on center stage, he has spoken no lines. And save for one passing reference to him (13:55), Joseph will now disappear from the pages of Matthew's gospel. Joseph has quietly and faithfully played his role, becoming a father and protector of Jesus, and now leaves the stage so that the next act may begin.

For reflection: What can I learn from the example of Joseph?

COMMENT: MATTHEW AND LUKE ON THE BIRTH OF JESUS   In telling how Jesus was conceived and born, Matthew and Luke agree on the essential elements. Jesus was conceived in the virgin Mary through the Holy Spirit; Jesus is the Son of God. Jesus is also the Son of David through Joseph's acceptance of him as his legal son. Jesus was born in Bethlehem but grew up in Nazareth. Yet Matthew and Luke differ when it comes to fleshing out the story of Jesus' birth. Each relates events not mentioned by the other; for example, magi pay homage in M atthew, shepherds in Luke. Sometimes the differences between their accounts are difficult to smooth over. One difference, for example, concerns the place of residence. Matthew portrays Joseph and Mary apparently living in Bethlehem for more than a year after Jesus is born, and then relocating to Nazareth after a sojourn in Egypt. Luke portrays Mary and Joseph living in Nazareth when Jesus is conceived, and on a visit to Bethlehem when Jesus is born; they return to Nazareth with no detour to Egypt. The differences between Matthew and Luke's accounts remind us that neither Matthew nor Luke provide their readers with a video recording of events surrounding the birth of Jesus. Both accounts proclaim who Jesus is; both accounts link Jesus with what God has done in the past; and both accounts foreshadow what God will do through Jesus in the future. The church accepts both accounts as inspired Scripture, despite the differences. In reading their accounts as Scripture, our primary focus should be on what they proclaim about Jesus. We should not try to force Matthew's account into Luke's mold, nor Luke's account in Matthew's mold— much less force the two of them into a mold of our own contriving.

CHAPTER 3

ORIENTATION: *After telling of Joseph settling his family in Nazareth (2:19-23), Matthew provides no further information about Jesus' early life. Matthew skips ahead to the ministry of John the Baptist in order to set the scene for Jesus.*

John the Baptist
¹ In those days John the Baptist appeared, preaching in the desert of Judea ² [and] saying, "Repent, for the kingdom of heaven is at hand!" ³ It was of him that the prophet Isaiah had spoken when he said:

**"A voice of one crying out in the desert,
'Prepare the way of the Lord,
make straight his paths.'"**

⁴ John wore clothing made of camel's hair and had a leather belt around his waist. His food was locusts and wild honey. ⁵ At that time Jerusalem, all Judea, and the whole region around the Jordan were going out to him ⁶ and were being baptized by him in the Jordan River as they acknowledged their sins.
> Gospel parallels: Mark 1:2-6; Luke 3:1-6; John 1:22-23
> OT:Isaiah 40:3

1 **In those days John the Baptist appeared:** Matthew does not specify a date for **John the Baptist** coming on the scene nor does he provide any background information about him. Matthew's expression **in those days** might imply that, in God's plan, John's appearance continues what began with the birth of Jesus (2:1-23). Matthew may also have wanted to trigger some associations for his Jewish Christian readers by using **in those days** to introduce John the Baptist. The expression echoes Old Testament expressions for a "day of the Lord" when God will act to vanquish evil, and John's preaching will have this theme (3:7-12).
> The day of the Lord: See page 48

John appears **preaching in the desert of Judea,** a desolate region stretching from the outskirts of Jerusalem east and south to the Jordan River and the Dead Sea. John's baptizing takes place in the Jordan (see verse 6).

2 The message John preaches is **Repent, for the kingdom of heaven is at hand!** To **repent** means to turn away from sin and to God. True repentance involves a reorientation of one's thinking and values as well as changes in behavior. John calls upon his listeners to change the direction of their lives.

> *For reflection: Do I need to make a change in the direction of my life? What do I need to turn away from in order to turn more completely to God?*

John the Baptist tells his listeners that the reason why repentance is necessary is that **the kingdom of heaven is at hand.** The **kingdom of heaven** is the same as the kingdom of God (Jews avoided the use of God's name out of reverence, substituting instead a word like "heaven"; Matthew usually follows this custom in his gospel in references to God's kingdom). **The kingdom of heaven** means God establishing his sovereign reign over everyone and everything, vanquishing all evil. John proclaims that the decisive reign of God **is at hand:** God is about to act. There isn't much time left to prepare oneself for it; therefore, it is urgent that John's listeners **repent.**

Kingdom of heaven: See page 266

John's words foreshadow Jesus' preaching: Jesus will begin his ministry with the proclamation, "Repent, for the kingdom of heaven is at hand" (4:17). John will not say much about the nature of the kingdom of heaven; John's emphasis is on repentance in preparation for its coming. Jesus will devote a good part of his teaching to explaining what the kingdom of heaven is like and how one lives under the reign of God.

BACKGROUND: REPENTANCE In the Old Testament, the Hebrew verb used for "repent" means to turn back or return: "Return, O Israel, to the LORD, your God" (Hosea 14:2). The New Testament expresses repentance differently: the Greek word translated "repentance" literally means "a change of mind." A change of mind means recognizing that one's views are wrong or inadequate. If wrong views lead to wrong actions, then a change of mind should result in a change of behavior. Summing up all of this is the notion of conversion, a profound reorientation of oneself. When John the Baptist and Jesus call for repentance, they are calling for an acceptance of the messages they proclaim and for life changes on the basis of their messages. Repentance is not simply a matter of feeling sorry but also of adopting new attitudes and new behavior.

3 If a person were to claim that he or she knows what God is about to do, we would want to know what credentials the person has for making such a claim. Matthew provides credentials for John the Baptist by invoking a prophecy of Isaiah: **It was of him that the prophet Isaiah had spoken when he said: "A voice of one crying out in the desert, / 'Prepare the way of the Lord, / make straight his paths.'"** Matthew identifies John as the one Isaiah prophesied about.

> *A voice cries out:*
> *In the desert prepare the way of the LORD!*
> *Make straight in the wasteland*
> *a highway for our God!*
> *Isaiah 40:3*

Isaiah announced that Israel's exile in Babylon was nearing an end and called for a straight highway through the wilderness between Babylon and Jerusalem so that God could lead his people back to Jerusalem (Isaiah 40:9-11). Matthew repunctuates Isaiah's prophecy in order to apply it to John, making "the desert" the place where the voice is crying out rather than part of what the voice says. Matthew understands **the Lord** to be Jesus. Matthew identifies John the Baptist as the one who goes before Jesus, preparing the way for him. In light of verse 2, this implies that the coming of God's reign is tied up with the person and work of Jesus.

Lord: See page 133

4 John wore clothing made of camel's hair and had a leather belt around his waist. His food was locusts and wild honey. John's attire and diet were not unusual for those who lived and foraged in wilderness areas. His garb is reminiscent of how Elijah the prophet dressed (2 Kings 1:7-8), and in Matthew's gospel, Jesus will identify John the Baptist with Elijah (11:11-14; 17:10-13). John's living in the harsh Judean wilderness and scavenging for food indicates that he is convinced that the kingdom of heaven is indeed at hand (verse 2), not a far-off prospect that allows for life to go on as usual.

5 At that time Jerusalem, all Judea, and the whole region around the Jordan were going out to him. Although John proclaimed his message in a sparsely inhabited region, it was near a trade route. Many Jews came to John in the wilderness and accepted his message of repentance.

Jerusalem: See page 440

Judea: See page 397

6 Those who came to John **were being baptized by him in the Jordan River as they acknowledged their sins.** The Greek word for **baptized** simply meant to immerse, dip, plunge, or wash; it did not yet carry a specific religious meaning. John's baptism probably involved immersing people in water, but the essential note is that it was a washing—a washing of the body as a symbol for a washing away of sins.

Baptism: See page 669

John's washing gave concrete expression to the repentance of those who **acknowledged their sins.** The first step in repentance is to acknowledge one's sins—to admit that one needs to repent. Some find this first step difficult, just as we might find it difficult to admit that a lump in our body needs medical attention. Both physical and spiritual well-being require that we acknowledge our need for healing when we are sick.

For reflection: Do I find it hard to admit my sins? If so, why?

The Coming One

[7] When he saw many of the Pharisees and Sadducees coming to his baptism, he said to them, "You brood of vipers! Who warned you to flee from the coming wrath? [8] Produce good fruit as evidence of your repentance. [9] And do not presume to say to yourselves, 'We have Abraham as our father.' For I tell you, God can raise up children to Abraham from these stones. [10] Even now the ax lies at the root of the trees. Therefore every tree that does not bear good fruit will be cut down and thrown into the fire. [11] I am baptizing you with water, for repentance, but the one who is coming after me is mightier than I.

"I am not worthy to carry his sandals. He will baptize you with the holy Spirit and fire. [12] His winnowing fan is in his hand. He will clear his threshing floor and gather his wheat into his barn, but the chaff he will burn with unquenchable fire."

Gospel parallels: Mark 1:7-8; Luke 3:7-18; John 1:26-31

OT:Ezek 36:25-27; Zeph 1:14-18

7 When he saw many of the Pharisees and Sadducees coming to his baptism: the sense of **coming to his baptism** is coming to be baptized. There were a number of Jewish groups, each with its own agenda, within the broad stream of first-century Judaism. One group was the **Pharisees,** who had developed traditions for applying the law of Moses in everyday life; among their particular concerns were maintaining ritual purity and observing the Sabbath. The **Sadducees** were a priestly and aristocratic leadership elite centered in Jerusalem. Sadducees rejected the traditions of the Pharisees: their coming with the Pharisees to John did not mean they and the Pharisees were allies (see Acts 23:6-10).

Pharisees: See page 231
Sadducees: See page 476

John the Baptist had strong views about the Pharisees and Sadducees: **he said to them, "You brood of vipers!"** To call others "offspring of deadly snakes" may have been a common insult (Jesus will use the same expression: 12:34; 23:33). **Who warned you to flee from the coming wrath?** The implication of John's question is that Pharisees and Sadducees would experience God's **wrath** when he established his rule on earth (3:2). John is a prophet (11:9; 14:5; 21:26); earlier prophets warned that sinners would be

---

BACKGROUND: JEWISH RELIGIOUS DIVERSITY AT THE TIME OF JESUS While all Jews shared certain fundamental beliefs and observances, there was considerable diversity when it came to specific views and practices. All Jews revered the law of Moses and the Temple, but different groups, such as the Pharisees, Sadducees, and Essenes, developed different traditions for observing the law. These groups also had differing views on such matters as the kind of messiah or messiahs God would send and whether there would be an afterlife or resurrection of the dead. The vast majority of Jews belonged to no religious group or party. Pharisees, the largest and most influential party, numbered only about six thousand. There were also degrees of compliance with God's laws, however these laws were interpreted. Zealous groups, such as the Pharisees and Essenes, developed and followed traditions for strictly living out God's laws. On the other end of the spectrum were those universally considered sinners because they violated some of God's basic commands. Most Jews fell somewhere in the middle, observing the law as best as their circumstances allowed but without adopting the practices of the Pharisees. The Judaism of today has roots in the Pharisees of the time of Jesus but reflects a considerable development of traditions and practices. *Related topics: Essenes (page 238), Pharisees (page 231), Sadducees (page 476).*

punished on a "day of the LORD" (Amos 5:18-20), and although John does not use this expression, he seems to have this day of judgment in mind.

The day of the Lord: See page 48

> Near is the great day of the LORD,
>   near and very swiftly coming. . . .
> A day of wrath is that day,
>   a day of anguish and distress,
> A day of destruction and desolation,
>   a day of darkness and gloom.
> Zephaniah 1:14, 15

8 Being baptized by John was a sign of repentance, and although Pharisees and Sadducees have come to John for baptism, he judges their repentance to be superficial. He tells them, **Produce good fruit as evidence of your repentance.** Otherwise, they could not hope to escape God's wrath. **Fruit** is a biblical metaphor for deeds that flow from one's inner disposition; **good fruit** means good deeds (see 7:16-20). One's behavior reveals whether one has truly repented.

For reflection: What fruit am I producing?

9 John warns them, **do not presume to say to yourselves, "We have Abraham as our father."** Being a member of the chosen people will not exempt Jews from God's judgment. Complacently reassuring oneself that one is right with God is dangerous.

For reflection: Am I in any way complacent in my relationship with God?

For I tell you, God can raise up children to Abraham from these stones. Behind John's words there may be a pun: the Aramaic words for **children** and **stones** are similar. God is quite capable of populating his kingdom with whomever he chooses, transforming them so that they can enter it. If God can raise up **children** from **stones,** he can also transform sinners and Gentiles into his children. John's words would have been of reassurance to Matthew's Gentile Christian readers, and can be of reassurance to those of us with stony hearts today.

For reflection: What reassurance do I find in John's words?

10 **Even now the ax lies at the root of the trees. Therefore every tree that does not bear good fruit will be cut down and thrown into the fire.** Trees were grown for the fruit they produced; olive and fig trees were the most common. A fruit tree that did not bear good fruit wasted water and space; such trees were chopped down for firewood. John demands good fruit as evidence of repentance (verse 8); those not bearing good fruit will be as barren trees cut down at God's judgment and **thrown into the fire.** The cooking-fire fate of fruitless trees is a metaphor for the fires of punishment. Jesus will use the same metaphor (7:19).

John announces that **even now the ax lies at the root of the trees.** Judgment was not a distant possibility but was already beginning, for the kingdom of heaven was at hand (3:2). Hence the urgency of John's call to repent and bear fruit: there is no time to lose!

Judgment: See page 557

For reflection: How urgent is it for me to change my life and bear better fruit?

11 John turns his attention from the Pharisees and Sadducees to those whom he is baptizing and tells them, **I am baptizing you with water, for repentance, but the one who is coming after me is mightier than I. I am not worthy to carry his sandals. He will baptize you with the holy Spirit and fire.** John contrasts the baptism he administers with a baptism to be administered by **the one who is coming after** him. John recognized Jesus as the coming one (3:14), but later may have had doubts (11:2-3).

John says that this coming one **is mightier than I** and can accomplish far more. The superiority of the coming one over John is so great that John is not even worthy to perform a slave's task—carrying **his sandals.** The coming one **will baptize you with the holy Spirit and fire.** John's baptism immerses and cleanses people in water; the coming one will immerse and cleanse people in the **holy Spirit.** Ezekiel used images of water and cleansing in speaking of God's sending his Spirit to his people (Ezek 36:25). John announced that the kingdom of heaven was at hand (3:2); being baptized with the Spirit is thus linked with becoming part of God's reign.

The Spirit: See page 21

For reflection: What is my experience of and relationship with the Holy Spirit?

John says that the coming one will baptize with the Holy Spirit **and fire.** This **fire** is probably not an allusion to the tongues of fire that will signal the outpouring of the Holy Spirit on Pentecost (Acts 2:3) or to a refining fire that will purify us from our sins (Mal 3:2-3). Probably the **fire** John speaks of is the fire of punishment, like the fire that consumes fruitless trees (verse 10) and chaff (verse 12). John expects that the one coming after him will be an agent of God's judgment and fiery wrath.

Jesus is the one who will come after John to immerse women and men in the Holy Spirit, but Jesus will not immediately execute judgment and punishment as John expects. In later Christian tradition, the fire of the Holy Spirit is the fire of divine love.

12 **His winnowing fan is in his hand. He will clear his threshing floor and gather his wheat into his barn, but the chaff he will burn with**

BACKGROUND: THE DAY OF THE LORD   Old Testament prophecy is filled with expectations that God will act to vanquish evil. Some expectations are expressed in terms of "the day of the Lord" or "that day" or "the day when" God will act, or similar expressions. Originally "the day of the Lord" meant a time when God would vindicate his people by defeating their enemies, but Amos proclaimed that it would be a time when God would judge his own sinful people (Amos 5:18-20). Other prophets issued similar warnings, sometimes with the promise that God would restore his people after punishing them. Some prophecies use cosmic imagery to convey how momentous "the day of the Lord" will be (Isaiah 13:9-10; Joel 2:10-11; 3:3-4). Isaiah prophesied that that day would have worldwide consequences, not only restoring Israel but bringing a reign of justice to all nations (Isaiah 2:2-4; 19:18-25; 25:6-9). Most prophecies envision "the day of the Lord" as a time when God will act directly; a few prophecies portray God raising up a descendant of David to rule God's people (Isaiah 11:10; Jer 23:5-6; 30:7-9; 33:14-18; Zech 3:8-10). "The day of the Lord" thus carries a range of meanings in the Old Testament, some of which influenced expectations of the Messiah and the establishment of the kingdom of God (although "the day of the Lord" prophecies do not use these terms). In the letters of the New Testament, "the day of the Lord" takes on the meaning of "the day of the Lord Jesus Christ," when he will judge the human race and establish the final reign of God (see 1 Cor 1:8; Phil 1:6, 10; 2:16). *Related topics: Cosmic signs (page 530), Jewish expectations at the time of Jesus (page 515), Judgment (page 557).*

---

unquenchable fire. After reaping, stalks of grain were laid on a **threshing floor**—a flat outdoor area—and beaten with flails to detach the grain from the stalk. Then the grain and stalks were tossed into the air with **a winnowing fan** (or pitchfork), and the wind blew aside the stalks while the heavier grain fell back onto the threshing floor. The grain was swept up and stored, and the chaff collected as fuel for cooking fires. The process provides an image for good being sorted out from evil. John expects the one coming after him to do the sorting: **His winnowing fan is in his hand.** The coming one will gather the good to himself, gathering **his wheat into his barn.** The evil will be as **chaff** that **he will burn with unquenchable fire.** John characterizes the fire not as a short-burning cooking fire but as **unquenchable.** John proclaims the urgency of preparing oneself for imminent judgment, as on "the day of the Lord," and warns of a fiery fate for the unrepentant.

For reflection: Do I look ahead to God's judgment with hope or dread?

God's Beloved Son
13 Then Jesus came from Galilee to John at the Jordan to be baptized by him. **14** John tried to prevent him, saying, "I need to be baptized by you, and yet you are coming to me?" **15** Jesus said to him in reply, "Allow it now, for thus it is fitting for us to fulfill all righteousness." Then he allowed him. **16** After Jesus was baptized, he came up from the water and behold, the heavens were opened [for him], and he saw the Spirit of God descending like a dove [and] coming upon him. **17** And a voice came from the heavens, saying, "This is my beloved Son, with whom I am well pleased."

> Gospel parallels: Mark 1:9-11; Luke 3:21-22
> OT:Psalm 2; Isaiah 11:1-2; 42:1-4; 61:1
> NT:Matt 17:5; John 1:32-34; 2 Cor 5:21

13 **Then Jesus came from Galilee to John at the Jordan to be baptized by him.** Jesus' first act in the Gospel of Matthew is to come to John **to be baptized by him**—not merely to observe what John is doing or to speak with John. Matthew does not tell his readers why Jesus chooses to come for John's baptism at this time, after having lived an apparently unremarkable life in Nazareth (see 13:54-57). Jesus' first public appearance is not as the divine judge that John has expected (3:11-12), but as one who lines up with sinners for John's baptism.

Baptism: See page 669

14 **John tried to prevent him, saying, "I need to be baptized by you, and yet you are coming to me?"** John recognizes Jesus as the coming one who will baptize with the Holy Spirit (3:11) and acknowledges that he needs Jesus' baptism: **I need to be baptized by you.** Why is someone whose sandals John was not worthy to carry (3:11) **coming to** John for baptism? John cannot fathom Jesus' motives and tries **to prevent** Jesus from doing what Jesus wants to do.

> *For reflection: Am I sometimes baffled by how Jesus comes to me? Do I try to prevent Jesus from doing what he wants to accomplish with me?*

The New Testament proclaims that Jesus was without sin (2 Cor 5:21; Heb 4:15; 1 Pet 2:22), but Jesus' sinlessness does not seem to have been the reason John draws back from baptizing Jesus. Rather, John hesitates to baptize someone whom he acknowledges to be the far more powerful baptizer.

15 **Jesus said to him in reply, "Allow it now, for thus it is fitting for us to fulfill all righteousness."** In Matthew's gospel, **righteousness** usually refers to moral conduct (see 6:1), but can also mean the saving action of God (see 5:6). **To fulfill all righteousness** means to accomplish God's plan of salvation, to do God's will. In God's plan, it is **fitting** for Jesus to join with those being baptized. Jesus is God-with-us (see 1:23) even in our sinful condition and takes our infirmities upon himself (see 8:17). Paul will write that God made Jesus "to be sin who did not know sin, so that we might become the righteousness of God in him" (2 Cor 5:21).

> *For reflection: What does Jesus' submitting himself to baptism tell me about him?*

Jesus tells John to **allow** him to receive baptism because that is fitting for **us**: God's plan involves John as well as Jesus. God invites and requires our cooperation, as well; we must **allow** God to carry out his saving activity in and through us. **Then he allowed him:** John accepts Jesus' words and acts in accordance with them.

For reflection: What is God asking that I allow him to accomplish in and through me?

16 **After Jesus was baptized, he came up from the water.** Matthew passes rather quickly over Jesus' immersion in the Jordan River; what happens next is more important. **The heavens were opened:** the Old Testament speaks of the heavens being opened when God reveals himself or acts on behalf of his people (Ezek 1:1; Isaiah 63:19). Some ancient manuscripts of Matthew's gospel read that the heavens are opened **for him,** as if only Jesus sees it happen. Jesus **saw the Spirit of God descending like a dove [and] coming upon him.** This is not Jesus' first contact with the **Spirit,** for Jesus was conceived through the power of the Holy Spirit (1:20). He who will baptize with the Holy Spirit is the Spirit-filled Messiah (Isaiah 11:2; 61:1).

The Spirit: See page 21

The Holy Spirit appearing **like a dove** is unique to the baptism of Jesus; nowhere else in Scripture is the Spirit represented as a dove. Matthew's Jewish Christian readers might have detected a faint echo of Genesis's account of creation. When the earth was a formless waste shrouded in darkness "a mighty wind swept over the waters" (Gen 1:2): the Hebrew can also be translated "a spirit of God hovered over the waters"—hovering like a dove, according to one late first-century rabbi. Thus, the descent of the Spirit like a dove on Jesus may symbolize God beginning a new act of creation through Jesus.

17 **And a voice came from the heavens, saying, "This is my beloved Son, with whom I am well pleased."** God proclaims to all present—and to all who read Matthew's gospel—**This is my beloved Son.** Jesus, begotten through the Holy Spirit (1:18, 20) is God's **Son.** Jesus is God's **beloved** Son: the relationship between God and Jesus is one of love. The Greek word for **beloved** can convey the notion of "only" or "only beloved": there is a unique relationship between Jesus and God. God proclaims that he is **well pleased** with Jesus; God looks upon Jesus with affection and delight.

The voice from heaven echoes two Old Testament passages. **This is my beloved Son** recalls Psalm 2, in which God tells an Israelite king as he takes the throne, "You are my son; today I am your father" (Psalm 2:7). Verse 2 of this psalm speaks of this king as God's "anointed" (*messiah* in

Hebrew) who faces opposition from other kings and princes. **With whom I am well pleased** echoes a prophecy of Isaiah in which God proclaims, "Here is my servant whom I uphold, / my chosen one with whom I am pleased." This servant of God is endowed with God's Spirit (Isaiah 42:1). Another passage in Isaiah will speak of God's servant accepting suffering and death for the sake of others (Isaiah 52:13–53:12).

Jesus' baptism reveals his identity and foreshadows what lies ahead. Accepting John's baptism is a sign that Jesus is one with sinful humanity at the same time that he is uniquely God's Son. And although Jesus is God's beloved Son, he is also God's servant, who will suffer in order to carry out God's will. Jesus is anointed with the power of God's Spirit, but he will arouse opposition and be put to death.

For reflection: What are the implications for me of Jesus being the Son of God?

What happens after Jesus' baptism provides a glimpse of the Trinity. God speaks as the Father, proclaiming Jesus to be his Son; the Holy Spirit descends upon Jesus. Jesus' baptism reveals the meaning of our own

---

BACKGROUND: SON OF GOD The title "son (or "sons") of God" carries a variety of meanings in the Old Testament. It is applied to angels and members of the heavenly court (Job 1:6; 2:1; 38:7). It is used to refer to the people of God (Exod 4:22; Deut 14:1). A king could be referred to as a son of God (2 Sam 7:14; Psalm 2:7), as could a devout Israelite (Wisd 2:18). It is not, however, a title explicitly associated with the Messiah: no prophecy refers to the Messiah as the Son of God. When the title "Son of God" is applied to Jesus in the gospels or in Paul's letters, it carries a far greater meaning than in the Old Testament, since it refers to Jesus' unique relationship with God as his Father. This is particularly developed in the Gospel of John. Paul focuses on what Jesus is able to do to bring us salvation because he is the Son of God (Rom 5:10; 8:3, 32; Gal 4:4-5; Col 1:13). In later centuries, the church reflected on what Jesus' sonship meant in terms of his divinity. The Council of Nicaea in 325 proclaimed that the "Lord Jesus Christ, the Son of God" is "true God from true God, begotten not made, consubstantial with the Father"—"one in Being with the Father" in the current English wording of the Nicene Creed used in the liturgy. The Council of Chalcedon, held in 451, proclaimed that Jesus Christ is one person with two natures, a divine nature and a human nature, so he is both fully divine and fully human.

---

baptism. In baptism we receive the Spirit who manifested himself at the baptism of Jesus. Each of us is adopted to become what Jesus is: a child of our heavenly Father (see Rom 8:14-17; Gal 4:4-7). Jesus' final instruction to his followers will be to "make disciples of all nations, baptizing them in the name of the Father, and of the Son, and of the holy Spirit" (28:19).

For reflection: What does it mean for me that I am a child of God?

CHAPTER 4

ORIENTATION: *God has proclaimed that Jesus is his Son (3:17). But what kind of Son is he? Satan tests Jesus' identity as the Son of God.*

The Testing of the Son of God

[1] Then Jesus was led by the Spirit into the desert to be tempted by the devil. [2] He fasted for forty days and forty nights, and afterwards he was hungry. [3] The tempter approached and said to him, "If you are the Son of God, command that these stones become loaves of bread." [4] He said in reply, "It is written:

'One does not live by bread alone,
    but by every word that comes forth
        from the mouth of God.'"

[5] Then the devil took him to the holy city, and made him stand on the parapet of the temple, [6] and said to him, "If you are the Son of God, throw yourself down. For it is written:

'He will command his angels concerning you'
    and 'with their hands they will support you,
  lest you dash your foot against a stone.'"

[7] Jesus answered him, "Again it is written, 'You shall not put the Lord, your God, to the test.'" [8] Then the devil took him up to a very high mountain, and showed him all the kingdoms of the world in their magnificence, [9] and he said to him, "All these I shall give to you, if you will prostrate yourself and worship me." [10] At this, Jesus said to him, "Get away, Satan! It is written:

'The Lord, your God, shall you worship
  and him alone shall you serve.'"

[11] Then the devil left him and, behold, angels came and ministered to him.
    Gospel parallels: Mark 1:12-13; Luke 4:1-13
    OT:Exod 34:28; Deut 6:13, 16; 8:2-3; Psalm 91:11-12
    NT:Heb 4:15

1 Matthew wrote his gospel as a continuous account without chapter breaks. Chapter divisions were introduced later, and they sometimes interrupt the flow of Matthew's account, as happens here. The Spirit descended upon Jesus, God proclaimed Jesus to be his Son (3:16-17), and **then Jesus was led by the Spirit into the desert to be tempted by the devil.** The Holy Spirit leads Jesus to a surprising destination for a surprising purpose. We might think that the role of the Holy Spirit should be to steer Jesus—and us—through green valleys and away from temptations. But the Spirit leads Jesus **into the desert,** where Israel was tested (Deut 8:2), so that Jesus may **be tempted** and tested. The **devil** is also known as Satan, a name that means "accuser" or "adversary." God has proclaimed Jesus to be his beloved Son (3:17); now Jesus' sonship will be put to the test. Jesus is not immune to temptations and testing; the letter to the Hebrews states that Jesus was "tested in every way" that we are tested (Heb 4:15).

The Spirit: See page 21

For reflection: Do I accept that Jesus experienced temptations?

Jesus was **led** by the Spirit into the desert: the Greek literally reads "led up." Geographically, the Judean wilderness lies at a higher elevation than the Jordan River, where Jesus was baptized (3:13).

BACKGROUND: SATAN In Hebrew, the word *satan* means "adversary" or "accuser." Satan (literally "the satan," "the accuser") appears in the Book of Job as an angelic prosecuting attorney who puts humans to the test (Job 1:6-12; 2:1-7). In Job this accuser is a member of God's heavenly court, not an evil spirit opposed to God (see also Zech 3:1-2). In late Old Testament times, however, Satan began to be thought of as an evil spirit (see 1 Chron 21:1). Nonbiblical writings from shortly before the time of Jesus describe the fall of some angels, the chief of whom is variously called Mastema, Satan, and Belial or Beliar. In the New Testament, this evil spirit is likewise called a variety of names, including "Satan," "the devil," "Beelzebul" (Matt 12:24-27; Mark 3:22; Luke 11:15-19), and "Beliar" (2 Cor 6:15), and is portrayed as the chief of evil spirits and demons (Matt 12:24; Luke 11:15). While demons are inferior to God, they can influence or control individuals and events. The gospels present Satan as the ruler of this world (Matt 4:8-9; Luke 4:5-6; John 12:31; 14:30; 16:11; see also 1 John 5:19); the coming of God's kingdom abolishes the reign of Satan. *Related topics: Demons, unclean spirits (page 177), Nonbiblical writings (page 198).*

---

2 Jesus is not immediately tested by the devil. First **he fasted for forty days and forty nights.** Forty is a biblical round number indicating an extended period. It is not obvious why Jesus **fasted.** Jews fasted when too grief stricken to eat, but Jesus had nothing to mourn. Jews fasted also as an act of penitence, but Jesus hardly needed to do penance for his sins. Fasting had become a pious practice for many Jews, and Jesus approved of such fasting if done properly (6:16-18). Yet during his public ministry Jesus apparently neither fasted (11:18-19) nor required his disciples to fast (9:14). Perhaps Matthew's choice of words provides a clue to the nature of Jesus' fast: Jesus **fasted for forty days and forty nights.** This expression echoes Exodus's account of Moses being in God's presence on Mount Sinai: "Moses stayed there with the LORD for forty days and forty nights, without eating any food or drinking any water" (Exod 34:28). If one could be too grief stricken to eat, so might one be so caught up in the presence of God that no thought is given to matters like eating. I interpret Jesus' fasting as a by-product of his communion with God, after God declared him to be his beloved Son (3:17). I also interpret Matthew's next words in this light: **and afterwards he was hungry.** Jesus was not aware of hunger during his time of communion with his Father but **afterwards** noticed that **he was hungry.**

Fasting: See page 113

For reflection: How do I understand the purpose of Jesus' fast?

3 **The tempter approached:** Matthew characterizes the devil as **the tempter,** indicating that the devil's function is to tempt and test (see also 1 Thess 3:5). In Matthew's account, **the tempter approached** Jesus after Jesus had fasted for forty days and nights (verse 2). The devil waits to tempt Jesus until Jesus' time of special communion with his Father is over and Jesus is physically weakened by hunger.

The tempter **said to him, "If you are the Son of God, command that these stones become loaves of bread."** The tempter's **if** does not mean that the tempter does not know whether Jesus is **the Son of God:** that has been publicly proclaimed (3:17; see also 8:28-29). Rather, the tempter's words imply that since Jesus is the Son of God, he should use his power for his own advantage. He is hungry, so he should **command that these stones become loaves of bread** for him to eat.

Son of God: See page 52

56

4 He said in reply, "It is written: 'One does not live by bread alone, but by every word that comes forth from the mouth of God.'" Jesus' response is consistent with his not eating because he was wrapped up in communion with his Father. Jesus quotes a passage from Deuteronomy: **One does not live by bread alone** (see Deut 8:3). The word translated **one** means "a human being"; the Son of God shares our human condition. Human beings do **not live by bread alone, but by every word that comes forth from the mouth of God.** Human life is not merely a matter of satisfying bodily needs and of physically surviving: God created humans to enter into relationship with him. Our needs are an opportunity to trust in God's care for us, as Jesus will teach his followers (6:25-34). Jesus is hungry, but he will not capitalize on his status as the Son of God to provide a banquet for himself, or even a simple meal of bread. His sonship means trusting in his Father's care for him.

> Remember how for forty years now the LORD, your God, has directed all your journeying in the desert, so as to test you by affliction and find out whether or not is was your intention to keep his commandments. He therefore let you be afflicted with hunger, and then fed you with manna, a food unknown to you and your fathers, in order to show you that not by bread alone does man live, but by every word that comes forth from the mouth of the LORD.
>
> Deuteronomy 8:2-3

> For reflection: Do my needs distract me from God or help me grow in trust in him?

5 Since Jesus trusts in God's care for him, the tempter tests Jesus' trust. **Then the devil took him to the holy city, and made him stand on the parapet of the temple.** The **holy city** is Jerusalem (Isaiah 52:1), holy because of God's special presence in **the temple.** The **parapet** of the Temple cannot be identified precisely. Herod's expansion of the Temple complex created towering buildings and walls, a fall from which would be fatal.

Jerusalem: See page 440
Temple: See page 442

6 The devil **said to him, "If you are the Son of God, throw yourself down."** Leap from the parapet, he says. Let's see if you really trust God! The tempter

tries to twist Jesus' trust into presumption—into a demand that God follow one's stage directions. **If you are the Son of God,** prove it with a spectacular display and gain the adulation of all who witness it. Jesus will face much the same temptation again, from the cross (27:39-44).

Since Jesus is guided by Scripture (verse 4), the devil bolsters his temptation with a quote from Scripture: **For it is written: "He will command his angels concerning you" / and "with their hands they will support you, / lest you dash your foot against a stone."** Psalm 91 poetically proclaims God's care of his people; the devil invites Jesus to use Scripture to manipulate God.

Angels: See page 33

> For God commands the angels
> to guard you in all your ways.
> With their hands they shall support you,
> lest you strike your foot against a stone.
> Psalm 91:11-12

For reflection: Do I trust God to care for me? Have I ever tried to manipulate God?

7 **Jesus answered him, "Again it is written, 'You shall not put the Lord, your God, to the test.'"** Jesus quotes a verse of Deuteronomy that refers to Israel's time in the desert, where Israel put God to the test (Deut 6:16; see also Exod 17:1-7). Jesus will not use his status as the Son of God to preserve his life (26:53) or work wonders simply to amaze the crowds (9:23-25). Nor will he, even as the Son of God, try to force God's hand and put God to the test.

> You shall not put the LORD, your God, to the test.
> Deuteronomy 6:16

8 If the tempter cannot get Jesus to capitalize on his sonship, perhaps he can get him to abandon his sonship. **Then the devil took him up to a very high mountain, and showed him all the kingdoms of the world in their magnificence.** There is no mountain from which one can see all the kingdoms of the world, making this temptation easier to understand as a vision.

9 **and he said to him, "All these I shall give to you."** The devil speaks as if it is in his power to grant kingdoms to whomever he wishes (John's gospel calls Satan "the ruler of this world"—John 12:31; 16:11). In the view of the gospels, one is either part of the reign of God or of the reign of Satan; there is ultimately no neutral middle ground. I will give you the kingdoms of the world, Satan tells Jesus, **if you will prostrate yourself and worship me.** Satan no longer begins his temptation by saying to Jesus, "If you are the Son of God," for he is inviting Jesus to renounce his divine sonship and to switch his allegiance to Satan. Satan offers Jesus all he can as a payoff: power over all the kingdoms of the world. Jesus will receive all power in heaven and on earth (28:18), but from his Father, not from Satan, and Jesus will receive it by undergoing crucifixion and resurrection.

10 **At this, Jesus said to him, "Get away, Satan!"** Jesus commands Satan to depart. Not only is Jesus able to withstand Satan's temping, but he has the authority to order Satan away. Jesus again turns to Scripture—and again to the Book of Deuteronomy—as an expression of God's will for him. **It is written: "The Lord, your God, shall you worship / and him alone shall you serve."** The words **worship** and **serve** are parallel terms, each throwing light on the meaning of the other. We express worship of God by serving God, and we serve God as an act of worship. As the Son, Jesus worships and serves God, giving his allegiance to God alone. He will serve God to the point of giving up his life (20:28).

> The LORD, your God, shall your fear; him shall you serve, and
> by his name shall you swear.
>
> Deuteronomy 6:13

For reflection: How do I worship God? serve God?

Jesus' testing in the desert reveals him to be a faithful and obedient Son who will not use his status for his own advantage or to manipulate God; Jesus is a Son who is wholeheartedly set on serving God. We also face temptations to seek our own comfort, to manipulate God, to be in charge; how we respond to these temptations reveals what kind of daughters and sons of God we are.

For reflection: What temptations test me? How do my values and choices demonstrate that I am a child of God?

11 **Then the devil left him and, behold, angels came and ministered to him.** Satan goes away, as Jesus ordered him. Angels **ministered** to Jesus: the expression can also be translated "served" and can mean serving food (see 8:15). While the angels might have given Jesus spiritual consolation, Matthew's account can also mean that they brought Jesus food, as angels had brought food to Elijah in the desert (1 Kings 19:5-8).

ORIENTATION: *Matthew tells his readers that Jesus moves from Nazareth to Capernaum but is silent about many things we would expect an author to include if he were writing a biography. Matthew focuses on the significance of Jesus' settling in Capernaum.*

Light Rises on Capernaum
12 When he heard that John had been arrested, he withdrew to Galilee. **13** He left Nazareth and went to live in Capernaum by the sea, in the region of Zebulun and Naphtali, **14** that what had been said through Isaiah the prophet might be fulfilled:

> **15** "Land of Zebulun and land of Naphtali,
>   the way to the sea, beyond the Jordan,
>   Galilee of the Gentiles,
> **16** the people who sit in darkness
>   have seen a great light,
> on those dwelling in a land overshadowed by death
>   light has arisen."

Gospel parallels: Mark 1:14; Luke 4:14, 31
OT:2 Kings 15:29; Isaiah 8:23–9:6

12 **When he heard that John had been arrested, he withdrew to Galilee.** Matthew mentions the arrest of John the Baptist in passing; he will later recount John's death (14:3-12). Matthew does not tell us how much time has passed after Jesus' days in the desert (4:1-11) before Jesus learns of John's arrest. Nor does Matthew indicate where Jesus is during this time, other than somewhere outside of Galilee. **When he heard** of John's arrest, Jesus **withdrew to Galilee.** John's arrest leads Jesus to go to Galilee, but why Jesus would do so is unclear: John was arrested by Herod Antipas (14:3), who ruled Galilee.

Galilee: See page 68

13 **He left Nazareth and went to live in Capernaum by the sea, in the region of Zebulun and Naphtali.** Matthew continues to sketch Jesus' moves without filling in the whole picture. Jesus returns to **Nazareth,** where he had grown up (2:23), but we are not told how long he stays there or his reasons for leaving (13:54-58 may shed some light). Jesus **went to live in Capernaum.** He will make Capernaum his base of operations in Galilee (9:1). What motivates Jesus to choose Capernaum is not explained. Matthew notes that Capernaum is **by the sea**—it is on the shore of the Sea of Galilee—and **in the region of Zebulun and Naphtali.** Zebulun and Naphtali were two of the twelve tribes of Israel, but their tribal presence was a distant memory. Capernaum was in the area that had been allocated to the tribe of **Naphtali** (Joshua 19:32-39). The tribal lands of **Zebulun** were to the southwest (Joshua 19:10-16), where Nazareth lay. In the time of Jesus, these regions were simply part of Galilee. To

BACKGROUND: CAPERNAUM lay on the northwest shore of the Sea of Galilee, along a road that led from the Mediterranean to Bethsaida and ultimately to Damascus. Since Capernaum was near the border between the territory governed by Herod Antipas and the territory governed by Philip, there was a customs post there to collect taxes on goods being transported between the territories. Capernaum was a fishing and farming village covering about twenty-five acres, with a population estimated to have been between six hundred and fifteen hundred. Its houses were one story and small, with walls of unworked stones and flat thatched roofs; its narrow winding streets of packed earth would have been muddy during the rainy season and dusty the rest of the year. Archaeologists have not found signs of wealth in any of its houses; Capernaum was a village of ordinary rural Galileans. Nor have they found evidence of public buildings, other than what seems to be the remains of a synagogue, which probably served as a community center. Jesus moved from Nazareth to Capernaum and made Capernaum his base of operations for his public ministry; Mark and Matthew indicate that he stayed in the house of Peter. In later centuries there was a continuing Christian presence in Capernaum, alongside its Jewish population. Capernaum was abandoned in the seventh century, following the Islamic conquest of Palestine. *Related topics: Farming (page 263), Fishing (page 65), Galilee (page 68), Peter's house (page 148).*

mention their ancient names was akin to a resident of Missouri saying today, "I live in the Louisiana Purchase."

Nazareth: See page 38

14 Matthew had a reason for associating Capernaum with ancient geographical designations. Whatever Jesus' motives for moving to Capernaum might have been, Matthew understands his settling in Capernaum as the fulfillment of a prophecy. Jesus went to live in Capernaum **that what had been said through Isaiah the prophet might be fulfilled:**

15 **Land of Zebulun and land of Naphtali, / the way to the sea, beyond the Jordan, / Galilee of the Gentiles.** Around 732 B.C. Assyria invaded the kingdom of Israel and annexed its northern portion—including the lands of **Zebulun** and **Naphtali**—into the Assyrian Empire (2 Kings 15:29). Assyria deported a number of Israelites and brought in foreigners to replace them, giving the region a mixed Jewish-Gentile population as indicated by the designation, **Galilee of the Gentiles.** In the time of Jesus, Galilee had a predominantly Jewish population, but mention of its Gentile past foreshadows Jesus' mission being extended to Gentiles (see 28:19; the word here translated as "Gentiles" is the same word translated as "nations" in 28:19).

After Assyria's invasion and annexation, Isaiah prophesied that a child would be born into David's royal family, a "Prince of Peace," who would take the throne and liberate the lands of Zebulun and Naphtali from Assyrian rule, bringing light and joy to those who were living in the gloom of foreign occupation. He would rule justly, fulfilling hopes that God's people would enjoy peace under the rule of an ideal king.

First he degraded the land of Zebulun and the land of Naphtali;
but in the end he has glorified the seaward road, the land west of
the Jordan, the District of the Gentiles. . . .

The people who walked in darkness
have seen a great light;
Upon those who dwelt in the land of gloom
a light has shone. . . .
For a child is born to us, a son is given us;
upon his shoulder dominion rests.

> They name him Wonder-Counselor, God-Hero,
>> Father-Forever, Prince of Peace. . . .
> From David's throne, and over his kingdom,
>> which he confirms and sustains,
> By judgment and justice,
>> both now and forever.
>> > Isaiah 8:23; 9:1, 5-6

16 By settling in Capernaum, Jesus fulfills Isaiah's prophecy of light shining on those living in this region: **The people who sit in darkness / have seen a great light, / on those dwelling in a land overshadowed by death / light has arisen.** Matthew does not quote Isaiah's entire prophecy, but his Jewish Christian readers would have known that it spoke of a "Wonder-Counselor, God-Hero, Father-Forever, Prince of Peace" who would reign over David's kingdom (Isaiah 9:5-6). Jesus, the Son of David (1:1), fulfills Isaiah's prophecy by filling it with greater meaning: Jesus will establish the kingdom of God. Matthew proclaims that Jesus is a **great light** that dispels the **darkness.**

For reflection: What might I learn from what Matthew chooses to omit and chooses to include in his account of Jesus' moving to Capernaum?

ORIENTATION: *Jesus begins his public ministry by announcing that the kingdom of God is at hand and inviting people to enter it.*

Jesus Calls Disciples

[17] From that time on, Jesus began to preach and say, "Repent, for the kingdom of heaven is at hand."

[18] As he was walking by the Sea of Galilee, he saw two brothers, Simon who is called Peter, and his brother Andrew, casting a net into the sea; they were fishermen. [19] He said to them, "Come after me, and I will make you fishers of men." [20] At once they left their nets and followed him. [21] He walked along from there and saw two other brothers, James, the son of Zebedee, and his brother John. They were in a boat, with their father Zebedee, mending their nets. He called them, [22] and immediately they left their boat and their father and followed him.

Gospel parallels: Mark 1:14-20; Luke 5:1-11
NT: John 1:35-42

17 **From that time on:** Matthew dates the beginning of Jesus' public ministry to his settling in Capernaum (4:13). **From that time on** indicates that Jesus is embarking on a new stage of his life (Matthew will later use the same expression to indicate another major turning point: 16:21). After moving to Capernaum **Jesus began to preach:** he had not previously preached. Jesus begins his mission with the message, **Repent, for the kingdom of heaven is at hand,** and this message will be the keynote of his entire ministry. Jesus does not immediately explain what he means by his call to **repent,** nor does he offer a description of the **kingdom of heaven.** The meaning of Jesus' message about God's kingdom will unfold in the course of Mathew's gospel. Repentance means a changed life, and the kingdom of heaven means the active rule of God. But is a changed life a condition for entering into the reign of God, or is a changed life a consequence of God actively reigning—or are there elements of both views in Jesus' message?

Repentance: See page 42

Kingdom of heaven: See page 266

For reflection: What do Jesus' words, "Repent, for the kingdom of heaven is at hand," mean to me?

18 **He was walking by the Sea of Galilee,** a freshwater lake thirteen miles long and seven miles at its widest. Since Jesus has moved to Capernaum, a fishing and farming village on the northwest shore of the Sea of Galilee (4:13), he is apparently walking along the lakeshore near Capernaum. **He saw two brothers, Simon who is called Peter, and his brother Andrew, casting a net into the sea; they were fishermen.** Jesus will not give Simon the name "Peter" until later (16:18), but Matthew usually calls him Peter because that name was more familiar to his readers. **Peter** and **his brother Andrew** were **fishermen.** Commercial fishing provided only a modest income, for catches were heavily taxed. Peter and Andrew were **casting a net into the sea;** Matthew's Greek word for **net** indicates a circular net thrown by hand. Jesus comes to Peter and Andrew while they are going about their everyday lives.

Sea of Galilee: See page 153

19 **He said to them, "Come after me."** Jesus takes the initiative; Peter and Andrew do not approach Jesus and volunteer. **Come after me** is not an invitation to be Jesus' casual traveling companion but a call to discipleship,

involving not only learning from Jesus but imitating him. Jesus' statement **I will make you fishers of men** promises Peter and Andrew a share in Jesus' mission; they will draw others into the kingdom of God as a fisherman gathers fish in a net. Sharing Jesus' mission is an essential element of being a disciple of Jesus. This is not something that Peter and Andrew are equipped to do: Jesus will have to **make** them into fishers of men and women, transforming them to carry out his work.

In Matthew's account, the first thing Jesus does after announcing that the kingdom of heaven is at hand (4:17) is to call individuals to become his disciples. His calling disciples indicates that the kingdom of heaven is a not a physical location but men and women in relationship with God through Jesus.

For reflection: How did Jesus call me to be his disciple? What share has Jesus given me in his mission?

20 The response of Peter and Andrew to Jesus' invitation is immediate and complete: **at once they left their nets** and their old way of life **and followed him.** Matthew presents Jesus' call as abrupt and their responses as equally abrupt: it is as if their first meeting with Jesus changes their lives.

BACKGROUND: FISHING   In the first century, the Sea of Galilee was ringed with villages with harbors and was commercially fished—as it has been from ancient until modern times. Commercial fishing activities, rather than sport-fishing, are reflected in the gospels. There were about twenty species of fish in the Sea of Galilee, and three made up the bulk of commercial catches: the sardine, the carp, and the musht (*Tilapia galilea*). Musht feed on plankton and must be caught with nets, not with hooks and bait. Musht weigh up to three pounds and swim in schools; the great nettings of fish reported in the gospels were probably catches of musht. Fishermen used various forms of nets, including nets that could be cast and dragnets that were deployed from boats. Remains of a first-century fishing boat were discovered in 1986 buried in the mud near the shore of the Sea of Galilee at Ginnosar (ancient Gennesaret), an area Jesus visited (Matt 14:34; Mark 6:53). This boat, 26 1/2 feet long, 7 1/2 feet wide, and 4 1/2 feet high, was apparently typical of the fishing boats mentioned in the gospels. It had a rounded stern and may have had decks fore and aft. It would have had a small square sail and a crew of four rowers and a rudder man. It could have carried an additional ten to twelve passengers when it was not transporting nets and fish.

Matthew skips over any previous encounters they might have had in order to focus on the most important elements of their discipleship: Jesus called, and they responded. They **followed him,** an expression that means they became his disciples (see 8:19, 22; 9:9; 10:38; 16:24; 19:21). For Peter and Andrew to follow Jesus meant to travel with him, and this necessarily required leaving things like nets behind. Peter will later say, "We have given up everything and followed you" (19:27).

21 **He walked along from there**—along the shore of the Sea of Galilee—**and saw two other brothers, James, the son of Zebedee, and his brother John. They were in a boat, with their father Zebedee, mending their nets.** Matthew uses a different word for nets here; they were possibly dragnets, deployed from a boat. We are not told whether Jesus had had previous contact with James and John; the essential point is that **he called them,** inviting them to become his disciples. The initiative once again rests with Jesus, choosing whom he chooses. (Why didn't Jesus invite Zebedee to be a disciple? Matthew doesn't tell us.)

22 **and immediately they left their boat and their father and followed him.** As did Peter and Andrew, James and John respond **immediately** and completely. They leave behind not only their nets and boat but their **father,**

BACKGROUND: DISCIPLE Generally, a first-century Jewish disciple was someone who studied for a period of time under a teacher. Once this training was complete, the disciple could in turn become a teacher, gathering disciples and passing on to them what he had learned. However, Jesus' call of men and women to follow him involved more than their studying under him. Jesus invited them into a lifelong personal relationship with him, not a temporary apprenticeship. Being a disciple of Jesus meant sharing his life and accompanying him as he traveled about, taught, and healed. Hence Jesus issued his invitations to discipleship by saying, "Come after me" (Mark 1:17) or "Follow me" (Mark 2:14). At the same time, some of Jesus' disciples did not accompany him in his travels: the gospels of Luke and John portray Martha, Mary, and Lazarus as remaining at home and extending hospitality to Jesus. The gospels show Jesus taking the initiative in inviting men and women to become his disciples, rather than would-be followers taking the first step toward discipleship. Becoming a disciple of Jesus could involve some break with one's family and livelihood, and potentially even giving up one's life. That was the cost of sharing the life of the one who would lay down his life for the sake of others.

Zebedee, as well: the call of Jesus takes priority over all else and all others (see 10:35-37). Jesus' call to repent because of the coming of the reign of God (verse 17) is a call demanding a total response.

In the course of his public ministry Jesus will call many to be his disciples; Matthew relates the calls of only five: the four fishermen and later Matthew (9:9). These examples highlight what is at the heart of all discipleship: Jesus' personal call and our response.

For reflection: How did I first respond when Jesus invited me to be his follower? What is my response to him today?

ORIENTATION: *Matthew provides a preview of Jesus' public ministry as an introduction to the next five chapters of his gospel.*

Jesus Proclaims Good News by Word and Deed
[23] He went around all of Galilee, teaching in their synagogues, proclaiming the gospel of the kingdom, and curing every disease and illness among the people. [24] His fame spread to all of Syria, and they brought to him all who were sick with various diseases and racked with pain, those who were possessed, lunatics, and paralytics, and he cured them. [25] And great crowds from Galilee, the Decapolis, Jerusalem, and Judea, and from beyond the Jordan followed him.
Gospel parallels: Mark 1:28, 39; 3:7-11; Luke 4:44; 6:17-19

23 **He went around all of Galilee:** Jesus used Capernaum as his base (4:13) but traveled through **all of Galilee,** where most of his public ministry takes place in Matthew's account. Matthew summarizes Jesus' activities as **teaching in their synagogues, proclaiming the gospel of the kingdom, and curing every disease and illness among the people.**

Matthew lists **teaching** first among the activities of Jesus. Matthew's gospel highlights the teachings of Jesus, gathering them together by topic or theme. The first collection of Jesus' teachings will begin in a few verses and fill three chapters (chapters 5–7, the Sermon on the Mount).

For reflection: Am I prepared to hear and heed what Jesus teaches?

Jesus taught **in their synagogues:** Jews assembled every Sabbath (Saturday) for Scripture reading, teaching, and prayer, and these assemblies provided occasions for Jesus to teach. Since assemblies normally took place only on the Sabbath (the rest of the week being taken up with work for the majority of Galileans, who struggled to get by), Jesus' teaching in **synagogues** implies that he did so over a period of time. Matthew's expression **their synagogues** is a bit odd, for we can wonder who **their** refers to. In context, it could mean those who lived in Galilee. But here and elsewhere where Matthew's gospel makes references to **their synagogues** (9:35; 10:17; 12:9; 13:54; see also 23:34), the phrase may reflect conditions at the time of Matthew, when synagogues increasingly came under the control of leaders who rejected Jesus as the Messiah: Matthew's Jewish Christian readers may have thought of synagogues as "their synagogues" rather than "our synagogues."

Synagogue: See page 104

Matthew lists as the second component of Jesus' public ministry **proclaiming the gospel of the kingdom.** Listing this activity between **teaching**

BACKGROUND: GALILEE was the northern region of ancient Palestine. Most of the Galilean sites mentioned in the gospels were in what was considered lower Galilee in the time of Jesus: a roughly circular area twenty to twenty-five miles across, with the Sea of Galilee on the east and the coastal hills of the Mediterranean on the west. Nazareth was near the southern edge of lower Galilee, and Capernaum was in the northeast. The general character of Galilee was rural: the two most significant cities in lower Galilee—Sepphoris and Tiberias—seem to have had little cultural impact on those who did not live within them. Most of the inhabitants of Galilee made their living as farmers or fishermen and lived in villages or small towns. Galilee contained the estates of its ruler, Herod Antipas, and his wealthy supporters, and some Galileans worked as tenant farmers or day laborers on these estates. There was not much of a middle class in Galilee: there was a small wealthy elite and many ordinary and rather poor people. The Galilee of Jesus was primarily the Galilee of ordinary people: while Jesus' message reached members of the upper class, the gospels never describe Jesus going into Sepphoris or Tiberias, even though Sepphoris lay only four miles from Nazareth, and Tiberias seven miles from Capernaum. Galilee during the ministry of Jesus has sometimes been described as a paganized area, a region of lax religious observance, and a hotbed of revolutionary nationalism, but none of these characterizations is accurate. In general, the Jews of rural Galilee were traditional in their religious practices, relatively uninfluenced by Greek culture, and slow to heed calls to revolution. *Related topic: Herod Antipas (page 298).*

and **curing** indicates that it is central to the mission of Jesus: Jesus' activities in word and deed were integral aspects of his **proclaiming** that the kingdom of heaven was at hand (4:17). Jesus taught women and men how to live under God's reign, and he freed them from the effects of evil. Matthew characterizes Jesus' message of the kingdom as **the gospel,** a word that means "good news." It is good news that the reign of God is being established through Jesus' teaching and healing. Matthew's Jewish Christian readers might have recalled a prophecy of Isaiah that spoke of the "good news" that "your God is King!" (Isaiah 52:7).

Gospel: See page 211

For reflection: Do I embrace the message of Jesus as good news for me?

Matthew lists the third characteristic activity of Jesus' public ministry: he went about **curing every disease and illness among the people.** Matthew literally speaks of Jesus curing **every disease** and *every* **illness:** there was no affliction beyond the scope of his healing power. Matthew will recount examples of Jesus' healings in chapters 8 and 9. His healings were acts of compassion, but they had additional significance. Sickness was thought of as the consequence of sin (see John 9:1-2) or the result of demonic activity. As part of establishing the reign of God, Jesus conquers the powers of sin and evil (see 12:28) and repairs the damage they have caused.

For reflection: Do I consider any of my afflictions to be beyond Jesus' healing power?

Matthew's summary in verse 23 is repeated in 9:35 as a sign that the intervening chapters spell out how Jesus proclaimed the reign of God in word (chapters 5-7) and deed (chapters 8-9).

24 **His fame spread to all of Syria:** word of Jesus' healings and teachings spread to **Syria,** which lay to the north and east of Galilee. If Matthew's gospel was written in Syria, Matthew's first readers might have understood Jesus' fame spreading to Syria as a foreshadowing of the gospel message coming to them.

Because of Jesus' **fame** as a healer, **they brought to him all who were sick with various diseases and racked with pain.** The sick are **brought** to

Jesus if they are too infirm to come on their own. The expression **various diseases** is a general term covering many afflictions; **racked with pain** is a vivid description of their effect. Matthew lists a sampling of the specific afflictions of those brought to Jesus: **those who were possessed, lunatics, and paralytics.** The **possessed** are under the influence of evil spirits. The English word **lunatics** (see also 17:15) is from the Latin word for moon, *luna*. Lunatics is a translation of a Greek word that means "moonstruck." In ancient times, it was thought that phases of the moon had an effect on maladies such as seizures; Psalm 121 promises God's protection from the moon's harm (Psalm 121:6). **Paralytics** are spoken of in the same breath as those suffering demonic possession and lunacy, as if paralysis was also an affliction with evil causes. Whatever the affliction of those brought to Jesus, **he cured them:** Jesus has the power to overcome every evil.

25 **And great crowds from Galilee, the Decapolis, Jerusalem, and Judea, and from beyond the Jordan followed him.** Jesus' fame spread from Galilee to the surrounding regions, and **great crowds** came to him. The **Decapolis** was a largely Gentile region east of Galilee; Matthew does not specify whether those who came to Jesus from the Decapolis were Jews or Gentiles. Matthew puts **Jerusalem** in the middle of his list, hinting at its centrality for Jews. **Judea** was the region around Jerusalem, and **beyond the Jordan** refers to a territory to the east of the Jordan River that was ruled by Herod Antipas. These five areas were once ruled by King David; the Son of David attracts crowds from the historical lands of the kingdom of David. The crowds who came to Jesus followed him. Following Jesus is a term for discipleship (4:20, 22); these crowds respond favorably to Jesus. They will be a prime fishing ground when the disciples undertake their mission as fishers of men (4:19; see also 9:36-38; 10:6).

Decapolis: See page 156
Jerusalem: See page 440
Judea: See page 397

CHAPTER 5

ORIENTATION: *In chapters 5 through 7, Jesus teaches how to live under the reign of God now in order to be part of the kingdom of God when it is established in its fullness. This collection of teachings is popularly known as the Sermon on the Mount.*

The Beatitudes
1 When he saw the crowds, he went up the mountain, and after he had sat down, his disciples came to him. 2 He began to teach them, saying:

> **3 "Blessed are the poor in spirit,**
>   **for theirs is the kingdom of heaven.**
> **4 Blessed are they who mourn,**
>   **for they will be comforted.**
> **5 Blessed are the meek,**
>   **for they will inherit the land.**
> **6 Blessed are they who hunger and thirst for righteousness,**
>   **for they will be satisfied.**
> **7 Blessed are the merciful,**
>   **for they will be shown mercy.**
> **8 Blessed are the clean of heart,**
>   **for they will see God.**
> **9 Blessed are the peacemakers,**
>   **for they will be called children of God.**
> **10 Blessed are they who are persecuted for the sake of righteousness,**
>   **for theirs is the kingdom of heaven.**

11 Blessed are you when they insult you and persecute you and utter every kind of evil against you [falsely] because of me. 12 Rejoice and be glad, for your reward will be great in heaven. Thus they persecuted the prophets who were before you."

Gospel parallels: Luke 6:20-23
OT:Psalm 37:11; Isaiah 61:1-2, 7

1 **When he saw the crowds:** Matthew has told of great crowds coming to Jesus to be healed (4:24-25). Seeing these crowds, Jesus **went up the mountain.** God's revelation to Moses took place on a mountain (Exod

71

19:3; 24:18; 34:4), and God's revelation through Jesus will also take place on a mountain (possibly one of the high hills overlooking the Sea of Galilee, but its location is not important for Matthew). Jesus **sat down:** Jewish teachers normally taught while seated. Jesus' **disciples came to him.** Matthew has described the call of four disciples (4:18-22), but his account reads as if Jesus had also invited others to follow him (see also 10:1).

Disciple: See page 66

2 **He began to teach them.** Jesus instructs his disciples, but his teachings are not addressed exclusively to them: the crowds (verse 1) overhear what Jesus teaches (see 7:28-29). Matthew has told his readers that Jesus went about "proclaiming the gospel of the kingdom" (4:23), but Matthew has quoted only two utterances of Jesus since he began his public ministry: "Repent, for the kingdom of heaven is at hand" (4:17) and "Come after me" (4:19). Now Matthew presents teachings that are part of the "gospel of the kingdom," teachings that spell out what it means to repent and to come after Jesus. Jesus speaks to his disciples and describes the life they are called to live, but allows the crowd to listen as an invitation for them to join the disciples in living under God's reign. Matthew intends his readers to likewise listen to Jesus' words as an instruction to them.

3 Jesus begins by proclaiming, **Blessed are the poor in spirit, / for theirs is the kingdom of heaven.** Pronouncing someone **blessed** or happy was an established pattern of speech in the biblical world, a way of congratulating or praising someone (see Luke 11:27-28). Today we label these pronouncements "beatitudes."

Jesus proclaims that **the poor in spirit** are very fortunate and blessed. There are different Hebrew and Greek words for different classes of poor people. The word used here is not the word for the working poor, who made up the bulk of the population of Galilee. The word **poor** here means those with no means of support, beggars at the bottom of the social order. Such **poor** had to depend on others to survive, and this engendered an attitude of dependence. In the Psalms, the poor and afflicted cry out to God for help (Psalms 70:6; 86:1). The expression **poor in spirit** highlights the attitude of helplessness and dependence that comes from being destitute—or from recognizing one's fundamental and absolute dependence on God—an attitude that is the opposite of self-assuredness and arrogance. The **poor in spirit** realize their own fragility and emptiness and turn to God.

72

Jesus pronounces the **poor in spirit** to be in a **blessed** and happy condition; they are fortunate because **theirs is the kingdom of heaven.** The word **theirs** can have the connotation of "theirs *alone.*" Jesus' listeners would generally have understood the **kingdom of heaven** to be God ruling over everything at the end of this age. Jesus proclaims that the **poor in spirit** are **blessed** because they will be part of God's reign when it is established. But Jesus says more than that: he says that the poor in spirit are in a blessed condition now because theirs **is** the kingdom of heaven. The poor in spirit already participate in God's reign because their recognition that they are fragile and empty allows God to have unimpeded reign in their lives.

Kingdom of heaven: See page 266

Jesus' pronouncement is a shocking reversal of our usual way of thinking. We do not enter into God's reign by what we have or do, but by realizing what we do not have and cannot do, and by our turning to God in our emptiness.

For reflection: When have I turned to God in my emptiness?

4 **Blessed are they who mourn, / for they will be comforted.** Jesus does not specify what those who mourn are mourning about, but a key to understanding their mourning may be found in the other beatitudes. The eight

---

BACKGROUND: BEATITUDES A beatitude praises or congratulates someone for being fortunate, telling why or how they are fortunate. "A woman from the crowd called out and said to him, 'Blessed is the womb that carried you and the breasts at which you nursed.' He replied, 'Rather, blessed are those who hear the word of God and observe it'" (Luke 11:27-28). There are about sixty beatitudes in the Old Testament and (by one count) twenty-eight beatitudes in the New Testament. Psalm 1 is an extended beatitude. It begins with an exclamation, "Happy the man," or "the person," and then lays out the basis of the person's happiness: he or she avoids bad company and spends time meditating on Scripture (Psalm 1:1-2). By explaining why the person is fortunate, the beatitude usually encourages the behavior that is the basis of the person's happiness. Beatitudes may also describe the nature of the person's happiness; Psalm 1, for example, speaks of flourishing even in difficult circumstances (Psalm 1:3). Beatitudes are sometimes translated "Blessed is so and so," but a beatitude does not call down God's blessing on a person; it declares that the person is already fortunate in the eyes of God because of what the beatitude praises him or her for being or doing.

beatitudes do not refer to eight different groups of people but to eight characteristics shared by those who enter the reign of God. Those **who mourn** are poor in spirit (verse 3). Their mourning, then, is because of their deprivation and emptiness—and they may mourn as well God's seeming slowness in rescuing them. Despite their mourning, Jesus proclaims them to be fortunate, **for they will be comforted.** The grammatical construction used here (and in later beatitudes) implies that they will be comforted by God. Jesus is not saying that unhappy people are really happy even if they don't realize it; he knew sorrow himself (26:37-38). Jesus proclaims that when God establishes his reign, God will comfort those who grieve (see Rev 21:1-4).

> *For reflection: What has been my greatest grieving? What comforted me, or could comfort me?*

5 **Blessed are the meek, / for they will inherit the land.** Matthew's Jewish Christian readers would have heard a clear echo of Psalm 37: "The poor will possess the land" (Psalm 37:11). Some translations of Psalm 37 read, "The meek will possess the land." In the context of Psalm 37, **the land** they will possess is the land promised to the descendants of Abraham (Gen 12:7). All too often this land was seized by the powerful and greedy, leaving others landless and in need. Psalm 37 promises a reversal: the wicked will vanish, allowing the poor to take possession of the land and enjoy prosperity (Psalm 37:10-11).

> *Wait a little, and the wicked will be no more;*
> *look for them and they will not be there.*
> *But the poor will possess the land,*
> *will delight in great prosperity.*
> *Psalm 37:10-11*

Jesus' beatitude also promises a reversal. The **meek** are not mild-mannered or shy people; the meek are those who recognize their powerlessness—the poor in spirit. The **land** they will inherit is not a geographical territory but, in the context of the beatitudes, the kingdom of heaven (verses 3, 10). The meek will **inherit** it, as a bequest or gift. It is not something that they can earn: the poor in spirit have no earning power, materially or spiritually.

For reflection: In what ways am I meek? In what ways am I not meek?

Matthew's Jewish Christian readers would likely have heard echoes of a prophecy of Isaiah in the first three beatitudes. Isaiah spoke of someone being anointed with the spirit of God to proclaim glad tidings to the lowly and to comfort those who mourn. The prophecy goes on to promise a double inheritance of the land to those who had known shame and disgrace. Jesus, upon whom the Spirit descended (3:16), fulfills Isaiah's prophecy by proclaiming good news to those who are meek and mourning and poor in spirit: theirs is the kingdom of heaven.

> *The spirit of the Lord GOD is upon me,*
> *because the LORD has anointed me;*
> *He has sent me to bring glad tidings to the lowly,*
> *to heal the brokenhearted . . .*
> *to comfort all who mourn . . .*
> *Since their shame was double*
> *and disgrace and spittle were their portion,*
> *They shall have a double inheritance in their land,*
> *everlasting joy shall be theirs.*
> *Isaiah 61:1, 2, 7*

6 **Blessed are they who hunger and thirst for righteousness, / for they will be satisfied.** To **hunger** and **thirst** for something means to yearn intensely for it, as a starving person longs for food and someone dying of thirst craves water. **Righteousness** has different shades of meaning. It can be God's saving activity or humans doing God's will in response to God's saving activity. If those **who hunger and thirst for righteousness** are the poor in spirit, the meek and mourning, what are they hungering and thirsting for? They may long for God to set things right, vanquishing all that oppresses them. They may long to be set right themselves, so that they can live out God's will for them. Perhaps we cannot decide whether the accent in this beatitude falls on God's **righteousness** or on human **righteousness;** perhaps the **hunger and thirst** is for God to make all things right, including the one who hungers and thirsts. Their yearning is ultimately for God's kingdom to come.

For reflection: What are my most heartfelt longings?

Jesus promises that those who hunger and thirst for righteousness **will be satisfied;** the implication is "satisfied *by God*." Satisfaction comes through being included in God's plan of salvation. Being part of God's reign is the fulfillment of the deepest human longings.

7 **Blessed are the merciful, / for they will be shown mercy.** The poor in spirit realize their own affliction and fragility and can have sympathy and compassion for others who are afflicted and fragile. Being **merciful** includes helping those in need and forgiving those who harm us. The **merciful** are blessed, **for they will be shown mercy** by God. The beatitude does not imply that our mercy to others is the cause of God's mercy to us: God is merciful by nature (Exod 34:6). Our being unmerciful can, however, block God's mercy (6:12, 14-15). In the context of the beatitudes, the merciful will receive mercy when God establishes his reign. This will involve a judgment that sorts out good from evil; the merciful will be judged mercifully (25:31-40).

For reflection: What is the measure of my mercy?

8 **Blessed are the clean of heart, / for they will see God.** In the biblical view, the **heart** was the inner self, the seat of thinking, willing, and feeling. To be **clean of heart** means to be a person of integrity, wholeheartedly and single-mindedly devoted to God, without self-deception and mixed motives. Those who are **clean of heart,** who love God with their whole heart and soul and mind (22:37), **will see God.** To **see God** is an idiom for being united with God (see also 1 Cor 13:12; 1 John 3:2; Rev 22:4). In the context of the beatitudes, the clean of heart will see God when God fully establishes his reign at the end of this age. (In traditional Catholic theology, being united with God in eternity is called the "beatific vision.") Jesus announces that the reign of God is at hand (4:17), and those who seek God wholeheartedly can glimpse God revealed in and through Jesus (11:27; 12:28).

For reflection: How completely is my heart set on seeing God?

9 **Blessed are the peacemakers, / for they will be called children of God.** Being **peacemakers** is not simply a matter of living peacefully; peacemakers strive to bring about reconciliation and peace. The biblical notion of

peace encompasses well-being and wholeness as well as an absence of strife. Peacemakers work to establish justice and harmony. They do not respond to violence with violence (5:38-48); by absorbing violence **peacemakers** can act as circuit breakers in the spiral of revenge. There is no guarantee that their peacemaking will succeed: only when God's kingdom is fully established will violence be vanquished and complete peace reign. Jesus pronounces peacemakers to be **blessed,** even if they suffer violence, **for they will be called children of God.** As in other beatitudes, God's action is implied: peacemakers will be called children of God by God (see 5:44-45). **Children of God** (literally, sons of God) is an Old Testament expression with different shades of meaning. Here it conveys that when God establishes his reign, God will claim as his own and have special affection for those who are **peacemakers.** Just as God proclaimed Jesus to be his beloved Son (3:17), so too God looks upon those who sacrifice themselves for peace as beloved sons and daughters. (Other New Testament writings also speak of what it means to be children of God: Rom 8:14-17; Gal 4:4-7; 1 John 3:1-2.)

For reflection: Have I been a peacemaker? How could I be a peacemaker?

10 **Blessed are they who are persecuted for the sake of righteousness, / for theirs is the kingdom of heaven.** Here **righteousness** means doing God's will and playing one's role in God's plan of salvation. Experiencing some form of persecution is a real possibility for those whose allegiance is to God. Jesus proclaims them **blessed** and fortunate even if they are **persecuted for the sake of righteousness, / for theirs is the kingdom of heaven.** The promise that the persecuted will be welcomed into the reign of God is the same promise made to the poor in spirit (verse 3) and is the implicit promise of all the beatitudes.

For reflection: What have I done out of faithfulness to God that has aroused the greatest opposition?

11 Jesus continues with a ninth beatitude that is an expansion and application of the eighth. He switches from speaking of "they" to explicitly addressing his disciples as "you." Jesus tells them, **Blessed are you when they insult you and persecute you and utter every kind of evil against you [falsely] because of me.** The accent falls on verbal abuse in Jesus' expanded version of the eighth beatitude. Some will **insult** the disciples of Jesus and **utter every kind of evil against** them. (By printing **falsely** in brackets, the New American Bible indicates that this word is not found in all ancient manuscripts of Matthew's gospel.) Jesus says that insult and slander and even persecution will befall the disciples **because of me:** life has some hard knocks for everyone, but Jesus addresses what his disciples endure because of their allegiance to him. He tells them that they are **blessed** and fortunate despite whatever abuse comes to them because they are his disciples. Matthew probably intends his readers to include themselves among the "you" who are addressed by this beatitude: suffering for the sake of Jesus will not be limited to his first disciples.

12 Jesus explains why his disciples should consider themselves blessed to suffer for him: **Rejoice and be glad, for your reward will be great in heaven.** While the beatitudes implicitly invite us to imitate what they praise, they contain only two direct commands: **rejoice** and **be glad.** Jesus tells his disciples to be joyful even when they are abused and slandered because of him, **for your reward will be great in heaven.** Matthew's words can literally be translated "in the heavens"; the upper part of the heavens (or sky) were thought of as the abode of God (see 3:16-17). To receive a reward **in heaven** means that one has been brought into the presence of God; there those who endure suffering for the sake of Jesus will receive a **great** reward from God.

Jesus adds, **Thus they persecuted the prophets who were before you.** The abuse heaped on disciples of Jesus will be nothing new. Most of the prophets sent by God had a tough time (Jeremiah was quite vocal about what he suffered for God: Jer 15:10-18; 20:7-18). Late Old Testament writings characterize prophets as being rejected and even killed (2 Chron 36:16; Neh 9:26). What happens to Jesus' disciples will be in line with what happened in the past to those who served God.

Three general observations on the beatitudes as a whole: First, the beatitudes can be a mirror in which we see Jesus. They portray what one is like who lives under the reign of God, and Jesus is the perfect example of living one's life completely for God. We can meditate on each of the beatitudes for what it tells us about Jesus.

Second, the beatitudes proclaim a profound reversal of values. If the beatitudes reflected conventional thinking they would read, "Happy are the wealthy, the powerful, the good-looking, the physically fit." Jesus proclaims, happy are those who realize their fragility and emptiness and wholeheart-edly turn to God. Jesus' call to repent (4:17) is a call to change our atti-tudes and values.

Third, the beatitudes are like an overture to an opera, sounding the themes that will be developed in the course of Jesus' teachings. Some of these teachings make high demands on those who want to follow Jesus. The beatitudes proclaim from the very beginning: Blessed and happy and truly fortunate are those who hear Jesus' words and act on them (7:24).

Parables of Discipleship
13 **"You are the salt of the earth. But if salt loses its taste, with what can it be seasoned? It is no longer good for anything but to be thrown out and trampled underfoot. ¹⁴ You are the light of the world. A city set on a mountain cannot be hidden. ¹⁵ Nor do they light a lamp and then put it under a bushel basket; it is set on a lampstand, where it gives light to all in the house. ¹⁶ Just so, your light must shine before others, that they may see your good deeds and glorify your heavenly Father."**
Gospel parallels: Mark 4:21; 9:50; Luke 8:16; 11:33; 14:34-35

13 Jesus has just spoken of his disciples being slandered and persecuted (5:11-12) but tells them, **You are the salt of the earth.** Jesus compares his disci-ples to **salt** in what can be taken as a very brief parable. (A parable is basi-cally a comparison. The meaning of parables is often elusive, inviting reflection.) **Salt** was used to season and preserve food, among other uses, but Jesus does not specify any particular use of salt as the basis for compar-ing his disciples to salt. **The earth** has the sense here of the whole earth, parallel to the expression "the world" in the next verse. Matthew's Greek emphasizes the word **you:** Jesus tells his disciples, **you** who are abused and persecuted, **you are the salt of the earth.** Despite your lowliness you have a usefulness for the whole earth, just as salt is useful. What their usefulness is—their saltiness—is not yet spelled out.

Parables: See page 262

But if salt loses its taste, with what can it be seasoned? Salt is inher-ently salty, and cannot lose **its taste** without ceasing to be salt. But should the impossible happen and salt no longer be salty, **with what can it be sea-soned?** How do you salt salt if all your salt is unsalty? **It is no longer good for anything but to be thrown out and trampled underfoot.** Unsalty salt

79

is useless, and can be **thrown out** into the street like any other refuse **and trampled underfoot** (first-century garbage disposal would not satisfy modern standards). One implication of Jesus' comparing his disciples to salt emerges: his disciples must remain faithful to their identity if they are to be of any use to anyone. For disciples to lose their discipleness would be like salt losing its saltiness.

> *For reflection: If Jesus said to me, "You are the salt of the earth," how would I understand his words?*

14 Jesus provides a second comparison: **You are the light of the world.** Jesus does not immediately explain how his disciples are like **light,** but Matthew's readers might recall that Jesus himself is a light shining on those in darkness (4:16). Jesus tells his followers, **you** (again, an emphatic **you**) are the light **of the world.** This is a big claim to make for the small band of disciples gathered around Jesus—particularly if they are the poor and persecuted of the beatitudes. Jesus' words echo Isaiah's prophecies of a servant of God who is a light to the nations (Isaiah 42:6; 49:6). By sharing in Jesus' mission (4:19), his disciples will be a light for the entire world (28:19-20).

In case the disciples are puzzled over how they could have much impact, Jesus adds another comparison: **A city set on a mountain cannot be hidden.** Jesus has no particular city in mind; any city or even a village resting atop a hill is visible for miles. By comparing his disciples to **a city,** Jesus indicates that they will be visible as a group rather than as individuals. It will be as church that they will be the light of the world.

15 Just as salt must be salty, so light must shine: **Nor do they light a lamp and then put it under a bushel basket.** The kind of **lamp** used at the time was a small pottery container filled with olive oil; a wick dipped in the oil burned with a candle-like flame. A **bushel basket** was used to measure grain and held about two gallons. Anyone who would **light a lamp** did so for its light; it made no sense to **put it under a bushel basket** where its light would be blocked. Rather, **it is set on a lampstand, where it gives light to all in the house.** The houses of ordinary Galileans were often a single room; in such houses, an oil lamp flame could be seen by **all.**

16 Jesus draws a consequence of his disciples' being light. **Just so, your light must shine before others, that they may see your good deeds and glorify**

your heavenly Father. Just as lamps produce light (verse 15), so disciples are to produce **good deeds** that lead others to **glorify** the **heavenly Father** of the disciples. Some **good deeds** are praised in the beatitudes (showing mercy, making peace), and Jesus will discuss others in the course of the Sermon on the Mount. Salt must be salty, light must shine, and disciples must manifest their identity by what they do. Disciples are to behave in a way that does not call attention to themselves but reveals that they are living under the reign of God, so that God gets the credit. This fits in with the disciples being poor in spirit—so that they can be transparent to God's presence and power.

For reflection: What have I done that has given others a glimpse of God?

For the first time in Matthew's gospel, Jesus speaks of God to his disciples as **your heavenly Father.** God is in a unique sense the Father of Jesus (3:17), but God is also **Father** to those who are disciples of Jesus. God is their **heavenly** Father: the fatherhood of God transcends human fatherhood, even if human fatherhood provides a basis for understanding God's relation to humans. (Human motherhood also provides a basis for understanding God's relationship to us, but this is far less explored in the gospels.)

For reflection: Do I find it easy or difficult to think of God as my heavenly Father? Why?

BACKGROUND: HOUSES First-century Palestinian houses ranged from the very small to the truly sumptuous. Ordinary people often lived in one-room houses that usually shared an open courtyard with other one-room houses. Much of life was lived outdoors; cooking was done in the courtyard. Rooms were dark and sometimes windowless and used for sleeping and shelter from the elements. In eastern Galilee (for example, in Capernaum), house walls were built of basalt, a volcanic stone common in the area. Floors were made of basalt cobblestones; roofs were made of beams overlaid with thatch and clay. In Jericho, a city in the lower Jordan River valley, mud brick was used for the walls of ordinary dwellings. The wealthy elite lived in fine houses with mosaic floors, frescoed (painted plaster) walls, and elegant columns. The remains of several mansions belonging to the wealthy have been excavated in Jerusalem. One of these houses had several stories and more than six thousand square feet under its roof; it probably belonged to a member of a high-priestly family.

ORIENTATION: *Jesus solemnly assures his listeners that his teachings are the ful-fillment, and not a repudiation, of all that God has revealed in the past.*

The Fulfillment of Law and Prophecy

¹⁷ "Do not think that I have come to abolish the law or the prophets. I have come not to abolish but to fulfill. ¹⁸ Amen, I say to you, until heaven and earth pass away, not the smallest letter or the smallest part of a letter will pass from the law, until all things have taken place. ¹⁹ Therefore, whoever breaks one of the least of these commandments and teaches others to do so will be called least in the kingdom of heaven. But whoever obeys and teaches these commandments will be called greatest in the kingdom of heaven. ²⁰ I tell you, unless your righteousness surpasses that of the scribes and Pharisees, you will not enter into the kingdom of heaven."

Gospel parallels: Luke 16:16-17

17 Lest there be any misunderstanding of what he will go on to teach (5:21-48), Jesus proclaims, **Do not think that I have come to abolish the law or the prophets.** The **law** and the **prophets** represent the Hebrew Scrip-tures and God's revelation through these Scriptures. Jesus' mission is not to **abolish** or repeal God's revelation. Rather, Jesus assures his listeners, **I have come not to abolish but to fulfill.** The words **I have come** convey that Jesus is on a mission. His mission is **to fulfill** the law and the proph-ets. Matthew has told his readers that Jesus fulfilled the words of **proph-ets** (1:22-23; 2:6, 15, 17-18, 23; 4:13-16). For Jesus to **fulfill** the **law** means that he not only obeys it but brings it to completion through his interpretation and teaching.

18 **Amen, I say to you:** the word **amen** means "truly" and was used as an ex-clamation at the end of prayers (1 Chron 16:36). Jesus prefaces a statement with the word **amen** to indicate its importance. **Amen, I say to you** signals that Jesus is making a solemn declaration. **Until heaven and earth pass away:** for **heaven and earth** to **pass away** means this age coming to an end and a new age beginning—the age to come, when the kingdom of God is fully established. Until this age ends, **not the smallest letter or the smallest part of a letter will pass from the law, until all things have taken place.** The phrase **until all things have taken place** is best understood to refer to

heaven and earth passing away. The law will remain in effect as long as this universe endures—the law as interpreted by Jesus.

The age to come: See page 250

19 If God's law is not abolished by Jesus but remains in effect, then it must be obeyed and taught. Therefore, **whoever breaks one of the least of these commandments and teaches others to do so will be called least in the kingdom of heaven.** There were numerous commands in the Mosaic law—613 by a later count. Some were less weighty than others (see Deut 22:6-7). Those who break even the **least of these commandments** or lead others to break them will be called **least in the kingdom of heaven.** To be the least does not mean that one is excluded. On the other hand, **whoever obeys and teaches these commandments will be called greatest in the kingdom of heaven.** Matthew's readers can understand these commandments to be what Jesus teaches in the rest of the Sermon on the Mount as his interpretation of the law of Moses. **Obeys and teaches:** Jesus will stress that it is necessary to do God's will to enter the kingdom of heaven (7:21); after his resurrection he will commission his disciples to teach all that he has commanded (28:20).

Kingdom of heaven: See page 266

20 Jesus will authoritatively interpret the law of Moses, not abolishing it but drawing out its deeper meaning. As an introduction to his interpretation he proclaims to his disciples, **I tell you, unless your righteousness surpasses that of the scribes and Pharisees, you will not enter into the kingdom of heaven.** Jesus interacted with **scribes** (religious scholars) and **Pharisees** (a Jewish religious group) during his public ministry; Matthew's Jewish Christian readers would have understood **scribes** and **Pharisees** as representing the leaders of a rival movement within Judaism (see "Jewish religious diversity at the time of Matthew"—page 529). **Righteousness** in this context means obedience to God's laws. If disciples of Jesus are to enter into the reign of God, they will have to be more obedient than are the scribes and Pharisees. Jesus will go on in the Sermon on the Mount to provide examples of the **righteousness** or behavior required to **enter into the kingdom of heaven.**

Scribes: See page 138
Pharisees: See page 231

For reflection: How seriously do I take God's laws—even the least demanding of them?

Jesus' teachings in verses 17 to 20 had particular importance for Matthew's church, which was engaged in external and internal debates over the law of Moses. Externally, the successors of the "scribes and Pharisees" were developing their own application of the Mosaic law. These verses counter any charge that the church, by upholding Jesus' interpretation of the Mosaic law, has abandoned the law and its Jewish heritage. Internally, Matthew's church was working through the complex question of how the Mosaic law was binding on Gentile converts. These verses do not resolve all issues, but they establish the principle that the law of Moses is to be interpreted in light of Jesus.

ORIENTATION: *Jesus provides a series of examples of the righteousness or behavior required to enter the kingdom of heaven. Jesus invokes the law of Moses but proclaims a higher standard.*

Anger and Reconciliation

21 "You have heard that it was said to your ancestors, 'You shall not kill; and whoever kills will be liable to judgment.' 22 But I say to you, whoever is angry with his brother will be liable to judgment, and whoever says to his brother, 'Raqa,' will be answerable to the Sanhedrin, and whoever says, 'You fool,' will be liable to fiery Gehenna. 23 Therefore, if you bring your gift to the altar, and there recall that your brother has anything against you, 24 leave your gift there at the altar, go first and be reconciled with your brother, and then come and offer your gift. 25 Settle with your opponent quickly while on the way to court with him. Otherwise your opponent will hand you over to the judge, and the judge will hand you over to the guard, and you will be thrown into prison. 26 Amen, I say to you, you will not be released until you have paid the last penny."

Gospel parallels: Luke 12:58-59
OT: Exod 20:13; Deut 5:17

21 **You have heard that it was said to your ancestors, "You shall not kill; and whoever kills will be liable to judgment."** Jesus continues to address his disciples as **you**, and reminds them of something that they **have heard**—heard read from Scripture (most ordinary Jews were illiterate, and

their knowledge of Scripture came from hearing it read in a synagogue). The expression **it was said** implies that it was said by God. **Your ancestors** were the Israelites present at Mount Sinai when God gave his law; one of its basic commands is **You shall not kill** (Exod 20:13; Deut 5:17). The law of Moses does not explicitly state that **whoever kills will be liable to judgment,** but does command that murderers be punished (Exod 21:12-14; Lev 24:17; Num 35:16-18).

22 **But I say to you:** the I is emphatic; Jesus is proclaiming something on his own authority. Not only murderers but also **whoever is angry with his brother will be liable to judgment.** At issue is consciously harbored anger, not an unbidden and passing emotion. Deliberate anger can lead to murder; by prohibiting anger Jesus eliminates a source of murder. But what about when we think we have cause to be angry? Jesus does not seem to leave room for "righteous anger," which is often really "self-righteous anger," anger we wish to justify. Jesus' condemnation of anger is sweeping and covers **whoever is angry.** Matthew's first readers would have understood the word **brother** to mean a member of the church. For Christians to be angry with each other impairs the mission of the church to be the light of the world, which requires behaving in a way that leads others to glorify God (5:14, 16).

Jesus takes up verbal expressions of anger: **and whoever says to his brother, "Raqa," will be answerable to the Sanhedrin.** The Aramaic word

---

BACKGROUND: THE EARLY CHURCH AND THE LAW OF MOSES Jesus' first disciples were Jews, and they continued to follow the law of Moses after Jesus' resurrection. As Gentiles began to join the church, questions arose over the applicability of the law of Moses. Did Gentiles have to become Jews to become Christians, with males accepting circumcision? Could Christians who observed Jewish food laws eat with (and share a eucharistic meal with) Christians who did not observe Jewish food laws? Some Jewish Christians and their Gentile converts insisted that the law of Moses was fully binding on all Christians, Gentiles as well as Jews. Others thought that Jewish observances had no significance for any Christian. Church leaders such as Peter, Paul, and James took middle stances (although with some disagreements: Gal 2:11-14) and maintained that some but not all of the law of Moses was binding on Gentile converts. Since Jesus had not settled all questions during his public ministry, the church had to work out solutions based on what Jesus had taught and the guidance of the Holy Spirit (see Acts 15).

---

raqa is roughly equivalent to "blockhead"—an insult, but not the worst thing someone can be called. Those who hurl this insult **will be answerable to the Sanhedrin,** which was the highest Jewish executive and judicial council. Similarly, **whoever says, "You fool," will be liable to fiery Gehenna.** The expression **you fool** is equivalent to **raqa,** not a worse insult; yet those who call another a **fool** will end up in **fiery Gehenna.** Some Jewish writings used **Gehenna** (the Hinnom Valley on the south and west sides of Jerusalem) as a symbol of punishment in the age to come. Jesus' words might be paraphrased in modern terms as, "A disciple who insults another disciple will be hauled before the Supreme Court in this life and go to hell in the next." Jesus seems to be exaggerating to make the point that abusive speech is a far more serious matter than one might think. (See 7:3-5 for another example of Jesus using exaggeration to make a point.)

Sanhedrin: See page 601

Gehenna: See page 88

For reflection: What is my reaction to Jesus' words about anger and abusive speech?

23 Jesus turns from forbidding anger and abusive speech to commanding reconciliation. **Therefore, if you bring your gift to the altar:** Jesus' words presume that his listeners are Jews who come to the Temple in Jerusalem with sacrificial offerings. If in the course of making an offering at the altar you **there recall that your brother has anything against you:** at issue is someone having a grievance against you, not you having a grievance against another.

24 Jesus says that resolving a grievance against you is so important that you should **leave your gift there at the altar,** interrupting your worship, and **go first and be reconciled with your brother, and then come** back to the Temple **and offer your gift.** Jesus' words are best understood as an example with a message for everyone rather than an instruction that applied only to Jews making offerings at the Temple. The point is that reconciliation with someone who has a grievance against us takes precedence over worship of God. In order to be reconciled with God, we must be reconciled with each other (see also 6:12, 14-15). We must not only avoid anger ourselves; we must do what we can to soothe the anger of others by addressing the grievances they have against us.

For reflection: Does anyone have a grievance against me? How could I pursue reconciliation?

25 **Settle with your opponent quickly while on the way to court with him. Otherwise your opponent will hand you over to the judge, and the judge will hand you over to the guard, and you will be thrown into prison.** It is conventional wisdom that out-of-court settlements and plea bargains are often preferable to going to trial and risking greater penalties.

26 But Jesus is not simply passing on conventional wisdom. His **Amen, I say to you** signals that he is trying to convey a more important lesson. **You will not be released until you have paid the last penny** refers not to a court-imposed fine but to being imprisoned until one has paid off a debt. Keeping debtors in prison until family or friends paid off the debts was a Roman rather than Old Testament practice. Jesus uses this practice as a comparison for what happens to those who face God's judgment without having been reconciled with others (see 18:33-35 for another use of this comparison). Being required to pay off debts down to **the last penny** means being held accountable by God for all that we do or fail to do. A failure to seek reconciliation with those who have something against us will not go unnoticed when we stand before God's judgment.

Jesus sets high standards, forbidding deliberate anger and abusive speech and commanding reconciliation with those who have something against us. We might think that Jesus' demands are unrealistic: only in heaven will there be no anger or divisions. But that is Jesus' point. To enter heaven, we must live in a heavenly manner; we must live under God's reign now if we expect to enter it in the future.

Adultery and Lust

27 "You have heard that it was said, 'You shall not commit adultery.' **28** But I say to you, everyone who looks at a woman with lust has already committed adultery with her in his heart. **29** If your right eye causes you to sin, tear it out and throw it away. It is better for you to lose one of your members than to have your whole body thrown into Gehenna. **30** And if your right hand causes you to sin, cut it off and throw it away. It is better for you to lose one of your members than to have your whole body go into Gehenna."

Gospel parallels: Mark 9:43-48
OT: Exod 20:14; Deut 5:18
NT: Matt 18:8-9

27 **You have heard** when Scripture is read **that it was said, "You shall not commit adultery"**—another basic command of the law of Moses (Exod 20:14; Deut 5:18). In the Old Testament, **adultery** means a married or betrothed woman's having sexual relations with a man other than her husband (see Deut 22:22-24); adultery was an offense against her husband, a violation of his rights.

28 **But I say to you:** Jesus again makes a proclamation based on his own authority. **Everyone who looks at a woman with lust has already committed adultery with her in his heart.** That the sin is **adultery** might imply that Jesus is speaking about lust for a married woman, because a man having sexual relations with an unmarried woman was not considered adultery. Yet Jesus seems to have in mind all **women,** married or not. **Everyone who looks at a woman with lust:** Jesus is not talking about a casual glance but a man desiring to have sexual relations with a woman. Jesus characterizes such desire as committing **adultery with her in his heart.** The heart in biblical idiom is the seat of emotions and desires and the source of human actions (see 15:18-19). Not only is adultery forbidden but also the lustful desires that lead to adultery. Jesus' teaching is foreshadowed in the law of Moses: "You shall not covet your neighbor's wife" (Exod 20:17; Deut 5:21).

BACKGROUND: GEHENNA is a transliteration of the Greek form of the Hebrew name for the Hinnom Valley, a steep ravine on the western and southern sides of Jerusalem. In Old Testament times the Hinnom Valley was the setting for idolatrous worship (called "Ben-hinnom"—Jer 7:31; 19:1-6), which took place at sites that may have been considered entrances to the underworld. The Hinnom Valley was also used for burials and as a refuse dump. As the ideas of judgment after death and the punishment of the wicked developed, some nonbiblical writings portrayed the Hinnom Valley as a place of fiery punishment—perhaps because of its smoldering refuse and associations with death and idolatry. When Jesus spoke of Gehenna as a place of everlasting punishment, he was using imagery familiar to his listeners. *Related topics: Judgment (page 557), Nonbiblical writings (page 198).*

Jesus' words were specifically addressed to men but can easily be extended to women. They are a warning to both women and men of the dangers of lustful desires and fantasies.

For reflection: How seriously do I take the dangers of sexual temptations?

29 **If your right eye causes you to sin, tear it out and throw it away.** Eyes are used for lustful glances (verse 28) but blinding oneself would not insure chastity; the root of sin lies in the inner self. Hence Jesus' words are not to be taken literally; they are simply a graphic opening to Jesus' warning about the danger of lust. The **right eye** might be considered the more valuable eye (on the basis of the right hand being the more valuable hand for right-handed people—see verse 30), and losing it, a greater sacrifice than losing the left eye. **It is better for you to lose one of your members**—such as an eye—**than to have your whole body thrown into Gehenna,** a symbolic way of speaking about punishment after death. It is better to endure even a great loss than the loss of everything; it is better to go through this life maimed than to suffer eternal loss. Jesus' words are not an endorsement of maiming but a sobering warning of the eternal consequences of our actions (see also 18:8-9).

30 Jesus adds a second comparison for emphasis. **And if your right hand causes you to sin, cut it off and throw it away. It is better for you to lose one of your members than to have your whole body go into Gehenna.** The loss of one's right hand is a great hardship, especially for a right-handed person. Similarly, restraining one's desires may be a great hardship but is preferable to suffering punishment in the next life.

Jesus' comparisons make the point, Whatever causes you to sin, whatever leads you into sin—whatever it is, get rid of it! It's not worth it in the long run.

For reflection: What messages do Jesus' comparisons have for me?

Divorce
31 "It was also said, 'Whoever divorces his wife must give her a bill of divorce.' 32 But I say to you, whoever divorces his wife (unless the marriage is unlawful) causes her to commit adultery, and whoever marries a divorced woman commits adultery."

Gospel parallels: Luke 16:18
OT:Deut 24:1-4
NT:Matt 19:3-9; Mark 10:2-12

31 **It was also said, "Whoever divorces his wife must give her a bill of divorce."** The Old Testament presumes that a husband has the right to divorce his wife (a Jewish wife did not have the right to divorce her husband), but requires him to give her a written **bill of divorce** (Deut 24:1-4). This document established that her husband had relinquished his rights over her and another man was thus free to marry her.

> When a man, after marrying a woman and having relations
> with her, is later displeased with her because he finds in her
> something indecent, and therefore he writes out a bill of divorce
> and hands it to her, thus dismissing her from his house. . . .
> *Deuteronomy 24:1*

32 **But I say to you, whoever divorces his wife (unless the marriage is unlawful) causes her to commit adultery.** Jesus assumes that a divorced wife would remarry: allowing her to do so was the point of the bill of divorce. But Jesus proclaims that such remarriage is **adultery.** In the law of Moses, adultery is an offense against a husband, a violation of his rights to his wife (Lev 20:10; Deut 22:22). If Jesus proclaims that a woman's second marriage **causes her to commit adultery,** this means that she is still married to her first husband and is committing adultery against him. Jesus thus declares that a marriage is not dissolved by divorce. Jesus will later explain why the bond of marriage is permanent (19:3-9). Jesus adds, **and whoever marries a divorced woman commits adultery**—that is, violates the rights of her first husband, to whom she is still married despite the bill of divorce.

There seems to be an exception to divorce and remarriage being adultery: **(unless the marriage is unlawful).** There are two question about this exception: whose words are they, and what do they mean? The likeliest interpretation is that these words are a comment inserted by Matthew to apply Jesus' words to the situation of his church. (For another example of a gospel author inserting a comment to clarify a teaching of Jesus, see Mark 7:19, where the final observation is Mark's.) Some of the Gentile converts who were joining Matthew's church were apparently married to close relatives, a practice tolerated in the Greek and Roman world but not by Jews (Lev 18:6-18) or by the church (Acts 15:20, 29; 21:25). By adding the parenthetical remark **(unless the marriage is unlawful)**, Matthew indicates that dissolving such forbidden unions is not a violation of Jesus' teaching on divorce.

Unlawful marriages: See page 401

Jesus' prohibition of divorce remains a hard saying: Jesus sets high standards for living under the reign of God. See the exposition of Matthew 19:1-12 for further consideration of this pastorally difficult subject. The Catholic Church upholds the permanence of marriage but declares a marriage null when it can be determined that a marriage bond did not exist.

For reflection: What is my reaction to Jesus' prohibition of divorce?

Oaths and Truthfulness

33 "**Again you have heard that it was said to your ancestors, 'Do not take a false oath, but make good to the Lord all that you vow.' 34 But I say to you, do not swear at all; not by heaven, for it is God's throne; 35 nor by the earth, for it is his footstool; nor by Jerusalem, for it is the city of the great King. 36 Do not swear by your head, for you cannot make a single hair white or black. 37 Let your 'Yes' mean 'Yes,' and your 'No' mean 'No.' Anything more is from the evil one.**"

OT: Exod 20:7; 22:10; Lev 19:12; Deut 5:11; 23:22-24
NT: Matt 23:16-22; James 5:12

33 **Again you have heard that it was said to your ancestors, "Do not take a false oath, but make good to the Lord all that you vow."** An oath invokes God's name or calls upon God as the witness to the truth of what one is saying (Exod 22:10); a **vow** is a promise made to God or a promise made solemn by invoking God. The law of Moses allowed oaths and vows, but required that oaths be truthful (Lev 19:12) and vows be kept (Num 30:3; Deut 23:22-24). To swear falsely is to take God's name in vain (Exod 20:7; Deut 5:11).

> *[T]he custodian shall swear by the LORD that he did not lay hands on his neighbor's property; the owner must accept the oath.*
> *Exodus 22:10*

You shall not swear falsely by my name, thus profaning the name of your God.

Leviticus 19:12

34 But I say to you, do not swear at all. Oaths back up our words by invoking God, but Jesus tells us to leave God out of it! **Do not swear** by God or use God's name to persuade people that you are telling the truth. Jesus' prohibition is absolute: do not swear **at all.** Do not even swear using euphemisms for God. Jesus gives examples of such euphemisms: **not by heaven, for it is God's throne.** Just as the expression "kingdom of heaven" means "kingdom of God," so swearing by heaven is a way of swearing by God.

35 nor by the earth, for it is his footstool. Jesus' words echo Isaiah's prophecy, "Thus says the LORD: / The heavens are my throne, / the earth is my footstool" (Isaiah 66:1). **Nor by Jerusalem, for it is the city of the great King** echoes Psalm 48:3. Don't swear by invoking God's dwelling place or God's creation or God's city as a way of invoking God without using his name.

36 Do not swear by your head. If one cannot invoke God in an oath, can one invoke oneself? Jesus rules out even such oaths, **for you cannot make a single hair white or black.** God has numbered the hairs on our heads (10:30), and we can't keep them from turning gray and falling out. If we can't prevent even **a single hair** from turning gray (Dye doesn't count!), then swearing by our heads adds not a hair's weight to what we say.

37 Let your "Yes" mean "Yes," and your "No" mean "No." Simply speak honestly; oaths are unnecessary for those living under God's reign. All that is necessary is to tell the truth, without trying to give our words greater weight by invoking God as the guarantor of our truthfulness. **Anything more is from the evil one.** Oaths are not only unnecessary but prone to abuse (23:16-22) and even dangerous. Invoking God as our guarantor can be a way of trying to manipulate God or of manipulating others by our invocation of God. There can be no lies or manipulation in the kingdom of God. The **evil one** is Satan (6:13; 13:19, 38); lies and manipulation play into his hands.

For reflection: When am I most tempted to be less than fully truthful?

Jesus' teaching about oaths and truthfulness is echoed in the Letter of James (James 5:12), but has generally not been interpreted by Christians as an absolute prohibition of all oaths in all circumstances. Citing 2 Corinthians 1:23 and Galatians 1:20, the *Catechism* states that "following St. Paul, the tradition of the church has understood Jesus' words as not excluding oaths made for grave and right reasons (for example, in court)" (*Catechism of the Catholic Church*, 2154).

Nonresistance and Vulnerability

38 "You have heard that it was said, 'An eye for an eye and a tooth for a tooth.' **39** But I say to you, offer no resistance to one who is evil. When someone strikes you on [your] right cheek, turn the other one to him as well. **40** If anyone wants to go to law with you over your tunic, hand him your cloak as well. **41** Should anyone press you into service for one mile, go with him for two miles. **42** Give to the one who asks of you, and do not turn your back on one who wants to borrow."

Gospel parallels: Luke 6:29-30, 34-35
OT: Exod 21:23-25; Lev 24:19-20; Deut 19:21

38 **You have heard that it was said, "An eye for an eye and a tooth for a tooth."** The law of Moses set a standard of strict justice, requiring that the punishment fit the crime (Exod 21:23-25; Lev 24:19-20; Deut 19:21). Excessive retribution was outlawed, for example, the seventy-sevenfold revenge of Lamech's boast (Gen 4:23-24). A just proportion between punishment and crime is a basic principle of all criminal and civil law. In the time of Jesus, those injured normally received monetary compensation instead of their assailants' being mutilated.

> *Anyone who inflicts an injury on his neighbor shall receive the same in return. Limb for limb, eye for eye, tooth for tooth! The same injury that a man gives another shall be inflicted on him in return.*
>
> *Leviticus 24:19-20*

39 **But I say to you:** Jesus again makes a proclamation on the basis of his own authority. The law of Moses limited retribution, but Jesus goes further: **offer no resistance to one who is evil.** Jesus' words are directed to those who would live under the reign of God, but Jesus acknowledges that not everyone is committed to God: there are those who are **evil** and harm others. Jesus tells his followers, **offer no resistance** to those who injure you. Jesus does not explain what this will accomplish. But Jesus is addressing the poor in spirit (5:3), the lowly and vulnerable, and part of what it means for them to be peacemakers (5:9) may be for them to absorb violence without retaliating. There is no guarantee their nonresistance will leave them unscathed: Jesus' nonresistance led him to the cross.

For reflection: What is my reaction to Jesus' words, "offer no resistance"?

Jesus provides examples of nonresistance. **When someone strikes you on [your] right cheek, turn the other one to him as well.** A right-handed person would normally strike another person on the left side of the face; being struck on the **right cheek** seems to describe a backhanded slap, more an insult than an injury. When struck, the poor in spirit are to accept additional blows and insult without striking back.

Jesus' demand that his disciples not respond to violence with violence challenges our deep-seated instincts. Had Jesus taught, "If anyone strikes you, you have a right to defend yourselves," we would have nodded in agreement. But that is not what Jesus said. How we respond to Jesus' commands to offer no resistance and to turn the other cheek may reveal whether we are more set on our ways or on God's ways. We should note, however, that the Catholic Church does not interpret Jesus' teaching as requiring non-resistance in every circumstance; sometimes defending oneself or others is legitimate or even necessary (*Catechism of the Catholic Church*, 2263–2265).

For reflection: How do I understand Jesus' command to turn the other cheek? What opportunities have I had to obey this teaching?

40 A second example of nonresistance: **If anyone wants to go to law with you over your tunic, hand him your cloak as well.** Having someone **go to law with you** over a possession means having someone ask a court to enforce a claim against you. The minimum possessions that the abjectly poor have are their clothes, so demanding clothing means demanding virtually everything. The two pieces of clothing worn at the time were a **tunic** under a **cloak**. Since the law of Moses treated a cloak, which is necessary for survival, as an almost inalienable possession (Exod 22:25-26; Deut 24:12-13),

it is the **tunic** that is demanded in the lawsuit. Jesus does not rule on the merits of the case—whether someone has a valid claim to your tunic or not. Jesus simply says that if someone wants to sue you for your tunic, **hand him your cloak as well.** Taken literally, this leaves one naked.

41 Third example: **Should anyone press you into service for one mile, go with him for two miles.** Roman soldiers had the authority to conscript Jewish civilians as temporary beasts of burden, forcing them to carry baggage or other burdens for up to one mile. (Simon of Cyrene will thus be "pressed into service" to carry Jesus' cross: 27:32.) The practice was hardly popular with Jews. But **should anyone press** a disciple of Jesus **into service for one mile,** the disciple is to **go with him for two miles.** As with turning the other cheek and handing over the tunic, Jesus provides no rationale for behaving as he commands—no explanation of why a disciple should go the extra mile or of what it may accomplish. Jesus simply tells those who would live under the reign of God to be so nonresistant that they willingly do twice as much as is demanded of them.

For reflection: How do I respond to demands made upon me?

42 Fourth example: **Give to the one who asks of you, and do not turn your back on one who wants to borrow.** It is uncertain whether **the one who asks of you** is asking for an outright gift or (as in the second part of the verse) for a loan. If we take **asks of you** to mean "asks for a gift," then Jesus is saying that his disciples should give whatever is asked of them, whether as an outright gift or a temporary loan. Jesus does not provide for exceptions; he does not say, "Give to the one who asks of you if you can

---

BACKGROUND: CLOTHING The two basic items of clothing at the time of Jesus were the tunic and the cloak. The tunic was an inner garment often made by folding a rectangle of cloth (sometimes linen) over on itself and stitching the sides, with openings for the head and arms. The cloak (often wool) was an outer garment, perhaps a loose-fitting robe or a rectangular cloth that one draped around oneself. These garments were worn by both men and women, with only color and decoration distinguishing them. A Jewish man's cloak would have tassels (Num 15:37-40; Deut 22:12). Belts were used to cinch tunics and cloaks. A head covering could be simply a cloth draped or tied around the head; leather sandals protected the feet. The upper class could afford imported silk and dyes, and their clothing proclaimed their status.

---

spare it," or "Make loans to those who can be counted on to pay you back." Since this example is an instance of what it means to "offer no resistance to one who is evil" (verse 39), the one asking for a gift or a loan may be someone who insults us (verse 39), takes us to court (verse 40) and imposes on us (verse 41). Jesus' words are nevertheless unconditional, making us vulnerable to the demands of others: **give** and **do not turn your back.**

For reflection: How have I made myself vulnerable to the demands of others?

The Perfection of Love

43 "You have heard that it was said, 'You shall love your neighbor and hate your enemy.' **44** But I say to you, love your enemies, and pray for those who persecute you, **45** that you may be children of your heavenly Father, for he makes his sun rise on the bad and the good, and causes rain to fall on the just and the unjust. **46** For if you love those who love you, what recompense will you have? Do not the tax collectors do the same? **47** And if you greet your brothers only, what is unusual about that? Do not the pagans do the same? **48** So be perfect, just as your heavenly Father is perfect."

Gospel parallels: Luke 6:27-28, 32-36
OT: Lev 19:18
NT: Matt 19:19; 22:39

43 You have heard that it was said, "You shall love your neighbor and hate your enemy." Jesus' listeners may well have heard this said, but only the command **you shall love your neighbor** is found in Scripture (Lev 19:18). Nowhere does the Old Testament explicitly command that you shall **hate your enemy.** Yet it is easy to understand why hatred of enemies might become paired with love of neighbor. In the Old Testament, one's **neighbor** meant a fellow Israelite. If some who are outside our group are opposed to our group, then it is all too easy to think that we are justified in hating them as enemies. The Old Testament contains ample expressions of hatred of enemies (for example, Psalms 137:8-9; 139:21-22).

Take no revenge and cherish no grudge against your fellow countryman. You shall love your neighbor as yourself.

Leviticus 19:18

One of the Dead Sea Scrolls—the library of a Jewish community—urges community members to "love all the sons of light" (members of the community) and "hate all the sons of darkness" (enemies of the community). Jesus may not have read this scroll, but the idea that one was justified in hating outsiders and enemies was not unique to the Dead Sea Scrolls.

44 **But I say to you:** Jesus again authoritatively pronounces what his disciples are to do. **Love your enemies, and pray for those who persecute you.** Jesus acknowledges that we may have **enemies** who harm us and **persecute** us (see 5:10-12), but we nonetheless must **love** them. The **love** that Jesus commands is not a warm feeling but love in action, deeds of love. If our enemies reject what we do for them in love, we can at least and always **pray** for them. Jesus gives no assurance that our love will convert enemies into friends or stop them from making our lives miserable, but we must love them anyway.

Jesus' admonition to love enemies would have been a demanding command for Matthew's first readers, who had experienced some degree of

---

BACKGROUND: DEAD SEA SCROLLS In 1947, a Bedouin shepherd boy came across some clay jars in a cave overlooking the Dead Sea. The jars contained seven ancient scrolls, including the Book of Isaiah. Over the next nine years more scrolls were found in ten other caves in the area. Over nine hundred different scrolls have been discovered, virtually all of them incomplete and decayed, in more than one hundred thousand fragments. The process of assembling and translating the fragments has taken scholars many years. The scrolls were copied between roughly 200 B.C. and A.D. 68 and represent an entire library. About two hundred of the scrolls were copies of books of the Old Testament, including thirty-six copies of the Psalms. Also discovered were copies of nonbiblical religious writings, including about ten copies of 1 Enoch and fifteen copies of Jubilees, as well as scrolls of religious writings that had been previously unknown to modern scholars. Along with these works, which had been in general circulation among Jews at the time of Jesus, were a number of works that pertained to the religious community that owned the library. Some of these scrolls were community rules, hymns used in the community, and commentaries on books of the Old Testament written from the community's perspective. The community that owned this library is commonly identified as the Essenes, a sect headquartered at Qumran, on the shore of the Dead Sea, where the scrolls were found. *Related topics: Essenes (page 238), Nonbiblical writings (page 198).*

persecution (see 5:10-12; 10:21-23). It is likewise a demanding command for all Christians of all times who suffer harm at the hands of others.

For reflection: What is the greatest harm another person has done me? How have I responded to that person?

If we have to love enemies, we have to love everyone! Jesus abolishes the boundaries limiting our love.

For reflection: What are the limits of my love?

45 Jesus tells his disciples that they must love their enemies so **that you may be children of your heavenly Father.** Jesus earlier said that peacemakers "will be called children of God" (5:9). Peacemakers strive for peace, not only through their nonresistance (5:38-42) but by their love for those who harm them. For Jesus' disciples to be **children** (literally, sons) of their **heavenly Father** means having a relationship with God parallel to the relationship that Jesus enjoyed as God's beloved Son (3:17). Jesus has been giving examples of the behavior required to live under the reign of God (5:20-48); he now expresses the reality of living under God's reign as being **children of your heavenly Father.** God's kingdom is not an impersonal bureaucracy but a family united in love.

How is it that loving our enemies makes us children of God? Because that is the way God acts, **for he makes his sun rise on the bad and the good, and causes rain to fall on the just and the unjust.** Many in Jesus' audience were farmers, and they well knew that sunshine and rainfall were necessary for crops. God provides sunlight and rain for the crops of everyone, the **bad** as well as the **good, the just and the unjust.** Crops are necessary to sustain life; God provides crops and life even for those who hate him! To be children of God means to behave as God behaves, loving and doing good for even the unlovable.

46 **For if you love those who love you, what recompense will you have?** It is natural to love those who love us—and no great achievement. **Do not the tax collectors do the same?** Since **tax collectors** were scorned as corrupt parasites, to love no more than they loved hardly merited any **recompense** or reward.

Tax collectors: See page 163

47 **And if you greet your brothers only, what is unusual about that?** To **greet** someone meant more than saying hello; a Jewish greeting wished peace and blessings upon the one greeted (see 10:12). **Brothers** broadly means those we are linked with through kinship or friendship; for Matthew's first readers it included fellow Christians. It is natural to wish that those we are linked with enjoy blessings and peace—but **do not the pagans do the same?** The word **pagans** means "non-Jews"; it doesn't require God's revelation for human beings to be nice to those who are nice to them.

Jesus' point is that it takes more than normal human behavior—more than what even tax collectors and pagans do—to live under God's reign. When Jesus asks **what is unusual about** greeting a brother, the Greek word Matthew uses for **unusual** is related to the word that is translated "surpasses" when Jesus says, "unless your righteousness surpasses that of the scribes and Pharisees, you will not enter the kingdom of heaven" (5:20). The unusual and surpassing behavior Jesus asks of us is to love our enemies, which is to love as God loves.

48 Jesus concludes, **So be perfect, just as your heavenly Father is perfect.** We often understand perfection as freedom from faults, but Jesus puts the accent on love: to **be perfect just as your heavenly Father is perfect** means to love as God loves, loving those who do not return our love, loving even those who harm us. In the Greek of Matthew's gospel, Jesus literally says "*you* be perfect"—an emphatic and plural "you," addressed first to Jesus' disciples and then to all who read Matthew's gospel. Jesus' words are an invitation to become children of God by loving as God loves, thereby living under God's reign now so as to be part of God's reign when it is fully established.

For reflection: How do I respond to Jesus' asking me to be perfect?

Matthew does not record any immediate reaction by the disciples or the crowd to Jesus' words. We can well imagine that some of them thought, "Surely you exaggerate!" That might be our reaction as well. Some of Jesus' examples demand the difficult but not the impossible: quelling anger and seeking reconciliation (5:21-26), curbing lust (5:27-30), avoiding oaths and speaking truthfully (5:33-37). But Jesus' prohibition of divorce (5:31-32) and his requirement of nonresistance (5:38-42) and love of enemies (5:43-48) are even harder to follow. Being perfect as God is perfect (5:48) seems an unrealistic and impossible ideal. Yet Jesus gives no indication that his demands are not real demands. Rather, he puts forth these demands as examples of the righteousness required to enter the kingdom of heaven (5:20). He will shortly exclaim, "How narrow the gate and constricted the road that leads to life. And those who find it are few" (7:14). Jesus recognizes that his demands are demanding. It is best that we also acknowledge that Jesus asks a lot of us, rather than try to tame or explain away his words.

At the same time, Jesus' demands must be understood in the context of his entire mission and ministry. In Matthew's gospel, Jesus went about proclaiming the good news of the kingdom and curing every disease and illness (4:23-24) before setting forth the demands of the Sermon on the Mount. The mission of Jesus is to enable women and men to live under God's reign and experience its joy and blessedness. The ultimate healing he bestows is from sin (see 1:21; 26:28) and from all that prevents us from entering through the gate of eternal life.

CHAPTER 6

ORIENTATION: *Jesus told his disciples to let their light shine before others (5:16); now he warns against doing it to win praise. Jesus uses three religious practices as examples.*

A Warning

¹ "[But] take care not to perform righteous deeds in order that people may see them; otherwise, you will have no recompense from your heavenly Father."

1 **[But] take care not to perform righteous deeds in order that people may see them.** While the word **but** is not found in all ancient manuscripts of Matthew's gospel, Jesus' warning is in any case connected with what he has just taught. His disciples are to behave righteously (5:20-48) and let their good deeds be seen by others (5:16)—**but** they are not to **perform righteous deeds in order that people may see them.** Jesus makes an important distinction. Even if our righteous deeds are to be seen by others, we are not to do them **in order** to have them seen by others. Disciples' good deeds are to be seen so that others might "glorify your heavenly Father" (5:16). Doing good **in order** to be seen doing good means trying to win glory for ourselves, not for God. Those who strive after adulation and glory **will have no recompense from your heavenly Father**—that is, no reward when God establishes his kingdom (see 5:12, which speaks of reward in heaven). God will not glorify those who glorify themselves.

Jesus goes on to give three examples of what he is talking about.

First Example: Almsgiving

² "When you give alms, do not blow a trumpet before you, as the hypocrites do in the synagogues and in the streets to win the praise of others. Amen, I say to you, they have received their reward. ³ But when you give alms, do not let your left hand know what your right is doing, ⁴ so that your almsgiving may be secret. And your Father who sees in secret will repay you."

OT:Tobit 12:8-9

2 Prayer, fasting, and almsgiving became customary practices for many pious Jews toward the end of the Old Testament era. Jesus uses these practices as

examples to flesh out his warning (6:1), beginning with almsgiving—giving money or showing mercy to the poor. **When you give alms, do not blow a trumpet before you, as the hypocrites do in the synagogues and in the streets to win the praise of others.** Jesus wants his disciples to help those in need (see 19:21; 25:34-40), but he does not want them to do it **to win the praise of others.** Those who help the poor should not call attention to their generosity. To **blow a trumpet** while making a donation is a vivid image for making a big show of it. Those who make a show of their almsgiving are **hypocrites.** The Greek word **hypocrite** originally referred to a stage actor; Jesus uses it to mean someone putting on a performance. To make a show of being generous, whether in a synagogue or out on the street, is not so much giving money to the poor as it is buying **praise** for oneself. Jesus warns, **Amen, I say to you, they have received their reward.** Those who buy the praise of others can expect nothing more for their money.

> *Prayer and fasting are good, but better than either is almsgiving accompanied by righteousness.*
>
> Tobit 12:8

3 **But when you give alms, do not let your left hand know what your right is doing.** Not letting one's left hand know that one's right hand is giving alms is an image for keeping one's generosity as secret as possible—the opposite of blowing a trumpet while making a donation (verse 2). Don't give so that you will receive praise, not even self-praise: not letting your left hand know makes it impossible to applaud yourself. Give for the sake of others, not for your own sake.

BACKGROUND: ALMS are money given to help those in need. A clue to the meaning of "alms" is found in the Greek word used in the gospels for "alms," for it is derived from the verb that means to show mercy. There is no mention of giving alms in the early Old Testament era, because money had not yet been invented. In a farming economy, mercy could be exercised by feeding the hungry with what one raised or letting the poor glean crops from one's fields (Lev 19:9-10; Deut 15:11). As coins came into use, the hungry could be also helped by giving them money to buy food and to meet their other needs. Almsgiving—the showing of mercy by giving money—is praised in the books of Tobit (Tobit 4:7-11, 16; 12:8-9) and Sirach (Sirach 3:29; 7:10), among the last books of the Old Testament to be written.

4 Give surreptitiously, **so that your almsgiving may be secret. And your Father who sees in secret will repay you.** Even if we can keep our generosity a secret from others, there are no secrets from God. God **will repay** our merciful acts when he establishes his kingdom (see also 25:31-40). Jesus speaks of God as **your Father,** which can convey that the reward we receive is an inheritance given to sons and daughters rather than a wage paid to servants. God gives us far more than we earn.

If alms are to be given secretly, what then of Jesus' charge to let our light shine before others, so that they may see our good deeds and glorify God (5:16)? Even if we are quiet about it, those whom we are personally assisting will know of our acts of mercy. If they are able to sense that we are really concerned for them (rather than doing good so that we can feel good about ourselves) they may perceive us as channels of God's love and glorify God.

> *For reflection: How generous am I to those in need? What can I do to practice quiet generosity?*

Second Example: Personal Prayer
5 **"When you pray, do not be like the hypocrites, who love to stand and pray in the synagogues and on street corners so that others may see them. Amen, I say to you, they have received their reward. ⁶ But when you pray, go to your inner room, close the door, and pray to your Father in secret. And your Father who sees in secret will repay you."**

OT:Psalm 55:17-18; Dan 6:11

5 **When you pray, do not be like the hypocrites**—like actors putting on a performance—**who love to stand and pray in the synagogues and on street corners so that others may see them.** Jesus is not talking about prayer offered by a congregation as a part of Temple or synagogue services, but personal prayer. Many devout Jews had adopted the custom, perhaps based on Psalm 55:18, of praying three times a day. To **stand and pray** was not in itself ostentation: both standing (Neh 9:4; Psalm 134:1) and kneeling (Ezra 9:5; Dan 6:11) were Jewish postures of prayer. The Book of Daniel describes Daniel going to his room to offer thrice-daily prayers (Dan 6:11), but those whose motive in prayer was **so that others may see them** chose public places for their private prayers: **in the synagogues and on street corners.** Offering one's personal prayers in a synagogue ensured an audience,

as did standing in a busy intersection (the Greek word here for **street** means a wide, main street). **Amen, I say to you, they have received their reward.** Such prayers are not prayers directed to God but a performance put on for an audience. God does not **reward** performers.

> But I will call upon God,
>   and the LORD will save me.
> At dusk, dawn, and noon,
>   I will grieve and complain,
>   and my prayer will be heard.
>   Psalm 55:17-18

6 **But when you pray:** in Matthew's Greek, **you** is singular and emphatic; Jesus is speaking to individuals about personal prayer. To offer personal prayer, **go to your inner room, close the door, and pray to your Father in secret.** The Greek word translated **inner room** can refer to a storage room or shed for tools and crops. It afforded privacy, but was hardly a chapel or

---

BACKGROUND: SYNAGOGUE The original meaning of the Greek word *synagogue* was a gathering or an assembly, but it came to mean the *place* of assembly—the building that served as a Jewish community center and place of prayer and study. Synagogues may have originated during the Exile, when Jews were deprived of Temple worship. At the time of Jesus, synagogues, at least in the sense of assemblies, were common in Galilee, in Jerusalem, and wherever Jews resided outside of Palestine. Synagogues were used for Scripture reading and prayer; sacrifices were offered only in the Temple in Jerusalem. Synagogues were also used for religious education and community gatherings, which sometimes included communal meals. After the time of Jesus, synagogues became more exclusively used for religious activities and less as general-purpose community centers. Archaeologists have discovered the remains of a few first-century synagogues. They typically consisted of a large room with tiers of stone benches around the walls. Anything done in such a synagogue—such as Jesus' healings and exorcisms—would have been visible to the whole congregation. Ruins of a third- or fourth-century synagogue built of limestone can be found in Capernaum today; beneath the ruins are what seem to be the remains of a first-century synagogue built of basalt blocks—apparently the synagogue in which Jesus taught and healed.

sacred place. There, with door closed, Jesus' disciples should **pray** with no one watching. Jesus tells his disciples to pray **to your Father:** Jesus will shortly teach his disciples how to pray to their Father (6:7-15). **Your Father in secret** means your Father "*who is* in secret," and perhaps conveys that the God we pray to is a hidden God, a God who is beyond our natural means of perceiving and knowing. **And your Father who sees in secret will repay you.** When we are by ourselves we are not alone: God is present even in storage sheds, and hears the prayers and silent cries of our hearts.

For reflection: Where do I pray best? How do I pray?

Jesus' teaching does not rule out praying with others; that too is a part of the Christian life (see 18:19-20). Jesus' warning is directed against making a public display of private piety in order to gain the admiration of others.

ORIENTATION: *Before going on to a third example of piety practiced for the sake of praise, Jesus expands his teaching on prayer.*

How and How Not to Pray
[7] "In praying, do not babble like the pagans, who think that they will be heard because of their many words. [8] Do not be like them. Your Father knows what you need before you ask him.
[9] "This is how you are to pray:

Our Father in heaven,
    hallowed be your name,
      [10] your kingdom come,
your will be done,
    on earth as in heaven.
  [11] Give us today our daily bread;
  [12] and forgive us our debts,
    as we forgive our debtors;
  [13] and do not subject us to the final test,
    but deliver us from the evil one.

[14] If you forgive others their transgressions, your heavenly Father will forgive you. [15] But if you do not forgive others, neither will your Father forgive your transgressions."

Gospel parallels: Luke 11:1-4
OT:Sirach 28:1-5
NT:Mark 11:25

7 Jesus continues to tell his disciples how not to pray: **In praying, do not babble like the pagans, who think that they will be heard because of their many words.** The word **pagans** means those who are not Jews and have not benefited from God's revelation to the Israelite people. Pagans have their gods (or their ideas of God: Rom 1:18-23). According to pagan notions, gods must be cajoled into answering prayers. Petitioners must make their needs known and overcome any reluctance on the part of the one who can grant their wishes; pagans try to inform and persuade the gods with **many words.** Disciples of Jesus might devote significant time to prayer (just as Jesus will spend a night in prayer: 14:23-25), but not because God has to be nagged.

8 **Do not be like them.** Jesus' disciples are not to pray like pagans, because God is not like pagans imagine. **Your Father knows what you need before you ask him:** Jesus characterizes God in relation to his disciples as **your Father,** concerned for them as his children. There is no need to use a torrent of words to win God's favor: God is not aloof and indifferent but loves his children. Nor is God ignorant of the disciples' needs: **your Father knows what you need before you ask him.** Prayer is not a matter of informing God of what he does not know nor of motivating him to be more loving.

Why pray if God already knows our needs and loves us? Prayer is our acknowledgement that God is our loving Father; prayer is an expression of our trust in God's care for us (see 6:25-32; 7:7-11). Petitionary prayer ultimately asks nothing more of God than that God be God.

For reflection: How do I pray when there is something I dearly want God to do? What do my prayers reveal about my notion of God?

9 **This is how you are to pray.** Jesus has spoken of wrong ways to pray (verses 5-8) and now tells his disciples **how you are to pray.** Jesus gives his disciples a model prayer—not so much a prayer to be memorized as a pattern

to follow: note the differences in wording among verses 9-13, Luke 11:2-4, and the Lord's Prayer as we recite it. The different versions of the Lord's Prayer have different nuances of meaning. The following exposition focuses on the Lord's Prayer as presented by Matthew, which may reflect the version of the prayer familiar to his church community.

Jesus' disciples are to address God as **our Father in heaven.** It was not unheard of for Jews to speak of or pray to God as **Father** (Tobit 13:4; Wisd 2:16; 14:3; Sirach 23:1, 4; 51:10), but it was not the ordinary way of addressing God at the time of Jesus. Jesus, however, characteristically prayed to God as his Father and spoke of God as Father (for example, 11:25-27; 26:39, 42). Mark's gospel recounts Jesus praying to God as "Abba, Father" (Mark 14:36); *Abba* is an Aramaic word that children, even grown children, would use for their father. *Abba* is an intimate and affectionate word for father; the nearest English equivalent might be "dad." Jesus tells his disciples that they are to call upon his Father as their Father—praying to him in their native Aramaic as their Abba (see also Rom 8:15; Gal 4:6). Jesus' disciples are to share in the intimate and affectionate relationship that Jesus the Son of God has with his Father. They are to pray **our** Father because having God as their Father makes them sisters and brothers.

Although the disciples of Jesus can affectionately call God their Father, God is nevertheless their **Father in heaven.** The expression **in heaven** does not merely distinguish God from fathers on earth; it more importantly signals the awesome status of God. **Our Father in heaven** is the God who created the universe, a hundred billion galaxies each with its billions of stars. Such a God is beyond human comprehension—yet Jesus authorizes his disciples to call upon him as their Father, their loving Dad!

Not all find it easy to pray to God as Father, much less as Dad. Some have had horrible fathers, and their experience of human fatherhood provides a poor basis for turning to God as their heavenly Father. Others rightly insist that God is neither male nor female, or advocate maternal images for a loving God (see Isaiah 49:15; 66:13). Still, we should not lose sight of the legacy Jesus left us. He invited us to share in his intimate relationship with God, a relationship expressed by calling upon his Father as **our Father.**

For reflection: Do I think of and pray to God as Father? How do I most naturally address God?

After addressing God as their Father, disciples are to pray **hallowed be your name.** When we pray these words, we might have in mind that God's name be respected by everyone. But there is a deeper significance to this petition. In the biblical view, names were not arbitrary labels but were virtually equivalent to what they named: the **name** of God represents the person of God (see Isaiah 29:23; Ezek 36:23). The word "hallow" means to make holy or sanctify. The Greek verb translated as **hallowed be** conveys one-time action rather than continued action, and conveys as well that God is the one being called upon to carry out the action. **Hallowed be your name** is a petition that asks God to sanctify his name once and for all. This is not a request that God make his name or himself any holier but that God manifest his holiness by manifesting who he is. How does God provide a definitive demonstration of who he is? That is taken up in the next petition.

10 **Your kingdom come:** God will definitively demonstrate who he is by completing his work of creation and redemption, vanquishing evil and bringing men and women into his **kingdom.** Jesus by his public ministry and his death and resurrection inaugurated the reign of God on earth. But God does not yet rule completely over everyone and everything: the world is still shot through with evil and suffering. The petition **your kingdom come** asks God to fully establish his reign, once and forever. That is how God will hallow his name.

Kingdom of heaven: See page 266

What does it mean for God's kingdom to come? This is taken up by the third petition: **your will be done, on earth as in heaven.** God's will is perfectly accomplished in heaven; this petition asks that God also accomplish his will on earth once and for all. God's will means God's plan in creating the universe and in sending his Son. This petition, like the other two petitions, asks God to act and to act definitively, establishing his kingdom in its fullness, making it clear that God is indeed God. We might pray "your will be done" as a way of expressing our submission to God's will, and that is certainly a valid prayer. But in the context of the Lord's Prayer, "your will be done" is a petition that God completely carry out his sovereign will: the accent falls on what God does, not on what we are willing to do.

The first three petitions of the Lord's Prayer make the same basic request of God but in different words. These petitions ask God to complete his work of creation and redemption, bringing everything to fulfillment, establishing his definitive reign. They ask God to be God. At the same time, these petitions have implications for the one praying them. They can be expressions of our reverence for God and God's name, of our longing and striving to live under God's reign, and of our submission to God's will for us.

For reflection: What do the first three petitions of the Lord's Prayer mean to me when I pray them?

11 The first three petitions ask God to establish his definitive reign; the remaining petitions focus on our needs. **Give us today our daily bread.** In Matthew's gospel, the meaning of praying for **daily** bread is not completely clear: the word translated **daily** is an extremely obscure Greek word of uncertain meaning. The easiest course is to accept the traditional translation. Asking God for our **daily bread** may seem a simple request— too simple for many of us to pray with literal meaning, since we have food on our shelves to last us a number of days. It would have been a meaningful petition, however, for some who first heard these words and who may not have known where their next meal was coming from. And it is a meaningful petition for those who take to heart Jesus' teaching that they should not worry about what they will eat or drink for they will be provided for by a loving Father (6:25, 31-33). Since **bread** was the staple food at the time of Jesus, **bread** can stand for all we need to sustain us physically and, by extension, what we need to sustain us in all aspects of our lives. Praying for our **daily bread** can be an expression of our trust that God takes care of us, day by day. It too can be a way of asking that God be God.

Bread: See Diet, page 304

For reflection: What am I asking for when I pray, "Give us this day our daily bread"?

12 **and forgive us our debts, as we forgive our debtors.** If read outside of the context of the Lord's Prayer, the language of this petition sounds like something we might say in court to a bankruptcy judge: please forgive all

that I owe, as I am forgiving what is owed me. But in Aramaic, the word **debts** was also used for sins; our sins create, as it were, a debt we owe God—damages owed to him. We pray that God will forgive us what we owe him, just as we forgive those who have harmed us and owe us recompense. Like the first three petitions, this petition might have God's final establishment of his reign in mind: we are asking God to forgive us when we stand before him in judgment on the last day. But as in asking for daily bread, we can also be asking for God's daily forgiveness. Asking God to forgive our debts **as we forgive our debtors** might seem to make God's forgiveness of us a consequence of our forgiving others, as if we earn God's forgiveness by forgiving. However, God's forgiveness always comes first. We cannot earn God's forgiveness; we can however block God's forgiveness of us by refusing to forgive others—a point Jesus will emphasize shortly (verses 14-15) and teach about again (18:21-35).

> *For reflection: In what area of my life do I stand in greatest need of God's forgiveness?*

13 **and do not subject us to the final test:** the Greek word that the New American Bible translates as **final test** has several meanings. It can mean temptation or enticement to sin (which is how it is translated when we pray, "lead us not into temptation"). It can also mean a **test** or trial. A test in turn could be ordinary difficulties that try us, or it could be the testing that was expected before the end of this age (see 24:7-13). The New American Bible follows the latter interpretation and characterizes the testing as **the final test.** We pray that God **not subject us to the final test,** that is, that God preserve us through the afflictions and difficulties that will occur as this age is wrapped up. The first three petitions ask God to establish his definitive reign; this petition asks that we be kept safe when it happens. (This concern is echoed in the Book of Revelation, which has the promise "I will keep you safe in the time of trial that is going to come to the whole world to test the inhabitants of the earth"—Rev 3:10.) When we pray the Our Father, though, we probably have in mind God preserving us from the temptations that now afflict us.

But deliver us from the evil one. The final petition can also be interpreted in more than one way. It literally asks that we be delivered from "the evil," which could mean evil in general (the familiar wording of the Lord's Prayer asks, "Deliver us from evil"). However, in Matthew's gospel, "the evil" usually means **the evil one,** or Satan (5:37; 13:19, 38). This petition can have the end of this age in view and ask that we be delivered, or rescued, from Satan and brought safely into the kingdom of heaven. We can also pray it as a prayer for daily protection from Satan's harm, as we await the final coming of the kingdom of God.

Satan: See page 55

For reflection: What do I understand I am asking for when I pray, "And lead us not into temptation but deliver us from evil"?

The oldest known text of the Lord's Prayer outside the gospels is found in the *Didache*, a very early Christian writing. The *Didache* presents the Lord's Prayer as it is found in Matthew and adds the doxology, "For thine is the power and the glory for ever and ever." Then it urges, "Say this prayer three times a day" (*Didache* 8).

The *Didache*: See page 129

We can note that the Lord's Prayer is in the middle of the Sermon on the Mount (chapters 5 to 7 of Matthew's gospel), as if prayer is at the heart of Jesus' teachings. Jesus' disciples are to pray that God be God and establish his reign, even as they try to live in God's reign by following Jesus' teachings.

14 In order to emphasize the importance of one of the petitions in the prayer Jesus has taught his followers, Jesus expands upon it: **If you forgive others their transgressions, your heavenly Father will forgive you.** To receive the forgiveness we need from God we must forgive those who have harmed us.

15 To refuse to forgive others blocks our being forgiven: **But if you do not forgive others, neither will your Father forgive your transgressions.** Jesus will later put God's forgiveness of us and our forgiveness of others in perspective (18:21-35), making it clear that God extends his forgiveness first, and that the forgiveness we receive from God far outweighs all the forgiveness we will ever grant. Here Jesus is content to emphasize that we cannot expect God to forgive us if we refuse to forgive others. Two centuries earlier Sirach had linked receiving God's forgiveness with our forgiving others (Sirach 28:1-5), and Jesus upholds this view.

Forgive your neighbor's injustice;
> *then when you pray, your own sins will be forgiven.*
Should a man nourish anger against his fellows
> *and expect healing from the LORD?*
Should a man refuse mercy to his fellows,
> *yet seek pardon for his own sins?*

> Sirach 28:2-4

For reflection: Who do I find it most difficult to truly forgive? What step might I take to extend forgiveness to that person?

ORIENTATION: *After teaching his disciples how to pray, Jesus returns to examples of pious practices that can be done for show.*

Third Example: Fasting
16 "When you fast, do not look gloomy like the hypocrites. They neglect their appearance, so that they may appear to others to be fasting. Amen, I say to you, they have received their reward. **17** But when you fast, anoint your head and wash your face, **18** so that you may not appear to be fasting, except to your Father who is hidden. And your Father who sees what is hidden will repay you."

16 **When you fast:** fasting—abstaining from all food—was commanded only on the annual Day of Atonement (Lev 16:29). Jesus is speaking of voluntary fasting, done as a personal act of piety. Such fasting had became a customary practice for many devout Jews. Jesus first addresses how such fasting should not be done: **do not look gloomy like the hypocrites.** Some put on a show of appearing dismal and sad when they fast (recall that the word "hypocrite" means "actor"). **They neglect their appearance, so that they may appear to others to be fasting.** By **neglect their appearance** Jesus may mean they were disheveled or that they wore sackcloth and ashes (see 1 Macc 3:47; Dan 9:3). In any case, they altered their **appearance** so that they would **appear to others to be fasting.** They wanted the admiration of others for their fasting—and that is all that they will get from their fasting for display: **Amen, I say to you, they have received their reward.** God disregards playacting.

17 **But when you fast, anoint your head and wash your face.** This might mean that you should go about your usual routine of washing up so that you will appear normal while you fast. There is another possibility. Anointing oneself with oil was a pleasant experience (Psalms 23:5; 104:15), perhaps like the use of body lotion today. The popular practice of fasting may have included not washing or anointing oneself (see 2 Sam 12:20-21; 14:2), which would have been a sign that one was fasting.

18 Jesus' disciples are to wash up and anoint themselves **so that you may not appear to be fasting:** they should act and look no differently when fasting than when not fasting. They will not appear to anyone to be fasting **except to your Father who is hidden.** An act of personal piety like fasting should be as hidden as God is hidden. **And your Father who sees what is hidden will repay you.** God takes note of all that we do out of devotion to him.

For reflection: What role does fasting play in my spiritual life?

BACKGROUND: FASTING   In both the Old and New Testaments, fasting means abstaining from all food for a period of time. In its origins, fasting may have been a sign of mourning: David fasted following the deaths of Saul, Jonathan, and Abner (2 Sam 1:12; 3:31-35), and Judith fasted after the death of her husband as part of her mourning (Judith 8:2-6). Fasting out of grief was not necessarily a religious practice but a mark that one was so deeply sorrowful that he or she had lost all appetite for food. Fasting as an expression of sorrow may have evolved to include fasting as an expression of sorrow for sin (Joel 2:12-13). The Day of Atonement is the only annual fast day prescribed in the Old Testament (Lev 16:29). Fasts could also be called in times of national crisis, as part of prayers of supplication (Joel 1:14). Prophets such as Isaiah warned that fasting was no substitute for upright and merciful conduct (Isaiah 58). Eventually fasting became a pious act, done not only in times of sorrow or crisis but also simply as an act of devotion. The Book of Tobit, written about two centuries before Jesus, lists fasting, prayer, and almsgiving as three pious Jewish practices (Tobit 12:8). Different Jewish groups at the time of Jesus had their own traditions of fasting. The *Didache,* a Christian writing dating from about a century after Jesus, speaks of Jews fasting on Mondays and Thursdays and advises Christians to fast instead on Wednesdays and Fridays. *Related topic: The* Didache *(page 129).*

Jesus used almsgiving (6:2-4), prayer (6:5-8), and fasting (6:16-18) as examples of "righteous deeds" that should be done privately rather than for show (6:1). Since these were three characteristic Jewish pious practices of the time (Tobit 12:8), they can stand for all pious practices and private devotions. What we do out of devotion to God should be done out of devotion to God, not to win the admiration of others, not to win even self-admiration.

What then of letting our light shine before others so that they see our good deeds and glorify God (5:16)? It would seem that not every "righteous deed" (6:1) qualifies as a deed meant to be seen by others. Fasting and private prayer are matters between us and God. So too may be other devotional acts we perform. There is a difference between bearing witness and showing off.

For reflection: What do I do to draw closer to God? How quietly do I go about it?

ORIENTATION: *Jesus has contrasted seeking praise from others and receiving reward from God (6:1-6, 16-18). Jesus goes on to contrast seeking wealth on earth and having wealth in heaven.*

No Divided Loyalties
[19] "Do not store up for yourselves treasures on earth, where moth and decay destroy, and thieves break in and steal. [20] But store up treasures in heaven, where neither moth nor decay destroys, nor thieves break in and steal. [21] For where your treasure is, there also will your heart be.

[22] "The lamp of the body is the eye. If your eye is sound, your whole body will be filled with light; [23] but if your eye is bad, your whole body will be in darkness. And if the light in you is darkness, how great will the darkness be.

[24] "No one can serve two masters. He will either hate one and love the other, or be devoted to one and despise the other. You cannot serve God and mammon."

Gospel parallels: Luke 11:34-36; 12:33-34; 16:13
OT: Tobit 4:7-11; Sirach 29:8-12
NT: James 5:1-3

19 **Do not store up for yourselves treasures on earth** by hoarding money and luxuries such as fine clothing, for **moth and decay destroy** such possessions **and thieves break in and steal** them. Nothing **on earth** is completely secure or offers true security. (The Letter of James will echo Jesus' words: James 5:1-3.)

20 **But store up treasures in heaven, where neither moth nor decay destroy, nor thieves break in and steal.** Moths, decay, and thieves will not be a problem **in heaven.** Jesus does not spell out here how we **store up treasures in heaven,** but we might associate **treasures in heaven** with Jesus' earlier words about reward in heaven (5:10-12) and repayment by God (6:4, 6, 18). Living by Jesus' teachings in the Sermon on the Mount stores up treasures in heaven. Another association: Jesus has taught about almsgiving (6:2-4), and late Old Testament writings spoke of almsgiving as storing up treasure for oneself (Tobit 4:7-11; Sirach 29:8-12).

> For reflection: What am I storing up on earth? What am I storing up in heaven?

21 **For where your treasure is, there also will your heart be.** In biblical idiom the **heart** is the inner self. If we ignore Jesus' admonition (verse 19) and store up treasures on earth, we will remain earthbound and will, like our treasures, decay. If we follow Jesus' admonition to store up treasures in heaven (verse 20), then we are destined for the kingdom of heaven, beyond the decay of this earth. **Where** we put our treasures, **there** we will be.

> For reflection: Where am I putting my long term investments?

22 **The lamp of the body is the eye. If your eye is sound, your whole body will be filled with light.** We understand our eyes as organs that admit light and enable us to see the world around us. We might think that an **eye** that **is sound** is like a window that allows, as it were, the **whole body** to be **filled with light.** But some ancient peoples, including Jews, had a different impression of how eyes worked. Eyes were thought of as having a light or fire within them that made sight possible; eyes were not like windows but lamps. In extreme cases eyes could be imagined as being like "fiery torches" (Dan 10:6) or a "fiery flame" (Rev 1:14; 2:18; 19:12); the eyes of God are "ten thousand times brighter than the sun" (Sirach 23:19).

115

It is in line with this notion of eyesight that Jesus says **the lamp of the body is the eye.** Jesus speaks of an **eye** as a **lamp** that shines not only outwardly onto the world but inwardly into the **body** as well. **If your eye is sound**—if it provides light—**your whole body will be filled with light.**

23 **But if your eye is bad**—if the lamp of your eye does not shine light into your body—then **your whole body will be in darkness. And if the light in you is darkness,** if what should have been light within you is instead darkness, then **how great will the darkness be.** A defective eye leaves one in inner darkness, just as a doused lamp leaves a room in darkness.

Jesus is making a comparison—telling a parable—based on how eyes were thought to function. The point Jesus wishes to make is not easily apparent; some of Jesus' parables are riddles. The meaning of this parable may hinge on a pun. When Jesus says, "If your eye is sound" (verse 22), the word translated as "sound" can mean "single-minded" and "generous," as well as "healthy." Just as a healthy eye means one is filled with light and a bad eye means inner darkness, so being single-minded and generous means that one is full of light, and having divided loyalties or being greedy means that one is full of darkness. Jesus has contrasted hoarding treasure on earth with having treasure in heaven (verses 19-21), and he will go on to speak about serving God or serving wealth (verse 24). In context, Jesus' parable challenges his listeners: Are you single-minded in serving God and laying up treasure in heaven? Are you generous in giving alms? Or are you beset by greed and other wrong allegiances? Are you filled with light or darkness?

For reflection: Am I filled with light or darkness or mottled gray? What message does Jesus' parable have for me?

24 **No one can serve two masters.** The word translated **serve** literally means "to be the slave of"; the word **masters** is used for those who own slaves. Jesus says that one cannot be the slave of two owners. This is not strictly true: some slaves were the property of two or more owners (see Acts 16:16, 19). But shared ownership of a slave creates divided loyalties: the slave **will either hate one** master **and love the other, or be devoted to one and despise the other.** Here **hate** has the connotation of "neglect," and **love** the meaning of "prefer"; **devoted** conveys "loyal attention," and **despise** conveys "disregard." A slave with two masters will inevitably give his or her primary allegiance to one master rather than the other.

Jesus is providing a comparison or parable: just as a slave cannot **serve two masters,** so **you cannot serve God and mammon.** In the phrase **serve God,** the word **serve** again means "to be the slave of." **Mammon** is an Aramaic word for wealth or property; it has no inherently bad connotations but simply means what one owns. Jesus tells his disciples that they cannot give their complete allegiance both to God and to what they own: one has to come first and the other be subordinate. Jesus' words are an implicit injunction to put God ahead of wealth and everything else: God wants our total, undivided commitment. Wealth will decay like all things of this earth (verse 19); giving our allegiance to God and using our resources to **serve God** will lay up treasure for us in heaven (verses 20-21).

For reflection: What would an examination of my checking account or charge card records reveal about my priorities and allegiances?

ORIENTATION: *After telling his disciples not to lust for wealth (6:19-24), Jesus addresses anxieties over simple survival.*

Anxiety and Trust

25 "Therefore I tell you, do not worry about your life, what you will eat [or drink], or about your body, what you will wear. Is not life more than food and the body more than clothing? **26** Look at the birds in the sky; they do not sow or reap, they gather nothing into barns, yet your heavenly Father feeds them. Are not you more important than they? **27** Can any of you by worrying add a single moment to your life-span? **28** Why are you anxious about clothes? Learn from the way the wild flowers grow. They do not work or spin. **29** But I tell you that not even Solomon in all his splendor was clothed like one of them. **30** If God so clothes the grass of the field, which grows today and is thrown into the oven tomorrow, will he not much more provide for you, O you of little faith? **31** So do not worry and say, 'What are we to eat?' or 'What are we to drink?' or 'What are we to wear?' **32** All these things the pagans seek. Your heavenly Father knows that you need them all. **33** But seek first the kingdom [of God] and his righteousness, and all these things will be given you besides. **34** Do not worry about tomorrow; tomorrow will take care of itself. Sufficient for a day is its own evil."

Gospel parallels: Luke 12:22-31

25 **Therefore I tell you:** Jesus' **therefore** indicates that what he says flows from his admonition, "you cannot serve God and mammon" (6:24). Some might think this admonition applies only to those set on accumulating wealth. But anxiety over the necessities of life can also distract from singe-minded service of God. **Therefore,** Jesus tells his disciples, **do not worry about your life, what you will eat [or drink], or about your body, what you will wear.** The word **life** has the connotation of our livingness, our being alive. Jesus does not deny that humans need food and drink and clothing to stay alive, but he tells his followers, **do not worry**—do not be anxious—about the necessities of life. In the context of the previous verse this means to set yourself on the service of God rather than on simply staying alive. **Is not life more than food and the body more than clothing?** Jesus previously quoted the Scripture passage, "One does not live by bread alone, / but by every word that comes forth from the mouth of God" (4:4; Deut 8:3). Our **life,** our very existence comes from God and cannot be reduced to the calories we consume or the clothing we wear.

For reflection: What are my greatest anxieties?

26 Jesus provides a parable or comparison: **Look at the birds in the sky; they do not sow or reap, they gather nothing into barns.** Bread, the staple food of Jesus' audience, was made from grain, which required sowing and reaping. Birds don't raise grain or other crops, **yet your heavenly Father feeds them.** It was commonly accepted that God sustained all life on earth (Psalm 104), providing birds with food (Job 38:41; Psalm 147:9). **Are not you more important than they?** If God sustains the life of birds, how much more so will their **heavenly Father** sustain the life of Jesus' disciples.

For reflection: How important do I consider myself to be in the eyes of my heavenly Father?

27 Jesus is not saying that his disciples are excused from the human condition of needing to work to provide for their needs (Gen 2:15; 3:19; Psalm 104:23), but he wants to put their efforts in perspective. He asks, **Can any of you by worrying add a single moment to your life-span?** Our **life-span** is in the hands of God (see Psalm 39:5-6). We can shorten it by self-destructive behavior but not lengthen it by **worrying.** Anxieties over the fragility of our lives betray a lack of trust in God who gives us life; anxieties do nothing to make our lives less fragile.

28 **Why are you anxious about clothes?** Jesus spoke of anxieties over nourishment and clothing (verse 25) and provided a parable, or comparison, about nourishment (verse 26); now he provides a parable about clothing. **Learn from the way the wild flowers grow. They do not work or spin.** Humans do have to **work** and **spin** in order to clothe themselves—spinning thread, weaving cloth, and making garments. **Wild flowers** do not perform such labors.

29 **But I tell you that not even Solomon in all his splendor was clothed like one of them.** The **splendor** of **Solomon** was proverbial; he is the greatest biblical example of luxurious living and conspicuous consumption (1 Kings 10:4-5, 14-25). Yet wild flowers have a beauty that not even Solomon in his royal robes could match.

30 **If God so clothes the grass of the field:** the beauty of flowers and plants is God's handiwork. But however exquisite, this beauty is fleeting: grass **grows today and is thrown into the oven tomorrow,** used as fuel for cooking. Jesus tells his disciples that if God beautifully adorns plants, **will he not much more provide** clothing **for you, O you of little faith?** Jesus' followers rank a lot higher than flowers in the eyes of God. Jesus addresses his disciples as **you of little faith.** This means that they have less faith than they should rather than no faith at all. **Faith** here means confidence that their lives are in the hands of God and that their heavenly Father will care for them. Jesus invites them to have greater faith—an invitation to the readers of Matthew's gospel as well.

For reflection: If faith means confidence in God's care for me, how little or great is my faith?

31 **So**—therefore—**do not worry and say, "What are we to eat?" or "What are we to drink?" or "What are we to wear?"** The questions are natural; it is not the questions but the frame of mind and tone of voice in asking them that concerns Jesus. He tells his disciples, **do not worry:** do not anxiously wail, "Oh, what will I eat?" as if starvation is certain; do not lament, "What

will I have to drink?" as if you are dying of thirst; do not worry, "What will I wear?" as if you have no clothes.

32 **All these things the pagans seek.** By **pagans** (another translation would be Gentiles) Jesus refers to those who have not benefited from God's revelation to Israel. Those without this knowledge of God may think that they have to make it through life on their own, providing for themselves what they need to survive. While **pagans seek** these **things,** Jesus' disciples should think and behave differently. Disciples should realize that they are not on their own; they are able to turn to God as their heavenly Father. Jesus tells his disciples that **your heavenly Father knows that you need** the necessities of life. Jesus has previously taught them that they were not to pray as pagans prayed, for "Your Father knows what you need before you ask him" (6:8). Now he tells his disciples that they do not need to be anxious about the necessities of life as pagans might. The God who gives life knows perfectly well what is needed to sustain life; God cares for the disciples of Jesus as a **Father** for his children.

33 The disciples therefore do not make survival their top concern. Jesus tells them to **seek first the kingdom [of God] and his righteousness.** Seeking these **first** does not mean not seeking anything else; it is a matter of priorities. Jesus' disciples are to seek God's kingdom and righteousness above everything else. The word **seek** has the connotation *keep* seeking, as on a permanent quest. The **kingdom** of God is the reign of God, inaugurated by Jesus and to be brought to fulfillment at the end of this age. Jesus' disciples are to strive to live under God's reign now so that they can enter into its fullness. The **righteousness** of God can have two senses. It can mean God's making things right, as he has begun to do through Jesus and will do definitively at the end of this age. Righteousness can also mean the human response to what God is doing: living as God requires, obeying the teachings of Jesus as the law of God's realm. Perhaps both senses are included in Jesus' exhortation to seek righteousness: Jesus' disciples are to live according to his teachings with their eyes on their final goal (see 5:20). They are to "hunger and thirst for righteousness" (5:6); they are to pray to their Father, "your kingdom come, your will be done" (6:10).

Kingdom of God: See Kingdom of heaven, page 266

For reflection: What I am seeking first in life?

Jesus tells his disciples that if they make living in the reign of God their top priority, then **all these things** that they need to sustain their lives **will be given you besides.** The expression **will be given you** has the connotation "will be given you *by God.*" God as a Father knows their needs (verse 32) and will make provision for them. Jesus' disciples will not be absolved from work, but their primary goal in life will be serving God rather than taking care of their own needs. Jesus invites his disciples to put God first and to trust God for the rest.

For reflection: How confident am I that God will provide for my needs if I put him first?

34 **Do not worry about tomorrow:** the Greek text literally reads, "*Therefore,* do not worry about tomorrow"—connecting Jesus' final observations with what he has just taught. Since God will provide for their survival (verse 33), Jesus' disciples do not need to **worry about tomorrow** and their future needs. **Tomorrow will take care of itself.** The Greek text has a play on words: "Do not be anxious about tomorrow, for tomorrow will be anxious about itself." The sense seems to be, You have enough to do today; don't add tomorrow's anxieties to today's concerns; let tomorrow worry about itself. **Sufficient for a day is its own evil.** The word **evil** probably has the sense of the troubles and misfortunes that are an inescapable part of life. God's care does not mean that Jesus' disciples will never experience misfortune; God's care does mean that disciples should face the future without anxiety. Those who are confident in God's care for them can live each day to its fullest, putting themselves and their future in the hands of God.

For reflection: Do I brood over the future, or am I able to put it in the hands of God?

Paul offers what can be read as an exhortation based on Jesus' teachings about anxiety and trust: "Have no anxiety at all, but in everything, by prayer and petition, with thanksgiving, make your requests known to God. Then the peace of God that surpasses all understanding will guard your hearts and minds in Christ Jesus" (Phil 4:6-7).

CHAPTER 7

ORIENTATION: *The Sermon on the Mount is a collection of Jesus' teachings. There are fewer logical connections among the teachings in chapter 7 than in the preceding two chapters. The ultimate aim of Jesus' teachings remains how to live under the reign of God now in order to be part of the kingdom of God when it is established in its fullness.*

Faultfinding

[1] "Stop judging, that you may not be judged. [2] For as you judge, so will you be judged, and the measure with which you measure will be measured out to you. [3] Why do you notice the splinter in your brother's eye, but do not perceive the wooden beam in your own eye? [4] How can you say to your brother, 'Let me remove that splinter from your eye,' while the wooden beam is in your eye? [5] You hypocrite, remove the wooden beam from your eye first; then you will see clearly to remove the splinter from your brother's eye."

Gospel parallels: Mark 4:24; Luke 6:37-42

1 **Stop judging, that you may not be judged.** Making judgments about people is inescapable (see 7:15-20). Should I lend this person money? Do I trust this doctor? What then does Jesus have in mind when he commands **stop judging**? Further, Jesus tells his disciples not to judge so **that you may not be judged,** meaning not be judged *by* God. But every human will face God's final judgment. How can Jesus speak of anyone not being judged by God?

The key to understanding what Jesus has in mind lies in the various connotations of the word **judging.** We do not label someone as judgmental because they say nice things about others! All too often our judgments are not objective appraisals but biased condemnations. **Judging,** in this sense, means focusing on the flaws of others (verse 3) and ignoring their virtues, attributing bad motives to others, faultfinding. Jesus warns that those who judge in order to condemn will themselves **be judged** and condemned.

2 Jesus makes it explicit: **For as you judge, so will you be judged** by God at the last judgment. Unlike our judging, God's judging is always just. Those who appraise fairly will be fairly appraised; those who give others the

benefit of the doubt will be judged leniently by God. Those who are eager to condemn others bring condemnation on themselves, just as those who refuse to forgive others cut themselves off from God's forgiveness (6:12, 14-15). **The measure with which you measure will be measured out to you.** At the time of Jesus a **measure** would have been, for example, a basket used to measure grain. A dishonest merchant might use a smaller than standard basket to cheat customers—a practice repeatedly condemned in the Old Testament (Lev 19:35-36; Deut 25:13-16; Ezek 45:10-12; Micah 6:10-11). Jesus warns that shortchanging others in our assessment of them will boomerang: the measure we use in judging others will be the measure God uses in judging us.

For reflection: What is the measure of my sympathy for others? How sympathetic do I hope that God will be toward me?

3 Jesus provides a vivid illustration. **Why do you notice the splinter in your brother's eye, but do not perceive the wooden beam in your own eye?** Jesus, growing up in a carpenter's shop (13:55), presumably knew what it felt like to get a speck of sawdust or splinter of wood in his eye, and how a watering eye affected one's vision. Jesus exaggerates this experience to make a point: he questions how one who has an entire log in his or her eye is able to see a splinter in a the eye of another. Before appraising others, look in a mirror. During Jesus' public ministry, a **brother** would have been a fellow disciple; for Matthew's readers, a brother was a member of the church. Chronic faultfinding corrodes personal relationships and erodes bonds of love within the community.

4 An overdeveloped sensitivity to the shortcomings of others is often accompanied by an exaggerated sense of one's abilities to set others right. This too Jesus challenges: **How can you say to your brother, "Let me remove that splinter from your eye," while the wooden beam is in your eye?** Removing a splinter from the eye of another is a delicate affair, liable to cause injury if done clumsily. Those with logs in their eyes should not purport to be eye surgeons.

5 **You hypocrite:** Jesus applies the word **hypocrite** to his followers, for they too can put on a show of superior moral standing. **Remove the wooden beam from your eye first; then you will see clearly to remove the splinter**

from your brother's eye. Jesus does not rule out all brotherly and sisterly correction or all attempts to help others surmount their difficulties. But he makes correcting one's own faults a prior concern. Before trying to set others right, first set yourself right.

For reflection: Am I more alert to faults in others than to these same faults in myself?

Jesus implicitly calls upon his followers to adopt the attitude that whatever the faults of others, his followers' first concern must be their own faults. Should anyone argue, But there are greater sinners than I, Jesus might reply, How can you tell with a plank in your eye?

A Proverb

6 "Do not give what is holy to dogs, or throw your pearls before swine, lest they trample them underfoot, and turn and tear you to pieces."

6 **Do not give what is holy to dogs.** In the Old Testament, the term **holy,** or sacred, was applied to sacrificial offerings; a portion of some sacrifices was eaten in a sacred meal (Exod 29:31-33; Lev 22:4-16; Num 18:8-10). Virtually all references to **dogs** in the Old Testament regard them as wild scavengers (Exod 22:30; 1 Kings 21:23-24; 2 Kings 9:33-36). To take **what is holy**—flesh from a sacrificial animal that was to be consumed in a sacred meal—and throw it to scavenging **dogs** was an abomination.

Or throw your pearls before swine. In the ancient world, **pearls** were more valued than they are today and were extremely expensive (see 13:45-46). **Swine** were considered to be unclean (Lev 11:6-8; Deut 14:8). To **throw** valuable **pearls** to **swine** was an act of contemptuous squander; swine were liable to **trample them underfoot,** crushing them and making them worthless. We might think of flushing diamonds down a toilet.

Jesus adds that they might **turn and tear you to pieces.** Swine are capable of such violence. The structure of the verse, however, can convey that it is the **dogs** who will **turn** and **tear to pieces** the one who gave them what was holy. It is risky to throw a piece of meat to a pack of scavenging dogs; they may hunger for a larger meal.

This saying does not seem to tie in with what either precedes or follows it in the Sermon on the Mount. Since Jesus' disciples were unlikely to desecrate sacrificial offerings or be wealthy enough to own pearls, Jesus' words should be taken as a proverb that speaks of specifics in order to convey a general message: what is holy should not be profaned and what is valuable should not be wasted; to do so puts one at risk. Does Jesus have an application in mind? Many interpretations have been suggested, none completely convincing: Jesus is warning against preaching the gospel to unappreciative audiences, or being too accommodating to apostates, or taking church disputes outside the community of believers. We can best take Jesus' words as a general warning against wasting what is precious and holy, and make our own applications. The *Didache*, an early second-century Christian writing, applied Jesus' words to the Eucharist: "No one is to eat or drink of your Eucharist but only those who have been baptized in the name of the Lord; for the Lord's own saying applies here: 'Give not that which is holy unto dogs'"(*Didache* 9:5).

The *Didache*: See page 129

For reflection: What application can I make of Jesus' warning?

Asking a Father

7 **"Ask and it will be given to you; seek and you will find; knock and the door will be opened to you. ⁸ For everyone who asks, receives; and the one who seeks, finds; and to the one who knocks, the door will be opened. ⁹ Which one of you would hand his son a stone when he asks for a loaf of bread, ¹⁰ or a snake when he asks for a fish? ¹¹ If you then, who are wicked, know how to give good gifts to your children, how much more will your heavenly Father give good things to those who ask him."**

Gospel parallels: Luke 11:9-13

NT: Matt 18:19; 21:22; James 4:3; 1 John 5:14-15

7 **Ask and it will be given to you; seek and you will find; knock and the door will be opened to you.** Jesus is not talking about asking, seeking, and knocking in general, but about asking, seeking, and knocking within the context of our relationship with God. To **ask, seek,** and **knock** can stand for all the ways that we turn to God with our needs, but Jesus has provided some examples. Jesus taught his followers to ask, "Give us today our daily bread" (6:11), addressing their petitions to a Father who knows their needs (6:8, 32): **ask and it will be given to you** by God. Jesus told his disciples, "Seek first the kingdom [of God] and his righteousness" (6:33): **seek and you will find** what you are seeking. Jesus will shortly urge his followers to

enter the kingdom through its narrow gate (7:13): **knock and the door** of the kingdom **will be opened to you** by God.

The three verbs, "ask," "seek," and "knock" are imperatives: Jesus is commanding his disciples to ask for what they need, to seek God's reign and righteousness, to knock at the door of God's realm. These verbs are in the present tense, signifying repeated or continual actions: keep on asking, keep on seeking, keep on knocking. Discipleship is not a passive state but requires initiative and perseverance, even in one's relationship with God.

For reflection: What do I ask God for? What am I seeking?

8 Jesus repeats his teaching, now with an emphasis on the results of asking, seeking, knocking. **For everyone who asks, receives; and the one who seeks, finds; and to the one who knocks, the door will be opened.** Jesus' words ring with assurance, but they should not be interpreted simplistically. Will not Jesus ask his Father to be excused from suffering (26:39) and have his request denied? Will not Jesus' own prayer ultimately be, "Your will be done!" (26:42)? New Testament writers will warn that our asking must not be for sensual pleasures (James 4:3) and must be in accord with God's will (1 John 5:14). Yet to focus on the fine print risks missing Jesus' main point: our asking, seeking, and knocking will not be in vain (see also 18:19; 21:22). Jesus assures us that when we turn to God, we will receive and we will find and the door will be opened.

For reflection: How has God answered me when I asked, sought, knocked?

9 As if to address skepticism about God's responsiveness, Jesus makes a comparison. **Which one of you would hand his** or her **son a stone when he asks for a loaf of bread?** Bread, the staple food of the time, was often baked in small round loaves that might resemble stones. To refuse a son bread was to refuse him nourishment; to substitute a tooth-breaking stone was malicious. What parent in his or her right mind would do that?

Bread: See Diet, page 304

10 **or** hand a son **a snake when he asks for a fish?** Some eel-like fish might resemble snakes, but handing a hungry child a venomous snake instead of a fish would be malicious indeed. What kind of parent would do such a thing to a child?

11 Jesus draws a parallel between how his listeners behave and how God behaves. **If you then, who are wicked**—wicked certainly in comparison with God—**know how to give good gifts to your children, how much more will your heavenly Father give good things to those who ask him.** God gives **good things**—bread, not stones—**to those who ask.** If we take care of our children, **how much more** will God provide for us as our **heavenly Father** (see 6:31-33).

For reflection: What are the good things my heavenly Father has given me?

Jesus' basic point is that his disciples are to relate to God as their Father in heaven, turning to God with the trust that a child has for loving parents. Our asking, our seeking, our knocking are not done to arouse a distant and disinterested God. We can approach God with trust and confidence because Jesus authorizes his followers to call upon his Father as their Father (6:9).

For reflection: How confident am I in God's love and care for me?

The Golden Rule
12 **"Do to others whatever you would have them do to you. This is the law and the prophets."**
Gospel parallels: Luke 6:31
OT: Lev 19:18; Tobit 4:15
NT: Matt 19:19; 22:37-40

12 **Do to others whatever you would have them do to you.** The injunction to treat others as we want to be treated is commonly known as the Golden Rule. Different versions of this rule circulated in the centuries before Jesus. The rule was often formulated negatively: "Do to no one what you yourself dislike" (Tobit 4:15). A prominent Jewish teacher named Hillel, who lived shortly before Jesus, taught, "Whatever is displeasing to you do not do to your neighbor; that is the entire law, and the rest is commentary."

In its negative formulation, the Golden Rule might be taken as simple self-interest: do no harm to others, lest they harm you in return. Jesus' formulation goes far beyond self-interest. Jesus' command is framed positively: **Do to others.** It is not enough to be passive and avoid doing hateful things; the disciples of Jesus must take the initiative and act for the good of others, doing to others **whatever you would have them do to you.** No detailed checklist of what this entails is necessary: we each know how we like to be treated. We want to be esteemed and loved, and forgiven when necessary. **Do** so **to others,** loving them (even enemies—5:44), forgiving them if they harm you (6:12, 14-15).

Jesus, like Hillel, connects this rule of conduct with God's law: **This is the law and the prophets.** Jesus said that he came not to abolish the law and prophets but to fulfill them (5:17). Behaving lovingly toward others fulfills the requirements revealed in the law and prophets. The law commanded, "You shall love your neighbor as yourself" (Lev 19:18), and Jesus will cite this commandment (19:19; 22:39) as a basis of "the whole law and the prophets" (22:40). In the Golden Rule, Jesus broadens the command to love one's neighbors to include all **others,** not just one's fellow Israelites or fellow disciples.

Such a simple rule of life: treat others as you wish to be treated. But so sweeping in its compass, and so demanding in its application!

For reflection: Do I treat others as well as I want to be treated? As well as I treat myself?

ORIENTATION: *The Sermon on the Mount concludes with a series of contrasts that serve as exhortations to live according to Jesus' teachings.*

Two Ways
13 "**Enter through the narrow gate; for the gate is wide and the road broad that leads to destruction, and those who enter through it are many. 14 How narrow the gate and constricted the road that leads to life. And those who find it are few.**"

Gospel parallels: Luke 13:23-24
OT: Deut 30:15-20; Psalm 1; Jer 21:8
NT: Matt 22:14

13 Enter through the narrow gate: Jesus exhorts his disciples to **enter** into the reign, or realm, of God. To do so they must pass through a **narrow gate.** Jesus told his disciples, "unless your righteousness surpasses that of the scribes and Pharisees, you will not enter into the kingdom of heaven" (5:20). Living by a higher righteousness is the **narrow gate** through which one enters the kingdom. Narrow gates are more difficult to pass through than broad gates, but they are passable nonetheless. Living the kind of life necessary to enter the kingdom of heaven may be difficult, but Jesus does not present it as an impossible demand.

The alternative is unappealing in the long run: **for the gate is wide and the road broad that leads to destruction.** Here **gate** and **road** are images for the direction our lives take, leading to our final destination. There are easier ways of life than following the teachings of Jesus, but they lead to **destruction,** to ultimate ruin. Jesus adds somberly that **those who enter through it are many:** there are many who are on a path to destruction.

14 In comparison to the easy way, **how narrow the gate and constricted the road that leads to life.** Here **life** means eternal life (see 18:8-9; 19:16-17), life in the kingdom of God. Jesus has already said that the **gate** that leads to life is **narrow** (verse 13) and now uses a **constricted road** as another image for the same reality. The word **constricted** means "narrow," but it also has associations of afflictions and tribulations. Obeying Jesus' teachings

---

BACKGROUND: THE DIDACHE Even as the last books of the New Testament were being written, the early church produced other writings. One of these books is titled *The Teaching of the Lord to the Gentiles by the Twelve Apostles* and is commonly called the *Didache* (the Teaching). It was apparently composed in stages, and some of its material may predate Matthew's gospel. The *Didache* is a book of church instruction—the very first catechism, as it were. The first six chapters deal with individual conduct; the next nine address church practice in baptizing, fasting and prayer, celebrating the Eucharist and the Lord's day, and the treatment of apostles and prophets. A final chapter deals with the second coming of Christ. The opening chapters are patterned on the "two ways" and draw either on Matthew's gospel or traditions used by Matthew. The *Didache* begins, "There are two ways: a way of life and a way of death, and the difference between these two ways is great. The way of life is this: You shall love the Lord your creator, and secondly your neighbor as yourself; and you shall do nothing to anyone that you would not want done to yourself. What you may learn from these words is to bless them that curse you, to pray for your enemies, and to fast for your persecutors. For where is the merit in loving only those who return your love? Even the pagans do as much." Although not part of Scripture, the *Didache* was widely used for instruction by the early church, and elements of it were incorporated into later collections of church teachings.

---

and following him along the path of discipleship may involve hardships and persecution (5:10-12; 10:16-39). Yet this path, whatever its difficulties, **leads to life.**

For reflection: If I continue along the path I am on, where do I expect to end up?

Jesus again adds a somber note: **And those who find it are few**—only a few are following the path leading to eternal life. Jesus will say something similar on a later occasion (22:14). But he will also speak of "many" entering the kingdom of heaven (8:11) and of his giving his life for the sake of "many" (20:28). It is best to interpret Jesus' words about **few** finding life as an acknowledgment that most who have heard him preach have not wholeheartedly embraced his message. That should not discourage or deter his disciples; rather, it should spur them to be among those who do live according to his teachings and enter through the narrow gate that leads to life. The choice is theirs.

Jesus is echoing a strand of Jewish teaching known as the "two ways," with roots in the Old Testament. In Deuteronomy, Moses tells the Israelites, "I have today set before you life and prosperity, death and doom" (Deut 30:15) and urges them to "choose life" (Deut 30:19). Jeremiah echoes Deuteronomy: "Thus says the LORD: See, I am giving you a choice between life and death" (Jer 21:8—literally, "the way of life" and "the way of death"). Psalm 1 contrasts two ways: "The LORD watches over the way of the just, / but the way of the wicked leads to ruin" (Psalm 1:6). Jesus also contrasts two ways—a broad way leading to destruction and a narrow way leading to life—in order to make the same point as Moses: choose the way of life. The early church will use the "two ways" in its catechetical instruction, as evidenced by the *Didache*.

Two Kinds of Fruit

¹⁵ **"Beware of false prophets, who come to you in sheep's clothing, but underneath are ravenous wolves.** ¹⁶ **By their fruits you will know them. Do people pick grapes from thornbushes, or figs from thistles?** ¹⁷ **Just so, every good tree bears good fruit, and a rotten tree bears bad fruit.** ¹⁸ **A good tree cannot bear bad fruit, nor can a rotten tree bear good fruit.** ¹⁹ **Every tree that does not bear good fruit will be cut down and thrown into the fire.** ²⁰ **So by their fruits you will know them.**

[21] "Not everyone who says to me, 'Lord, Lord,' will enter the king-dom of heaven, but only the one who does the will of my Father in heaven. [22] Many will say to me on that day, 'Lord, Lord, did we not prophesy in your name? Did we not drive out demons in your name? Did we not do mighty deeds in your name?' [23] Then I will declare to them solemnly, 'I never knew you. Depart from me, you evildoers.'"

Gospel parallels: Luke 6:43-46; 13:25-27
OT:Psalm 6:9

15 **Beware of false prophets:** Jesus foresees the gift of prophecy being exer-cised in the early church (10:41; 23:34) but recognizes that there will also be **false prophets** (24:11, 24) who claim to speak for God but do not. Je-sus uses imagery to characterize false prophets as coming **in sheep's cloth-ing, but underneath are ravenous wolves.** Wolves kill sheep; "wolves who look like sheep" is an image for something dangerous that appears to be harmless. False prophets may appear to be delivering messages from God, but their fraudulent messages are as dangerous to the flock of God's people as wolves in sheep's clothing are to sheep.

16 If false prophets can appear to be true prophets, then how can false prophets be distinguished from true prophets? Jesus switches to imagery from the plant world and says that **by their fruits you will know them.** John the Baptist and Jesus use **fruits** as a metaphor for deeds or behavior (3:8; 12:33; 21:43). How a person behaves reveals who she or he is. Jesus appeals to his listeners' experience: **Do people pick grapes from thorn-bushes, or figs from thistles?** Grapes and figs were commonly cultivated in Palestine, and they certainly weren't harvested from thornbushes and thistles. The nature of a plant determines its produce: thornbushes and thistles produce prickly spikes, not edible grapes or figs.

17 **Just so, every good tree bears good fruit, and a rotten tree bears bad fruit.** Again, the nature of a plant determines what it produces: good trees produce good fruit and rotten trees produce bad fruit.

18 Jesus has stated what good and bad trees produce, and now he states what they cannot produce: **A good tree cannot bear bad fruit, nor can a rot-ten tree bear good fruit.** Good fruit only comes from good trees, and bad

fruit only comes from bad trees. The quality of the fruit is therefore evidence of the quality of the tree.

19 Jesus adds as an aside, **Every tree that does not bear good fruit will be cut down and thrown into the fire.** Since fruit trees were cultivated for the fruit they produced, a fruit tree that did not produce a good crop wasted space and water, and would be cut down and used for firewood. John the Baptist used this as an image for God's fiery punishment of those who did not produce good fruit of repentance (3:8, 10), and Jesus' words have a similar connotation, as verse 23 will make clear.

20 Jesus returns to his main point: **So by their fruits you will know them** (see verse 16). If fruit is evidence of the quality of a tree, so too deeds and behavior are evidence of the quality and character of a person. Specifically, a prophet's behavior is a reliable index of whether he or she is a true prophet or a false prophet. A prophet may proclaim something as a message from God, but the prophet's life is a more fundamental proclamation. In the context of the Sermon on the Mount, what is at issue is whether a prophet lives up to what Jesus commands, for Jesus' words reveal God's will (verse 21). A person who claims to speak for God but does not obey Jesus' teachings is a false prophet, a wolf in sheep's clothing, a danger to the flock of Jesus' followers.

21 The principle that behavior reveals character and identity can be applied to all followers of Jesus, distinguishing true disciples just as it distinguishes true prophets: **Not everyone who says to me, "Lord, Lord," will enter the kingdom of heaven, but only the one who does the will of my Father in heaven.** The word **Lord** has a range of meanings. It can simply be a polite form of address, roughly equivalent to "sir." It has a much more profound meaning when God is called "Lord" in acknowledgment of his sovereign majesty. Early Christians called Jesus "Lord" as a profession of his exalted status (Rom 10:9; 1 Cor 12:3; Phil 2:11). In this passage in Matthew's gospel, **Lord** bears its more profound meaning: Jesus is called "Lord" as God is called "Lord." Jesus warns that **not everyone** who solemnly acknowledges him as **Lord** will enter the kingdom of heaven. Words, even correct words sincerely spoken, are not enough. The **kingdom of heaven** means God's rule established in its fullness at the end of this age.

Kingdom of heaven: See page 266

Not everyone who calls upon Jesus as their Lord will enter the kingdom of heaven **but only the one who does the will of my Father in heaven.** Jesus in the Sermon on the Mount teaches what God's **will** is for us, how we are to behave, the kind of lives we are to lead. Only the one who **does the will** of God will enter the kingdom of heaven; doing God's will is the righteousness required to enter God's reign (5:20). In the immediate context, doing the will of God means bearing good fruit as the entrance requirement of the kingdom; not doing God's will means bearing bad fruit and being consigned to fire at God's judgment (verse 19). Jesus speaks of God as **my Father in heaven**—the first time in Matthew's gospel that Jesus refers to God as **my Father.** Matthew's readers know that Jesus is uniquely the Son of God (3:17), but it will be some time before the disciples understand the implications of Jesus' speaking of God as **my Father.** That Jesus does so now is perhaps a hint that his role as judge (verses 22-23) is part of his mission as the Son of God. Jesus was sent by the Father to make known his Father's will; Jesus will judge us on whether we have lived according to what he has taught us (see also 16:27; 25:31-32).

For reflection: If Jesus' teachings in the Sermon on the Mount lay out God's will, are there ways in which I am failing to do the will of God?

BACKGROUND: LORD The Greek word for "lord" is *kyrios,* familiar to many in the form in which it occurs in the petition *Kyrie, eleison* (Lord, have mercy)—Greek words in the Roman liturgy. A kyrios, or lord, is someone who has power and authority; thus the word has wide application. The owner of a property could be called its *kyrios* (the "owner of the vineyard" in Mark 12:9 is literally the "lord of the vineyard"). A master would be addressed as "lord" by his servants, but anyone could also use "lord" as a polite form of address to a man, much as the English word "sir" is used (see John 12:21). At the other extreme, Greek-speaking Jews used the word *kyrios*—"Lord"—as a title for God (Tobit 3:2, 11-12), as did New Testament writers (Luke 1:32; Rev 1:8). Because of this range of usage, when Jesus is called *kyrios* by someone in the gospels, it can simply be a respectful form of address (translated as "sir" in John 4:19) or an acknowledgment that he is someone with authority (the meaning of "Lord" in Matt 8:21 and Luke 7:6) or a declaration that he can be called "Lord" as God is called "Lord" (the meaning of "Lord" in John 20:28 and Phil 2:11).

22 **Many will say to me on that day:** the expression **that day** recalls Old Testament prophecies of a "day of the Lord" when God will set things right. For the early church, **that day** was "the day of our Lord Jesus" when he will establish God's reign in its fullness (1 Cor 1:8). Jesus says that **on that day,** the day of judgment, **many will say to me . . . "Lord, Lord,"** appealing to Jesus and pointing out what they have done for him: **Did we not prophesy in your name? Did we not drive out demons in your name? Did we not do mighty deeds in your name?** Jesus will empower disciples to "cure the sick, raise the dead, cleanse lepers, drive out demons" (10:8), and the exercise of these gifts will continue in the early church. To do these deeds in the **name** of Jesus means to do them on behalf of him and with his authority. Surely those who call upon Jesus as their Lord and are empowered by him to prophesy, drive out demons, and perform mighty deeds will be embraced by him on the day of judgment?

The day of the Lord: See page 48

23 Not necessarily. Jesus warns, **Then I will declare to them solemnly, "I never knew you."** Jesus won't deny that they have done mighty deeds on his behalf. Yet he will solemnly declare, **I never knew you**—I do not recognize you as one of my own. Despite their calling upon him as Lord, despite all the great works that they have done in his name, Jesus will order them, **Depart from me, you evildoers.** Why Jesus will make this pronouncement lies in the meaning of **evildoers:** it is literally "workers of lawlessness." God's law is at issue, God's will as proclaimed by Jesus in the Sermon on the Mount. Only those who do the will of God will enter the kingdom of heaven (verse 21); those who fail to obey God's law as proclaimed by Jesus will be banished from the kingdom on the day of judgment. Not even the exercise of gifts like exorcism and healing excuses one from keeping God's laws. Jesus adopts words from Psalm 6 for his pronouncement: **Depart from me, you evildoers** (see Psalm 6:9). This will not be the last time that Jesus will refer to those who are turned away on the day of judgment (13:40-42, 49-50; 22:11-13; 25:41-46).

Away from me, all who do evil!
Psalm 6:9

Jesus does not address here all issues pertaining to our salvation; he does not speak of the role of faith or about God's grace enabling us to keep

God's law. What Jesus does say is clear. We will be judged on our conduct, on the fruit we have produced, on what we have done and not done. We will repeatedly hear this teaching in the course of our reading of Matthew's gospel.

For reflection: What kind of fruit am I producing?

Two Builders

24 "Everyone who listens to these words of mine and acts on them will be like a wise man who built his house on rock. **25** The rain fell, the floods came, and the winds blew and buffeted the house. But it did not collapse; it had been set solidly on rock. **26** And everyone who listens to these words of mine but does not act on them will be like a fool who built his house on sand. **27** The rain fell, the floods came, and the winds blew and buffeted the house. And it collapsed and was completely ruined."

28 When Jesus finished these words, the crowds were astonished at his teaching, **29** for he taught them as one having authority, and not as their scribes.

Gospel parallels: Luke 6:47-49
NT: Mark 1:21-22; Luke 4:31-32; James 1:22-25

24 Everyone who listens to these words of mine and acts on them: Jesus' **everyone** is inclusive, covering his first disciples, members of the early church, and those today who listen and act. **These words of mine** are his teachings in the Sermon on the Mount and, more broadly, all his teachings. Jesus speaks of the person who not only **listens** to his teachings but **acts on them**, doing the will of Jesus' Father (7:21). That person **will be like a wise man who built his house on rock.** The Greek word for **wise** could also be translated as "prudent" (see 24:45); this man's prudence lay in his choice of a site to build his house (real estate has always been a matter of location, location, location). Galilee is dotted with limestone hills covered by an uneven layer of soil. Houses commonly had stone walls; an outcropping of rock provided a stable base for such walls. This wise builder picked a site where he could build his house **on rock.**

Houses: See page 81

135

25 **The rain fell, the floods came, and the winds blew and buffeted the house. But it did not collapse; it had been set solidly on rock.** The rocky hills of Galilee do not readily absorb rain; a heavy rainfall can become a flood of water crashing down hillsides and filling ravines. A stone house built on rock can withstand floods and windstorms.

Jesus says that those who listen to his teachings and act on them "will be like" (verse 24) a wise builder whose house withstands a storm; the phrase "will be like" points to something that will happen in the future. Prophets used storms as an image for God's judgment (Isaiah 28:2; 29:6; 30:30; Ezek 13:10-16). Jesus is again speaking of the last judgment (see verses 13-14, 19, 21-23), now by means of a comparison or parable. Those who take Jesus' words to heart and act on them will withstand God's judgment, just as a house built on rock withstands a storm.

26 **And everyone who listens to these words of mine but does not act on them will be like a fool who built his house on sand.** Rain flushed soil and sand down from hills to the floors of valleys and ravines, providing some temptingly level places to build a house. A foolish builder might choose such a site, laying the lowest course of house walls directly on **sand.**

27 **The rain fell, the floods came, and the winds blew and buffeted the house.** Storm runoff surged against the house, washing away the sand beneath its walls and undermining them, and the house **collapsed and was completely ruined.** Just as a house built on sand will collapse in a flood, so those who do not live according to Jesus' teachings will face utter ruin at the last judgment.

For reflection: Upon what am I basing my life?

Jesus uses the parable of two builders and their house sites to teach the importance of not only listening to his teachings but putting them into practice. The Letter of James uses a different comparison to make the same point: "Be doers of the word and not hearers only, deluding yourselves. For if anyone is a hearer of the word and not a doer, he is like a man who looks at his own face in a mirror. He sees himself, then goes off and promptly forgets what he looked like" (James 1:22-24).

For reflection: Where might my doing fall short of my hearing?

Jesus' series of contrasts—two ways (verses 13-14), two kinds of fruit (verses 15-23), two builders (verses 24-27)—serve as exclamation points at the end of the Sermon on the Mount. Jesus' disciples must follow his teachings to gain entrance to God's kingdom at the final judgment.

28 **When Jesus finished these words**—the Sermon on the Mount—**the crowds were astonished at his teaching.** The crowds who had come to Jesus (4:25) and listened as he began to instruct his disciples (5:1-2), were **astonished at his teaching.** They were amazed by the way Jesus taught (verse 29); were they amazed as well by what he taught? Jesus has said some astonishing things, for example, that we must love our enemies (5:44) and that we must be perfect as God is perfect (5:48). Jesus has presented his teachings as the entrance requirements of the kingdom of heaven. If someone wasn't astonished by Jesus' words, were they really listening?

For reflection: What most astonishes me as I read the Sermon on the Mount?

29 The manner in which Jesus taught was astonishing, **for he taught them as one having authority.** He reminded his listeners what was written in God's law and then said, "But I say to you" (5:22, 28, 32, 34, 39), conveying that it was within his authority to interpret and extend God's law. Jesus referred to God as "my Father" and spoke of himself as the judge of whether a person satisfied the entrance requirements of God's kingdom (7:21-23). Jesus teaches as if he has the **authority** to require what he requires. The crowd noted that Jesus taught **not as their scribes** taught. **Scribes** were religious scholars who passed on and interpreted teachings and traditions they had received from others. Their authority was based on the tradition that they were handing on and on their training and expertise in that tradition. In contrast to them Jesus did not appeal to earlier authorities; Jesus taught **as one having** the **authority** to pronounce what God wants.

For reflection: What glimpse into Jesus' identity am I given by the manner in which he taught?

The Sermon on the Mount does not stand on its own as an independent tract, but must be interpreted in the context of Matthew's gospel. At the beginning of the gospel, Joseph was told that Jesus will "save his people from their sins" (1:21). If Jesus demands that his followers live upright lives, he also rescues them from their failures to do so. Jesus enables his disciples to relate to his Father (3:17) as their loving Father (6:9); the Sermon on the Mount describes how one lives out this relationship. Jesus began his public ministry with the proclamation, "Repent, for the kingdom of heaven is at hand" (4:17). The Sermon on the Mount spells out the requirements of repentance and how a person lives under the reign of God. Jesus released men and women from the grasp of evil (4:23-24; see also 8:1-17, 28-32), freeing them to do the will of God. Jesus lived out what he taught in the Sermon on the Mount; his teachings describe how his disciples are to imitate him.

BACKGROUND: SCRIBES   The scribes encountered in the gospels are scholars and teachers of the law of Moses, but the profession of scribe included others as well. A scribe was literally someone who could write, a literate person in a largely illiterate society. Scribes ranged from village scribes who handled routine correspondence and record keeping to high-ranking officials in governmental administrative positions. (Today we apply the title "secretary" both to a typist and to the secretary of state.) In the gospel accounts, scribes are men who specialize in studying and teaching the law of Moses and are centered in Jerusalem. When Jesus proclaimed interpretations of the law different from those of scribes, conflicts arose between scribes and Jesus. Some scribes (a professional group) were Pharisees (a religious group), but not all scribes were Pharisees, and not all Pharisees were scribes. Likewise, some Jerusalem priests were also scribes, and some scribes were Sadducees (an aristocratic elite). Eventually some scribes took part in the reshaping of Judaism after the destruction of Jerusalem by Rome in A.D. 70 and were among those who became known as rabbis. *Related topics: Pharisees (page 231), Sadducees (page 476).*

CHAPTER 8

ORIENTATION: *Matthew summarized Jesus' activities as teaching and proclaiming the gospel, and "curing every disease and illness" (4:23). In chapters 5 to 7, Matthew provided a collection of Jesus' teachings; in chapters 8 and 9 he presents accounts of Jesus' healings.*

Jesus Cleanses a Man of Leprosy

1 When Jesus came down from the mountain, great crowds followed him. **2** And then a leper approached, did him homage, and said, "Lord, if you wish, you can make me clean." **3** He stretched out his hand, touched him, and said, "I will do it. Be made clean." His leprosy was cleansed immediately. **4** Then Jesus said to him, "See that you tell no one, but go show yourself to the priest, and offer the gift that Moses prescribed; that will be proof for them."

Gospel parallels: Mark 1:40-45; Luke 5:12-16
OT:Lev 13–14

1 **When Jesus came down from the mountain**—after delivering the Sermon on the Mount (chapters 5-7)—**great crowds followed him.** These **crowds** had come to Jesus for healing (4:24-25) and had heard his teaching on the mountain (5:1; 7:28). Now Jesus is making his way to Capernaum (8:5) and the crowds **followed** along after him. While following Jesus characterizes discipleship (see 4:20, 22), the crowds are not yet disciples. They are potential disciples: they have been impressed by Jesus' words (7:28-29). Getting to know Jesus and his message is the first step toward discipleship.

2 **And then a leper approached.** The **leper** suffered from a disfiguring skin condition, possibly but not necessarily what is diagnosed as leprosy today. Whatever the precise malady, his condition made him ritually unclean, and he had to live apart lest he infect others with his ritual impurity.

> *The one who bears the sore of leprosy shall keep his garments rent and his head bare, and shall muffle his beard; he shall cry out, "Unclean, unclean!" . . . He shall dwell apart, making his abode outside the camp.*
> *Leviticus 13:45-46*

Yet this man with leprosy **approached** Jesus, reaching across the barrier that kept them apart. He did Jesus **homage,** prostrating himself before Jesus as had the magi (2:11). Kings received such homage (1 Kings 1:16, 23, 31), as did God (the word for "worship" in 4:10 is the same word translated here as **homage).** The man with leprosy does Jesus homage as an act of supplication and in recognition that Jesus has the power to heal. He tells Jesus, **Lord, if you wish, you can make me clean.** A lord was someone with authority and power; the man with leprosy called Jesus **Lord** in acknowledgment of his power to heal him: **you can make me clean.** Matthew's readers hailed Jesus as Lord with more profound meaning: Jesus could be called "Lord" as God is called "Lord" (see Phil 2:9-11). Since Jesus could heal leprosy, the only question was whether he was willing to do so: the man told him, **if you wish,** you can make me clean.

Lord: See page 133

For reflection: What does Jesus have the power to do for me? Where do I need to be made clean?

3 **He stretched out his hand, touched him.** The man had approached Jesus and had fallen on the ground before him; Jesus bridges the remaining distance between them, stretching out his hand to him, touching him. Those with leprosy were untouchables; any who touched them became unclean (see Lev 5:3). But Jesus' touch is healing, removing untouchableness. Jesus

---

BACKGROUND: LEPROSY In the Old and New Testaments, "leprosy" refers to a variety of skin conditions and infections, one of which might have been what is called leprosy today (Hansen's disease). Some of these skin conditions went away in time; some did not. A skin condition that resulted in abnormal appearance made the afflicted person ritually impure, or unclean, since purity was associated with normality, and impurity with abnormality. Old Testament regulations specified that priests were to determine whether a skin condition was leprosy; if it was, the person with the skin disease was excluded from the community as unclean (Lev 13). Priests likewise judged whether a person's leprosy had gone away, in which case the person underwent purification rituals before rejoining the community (Lev 14). These procedures indicate that what was at stake was ritual purity. Exclusion of the afflicted person from the community prevented the spread of uncleanness; there was little understanding of the nature of diseases or of how they were spread.

said, "I will do it. Be made clean." Jesus wants to heal the man and commands that it happen. His leprosy was cleansed immediately. His skin was cleansed of leprosy as grime is washed away; he was, at the same time, cleansed from the cause of his ritual uncleanness.

For reflection: How have I experienced Jesus' healing touch?

4 Yet further steps were necessary for the man's cleansing to be certified and for him to be able to rejoin society. Jesus tells him to take these steps. Then Jesus said to him, "See that you tell no one, but go show yourself to the priest." The law of Moses assigned priests the role of declaring whether or not a person had been healed of leprosy (Lev 14:2-3). See that you tell no one probably does not mean that the man should keep his healing a secret: how could he, with a crowd present (verse 1) who had apparently witnessed his encounter with Jesus? Further, when the man rejoined his family and village, he would have to explain how he came to be free of leprosy. Jesus' instruction tell no one might mean, "Don't dally on the way, but go directly to a priest." After a priest had certified the man healed, he was to offer the gift that Moses prescribed. The gift was a sacrificial offering of animals (Lev 14:4-32), which would have been done at the Temple in Jerusalem. Jesus adds, that will be proof for them, but the meaning of this final instruction is unclear. What is the proof and what does it prove? Does them refer to priests or to people in general? Perhaps

---

BACKGROUND: PRIESTS in the time of Jesus were primarily responsible for offering sacrificial worship in the Temple. During the Old Testament era, priests also instructed the people in the law of Moses, but in time this function largely passed to scribes as professional scholars and teachers (some priests were also scribes). The office of priesthood was hereditary. All priests were members of the tribe of Levi, but not all members of this tribe were priests: some served in the Temple in secondary roles as Levites. At the time of Jesus there were perhaps seven thousand priests and ten thousand Levites, out of a total Jewish population in Palestine of a half million to a million. Some priests, especially those from high priestly families, lived in Jerusalem and were in charge of the Temple. Most priests lived in other towns, and only served in the Temple a week at a time on a twenty-four-week rotation. There was a considerable gap in income and influence between the Jerusalem high priestly families and ordinary priests living outside Jerusalem.

Jesus is referring to his having the man follow the procedures laid down in the law of Moses: Jesus means that this is proof that he has come to fulfill rather than abolish the law (5:17).

In the first healing described in Matthew's gospel, Jesus not only cures a man of a physical affliction but enables him to rejoin society. This is a hint that Jesus' healings are an aspect of his bringing women and men into the reign of God.

A Gentile's Amazing Faith
5 **When he entered Capernaum, a centurion approached him and appealed to him,** **6** **saying, "Lord, my servant is lying at home paralyzed, suffering dreadfully."** **7** **He said to him, "I will come and cure him."** **8** **The centurion said in reply, "Lord, I am not worthy to have you enter under my roof; only say the word and my servant will be healed.** **9** **For I too am a person subject to authority, with soldiers subject to me. And I say to one, 'Go,' and he goes; and to another, 'Come here,' and he comes; and to my slave, 'Do this,' and he does it."** **10** **When Jesus heard this, he was amazed and said to those following him, "Amen, I say to you, in no one in Israel have I found such faith.** **11** **I say to you, many will come from the east and the west, and will recline with Abraham, Isaac, and Jacob at the banquet in the kingdom of heaven,** **12** **but the children of the kingdom will be driven out into the outer darkness, where there will be wailing and grinding of teeth."** **13** **And Jesus said to the centurion, "You may go; as you have believed, let it be done for you." And at that very hour [his] servant was healed.**

Gospel parallels: Luke 7:1-10; 13:28-29; John 4:46-54
OT:Isaiah 25:6-8; Jer 3:17-18

5 **When he entered Capernaum:** Jesus had moved from Nazareth to Capernaum (4:13), and used Capernaum as his base of operations during his public ministry. As he came into town, **a centurion approached him and appealed to him.** A centurion usually commanded one hundred soldiers but sometimes fewer. Although centurion was a rank in the Roman army, other armies also had centurions. (*Lieutenant* is a French word, but this does not mean that everyone with this rank is French.) **Capernaum** was in Galilee, a region ruled by Herod Antipas; Roman centurions did not serve under Jewish rulers such as Herod. Herod's armed forces were recruited locally or from neighboring Syria, and included both Jews and

Gentiles. Verse 10 will indicate that this **centurion** is a Gentile. Matthew does not tell us that this centurion was stationed at Capernaum, but Herod did post troops there. Capernaum lay on the border of Herod's realm and had a customs post (9:9); the presence of soldiers facilitated the collection of Herod's taxes.

Capernaum: See page 61
Herod Antipas: See page 298

This centurion **approached** Jesus **and appealed to him.** Jesus did not seek him out; he came to Jesus.

6 He told Jesus, **Lord, my servant is lying at home paralyzed, suffering dreadfully.** The centurion addresses Jesus as **Lord,** for he views Jesus as a person with superior power and authority (verses 8-9). The Greek word translated **servant** can mean "son" or "servant"; the New American Bible interprets it to mean "servant" in this passage. The servant is bedridden and terribly tortured by his affliction. The centurion comes to Jesus in the hope that Jesus will heal him: his telling Jesus about his sick servant is an implied request for healing.

Lord: See page 133

For reflection: What are my hopes when I bring my needs to Jesus?

7 **He said to him, "I will come and cure him."** Jesus' words could also be translated as a question—"Am I to come and cure him?"—and interpreted as a rebuff (biblical Hebrew and Greek manuscripts lack punctuation such as questions marks, and it is sometimes uncertain whether a sentence should be translated as a statement or a question). Jesus will later turn aside another Gentile's request, saying that his mission is only to Jews (15:24). The New American Bible interprets Jesus' words to be an offer to go to the sick servant and heal him. The centurion's response (verses 8-9) makes sense as a reaction to either a question or a statement by Jesus, and it is the centurion's response that is the focal point of this passage.

8 **The centurion said in reply, "Lord, I am not worthy to have you enter under my roof."** Several factors likely lie behind the centurion's words. Despite being a man with authority (verse 9), the centurion considers himself of little consequence compared to Jesus. Someone with Jesus' status,

who can be called **Lord,** should hardly be expected to make house calls. Second, this Gentile centurion may have thought that Jesus would incur ritual impurity by entering his house (see Acts 10:28; 11:2-3), and was considerate of Jesus. Third, there was no need for Jesus to enter his house to heal his servant: the centurion told Jesus, **only say the word and my servant will be healed.** Jesus does not need to touch the servant to heal him, or even be in the same room with him. The centurion believes that a mere healing **word** uttered by Jesus is sufficient for his servant to be **healed.**

9 The centurion uses himself as a comparison to explain his faith in the power of Jesus to command illness away with a word. **For I too am a person subject to authority, with soldiers subject to me:** the centurion is in a chain of command. His being under the authority of Herod Antipas means that he is authorized to issue orders to Herod's soldiers under him. He is used to having his orders carried out: **I say to one, "Go," and he goes; and to another, "Come here," and he comes.** The centurion also has authority over a slave he owns: he can say to his **slave, "Do this," and he does it.** Verbal commands are all it takes to have those subject to the centurion do what he wants. He implies that it is the same with Jesus: Jesus can utter a word of command to anyone or anything subject to him, and his command will be obeyed. The centurion believes that Jesus has authority over illnesses, and therefore it will take no more than a word from Jesus for his servant to be healed.

10 **When Jesus heard this, he was amazed**—the only time in Matthew's gospel that Jesus is amazed or surprised. Jesus is so amazed that he comments on his amazement. He turns from the centurion and says **to those following him, "Amen, I say to you, in no one in Israel have I found such faith."** Jesus notes the **faith** of the centurion—the centurion's confidence that Jesus has such authority over afflictions that he is able to heal with a simple word of command. This is the first mention of or praise of a person's **faith** in the Gospel of Matthew—and the faith-filled person is not a Jew but a Gentile centurion. **No one in Israel**—that is, no Jew—has demonstrated such faith in Jesus as has this Gentile centurion. Jesus' disciples, whom he is now addressing, are included in the **no one:** they have a "little faith" (6:30) but not such faith as has the centurion. Jesus is **amazed** that he has found such great faith in a Gentile.

11 Jesus continues with a prophetic pronouncement: **I say to you, many will come from the east and the west, and will recline with Abraham, Isaac, and Jacob at the banquet in the kingdom of heaven.** Jesus invokes several Old Testament themes. The Old Testament speaks of two groups coming **from the east and the west** or from afar: Israelites returning home from exile (Psalm 107:2-3; Isaiah 43:5-6; Baruch 4:36-37; Zech 8:7-8) and Gentiles coming to Jerusalem to give homage God (Isaiah 2:2-3; Zech 8:20-23). Jeremiah speaks of both Jews and Gentiles coming to Jerusalem (Jer 3:17-18). Verse 12 indicates that Jesus has Gentiles in mind. They will come from the ends of the earth to **recline with Abraham, Isaac, and Jacob at the banquet in the kingdom of heaven.** A **banquet** was not an ordinary meal but a feast; Jews adopted the Greek custom of reclining at banquets. Isaiah used a feast as an image for God's abundant care for his people at the end of this age (Isaiah 25:6-8); Jesus adopts Isaiah's image and will teach that the kingdom of heaven is like a feast (22:1-14). **Abraham, Isaac, and Jacob** were revered as the ancestors of the Jewish people. Jews who believed in an afterlife presumed that these patriarchs were with God and that those who will be rewarded in the next life will join them (see Luke 16:22-26). In Jesus' prophetic pronouncement, it is Gentiles who will enjoy **the banquet in the kingdom of heaven** in the company of Abraham, Isaac, and Jacob.

Banquets: See page 464

Kingdom of heaven: See page 266

On this mountain the LORD of hosts
   will provide for all peoples
A feast of rich foods and choice wines,
   juicy, rich food and pure, choice wines.
Isaiah 25:6

12 **but the children of the kingdom:** the **children of the kingdom** are its natural heirs: Jews, who have been blessed with God's revelation and should be part of God's reign when it is established. But Jesus proclaims that they (at least some of them) will not be part of the heavenly banquet; they **will be driven out into outer darkness, where there will be wailing and grinding of teeth.** Wailing and grinding of teeth is an idiom for being in great distress (see 13:41-42, 49-50; 22:13; 24:51; 25:30).

Jesus' pronouncement is a shocking reversal of Jewish expectations. Jews thought that they would be at the head of the line entering into God's banquet; Gentiles, if they acknowledged God and were admitted at all, would be at the end of the line. Jesus tells his Jewish audience that Gentiles will dine with Abraham, Isaac, and Jacob while Jews will be refused admittance. His pronouncement should be understood as a prophetic warning, akin to his saying that only a few will enter through the narrow gate to life (7:13-14). Jesus does not say how many Gentiles will be admitted to the heavenly banquet or how many Jews will be excluded; his words cannot be taken as a statement of what will happen to all Gentiles and to all Jews. His words warn against feeling assured that one will be automatically included in God's heavenly banquet—a warning for Jesus' Jewish listeners, and a warning that Matthew wants his readers, both Jewish and Gentile Christians, to take to heart.

For reflection: What is the lesson of Jesus' warning for me?

13 Jesus turns his attention back to the centurion. **Jesus said to the centurion, "You may go; as you have believed, let it be done for you."** The centurion **believed** that Jesus could heal his servant with a word (verse 8); Jesus responds by saying **let it be done for you.** That is all it takes: **And at that very hour [his] servant was healed.** Matthew provides no additional details about the healing. The focus in Matthew's account is on the faith of the centurion rather than the healing itself.

Jesus' first healing recounted in Matthew's gospel was of a man with leprosy, an outcast from Jewish society (verses 1-4). The second healing Matthew recounts is worked on behalf of another person who was excluded from God's people: a Gentile centurion. Jesus speaks of many Gentiles entering into the heavenly banquet, while Jews ("children of the kingdom"—verse 12) will be excluded. The church for which Matthew wrote his gospel was initially made up of Jewish Christians, but was increasingly receiving Gentile converts. Jesus' praise for the centurion's faith and his pronouncement that many will come from east and west into God's banquet conveyed that Gentiles as well as Jews could receive salvation through faith. Gentile members of Matthew's church could look back on the centurion as one of their ancestors in faith. Both Jewish Christians and Gentile Christians could take the centurion's absolute confidence in Jesus as a model for their own faith.

For reflection: In what ways is the centurion a model for me?

Jesus Heals the Afflicted

14 Jesus entered the house of Peter, and saw his mother-in-law lying in bed with a fever. **15** He touched her hand, the fever left her, and she rose and waited on him.

16 When it was evening, they brought him many who were possessed by demons, and he drove out the spirits by a word and cured all the sick, **17** to fulfill what had been said by Isaiah the prophet:

> "He took away our infirmities
>   and bore our diseases."

Gospel parallels: Mark 1:29-34; Luke 4:38-41
OT:Isaiah 53:4

14 Having come into Capernaum (8:5), **Jesus entered the house of Peter.** This is the only explicit mention of **the house of Peter** in the Gospel of Matthew. Peter had accepted Jesus' invitation to "Come after me" (4:18-20), but following Jesus did not mean that Peter became homeless. It rather seems that Jesus came to live in Peter's house in Capernaum (see 13:1, 36; 17:24-25; Mark 1:21, 29-35; 2:1; 3:20; 9:33). Having entered Peter's house, Jesus **saw his mother-in-law lying in bed with a fever.** Peter was married; Paul indicates that Peter's wife later accompanied him on his missionary travels (1 Cor 9:5). Extended families lived together, making it no surprise that Peter's **mother-in-law** might be found in his house. Matthew does not specify the cause of her **fever;** one possibility would be malaria, which was common, and often fatal, in northern Palestine until the twentieth century. Jesus **saw** that she was feverish and bedridden.

15 Jesus takes the initiative to heal her, without being asked: **He touched her hand** and **the fever left her.** Matthew's account is sparse, foregoing details in order to focus on essentials. Jesus sees the woman's suffering and need; he reaches out to touch her and heal her of her malady.

For reflection: What does Jesus see when he gazes on me? How am I most in need of his healing touch?

Freed of her affliction, **she rose and waited on him.** Her getting up from her bed was a sign that she had been healed. She **waited on** Jesus: the expression can mean that she served Jesus a meal, and this is probably the

147

meaning here. The Greek for "waited on" could also be translated "served" and carry broader meaning. Jesus will call his disciples to be servants of one another (20:26-27; 23:11) just as he came to serve (20:28). Peter's mother-in-law is the first person in Matthew's gospel to put Jesus' teaching into practice. She waits on **him:** her efforts are directed to Jesus, doing what she can for him in gratitude for what he has done for her.

For reflection: How am I able to serve Jesus?

16 **When it was evening, they brought him many who were possessed by demons, and he drove out the spirits by a word and cured all the sick.** Jesus attracts people with needs (see also 4:23-25). Matthew says that when those who were **possessed by demons** were brought to Jesus, he **drove out**

BACKGROUND: PETER'S HOUSE In Capernaum, archaeologists have found the remains of an ancient neighborhood of houses clustered around courtyards. An octagonal church was erected over some of the ruins in the fifth century; octagonal or circular churches were built to mark holy places. Beneath the center of the church are the remains of a room that was built around 65 B.C. Its walls and floor were made of unworked basalt stones (basalt is black volcanic rock) and would have supported a roof of beams and tree branches covered with thatch and earth. The interior of this room measured about twenty by twenty feet, and it shared a courtyard with other rooms. Archaeologists have found evidence (fishhooks, broken kitchenware) indicating that it was used as a family home at the time of Jesus. Later in the first century this room was set aside for special use. Its walls and floor were plastered (unlike other houses discovered in Capernaum), and Christians began carving prayers in the plaster, which suggests that it was a venerated site and a place for Christian gatherings. An arch was added in the fourth century to support a more durable roof. Egeria, a European nun who came on pilgrimage to the Holy Land sometime around 390, wrote in her travel notes, "In Capernaum a house church was made out of the house of Peter, and its walls still stand today." Egeria's words and the archaeological evidence make it very probable that the venerated room was the house of Peter. Subsequently the octagonal church was built over the site. This church was destroyed in the seventh century, perhaps during a Persian invasion. Capernaum went into a steady decline after an eighth-century earthquake and was abandoned in the eleventh century. A modern church was dedicated in 1992, with a glass floor that allows worshipers to gaze down on the remains of Peter's house.

the spirits and **cured all the sick:** Matthew does not draw a clear distinction between demon possession and illness. Whatever the afflictions and their root causes, Jesus is able to free men and women from them. **Many were brought to Jesus, and he cured all of them:** he turned no one away nor sent anyone away unhealed. Jesus healed **by a word,** just as he was able to heal the centurion's servant with a word (8:8). In chapters 5 to 7, Matthew presented the teaching word of Jesus; in chapters 8 and 9 Matthew gives examples of Jesus' healing word.

Demons, unclean spirits: See page 177

17 Jesus' healings are not simply acts of compassion and demonstrations of his power; they are part of God's plan revealed in Scripture. Jesus' healings **fulfill what had been said by Isaiah the prophet: "He took away our infirmities / and bore our diseases"** (Isaiah 53:4). The Greek word for **bore** has the senses of "remove" and "endure." This passage occurs in a prophecy that speaks of a servant of God who frees others from sin and suffering by suffering in their place and giving his life (Isaiah 52:13–53:12). Matthew does not quote the full prophecy as a foreshadowing of Jesus' suffering and crucifixion. He is content to proclaim that Jesus fulfills Isaiah's words about a servant of God who takes away and bears the infirmities of others.

> Yet it was our infirmities that he bore,
>   our sufferings that he endured,
> While we thought of him as stricken,
>   as one smitten by God and afflicted.
>   Isaiah 53:4

For reflection: What insight into Jesus do I find in Isaiah's words?

ORIENTATION: *The setting apparently shifts to a new day, with Jesus no longer in Peter's house (8:14-17) but somewhere on the western shore of the Sea of Galilee.*

The Demands of Discipleship
18 When Jesus saw a crowd around him, he gave orders to cross to the other side. **19** A scribe approached and said to him, "Teacher, I will follow you wherever you go." **20** Jesus answered him, "Foxes have dens and

birds of the sky have nests, but the Son of Man has nowhere to rest his head." ²¹ Another of [his] disciples said to him, "Lord, let me go first and bury my father." ²² But Jesus answered him, "Follow me, and let the dead bury their dead."

²³ He got into a boat and his disciples followed him. ²⁴ Suddenly a violent storm came up on the sea, so that the boat was being swamped by waves; but he was asleep. ²⁵ They came and woke him, saying, "Lord, save us! We are perishing!" ²⁶ He said to them, "Why are you terrified, O you of little faith?" Then he got up, rebuked the winds and the sea, and there was great calm. ²⁷ The men were amazed and said, "What sort of man is this, whom even the winds and the sea obey?"

Gospel parallels: Mark 4:35-41; Luke 8:22-25; 9:57-60

18 **When Jesus saw a crowd around him:** Jesus attracted crowds who came to him for healing (4:23-25; 8:1-2, 16). **He gave orders to cross to the other side.** Matthew does not indicate why Jesus wanted to cross the Sea of Galilee; perhaps the implication of Jesus seeing the **crowd around him** is that he wanted to get away from their demands for a while. Jesus gave orders **to cross**—literally, gave orders "to go" or "to go off"; the notion of going will come up again.

19 **A scribe approached:** a **scribe** in the gospels is someone who studied and interpreted the law of Moses. This scribe **said to him, "Teacher, I will follow you wherever you go."** Scribes received their training from those who had achieved some mastery of the law of Moses and thus could be teachers; this scribe addresses Jesus as **Teacher,** indicating that he looks upon Jesus as having superior knowledge of the law. He wants to study under Jesus and be his disciple: that is the meaning of telling Jesus, **I will follow you.** It was normal Jewish practice for students to choose their teachers; Jesus on the other hand took the initiative in choosing his disciples (4:18-22). The scribe tells Jesus, **I will follow you wherever you go.** Jesus has just ordered his disciples to cross the Sea of Galilee; this scribe wants to **go** with them.

Scribes: See page 138

20 **Jesus answered him, "Foxes have dens and birds of the sky have nests, but the Son of Man has nowhere to rest his head."** Much of Jesus' public ministry was spent on the road (4:23; 9:35). When he sends his disciples

out on missions, he instructs them to rely on the hospitality of others (10:9-11), and this presumably mirrors Jesus' own practice. When in Capernaum, Jesus apparently relied on the hospitality of Peter (8:14; 13:1, 36; 17:24-25). Jesus had **nowhere** of his own **to rest his head;** even **foxes** and **birds** had more assured accommodations. For the first time in Matthew's gospel, Jesus refers to himself as **the Son of Man.** This enigmatic title may simply mean here that Jesus shares the human condition. But while most men and women have a place to call home, Jesus has relinquished this security.

When the scribe called Jesus "Teacher" (verse 19), he indicated his respect for Jesus' knowledge. But Jesus is far more than a teacher, and those who are his disciples must be more than students. Jesus invites his disciples to share his life, including his life on the road with its uncertainties. Jesus' implicit question to the scribe is, "Are you willing to take on my lifestyle as well as learn my teachings?" Matthew does not tell us how the scribe responded. Did he turn away discouraged? Did he reaffirm his commitment to follow Jesus wherever he went? Perhaps Matthew leaves the matter unresolved to invite his readers to examine their own response to Jesus. Are we willing to imitate Jesus as well as learn his teachings?

Disciple: See page 66

BACKGROUND: SON OF MAN Jesus uses the expression "Son of Man" about eighty times in the four gospels; it is found only four times in the rest of the New Testament. In its origin it is a Hebrew and Aramaic idiom that means "human being": Ezekiel, for example, is repeatedly addressed by God as "son of man" (Ezek 2:1; 3:1; 4:1). It seems to have the same meaning in some passages where Jesus refers to himself as the Son of Man; that is, it simply means that he shares the human condition. Jesus also employs the expression as a way of referring to himself during his public ministry, even when he is doing things that by human standards are extraordinary, for example, forgiving sins (Mark 2:10). In other passages, Jesus uses the expression "Son of Man" when speaking of his coming suffering and death. In still other passages, the Son of Man is the risen Jesus returning in glory at the end of time. These last instances echo the use of "one like a son of man" in Daniel 7:13-14. Neither in Daniel nor in any other Jewish writing from before the time of Jesus is "Son of Man" used as a title for the Messiah. Jesus' referring to himself as the Son of Man was distinctive: others did not call him the Son of Man. It is also enigmatic: scholars have endlessly debated the complexities of this title.

For reflection: Can I say to Jesus, I will follow you wherever you lead me? Am I willing to forsake security to be his disciple?

21 Another of [his] disciples said to him, "Lord, let me go first and bury my father." This disciple addresses Jesus as **Lord,** which on his lips is an acknowledgement that Jesus is more than a teacher. He too wants to go with Jesus across the Sea of Galilee, but not immediately. He asks Jesus, **let me go first and bury my father.** It would seem that his father has just died and is about to be buried (Jewish burials took place on the day of death: see Acts 5:5-6, 10). Burying one's father was a son's special obligation (see Tobit 4:3-4); later Jewish tradition considered it a duty that took precedence over other requirements of the law of Moses. This disciple makes what seems to be a perfectly reasonable request of Jesus: let me first bury my father, and then I will go with you.

22 But Jesus answered him, "Follow me, and let the dead bury their dead." Jesus' response seems anything but reasonable, for he demands the impossible: corpses cannot bury other corpses. Trying to transform Jesus' demand into something reasonable creates as many problems as it solves. Suggesting, for example, that Jesus means "let the spiritually dead bury the physically dead" would imply that Jesus considered everyone who was not his disciple to be spiritually dead, which is not how Jesus viewed the centurion (8:10-13). It is better to take Jesus' words as a provocative demand, meant to convey that responding to his call to **follow me** must take precedence over all else, including family and social obligations. For a disciple, nothing is more urgent than following Jesus. Matthew does not recount the disciple's response, perhaps again so that his readers will ponder whether they have put their own following of Jesus ahead of all else.

For reflection: What do I need to leave behind if I am to follow Jesus?

23 He got into a boat: someone has noted that in the gospels there always seems to be a boat handy when Jesus needs one, as a fringe benefit of having fishermen as disciples (4:18-22). **His disciples followed him:** the nature of discipleship is indicated even in the simple matter of boarding a boat: Jesus got in first, and his disciples **followed him.** Jesus goes ahead; disciples follow after, going where he goes.

Boat: See Fishing, page 65

24 **Suddenly a violent storm came up on the sea:** storms can spring up suddenly on the Sea of Galilee and be quite violent, but Matthew's choice of words indicates that he is not just providing a weather report. The Greek word translated **storm** literally means "shaking" and is normally applied to an earthquake. Earthquakes are part of the biblical imagery for "the day of the Lord" (Isaiah 13:9-13; 24:18-21) and for the tribulations prior to the end of this age (24:7; see also Rev 6:12; 8:5; 11:13, 19; 16:18); Matthew may present this storm as a foreshadowing of trials that Jesus' disciples will face. The storm that engulfs the disciples is so violent **that the boat was being swamped by waves** and was on the verge of sinking. Despite the raging storm, Jesus **was asleep**—perhaps an indication that he was very tired. But there is another meaning to Jesus' being able to sleep despite the storm: it is an index of his complete confidence in God's care for him (see Psalms 3:6; 4:9).

The day of the Lord: See page 48

25 **They came and woke him, saying, "Lord, save us! We are perishing!"** The disciples included professional fishermen well acquainted with the perils of storms on the Sea of Galilee, and their cry **We are perishing!** reveals that they thought their situation was desperate. They appeal to Jesus, **Lord, save us!** Calling Jesus **Lord** acknowledges that he has authority and power. The disciples ask Jesus to **save** them from drowning; their plea indicates they believe that Jesus has the power to do so. Matthew's readers can also cry out to Jesus, **Lord, save us,** but with fuller meaning. Jesus is **Lord** as God is Lord; Jesus is able to "save his people from their sins" (1:21).

Lord: See page 133

BACKGROUND: SEA OF GALILEE Luke aptly calls the Sea of Galilee a lake (Luke 5:1; 8:22), for it is a freshwater body thirteen miles long and seven miles wide at most, with a maximum depth of two hundred feet. The Jordan River empties into the northern end of the lake and flows out from its southern end. In the time of Jesus the lake was ringed with fishing villages, and it is still commercially fished today. The Sea of Galilee lies seven hundred feet below sea level and is bordered by high hills that are cut by steep valleys. Strong winds can blow through these valleys and down onto the Sea of Galilee and stir up sudden storms. The Sea of Galilee is called the Sea of Chinnereth (or Kinneret) in the Old Testament, the Sea of Tiberias by John, and the Lake of Gennesaret by Luke.

For reflection: When I pray to be saved, what am I asking to be saved from?

26 Jesus does not immediately get up and calm the storm. Instead, as the winds still howl and the waves rage and the boat flounders, **he said to them, "Why are you terrified, O you of little faith?"** They had faith that Jesus could save them, but only a **little faith,** as was evident from their being **terrified** (verse 25). Fears and anxieties are symptoms of inadequate faith (6:30-31; 14:30-31). There may be good reason to be fearful, but firm faith overcomes fear. In this situation, despite being on the verge of drowning, the disciples should have had more faith that Jesus would preserve them.

For reflection: What do my fears and anxieties reveal about my faith?

Matthew presents this incident as a lesson for his readers. Following Jesus in the company of other disciples is no guarantee of smooth sailing. As the church awaits "the day of our Lord Jesus" (1 Cor 1:8) and the end of this age, it may be buffeted by storms and in danger of floundering. Jesus may seem asleep, doing nothing to calm the storms. Matthew's readers are to remain firm in their faith despite whatever storms may rage.

For reflection: What are the greatest storms I have endured? How did my faith sustain me?

Only after inviting his disciples to greater faith does Jesus take action. **Then he got up, rebuked the winds and the sea, and there was great calm.** At the word of Jesus (see 8:8, 16) the violent storm (verse 24) is replaced by **great calm.**

27 **The men were amazed and said, "What sort of man is this, whom even the winds and the sea obey?"** The disciples had witnessed Jesus freeing people of sickness and evil spirits (4:23-24; 8:14-16) but are now **amazed** that **even the winds and the sea obey** him. The Old Testament spoke of God controlling the seas (Job 38:8-11; Psalms 33:6-7; 65:8; 89:10; 106:9; 107:29; Isaiah 51:10), but **what sort of man is this** who wields such godlike power? The disciples are growing in their understanding of Jesus, but their amazement shows that they have not fully comprehended who he is. Readers of Matthew's gospel know that Jesus is the Son of God (3:17); it will take another storm to bring the disciples to this realization (14:22-33).

While the incident of the storm at sea provides a glimpse of **what sort of man** Jesus is, Matthew's focus in recounting it is on what sort of disciples Jesus wants. Jesus invites his disciples to be with him wherever he goes, sharing his life and enduring the hardships he endures (verses 19-20). His disciples must put following him above all else (verses 21-22). They must remain firm in their faith, no matter what storms rage about them (verses 23-26). An ordinary teacher deserves respect; a Lord who has the authority to command winds and seas deserves absolute, unwavering commitment.

For reflection: What does being Jesus' disciple demand of me at this point in my life?

The Son of God Vanquishes Evil Spirits

28 When he came to the other side, to the territory of the Gadarenes, two demoniacs who were coming from the tombs met him. They were so savage that no one could travel by that road. **29** They cried out, "What have you to do with us, Son of God? Have you come here to torment us before the appointed time?" **30** Some distance away a herd of many swine was feeding. **31** The demons pleaded with him, "If you drive us out, send us into the herd of swine." **32** And he said to them, "Go then!" They came out and entered the swine, and the whole herd rushed down the steep bank into the sea where they drowned. **33** The swineherds ran away, and when they came to the town they reported everything, including what had happened to the demoniacs. **34** Thereupon the whole town came out to meet Jesus, and when they saw him they begged him to leave their district.

Gospel parallels: Mark 5:1-20; Luke 8:26-39

28 **When he came to the other side** of the Sea of Galilee, **to the territory of the Gadarenes:** Gadara was a town about five miles southeast of the Sea of Galilee. Its **territory** extended to the Sea of Galilee. Gadara was part of the Decapolis, a confederation of ten Gentile cities. Jesus has left Galilee and entered a predominantly pagan region. **Two demoniacs**—men under the control of evil spirits—**who were coming from the tombs met him.** Matthew does not tell his readers whether the two men were Gentiles or Jews; some Jews did live in the region. **Tombs** hewn out of rock could provide shelter for desperate outcasts from society, such as these two men.

155

They were so savage that no one could travel by that road: their uncontrollable violence made them a public menace.

29 **They cried out:** the demons who controlled the men cried out through them. They asked Jesus, **What have you to do with us?**—a biblical idiom meaning "Mind your own business!" (see 2 Sam 16:10; 19:23). They recognize who Jesus is and address him as **Son of God** (see 4:3, 6). They know he has power over them and want to know, **Have you come here to torment us before the appointed time?** The **appointed time** refers to the end of this age. Nonbiblical Jewish writings in circulation at the time of Jesus speak of evil spirits being confined in a place of punishment when the present age comes to an end (see also 25:41; Rev 20:10). The demons fear that the arrival of the **Son of God** means they will be punished, even though the present age had not yet come to an end. Or had it? Did the coming of the Son of God mean this age was reaching its end?

Nonbiblical writings: See page 198

30 **Some distance away a herd of many swine was feeding.** The presence of **a herd of many swine** is an indication that Jesus has entered a Gentile area, for Jews were forbidden to eat—and presumably did not raise—pigs (Lev 11:6-8; Deut 14:8).

31 **The demons pleaded with him, "If you drive us out, send us into the herd of swine."** The demons want a place to reside (see 12:43-45) and beg Jesus to not leave them homeless. Their plea can have the sense, "Since you are going to expel us from these men, allow us to use the herd of swine as our new home."

Demons, unclean spirits: See page 177

BACKGROUND: DECAPOLIS The Greek word *decapolis* means "ten cities," and it originally referred to a confederation of ten cities chiefly situated east of the Jordan River. At the time of Jesus the Decapolis was an administrative district attached to the Roman province of Syria. The cities of the Decapolis had a predominantly or entirely Gentile population, were Greek in their culture and religion, and were wealthy compared with the Jewish villages of Galilee. Archaeologists have uncovered colonnaded, paved streets, as well as theaters, temples, sports facilities, and other evidence of Greek lifestyle in cities of the Decapolis.

32 **And he said to them, "Go then!"** In Capernaum Jesus had driven out demons "by a word" (verse 16), and he needs no more than a word to do so again. He commands the demons, **Go** (the Greek could also be translated "go away"—4:10). The New American Bible interprets Jesus' command as permission for the demons to enter the swine: **Go then** into the swine, as you requested. That is what they do: **They came out and entered the swine, and the whole herd rushed down the steep bank into the sea where they drowned.** Jesus' word of command produces dramatic results; there can be no doubts whether the demons have departed. Matthew does not explicitly tell his readers that the two men regained control of themselves, nor does he spell out what became of the demons when the swine drowned. Matthew's focus is on the Son of God (verse 29) vanquishing demons with a word; the final state of the men and the demons is of less interest to him.

33 **The swineherds ran away:** Matthew tells his readers that the swineherds fled but not why they did so. **When they came to the town they reported everything, including what had happened to the demoniacs.** Those who had been tending the swine made a connection between what had happened to their herd and **what had happened to the demoniacs,** and we can speculate that this is what prompted them to run away. They saw that Jesus could command demons to move from men to swine, and it was safer to flee from such a man than to stick around to see what he would do next. The swineherds came into **the town** (presumably Gadara—see verse 28) and **reported everything.**

34 **Thereupon the whole town came out to meet Jesus,** but not to thank him for freeing the men from demons and making road travel safer (see verse 28). Rather, **when they saw him they begged him to leave their district.** Matthew does not explain why they wanted Jesus to go away, but we can speculate that the reaction of the townspeople was the same as the apparent reaction of the swineherds: someone who could tame dangerous demoniacs by sending their demons into a herd of pigs was himself too dangerous to have around. They knew little or nothing about Jesus and his teachings, but they recognized that he had amazing power. Presumably those who owned the large herd of swine were upset by their loss, but this is a matter Matthew leaves unsaid. Whatever the reason for asking Jesus

157

to leave, **the whole town** wants Jesus to go away. Jesus complies with their request and returns by boat to Capernaum (9:1).

For reflection: How comfortable am I with Jesus' power?

Matthew has mentioned that Jesus cast out demons (4:24; 8:16), but this is Matthew's first account of an exorcism. It is a very sparse account, stingy on details (Matthew devotes but seven verses to what Mark recounts in twenty: Mark 5:1-20). This is Jesus' first venture into a predominantly Gentile region, but it is a brief visit with mixed results. Two men have been freed of demons, but Matthew doesn't dwell on their restored state. Instead Matthew cuts rather quickly to the end of the story, where Jesus is asked to leave. The brevity of Matthew's account serves to highlight several of its features. Matthew has recounted Jesus' authority over illnesses (8:1-17) and over nature (8:23-27); now there is a demonstration of his authority over demons. In every case he is able to exercise his authority with a simple word of command (8:8, 16, 32). His disciples wondered, "What sort of man is this, whom even the winds and the sea obey?" (8:27). The demons recognize what sort of man Jesus is: he is the Son of God (8:29), with authority over them. The identity and power of Jesus is being progressively manifested to Matthew's readers.

For reflection: How do I answer the disciples' question, "What sort of man is this?" What sort of man is Jesus for me?

CHAPTER 9

Jesus' Authority to Forgive Sins

1 He entered a boat, made the crossing, and came into his own town. **2** And there people brought to him a paralytic lying on a stretcher. When Jesus saw their faith, he said to the paralytic, "Courage, child, your sins are forgiven." **3** At that, some of the scribes said to themselves, "This man is blaspheming." **4** Jesus knew what they were thinking, and said, "Why do you harbor evil thoughts? **5** Which is easier, to say, 'Your sins are forgiven,' or to say, 'Rise and walk'? **6** But that you may know that the Son of Man has authority on earth to forgive sins"—he then said to the paralytic, "Rise, pick up your stretcher, and go home." **7** He rose and went home. **8** When the crowds saw this they were struck with awe and glorified God who had given such authority to human beings.

Gospel parallels: Mark 2:1-12; Luke 5:17-26

1 **He entered a boat, made the crossing, and came into his own town.** The Gadarenes had begged Jesus to go away (8:34), and Jesus complied. Jesus' **own town** is Capernaum (4:13) on the northwest shore of the Sea of Galilee. **Crossing** to it from the territory of the Gadarenes (8:28) on the southeast shore is a boat ride of about twelve miles.

Capernaum: See page 61

2 **And there people brought to him a paralytic lying on a stretcher.** Matthew leaves the setting vague, not telling his readers whether Jesus is indoors or outdoors when the paralytic is brought to him. As in the previous incident (8:28-34), Matthew forsakes details to focus on essentials. The **paralytic** was unable to walk; he could not come to Jesus on his own for healing but was brought by others. Their coming to Jesus indicates that they believe that Jesus can heal the paralytic, and Jesus perceives this: **Jesus saw their faith.** What Jesus did next is surprising: **he said to the paralytic, "Courage, child, your sins are forgiven."** Some Jews considered sickness to be a consequence and sign of sin (see John 9:2), but Matthew does not characterize the paralyzed man as a sinner or say that his paralysis was caused by sin. Yet Jesus treats this man as if his greatest need was for spiritual rather than physical healing. Jesus speaks to him gently even if he is a sinner, telling him to have **courage** (take heart, don't be afraid) and calling him **child,** an affectionate term that could be used

159

regardless of a person's age. **Your sins are forgiven** is in the present tense: the paralyzed man is forgiven even as Jesus speaks. Is Jesus saying, "The LORD on his part has forgiven your sin" (as Nathan announced God's forgiveness to David: 2 Sam 12:13), or is Jesus himself forgiving the man's sins? The next verse indicates that those who heard Jesus understood him to pronounce forgiveness on his own authority.

For reflection: Where am I in greatest need of Jesus' healing? Do I believe that Jesus speaks to me gently and affectionately even if I am in sin?

3 **At that, some of the scribes said to themselves, "This man is blaspheming."** There were some **scribes** present who overheard Jesus' words to the paralyzed man. Scribes were religious scholars, and they knew that there was no precedent in the Old Testament or Jewish tradition for a man to pronounce forgiveness of sins on his own authority. They reacted to Jesus' words as blasphemy, in the sense that Jesus was claiming to do what only God could do. This is the first time in Matthew's gospel that there is friction between religious leaders and Jesus. Jesus will be charged with blasphemy again, on the eve of his death (26:65).

Scribes: See page 138

4 **Jesus knew what they were thinking, and said, "Why do you harbor evil thoughts?"** Matthew does not write that Jesus shrewdly deduced what the scribes were thinking but that he **knew**. Jesus knew the spiritual condition of the paralytic (verse 2) and he knew what the scribes were thinking. The Greek words translated as **harbor evil thoughts** literally mean "to think evil in your hearts." God sees into the human heart (1 Sam 16:7; 2 Chron 6:30), and Jesus can as well (see 12:25; 22:18). Jesus characterizes the scribes' thinking as not merely mistaken but **evil**. These scribes had closed their hearts to Jesus and were not willing to consider the possibility that Jesus acted on behalf of God.

5 Jesus addresses the scribes' disbelief: **Which is easier, to say, "Your sins are forgiven," or to say, "Rise and walk"?** Jesus has already said to the paralyzed man, **Your sins are forgiven** (verse 2). Would it be **easier** or harder for Jesus to also tell him, **Rise and walk**? There is a difference between easier to say and easier to accomplish. A physical healing, even if miraculous, falls short of granting divine forgiveness. Yet it is easier to claim

that one can forgive sins than to claim that one can heal a paralytic: for-giveness cannot be seen, but a paralyzed man's rising up certainly can.

6 Since Jesus cannot physically display the man's forgiveness, he performs a physical healing as its sign, so **that you may know that the Son of Man has authority on earth to forgive sins.** Jesus often refers to himself as **the Son of Man,** a title that has different nuances of meaning. It indicates that Jesus shares the human condition, and it is also an echo of the "one like a son of man" in the Book of Daniel who receives authority from God (Dan 7:13-14). Jesus exercises God's authority **on earth,** as God's unique agent. **That you may know** echoes Old Testament texts in which God says that he is going to do something that will demonstrate his might (Exod 8:18; 9:14); Jesus is about to make a demonstration of his **authority on earth to forgive sins.** Matthew intends his readers to be among the **you** who know Jesus' authority to forgive.

Son of Man: See page 151

Jesus **then said to the paralytic, "Rise, pick up your stretcher, and go home."** The three acts that Jesus commands are quite easy to do—unless one is paralyzed! Jesus speaks to the man as if he is no longer paralyzed.

7 **He rose and went home,** presumably carrying his stretcher as Jesus told him, demonstrating that he had been healed. The healing itself is glossed over; we are only shown its results. Nothing further is said about the man's sins having been forgiven, but his rising from his stretcher is a visi-ble sign of his spiritual healing. The man's obedience to Jesus is a model for all disciples: do what Jesus asks of you, even if you have previously been unable to do it.

For reflection: Has Jesus ever asked me to do something I was previously unable to do? How did he enable me to do it?

8 **When the crowds saw this they were struck with awe.** This is the first mention of **crowds** being present and witnessing what was happening. The Greek for **were struck with awe** can also be translated "became afraid." The people of Capernaum had already seen Jesus heal many peo-ple (8:14-17), so we can ponder why this particular healing aroused awe and fear. Its only unique feature was that it was done as a sign that Jesus had

the authority to forgive sins. The crowd was **struck with awe** that Jesus had demonstrated that he had such authority; Jesus was a man who could forgive as God could forgive. Joseph had been told that Jesus would "save his people from their sins" (1:21), and the people of Capernaum had just witnessed a down payment.

Consequently they **glorified God who had given such authority to human beings.** They recognized that Jesus' authority to forgive sins came from God, for only God could forgive sins. They **glorified** God for sharing his authority with Jesus, bringing his forgiveness to earth (verse 6). Matthew writes that they glorified God for giving authority to forgive sins **to human beings** rather than simply to Jesus. Matthew's wording foreshadows Jesus' sharing his authority to forgive sins with his disciples and the church (see 16:19; 18:18; James 5:16). Matthew's first readers experienced forgiveness of sins through the church, and they could join in glorifying God for giving such **authority to human beings.**

For reflection: How have I experienced Jesus' forgiveness through the church? Where am I most in need of forgiveness?

The disciples had wondered about Jesus, "What sort of man is this?" (8:27), and more pieces of the answer are falling into place. Jesus not only has authority over disease (8:1-17), over the physical world (8:23-27), and over demons (8:28-34); he also sees into human hearts (verses 2, 4) and has the authority to forgive sins (verse 6).

Jesus' Mission of Mercy

9 As Jesus passed on from there, he saw a man named Matthew sitting at the customs post. He said to him, "Follow me." And he got up and followed him. **10** While he was at table in his house, many tax collectors and sinners came and sat with Jesus and his disciples. **11** The Pharisees saw this and said to his disciples, "Why does your teacher eat with tax collectors and sinners?" **12** He heard this and said, "Those who are well do not need a physician, but the sick do. **13** Go and learn the meaning of the words, 'I desire mercy, not sacrifice.' I did not come to call the righteous but sinners."

Gospel parallels: Mark 2:13-17; Luke 5:27-32
OT: Hosea 6:6
NT: Matt 10:3; 11:19; 12:7

9 **As Jesus passed on from there:** Jesus had been in Capernaum, where he forgave and healed a paralyzed man (9:1-8). He may now be walking along a road that ran past Capernaum, for **he saw a man named Matthew sitting at the customs post.** Capernaum was in a territory governed by Herod Antipas, near its border with the territory governed by Antipas's half brother, Philip. A duty was imposed on merchandise passing between territories; hence the **customs post.** Sitting at it was **a man named Matthew,** collecting taxes for Herod Antipas. Jesus **saw** Matthew going about his work and **said to him, "Follow me."** Jesus takes the initiative, singling Matthew out and inviting him to be his disciple just as he had earlier called others (4:18-22). This is the first mention of Matthew in the gospel; we do not know how much previous contact Matthew might have had with Jesus. Matthew immediately responds to Jesus' invitation: **he got up and followed him,** becoming his disciple. Matthew also becomes a model for us in responding to Jesus, even if it means forsaking security and venturing out on a new way of life.

10 **While he was at table in his house:** the Greek literally reads that Jesus was "reclining" in the house. Reclining on cushions around a low table was customary at formal meals and banquets (see 26:20). Diners leaned on one elbow while eating with the free hand. It is unclear in whose **house** the meal was being held. Matthew may have had sufficient income to afford a large home, suitable for hosting banquets. **Many tax collectors and**

BACKGROUND: TAX COLLECTORS   Those who collected taxes were almost universally scorned by Jews at the time of Jesus and were spoken of in the same breath with sinners (Matt 11:19). They were despised for several reasons. First, the tax system lent itself to abuse. One arrangement was to auction off the right to collect taxes to the highest bidder and then allow the tax collector to keep anything he could collect over that amount. It was a license for greed and extortion, and many tax collectors took advantage of it. Second, there were many forms of taxation, and together they extracted a sizeable portion of the income of ordinary people—up to 40 percent, by some estimates. Third, Jewish tax collectors were agents, directly or indirectly, of Rome. After about a century of Jewish self-rule, Rome had taken away Jewish independence in 63 B.C. and had imposed tribute or taxes. As a result of these factors, tax collectors were considered unscrupulous extortionists who worked on behalf of a foreign power and drained people's livelihoods.

---

sinners came and sat with Jesus and his disciples. If many were at the meal, it was quite a banquet! Tax collectors and sinners has the connotation of tax collectors and *other* sinners. Since tax collectors worked directly or indirectly for Rome, an occupying foreign power, they were viewed by many people as corrupt parasites. Sinners were those guilty of serious sins like fraud, adultery, extortion, prostitution, theft and the like, and not merely those careless about ritual purity.

Banquets: See page 464

Jesus lived in a culture where sharing a meal had much greater significance than in modern, eat-on-the-run cultures. To eat together expressed acceptance, fellowship, even intimacy. Yet Jesus and his disciples share a meal with many of these disreputable tax collectors and sinners. Jesus' eating with sinners was a sign of his welcoming them to himself and his willingness to be associated with them. Jesus has even invited a tax collector to be his disciple! Matthew doesn't tell us how the other disciples reacted to Jesus inviting a tax collector to join them, but it may have taken some adjustment on their part.

For reflection: What does Jesus' welcoming sinners and outcasts to himself mean for me? What light might his sharing a banquet with sinners throw on the celebration of the Eucharist?

11 Jesus' acceptance of disreputable dinner companions did not go unnoticed. The Pharisees saw this and said to his disciples, "Why does your teacher eat with tax collectors and sinners?" The Pharisees were a group whose aim was strict observance of God's laws; this is the first time in Matthew's gospel that they appear on the scene during Jesus' public ministry. The name Pharisee may come from a word that means "separated" and may indicate their zeal to separate themselves from uncleanness and sinners. Jesus does the opposite by eating with tax collectors and sinners. The Pharisees voice their concern to Jesus' disciples, referring to Jesus as your teacher: Jesus is not *their* teacher. Why does your teacher eat with tax collectors and sinners? The Pharisees' question is really an accusation. In their minds, table fellowship with sinners expressed tolerance of their sins and thus disregard for God's laws.

Pharisees: See page 231

12 He heard this and said, "Those who are well do not need a physician, but the sick do." Jesus may be quoting a proverb familiar to his listeners. It is the duty of physicians to help those who are ill; no one should be surprised to find a physician in the company of sick people. The work of physicians serves as a comparison or parable for Jesus' mission. Not only does Jesus heal the physically ill (8:1-17); he also brings healing to the spiritually ill (9:1-8).

13 Jesus tells those questioning his actions, **Go and learn the meaning of the words, "I desire mercy, not sacrifice."** The quotation is from the prophet Hosea (Hosea 6:6), and **go and learn** is an idiom that means to seek the meaning and application of a text of Scripture. **Mercy** translates a Hebrew word for faithful-loving-kindness; **sacrifice** means sacrificial offerings in the Temple. In God's eyes, showing **mercy** is even more important than acts of worship. Performing works of mercy, even for unsavory sinners, is God's **desire,** and Jesus carries out God's desires. Jesus has come to fulfill the law and the prophets (5:17); he fulfills Hosea's prophecy by showing mercy to sinners. No one should be surprised to find Jesus in the company of the scruffy, the disreputable, even the wicked.

> For it is love that I desire, not sacrifice,
> and knowledge of God rather than holocausts.
> *Hosea 6:6*

Jesus' disciples should also **go and learn** how to apply Hosea's prophecy through their own acts of mercy. Jesus proclaimed, "Blessed are the merciful, for they will be shown mercy" (5:7).

For reflection: How do I respond in my daily life to God saying, "I desire mercy, not sacrifice"?

Jesus' mission is to show God's mercy to those who need mercy. He tells his critics, **I did not come to call the righteous but sinners.** The **righteous** are those who are right with God; they have no need to be rescued from their condition. Jesus came for the sake of **sinners,** of those who do need to be rescued—saved. Jesus is a physician who cures sinners of their sins, as he demonstrated by forgiving the paralyzed man (9:1-8). Jesus has **come** on a mission of bringing God's love and mercy to those who need it most. Jesus has come to **call** sinners to changed lives (4:17) and to discipleship, as he has called Matthew (verse 9). Jesus welcomes sinners not only to this banquet with his disciples but calls them to the "banquet in the kingdom of heaven" (8:11). Another piece of the answer to the question, "What sort of man is this?" (8:27) has fallen into place: Jesus is a man on a mission of mercy from God, calling sinners to new life.

For reflection: What is Jesus' call to me?

The Old and the New

¹⁴ Then the disciples of John approached him and said, "Why do we and the Pharisees fast [much], but your disciples do not fast?" ¹⁵ Jesus answered them, "Can the wedding guests mourn as long as the bridegroom is with them? The days will come when the bridegroom is taken away from them, and then they will fast. ¹⁶ No one patches an old cloak with a piece of unshrunken cloth, for its fullness pulls away from the cloak and the tear gets worse. ¹⁷ People do not put new wine into old wineskins. Otherwise the skins burst, the wine spills out, and the skins are ruined. Rather, they pour new wine into fresh wineskins, and both are preserved."

Gospel parallels: Mark 2:18-22; Luke 5:33-39
OT:Isaiah 53:8
NT:Matt 6:16-18; 11:2, 18-19

14 Jesus' eating habits aroused comment (9:10-11) and continue to do so. **Then the disciples of John approached him.** Some whom **John** baptized had become his **disciples** (11:2; 14:12); John was now in prison (4:12). His disciples ask Jesus, **Why do we and the Pharisees fast [much], but your disciples do not fast?** Jesus had been criticized for eating with the wrong people (9:11), and now he is criticized for letting his disciples eat too much! For Jews, to **fast** meant to abstain from all food for a period of time. The law of Moses required fasting only on the annual Day of Atonement (Lev 16:29); some Jews undertook additional fasts, which are at issue here. John's disciples fasted in imitation of him (see 11:18), perhaps as an expression of sorrow for sin in preparation for God's judgment (3:8-12). Some **Pharisees** fasted twice a week (see Luke 18:12); an ancient Christian writing called the *Didache* speaks of a Jewish practice of fasting on Mondays and Thursdays (*Didache* 8:1). Some manuscripts of

166

Matthew's gospel read that the disciples of John and the Pharisees fasted **much**, meaning "often."

Fasting: See page 113
Pharisees: See page 231
The *Didache*: See page 129

The question put to Jesus indicates that his disciples **do not fast.** Since disciples obey and imitate their teachers, this implies that Jesus neither instructed his disciples to fast nor fasted himself during his public ministry. Indeed, Jesus will later be accused of being "a glutton and a drunkard" (11:19). Yet Jesus did fast before his ministry (4:2), and he taught his disciples how fasting should be done (6:16-18). In Jesus' mind, when is fasting appropriate and when is it inappropriate?

15 **Jesus answered them, "Can the wedding guests mourn as long as the bridegroom is with them?"** Fasting can be done for a variety of reasons, but in its origins fasting seems to have been an act of mourning (Judith fasted to mourn the death of her husband: Judith 8:6). A **wedding**, on the other hand, was a joyous occasion. There was no wedding ceremony as such, but simply a feast celebrating the bride's moving into the bridegroom's house (see 22:1-14; 25:1-13). To fast and **mourn** during the merriment of a wedding feast would be completely out of place.

Marriage practices: See page 479

Jesus speaks of the wedding feast in terms of the presence of the **bridegroom;** mourning in the presence of the bridegroom would be unthinkable. There is an implicit identification of Jesus as the **bridegroom** and of his disciples as **wedding guests.** They cannot fast and mourn while Jesus is with them: his presence demands celebration. **Bridegroom** was not previously a title for the Messiah, but Jesus' comparison of himself to a bridegroom will provide an image for his relationship with the church (2 Cor 11:2; Eph 5:25-32; Rev 19:7).

Jesus goes on to make his identification as the bridegroom more explicit: **The days will come when the bridegroom is taken away from them, and then they will fast.** Normally the bridegroom remains and the guests leave when the wedding feast is over, but Jesus speaks of the bridegroom being **taken away.** Although Matthew does not comment on it, this expression is a faint echo of a prophecy of Isaiah that describes a servant of God who is "taken away" in death as an offering for the sins of others (Isaiah 53:8). This is the first time in Matthew's gospel that Jesus speaks of his coming death.

> *Oppressed and condemned, he was taken away,*
> *and who would have thought any more of his destiny?*
> *When he was cut off from the land of the living,*
> *and smitten for the sin of his people.*
>
> Isaiah 53:8

The days will come when Jesus is taken away, and afterward his disciples **will fast.** The risen Jesus will assure his disciples that he will always be with them (28:20), but not visibly present in bodily form. Fasting was inappropriate during his public ministry, but fasting will be adopted as an ongoing practice by the early church (see Acts 13:2-3; 14:23). The *Didache* will advise Christians to fast on Wednesdays and Fridays (*Didache* 8:1).

For reflection: What do I do to celebrate Jesus' presence? What do I do to mourn his absence?

16 Fasting is inappropriate at a feast, and Jesus goes on to tell two parables about other inappropriate combinations. He notes that **no one patches an old cloak with a piece of unshrunken cloth, for its fullness pulls away from the cloak and the tear gets worse.** New cloth shrinks when washed; to sew an **unshrunken** piece of **cloth** on an **old,** already washed and shrunken **cloak** will result in the patch's tearing away the next time the cloak is washed, leaving the cloak in **worse** shape than before it was patched.

17 Similarly, **people do not put new wine into old wineskins.** Here the problem is expansion rather than shrinkage. **Old** leather **wineskins** become brittle; **new wine** is grape juice that is still fermenting. Because of the pressure resulting from fermentation, **the skins burst, the wine spills out, and the skins are ruined.** Jesus places as much or more emphasis on the old wineskins bursting and being ruined than on loss of the new wine. **Rather** than have this happen, **they pour new wine into fresh wineskins, and both are preserved.** New **wineskins** made from **fresh** leather are flexible enough to accommodate the fermenting new wine. The **both** that **are preserved** seem to be the old wineskins and the

new wine (it makes little sense to speak of a fresh wineskin being preserved by new wine).

Jesus speaks of new cloth and new wine as comparisons for his mission.
There is a radical newness to what Jesus does, evident in his forgiving sins
(9:2), associating with sinners (9:11), and not fasting like other devout Jews
(9:14). Jesus uses the old cloak and old wineskins as comparisons for the
Judaism of his day, and in both examples he shows concern for the old. He
does not want the cloak to tear or the old wineskins to burst and be ruined. Jesus has come to fulfill rather than abolish the old (5:17), but the
fulfillment he brings cannot be confined within the limits of the old.

Jesus' parables highlight the challenge of getting on with the new
while preserving the old, but do not provide a blueprint for what to do in
specific situations. Matthew's church was faced with the challenge of remaining faithful to its Jewish roots even as it welcomed Gentile converts.
For Matthew's community, Jesus' parables indicate that forcing Gentile
converts to fully conform to Jewish patterns of life would tear apart the
church. Rather, the new wine of Gentile converts calls for new patterns
of life, so that both old Jewish wineskins and new Gentile wine may be
preserved.

*For reflection: Am I more comfortable with the old or eager for the new?
What is the message of Jesus' parables for me?*

ORIENTATION: *Matthew recounts a series of incidents that highlight the faith of
those who come to Jesus for healing.*

Faith, Healing, Life

¹⁸ While he was saying these things to them, an official came forward,
knelt down before him, and said, "My daughter has just died. But come,
lay your hand on her, and she will live." ¹⁹ Jesus rose and followed him,
and so did his disciples. ²⁰ A woman suffering hemorrhages for twelve
years came up behind him and touched the tassel on his cloak. ²¹ She
said to herself, "If only I can touch his cloak, I shall be cured." ²² Jesus
turned around and saw her, and said, "Courage, daughter! Your faith
has saved you." And from that hour the woman was cured.

²³ When Jesus arrived at the official's house and saw the flute play-
ers and the crowd who were making a commotion, ²⁴ he said, "Go away!
The girl is not dead but sleeping." And they ridiculed him. ²⁵ When the

crowd was put out, he came and took her by the hand, and the little girl arose. **²⁶** **And news of this spread throughout all that land.**

Gospel parallels: Mark 5:21-43; Luke 8:40-56

OT:Dan 12:2-3

18 Jesus is in Capernaum (9:1). He has been speaking with disciples of John the Baptist (9:14-17), and **while he was saying these things to them, an official came forward** and **knelt down before him.** Matthew skimps on details such as the official's name and the office he held. Whatever his office, this **official** was a person of some authority. Nevertheless, he came to Jesus and **knelt down before him,** a position of homage and supplication (see 8:2, where the same Greek word is translated "did him homage"). He told Jesus, **My daughter has just died. But come, lay your hand on her, and she will live.** An amazing declaration! Jesus had performed many healings in Capernaum (8:5-17; 9:1-8), but restoring a dead person to life is a far greater feat than curing the sick. Yet this official has confidence that even though his daughter has **died,** at Jesus' touch **she will live.** He asks Jesus, **lay your hand on her.** There is no mention in the Old Testament of healing through the laying on of hands, but this practice is mentioned in one of the Dead Sea Scrolls (writings from the time of Jesus), and it may have been a common way of praying for a person to be healed (see Acts 9:17; 28:8). The official invites Jesus to **come** to his house where his daughter lies dead.

Dead Sea Scrolls: See page 97

For reflection: How firm is my faith that Jesus can bring the dead to life?

19 **Jesus rose:** he was apparently still dining with Matthew and other tax collectors and sinners (9:9-10) and now rises from reclining at the meal. Jesus **followed him, and so did his disciples,** going with the official to his home. Jesus says nothing in praise of the official's faith, even though he had earlier praised the faith of the centurion (8:10); and yet, it would seem that believing that Jesus can bring a dead person back to life signifies greater faith than believing that Jesus can restore a sick person to health with his word (8:8-9). Jesus nevertheless does something worth noting for the official: Jesus **followed** him. This is the only mention in Matthew's gospel of Jesus' following anyone; elsewhere Jesus is always in the lead, even in such a simple matter as boarding a boat (8:23). Perhaps Jesus' following of the official is an acknowledgment by deed, rather than word, of the official's faith.

20 While Jesus was on the way to the official's house, **a woman suffering hemorrhages for twelve years came up behind him and touched the tassel on his cloak.** This woman suffered from chronic vaginal bleeding, which made her ritually unclean according to the law of Moses (Lev 15:25); anyone who had physical contact with her or with articles she touched also became unclean (Lev 15:19-27). Her condition meant that she could not worship in the Temple or have sexual intercourse if she was married (Lev 20:18). She had been in this condition **for twelve years.** She may have been concerned that Jesus would become ritually unclean if she touched him, so she **came up behind him,** perhaps hoping to escape notice, **and touched the tassel on his cloak,** minimizing her contact with him. The law of Moses commanded Jewish men to wear tassels on the four corners of their cloaks as a reminder to keep God's commandments (Num 15:37-39; Deut 22:12); Jesus obeyed the Mosaic law.

> For reflection: How hesitant or bold am I in approaching Jesus with my needs?

21 The woman thought that even minimal contact with Jesus could heal her. **She said to herself, "If only I can touch his cloak, I shall be cured."** The centurion had faith that his servant would be healed if Jesus "only" said the word (8:8); this woman has faith that her **only** touching the fringes on his cloak will be sufficient. (Others will touch a tassel on Jesus' cloak and be healed—14:36.)

22 **Jesus turned around and saw her, and said, "Courage, daughter! Your faith has saved you."** Jesus did not simply feel a tug on his cloak and turn around to see who was tugging. Rather, Jesus speaks to her as if he completely understands her need and her reasoning in touching his cloak. He calls her **daughter,** a term of endearment, and tells her to have **courage,** to take heart. She has nothing to fear from him. On the contrary, he tells her, **Your faith has saved you.** Her **faith** was her belief that Jesus could heal her, and that it would take only her touching the tassel of his cloak to be healed. There was nothing magical about the tassel; it was her **faith** that **saved her.** The Greek verb translated **saved** is the same verb that is translated **cured** in the previous verse. The word means to be saved from death or to be kept alive and can broadly refer to any rescue from danger and distress. (The disciples had cried to Jesus, "Lord, save us!" during the

storm at sea—8:25.) The woman's faith in Jesus resulted in her being saved from her malady, and this is a foreshadowing of Jesus' saving from sin and eternal death (1:21; 10:22; 16:25; 19:25-26).

And from that hour the woman was cured. The expression **from that hour** is an idiom meaning "from that time" (see 8:13; 15:28; 17:18): she was cured from the moment Jesus told her that her faith had saved her. She **was cured:** the same Greek verb for "saved" or "healed" is used again.

We can note parallels between this woman and the paralyzed man who was brought to Jesus (9:2-7). In each situation Jesus sees the faith of those who approach him. In each situation Jesus tells the afflicted person to have courage, addressing them affectionately as child or daughter. In each situation Jesus sees into their hearts and knows their needs. The incidents are two snapshots of Jesus carrying out his mission, healing from sickness and sin, restoring life, and saving.

For reflection: How have I experienced Jesus saving and healing me?

23 **When Jesus arrived at the official's house and saw the flute players and the crowd who were making a commotion:** it was customary in Jewish culture (and some other ancient cultures) to hire **flute players** to accompany the dirges sung at a funeral. Women to wail and sing dirges (see Jer 9:16-21) might also be hired; the **crowd** that was **making a commotion** could have included family, friends, and professional mourners. The scene that greeted Jesus when he arrived at the **official's house** was the normal noisy display of grief after a death. The official had presumably taken leave of the mourners and gone to Jesus, confident that he could bring his daughter back to life.

24 Jesus tells the mourners, **Go away! The girl is not dead but sleeping.** Jesus uses **sleeping** as a metaphor for death. He does not deny that the girl is dead, but her being dead is a temporary state like sleep. Jesus can raise the dead as easily as one can awaken a person who is sleeping. The Book of Daniel characterizes death as sleep and promises awakening through resurrection (Dan 12:2-3); Jesus has a more immediate awakening in mind for this girl. The crowd of mourners greet Jesus' words with jeers: **they ridiculed him.** They took Jesus' claim that the girl was sleeping as a literal statement instead of a metaphor, and they knew she was not asleep. She was dead, and that was why they were gathered to mourn

her. Unlike the girl's father, they had no faith that Jesus could do anything for the girl.

25 Jesus nevertheless prevails and gets the mourners to disperse. **When the crowd was put out, he came** and entered the room where the girl's body lay **and took her by the hand.** Entering a house with a corpse inside or touching a corpse made one ritually unclean for seven days (Num 19:14), but Jesus shows no hesitation in going to the girl and taking her hand. Jesus' touch removes the source of uncleanness, whether leprosy (8:2-3) or blood flow (verses 20-22) or even death. Jesus **took her by the hand, and the little girl arose.** Just as his saving, or healing, of the woman suffering from a hemorrhage foreshadowed his saving, or healing, from sin and all that threatens life, so his raising of this girl back to this life foreshadows his raising up women and men to resurrected life. Another snapshot of Jesus carrying out his mission.

> For reflection: What hope does the image of Jesus' raising of the girl hold for me?

26 Matthew does not dwell on the restored condition of the girl or tell the reactions of her family or of Jesus' disciples to his bringing her back to life. Matthew provides a bare-bones account to throw the spotlight on what Jesus does in response to faith. Matthew wraps up the incident by simply noting that **news of this spread throughout all that land.** Jesus' fame as one who could heal and expel demons had already spread well beyond Galilee (4:24-25); now he is known to have brought a dead person back to life.

> For reflection: What lessons can I learn from the faith of the woman with a hemorrhage and the faith of the official?

ORIENTATION: *Matthew concludes his series of stories about men and women who have faith in Jesus' healing power (9:18-31).*

Blind Faith

27 And as Jesus passed on from there, two blind men followed [him], crying out, "Son of David, have pity on us!" **28** When he entered the house, the blind men approached him and Jesus said to them, "Do you believe that I can do this?" "Yes, Lord," they said to him. **29** Then he touched their eyes and said, "Let it be done for you according to your faith." [30] And their eyes were opened. Jesus warned them sternly, "See that no one knows about this." [31] But they went out and spread word of him through all that land.

NT: Matt 20:29-34

27 The setting remains Capernaum (9:1). **And as Jesus passed on from there,** from the house of the official whose daughter Jesus had raised to life (9:23-25), **two blind men followed [him].** To be blind in the ancient world generally meant not being able to work. Those without a family to support them had to beg to survive and were among the abject poor. These **two blind men followed** Jesus—not an impossible feat for those used to getting around without sight but nonetheless more difficult than for those with sight. To follow Jesus is an image of discipleship (4:20, 22; 9:9); these two blind men are not disciples, but their following of Jesus may nevertheless bear a message about discipleship. As they **followed** Jesus they were **crying out, "Son of David, have pity on us!"** Those who were blind might ask others to have pity on them by giving alms, but these men are **crying out** for more than money. They address Jesus as **Son of David,** the first time in Matthew's gospel that anyone calls Jesus by this title during his public ministry. **Son of David** was not a common title for the Messiah and could have other connotations. Jesus was a descendant of David through Joseph's legal parentage (1:6-16) and thus could be called a son of David just as was Joseph (1:1, 20). The two men might have been appealing to Jesus as Son of David because he cast out demons and healed, works that Jewish tradition ascribed to Solomon, the son of David. **Have pity** is a form of the word translated "mercy" in Hosea's prophecy, "I desire mercy, not sacrifice" (9:13; Hosea 6:6).

Son of David: See page 16

Jesus does not stop and heal them! Rather, he continues on to his destination (verse 28), with the blind men following after him **crying out** for him to **have pity.** It is a disturbing picture. Even though Jesus immediately healed others who came to him, and even though he proclaimed that God places the highest value on mercy, or pity (9:13), he inexplicably ignores these men and their pleas for pity. They are left to follow Jesus blindly, with no word of encouragement from him.

For reflection: Has my own following of Jesus ever meant walking in darkness, with Jesus seemingly deaf to my pleas?

28 **When he entered the house:** Matthew does not make it clear whose house is **the house** that Jesus **entered;** one possibility is the house of Peter (8:14), where Jesus stays when he is in Capernaum. When Jesus stopped at his destination, **the blind men** caught up with him and **approached him.** He has been aware of them and their pleas, for now **Jesus said to them, "Do you believe that I can do this?"** The men want to be able to see, and Jesus knows that **this** is what they want. He asks them whether they **believe** that he **can do this.** This is the only time in Matthew's gospel (or in any gospel) that Jesus asks anyone whether they believe that he is able to heal them. **"Yes, Lord," they said to him.** Calling Jesus **Lord** is an acknowledgment of his authority; the men who are blind **believe** that Jesus has the authority and power to give them sight. Their faith has been demonstrated by their following Jesus and crying out to him, even though he seemed to ignore them.

Lord: See page 133

29 **Then he touched their eyes and said, "Let it be done for you according to your faith."** Jesus' touch is a healing touch (8:3, 15; 9:25), which he now extends to them because of their **faith.** Just as Jesus told the centurion, "as you have believed, let it be done for you" (8:13), he tells these two men, **Let it be done for you according to your faith** (for other examples of faith that leads to healing see 9:2, 18, 21).

For reflection: What have I received from Jesus in response to my faith in him?

30 **And their eyes were opened:** they are given sight by Jesus. Their persistent faith has led to their healing. Why did Jesus not heal them at their first pleas? Why did they have to follow him blindly? If Jesus' questioning them about their faith (verse 28) indicates that he was testing their faith, then why were *they* tested but not others whom Jesus healed immediately? Matthew's account provides no answer. Similarly, there is sometimes no apparent explanation for why we have to follow Jesus in darkness, for why our pleas and prayers are not answered, for why the only faith available to us is blind faith. Those in such darkness can nevertheless take heart from the image of the two men who blindly followed Jesus through the streets of Capernaum: their faith was not in vain.

Matthew's account ends with additional inexplicable elements. After healing them, **Jesus warned them sternly, "See that no one knows about this."** The Greek word translated **sternly** has connotations of a very strong, even angry, emotion. There is nothing in Matthew's account to explain why Jesus would speak to them **sternly** after healing them because of their faith. It is also unclear why Jesus would command them, **See that no one knows about this.** How could men who had been blind keep their sight a secret? Why would Jesus want it kept secret, since he was already known far and wide as a person who could heal (4:24-25) and even raise the dead back to life (9:26)? I do not know a satisfactory explanation for why Jesus' command of silence appears in Matthew's account.

31 **But they went out and spread word of him through all that land.** The two men who had been given sight seem to go out of their way to publicize their healing, despite Jesus' stern warning. We could understand their inability to keep their healing a secret, but why would they go **out and spread word through all that land**? Had they no deference to Jesus' wishes out of gratitude? Are they unfortunately a model for how we sometimes respond to Jesus?

For reflection: How do I understand the significance of Jesus' command that the men be silent and their disobeying his command?

Mixed Reactions to Jesus
32 As they were going out, a demoniac who could not speak was brought to him, **33** and when the demon was driven out the mute person spoke. The crowds were amazed and said, "Nothing like this has ever been seen in Israel." **34** But the Pharisees said, "He drives out demons by the prince of demons."
NT: Matt 12:22-24; 15:31

32 **As they were going out**—as the two men whom Jesus had given sight were leaving the house in which Jesus had healed them (9:27-31)—**a demoniac who could not speak was brought to him.** Jesus is constantly besieged by people with needs; as those he has healed leave, another afflicted person is brought to him. The man's inability to **speak** is attributed to his being

demon possessed. Implicit in his being **brought** to Jesus is belief that Jesus can free him of his affliction.

33 Matthew skips over whatever Jesus did to expel the demon and simply notes the result: **when the demon was driven out the mute person spoke.** Matthew then shifts attention away from the formerly mute person and Jesus; Matthew's interest in recounting the episode is in how various people reacted to it. Many were quite impressed by Jesus: **The crowds were amazed and said, "Nothing like this has ever been seen in Israel."** Jesus was not the only one who cast out evil spirits (see 12:27), so the crowd's claim that **nothing like this has ever been seen in Israel** probably refers to more than this particular incident. The crowd may be **amazed** by all that Jesus has done to free people from their afflictions (see 15:31), capped off by this most recent exercise of his healing power. The crowds' saying that nothing like this has been seen **in Israel** reflects the fact that Jesus' public ministry is directed toward Jews, the people of Israel (see 15:24). Those who make up the **crowds** are not disciples, but their acknowledgement that Jesus is doing amazing things for God's people makes them potential followers of Jesus.

For reflection: What amazes me most about Jesus?

34 Not everyone is favorably impressed. **But the Pharisees said**—apparently to the crowds in response to their admiration of Jesus—**He drives out demons**

BACKGROUND: DEMONS, UNCLEAN SPIRITS The New Testament takes the existence of demons for granted but does not describe their origin and says little about their nature. The chief emphasis lies on their influence and effects on human beings. Both mental and physical illnesses (including epilepsy, blindness, deafness, muteness, and curvature of the spine) are sometimes ascribed to the influence of demons, and healing takes place through casting out the demon causing the illness. But not every illness is attributed to the influence of demons, and some healings are presented simply as healings. Likewise, some exorcisms are simply exorcisms, with no mention of any accompanying physical healing. Demons are also referred to as unclean spirits and evil spirits, and they are under the authority of Satan (also called Beelzebul). Jesus' casting out of demons was an assault on the kingdom of Satan and evidence that the kingdom of God was breaking into this world through the power of Jesus. *Related topic: Satan (page 55).*

---

by the prince of demons. The Pharisees cannot deny that Jesus **drives out demons:** a man who had not been able to speak because of a demon can now speak. Jesus' extraordinary power has to come from somewhere. These **Pharisees** do not recognize that it comes from God; they attribute Jesus' power to his operating in collusion with the **prince of demons,** Satan, who has power over other evil spirits. The Pharisees make this charge to sway the crowds against Jesus. This is the most serious charge lodged against Jesus to this point in Matthew's gospel; opposition to Jesus is growing, even as he is gaining the admiration of many. Matthew does not recount Jesus making any response to the Pharisees' charge; this will be done on a later occasion (12:24-32).

Pharisees: See page 231
Satan: See page 55

Matthew's first readers might have understood this incident as a fore-shadowing of their own experiences. At the time Matthew wrote, many Jews (represented by the crowds in this incident) may have had an open mind about Jesus, but some Jewish leaders (represented by their forerunners the Pharisees) had rejected Jesus and were trying to sway undecided Jews against him. Matthew's church was caught up in a conflict that had its roots in the public ministry of Jesus.

ORIENTATION: *Matthew summarizes how Jesus has been carrying out his mission. Jesus will shortly authorize his disciples to take on his mission themselves.*

The Compassion of Jesus
35 Jesus went around to all the towns and villages, teaching in their synagogues, proclaiming the gospel of the kingdom, and curing every disease and illness. 36 At the sight of the crowds, his heart was moved with pity for them because they were troubled and abandoned, like sheep without a shepherd. 37 Then he said to his disciples, "The harvest is abundant but the laborers are few; 38 so ask the master of the harvest to send out laborers for his harvest."

Gospel parallels: Mark 6:34; Luke 8:1; 10:2
NT: Matt 4:17, 23; John 4:35

35 **Jesus went around to all the towns and villages, teaching in their synagogues, proclaiming the gospel of the kingdom, and curing every disease and illness.** Matthew earlier gave his readers a preview of Jesus' public ministry (4:23), and he now uses virtually identical words to summarize what Jesus has been doing. Jesus' public ministry took place largely in Galilee, in **towns and villages** that were within a one- or two-day walk from Capernaum. Matthew summarizes Jesus' activities under three headings: **teaching, proclaiming,** and **curing.** Jews gathered in synagogues every Sabbath for Scripture reading, prayer, and teaching; these gatherings were opportunities for Jesus to teach. Matthew's gospel presents collections of Jesus' teachings; chapters 5 to 7 (the Sermon on the Mount) make up the first collection. Jesus also cured every disease and illness: there is no affliction Jesus cannot heal. In chapters 8 and 9 Matthew recounts a representative sampling of Jesus' healings. The context for Jesus' **teaching** and **curing** was his **proclaiming the gospel of the kingdom.** The word "gospel" means "good news"; Jesus proclaimed the good news that "the kingdom of heaven is at hand" (4:17). By his teaching, Jesus instructed women and men how to enter into God's reign; by his curing, Jesus freed men and women from the grip of evil. Jesus' mission is good news in word and deed.

Galilee: See page 68
Synagogue: See page 104
Gospel: See page 211

36 Jesus' travels brought him into contact with many people, and he observed their condition and needs. **At the sight of the crowds, his heart was moved with pity for them.** The Greek word translated **his heart was moved with pity** has the connotation of being profoundly moved by a gut reaction of compassion. This is the first time Matthew describes Jesus' emotional state. Jesus sees the condition of the people he encounters and is profoundly moved **because they were troubled and abandoned.** Those Jesus encounters are hurting, and Jesus hurts for them. The expression **troubled and abandoned** could also be translated "harassed and helpless." The people were **like sheep without a shepherd,** an image for being vulnerable (Num 27:17; 1 Kings 22:17). This expression may convey that the shepherds—the leaders of God's people—have neglected their flock (Ezek 34:1-6), but the primary meaning here is that those with whom Jesus came into contact were helpless. At the **sight** of their being distressed and helpless, Jesus **was moved with pity for them.**

*For reflection: What distress does Jesus see when he looks at me? Do I be-
lieve that his attitude toward me is profound compassion?*

37 Jesus has been proclaiming the good news of the kingdom of God (verse
35) to people whose helplessness filled him with compassion (verse 36).
There are many who desperately need to hear the good news and be
brought into the reign of God, but Jesus can't speak to and heal every individual himself. **Then he said to his disciples, "The harvest is abundant
but the laborers are few."** In the context of Jesus proclaiming the good
news of the kingdom to the troubled and healing them (verses 35-36) the
harvest is an image for bringing men and women into the reign of God.
Jesus has been the laborer bringing in this harvest, but the **harvest** is
more **abundant** than Jesus can bring in by himself.

38 Because the harvest is abundant but the harvesters few, Jesus in his compassion tells his disciples to **ask the master of the harvest to send out laborers for his harvest.** The **master of the harvest** is God, and it is **his
harvest**—his people—that is to be brought in. The disciples are to **ask** and
pray that God will **send** additional **laborers** to bring men and women
into the reign of God.

Asking God to send laborers has different applications in different
contexts. Jesus will give twelve disciples the authority to preach and heal
as he has been doing, and he will send them out to carry on his mission
(10:1-8). This will be the first step in involving more laborers in Jesus'
mission of bringing women and men into the reign of God. But what
were twelve workers in the face of the thousands upon thousands who
needed to hear the good news and be freed from evil? Jesus' disciples were
to pray that God would send other workers to join them. This request
will be the prayer of the church when Matthew writes his gospel, and it is
the prayer of the church today. It is a prayer offered out of compassion
for those who are troubled and helpless: laborers are needed to lift their
burdens and bring them "the gospel of the kingdom" (verse 35).

For reflection: Where are laborers for the harvest most needed today?

CHAPTER 10

ORIENTATION: *Chapter divisions were not introduced into Matthew's gospel until centuries after it was written, and they sometimes break up the flow of Matthew's account. That is the case here. In order to extend his compassion and bring women and men into the reign of God (9:35-38), Jesus involves his disciples in his mission (10:1-8).*

Jesus Shares His Authority With Twelve Disciples
1 Then he summoned his twelve disciples and gave them authority over unclean spirits to drive them out and to cure every disease and every illness. 2 The names of the twelve apostles are these: first, Simon called Peter, and his brother Andrew; James, the son of Zebedee, and his brother John; 3 Philip and Bartholomew, Thomas and Matthew the tax collector; James, the son of Alphaeus, and Thaddeus; 4 Simon the Cananean, and Judas Iscariot who betrayed him.
            Gospel parallels: Mark 3:13-19; Luke 6:12-16
            NT: Matt 19:28; Acts 1:13

1 **Then,** after noting that laborers were needed for the harvest (9:37-38), **he summoned his twelve disciples.** Matthew has recounted the call of only five disciples (4:18-22; 9:9), but Jesus has called at least twelve. The number **twelve** corresponds to the twelve tribes of Israel. Ten of the tribes disappeared after Assyrian deportations eight centuries earlier, but there were hopes that God would restore these tribes and reunite his people (Sirach 36:10-11). Jesus' summoning of **twelve** for a special role symbolizes Jesus' renewal and restoration of Israel (see 19:28). Jesus was not replacing what God had done in the past with the people of Israel but bringing it to fulfillment.

    Jesus **gave them authority over unclean spirits to drive them out and to cure every disease and every illness.** Matthew summarized Jesus' healing ministry as "curing every disease and illness" (literally, every disease and *every* illness—4:23; 9:35). Jesus now shares his **authority** over unclean spirits and disease with the twelve so that they can heal as he has healed. Jesus **gave** them authority to do what they could not do on their own. Participating in Jesus' mission is not simply a matter of being a good-hearted volunteer; empowerment by Jesus is necessary.

For reflection: How has Jesus equipped me to carry out his work?

2 **The names of the twelve apostles are these:** the Greek word for **apostles** literally means "ones sent." Apostles are those sent on a mission as representatives or messengers; they share in the authority of the one sending them out. Jesus has just given **the twelve** his authority, and he will shortly send them out (10:5), so they can rightly be called **apostles.** This is the only time that Matthew will refer to the Twelve as apostles. He prefers to call them disciples (see 11:1), perhaps to suggest that every disciple of Jesus has a share in his mission. (Even though we may think of them as "the twelve apostles," this title is found only here in the four gospels and only once elsewhere in the New Testament—Rev 21:14.)

Matthew names the Twelve by pairs, beginning with **first, Simon called Peter, and his brother Andrew.** Simon and Andrew were the first disciples called by Jesus (4:18-20), but that is not what Matthew means when he writes, **first, Simon called Peter.** In the Greek, **first** is an adjective characterizing Simon, not an adverb indicating that he was the first to be called. Simon will rank first among the disciples and be given a special role (16:18-19). **Simon** is a form of the name Simeon, one of the twelve sons of Jacob. Matthew notes that **Simon** is **called Peter** (see also 4:18); Jesus will not give Simon the name Peter until later (16:17-18). **Andrew** is a Greek name, without a Hebrew equivalent. The next disciples in Matthew's listing are **James, the son of Zebedee, and his brother John,** who were the second pair called by Jesus (4:21-22); along with Peter, they will be Jesus' closest companions (17:1; 26:37). **James** is from the Greek form of the Hebrew name Jacob, the father of the twelve ancestors of the tribes of Israel. **John** comes from the Hebrew for "Yahweh has been gracious" ("Yahweh" is God's personal name, rendered as "LORD" in the New American Bible—Exod 3:15).

BACKGROUND: APOSTLE The Greek word for apostle comes from a verb meaning to send out. In secular usage, an apostle was an ambassador or a messenger. Jesus was sent by God (Mark 9:37; John 20:21), and so the Letter to the Hebrews calls Jesus an apostle (Heb 3:1). Jesus in turn sent out twelve specifically chosen followers as his envoys, commissioned to bear his message and carry out his work. The gospels often refer to this group as "the Twelve"; their significance lay in their being a symbol of Jesus' restoration of all Israel, which was made up of twelve tribes (Matt 19:28). The early church will use the term "apostle" for a select few of those who went out on mission for Christ (Rom 1:1; 16:7).

3 **Philip and Bartholomew** are listed next; the name **Philip,** like the name Andrew, is a Greek name. **Thomas** is Aramaic for "twin" and is a nickname; we do not know whose twin he is. We have been told of the call of **Matthew the tax collector** (9:9); **Matthew** comes from the Hebrew for "gift of Yahweh." "James" was a popular name, and a second **James** among the twelve is identified as **the son of Alphaeus** to distinguish him from James the son of Zebedee. **Thaddeus** is a name of uncertain meaning.

4 Simon was also a popular name, and a second **Simon** is identified as **the Cananean** to distinguish him from Simon Peter. **Cananean** means neither that he was from Cana nor that he was a Canaanite; it is an Aramaic word meaning "zealot." Calling Simon a Cananean probably indicates that Simon was intensely zealous about obeying the law of Moses and in insisting that others obey it. A violent revolutionary group known as the Zealots will not form until some decades later, during the Jewish revolt against Roman rule. Last on the list of the twelve is **Judas Iscariot who betrayed him.** The name **Judas** is a form of "Judah," one of the twelve sons of Jacob. The word **Iscariot** may reflect the Hebrew for "man of Kerioth," a village thirtysome miles south of Jerusalem (mentioned in Joshua 15:25). Listing Judas as the one who **betrayed** Jesus is another foreshadowing that Jesus will be "taken away" (9:15).

The Twelve bear a mixture of names and nicknames drawn from several languages, perhaps symbolizing that they were a mixed group. A tax collector and a zealot for the Mosaic law would not normally be found at the same table (see 9:9-11). What these disciples had in common was their call by Jesus to be the Twelve, with authority to heal and drive out evil spirits. Serving Jesus can mean working with those who are quite different from us.

For reflection: When has my service to Jesus meant working with those I would otherwise avoid? What effect has this had on me?

Instructions for Mission
5 Jesus sent out these twelve after instructing them thus, "Do not go into pagan territory or enter a Samaritan town. 6 Go rather to the lost sheep of the house of Israel. 7 As you go, make this proclamation: 'The kingdom of heaven is at hand.' 8 Cure the sick, raise the dead, cleanse lepers, drive out demons. Without cost you have received; without cost you are

to give. [9] Do not take gold or silver or copper for your belts; [10] no sack for the journey, or a second tunic, or sandals, or walking stick. The laborer deserves his keep. [11] Whatever town or village you enter, look for a worthy person in it, and stay there until you leave. [12] As you enter a house, wish it peace. [13] If the house is worthy, let your peace come upon it; if not, let your peace return to you. [14] Whoever will not receive you or listen to your words—go outside that house or town and shake the dust from your feet. [15] Amen, I say to you, it will be more tolerable for the land of Sodom and Gomorrah on the day of judgment than for that town."

> Gospel parallels: Mark 6:7-11; Luke 9:2-5
> OT: Gen 18:16-33; 19:1-11, 23-28
> NT: Matt 4:17; 9:35; 15:24

5 Jesus sent out these twelve: apostles are those sent on a mission, and Jesus now sends out the **twelve.** Jesus has given them authority over unclean spirits and diseases (10:1) but sends them out only **after instructing them:** their authority must be exercised in line with his instructions. Matthew writes that Jesus sent the twelve after instructing them **thus:** Jesus' instructions will run to the end of chapter 10.

BACKGROUND: SAMARIA, SAMARITANS A region called Samaria lay south of Galilee, separating the predominantly Jewish areas of Galilee and Judea. In Old Testament times it was part of the northern kingdom of Israel after its split from the southern kingdom of Judah. The split between the kingdoms was religious as well as political: the northern kingdom established shrines as rivals to the Temple in Jerusalem. The northern kingdom was conquered by Assyria around 721 B.C.; some of its inhabitants were deported, and foreigners settled in their place (see 2 Kings 17 for a negative assessment of the events). The Samaritans of New Testament times were considered by the Jews of Judea and Galilee to be the descendants of the foreigners and Israelites left by the Assyrians, mixed in race and religion and ritually unclean. Sirach, writing around 180 B.C. called Samaritans "degenerate folk" whom he loathed with his whole being (Sirach 50:25-26). Samaritans, on the other hand, thought of themselves as true Israelites who rigorously followed the law set down in the five books of Moses (Genesis through Deuteronomy). They erected a temple to God in the heart of Samaria on Mount Gerizim, the place they believed God wanted to be worshiped. A Jewish ruler invaded and tore down the Samaritan temple around 110 B.C., increasing tensions between Samaritans and Jews (see John 4:20).

Jesus begins his instructions to those he is sending by telling them where not to go: **Do not go into pagan territory or enter a Samaritan town.** Galilee was a Jewish island in a non-Jewish sea. Walking west, north, or east from Galilee took one into predominantly Gentile regions. Samaria lay to the south; Jews considered Samaritans to be half-Jewish at best. The Twelve are not being sent to those who are not Jews.

6 The mission of the Twelve is to Jews: **Go rather to the lost sheep of the house of Israel.** The term **the house of Israel** is a biblical expression for the whole Jewish people (Ezek 34:30; Acts 2:36). **Lost sheep,** wandering in the wilderness, are in peril. We might interpret **the lost sheep of the house of Israel** to refer to straying Israelites but not all Israelites, and understand the mission of the Twelve to be only to "tax collectors and sinners" (9:10). But the expression **the lost sheep of the house of Israel** rather conveys that the *whole* **house of Israel** is **lost sheep** in need of rescue. Jesus' choice of twelve symbolized their mission to the twelve tribes, the entire people of Israel (10:1).

Jesus will later say, "I was sent only to the lost sheep of the house of Israel" (15:24); he now associates the Twelve with his mission to Israel. Only after his resurrection will Jesus enlarge their mission, commanding them to "make disciples of all nations" (28:19).

7 **As you go, make this proclamation: "The kingdom of heaven is at hand."** Jesus began his public ministry by proclaiming that "the kingdom of heaven is at hand" (4:17), making this announcement as "he went around all of Galilee" (4:23; see also 9:35). Jesus sends out the Twelve to make the same announcement. Jesus taught his followers to pray to their Father, "your kingdom come," asking God to reign over this earth as he reigns in heaven (6:10). The first priority for those whom Jesus was sending out was to proclaim that God was indeed establishing his reign. Their message did not center on themselves or on what they could do; the focus was on what God was doing.

Kingdom of heaven: See page 266

For reflection: What are the clearest signs of God at work in the world today? What am I able to announce that God is doing?

8 God's reign was being established on earth not only by what Jesus said but through what Jesus did, and it was to be the same for those who took on his mission. Jesus gave the Twelve "authority over unclean spirits to drive them out and to cure every disease and every illness" (10:1), and they were to use this authority to **cure the sick, raise the dead, cleanse lepers, drive out demons.** In chapters 8 and 9 of his gospel, Matthew recounted various examples of Jesus curing the sick, expelling demons, and raising a dead person to life. Jesus sends out his disciples to do the same, relying on the authority he has given them.

We can note that Jesus' ministry included teaching as well as healing and proclaiming the kingdom (9:35), but Jesus has not included teaching in his charge to his disciples. They will be commissioned by Jesus to teach only after his resurrection (28:20). Before they can teach, they have much to learn.

For reflection: What has Jesus authorized and sent me to do on his behalf? To whom have I been sent?

Jesus continues, **Without cost you have received; without cost you are to give.** His disciples have received something **without cost,** without making any payment: they **have received** his message of the kingdom, the call to be his disciples, and the authority to heal as he healed. If Jesus had not come into their lives, they would still be fishing and farming and collecting taxes. Now they are privileged to play a role in the coming of the kingdom of God.

Jesus tells his disciples, As you have received without cost, so **without cost you are to give.** Act toward others as I have acted toward you; pass on the generosity you have received. The disciples' power to heal and expel demons is a gift, to be used as a gift to others. They are not to charge others for what they themselves have not paid for.

For reflection: What have I received as free gifts from God? How have I used my gifts as gifts to others?

9 **Do not take gold or silver or copper for your belts:** the money of the time was in the form of coins minted in various metals, with **gold** coins the most valuable and **copper** coins the least. Coins were commonly carried in folds in **belts.** Matthew's Greek literally reads, "Do not *acquire* gold

or silver or copper." This can mean, "Don't procure traveling funds before setting out." In the context of what Jesus has just said, the meaning is also, "Do not acquire money by your preaching and healing; do not accept payment for your ministry." The Twelve are to pass on without charge what they received as a free gift; they are not to accept even the small change of copper coins.

10 Not only are the Twelve to forsake payment while traveling on mission; they also are to have **no sack for the journey, or a second tunic, or sandals, or walking stick.** A sack was a bag for bread and other provisions, carried by travelers at the time of Jesus. A **tunic** was the standard undergarment; the Twelve were to travel without a change of clothing. **Sandals** and a **walking stick** were indispensable for traveling any distance over rocky paths; a walking stick was also a defense against robbers and wild animals. Jesus instructed the Twelve to travel impractically light, without money or food, without sandals to ease their walking or a staff to protect themselves.

Clothing: See page 95

How were the Twelve to survive without money or provisions? Jesus tells them, **The laborer deserves his keep**—more literally, "the laborer deserves his *food*." Jesus is sending out the Twelve as laborers for the harvest (9:37-38). While they are not to accept payment for their work (verse 9), they may accept the hospitality of others (verses 11-13). They may eat the food their hosts set before them, but without a **sack** they will be unable to store up anything for the next day. Jesus told his disciples not to be anxious about what they would wear or eat and not to worry about tomorrow, trusting their heavenly Father to provide for their needs (6:25-34). So now Jesus sends them out on their mission depending on God and on those who would give them hospitality, rather than depending on their own resources.

The lifestyle of the disciples must be in line with their mission and message. They could not proclaim that the kingdom of heaven is at hand (verse 7)—which meant God making a radical change in the way the world operated—and yet continue in normal patterns of life. They could not cure the sick and raise the dead through their own resources; their lifestyle should manifest their complete dependence on God. Jesus, who had no place of his own to lay his head (8:20), asked his disciples to share his life and his reliance on God as well as his mission and his authority.

For reflection: How does the way I live bear witness to my mission from Jesus?

11 Jesus instructs his disciples how to receive hospitality as they travel. **Whatever town or village you enter, look for a worthy person in it, and stay there until you leave.** A **worthy person** in this context is someone who is willing to receive the disciples and the message they bear. They are to **stay** in the home of such a person, accepting the hospitality that is offered them. Staying in one house **until you leave** that **town** or **village** probably means not upgrading accommodations if a better offer comes along. The disciples' aim should not be getting the best lodgings and food but simply having their basic needs met.

12 **As you enter a house, wish it peace.** A guest might pronounce the blessing, "Peace be to this house," upon entering it. The biblical notion of **peace** was not simply the absence of conflict but a state of wholeness. The blessing would not be for the **house** as a building but for those who lived within it, the household. The disciples were to observe standard greeting customs but with a deeper meaning: they were bringing news of the coming of God's reign, the ultimate peace and wholeness for God's people.

BACKGROUND: HOSPITALITY The practice of welcoming guests, including strangers, into one's home for meals and lodging is common in the Old and New Testaments. Abraham provides an example of generous hospitality when he begs three traveling strangers to accept a snack from him but then serves them a banquet (Gen 18:1-8). Abraham's nephew Lot pleads with passing strangers to spend the night in his house rather than sleep in the town square (Gen 19:1-3). Job lists hospitality among his upright deeds: "no stranger lodged in the street, / but I opened my door to wayfarers" (Job 31:32). Those who traveled usually had to rely on the hospitality of others. Caravan inns on main routes provided shelter for travelers and animals (Luke 10:34-35), but there were no inns in ordinary towns and villages. Jesus depended on the hospitality of his followers, including Peter (Mark 1:29-34; 2:1) and Martha and Mary (Luke 10:38-42). Jesus included hospitality among his concerns on judgment day: "I was . . . a stranger and you welcomed me" (Matt 25:35). The practice of hospitality is evident in Acts (Acts 10:21-23; 16:15; 28:7), and the letters of the New Testament hold hospitality in high regard (Rom 12:13; 1 Tim 3:2; 5:10; Titus 1:8; Heb 13:2).

---

13 **If the house is worthy, let your peace come upon it.** The notion of **worthy** is again best understood as receptive. If a household is willing to accept the disciples as guests and accept their message, then **peace** will come upon that household. But not every household that the disciples approach will be receptive to them. **If not, let your peace return to you.** The disciples will lose nothing by wishing peace on an unreceptive household; if their **peace** is rejected, it will **return to** them, like a gift offered but spurned.

14 Jesus dwells on what his disciples are to do when they and their message are rejected, as if they might encounter more rejection than acceptance in the course of their mission. **Whoever will not receive you or listen to your words—go outside that house or town and shake the dust from your feet.** To **shake the dust from** one's **feet** is a symbolic gesture of disassociation (Acts 13:51), akin to washing one's hands (Matt 27:24). It conveys, "We have nothing further to do with you." The disciples are not expected to win everyone over and convince them of the message they bear. They are simply to do what Jesus asks of them, and move on to other opportunities if they are rejected.

> *For reflection: How do I react when my attempts to bear witness to Jesus are rebuffed?*

15 Those who reject the disciples and the message they proclaim do so to their detriment. **Amen, I say to you, it will be more tolerable for the land of Sodom and Gomorrah on the day of judgment than for that town.** The towns of **Sodom and Gomorrah** were proverbial examples of wickedness that was severely punished by God (Gen 18:20-21; 19:23-25; Deut 29:22; Isaiah 1:9; 13:19; Jer 49:18; 50:40; Amos 4:11). The people of Sodom were brutishly inhospitable to angels (messengers of God) visiting their town (Gen 19:1-11); towns that are inhospitable to messengers sent by Jesus will suffer a worse fate than Sodom and Gomorrah **on the day of judgment.** Jesus refers to the **judgment** that God will pass on every individual at the end of this age, when God definitively establishes his reign. Turning away messengers of Jesus would not merely violate cultural obligations to offer hospitality; it would be a rejection of their message that God's reign was at hand and a rejection of what God was doing.

Judgment: See page 557

What is the relevance of Jesus' mission instructions for us today? St. Francis took Jesus' demand to travel light quite literally, but our lives are far removed from such simplicity. Yet we can still make applications. "Without cost you have received; without cost you are to give" (verse 8) applies to our gifts. We can strive for a simpler lifestyle, with greater trust in God's care for us. We can acknowledge that we too have been sent to bring Jesus' message and healing to others, and shape our lives accordingly.

For reflection: What relevance and application do Jesus' mission instructions have for me?

ORIENTATION: *Jesus continues to instruct his disciples about going on mission. In the course of his instructions he addresses some situations that will not arise until after his resurrection.*

The Fate of Jesus' Disciples
[16] "Behold, I am sending you like sheep in the midst of wolves; so be shrewd as serpents and simple as doves. [17] But beware of people, for they will hand you over to courts and scourge you in their synagogues, [18] and you will be led before governors and kings for my sake as a witness before them and the pagans. [19] When they hand you over, do not worry about how you are to speak or what you are to say. You will be given at that moment what you are to say. [20] For it will not be you who speak but the Spirit of your Father speaking through you. [21] Brother will hand over brother to death, and the father his child; children will rise up against parents and have them put to death. [22] You will be hated by all because of my name, but whoever endures to the end will be saved. [23] When they persecute you in one town, flee to another. Amen, I say to you, you will not finish the towns of Israel before the Son of Man comes. [24] No disciple is above his teacher, no slave above his master. [25] It is enough for the disciple that he become like his teacher, for the slave that he become like his master. If they have called the master of the house Beelzebul, how much more those of his household!"

Gospel parallels: Mark 13:9-13; Luke 6:40; 10:3; 12:11-12; 21:12-19; John 13:16

OT: Deut 25:1-3

NT: Matt 5:10-12; 9:34; 12:24; 23:34; 24:9, 13, 30, 36; John 14:16, 26; 15:18-20, 26-27; 2 Cor 11:24

16 Jesus has spoken of the fate of those who will reject his messengers (10:14-15), and he now turns his attention to what will happen to the messengers themselves. He begins with the warning, **Behold, I am sending you like sheep in the midst of wolves.** Sheep are rather defenseless animals, easy prey for wolves. Jesus is **sending** his disciples into danger, like **sheep** sent to a pack of **wolves.** Those who take on the mission of Jesus cannot remain in the safety of a sheepfold; they must go out to those who may do them harm. Jesus prefaces his words with **behold:** his disciples are to take note of his warning.

Because the disciples are being sent into danger, Jesus tells them **so be shrewd as serpents and simple as doves.** Just as sheep and wolves are images of defenselessness and danger, so **serpents** and **doves** are images of shrewdness and innocence. "Now the serpent was the most cunning of all the animals that the LORD God had made" (Gen 3:1). Those being sent out by Jesus are to be **shrewd** as they carry out their mission. The Greek word translated as **shrewd** can also be translated as "prudent" (24:45) or "wise" (7:24; 25:2) but here probably has the connotation of "cunning." Yet at the same time they are also to be as **simple as doves.** The word translated **simple** literally means "unmixed" and has connotations of "pure and innocent"; Jesus' disciples are to be guileless.

Being both shrewd and simple—cunning and guileless—seems contradictory. Jesus may intend his words to be paradoxical in order to provoke reflection. His disciples can neither rely on shrewdness alone nor spurn all shrewdness. Jesus is sending them into danger, and they must exercise discernment.

For reflection: What does Jesus' admonition to be shrewd and simple mean to me?

17 **But beware of people:** the disciples will face opposition from several categories of **people.** Jesus first speaks of fellow Jews: **for they will hand you over to courts and scourge you in their synagogues.** The word **courts** covered both civil and religious tribunals; in this context it means local councils of Jewish leaders. The law of Moses allowed the community to have an offender whipped, but limited the whipping to forty lashes (Deut 25:1-3); Jewish practice reduced this to thirty-nine lashes to allow a margin for error (see 2 Cor 11:24). Jewish councils had authority only over Jews; Jesus' disciples risk being scourged in synagogues because

they are Jews proclaiming the message of Jesus to fellow Jews. None of the gospels describe Jesus' disciples being scourged during Jesus' public ministry; his words seem to address a later time. When Matthew wrote his gospel, synagogues were increasingly coming under the control of Jews who rejected Jesus as the Messiah, and Matthew's Jewish Christian readers may have thought of such synagogues as **their synagogues** rather than *our* synagogues. While there was no general Jewish persecution of Christians in the first century—or in any century—some Jewish Christians did encounter considerable hostility from some fellow Jews (see also 23:34).

Synagogue: See page 104

18 Those bearing Jesus' message will meet with opposition from those who are not Jews as well as from Jews: **and you will be led before governors and kings for my sake as a witness before them and the pagans.** Jesus initially sent the twelve disciples only "to the lost sheep of the house of Israel" (10:6). His words now clearly address a later time, when the disciples will bear witness to **pagans.** After his resurrection Jesus will commission his disciples to "make disciples of all nations" (28:19). **Governors and kings** represent civil authorities in the regions and nations in which the gospel will be preached. Jesus tells his disciples that they will be brought before civil authorities **for my sake.** Jesus' disciples may be arrested because of their preaching or simply because of their identification with Jesus. Being led before civil authorities will provide occasions for the disciples to bear **witness before them,** proclaiming the message of Jesus (as Paul will do—Acts 26). Being arrested should be viewed as an opportunity to give witness rather than a misfortune.

For reflection: What have I endured for the sake of Jesus? How have I made use of opportunities to bear witness to him?

19 **When they hand you over, do not worry about how you are to speak or what you are to say.** Jesus previously told his disciples not to worry about food and clothing; their heavenly Father would provide for them (6:25-34). Now he tells them not to **worry** when they are handed over to civil authorities and put on trial. Jesus' first disciples lacked status and education (see Acts 4:13), so being arrested could be a source of anxiety: "How will I defend myself?" Jesus tells them not to worry **about how you are to**

speak or what you are to say. There is no need for them to rehearse their defense beforehand: **you will be given at that moment what you are to say.** The implication of **will be given** is that they will be given by God. The right words will be provided **at that moment** when they are needed, not necessarily beforehand. Jesus' followers must **not worry** but trust that they will receive help in critical moments.

20 **For it will not be you who speak but the Spirit of your Father speaking through you.** Jesus was conceived through the Holy Spirit (1:18, 20); the presence of the Spirit was manifested after Jesus' baptism and led him (3:16; 4:1). This same **Spirit** will speak through the disciples of Jesus. This is the only promise by Jesus in Matthew's gospel of the Holy Spirit assisting or coming to his disciples. Jesus speaks of the Spirit as **the Spirit of your Father.** In the New Testament, the Spirit is sometimes identified with Jesus (Acts 16:7; Phil 1:19; 1 Pet 1:11) and sometimes, as here, with the Father—and sometimes with both in almost the same breath (Rom 8:9, 11). The church will grapple for centuries over how to speak of the relationships of the Father, Son, and Holy Spirit to one another. Jesus does not go into such matters here; his point is that the **Spirit** will speak through his disciples as they bear witness. They therefore do not need to worry about what they will say; their heavenly **Father** will, as always, provide for their needs.

The Spirit: See page 21

For reflection: How have I experienced inspirations from the Spirit helping me in difficult situations?

21 The disciples of Jesus will face opposition and persecution not only from strangers but from those closest to them: **Brother will hand over brother to death.** Here **hand over** means to betray a disciple of Jesus to civil authorities during a persecution, resulting in the disciple's **death.** There were sporadic Roman persecutions of Christians during the three centuries after Jesus; Nero's persecution of Christians in Rome during the sixties was particularly vicious. The word **brother** is used both for blood brothers (4:18, 21) and for members of the new family of Jesus (12:49-50; see also 7:3-5; 18:15, 21, 35; 23:8; 25:40). During Nero's persecution, some Christians succumbed to fear and torture and betrayed the names of other Christians, leading to their arrest and death. Some Christians were

betrayed by members of their own families: **brother handing over brother, and the father his child; children will rise up against parents and have them put to death.** Presumably family members who had not become followers of Jesus betrayed those who had. Jewish culture placed a high value on family relationships, making the prospect of being handed over to death by one's immediate family particularly distressing.

22 Jesus tells his disciples that they will not only be denounced by those closest to them, but **you will be hated by all because of my name.** The disciples will indeed be "like sheep in the midst of wolves" (verse 16), **hated by all** (see also 24:9). To be hated because of the **name** of Jesus means that the disciples will be hated because they will be identified with Jesus. This identification will lead to their becoming known by his name: "It was in Antioch that the disciples were first called Christians" (Acts 11:26; it is quite possible that Matthew wrote his gospel in Antioch). The Roman historian Tacitus (A.D. 56–118) wrote of a general antipathy toward Christians; many Romans considered them a superstitious sect with shameful practices.

Jesus' followers may face hatred and persecution, but **whoever endures to the end will be saved.** The phrase **to the end** can have different meanings. It might mean to the end of a particular persecution. It might mean to the end of one's life (verse 21). It might mean to the end of the present age, when Jesus will return (verse 23). Each of these possible meanings is linked with a corresponding meaning of being **saved.** If "the end" means the end of a persecution, then being saved means surviving it. If the end is the end of one's life, then being saved means receiving eternal life. If the end is the return of Jesus, then being saved means being rescued from the tribulation that was expected when this age comes to an end (see 24:29). It is not clear which meaning Jesus primarily intended for his listeners. Readers of Matthew's gospel today might best understand Jesus to be speaking of the end of their days on earth and take his words as a promise of eternal life if they endure in their faith.

For reflection: How do I understand Jesus' promise that the one who endures to the end will be saved?

23 **When they persecute you in one town, flee to another.** Jesus had told those he was sending out that if a town did not welcome them, they were to leave, shaking the dust from their feet (10:14). Now he addresses not

merely unfriendly reception but outright persecution. When persecuted, **flee** to another town. Perhaps one application of Jesus' admonition to be shrewd as serpents yet simple as doves might be, Don't endure persecution needlessly; go somewhere else where you can carry on your mission.

Amen, I say to you, you will not finish the towns of Israel before the Son of Man comes. These words are difficult to understand. If they are interpreted in light of Jesus' initial sending the twelve disciples on a mission to Israel (10:6), then their natural sense is that Jesus is proclaiming that they will not **finish** their mission in the **towns of Israel** before he, the **Son of Man, comes.** But that raises problems. To this point in Matthew's gospel Jesus has said nothing explicit about his leaving (9:15 is the only hint) and nothing at all about his coming again. Neither the disciples nor Matthew's readers have been prepared for understanding the significance of the coming of the Son of Man. When Jesus does speak of his coming (16:28; 24:30), he will speak of it as an event that will happen well after the initial sending out of the twelve disciples. Some biblical scholars suggest that when Jesus tells his disciples that they **will not finish the towns of Israel before the Son of Man comes,** he is speaking of a mission to Israel after his resurrection that will continue until he comes again. We will defer consideration of the timing of Jesus' coming until a later point in Matthew's gospel (see 24:32-36).

Son of Man: See page 151

24 Jesus' main concern has been to prepare his disciples to face persecution, and he now addresses the significance of their being persecuted. Taking on the mission of Jesus and being identified with him means sharing his fate. To make this point, Jesus begins with what may have been a common proverbial saying: **No disciple is above his teacher, no slave above his master.** In a school setting, no student is above the teacher; in a household, no slave is above his master. Jesus is the **teacher** and **master,** or "lord," of his disciples, and they should not expect to fare better than he does.

25 **It is enough for the disciple that he become like his teacher, for the slave that he become like his master.** A student is not expected to know more than a teacher but simply to learn what the teacher is able to impart and thereby become like the teacher. Likewise, while a slave will never be the equal of his or her owner, a slave can take on the owner's good qualities and become like the master.

Jesus draws a lesson from these observations about students and teachers, slaves and masters: **If they have called the master of the house Beelzebul, how much more those of his household!** Some Pharisees had accused Jesus of driving out demons by the prince of demons (9:34); **Beelzebul** was another name for Satan, the prince of demons. Jesus will face the same charge again (12:24). Jesus gives the twelve disciples authority over unclean spirits (10:1) and sends them out to expel demons (10:7). If the disciples perform the works of Jesus, they will face the same accusations he faces. If he as **master** is labeled **Beelzebul,** it will be even easier to make this charge against **those of his household,** or family (see 12:49-50).

Beelzebul: See Satan, page 55

Jesus does not speak of all the rejection and suffering he will face: that he will do later (16:21; 17:22-23; 20:18-19). He does indicate, however, that for his disciples to take on his mission means that they will face whatever opposition he faces. The persecutions they will endure are part of their serving him and becoming like him.

For reflection: What have I endured because of my identification with Jesus or because of my service of him?

Do Not Be Afraid
26 "Therefore do not be afraid of them. Nothing is concealed that will not be revealed, nor secret that will not be known. 27 What I say to you in the darkness, speak in the light; what you hear whispered, proclaim on the housetops. 28 And do not be afraid of those who kill the body but cannot kill the soul; rather, be afraid of the one who can destroy both soul and body in Gehenna. 29 Are not two sparrows sold for a small coin? Yet not one of them falls to the ground without your Father's knowledge. 30 Even all the hairs of your head are counted. 31 So do not be afraid; you are worth more than many sparrows. 32 Everyone who acknowledges me before others I will acknowledge before my heavenly Father. 33 But whoever denies me before others, I will deny before my heavenly Father."

Gospel parallels: Mark 8:38; Luke 9:26; 12:2-9
NT: Matt 7:21-23; 25:31-46

26 Jesus has just told his disciples that they will be rejected, persecuted, and killed (10:14-25); now he tells them, **Therefore do not be afraid of them,** of those who will persecute you. Jesus' disciples face fearful prospects; Jesus is sending them like lambs into the midst of wolves (10:16), yet he still tells them **do not be afraid.** Jesus does not ask blind courage of them, but goes on to explain why they should not be afraid.

Jesus' first reason for not being afraid is a bit cryptic. He assures his disciples that **nothing is concealed that will not be revealed, nor secret that will not be known.** The implication of **be revealed** and **known** is of being revealed and made known *by* God. In the context of Jesus' sending his disciples out to proclaim the kingdom of God (10:7), Jesus' assurance seems to mean that the message of the kingdom will get out and become known, despite whatever opposition and persecution the disciples face as its messengers. God's word does not go forth in vain (Isaiah 55:10-11), and those who proclaim it do not need to worry that they have undertaken a futile mission or **be afraid** of those who oppose their mission. Rejection and persecution of the messengers cannot stifle the message.

27 Therefore the disciples should boldly proclaim the message given them by Jesus. **What I say to you in the darkness, speak in the light; what you hear whispered, proclaim on the housetops.** Jesus invokes two pairs of contrasts, the second of which is easier to understand. **What you hear whispered** is literally, what you hear in the ear. The teachings that Jesus speaks privately to his disciples they are to **proclaim on the housetops.** House roofs were usually flat and accessible by a staircase or ladder; such roofs could be used as makeshift pulpits. The contrast between **darkness** and **light** also seems to stand here for the contrast between the private and the public: what Jesus tells his disciples privately they are to proclaim publicly. They are to be "the light of the world," as visible as a city set on a mountain (5:14). The message they bear cannot be whispered; it must be shouted, boldly and without fear.

28 Jesus provides a second reason for not being afraid: **And do not be afraid of those who kill the body but cannot kill the soul.** The Hebrew notion of **soul** was that it was one's life or self (the word that is translated **soul** in this verse is translated as "life" in 6:25 and 10:39). Jesus tells his disciples not to fear those who can only **kill the body** but are unable to **kill the soul,** that is, cannot annihilate the self, which will continue to exist after death. If Jesus' disciples are put to death (10:21), that will not be the end of them: martyrdom is the gateway to life in the age to come.

Life after death: See page 406

Still, it is easy to fear death, despite believing that there is life after death, and it is natural to **be afraid of those** who can kill us. Jesus does not tell his disciples to wave away such fears as if they were nothing; Jesus instead asks them to put their fears in proper perspective. They should not be concerned about those who can merely end their bodily lives but should **be afraid of the one who can destroy both soul and body in Gehenna.** Some Jewish nonbiblical writings used **Gehenna** (the Hinnom Valley around Jerusalem) as a symbol of punishment for the wicked after death. God is **the one who can destroy both soul and body in Gehenna.** He can **destroy** the wicked not in the sense of annihilating them but in the sense of punishing them. The disciples should not be afraid of those

---

BACKGROUND: NONBIBLICAL WRITINGS Other religious writings besides the books of the Old Testament were in circulation among Jews at the time of Jesus. Many of these texts had been written in the previous two centuries. Two of these writings, 1 Enoch and The Assumption of Moses, are quoted in the Letter of Jude (Jude 6, 9, 14-15). Other writings included Jubilees, Psalms of Solomon, and some of The Testaments of the Twelve Patriarchs, as well as other writings found among the Dead Sea Scrolls. Some of these writings claim to be revelations of how God will act to overcome evil and begin a new age. They differ considerably over what lies ahead. Various ideas about messianic figures, angels, the present age and the age to come, judgment, the resurrection of the dead, and life in the age to come are found in these writings, in more developed forms than they are found in the books of the Old Testament. It is uncertain how popular each of these writings was at the time of Jesus or how familiar the average Jew was with them. Yet at least some of their ideas and imagery, such as of Gehenna as a place of fiery punishment, were sufficiently familiar to first-century Jews for Jesus to invoke them in his teachings without having to explain them as if his listeners were hearing of them for the first time. These writings form part of the background for the gospels and help bridge the Old and the New Testaments, even though they are not part of inspired Scripture. *Related topics: Dead Sea Scrolls (page 97), Psalms of Solomon (page 354), Revelations of the end (page 518).*

---

who can harm them only in this life; the disciples are to be afraid of God, whose punishments know no such limit.

Gehenna: See page 88

To be **afraid of** or to fear God is a biblical idiom for an attitude of reverence and submission. "Fear of the LORD" is not sheer terror but encompasses love, service, hope, and trust (see Deut 10:12; Psalm 33:18-19). God can punish the wicked, but he is also a Father who provides for his children (6:25-34). Jesus' telling his disciples to be afraid of him who can destroy soul and body must be integrated with Jesus' telling them not to worry about their life (soul) or their body (6:25) because their heavenly Father cares for them (6:32).

For reflection: What kind of fear do I have of God?

29 To clarify what it means to be afraid of God, and to help the disciples understand why they should not be afraid of persecution and death, Jesus takes up another line of reasoning. He begins with an observation: **Are not two sparrows sold for a small coin?** Sparrows were the cheapest meat in the market. The Greek word translated **a small coin** designated a copper coin, akin to a penny. **Yet not one of them falls to the ground without your Father's knowledge.** The expression **falls to the ground** is an idiom for dying. In Greek, the end of the verse simply reads "without your Father;" the New American Bible interprets this to mean **without your Father's knowledge.** Despite sparrows being almost valueless, **not one of them** dies without the knowledge and consent of God. This has implications for how the disciples relate to God, who is the heavenly Father of the disciples, and for their being fearless in the face of persecution.

30 Before drawing a lesson from his observations about sparrows, Jesus makes another observation: **Even all the hairs of your head are counted.** It is implied that they are counted *by* God. Jesus does not spell out the implications of God numbering hairs, so we must ponder what the implications might be. A biblical idiom for God's protection of individuals has it that God would not let a single hair fall from their heads to the ground (1 Sam 14:45; 2 Sam 14:11; see also Luke 21:18; Acts 27:34). In the context of Jesus' telling his disciples not to be afraid, God's numbering the hairs on their heads may have the connotation that God will protect them.

199

Yet there is no guarantee that they will never suffer harm and death, for they will (10:21). There may also then be another implication of God's counting hairs on a head. How many hairs are there in a full head of hair? We cannot tally them—but God can. The Old Testament used examples of what God could count but humans couldn't to convey the fact that God's knowledge and plans are far above human comprehension (Job 38:37; Sirach 1:2). God is concerned about every aspect of us, down to our last hair, and it is no more possible for us to fully comprehend how God exercises his loving care for us than it is for us to number the hairs on our heads.

For reflection: How well does God know me? How well do I know God?

31 Jesus returns to his earlier observation about sparrows and draws its lesson. **So do not be afraid; you are worth more than many sparrows.** There is something wry about Jesus telling his disciples that they **are worth more than many sparrows,** for that's not saying much! Perhaps Jesus set the bar low and used two-for-a-penny sparrows as a comparison so that every disciple, even those with poor self-esteem, would find encouragement in his words. Jesus' main point is, If even the life of a lowly sparrow is in the hands of God, how much more are the lives of his disciples in his hands. They are certainly **worth more** to their Father than sparrows! **So do not be afraid,** Jesus tells his disciples. Because of your worth to God, do not be afraid of those who persecute you or put you to death. Fear only the one who has counted the hairs on your head; fear him with reverence and trust him as your heavenly Father who cares for you.

For reflection: What do I think I am worth to God?

32 Jesus adds a final reason for his disciples' carrying out the mission he gives them with confidence instead of fear. **Everyone who acknowledges me before others I will acknowledge before my heavenly Father.** Acknowledging Jesus **before others** broadly includes the disciples' public witness and more narrowly refers to their testimony before tribunals (10:17-18). Jesus speaks of his disciples acknowledging **me:** after his resurrection, the message his disciples will proclaim will center on Jesus more than on the coming of the kingdom (see Acts 2:36, for example). Jesus

promises that those who acknowledge him to others he **will acknowledge before** his **heavenly Father.** Jesus will make his acknowledgment at the last judgment, when God will sort out good from evil. Jesus will claim as his own those who acknowledged that they belonged to him. He adverts to his special standing with God, whom he speaks of as **my heavenly Father.** Jesus is not an ordinary defense witness but the beloved Son of the Father (3:17). Because Jesus will vouch for them at the last judgment, his disciples can proclaim him and his message without fear, despite whatever persecution they encounter.

Judgment: See page 557

For reflection: How have I acknowledged Jesus by my words? by my actions?

33 If Jesus will acknowledge those who acknowledge him, the reverse is also true. **But whoever denies me before others, I will deny before my heavenly Father.** If any say that they do not know Jesus or belong to him, at the last judgment he will take the same stance toward them: "I never knew you" (7:23). Jesus presents allegiance to him as a decisive factor at the last judgment, and this should be kept in mind in considering other teachings of Jesus about the final judgment (7:21-23; 25:31-46).

Tragically, one of the disciples who heard Jesus' warning about denying him before others will do exactly that: Peter will deny "in front of everyone" that he was with Jesus, swearing, "I do not know the man" (26:69-74). The fact that Peter will be forgiven tempers Jesus' warning that he will deny his deniers. Jesus offers forgiveness and reconciliation even to those who deny him.

For reflection: Have I ever denied or obscured my allegiance to Jesus out of fear or self-concern?

ORIENTATION: *Jesus continues to instruct the disciples he is sending out on mission (10:5), but his words apply to all his followers.*

The Price of Discipleship
34 "Do not think that I have come to bring peace upon the earth. I have come to bring not peace but the sword. 35 For I have come to set

a man 'against his father,
 a daughter against her mother,
 and a daughter-in-law against her mother-in-law;
   36 and one's enemies will be those of his household.'

37 "Whoever loves father or mother more than me is not worthy of me, and whoever loves son or daughter more than me is not worthy of me; **38** and whoever does not take up his cross and follow after me is not worthy of me. **39** Whoever finds his life will lose it, and whoever loses his life for my sake will find it."

> Gospel parallels: Mark 8:34-35; Luke 9:24; 12:51-53; 14:26-27; 17:33; John 12:25
> OT:Micah 7:6
> NT:Matt 10:21; 16:24-25

34 **Do not think that I have come to bring peace upon the earth.** The disciples might well have thought that Jesus had **come to bring peace upon the earth:** he has said that peacemakers are blessed (5:9), has forbidden violence (5:39), and has told his them to pronounce a blessing of peace on those whom they visit (10:12). Jesus retracts nothing he has taught about being peacemakers but addresses a different matter. **Do not think that I have come** has the sense of, Do not misunderstand the impact that my coming will have. **I have come to bring not peace but the sword.** Jesus speaks not of the *purpose* of his coming but of its *effect*. Just as a **sword** sunders, so Jesus will divide. Some will accept him but, as is already evident (9:3, 34), some will reject him. Jesus' disciples will be rejected as he is rejected (10:16-25), and it would be naive of them to think otherwise.

35 Even within a family, some will accept Jesus and some will reject him, tearing the family apart. Jesus borrows words from the prophet Micah to provide examples of family divisions that will arise because of him. **For I have come to set a man "against his father, / a daughter against her mother, / and a daughter-in-law against her mother-in-law."** The pairings reflect the culture of the time, in which men related primarily to men, women primarily to women. A son, possibly married but in any case living with his parents in the family home, will be set **against his father;** a **daughter,** unmarried and living at home, will be set **against her mother.** A **daughter-in-law,** living in the family home of her husband, will be set

against her mother-in-law. The divisions in these examples are between a younger and an older generation; these examples do not exhaust the possibilities for strife within a family over Jesus.

> For the son dishonors his father,
> > the daughter rises up against her mother,
> The daughter-in-law against her mother-in-law,
> > and a man's enemies are those of his household.
> > > > > Micah 7:6

36 Jesus uses the concluding words of Micah's prophecy as a generalization for conflicts within families over him: **one's enemies will be those of his household.** A **household** here means a family or extended family living together. Because of Jesus, "brother will hand over brother to death, and the father his child; children will rise up against parents and have them put to death" (10:21). The coming of Jesus is a sword that will divide families, as some members accept him while others reject him. Jesus lived in a culture that placed a high value on family loyalties, and to have those whom one looked to for support become **one's enemies** was a very sobering prospect.

> For reflection: Have I ever encountered rejection from family members because of my commitment to Jesus?

37 Some may face a choice between being a disciple of Jesus and preserving peace and unity with their families. Jesus tells his disciples that they must put him first if they wish to be his disciples. He proclaims, **Whoever loves father or mother more than me is not worthy of me.** The whoever covers all disciples of all time. Honoring one's **father** and **mother** is commanded by the law of Moses (Exod 20:12; Deut 5:16), a command Jesus upholds (15:4; 19:19). Jesus wants his disciples to love their parents, but they are to love him even more. Jesus says that whoever subordinates love for him to love for parents **is not worthy of me,** meaning that he or she does not deserve to be his disciple. Likewise, **whoever loves son or daughter more than me is not worthy of me.** If Jesus commands his disciples to love even their enemies (5:44), he certainly expects them to love their children. Yet as much as Jesus' disciples love their children, they are to have even greater love for him. Being Jesus' disciple does not mean loving others less; it means loving others more and loving Jesus most of all.

For reflection: How great is my love for Jesus?

38 Jesus asks a lot when he tells his disciples that their love for him must be greater than their love for their parents and children. He goes on to ask even more: **and whoever does not take up his cross and follow after me is not worthy of me.** Jesus invokes crucifixion as a metaphor for what his disciples must be willing to endure for his sake. His disciples knew what it meant for a person to **take up his cross:** crucifixions were not rare occurrences in first-century Palestine. A condemned person was forced to carry a crossbeam to the place of execution, where it was fastened to an upright beam already in place. To **take up** a **cross**—carry a crossbeam—meant being on one's way to the most painful and degrading form of death the ancient world could devise. For Jesus to demand that a disciple **take up his cross** and **follow after** him to be **worthy** of him means that his followers had to be willing to shoulder shame, suffering, and death as the price of discipleship. No sacrifice that one may have to make to be Jesus' disciple is too great, not even enduring the most horrible of deaths.

Crucifixion: See page 635

Jesus has not yet given any indication in Matthew's gospel that he will be crucified, but his words may hint at it: Jesus calls his disciples to take up a cross **and follow after me,** as if he is going ahead of them carrying a cross beam on the way to execution. Matthew's first readers knew that Jesus was crucified, for that was at the heart of the gospel message (see 1 Cor 2:2; 15:3-5). Being a disciple of Jesus means following him (4:19, 22; 8:19, 22, 23) and enduring what he endures (10:24-25), even death. While there was apparently no general persecution of Christians at the time Matthew wrote his gospel, many Christians had died, some by crucifixion, during a persecution in Rome twenty years earlier. Christians everywhere were vulnerable to sporadic persecution; to give one's life to Jesus meant being willing to give one's life for him. Taking up one's cross was not just a metaphor for Matthew's first readers.

For reflection: What cross do I bear for Jesus?

39 If the price one has to pay to be a disciple of Jesus is one's life, is it worth it? Yes! Jesus proclaims that **whoever finds his life will lose it, and whoever loses his life for my sake will find it.** The expression **finds his life** is

best understood as "tries to find" or "tries to hold onto." Those who grasp at **life** will inevitably find it slipping from their grip and **lose it.** "The way of all mankind" (1 Kings 2:2) is to the grave. But Jesus promises that **whoever loses his life** (which, assuredly, also means *her* life) **for my sake will find it**—find eternal life. Losing one's life **for** the **sake** of Jesus means dying because of allegiance to him. Paying the price of one's life on earth for the sake of Jesus results in receiving life in the age to come.

There is another shade of meaning to Jesus' promise. The Greek word translated as **life** is the same word translated as "soul" in 10:28 and can mean "one's self." To speak of finding and losing one's self means that those who live lives of self-indulgence harm themselves, while those who put aside self-concern for the sake of Jesus become their best and truest selves.

For reflection: What is the meaning for me of Jesus' promise that whoever loses his or her life for his sake will find it?

ORIENTATION: *Jesus had spoken of the fate of those who reject his messengers (10:14-15); now he promises that those who welcome his messengers will be rewarded.*

Reward for Hospitality

⁴⁰ "Whoever receives you receives me, and whoever receives me receives the one who sent me. ⁴¹ Whoever receives a prophet because he is a prophet will receive a prophet's reward, and whoever receives a righteous man because he is righteous will receive a righteous man's reward. ⁴² And whoever gives only a cup of cold water to one of these little ones to drink because he is a disciple—amen, I say to you, he will surely not lose his reward."

> Gospel parallels: Mark 9:41; Luke 10:16; John 13:20
> NT: Matt 10:5-13; 25:40

40 Jesus is instructing disciples whom he is sending out to carry on his mission (10:5-8). They are to travel light, relying on the hospitality of others (10:8-13). Jesus tells them that **whoever receives you**—provides you with food and lodging and accepts your message—**receives me.** The disciples represent their sender; receiving those sent by Jesus means receiving him. **And whoever receives me receives the one who sent me.** Just as Jesus sends his disciples, Jesus himself has been **sent.** Jesus does not say who sent him, but the disciples should realize by now that it is God, whom Jesus speaks of as "my heavenly Father" (10:32-33; see also 7:21). Jesus has said several times, "I have come," in speaking of his mission (5:17; 10:34-35; see also 9:13); now Jesus speaks of being **sent,** indicating that his mission is from God. Just as the disciples represent Jesus, Jesus represents God. **Whoever receives** those sent by Jesus thereby **receives** both Jesus and his Father. To open one's house to Jesus' messengers is to open oneself to God. This will be true not only during the disciples' first mission but for all future missions as well. **Whoever** welcomes and assists those who spread the gospel of Jesus are welcoming and assisting Jesus and his Father.

In the context of what follows, Jesus' words are an assurance to those who receive his messengers. But two points should be noted. Jesus speaks of himself as having been **sent** by God, and this is an essential characteristic of his identity and mission. Second, Jesus' words encourage his disciples to persevere in their mission, despite whatever hardships it might entail, for through them Jesus and his Father come to others.

41 **Whoever receives a prophet because he is a prophet will receive a prophet's reward.** Some in the early church will exercise the gift of prophecy (23:34; see also 7:22; 1 Cor 14). It is not clear, however, whether Jesus is referring to those who have the gift of prophecy or whether he is continuing to speak of those whom he is sending out. A **prophet** speaks on behalf of God—as do those whom Jesus is sending out, for Jesus has authorized them to proclaim his message (10:7), which God sent him to proclaim (verse 40). To **receive a prophet because he is a prophet** means to accept him or her as a messenger from God. **Whoever** does so **will receive a prophet's reward.** Jesus does not say how prophets will be rewarded; he simply promises that those who accept God's messengers will be no less rewarded by God than the messengers themselves.

Jesus continues, **and whoever receives a righteous man because he is righteous will receive a righteous man's reward.** The term **a righteous man** does not refer to any specific office or category of Christians in the early church. Rather, it seems to be another way of speaking of those whom Jesus is sending out. Jesus does not say here how the righteous will be rewarded, but other teachings of Jesus supply an answer. Jesus had warned his disciples that their righteousness needed to surpass that of the scribes and Pharisees if they were to enter the kingdom of heaven (5:20), and he will go on to speak of those who enter the kingdom of God as the righteous (13:43, 49; 25:37, 46). **Righteous** is a way of designating all those who do the will of God and enter his kingdom as their reward (7:21). **Whoever receives a righteous man because he is righteous** will receive the reward of the righteous, which the passages just cited indicate is entry into the kingdom of God.

42 And whoever gives only a cup of cold water to one of these little ones to drink because he is a disciple—amen, I say to you, he will surely not lose his reward. Jesus will later use the term **little ones** to designate the least important of his followers (18:6, 10, 14). Here **little ones** can also be a way of speaking of the disciples Jesus is sending out without money or provisions (10:9-10), in a manner that is "poor in spirit" (5:3) and dependent on others. Those who give them even minimal assistance, even **only a cup of cold water,** because they are disciples of Jesus will be rewarded. No act of kindness will go unnoticed, not even kindness extended to the most insignificant of Jesus' followers.

Throughout these promises the **whoever** extends beyond Galilee and the time of Jesus to encompass all who welcome and assist those bearing the message of Jesus. **Whoever** includes disciples of Jesus who do not go out on mission but remain home and give support to those who do go out. Even those giving the least bit of support, symbolized by a mere **cup of cold water,** will **surely not lose** their reward.

For reflection: How have I received those who proclaim the gospel? How have I assisted them?

CHAPTER 11

Jesus Resumes His Traveling Ministry
¹ When Jesus finished giving these commands to his twelve disciples, he went away from that place to teach and to preach in their towns.

1   When the Gospel of Matthew was divided into chapters, this verse became the first verse of chapter 11. It could just as well serve as the final verse of chapter 10, marking the end of Jesus' instructions to his disciples (10:5-42). **When Jesus finished giving these commands to his twelve disciples:** Matthew characterizes Jesus' instructions as **commands.** Jesus authorized the **twelve disciples** to carry on his mission (10:1, 7), and they must do so on his terms, obeying his commands.

Matthew told his readers that the Twelve were sent out (10:5), but does not tell what happened during their mission nor recount its conclusion. Perhaps Matthew omits mention of its conclusion to indicate that the mission of Jesus' disciples is ongoing. Jesus' commands (10:5-42) have a message not just for the first disciples but for all later disciples who take on the mission of Jesus.

After Jesus finished instructing his disciples, **he went away from that place to teach and to preach in their towns.** Jesus resumes his traveling ministry, picking up where he left off (see 9:35). Jesus goes from town to town **to teach and to preach,** and he continues to heal as well (see 11:4-5). Matthew does not name the **towns** Jesus visits, but three will be mentioned shortly (11:20-23).

Who is Jesus?
² When John heard in prison of the works of the Messiah, he sent his disciples to him ³ with this question, "Are you the one who is to come, or should we look for another?" ⁴ Jesus said to them in reply, "Go and tell John what you hear and see: ⁵ the blind regain their sight, the lame walk, lepers are cleansed, the deaf hear, the dead are raised, and the poor have the good news proclaimed to them. ⁶ And blessed is the one who takes no offense at me."

> Gospel parallels: Luke 7:18-23
> OT:Isaiah 35:5-6; 61:1
> NT:Matt 3:1-15; 4:12

2 **When John heard in prison of the works of the Messiah:** Matthew has mentioned the arrest of John the Baptist (4:12) and will describe its circumstances later (14:3-4). John heard about **the works of the Messiah,** about what Jesus was doing. It is Matthew, not John, who refers here to Jesus as **the Messiah.** Matthew spoke of Jesus as the Christ, or Messiah (the two mean the same), at the beginning of his gospel (1:1, 16–18) but neither John the Baptist nor any other contemporary of Jesus has called him the Messiah during his public ministry; Peter will be the first to say that Jesus is the Messiah (16:16). Matthew could have written that John heard of "the works of Jesus," but Matthew has a reason for referring to **the works of the Messiah,** as we will discuss shortly.

Messiah, Christ: See page 349

After John the Baptist heard of Jesus' deeds, **he sent his disciples to him.** Since John is in prison and cannot question Jesus personally, he sends his disciples (see 9:14; 14:12) to ask what, for John, is the all-important question.

3 John's disciples came to Jesus **with this question, "Are you the one who is to come, or should we look for another?"** John the Baptist proclaimed that God's judgment was at hand (3:10) and referred to the agent who would carry out God's judgment as "the one who is coming after me" (3:11). John did not speak of the coming one as the Messiah, for the Messiah was not expected to do what John said the coming one would do. The coming one would sort out good from evil; he would "gather his wheat into his barn, but the chaff he will burn with unquenchable fire" (3:12). When Jesus came to John to be baptized, John apparently thought that Jesus was the one who would come after him (3:14).

Now John has doubts whether Jesus is **the one who is to come,** for Jesus has not lived up to John's expectations. Jesus speaks of judgment as a future event rather than as what he is doing during his public ministry (7:21-23; 10:15, 28-33). Jesus is not sorting out the wheat from the chaff; Jesus is associating with the chaff, eating with tax collectors and sinners (9:10-11). Yet Jesus could not be dismissed as being of no account, for John has heard of the mighty works done by Jesus (verse 2; see 4:23-24). Hence John's question to Jesus: Are **you** the one I have been expecting, or should we wait for someone else?

4 Jesus said to them in reply, "Go and tell John what you hear and see." Jesus does not give John's disciples a yes or no answer. He instead tells them to report to John what they **hear** him teach and what they **see** him do. Matthew likewise wants his readers to hear what Jesus teaches and to recognize the activity of Jesus in their lives. Matthew will end his gospel with Jesus' promise that he will always be present with his disciples (28:20).

For reflection: What do I hear Jesus saying to me? What do I see him doing in my life?

5 In pointing out what he does, Jesus echoes and expands a prophecy from Isaiah, indicating that he is fulfilling prophetic hopes (see 5:17). John's disciples can see that **the blind regain their sight, the lame walk, lepers are cleansed, the deaf hear, the dead are raised.** Matthew recounts at least one example of each of these deeds (8:1-4; 9:1-8, 18-33; the Greek word for "mute" in 9:33 also means "deaf," as in 11:5).

> *Then will the eyes of the blind be opened,*
> *and the ears of the deaf be cleared;*
> *Then will the lame leap like a stag,*
> *then the tongue of the dumb will sing.*
> Isaiah 35:5-6

Jesus continues to stress the importance of hearing his words, this time by making them the climax of his deeds: **and the poor have the good news proclaimed to them.** This echoes Isaiah's prophecy of an agent of God who is anointed with the Holy Spirit to bring glad tidings to the lowly (Isaiah 61:1). Matthew has twice summarized Jesus' message as "the gospel of the kingdom" (4:23; 9:35); the word "gospel" means "good news." Jesus announces to the poor and lowly (5:3) the good news that God's kingdom is at hand (4:17). Jesus' words bring out the significance of his miracles: they are signs and aspects of the reign of God being established on earth.

> *The spirit of the Lord GOD is upon me,*
> *because the LORD has anointed me;*
> *He has sent me to bring glad tidings to the lowly,*
> *to heal the brokenhearted.*
> Isaiah 61:1

In response to John's question whether he is the one John was expecting, Jesus points to what he says and does. Jesus' response to John is in effect yes and no. Yes, Jesus is the mightier one John expected (3:11): Jesus' deeds manifest his might. But no, Jesus has not come to do what John expected the coming one to do. Jesus' mission is one of mercy (9:13), not wrathful judgment.

6 Jesus concludes his response to John's disciples with a surprising beatitude: **And blessed is the one who takes no offense at me.** Here to take **offense** means to trip and stumble over an obstacle. We might think that Jesus' healings and his bringing good news to the poor would win him nothing but praise, but that has not been the case (9:3, 11, 34). Jesus will face increasing opposition as some take offense at his words and deeds (13:57; 15:12). But happy, fortunate, **blessed** are those who can accept Jesus for who he is.

Beatitudes: See page 73

For reflection: Is anything that Jesus teaches or does an obstacle for me?

We can return to Matthew's reference to Jesus' words and deeds as "the works of the Messiah" (verse 2). A common expectation among Jews at the time of Jesus was that the Messiah would reestablish Jewish independence. This was not Jesus' mission. To help his readers understand what kind of Messiah Jesus is, Matthew characterizes what Jesus does as

---

BACKGROUND: GOSPEL The English word "gospel" comes from the Anglo-Saxon word *godspell*, which means "good news." "Good news" is in turn a literal translation of the Greek word *euangelion* used by gospel writers (Matt 4:23; 9:35; Mark 1:1, 14-15); *euangelion* gives us such English words as "evangelist" and "evangelization." New Testament authors did not invent the word *euangelion*; it is found in ancient Greek literature as a term for a message of victory or other message that brought joy. The Greek translation of Isaiah uses forms of this word: "Go up onto a high mountain, / Zion, *herald of glad tidings*; / Cry out at the top of your voice, / Jerusalem, *herald of good news*!" (Isaiah 40:9; emphasis added). Paul, whose letters predate the written gospels, was the first New Testament author to use the word *euangelion* as an expression for the message of Christ: "Our *gospel* did not come to you in word alone, but also in power and in the holy Spirit" (1 Thess 1:5; emphasis added).

"the works of the Messiah." Just as Jesus' bringing good news to the poor, curing those who were sick and raising the dead manifested Jesus' identity to John the Baptist, so these deeds manifest to Matthew's readers who Jesus is and what his mission is as the Messiah, the Christ.

For reflection: What do I think of as the works of Jesus? What does it mean to me to call him Christ?

Who is John?
[7] As they were going off, Jesus began to speak to the crowds about John, "What did you go out to the desert to see? A reed swayed by the wind? [8] Then what did you go out to see? Someone dressed in fine clothing? Those who wear fine clothing are in royal palaces. [9] Then why did you go out? To see a prophet? Yes, I tell you, and more than a prophet. [10] This is the one about whom it is written:

'Behold, I am sending my messenger ahead of you;
he will prepare your way before you.'

[11] Amen, I say to you, among those born of women there has been none greater than John the Baptist; yet the least in the kingdom of heaven is greater than he. [12] From the days of John the Baptist until now, the kingdom of heaven suffers violence, and the violent are taking it by force. [13] All the prophets and the law prophesied up to the time of John. [14] And if you are willing to accept it, he is Elijah, the one who is to come. [15] Whoever has ears ought to hear."

Gospel parallels: Luke 7:24-28; 16:16
OT: Mal 3:1, 23; Sirach 48:1-12
NT: Matt 3:1-12; 17:10-13; Mark 1:2

7 John the Baptist wanted to evaluate Jesus (11:2-3); now Jesus gives his evaluation of John. Some of Jesus' statements are cryptic. **As they were going off**—as the disciples of John the Baptist were leaving—**Jesus began to speak to the crowds about John.** Matthew did not mention **crowds** being present when John's disciples came to Jesus, but Jesus generally attracted crowds (4:25; 8:1, 18; 9:8, 33, 36). Jesus asks a series of rhetorical questions to remind his listeners of their attitudes toward John. **What did you go out to the desert to see?** Many had gone to the wilderness near the

southern end of the Jordan River where John was baptizing (3:1, 5-6). Did they go to see **a reed swayed by the wind?** Tall marsh grass grows along the banks of Jordan River and leans whichever way the wind is blowing, but the crowds had not gone to watch the grass sway. Nor had they gone to see a man who leaned whichever way the winds of expediency were blowing. John confronted religious leaders, calling them a "brood of vipers" (3:7), and he was in prison because he denounced the illicit marriage of Herod Antipas, the ruler of Galilee (14:3-4).

8 If they had not gone to the wilderness to see a crowd-pleaser, **then what did they go out to see? Someone dressed in fine clothing?** The Greek word translated "**fine** clothing" literally means "*soft* clothes" and has the connotation of luxurious apparel. John the Baptist "wore clothing made of camel's hair" (3:4), hardly soft or luxurious. Jesus' listeners knew that **those who wear fine clothing are in royal palaces.** Herod Antipas will throw a banquet to celebrate his birthday, and those attending it (14:6) will be dressed in fine clothing, reflecting their wealth and status.

Clothing: See page 95

9 If not to see a fashion show, **then why did you go out? To see a prophet?** The answer this time is **yes:** John the Baptist is a **prophet** (14:5; 21:26), a spokesman sent by God. No one had been recognized as a prophet for several centuries before John (see 1 Macc 4:46; 9:27; 14:41). That God was again speaking through a prophet indicated that something important was happening, something that God needed to make known to his people. John announced that someone was coming after him to execute God's judgment (3:11-12), for the kingdom of heaven was at hand (3:2). That was important news, and the one who announced it was rightly revered as a **prophet.** But Jesus proclaims that John is **more than a prophet.** John has more significance than did Isaiah or Jeremiah or any of the previous prophets.

10 Jesus explains why John is more than a prophet: **This is the one about whom it is written: "Behold, I am sending my messenger ahead of you; / he will prepare your way before you."** John is himself the fulfillment of prophecy; he is **written** about in Scripture. Jesus invokes a prophecy of Malachi in which God says that he is sending a messenger to prepare the way for his own coming to his people (Mal 3:1). Jesus identifies John the

Baptist as this **messenger.** In Malachi's prophecy the messenger is sent to prepare the way for God, but Jesus adapts the prophecy so that the messenger prepares **your way before you,** with the **you** being Jesus. John the Baptist is "more than a prophet" (verse 9) because he was sent to prepare the way for Jesus.

> *Lo, I am sending my messenger*
> *to prepare the way before me.*
> Malachi 3:1

11 **Amen, I say to you, among those born of women there has been none greater than John the Baptist.** The expression **born of women** is a biblical idiom for a human being (see Job 15:14; Sirach 10:18; Gal 4:4). From the beginning of the human race until John **there has been none greater than John** because of the role John carried out. But Jesus adds a qualification: **yet the least in the kingdom of heaven is greater than he.** John stands at the threshold of **the kingdom of heaven,** announcing its arrival (3:1); those who are part of God's reign, even the **least** significant of them, are **greater** than John because they possess what he announces. Jesus does not say that John will not be included in God's reign: Jesus only compares the greatness of the announcer and the greatness of those who experience what he announces. Even **the least in the kingdom of heaven,** those who barely sneak in (5:19), are greater than the greatest man who walked the earth before Jesus.

Kingdom of heaven: See page 266

For reflection: Do I consider entering the kingdom of heaven to be the greatest thing that could ever happen to me? Do I shape my life accordingly?

12 Jesus then makes one of the most enigmatic pronouncements to be found in the gospels: **From the days of John the Baptist until now, the kingdom of heaven suffers violence, and the violent are taking it by force.** The words **until now** refer to Jesus' ministry. The **violent are taking it by force** might also be translated "violent people plunder it." Scholars have proposed many different interpretations of Jesus' words. We might understand Jesus' meaning to be something like the following: John's baptizing and Jesus' public ministry mark the first stirrings of God's reign being established on earth. But God's reign is meeting resistance; those who are part of the coming of God's reign experience opposition and violence. John is in prison and will be beheaded (14:3-12); Jesus will also be executed. God's conquest of evil will be complete only when his reign is as fully established on earth as it is in heaven (6:10). At present **the kingdom of heaven suffers violence,** and Jesus' disciples will experience opposition and persecution (5:10-12; 10:16-36). Those who follow Jesus' teachings about living under God's reign—not striking back, not turning away those who make demands (5:38-42)—may find themselves plundered.

For reflection: What meaning do I find in these words of Jesus?

13 John the Baptist announced a turning point in God's plan for his people; what God did and revealed in the past was in preparation for what God is doing now. **All the prophets and the law prophesied up to the time of John.** Jews normally spoke of "the law and the prophets" (7:12; see also 5:17), since **the law** (God's covenant requirements for his people) came first and was the foundation for what God revealed through **the prophets.** By reversing the normal order, Jesus puts the accent on prophecy, on God's revelation of his plans. By saying that **all** of the prophets and the law **prophesied,** Jesus makes all that God has said and done in the past point to a future fulfillment, a next stage in God's plans. **Up to the time of John** is literally "until John." John's role was to prepare the way for Jesus (verse 10); Jesus will fulfill the law and the prophets (5:17), completing what God began through them.

14 **And if you are willing to accept it, he is Elijah, the one who is to come.** At the end of his life on earth, **Elijah** did not die but was taken up to heaven (2 Kings 2:11). Elijah was expected to return before "the day of the LORD" (Mal 3:23-24; Sirach 48:9-12). Jesus echoed Malachi's prophecy that God would send a messenger to prepare the way and identified this messenger as John the Baptist (verse 10; Mal 3:1). Malachi had already identified this messenger as Elijah (Mal 3:23). In light of Malachi's identification of the messenger as Elijah, Jesus now proclaims John to be **Elijah.** That is, John has done what Malachi prophesied Elijah would do: he prepared for "the day of the LORD," which now means the coming of the kingdom of God.

The day of the Lord: See page 48

> *Lo, I will send you*
> *Elijah, the prophet,*
> *Before the day of the LORD comes,*
> *the great and terrible day.*
> Malachi 3:23

Jesus tells his listeners that John is Elijah **if you are willing to accept it**—willing to understand what Jesus is talking about and believe it. It could be difficult to accept John as Elijah, because Elijah was revered as a prophet with awesome powers who "sent kings down to destruction" (Sirach 48:6), while John is now imprisoned by a ruler and seems rather powerless. Recognizing that John is carrying out Elijah's role means setting aside notions that God will establish his reign by means of might. If "the kingdom of heaven suffers violence" (verse 12), those who serve the kingdom suffer.

15 Accepting that the reign of God comes through suffering rather than earthly triumph is not easy. Hence Jesus concludes by saying **whoever has ears ought to hear,** that is, understand and take to heart. Some of what Jesus has said is difficult to understand, but it can be even more difficult to accept that embracing God's way for us can mean accepting suffering.

In speaking of who John is, Jesus has told his listeners about himself as well. If John's significance lies in his preparing the way for Jesus (verse 10), then how much more significant must be Jesus. If the least in the kingdom of heaven is greater than John (verse 11), then the one whose mission is to bring about the reign of God is even greater. John's mission means that all that was promised and foreshadowed by the prophets and in the law is about to be fulfilled (verse 13); Jesus is that fulfillment.

For reflection: What do Jesus' words about John tell me about Jesus?

ORIENTATION: *Not everyone accepted John despite his greatness, nor has everyone accepted Jesus (9:10-11, 34). Jesus addresses the rejection that he and John experience.*

Jesus Reacts to Rejection—Part One
16 "To what shall I compare this generation? It is like children who sit in marketplaces and call to one another, 17 'We played the flute for you, but

you did not dance, we sang a dirge but you did not mourn.' **¹⁸ For John came neither eating nor drinking, and they said, 'He is possessed by a demon.'** ¹⁹ The Son of Man came eating and drinking and they said, 'Look, he is a glutton and a drunkard, a friend of tax collectors and sinners.' But wisdom is vindicated by her works."

Gospel parallels: Luke 7:31-35
OT: Prov 1:20; 3:19; 8:22-31
NT: Matt 3:1-4, 10-12; 9:9-15; Luke 15:1-2

16 **To what shall I compare this generation?** The expression **this generation** could broadly mean all those alive at the time of Jesus, but Jesus often uses the expression as a way of referring to those who do not accept him (see 12:41-42, 45). **It is like children who sit in marketplaces and call to one another:** Jesus tells a parable comparing **this generation** to **children** at play in a public place. Some children have invited other children to join in their games.

Parables: See page 262

17 No matter what game is proposed, the other children refuse to play. **We played the flute for you, but you did not dance:** we invited you to a joyful game, a pretend wedding celebration, but you wouldn't join us in dancing. Since you weren't in a festive mood, we suggested a sad game and invited you to a make-believe funeral: **we sang a dirge but you did not mourn.** You wouldn't join in whether we were playing a happy game or a sad game. There's no pleasing you; you just don't want to play with us!

18 Jesus applies his parable to "this generation" (verse 16): **For John came neither eating nor drinking, and they said, "He is possessed by a demon."** John the Baptist lived in the wilderness (3:1), wore crude clothing and ate a meager diet (3:4), and taught his disciples to fast (9:14). To forswear **drinking** means John abstained from wine. Some looked at John's austere lifestyle and **said, "He is possessed by a demon."** Matthew does not elsewhere record this charge being made against John, but Jesus was similarly slandered (9:34; 12:24). John invited his listeners to repent in preparation for the coming judgment (3:2; 10-12), but some dismissed his call to repentance by writing him off as deranged fanatic, **possessed by a demon.**

19 The Son of Man came eating and drinking and they said, "Look, he is a glutton and a drunkard, a friend of tax collectors and sinners." Jesus refers to himself as **the Son of Man.** He did not fast during his public ministry or have his disciples fast (9:14-15). **Drinking** again means drinking wine. Jesus was as known for his **eating and drinking,** as was John for his fasting. Eating meals with others was a characteristic element of Jesus' public ministry, a means of his entering into personal relationships with men and women. Sharing meals was an expression of fellowship.

Son of Man: See page 151

For reflection: What does Jesus' sharing meals with others tell me about him? About what it means to be his disciple?

Jesus is accused of overeating and drinking too much wine: **he is a glutton and a drunkard.** Not only that, Jesus ate and drink with the wrong people, with **tax collectors and sinners.** Matthew has described one instance (9:10-11), but the charge implies that Jesus frequently ate with disreputable people. Jesus did so because he came to bring God's mercy to sinners (9:12-13). But for Jesus' critics, whatever Jesus had to say could be dismissed because he ate and drank too much, and did so with sinners.

BACKGROUND: WISDOM In the Old Testament, wisdom is the ability to discern and judge properly and to lead a successful life. Wisdom is a gift from God, the source of wisdom (Prov 2:6; Sirach 1:1). Some Old Testament writings speak of God's wisdom as if it were a person—a woman, perhaps because the Hebrew word for wisdom is a feminine noun: "Wisdom cries aloud in the street, / in the open squares she raises her voice" (Prov 1:20; see also Sirach 4:11-19). Wisdom is presented as the first of God's creations: "Before all ages, in the beginning, he created me, / and through all ages I shall not cease to be" (Sirach 24:9; see also Prov 8:22-26). Wisdom assisted God in creating the world (Prov 3:19; see also Wisd 9:9). The Book of Proverbs portrays wisdom as God's "craftsman" in the work of creation (Prov 8:27-30). Jesus' contemporaries would have been familiar with this view of wisdom as God's agent. The early church understood Jesus Christ in light of the Old Testament view of wisdom when it proclaimed that it was through him that God created the universe (1 Cor 8:6; Col 1:15-16; Heb 1:2; 2:10; Rev 3:14). This view of wisdom is also the background for John's writing, "In the beginning was the Word. . . . All things came to be through him, / and without him nothing came to be" (John 1:1, 3).

218

Those who reject John and Jesus are like the petulant children in the marketplace: they will neither mourn with John nor dance with Jesus the bridegroom (9:15). No matter whether the message is coming judgment (3:10-12) or God's mercy (9:12-13), they will not respond.

For reflection: Do I find ways to dismiss God's word to me, whether it is about judgment or mercy?

Jesus concludes with a cryptic comment: **but wisdom is vindicated by her works.** Jesus' statement must be understood in light of how **wisdom** is portrayed in the Old Testament. Wisdom is spoken of as a woman (Prov 1:20); hence Jesus refers to **her** works. Wisdom is God's first creation (Prov 8:22-26) and assists God in the creation of everything else (Prov 3:19; 8:27-31). Wisdom can therefore be thought of as God's agent, carrying out the works of God, and it is this notion of wisdom that Jesus invokes when he says **wisdom is vindicated by her works.** Jesus is speaking of himself as the **wisdom** or agent of God who does the **works** of God. These are the **works** that Jesus listed for the disciples of John the Baptist: "the blind regain their sight, the lame walk, lepers are cleansed, the deaf hear, the dead are raised, and the poor have the good news proclaimed to them" (11:5). Jesus is **vindicated**—shown to be God's agent—by these **works** or results of his ministry (see also 7:16, 20). He cannot be dismissed as a mere glutton and drunkard (verse 19); those who reject him are rejecting God's agent.

Jesus Reacts to Rejection—Part Two
20 Then he began to reproach the towns where most of his mighty deeds had been done, since they had not repented. **21** "Woe to you, Chorazin! Woe to you, Bethsaida! For if the mighty deeds done in your midst had been done in Tyre and Sidon, they would long ago have repented in sackcloth and ashes. **22** But I tell you, it will be more tolerable for Tyre and Sidon on the day of judgment than for you. **23** And as for you, Capernaum:

'Will you be exalted to heaven?
You will go down to the netherworld.'

For if the mighty deeds done in your midst had been done in Sodom, it would have remained until this day. **24** But I tell you, it will be more tolerable for the land of Sodom on the day of judgment than for you."

Gospel parallels: Luke 10:12-15

OT:Isaiah 14:12-15

NT:Matt 4:12-17; 10:14-15; 11:5-6, 19; 12:41-42; Mark 8:22-26;
Luke 9:10-17; John 1:44; 12:37

20 Jesus has spoken in general of those who reject him (11:16-19); now he singles out towns where he has met rejection. **Then he began to reproach the towns where most of his mighty deeds had been done, since they had not repented.** The **mighty deeds** were the "works" Jesus just mentioned (11:19), including healings and exorcisms. He goes on to identify **the towns** as Chorazin, Bethsaida, and Capernaum, all three near the north end of the Sea of Galilee. Jesus moved to Capernaum at the beginning of his public ministry (4:13) making it his "own town" (9:1). Chorazin was two miles north of Capernaum; Bethsaida was four miles northeast of Capernaum. Matthew writes that Jesus had performed **most of his mighty deeds** in these three neighboring towns.

They were not large towns: Capernaum had a population of less than 1,500; those living in Chorazin and Bethsaida numbered in the hundreds. Yet according to Matthew, **most** of Jesus' healings and exorcisms took place in these fishing and farming villages that lay within an hour's walk of one another. Larger cities or longer journeys would have given Jesus access to far larger audiences. But there was a personal dimension to Jesus' mission. Along with preaching to crowds, Jesus wanted opportunities to interact with housewives and children, fishermen and farmers—to share meals and befriend ordinary people in ordinary villages. Jesus was sent to the people of Israel (15:24) but to them as individuals, not anonymous faces in a crowd. Devoting time to three villages allowed him to have personal contact with the men, women, and children who lived in them.

For reflection: What are the implications for me of Jesus' devoting so much time to relatively few people?

Despite the personal attention Jesus gave the people of these towns and despite **the mighty deeds** he did for them, **they had not repented.** The keynote of Jesus' preaching was the call, "Repent, for the kingdom of heaven is at hand" (4:17). Repentance meant accepting his message about the reign of God and obeying Jesus' teachings, such as in the Sermon on the Mount (Matt 5–7). This the people of these towns had not done, to Jesus' great disappointment.

Repentance: See page 42

21 **Woe to you, Chorazin! Woe to you, Bethsaida!** Matthew has not re-counted Jesus being in these towns; this is the only mention of **Chorazin** and **Bethsaida** in Matthew's gospel. However, Matthew's gospel is not a complete record of all that Jesus did and said. The other gospels are like-wise selective, with only two passages that describe mighty deeds done at Bethsaida (Mark 8:22-26; Luke 9:10-17) and no accounts of Jesus being in Chorazin.

To declare **woe to you** is the opposite of proclaiming "blessed are you" (5:11). A beatitude recognizes and congratulates someone for being fortunate; a **woe** laments their unfortunate condition and reproaches them for it. Jesus reproaches the people of **Chorazin** and **Bethsaida** for not repenting and then makes a comparison to show how sorry their condition is: **For if the mighty deeds done in your midst had been done in Tyre and Sidon, they would long ago have repented in sackcloth and ashes.** The cities of **Tyre** and **Sidon** lay on the Mediterranean coast; today they are cities in southern Lebanon. They were Gentile cities that were denounced by prophets for their wealth and pride (Isaiah 23; Ezek 26–28). Had Jesus directed his mission to these Gentile cities and performed

---

BACKGROUND: CHORAZIN AND BETHSAIDA Chorazin was a small farming vil-lage on a hill about two miles north of Capernaum. Although excavated by archaeolo-gists, no significant remains from the time of Jesus have been discovered. The town was destroyed by an earthquake in the fourth century, rebuilt in the fifth century, and abandoned in the ninth century. Bethsaida, four miles northeast of Capernaum, was built on a hilltop near where the Jordan River flows into the northern end of the Sea of Galilee, allowing boats to be moored below the village. Archaeologists estimate that the population of Bethsaida at the time of Jesus was several hundred people. Some first-century houses have been discovered, several with evidence that their occupants were wealthy. Fishhooks and other fishing gear were found; the name "Bethsaida" may mean "house of the fisher." Bethsaida was apparently destroyed by an earth-quake in A.D. 115 and never rebuilt.

his **mighty deeds** there, the people of Tyre and Sidon **would long ago have repented in sackcloth and ashes.** Woven from goat or camel hair, **sackcloth** was used for bags. Wearing rough **sackcloth** and sitting in **ashes** were expressions of mourning, including mourning one's sins (Gen 37:33-34; Esther 4:1-3; Isaiah 58:5; Jonah 3:5-9). Jesus' words and deeds would have gotten a response from the people of Tyre and Sidon, even though they were pagans.

Woes: See page 499
Tyre and Sidon: See page 328

22 **But I tell you, it will be more tolerable for Tyre and Sidon on the day of judgment than for you.** Many Jews expected that there would be a **day of judgment** when God would sort out those who did good from those who did evil. Many Jews thought that pagans would not fare very well on the day of judgment, since they did not know and obey God's laws. But Jesus proclaims that **it will be more tolerable for Tyre and Sidon on the day of judgment** than for the people of Chorazin and Bethsaida. Those who have witnessed Jesus' mighty deeds but rejected him will be judged more severely than pagans who had no opportunity to respond to Jesus.

Judgment: See page 557

Jesus' words should be interpreted not simply as a prediction of what will happen to the people of Chorazin and Bethsaida on the day of judgment but also as a prophetic warning calling them to repentance. The prophet Jonah proclaimed to the people of Nineveh, "Forty days more and Nineveh shall be destroyed," but when the people of Nineveh repented in sackcloth and ashes God accepted their repentance and did not destroy Nineveh (Jonah 3:4-10). Similarly, Jesus' prediction is an exhortation to the people of Chorazin and Bethsaida to accept his message and change their ways.

For reflection: What mighty deeds has Jesus done for me? How have I responded to him?

23 **And as for you, Capernaum:** Matthew has recounted Jesus performing mighty deeds in and around Capernaum (8:5-17; 9:1-8, 18-34). Jesus' rhetorical question—**Will you be exalted to heaven?**—indicates the expectations of the people of Capernaum. Jesus tells them that the opposite will

happen: **You will go down to the netherworld.** Jesus echoes a prophecy of Isaiah condemning the pretensions of the king of Babylon (Isaiah 14:12-15). Isaiah's prophecy refers to the heavens and to the netherworld, the highest and lowest places in the world. The point of Isaiah's prophecy is that someone who exalts himself will be brought low. On Jesus' lips, however, the words of the prophecy take on a fuller meaning. The people of Capernaum may think that they will **be exalted to heaven** on the day of judgment, but because they have not repented they will **go down to the netherworld**—to the torments associated with Gehenna (see 5:22, 29-30; 10:28).

Capernaum: See page 61

> You said in your heart:
>   "I will scale the heavens;
> Above the stars of God
>   I will set up my throne. . . ."
> Yet down to the nether world you go
>   to the recesses of the pit!
>   Isaiah 14:13, 15

For if the mighty deeds done in your midst had been done in Sodom, it would have remained until this day. The city of **Sodom** was a proverbial example of extreme wickedness and depravity (Gen 18:20-21; 19:1-13). Jesus says that if his **mighty deeds** been done in Sodom, its citizens would have repented and been spared destruction, and the city **would have remained until this day.** Jesus would have received a better response from the wicked people of **Sodom** than he had from the people of his "own town" (9:1).

24 **But I tell you, it will be more tolerable for the land of Sodom on the day of judgment than for you.** Jesus said that those who were inhospitable to his disciples would fare worse than Sodom on the day of judgment (10:14-15), and the same will be true for those who reject him. Jesus is issuing a prophetic warning as a wake-up call for the people of Capernaum: their response to Jesus will have eternal consequences.

Not everyone in these three towns rejected Jesus; some became his disciples (4:18-22; 9:9; John 1:44). Jesus will continue to make Capernaum his home (17:24-25). Perhaps his prophetic warnings had an effect:

there is evidence of a Christian presence in Capernaum from the middle of the first century until the town was abandoned in the seventh century. But for the most part Jesus' mighty deeds did not yield results, and Jesus' solemn woes indicate his disappointment and sorrow.

ORIENTATION: *Jesus gives an extraordinary glimpse of his relationship with his Father and invites all to come to him.*

The Revelation of Jesus
25 At that time Jesus said in reply, "I give praise to you, Father, Lord of heaven and earth, for although you have hidden these things from the wise and the learned you have revealed them to the childlike. **26** Yes, Father, such has been your gracious will. **27** All things have been handed over to me by my Father. No one knows the Son except the Father, and no one knows the Father except the Son and anyone to whom the Son wishes to reveal him.
28 "Come to me, all you who labor and are burdened, and I will give you rest. **29** Take my yoke upon you and learn from me, for I am meek and humble of heart; and you will find rest for yourselves. **30** For my yoke is easy, and my burden light."

Gospel parallels: Luke 10:21-22
OT:Sirach 6:23-31; 51:23-27; Jer 6:16
NT:John 1:18; 3:35; 5:19-27; 7:28-29; 10:15; 14:9-11; 17:1-5, 25-26

25 Jesus has just spoken of being rejected (11:16-24), and **at that time Jesus said in reply;** that is, he spoke in response to rejection. Jesus addresses his words to God: **I give praise to you, Father, Lord of heaven and earth.** To call God the **Lord of heaven and earth** acknowledges God as the creator and ruler of the universe. Judith prayed to God as "LORD of heaven and earth, Creator of the waters, King of all you have created" (Judith 9:12; see also Tobit 10:14; Acts 17:24). But even as Jesus acknowledges God's sovereignty over all creation, he addresses God as **Father.** Mark's gospel indicates that when Jesus prayed to God as Father, he used the Aramaic word *Abba* for "Father" (Mark 14:36). A child—even a grown child—would call his or her father *Abba*; it is a familiar form of address, roughly equivalent to "Dad." Jesus and the **Lord of heaven and earth** enjoy an intimate relationship, such that Jesus can call God **Father.** Jesus' speaking of God as "my Father" (verse 27) indicates that he enjoys a unique relationship with God; his identity is bound up in his being related to God as Son to Father (see 3:17).

Lord: See page 133

For reflection: What does the way Jesus addresses God tell me about Jesus?

Jesus offers **praise** to his Father. The Psalms praised God by recounting his mighty deeds: "I will praise you, LORD, with all my heart; / I will declare all your wondrous deeds" (Psalm 9:2). Jesus states what God has done that is praiseworthy: **although you have hidden these things from the wise and the learned you have revealed them to the childlike.** We can understand **these things** to be Jesus' words and deeds (see 11:5, 20), the significance of which is **hidden** from those who reject him. The **wise** and the **learned** would include experts in the law of Moses. Jesus has been condemned by some of these experts (9:3, 34), and he views this as God's doing: God has **hidden** the significance of Jesus' words and deeds **from the wise and the learned.** As **Lord of heaven and earth,** God is in charge of the universe, and whatever happens can be attributed to him—even the hardening of hearts (Exod 7:3-5). This does not diminish human responsibility: those who reject Jesus will be held accountable (see 10:14-15; 11:20-24). The Bible does not reconcile God's sovereignty with human freedom but simply affirms both.

Along with hiding things from the learned, God has **revealed them to the childlike.** The **childlike** are the meek and poor in spirit (5:3, 5), the "little ones" who are Jesus' disciples (10:42). God has **revealed** the significance of what Jesus is doing to those who do not count for much in the eyes of the world. This reverses normal expectations: religious experts are presumed to know more about God's ways than uneducated people. Yet God chose **the childlike** and **revealed** to them what the wise and learned have not grasped.

For reflection: What are the implications for me of God choosing the childlike to receive his revelation?

26 **Yes, Father, such has been your gracious will.** Jesus reaffirms that the acceptance and even the rejection he has received are part of God's **gracious**

will. It has pleased God to have events unfold as they have; it has been God's choice that the childlike grasp the significance of Jesus' words and deeds.

This two-sentence prayer is one of three prayers of Jesus recounted in Matthew's gospel. The second prayer, also addressed by Jesus to his Father, will be offered in Gethsemane (26:39, 42); the third prayer will be a cry from the cross (27:46).

27 After his prayer Jesus explains how God's revelation has come to the childlike. He proclaims, **All things have been handed over to me by my Father.** Jesus speaks of God as **my Father** (see 7:21; 10:32-33) who has entrusted everything into his hands. Jesus has been given the authority to teach God's ways, to forgive sins and expel demons, to heal the sick and raise the dead. Matthew has provided examples of Jesus teaching with authority (chapters 5-7) and freeing those in bondage to spiritual and physical evil (chapters 8-9).

Jesus then makes an extraordinary claim about his relationship with God as his Father: **No one knows the Son except the Father, and no one knows the Father except the Son.** The biblical notion of knowing puts the accent on experiential and personal knowledge, such as spouses have of each other. That the Father **knows** the Son means they are intimately united with each other. Jesus refers to himself as **the Son,** indicating that he is uniquely the Son of God (see 3:17; 17:5). No one **knows the Son except the Father** because no one else has the intimate relationship with **the Son** that **the Father** has. Likewise, **no one knows the Father except the Son** because no one is intimately united with God as Jesus is. Jesus is not merely God's spokesman or agent; Jesus is uniquely related to God as **the Son** to **the Father.**

Son of God: See page 52

Because Jesus as **the Son** knows **the Father,** he is able to speak about his Father and make his Father known to **anyone to whom the Son wishes to reveal him.** The Father has handed all things over to Jesus; Jesus is the channel of God's revelation. God has revealed himself to the childlike (verse 25) through Jesus. John's disciples asked whether Jesus was the one whom John expected, and Jesus indicated that he was (11:2-6). Now Jesus tells more about his identity: he reveals that he is the revealer, **the Son** who is able to make **the Father** known. Those to whom Jesus makes

God known can pray to God as "our Father" (6:9) and depend on God as their Father (6:25-34).

For reflection: Who is Jesus for me? What revelation of who God is have I received from him?

Matthew does not describe the disciples' reaction to Jesus' speaking of himself as **the Son** who reveals **the Father.** Only later will Matthew present them grasping the implications of Jesus' words (14:33; 16:16-17).

The gospels rarely describe Jesus' emotions. I understand this scene to be a glimpse of Jesus' joy—perhaps his greatest joy. He is filled with joy because of his intimate and loving relationship with God as his Father, and his joy overflows in an outburst of prayer. He is filled with joy because he has been able to make his Father known to ordinary women and men; he finds joy in sharing with others the joy of being a child of God.

For reflection: Where do I find joy? What aspect of my relationship with God gives me the greatest joy?

In Matthew's gospel, Jesus will not again speak so directly of his unique relationship with God. Jesus' words about his relationship with his Father are a seed that sprouts into a full-grown plant in the Gospel of John (see John 1:18; 3:35; 5:19-27; 7:28-29; 10:15; 14:9-11; 17:1-5, 25-26).

28 Jesus invites his listeners to receive his revelation of God and the joy it brings: **Come to me, all you who labor and are burdened, and I will give you rest.** Jesus addresses his invitation to **all** women and men; no one is excluded. **Come to me** has the same meaning as "come after me" (4:19): it is an invitation to discipleship, to being with Jesus, to sharing his life. He speaks to those who **labor and are burdened.** His words cover all the burdens of life; later he will refer to excessive applications of the Mosaic law as unnecessary burdens (23:4). To all who come to him Jesus promises **I will give you rest.** Rest is an appealing prospect for those who are weary; **rest** also has a connotation of a state of well-being in fulfillment of God's promises (Exod 33:14; Sirach 6:29; Isaiah 28:12).

For reflection: How have I heard Jesus say, Come to me? What are my greatest burdens?

29 **Take my yoke upon you:** a **yoke** was a wooden frame placed on the neck of animals, harnessing them for work. A **yoke** served as a metaphor for submission to instruction (Sirach 6:25; 51:26) or obedience to the law of Moses (Acts 15:10; Gal 5:1). Jesus is inviting those who come to him to live by his teachings, which are the definitive interpretation of the law of Moses and present the way of life necessary to enter into the reign of God (5:17-20). Jesus calls upon his listeners to **learn from me** because he embodies what he teaches; discipleship means imitating Jesus. He invites his listeners to learn from him because he is **meek and humble of heart,** and therefore an unobstructed channel for God's revelation. Learning from Jesus means taking on his meek and humble way of life.

For reflection: What does Jesus invite me to learn from him?

Attached to Jesus' invitation to accept his yoke and learn from him is a promise: **and you will find rest for yourselves.** Jesus again offers **rest** (see verse 28), this time borrowing words from Jeremiah. God spoke through Jeremiah to promise "rest for your souls" to those who walked in his ways (Jer 6:16); Jesus promises **rest** to those who accept his yoke, his revelation of the ways of God.

30 For an animal to be yoked meant it was ready for work. The yoke of Jesus is also a yoke of service, but he can promise rest to those who accept it **for my yoke is easy, and my burden light.** The word translated **easy** also means "kind." There is a paradox in Jesus' characterizing his yoke as **easy** and his burden **light.** He makes great demands of his followers in the Sermon on the Mount (Matt 5–7); fully living up to his demands does not strike most of us as **easy.** Jesus also said that every disciple must take up his or her cross (10:38); most would not consider a cross to be a **light** burden. For Jesus to assure his listeners that his **yoke is easy** and his **burden light** reflects the paradox of discipleship. Jesus said, "Whoever finds his life will lose it, and whoever loses his life for my sake will find it" (10:39). Those who take up the seemingly difficult burden of discipleship will find rest and life. The meek and humble Jesus is compassionate (9:36), and out of compassion he teaches the best way for men and women to live, the way that leads to life (see 7:13-14), the way that leads to his Father.

For reflection: Have I experienced the yoke of Jesus as a light or heavy burden?

Jesus' Jewish audience and Matthew's Jewish Christian readers would likely have detected some echoes of wisdom writings in Jesus' words. Jesus spoke of himself as wisdom (11:19), referring to the Old Testament's portrayal of wisdom as God's firstborn who assists in the work of creation (Prov 8:22-31). Sirach invited his readers to "come aside to me" in order to be instructed in wisdom and urged them to "submit your neck to her yoke," referring to wisdom (Sirach 51:23, 26; see also Sirach 6:25). Those who attain wisdom find joy and rest (Sirach 6:29). Jesus carries out the role that the Old Testament assigned to wisdom, making known God and the ways of God.

CHAPTER 12

ORIENTATION: *Jesus, who promises an easy yoke and a light burden for those who come to him (11:30), demonstrates his mercy in two incidents that take place on the Sabbath, arousing opposition from Pharisees.*

Mercy for Hungry Disciples

¹ At that time Jesus was going through a field of grain on the sabbath. His disciples were hungry and began to pick the heads of grain and eat them. ² When the Pharisees saw this, they said to him, "See, your disciples are doing what is unlawful to do on the sabbath." ³ He said to them, "Have you not read what David did when he and his companions were hungry, ⁴ how he went into the house of God and ate the bread of offering, which neither he nor his companions but only the priests could lawfully eat? ⁵ Or have you not read in the law that on the sabbath the priests serving in the temple violate the sabbath and are innocent? ⁶ I say to you, something greater than the temple is here. ⁷ If you knew what this meant, 'I desire mercy, not sacrifice,' you would not have condemned these innocent men. ⁸ For the Son of Man is Lord of the sabbath."

Gospel parallels: Mark 2:23-28; Luke 6:1-5
OT: Exod 20:8-11; 34:21; Lev 24:5-9; Deut 23:26; 1 Sam 21:2-7;
   Hosea 6:6
NT: Matt 9:13

1 **At that time:** Matthew links what happens now with the teaching Jesus gave "at that time" (11:25); the chapter break introduced here into Matthew's gospel is artificial. Jesus invited those who were burdened to come to him (11:28-30); the incident that now follows is an example of his lightening burdens. **Jesus was going through a field of grain on the sabbath. His disciples were hungry and began to pick the heads of grain and eat them.** The law of Moses allowed those who were walking through a field of grain to eat some of the ripened grain but not to harvest the field. Jesus' **disciples** picked and ate grain because they were **hungry.**

> When you go through your neighbor's grainfield, you may pluck some of the ears with your hand, but do not put a sickle to your neighbor's grain.
>
> *Deuteronomy 23:26*

Grain crops ripen in springtime in Palestine, with harvesting stretching from Passover until Pentecost. This is the first indication Matthew's gospel provides of a time of the year during Jesus' public ministry. Since Jesus will be crucified at Passover (26:17), Jesus' public ministry took place over a span of at least a year, from one grain harvest until the next.

2 **When the Pharisees saw this, they said to him, "See, your disciples are doing what is unlawful to do on the sabbath."** The law of Moses commanded that the **sabbath** be a day of rest, when no work was to be done (Exod 20:8-11), even at harvest time (Exod 34:21). The law did not define what constituted work and provided only two examples of works forbidden on the Sabbath: lighting a fire (Exod 35:3) and gathering sticks (Num 15:32-36). Hence the prohibition of work had to be interpreted and applied. **Pharisees** were particularly concerned about Sabbath observance. Exodus 34:21 ruled out reaping on the Sabbath, and these Pharisees considered the disciples' plucking of heads of grain to be reaping. They accuse

---

BACKGROUND: PHARISEES were a group or movement, primarily of laymen, who developed particular traditions for how God's law was to be observed. They were influential but were only one group within first-century Judaism. An ancient historian reports that there were about six thousand Pharisees at the time of Jesus, out of a total Jewish population estimated at a half million to one million in Judea and Galilee. The Pharisees' traditions spelled out how a Jew should observe the Mosaic law, particularly regarding food, tithing, Sabbath observance, and ritual purity. Pharisees had their origin about 150 years before the birth of Jesus, and their rules for observing the law of Moses were handed on as "the tradition of the elders" (Mark 7:3, 5)—traditions established by earlier Pharisees. Pharisees accepted recent developments within Judaism, such as the belief in an afterlife (Acts 23:6-10). Jesus' outlook was closer to that of the Pharisees than to that of any other group we know of in first-century Judaism, but he also had some serious disagreements with them. These disagreements carried over into the early church, which found itself in competition with the Pharisees for the allegiance of Jews. Since the Pharisees were concerned with daily life rather than Temple worship, their influence survived the destruction of the Temple in A.D. 70, and they were among those who shaped the future course of Judaism. The Judaism of today is not identical to the Judaism of the Pharisees of the time of Jesus, but the traditions of the Pharisees are part of the roots of modern Judaism. *Related topic: Jewish religious diversity at the time of Jesus (page 45).*

Jesus of allowing his disciples to violate Sabbath law: **See, your disciples are doing what is unlawful to do on the sabbath.**

Sabbath: See page 233

> *For six days you may work, but on the seventh day you shall rest; on that day you must rest even during the seasons of plowing and harvesting.*
>
> *Exodus 34:21*

3 Jesus could have challenged the Pharisees' application of the law: casual snacking on the run is not the same as the hard toil of reaping. Jesus instead uses the opportunity to address more fundamental issues. **He said to them, "Have you not read what David did when he and his companions were hungry?"** When Jesus speaks about Scripture to ordinary people, who were likely illiterate, he says "You have heard," meaning, "You have heard the Scripture read to you" (5:21, 27, 33, 38). The Pharisees who challenge Jesus are able to read, so Jesus asks them, **Have you not read?** Jesus refers them to an incident in the life of David when **he and his companions were hungry** (1 Sam 21:2-7). Their hunger is only implicit in the text of 1 Samuel, but Jesus accents it in order to link his hungry disciples with David and his hungry companions.

4 Jesus reminds the Pharisees of how David **went into the house of God and ate the bread of offering, which neither he nor his companions but only the priests could lawfully eat.** At the time, **the house of God** was a shrine at Nob, near Jerusalem (1 Sam 21:2; Isaiah 10:32). The **bread of offering** was twelve loaves of bread that were baked on Friday and placed each Sabbath on a table in the house of God; priests ate the previous week's offering (Lev 24:5-9). Even though David and his companions were not priests and eating the bread of offering was reserved for priests, the author of 1 Samuel does not criticize David's actions.

Jesus cites David's actions as a precedent justifying the disciples' plucking of heads of grain on the Sabbath. Just as the hunger of David and his companions justified breaking the law governing who could eat the bread of offering, so the hunger of Jesus' disciples justified their plucking grain on the Sabbath. Human need takes precedence over regulations governing worship and the Sabbath. Jesus may be also implicitly comparing himself with David and conveying that he, the Son of David (1:1; 9:27), has authority just as David had authority.

5 Jesus provides a second justification for his allowing his disciples to pluck grain on the Sabbath. He again refers those who challenge him to what is written in Scripture: **Or have you not read in the law that on the sabbath the priests serving in the temple violate the sabbath and are innocent?** The law of Moses required priests to carry out certain acts on the Sabbath, such as setting out the bread of offering (Lev 24:8) and offering sacrifices (Num 28:9-10). Work was to cease on the Sabbath, but priestly work had to continue! There was thus justification in the law for setting aside requirements of the law: some laws took precedence over others. But how was this principle to be applied to the disciples' plucking grain on the Sabbath?

6 Jesus makes a solemn but enigmatic pronouncement: **I say to you, something greater than the temple is here.** The **temple** was the "house of God" (verse 4) where God was specially present, and the only place where Jews could offer sacrifices; the **temple** was the center of Jewish life and worship. Yet **something** even **greater than the temple is here** as Jesus is speaking—

BACKGROUND: SABBATH The Sabbath is the seventh day of the week in the Jewish calendar, our Saturday. "Sabbath" comes from a Hebrew verb that means to stop or cease, indicating an essential note of the Sabbath: it was a day on which all work was to cease. The third of the Ten Commandments spells this out: "Remember to keep holy the sabbath day. Six days you may labor and do all your work, but the seventh day is the sabbath of the LORD, your God. No work may be done then either by you, or your son or daughter, or your male or female slave, or your beast, or by the alien who lives with you" (Exod 20:8-10). Eventually the Sabbath became a day for prayer and study of Scripture as well as a day of leisure. By the time of Jesus, complex interpretations had been developed of what constituted work forbidden on the Sabbath, for example, walking more than roughly one thousand yards (the "sabbath day's journey" of Acts 1:12). Different Jewish groups had different interpretations of what constituted forbidden work, with the Essenes and some Pharisees taking a very rigorous approach. Jesus rejected rigorous Sabbath regulations as burdensome and instead emphasized the original meaning of the Sabbath, as a day of rest that God had given to his people. *Related topics: Essenes (page 238), Pharisees (page 231).*

---

an amazing pronouncement! But what is this **something greater?** Is it Jesus, who is uniquely the Son and revealer of God (11:27)? Is it the kingdom of heaven, the reign of God being made present through Jesus' teachings, healings, and exorcisms (4:17, 23; 11:5)? Is it the group of disciples gathered around Jesus? Jesus does not pin down what the **something greater** is. His words may be a wake-up call: Open your eyes and see what is happening! You are focused on grains of wheat and oblivious to **something greater than the temple** in your midst.

Temple: See page 442

For reflection: In what ways might I be overlooking great things that God is doing today?

Matthew's readers might understand Jesus to be the **something greater than the temple,** for they know that Jesus is God-with-us (1:23). God is more present through the person of Jesus than he is in the Temple. Since serving God's presence in the Temple supersedes Sabbath law (verse 5), how much more does attending to God's presence in Jesus take precedence over other concerns! If those walking with Jesus through a grain field are hungry (verse 1), it is better for them to relieve their hunger as they go, rather than stop following Jesus to get a meal.

7 Jesus provides a clearer application of the principle that some laws take precedence over others: **If you knew what this meant, "I desire mercy, not sacrifice," you would not have condemned these innocent men.** Jesus has previously quoted this prophecy from Hosea (9:13; Hosea 6:6); if Jesus had a store of favorite Scripture verses, Matthew's gospel indicates this was one of them. **Mercy** is response to need, whether God's mercy toward us in our need or our mercy for one another. Hosea's prophecy proclaims that **mercy** and loving-kindness are more important to God than animal **sacrifice.** If priests are able to violate the Sabbath rest to offer sacrifices (verse 5; Num 28:9-10), and if sacrifices themselves are less important in God's eyes than relieving human needs, then God puts relieving human needs over Sabbath laws. Hence in God's eyes the disciples who plucked grain on the Sabbath are **innocent,** just as priests offering sacrifices on the Sabbath are innocent (verse 5). If Jesus' critics had understood what Hosea's prophecy revealed about God's priorities, they would not have **condemned** the disciples for plucking grain.

> For it is love that I desire, not sacrifice,
>   and knowledge of God rather than holocausts.
>   Hosea 6:6

For reflection: What does this incident teach me about God's priorities? Is mercy my guiding principle in responding to the needs of others?

Because Jesus is merciful as his Father is merciful, the yoke Jesus places on his disciples is easy and the burden he asks them to bear is light (11:30). Jesus does not impose restrictive Sabbath regulations on his disciples; he gives them rest (11:28-29), accomplishing God's purpose in creating the Sabbath rest (Exod 20:10-11).

8 **For the Son of Man is Lord of the sabbath.** Just as the **Son of Man** has authority to forgive sins (9:6), so he is also **Lord of the sabbath,** able to teach how God wants the Sabbath observed. "All things have been handed over" to Jesus by his Father (11:27), making him the uniquely authorized interpreter of God's will, as is evident in the Sermon on the Mount (5:17-48).

Son of Man: See page 151
Lord: See page 133

Matthew's church was in a time of transition regarding Sabbath observance. Many Jewish Christian members observed the Sabbath (see 24:20), and they needed to know whether were they bound by the Pharisee's interpretations of how the Sabbath was to be observed. Both Jewish Christians and Gentile Christians met on the "first day of the week" (Acts 20:7), the "Lord's day" (Rev 1:10), to celebrate the Eucharist. Jesus' claim that he, not the Pharisees, had authority over Sabbath observance would have allowed Matthew's church to shape its Sabbath and Sunday observances in light of Jesus' teachings and example, which made mercy the priority.

For reflection: What do I do to observe Sunday as "the Lord's day"? What do I do to make it a day of rest? A day of mercy?

Mercy for a Man with a Crippled Hand

9 Moving on from there, he went into their synagogue. **10** And behold, there was a man there who had a withered hand. They questioned him, "Is it lawful to cure on the sabbath?" so that they might accuse him. **11** He said to them, "Which one of you who has a sheep that falls into a pit on the sabbath will not take hold of it and lift it out? **12** How much more valuable a person is than a sheep. So it is lawful to do good on the sabbath." **13** Then he said to the man, "Stretch out your hand." He stretched it out, and it was restored as sound as the other. **14** But the Pharisees went out and took counsel against him to put him to death.

Gospel parallels: Mark 3:1-6; Luke 6:6-11

OT: Exod 20:8-11

NT: Luke 13:10-17; 14:1-6

9 **Moving on from there,** from the field in which Jesus' disciples had plucked grain on the Sabbath (12:1), **he went into their synagogue.** For Matthew to refer to **their synagogue** might simply mean the synagogue in whatever village Jesus is visiting. On a Sabbath Jesus could expect to find a gathering of men and women in any synagogue, as "he went around all of Galilee, teaching in their synagogues" (4:23; see also 9:35). When Matthew wrote his gospel, synagogues were coming under the control of leaders who rejected Jesus as the Messiah, and Matthew's Jewish Christian readers may have thought of such synagogues as **their** synagogues. At the time of Jesus, synagogues were led by lay elders, some of whom were Pharisees, but Pharisees did not control all synagogues.

Synagogue: See page 104

10 **And behold, there was a man there who had a withered hand.** There is no indication that this man was looking for Jesus in the hope of being healed; he is simply among those present in the synagogue that Sabbath. A **withered hand**—paralyzed and atrophied—is a serious disability in a society in which most men made their living by some kind of manual labor.

They questioned Jesus: what follows indicates that **they** are Pharisees (verse 14). They asked, **"Is it lawful to cure on the sabbath?" so that they might accuse him.** They ask in order to snare Jesus into saying something that will be grounds for them to **accuse him** of not upholding the law of Moses, a charge they have just lodged, but without much success (12:2). They knew that Jesus did **cure** those who were afflicted and might cure

236

the man's withered hand; does Jesus consider it **lawful** for him to do so **on the sabbath,** when no work could be done (Exod 20:8-11)? Later rabbis would allow medical treatment on the Sabbath only when a life was in danger; the question these Pharisees pose to Jesus apparently indicates that they held this view. A withered hand was not life threatening; its cure could be deferred until after the Sabbath was over.

For reflection: Do I ask questions meant to embarrass or manipulate others?

11 Jesus responds to their question with a question. He said to them, **"Which one of you who has a sheep that falls into a pit on the sabbath will not take hold of it and lift it out?"** Jesus' question presumes that they would consider it lawful to rescue their sheep **on the sabbath.** Not all Jews of the time agreed: the Essenes, a Jewish group with some stricter views than the Pharisees, held that it violated the Sabbath to lift an animal that had fallen into a pit. Jesus may be subtly alluding to this Essene rule to convey to the Pharisees that there were those who would accuse Pharisees of holding a lax view of the Sabbath! In any case, Jesus reminds the Pharisees of their position regarding the welfare of their sheep and the Sabbath.

12 The Pharisees allow a sheep to be rescued on the Sabbath, but **how much more valuable a person is than a sheep.** Humans are more important than animals in the eyes of God (6:26; 10:31), and if doing good for animals is allowed on the Sabbath, then doing good for humans is even more justified. Jesus states the conclusion of his argument as a general principle: **So it is lawful to do good on the sabbath.** Healing an affliction like a withered hand is a **good** thing to do, **lawful . . . on the sabbath.** Jesus is "Lord of the sabbath" (12:8), able to declare on behalf of God (11:27) how the Sabbath is to be observed. God desires mercy (12:7), and the merciful thing to do for a man with a withered hand is to heal him. It is a misunderstanding of God's priorities to think that God wants mercy delayed because of the Sabbath.

For reflection: Do I find reasons to delay being merciful to those in need of my help?

13 **Then he said to the man, "Stretch out your hand."** Jesus' request is similar to his telling a paralyzed man to stand up (9:6). The man's hand is paralyzed and he is not able to open it or **stretch it out.** Jesus nevertheless commands him to do what he cannot do—and he is able to do it! **He stretched it out, and it was restored.** His once-withered hand is now completely healed and **as sound as** his **other** hand. The healing has required very little that could be considered work: Jesus did not touch him; the man only had to open his hand in response to Jesus' words. Matthew passes rather quickly over the healing, saying nothing about the man's gratitude or about the general reaction of those in the synagogue to this healing. Matthew's main interest is Jesus' pronouncement that it is lawful to do good on the Sabbath (verse 12).

For reflection: Do I view the Lord's Day as a day for doing good for others? How might I make doing good part of my Sunday observance?

BACKGROUND: ESSENES are not mentioned in the Bible. Ancient writers described them as a sect of Jews. Pliny the Elder (a Roman who lived from A.D. 23 to 79) wrote, "On the west side of the Dead Sea is the solitary tribe of the Essenes, which is remarkable beyond all the other tribes in the whole world, as it has no women and has renounced all sexual desire, has no money, and has only palm trees for company" (*Natural History,* 5:73). The Jewish historian Josephus described the Essenes as celibate men who lived at the Dead Sea and owned everything in common; he added that there were also other Essenes, some married, who lived throughout the land. Josephus numbered the Essenes at four thousand, several hundred of whom lived at their headquarters by the Dead Sea (in all likelihood at the site known today as Qumran). Most scholars identify the Essenes as the group who collected or wrote the Dead Sea Scrolls. Some scrolls show that the Essenes rejected the current high priests in Jerusalem as illegitimate and Temple worship as corrupt. Essenes determined religious feasts by a calendar different from the one used by the Temple. They expected God to act soon to vindicate them in a cosmic battle that would bring the end of this age; God would send two messiahs, one priestly and one royal. The Essenes carefully studied and rigorously observed the law of Moses and made daily ritual washings and communal meals part of their life. The gospels describe no encounters between Jesus and the Essenes, but Jesus was likely aware of them. Jesus and the Essenes would have agreed that God was about to act but would have differed over how. Rome destroyed Qumran in A.D. 68, and the Essenes disappeared from history. *Related topics: Dead Sea Scrolls (page 97), Jewish religious diversity at the time of Jesus (page 45).*

14 Matthew does recount the reaction of those who had questioned Jesus about healing on the Sabbath. **But the Pharisees went out and took counsel against him to put him to death.** The phrase, "put him to death" could also be translated, "destroy him." By doing good and showing mercy on the Sabbath, Jesus has put his own life in danger. This is the first notice in Matthew's gospel that Jesus has mortal enemies. It is deeply ironic that those who consider healing a violation of the Sabbath then hatch deadly plans on the Sabbath. Their motives are not completely clear. Does plucking grain and healing a hand on the Sabbath justify a death sentence? Perhaps these Pharisees were upset by Jesus' justification for his actions, his claim that he was Lord of the Sabbath (12:8). Either God had authorized Jesus to act on his behalf (as Jesus claimed—11:27) or Jesus was a religious imposter misleading the people. These Pharisees failed to recognize that God was at work through Jesus, and they wanted to do away with him.

Pharisees: See page 231

For reflection: What does the Pharisees' reaction to Jesus tell me about Jesus?

God's Servant

15 When Jesus realized this, he withdrew from that place. Many [people] followed him, and he cured them all, **16** but he warned them not to make him known. **17** This was to fulfill what had been spoken through Isaiah the prophet:

18 "Behold, my servant whom I have chosen,
my beloved in whom I delight;
I shall place my spirit upon him,
and he will proclaim justice to the Gentiles.
19 He will not contend or cry out,
nor will anyone hear his voice in the streets.
20 A bruised reed he will not break,
a smoldering wick he will not quench,
until he brings justice to victory.
21 And in his name the Gentiles will hope."

Gospel parallels: Mark 3:7-12
OT:Isaiah 42:1-4
NT:Matt 3:17; 8:16-17

239

15 **When Jesus realized this, he withdrew from that place:** when Jesus became aware that some Pharisees were plotting his death (12:14), he left from where he had healed a man's crippled hand (12:9-13). Jesus does not slacken the pace of his ministry, however: **many [people] followed him, and he cured them all.** While some Pharisees are now opposed to Jesus, **many** ordinary people come to him to be healed of their afflictions. Matthew notes that Jesus cured them **all:** Jesus sent no one away unhealed (see also 8:16).

> *For reflection: What might Jesus' example teach me about handling conflicts?*

16 **But he warned them not to make him known.** Jesus seemingly asks the impossible: he is already extremely well **known** (4:24) and attracts a crowd virtually everywhere he goes (4:25; 5:1; 8:1, 18; 9:8, 33, 36; 11:7). He previously asked some of those whom he healed not to talk about it (8:4; 9:30). Now he asks the crowds **not to make him known:** the Greek could also be translated "not to make him manifest." Jesus does not want publicity as a healer. Jesus' message is that the reign of God is at hand (4:17), and his healings are part of the coming of God's reign (12:28)—but only part. To focus too much on Jesus as a healer can distract from the larger picture of what God is doing through him.

17 **This was to fulfill what had been spoken through Isaiah the prophet.** Jesus said that he came to fulfill the law and prophets (5:17), and Matthew has pointed out how Jesus fulfills prophecy (1:22-23; 2:15, 23; 4:13-16; 8:16-17). When Matthew writes that **this** was to fulfill a prophecy, he refers to Jesus' withdrawing from open conflict (verse 15) and asking that he not be publicized (verse 16). Matthew sees these actions as a fulfillment of **what had been spoken through Isaiah the prophet.** The passage from Isaiah that Matthew quotes (Isaiah 42:1-4) is the longest Old Testament quotation in his gospel. Matthew translates Isaiah's Hebrew into Greek with some variations in wording.

> *Here is my servant whom I uphold,*
> *my chosen one with whom I am pleased,*
> *Upon whom I have put my spirit;*
> *he shall bring forth justice to the nations,*

> Not crying out, not shouting,
>> not making his voice heard in the street.
> A bruised reed he shall not break,
>> and a smoldering wick he shall not quench,
> Until he establishes justice on the earth;
>> the coastlands will wait for his teaching.
> *Isaiah 42:1-4*

18 Behold, my servant whom I have chosen, / my beloved in whom I delight. The Book of Isaiah has four prophecies about an unnamed **servant** of God (42:1-7; 49:1-7; 50:4-9; 52:13–53:12). Matthew has already quoted words from one of these prophecies and proclaimed them fulfilled by Jesus (8:17; Isaiah 53:4). Now Matthew declares that Jesus is the **servant** of God spoken of in prophecy. God has **chosen** Jesus and handed all things over to him; Jesus is the unique revealer of God (11:27). God looks upon Jesus as **my beloved in whom I delight.** In Matthew's Greek translation of Isaiah's prophecy, Matthew uses a word for **servant** that can also mean "son." A different Greek word meaning "son" was used in the passage about Jesus' baptism, but the quotation from Isaiah here may nonetheless remind Matthew's readers of the words of the voice from heaven in that earlier scene: "This is my beloved Son, with whom I am well pleased" (3:17). The next words from Isaiah—**I shall place my spirit upon him**— likewise bring to mind what happened after Jesus' baptism: "The heavens were opened [for him], and he saw the Spirit of God descending like a dove [and] coming upon him" (3:16).

> *For reflection: What does Isaiah's prophecy tell me about Jesus' identity?*
> *What does it mean for me that Jesus is the beloved servant and Son of God?*

While the opening words of Isaiah's prophecy found confirmation at the beginning of Jesus' public ministry, the following words seem to have little application to what Jesus has been doing: **and he will proclaim justice to the Gentiles.** Save for two incidents (8:5-13, 28-34), Jesus has directed his efforts to Jews, not to **Gentiles.** When he sent out the Twelve, he restricted their mission to Jews (10:5-6). Jesus will tell a Gentile woman that he "was sent only to the lost sheep of the house of Israel" (15:24). When Matthew applies these prophetic words concerning the Gentiles to Jesus, he has in mind what will happen after Jesus' resurrection, when Jesus sends his followers to "make disciples of all nations" (28:19; the Greek word translated "nations" there is translated "Gentiles" in our present passage). Jesus alluded to Gentiles when he spoke of many coming from east and west to join in the banquet of the kingdom of heaven (8:11).

Justice will be proclaimed to Gentiles. The Greek word translated **justice** has a range of meanings. It can mean "judgment"; "all the nations will be assembled" before Jesus at the last judgment (25:32). However, in this context, proclaiming **justice** might be equivalent to proclaiming the gospel message: the message of God's plan for the world will be preached to Gentiles. Matthew's own church, with its ever increasing number of Gentile converts, is evidence of this.

19 **He will not contend or cry out, / nor will anyone hear his voice in the streets.** The servant of God will not **contend** or wrangle; Jesus has just withdrawn from confrontation with Pharisees (verses 14-15). Jesus is meek and humble (11:29) and does not shout **in the streets** to attract notice. He has not let those whom he healed publicize him (verse 16). Jesus fulfills Isaiah's prophecy of a servant who carries out his mission quietly, without drawing attention to himself.

20 **A bruised reed he will not break:** reeds are fragile, and a **bruised** reed is easily broken. **A smoldering wick he will not quench:** an oil lamp used a fabric **wick;** a **smoldering** wick is at the point of going out. The servant of God abstains from violence even in the smallest matters, not breaking a bruised reed nor extinguishing a smoldering wick. Jesus taught his followers to be nonviolent (5:38-42), and he lived by his teaching. The **bruised reed** and **smoldering wick** can be images for those who are easily harmed, the wounded in body and spirit. Jesus heals the physically and spiritually afflicted; he welcomes sinners and outcasts to himself (9:9-13).

For reflection: Who are the bruised reeds and smoldering wicks in my life? What do I do to help them?

The servant's mission will continue **until he brings justice to victory.** Again, the Greek word translated **justice** has different meanings. If understood as judgment, then the prophecy proclaims that good will be rewarded and evil punished. But if **justice** is understood as God's plan for the world, then the prophecy promises that the servant's mission will culminate in the triumph of forgiveness and healing over evil and suffering.

21 **And in his name the Gentiles will hope.** The prophecy looks ahead to the time when **Gentiles** will experience God's saving action through Jesus. In biblical thought the **name** of a person is not an arbitrary label but is virtually equivalent with the person bearing the name. To have **hope in** the **name** of the servant of God means to hope in the servant. It is not the teachings and healings of Jesus that give salvation but Jesus himself. To hope in his name is to put ones hopes in Jesus.

> For reflection: What are my hopes in Jesus?

Matthew applied this prophecy to Jesus after Jesus avoided contention and publicity, but the words of the prophecy have broader fulfillment in Jesus and his mission. Jesus is the beloved servant and Son of God who will be the source of salvation for Gentiles as well as Jews. Matthew once again presents Jesus as the fulfillment of what God has said and done in the past, even as Jesus marks the next stage in God's plans.

ORIENTATION: *Matthew briefly told of Jesus' healing of a mute and demon-possessed man, a healing that evoked the charge that Jesus was in league with Beelzebul (9:32-34; 10:25). Now Matthew recounts a similar incident—or perhaps presents a fuller account of the earlier one.*

The Reign of God is Arriving
22 Then they brought to him a demoniac who was blind and mute. He cured the mute person so that he could speak and see. **23** All the crowd was astounded, and said, "Could this perhaps be the Son of David?" **24** But when the Pharisees heard this, they said, "This man drives out demons only by the power of Beelzebul, the prince of demons." **25** But he knew what they were thinking and said to them, "Every kingdom divided against itself will be laid waste, and no town or house divided against itself will stand. **26** And if Satan drives out Satan, he is divided against himself; how, then, will his kingdom stand? **27** And if I drive out demons by Beelzebul, by whom do your own people drive them out? Therefore they will be your judges. **28** But if it is by the Spirit of God

that I drive out demons, then the kingdom of God has come upon you.
 ^29 How can anyone enter a strong man's house and steal his property, unless he first ties up the strong man? Then he can plunder his house.
^30 Whoever is not with me is against me, and whoever does not gather with me scatters. ^31 Therefore, I say to you, every sin and blasphemy will be forgiven people, but blasphemy against the Spirit will not be forgiven. ^32 And whoever speaks a word against the Son of Man will be forgiven; but whoever speaks against the holy Spirit will not be forgiven, either in this age or in the age to come.

> Gospel parallels: Mark 3:22-30; Luke 11:14-23; 12:10
> NT: Matt 9:32-34; 10:25; Mark 9:40

22 **Then they brought to him a demoniac who was blind and mute.** Jesus continued to heal after he withdrew from where Pharisees were plotting his death (12:14-15); among those brought to him for healing is **a demoniac who was blind and mute.** The Greek word translated **mute** can also mean "deaf": in the ancient world, those who were congenitally deaf never

---

COMMENT: DEMONS AND SICKNESS It was taken for granted in the world of Jesus that the influence of demons could be experienced in everyday life. Evil spirits were sometimes understood as the cause of physical and mental illnesses (perhaps epilepsy and schizophrenia); hence curing these illnesses required the expulsion of such spirits. In the gospels of Matthew, Mark, and Luke, Jesus' casting out of demons is sometimes associated with healings, such as the healing of a woman with curvature of the spine (Luke 13:11-16). The line between healings and exorcisms in the gospels is not always clear. How should we understand Jesus' actions? Some points to keep in mind: First, the Catholic Church teaches that Satan exists and can cause spiritual harm and even, indirectly, physical harm (*Catechism of the Catholic Church,* 395), but the church urges care in distinguishing between demonic activity and physical or mental illness (*Catechism,* 1673). Second, although we understand more about the natural causes of sickness than people did in the first century, this does not change the effect that Jesus had on the sick people who came to him. They were healed. Jesus remains a healer. And even if we understand the effects of Satan differently from how they were understood in the first century, Jesus is the stronger one who overcomes him (Mark 3:27). Third, Jesus' exorcisms and healings were not merely done out of compassion for afflicted individuals but were also assaults on the forces of evil. Evil is still manifestly present in the world, and Jesus' overcoming of evil is no less a part of establishing God's reign today than it was in the first century.

learned to speak. A person who was **blind** and **mute** and deaf was cut off from society and normal life. By calling this man a **demoniac,** Matthew indicates that the man's blindness and muteness was caused by a demon. In the New Testament, illnesses are sometimes but not always understood as the work of evil spirits.

He cured the mute person so that he could speak and see. Matthew provides no details of how Jesus healed the man; Matthew's main interest lies in what follows. The man is freed of his afflictions—including his demon—and can now **speak and see.** Jesus enables him to see and converse with others and lead a more fully human life. Evil isolates us; Jesus' healing restores relationships.

23 **All the crowd was astounded**—literally "beside themselves"—**and said, "Could this perhaps be the Son of David?"** Everyone who witnesses the healing is amazed. Because Jesus freed the man from his afflictions, the crowd speculates that Jesus might be **the Son of David.** The *Psalms of Solomon,* a nonbiblical Jewish writing from the century before Jesus, called the Messiah **the Son of David,** but this was not a common title for the Messiah, even though the Messiah was expected to be a descendant of David. It is possible that the crowd thought of Jesus as **the Son of David** because Jesus had cast out a demon and healed a man, works that Jewish tradition ascribed to Solomon, the son of David (see also 9:27). Whatever specific meaning the crowd attached to the title **the Son of David,** they were amazed by what Jesus had done and thought he must be someone very significant.

Son of David: See page 16
Psalms of Solomon: See page 354
Nonbiblical writings: See page 198

24 **But when the Pharisees heard this, they said, "This man drives out demons only by the power of Beelzebul, the prince of demons."** The **Pharisees** were not present when Jesus cured the man, but they learn of it and react to the crowd's reaction. They **heard** that the crowd was speculating that Jesus might be the Son of David (verse 23), and they want to dampen any enthusiasm the crowd has for Jesus. Since they are determined to have Jesus killed (12:14), they certainly do not want him to have a following. To discredit Jesus they tell the crowds, **This man drives out demons only by the power of Beelzebul, the prince of demons.** The

Pharisees cannot deny that Jesus freed a man of a demon-inflicted condition, but they attribute his **power** to do so to **Beelzebul,** another name for Satan. As the chief evil spirit, Satan was **the prince of demons** with authority over other evil spirits. The Pharisees claim that Jesus is able to drive out demons **only** because he is in league with Satan and draws on Satan's power.

Pharisees: See page 231
Beelzebul: See Satan, page 55

25 **But he knew what they were thinking:** Jesus could have heard what the Pharisees were saying about him, just as the Pharisees had heard what the crowds were saying about Jesus (verse 24), but Matthew seems to indicate that Jesus knew the Pharisees' mind-set even without receiving a report (see also 9:4). In response to their charge, Jesus **said to them, "Every kingdom divided against itself will be laid waste, and no town or house divided against itself will stand."** He may be invoking a popular proverb or bit of wisdom. No political or social grouping can survive if it is **divided against itself,** whether it be a **kingdom** (the largest political entity), or a **town,** or a **house** (a family, the smallest social unit). Civil wars lay waste to kingdoms; divisions tear apart towns and families. Jews had lost their political independence a century earlier when Rome intervened in a Jewish civil war. Jesus' listeners likely knew from personal experience what happens when villages and families are torn by internal strife. They would have nodded agreement to Jesus' words.

26 **And if Satan drives out Satan, he is divided against himself; how, then, will his kingdom stand?** If Satan frees those under the control of evil spirits, Satan is working against himself and diminishing his influence over humans. The sway of Satan is characterized as the **kingdom** of Satan. It makes no more sense for Satan to enable Jesus to drive out evil spirits than it would make sense for a king to stir up a rebellion against his rule. The Pharisees' charge against Jesus (verse 24) defies common sense.

27 Jesus provides a second argument against the Pharisees' charge: **And if I drive out demons by Beelzebul, by whom do your own people drive them out?** Jesus is not the only person who drives out demons (see Mark 9:38; Acts 19:13). The expression **your own people** indicates that some

who perform exorcisms are Pharisees. If Jesus can be accused of driving out demons by the power of Beelzebul, then there is no reason why the same charge cannot be made against the Pharisees' own exorcists. These exorcists would undoubtedly be offended by such a charge and resent those who made it. **Therefore they will be your judges:** tell them they are operating by Satan's power, and see how they respond!

28 **But if it is by the Spirit of God that I drive out demons, then the kingdom of God has come upon you.** Jesus was conceived through the Holy Spirit (1:18, 20) and he saw the **Spirit of God** descending upon him after his baptism by John (3:16). Matthew has proclaimed that Jesus is the chosen servant of God prophesied by Isaiah, endowed with the Spirit (12:17-18). The **Spirit of God** is the power of God at work through Jesus, and it is **by the Spirit** that Jesus is able to **drive out demons.** Jesus' power comes from God, not Beelzebul.

The Spirit: See page 21

> *For reflection: How do I understand the relationship between Jesus and the Holy Spirit? How am I most aware of the working of the Holy Spirit in my life?*

It is of vital importance to recognize the source of Jesus' power, for **if it is by the Spirit of God** that Jesus frees women and men from demons and illnesses, **then the kingdom of God has come.** The expression **kingdom of God** has the same meaning as the expression "kingdom of heaven." It means God reigning over human affairs and all affairs. God's reign will not be established in its fullness until the end of this age (Matt 24-25). Yet Jesus proclaims to his listeners that if it is by the Spirit of God that he is overcoming demons and evil, then the kingdom of God **has come upon you.** The words **has come** mean "has arrived." God's reign does not lie only in the future; God's reign *has arrived* through the exorcisms and healings carried out by Jesus. Already the forces and effects of evil are being overcome; already the kingdom of Satan (verse 26) is being replaced by the **kingdom of God.** God's kingdom is being established when Jesus frees men and women from the grip of evil and brings them into God's reign; that is the profound significance of Jesus' deeds (4:23; 9:35; 11:5).

Kingdom of heaven: See page 266

247

For reflection: How has the kingdom of God come upon me? How in my daily life do I experience what it means to live in the reign of God?

29 Jesus tells a parable to help his listeners understand the significance of his exorcisms: **How can anyone enter a strong man's house and steal his property, unless he first ties up the strong man? Then he can plunder his house.** A thief cannot plunder a house guarded by a strong man unless he first overcomes and **ties up the strong man;** then the thief is free to take what he wants. This parable compares Satan to a strong man and Jesus to a thief. Satan's **property** or possessions are those who are possessed by demons. By driving out demons Jesus is plundering Satan of his possessions; the implication is that Jesus would not be able to do so unless he had subdued Satan. Jesus' exorcisms do not mean that he relies on Satan but the opposite: Jesus' exorcisms mean that he has overcome Satan. Jesus does not spell out when and how he has overcome Satan but presents his exorcisms as evidence that he has.

30 Driving out demons is beyond human powers; only God or Satan (the prince of demons—verse 24) can command demons. Those who witness Jesus' exorcisms must therefore attribute Jesus' power either to God or Satan. In this situation of having to make an either-or choice, Jesus proclaims, **Whoever is not with me is against me.** One must either recognize that Jesus drives out demons by the Spirit of God and join with Jesus, or attribute Jesus' powers to Satan and join with those who are against Jesus. When the kingdom of God is displacing the kingdom of Satan, there is no neutral corner to stand in. Jesus warns that **whoever does not gather with me scatters.** The image is that of a flock of sheep that is either gathered with a shepherd or scattered in the wilderness. Jesus' warning is an invitation to gather with him, to come to him (11:28) and enter into the reign of God.

Jesus proclaimed, **Whoever is not with me is against me,** in the context of his powers' being attributed either to Satan or to God. We should not take his words as an absolute edict covering all people in all situations. Mark recounts that Jesus said in another context, "Whoever is not against us is for us" (Mark 9:40; see also Luke 9:50; 11:23).

For reflection: How do I understand Jesus' two statements, "Whoever is not with me is against me" and "Whoever is not against us is for us"?

31 Jesus continues to address the issue of whether his powers come from Satan or from the Spirit of God. **Therefore, I say to you, every sin and blasphemy will be forgiven people.** His words **I say to you** indicate that Jesus is making a solemn pronouncement directed to the Pharisees who said that his power comes from Beelzebul (verse 24). **Every sin** might be interpreted as all sins against fellow human beings, and every **blasphemy** might broadly signify sins against God; together they would encompass all possible sins. Jesus solemnly assures his listeners that **every** sin **will be forgiven,** that is, forgiven by God. God's mercy and willingness to forgive are all encompassing; all sins are forgivable.

There is one exception: **but blasphemy against the Spirit will not be forgiven.** In a narrow sense, **blasphemy** is the sacrilegious use of God's name. **Blasphemy** here means to insult or slander **the Spirit** of God by ascribing the source of Jesus' power to Satan instead of the Spirit. Willful rejection of what the Spirit is doing through Jesus is a refusal to accept the healing and forgiveness he offers. Those who refuse to accept forgiveness **will not be forgiven.** God offers his mercy and forgiveness to everyone, no matter how horrible their sins, but refusing forgiveness means remaining unforgiven.

For reflection: Am I willing to let God's forgiveness reach into the dark corners of my life?

32 **And whoever speaks a word against the Son of Man will be forgiven.** Even those who reject and slander Jesus can be forgiven! Jesus is homeless (8:20) and meek and humble (11:29); some may fail to perceive that he is the Spirit-anointed Son of God and reject him out of ignorance (see Acts 3:13-17). Others may turn away from him and even curse him out of weakness and fear—a prominent example being Peter (26:74). They can be forgiven, **but whoever speaks against the holy Spirit will not be forgiven.** To speak against the Holy Spirit means the same as to blaspheme against the Spirit. Those who reject the forgiveness God offers through the Holy Spirit cut themselves off from forgiveness.

Son of Man: See page 151

Jesus says that whoever speaks against the Holy Spirit will not be forgiven **either in this age or in the age to come.** Jesus does not explain the nature of **the age to come.** Yet it is clear from his words that those who live in **this age** will continue to exist in **the age to come.** Whoever speaks against the Holy Spirit will never be forgiven, **either in this age or in the age to come.** But if all other sins can be forgiven (verse 31), then Jesus' words raise the possibility that they can be forgiven not only in this present age but also **in the age to come.** The Catholic Church cites this passage in support of its teaching that after we die there is the possibility of our being purified in preparation for being united with God, a purification it calls purgatory (*Catechism of the Catholic Church*, 1031).

For reflection: Will I ever be completely ready for death to usher me into God's presence? Do I hope to be forgiven and purified in the next life?

ORIENTATION: *Jesus continues to address Pharisees who accused him of drawing on the power of Satan to drive out demons (12:24).*

Words from the Heart

[33] "Either declare the tree good and its fruit is good, or declare the tree rotten and its fruit is rotten, for a tree is known by its fruit. [34] You brood of vipers, how can you say good things when you are evil? For from the

---

BACKGROUND: THE AGE TO COME There was no expectation of meaningful life after death in early Old Testament times; if God was to reward good and punish evil it had to be in this life. Most of the prophecies of the Old Testament share this perspective: God will rescue or punish his people through the events of history. Late in the Old Testament era a new perspective developed that is expressed in a first-century Jewish writing: "The Most High has made not one age but two" (4 Ezra 7:50—a book not in the Bible). God would bring an end to the present age and inaugurate a new age. The age to come was conceived of differently in different writings; there was general agreement that God would bring human history, with all its evils, to an end and reward good and punish evil at a judgment. This was often associated with God fully establishing his reign over his people and all peoples, but there were different expectations for how this would happen. Jesus spoke of the present age and the age to come (Mark 10:30) and proclaimed that the kingdom of God was at hand (Mark 1:15), which meant that the present age was drawing to an end (Matt 13:39-40, 49; 24:3; 28:20). Paul speaks of Christians as living in the present age (Rom 8:18; 12:2) and yet having been rescued from it (2 Cor 5:17; Gal 1:4): Jesus began establishing the reign of God, but we still await its fullness. *Related topics: Judgment (page 557), Kingdom of heaven (page 266), Life after death (page 406), Nonbiblical writings (page 198).*

fullness of the heart the mouth speaks. [35] A good person brings forth good out of a store of goodness, but an evil person brings forth evil out of a store of evil. [36] I tell you, on the day of judgment people will render an account for every careless word they speak. [37] By your words you will be acquitted, and by your words you will be condemned."

Gospel parallels: Luke 6:43-45
OT:Sirach 27:6
NT:Matt 7:16-20; James 3:2-12

33 Since the power to drive out demons can come only from God or from Satan (12:24-28), Jesus' exorcisms pose an unavoidable question: is Jesus an agent of God or an agent of Satan? There is no middle ground (12:30). Jesus calls upon the Pharisees to be consistent in judging him and his deeds, clothing his call in agricultural imagery: **Either declare the tree good and its fruit is good, or declare the tree rotten and its fruit is rotten, for a tree is known by its fruit.** Jesus has previously observed that good trees bear good fruit and rotten trees bear bad fruit, making the quality of fruit an index of the quality of a tree (7:16-18). Jesus invites his critics to judge him on the basis of what he accomplishes. If he produces the good fruit of expelling demons and curing the sick (12:22; see also 11:5), then he should be declared good. It is wrong minded to acknowledge that Jesus does good but then accuse him of being bad.

34 Jesus views his critics as being deliberately wrong minded and for the first time in Matthew's gospel launches a frontal attack on them. He calls them **You brood of vipers,** echoing John the Baptist's words (3:7). Jesus asks them, **How can you say good things when you are evil?** Just as fruit reveals the quality of a tree, so the Pharisees' evil accusation against Jesus (12:24) reveals their evil condition: they cannot **say good things** because they are **evil. For from the fullness of the heart the mouth speaks.** In biblical idiom, the **heart** is one's inner being, the seat of thinking and willing. Whatever one's heart is filled with overflows in one's words, and words as well as deeds reveal whether one is good or evil. Jesus' observations may echo a proverb about fruit and speech (Sirach 27:6).

> *The fruit of a tree shows the care it has had;*
>> *so too does a man's speech disclose the bent of his mind.*
>>> *Sirach 27:6*

35 Jesus rephrases his point that what is in our hearts overflows into our words: **A good person brings forth good out of a store of goodness, but an evil person brings forth evil out of a store of evil.** The Greek expression translated **store of goodness** is literally "good treasure," and **store of evil** is literally "evil treasure." The hidden treasure of the heart is revealed in speech. The person who has **a store of goodness** within herself or himself **brings forth goodness,** manifesting that she or he is **a good person.** The reverse is also true: **an evil person brings forth evil out of a store of evil.** Jesus' detractors cannot say good things because they are evil (verse 34).

The principle that words and actions manifest the one speaking and acting applies to Jesus, and to his detractors, and to the readers of Matthew's gospel. Jesus' exorcisms and healings reveal that he is God's agent, establishing the reign of God on earth (12:28). His accusers' charge that he is an agent of Satan reveals the evil that lies in their hearts (verse 34). The readers of Matthew's gospel must evaluate themselves according to their own words and deeds.

For reflection: How do my words and actions manifest who I am? What do they reveal about what is in my heart?

36 Jesus solemnly proclaims, **I tell you, on the day of judgment people will render an account for every careless word they speak.** Jesus' **I tell you** is addressed to Pharisees who said that he drives out demons by the power of Beelzebul (12:24). He has previously referred to **the day of judgment,** when every human will be judged by God (10:15; 11:22); Jesus will speak of it again (25:31-46). Here he notes that God's judgment will take into account what each person has said, even **every careless word they speak.** How much more will the Pharisees be held accountable for their charge against Jesus, for it is not mere carelessness but slander!

What about our **careless** words? Will we be condemned for our offhand comments and chitchat? Jesus may have a more substantial failing in mind. A **careless** word is literally an "idle" word. Jesus will use the word "idle" to describe laborers who should have been working but were standing around (20:3, 6); elsewhere the New Testament uses the word for those who are lazy, useless, unproductive. Small talk is not evil in itself but is a waste of time when there are important matters to talk about. If the kingdom of God is at hand and has been inaugurated by Jesus, then idle chatter distracts from what God is accomplishing through Jesus. **On the day of judgment people will render an account** for not paying proper attention to what God has done for them and for wasting their words—and lives—on trivialities.

Judgment: See page 557

37 **By your words you will be acquitted, and by your words you will be condemned. By your words** Jesus refers to the Pharisees' words; they will be **acquitted** or **condemned** on the basis of having said that Jesus' power is demonic (12:24). **Your words** covers our words as well. Our words help or harm others; our words reveal the condition of our hearts (verses 34-35). On the day of judgment our words will be evidence by which we can be **acquitted** or **condemned.**

> *For reflection: If my words will be the basis on which I will be judged, how do I expect to fare on the day of judgment?*

The Sign of Jonah

38 Then some of the scribes and Pharisees said to him, "Teacher, we wish to see a sign from you." 39 He said to them in reply, "An evil and unfaithful generation seeks a sign, but no sign will be given it except the sign of Jonah the prophet. 40 Just as Jonah was in the belly of the whale three days and three nights, so will the Son of Man be in the heart of the earth three days and three nights. 41 At the judgment, the men of Nineveh will arise with this generation and condemn it, because they repented at the preaching of Jonah; and there is something greater than Jonah here. 42 At the judgment the queen of the south will arise with this generation and condemn it, because she came from the ends of the earth to hear the wisdom of Solomon; and there is something greater than Solomon here."

Gospel parallels: Mark 8:11-12; Luke 11:16, 29-32
OT:1 Kings 10:1-13; Jonah 2-3
NT:Matt 16:1-4; John 2:18; 6:30

38 **Then some of the scribes and Pharisees said to him:** Jesus has been responding to **Pharisees** who accused him of relying on the power of Satan to drive out demons (12:24-37); this is the first mention of **scribes** being present. They tell him **Teacher, we wish to see a sign from you.** They

demand that Jesus do something that will authenticate him as God's agent who drives out demons by the Spirit of God (12:28). Just what kind of **sign** they have in mind is unclear. It was widely known that Jesus had raised a dead girl back to life (9:23-26), and if this was not enough to convince these scribes and Pharisees that Jesus was empowered by God, what would convince them? No matter what sign Jesus provided, would they want an even greater sign?

Scribes: See page 138
Pharisees: See page 231

39 Jesus knows that nothing will persuade those who dismiss his healings and exorcisms as works of Satan. **He said to them in reply, "An evil and unfaithful generation seeks a sign."** A **generation** can mean the people who were alive at the time of Jesus, but it also recalls an Old Testament generation that was hard-hearted and rejected God no matter what God did (Psalm 95:8-10). The connotation of **unfaithful** is "unfaithful to God." Those whose hearts are set on **evil** and who have turned away from God may demand that God do something spectacular before they change their ways. **But no sign will be given it except the sign of Jonah the prophet:** the implication of **will be given** is will be given by God. God will not provide an evil and unfaithful generation with a sign **except the sign of Jonah the prophet.**

40 **Just as Jonah was in the belly of the whale three days and three nights, so will the Son of Man be in the heart of the earth three days and three nights.** Called by God to preach to pagan Nineveh, Jonah tried to sail away from God's call, only to end up in the belly of a large fish (Jonah 2:1). The New American Bible has it that Jonah was in the belly of a **whale;** the Greek word Matthew uses could also mean "sea monster" or "huge fish." **Three days and three nights** may be a biblical idiom for a limited period of time (see Hosea 6:2) and need not mean precisely seventy-two hours. Jesus uses the expression **the Son of Man** as a way of referring to himself. Being in the **heart of the earth** means being buried in a grave and possibly has the connotation of being in the underworld, the abode of the dead. The "sign of Jonah" (verse 39) is **the Son of Man** being **in the heart of the earth** just as Jonah was in the belly of a large fish, and for a comparable period of time.

Son of Man: See page 151

What would the scribes and Pharisees have made of such a sign? Some Pharisees were plotting how Jesus might be put to death (12:14), and they might have taken Jesus' words as an indication that their plot would succeed. But Jonah did not remain in the belly of the great fish; did **the sign of Jonah** imply that the Son of Man would not remain in his grave? Scribes and Pharisees might have found **the sign of Jonah** a bit cryptic.

Matthew's readers would have understood **the sign of Jonah** in terms of Jesus' death and resurrection, which from the earliest days of the church were the core of the gospel message (1 Cor 15:1-4). Jesus alluded to his death when he spoke of himself as a bridegroom who would be taken away (9:15). **The sign of Jonah** is the second allusion to his death in Matthew's gospel, and for Matthew's readers it would have also signified his resurrection.

All of us would welcome more evident signs of God's presence and power in the world. The greatest—yet also most mysterious—sign that God has provided us is the death and resurrection of his Son. If we find ourselves demanding a sign from God, we can turn our eyes to Golgotha and the empty tomb.

For reflection: What is the significance of the sign of Jonah for me?

41 Jonah's mission and its outcome bears a lesson. **At the judgment, the men of Nineveh will arise with this generation and condemn it, because they repented at the preaching of Jonah.** The people of Nineveh **repented** in sackcloth and ashes in response to the **preaching of Jonah** (Jonah 3:4-9). They **will arise with this generation** in resurrection to face God's **judgment.** By **this generation** Jesus means those who willfully reject him (see 11:16-19). That the people of Nineveh will **condemn** this generation could mean that they will pass judgment on it, but in context it might simply mean that their example of repentance will be an implicit condemnation of those who have not repented. **They repented at the preaching of Jonah** while **this generation** has not repented despite there being **something greater than Jonah here.** The **something greater** broadly refers to the reign of God being established by Jesus. It is of greater importance to accept Jesus' message than it was for the people of Nineveh to accept the message of Jonah. Those who reject Jesus will be judged by the standard set by the people of Nineveh when they repented in response to Jonah.

Judgment: See page 557

42 **At the judgment the queen of the south will arise with this generation and condemn it, because she came from the ends of the earth to hear the wisdom of Solomon.** The **queen of the south** is called the queen of Sheba in Kings (1 Kings 10:1-13); Sheba lay on the southern end of the Arabian Peninsula, today's Yemen. "Having heard of Solomon's fame" (1 Kings 10:1), she came to Jerusalem **to hear the wisdom of Solomon** and was very impressed (1 Kings 10:4-9). Some of Jesus' contemporaries have been far less impressed with him, even though **there is something greater than Solomon here.** Jesus is the wisdom of God (see 11:19), able to reveal God (11:27). **At the judgment the queen of the south** will be raised by God and will serve as a standard for the response that should have been made to Jesus, who is far **greater than Solomon.** Judged by this standard of responsiveness to God's revelation, those who reject Jesus will be seen to be complete failures.

> *For reflection: What do the people of Nineveh and the queen of Sheba teach me about the response I should make to Jesus?*

Nineveh was the capital city of the Assyrians, the mortal enemies of Israel (which is why Jonah resisted his mission). The queen of Sheba was likewise not an Israelite. Yet at the judgment, these Gentiles will fare better than God's chosen people who reject Jesus. This favorable view of Gentiles would have been noted by Matthew's church, which was becoming increasingly Gentile in its makeup. Gentiles are included in God's plans.

The Parable of the Empty House
43 **"When an unclean spirit goes out of a person it roams through arid regions searching for rest but finds none. 44 Then it says, 'I will return to my home from which I came.' But upon returning, it finds it empty, swept clean, and put in order. 45 Then it goes and brings back with itself seven other spirits more evil than itself, and they move in and dwell there; and the last condition of that person is worse than the first. Thus it will be with this evil generation."**
Gospel parallels: Luke 11:24-26

43 Jesus tells a parable that provides a comparison for **this evil generation** (verse 45), meaning those who reject him. **When an unclean spirit goes out of a person:** Jesus is not talking about an unclean spirit leaving voluntarily

but being driven out, as when Jesus performs an exorcism (8:16, 31-32; 12:22). **It roams through arid regions searching for rest.** Wilderness areas were thought of as the haunt of demons (see Lev 16:10; Tobit 8:3; Isaiah 13:21; 34:11, 14). This unclean spirit searches for a place to settle down and **rest but finds none.**

44 Then it says, **"I will return to my home from which I came."** The unclean spirit thinks of the person from which it was expelled as a **home** or house. The spirit was evicted as an undesirable tenant but still regards it as **my home** and resolves to **return.** The unclean spirit might have thought that reoccupying the house would be a battle, **but upon returning, it finds it empty, swept clean, and put in order.** No one else has come to live in the house; it is **empty** and waiting for the unclean spirit to move in again.

45 Then it goes and **brings back with itself seven other spirits more evil than itself, and they move in and dwell there.** The unclean spirit shares its good fortune with other unclean spirits who are presumably homeless and searching for a place to rest. The other spirits are even **more evil** than the first one. The number **seven** symbolizes fullness and completeness: after the unclean spirit and its companions move into the empty house, it is completely filled with the worst possible tenants. Therefore **the last condition of that person is worse than the first.** Just as a house left empty is an invitation for undesirables to wander in and take over, so those who have had unclean spirits driven out of them but have not filled themselves with anything positive are liable to end up worse off than before. Jesus does not spell out what they should fill themselves with; we might think of the Holy Spirit, or faith in Jesus, or discipleship.

　　　Thus it will be with this evil generation. Jesus compares **this evil generation** to a person who has been freed from an unclean spirit but not filled with anything in its place. On the one hand, being freed from the sway of Satan does not in itself bring one into the kingdom of God. Entering the kingdom of God requires doing the will of God (7:21) as laid out by Jesus in such teachings as the Sermon on the Mount (Matt 5-7). On the other hand, there is no safe neutral ground in the battle between Satan and Jesus: empty houses do not stay empty. As Jesus has gone about teaching and healing and exorcising he has attracted large crowds (4:23-25; 8:1, 16; 9:35), but relatively few have fully accepted him and his message.

Some have dismissed him as a glutton and a drunkard (11:19). Even the towns where he performed most of his mighty deeds have not repented (11:20-24). Those who do not embrace Jesus will end up in the opposing camp (12:30), and their **last condition** will be **worse than the first.** Jesus' warning is addressed above all to Jewish leaders who attribute his exorcisms to the power of Satan rather than to the power of God (12:24, 28) and who seek his death (12:14): they are worse off than they would have been if Jesus had never come.

For reflection: What is the message of Jesus' parable for me? With what do I try to fill my emptiness?

The Family of Jesus
46 While he was still speaking to the crowds, his mother and his brothers appeared outside, wishing to speak with him. [**47** Someone told him, "Your mother and your brothers are standing outside, asking to speak with you."] **48** But he said in reply to the one who told him, "Who is my mother? Who are my brothers?" **49** And stretching out his hand toward his disciples, he said, "Here are my mother and my brothers. **50** For whoever does the will of my heavenly Father is my brother, and sister, and mother."

Gospel parallels: Mark 3:31-35; Luke 8:19-21
NT: Matt 7:21; 13:55-56; 26:42

46 **While he was still speaking to the crowds:** Matthew's last mention of **crowds** was at 12:23. **His mother and his brothers appeared outside.** Their being **outside** would imply that Jesus is inside a building, and Matthew will shortly indicate that Jesus is in a house (13:1). Jesus' **mother and his brothers** come to where Jesus is teaching, **wishing to speak with him.** Matthew gives no hint what they wanted to speak with Jesus about. Their intentions, like the details of the setting, are of secondary importance in what follows, and Matthew doesn't spell them out.

Brothers and sisters of Jesus: See page 294

47 **[Someone told him, "Your mother and your brothers are standing outside, asking to speak with you."]** The New American Bible prints this verse in brackets because it is missing in some of the oldest and best manuscripts

of Matthew's gospel. This might mean that Matthew wrote these words, but they were accidentally omitted by a copyist; or it might mean that Matthew didn't write these words, but a copyist, familiar with Mark 3:32, added them to make Matthew's account read more smoothly. In any case, this verse simply bridges between the preceding and following verses.

48 **But he said in reply to the one who told him, "Who is my mother? Who are my brothers?"** The answers to Jesus' questions would seem obvious: your mother and your brothers are the ones standing outside asking to speak with you! Yet Jesus nonetheless asks, **Who is my mother? Who are my brothers?** as if his relationship with those standing outside is in question. But how could this be? Family ties were very important in the culture in which Jesus lived; one's kinship formed an important component of one's identity. What is Jesus getting at by his questions?

49 **And stretching out his hand toward his disciples:** Jesus' **disciples** were last mentioned in the opening verses of chapter 12. By **stretching out his hand toward his disciples** Jesus draws attention to them. **He said, "Here are my mother and my brothers."** A startling pronouncement—but what does it mean? The first thing that might occur to us is that Jesus' **disciples** left behind their own families in order to follow Jesus (4:18-22; 8:21-22; 10:37; 19:27-29). Joined together in discipleship, they have become a new family gathered around Jesus.

50 But there is more to becoming a new family of Jesus than leaving old families behind. Jesus explains what this something more is: **For whoever does the will of my heavenly Father is my brother, and sister, and mother.** Jesus' **whoever** is all-encompassing, covering every woman and man of all time who **does the will of my heavenly Father.** Being a disciple of Jesus is not simply a matter of traveling with him as he goes about Galilee but of doing **the will** of his **heavenly Father.** Jesus taught that "not everyone who says to me 'Lord, Lord,' will enter the kingdom of heaven, but only the one who does the will of my Father in heaven" (7:21). Doing the will of his Father is Jesus' way of life; doing his Father's will is what makes one a disciple of Jesus and a member of the family gathered around him. Jesus calls them **my brother, and sister, and mother:** women are as fully included as men in Jesus' family.

For reflection: What does it mean to me that Jesus is my brother? How is my following of Jesus a matter of doing the will of his Father?

Jesus does not repudiate family ties (15:3-4), least of all to his own family. Their appearance **outside** (verse 46) provides an occasion for him to teach that his bond with his disciples is stronger than the bonds of blood kinship, a point he has earlier made (10:37).

Early Christians will call one another "brother" and "sister"; there are over 150 such references in the New Testament (for a sampling see Rom 1:13; 16:1; 1 Cor 7:15; Philm 1-2; James 2:14-15). Some of Matthew's first readers had been rejected by their families when they became Christians, and Jewish Christians were experiencing increasing alienation from some synagogues (10:17, 21, 35-36). Jesus' embrace of them as his brothers and sisters gave them new family ties, replacing the kinship they had given up to be his disciples.

For reflection: How strong are my bonds with other Christians simply because they are Christians? What might I do to express my bonds with them?

CHAPTER 13

ORIENTATION: *While some have accepted Jesus and become his new family (12:49-50) many have rejected him despite the mighty deeds he has performed (11:16-24). Some Jewish religious leaders seek his death (12:14) and attribute his powers to Satan (12:24). If the kingdom of God is at hand (4:17) and being established through Jesus (12:28), why is Jesus' mission not more successful? Jesus responds in parables.*

The Parable of the Seeds and the Harvest

¹ On that day, Jesus went out of the house and sat down by the sea. ² Such large crowds gathered around him that he got into a boat and sat down, and the whole crowd stood along the shore. ³ And he spoke to them at length in parables, saying: "A sower went out to sow. ⁴ And as he sowed, some seed fell on the path, and birds came and ate it up. ⁵ Some fell on rocky ground, where it had little soil. It sprang up at once because the soil was not deep, ⁶ and when the sun rose it was scorched, and it withered for lack of roots. ⁷ Some seed fell among thorns, and the thorns grew up and choked it. ⁸ But some seed fell on rich soil, and produced fruit, a hundred or sixty or thirtyfold. ⁹ Whoever has ears ought to hear."

Gospel parallels: Mark 4:1-9; Luke 8:4-8

1 **On that day, Jesus went out of the house and sat down by the sea.** By **that day** Matthew means the day whose events he has been recounting— events that begin with Jesus curing a mute and blind demoniac (12:22) and continue through his being in a house with his disciples (12:46-50). The chapter break between chapters 12 and 13 is artificial and interrupts Matthew's account. **Jesus went out of the house** where he had been with his disciples (possibly Peter's house: see 8:14-16; 9:28) **and sat down by the sea.** The **sea** is the Sea of Galilee, but Matthew gives no indication where along its shore-line Jesus might be. That Jesus **sat down** could indicate that he intended to teach: Jewish teachers as a rule sat while teaching (see 5:1-2; 26:55).

Sea of Galilee: See page 153

2 **Such large crowds gathered around him that he got into a boat:** Jesus had been "speaking to the crowds" (12:46), and they follow him to the seashore. The press of the crowds was so great **that he got into a boat,** giving himself some breathing room. What follows suggests that his disciples boarded the boat with him (13:10). He **sat down,** which might be expected for a passenger in a boat but, again, sitting is the posture for one who is teaching. **The whole crowd stood along the shore** with the boat pulled offshore a bit. Sound carries well over water; the boat provided a convenient way for Jesus to speak to a crowd, as a hillside had earlier (5:1–7:28).

3 **And he spoke to them at length in parables:** this is the first explicit mention of **parables** in Matthew's gospel. Parables can range from brief implied comparisons to rather developed stories. Jesus **spoke** to the crowds on the shore **at length** in parables: Matthew will recount a number of parables in the course of chapter 13 of his gospel.

Jesus begins his first parable, **A sower went out to sow.** Many in the crowd along the seashore were farmers or raised some crops; Galilee had an agricultural economy. The crowd would have been able to picture a sower sowing without Jesus' having to describe what was involved. Seeds were cast by hand and later plowed under; sowing of grain crops was done at the beginning of the annual rains that fell during wintertime.

BACKGROUND: PARABLES Jesus did not invent the idea of conveying a message by means of a parable (see 2 Sam 12:1-7 for an Old Testament example). The Greek word for parable means "setting beside, placing two things side by side for comparison." The Hebrew word for parable has a broader range of meanings, including "proverb," "riddle," "metaphor," "story," "fable," and "allegory." Jesus' parables range from pithy sayings ("No one pours new wine into old wineskins"—Mark 2:22) to miniature stories (the parable of the prodigal son—Luke 15:11-32). Jesus' parables often use examples from everyday life as comparisons that throw light on what God is doing through him or how one should respond to what God is doing. Jesus' parables are vivid but sometimes enigmatic. They are meant to be thought provoking, to stimulate the listener's reflection. Sometimes they confront the listener with a decision: Make up your mind—where do you stand? Some scholars have claimed that each parable makes only one point, but that is an artificial restriction. Some parables are like diamonds, revealing new facets of meaning when examined from different angles.

This parable is usually called the parable of the *sower* (see 13:18), but it devotes little attention to him. The focus is on where the seeds land and what happens to them.

4 **And as he sowed, some seed fell on the path.** Most Galilean farmers had to make do with rather small plots of farmable land and would sow every bit of such plots. Some hand-cast seeds might fall on a **path** bordering or cutting through (see 12:1) their fields. It would not be long before **birds came and ate it up:** seeds lying on a beaten path make easy pickings.

5 **Some fell on rocky ground, where it had little soil.** In Galilee the topsoil lies over an uneven limestone base and is very thin in places. A farmer cannot tell at a glance how thick or thin the soil is but casts seeds over his whole plot of land. After being plowed in, the seeds that landed on thin soil **sprang up at once because the soil was not deep.** Thin soil does not make seeds grow faster, but in shallow soil the seeds are near the surface after having been plowed in and hence break through the surface sooner than seeds plowed deeper into the soil.

6 **And when the sun rose it was scorched, and it withered for lack of roots.** Roots in thin soil have little room to grow and cannot sustain a mature

---

BACKGROUND: FARMING Farmers made up most of the population of rural Galilee. Unlike American farmers, who tend to live in isolated houses on their farms, Galilean farmers lived together in small towns and villages and went out to work their fields. They grew grain crops, including wheat and barley; fruits, such as grapes, olives, and figs; and vegetables, such as lentils, beans, peas, and cucumbers. Galilee contained some prime farmland in its valleys, including the broad valleys north and south of Nazareth. Much of the prime land had been expropriated by rulers (such as Herod Antipas at the time of Jesus), who either had it managed for them or entrusted it to their influential supporters. Some farmers worked as tenant farmers or day laborers on these estates. Most farmers owned their own plots of land, which were often small and were sometimes on a rocky hillside that had to be terraced to support crops. Farmers were subject to tithes and taxes on their crops, which by some estimates added up to 40 percent of their harvests. These farmers were better off than day laborers, but a few bad harvests could lead to indebtedness and loss of land. There was not much of a middle class in Galilee, and a wide gap separated the few wealthy people from the large number of ordinary farmers, craftspeople, and day laborers.

---

plant. Nor can thin soil retain much water, and as a result these sprouts wither in the sun. Thus the seeds in this second category were able to sprout but **withered** before they could produce any grain.

7 **Some seed fell among thorns, and the thorns grew up and choked it.** We might best picture these seeds not landing in the middle of thorn plants but being sown on soil that contains thorn seeds. The grain and the thorns **grew up** together, but the thorns **choked** out the grain plants. The grain in this category survived longer than that which sprouted in thin soil, but none of the seeds recounted so far have grown to maturity and produced a harvest.

8 **But some seed fell on rich soil**—literally, on good earth—**and produced fruit, a hundred or sixty or thirtyfold.** Farming in Galilee was inherently inefficient, with seeds landing in bad places, plants withering, and weeds choking out grain—not to mention the effects of insects and poor rains. Farmers nonetheless survived because some seeds grew into mature plants and produced a harvest, **a hundred or sixty or thirtyfold.** A hundredfold harvest was bountiful indeed, the best that might be expected (see Gen 26:12). But even a **sixty or thirtyfold** harvest was a good harvest, able to feed the farmer and his family until the next harvest. Despite the seeds that never produced a crop, the man who went out to sow went out again a few months later and reaped a good harvest.

9 **Whoever has ears ought to hear:** Jesus uses this admonition as an invitation for his listeners to understand the significance of what he has said (see 11:15). What is it that his listeners **ought to hear?** Jesus told a story about an ordinary farming experience, and some in his audience might have wondered, "Yeah, so? That's what happens when you raise grain: some seed is wasted but you get a crop anyway." That misses the point: Jesus told this story as a parable (verse 3), using an everyday experience as a comparison for something else. The significance of a parable lies in the comparison.

As is the case with most parables, more than one comparison can be drawn from the parable of the seeds and the harvest. Jesus will shortly explain this parable by drawing comparisons (13:18-23). Yet the readers of Matthew's gospel may at this point draw a lesson from this parable. Matthew has presented the parable being told "on that day" (verse 1) when Jesus met with rejection (12:24, 38) but pointed to his disciples as those who were doing God's will (12:49-50). This continues the pattern of Jesus' being rejected by some (11:16-24; 12:14) and embraced by others (11:25). Jesus' words and deeds have been like seeds that have fallen on a path and on thin soil and amidst thorns, producing no harvest. Yet his words and deeds have also fallen on good ground and are beginning to yield a harvest, evident in his disciples. Jesus' failures may seem to overshadow his successes, just as in the parable there are three examples of unproductive soil but only one of productive soil. Nevertheless, Jesus' mission will be accomplished; a harvest for the kingdom is assured.

For reflection: How do I understand Jesus' parable of the seeds and the harvest? What message or lesson do I find in this parable?

ORIENTATION: *Jesus' speaking to the crowd in parables (13:3) is interrupted by a question from his disciples and Jesus' extended response (13:10-23).*

Blessed Are Those Who See

10 The disciples approached him and said, "Why do you speak to them in parables?" **11** He said to them in reply, "Because knowledge of the mysteries of the kingdom of heaven has been granted to you, but to them it has not been granted. **12** To anyone who has, more will be given and he will grow rich; from anyone who has not, even what he has will be taken away. **13** This is why I speak to them in parables, because 'they look but do not see and hear but do not listen or understand.' **14** Isaiah's prophecy is fulfilled in them, which says:

'You shall indeed hear but not understand,
    you shall indeed look but never see.
15 Gross is the heart of this people,
    they will hardly hear with their ears,
        they have closed their eyes,
        lest they see with their eyes
    and hear with their ears
and understand with their heart and be converted,
    and I heal them.'

16 "But blessed are your eyes, because they see, and your ears, because they hear. **17** Amen, I say to you, many prophets and righteous people longed to see what you see but did not see it, and to hear what you hear but did not hear it."

> Gospel parallels: Mark 4:10-12, 25; Luke 8:9-10, 18; 10:23-24
> OT:Isaiah 6:9-10
> NT:Matt 11:4-6, 25-27; 25:29; John 12:39-40; Acts 28:25-27; Rom 11:8

10 **The disciples approached him:** the **disciples** were last mentioned being in a house with Jesus (12:46-50). Unless Matthew is inserting an incident that took place sometime later, we might best picture them now being in the boat with Jesus (13:2) and leaning toward him to ask, **Why do you speak to them in parables?** Jesus spoke to the crowd from the boat "at length in parables" (13:3); Matthew has recounted one of them (13:3-9). Although Jesus has previously used comparisons that could be considered parables (5:13-16; 7:24-25; 9:15-17; 10:16) most of his teaching has been done in a straightforward, instructive manner (see Matt 5–7; 10). Jesus'

BACKGROUND: KINGDOM OF HEAVEN The kingdom of heaven is the characteristic way Matthew's gospel refers to the kingdom of God, reflecting the Jewish practice of avoiding using the name "God" out of reverence. The central theme of Jesus' preaching was that God was establishing his kingly rule: "The kingdom of God is at hand" (Mark 1:15). When Jesus spoke of the kingdom of God, he invoked Old Testament images of God reigning as king (Psalm 97:1; Isaiah 52:7), and so his listeners would have had some grasp of what he was talking about. Yet the expression "the kingdom of God" never occurs in the Hebrew Scriptures and is rarely found in the New Testament except on the lips of Jesus. The coming of the kingdom of God meant the coming of God's final triumph over evil; it meant the coming of God's direct, manifest reign over everyone and everything. Jesus' listeners would not necessarily have understood this to mean the end of space and time, but they would at least have understood it as the end of the world as they knew it, the end of a world shot through with evil and suffering, a world in which God's people were in bondage to their sins and to foreign domination. The kingdom of God was anticipated as the fulfillment of hopes engendered by Old Testament prophecies and by nonbiblical writings of the two centuries before Jesus. But because of the richness and diversity of these prophecies and writings, Jesus' listeners had no single blueprint in mind for what the reign of God would be like. Some expected God to free them from Roman rule; others expected God to accomplish a good deal more. Jesus used parables to convey what the reign of God was like. *Related topics: Jewish expectations at the time of Jesus (page 515), Nonbiblical writings (page 198).*

---

present recourse to parables seems sufficiently out of keeping with his previous manner of teaching that the disciples want to know **why**.

11 **He said to them in reply, "Because knowledge of the mysteries of the kingdom of heaven has been granted to you."** The word **mysteries** has the connotation of the secret purposes or plans of God (Rom 11:25; Eph 3:9); God must reveal them in order for them to be known (Dan 2:28; Rom 16:25). The **mysteries of the kingdom of heaven** are God's plans to establish his reign. Jesus has been proclaiming "the gospel of the kingdom" (4:23; 9:35), the good news that the reign of God is at hand (4:17) and is being inaugurated by him (12:28). **Knowledge** of this **has been granted** by God (see 11:25) to the disciples through Jesus' teachings. The disciples would be in the dark about what God is doing if Jesus had not made it known. Others are still in the dark: **but to them it has not been granted** to know the mysteries of the kingdom of heaven.

For reflection: What would I know of God apart from the revelation brought by Jesus?

12 To help explain why God's revelation has been granted to the disciples but not to others, Jesus invokes a proverb akin to "the rich get richer and the poor get poorer." **To anyone who has, more will be given and he will grow rich; from anyone who has not, even what he has will be taken away.** The Greek expression translated **grow rich** means to have an abundance. In the context of speaking about some but not others receiving God's revelation, the proverb means that to **anyone who has** some "knowledge of the mysteries of the kingdom of heaven" (verse 11), **more** knowledge of these mysteries **will be given** by God until she or he has an abundance of understanding. Jesus' disciples fall into this category: even though they still need to grow in their understanding of God's plans, Jesus reveals God to them and has given them some understanding. But **anyone who has not** understood Jesus' revelation of God, **even** whatever understanding he or she has of God **will be taken away.** To fail to understand Jesus' revelation is to fail to understand God. A prime example would be the Pharisees who accused Jesus of driving out demons by the power of Satan (12:24): they willfully closed their minds to Jesus, and closed minds end up in darkness.

Jesus is not distinguishing among people on the basis of how smart they are (see 11:25!) but on the basis of their receptivity to him and his teachings. Those who welcomed his message of the kingdom of God and responded to it are able to receive increasing understanding and insight from him; those who reject Jesus and his message are cutting themselves off from God's revelation.

For reflection: How has my submission to the will of God enabled me to understand God's will?

13 **This is why I speak to them in parables:** the **them** Jesus refers to are those who reject or are indifferent to him. Many in the crowd on the seashore apparently fall into this category (the towns Jesus reproached in 11:20-24 lie on or near the Sea of Galilee). **Parables** carry a message but are riddles to those who have no interest in their meaning. Jesus speaks **to them in parables because "they look but do not see and hear but do not listen or understand."** Another translation would be, "because seeing they do not see and hearing they do not hear nor do they understand." Jesus implies that their not seeing or hearing or understanding is willful. Those who reject him see the good he does by his healings and exorcisms but refuse to see him as God's agent; they hear his teachings but do not hear them as revelations from God; they refuse to understand what Jesus is about. Therefore, in response to their blindness and deafness and refusal to understand, Jesus speaks to them in parables, in veiled speech, in words that will not be understood by those who have no interest in understanding him.

14 Jesus' speaking about those who "look but do not see and hear but do not listen or understand" (verse 13) echoes a prophecy of Isaiah, as is now made explicit. **Isaiah's prophecy is fulfilled in them, which says: "You shall indeed hear but not understand, / you shall indeed look but never see."** What Isaiah prophesied about **is fulfilled** in those who are willfully rejecting Jesus. Jesus goes on to quote the remainder of Isaiah's prophecy.

15 **Gross is the heart of this people**—a condition akin to hardness of heart. **They will hardly hear with their ears,** for they do not want to hear. **They have closed their eyes, / lest they see with their eyes** what they do not want to see **and hear with their ears / and understand with their heart and**

be converted. Were they to **see** and **hear** and **understand** and **be converted,** then God would **heal them.** Because they do not want to be converted and change their ways, they refuse to see what God is doing and to hear and understand his word to them; thus they will not be healed.

> *Go and say to this people:*
> *Listen carefully, but you shall not understand!*
> *Look intently, but you shall know nothing!*
> *You are to make the heart of this people sluggish,*
> *to dull their ears and close their eyes;*
> *Else their eyes will see, their ears hear,*
> *their heart understand,*
> *and they will turn and be healed.*
> *Isaiah 6:9-10*

In the context of Isaiah being called by God to be a prophet (Isaiah 6:1-8), this prophecy is God's warning to Isaiah that his words will fall on deaf ears (see Jer 7:25-27 for a similar warning that a prophet's message will be ignored). Matthew's gospel, written in Greek, quotes the Greek translation of Isaiah found in the Septuagint (the ancient Greek translation of the Old Testament used by Greek-speaking Christians). There are some differences in nuance between Isaiah's prophecy in Hebrew and its Greek translation. In the Greek translation the responsibility for not seeing and hearing and understanding rests with those who do not see and hear and understand.

16 The disciples of Jesus stand in sharp contrast to those who refuse to see and hear, and Jesus proclaims their happiness with a beatitude: **But blessed are your eyes, because they see, and your ears, because they hear.** The Greek of Matthew's gospel puts an emphasis on **your:** Jesus tells his disciples, *you* are blessed because *you* see and hear and understand. They have seen what Jesus does (11:4-6) and have heard his words; they have embraced him and his teachings (11:25; 12:49-50). Therefore they are **blessed,** fortunate, happy.

Beatitudes: See page 73

17 The disciples may not realize just how privileged they are. Jesus solemnly assures them, **Amen, I say to you, many prophets and righteous people**

longed to see what you see but did not see it, and to hear what you hear but did not hear it. The prophets and righteous people who lived before the time of Jesus longed for God to vanquish evil and establish his reign on earth. Jesus could have reminded his disciples of many Old Testament prophecies that spoke of God restoring his people. However, such prophecies were so familiar to every devout Jew that there was no need for Jesus to quote them. The prophets who delivered these prophecies and the righteous people who accepted them longed to see the fulfillment of what God had promised but did not see it. They longed to hear the announcement that the reign of God was at hand but did not hear it. Jesus' disciples are privileged and blessed indeed, because they are able to hear Jesus proclaim that the reign of God is at hand and see Jesus inaugurate God's reign (11:4-5; 12:28).

In explaining why he tells parables, Jesus has spoken about those who do not accept or understand him. His initial and final focus, however, is on those who do accept and understand him. They have been granted "knowledge of the mysteries of the kingdom of heaven," of God's plan to establish his reign (verse 11); they are blessed because they can see God's plan unfolding in Jesus (verses 16-17).

For reflection: What are my greatest blessings? Where does being a disciple of Jesus rank in my list of blessings?

Hearing the Word with Understanding

18 "Hear then the parable of the sower. 19 The seed sown on the path is the one who hears the word of the kingdom without understanding it, and the evil one comes and steals away what was sown in his heart. 20 The seed sown on rocky ground is the one who hears the word and receives it at once with joy. 21 But he has no root and lasts only for a time. When some tribulation or persecution comes because of the word, he immediately falls away. 22 The seed sown among thorns is the one who hears the word, but then worldly anxiety and the lure of riches choke the word and it bears no fruit. 23 But the seed sown on rich soil is the one who hears the word and understands it, who indeed bears fruit and yields a hundred or sixty or thirtyfold."

Gospel parallels: Mark 4:13-20; Luke 8:11-15
NT: Matt 13:3-9

18 Jesus continues to speak to his disciples about those who do and do not understand the mysteries of the kingdom of heaven (13:10-17). His parable about seeds falling on different kinds of ground (13:3-9) can apply to the mixed response Jesus has received. Jesus tells his disciples, **Hear then the parable of the sower.** Jesus refers to the parable as **the parable of the sower** not because the parable focuses on the sower but to identify it by its opening words (13:3). (Similarly, the Hebrew name for the Book of Genesis is its first word in Hebrew.) In the Greek of Matthew's gospel, Jesus' exhortation to his disciples begins with an emphatic *you* and has the sense, "You, therefore, hear and grasp the meaning of the parable of the sower." His disciples have been blessed with an understanding of how God is establishing his reign (13:11, 16-17); Jesus wants to increase their understanding.

19 **The seed sown on the path is the one who hears the word of the kingdom without understanding it:** the **word of the kingdom** is "the gospel of the kingdom" (4:23; 9:35), the good news Jesus brings that the kingdom of God is at hand (4:17). The **word of the kingdom** would broadly include all that Jesus preached and taught and, in the time of Matthew, the preaching and teaching of the church. Some hear this preaching and teaching **without understanding it:** Jesus has just spoken of those who do not understand because they do not want to understand (13:13-15). Anyone who **hears** Jesus' preaching and teaching **without understanding it** is like **the seed sown on the path** in the parable. Such seed made easy pickings for birds (13:4), and someone who does not understand and accept Jesus' message makes easy picking for Satan: **the evil one comes and steals away what was sown in his heart.** Even if **the word of the kingdom** was **sown in his heart,** it never penetrated because his heart was set against accepting Jesus' words. Some have heard Jesus' preaching and teaching but have not given him a hearing (11:19); his words and deeds have elicited no response (11:20-24).

Kingdom of heaven: See page 266

20 **The seed sown on rocky ground is the one who hears the word** of the kingdom **and receives it at once with joy.** This person not only **hears** but **receives** and accepts the message, doing so immediately and **with joy.** Fresh converts may be filled with great enthusiasm. So far, so good!

21 **But he has no root and lasts only for a time.** The joy of conversion cannot by itself sustain a converted life. Taking the message of Jesus to heart requires changing our hearts, our values, our priorities. Anyone who does not let the words of Jesus penetrate ever more deeply is like a sprout that **has no root;** he or she **lasts only for a time** as a disciple of Jesus. For **when some tribulation or persecution comes because of the word, he** or she **immediately falls away.** Jesus takes it for granted that his followers will face hardships. **Tribulation** can mean any kind of affliction, but Jesus' meaning is narrower: he refers to **tribulation or persecution** that **comes** to disciples **because** they have embraced **the word.** They suffer hardship and persecution precisely because they are disciples (see 5:10-12; 10:16-36). Anyone whose commitment to Jesus **has no root**—who will remain faithful as long as commitment means a comfortable life, who is carried along only by joy—**immediately falls away** when **some tribulation or persecution comes.** The Greek for **falls away** literally means "be tripped up by an obstacle." Shallow faith cannot surmount obstacles.

22 **The seed sown among thorns is the one who hears the word**—and, implicitly, accepts it—**but then worldly anxiety and the lure of riches choke the word and it bears no fruit.** Those who survive hardship and opposition may stumble over other obstacles. **Worldly anxiety** refers to concerns and worries about the things of this life. Jesus dealt with such anxieties, instructing his listeners, "Do not worry about your life, what you will eat . . . or about your body, what you will wear" (6:25) and "Do not worry about tomorrow" (6:34). Succumbing to worries reveals a lack of trust in our heavenly Father's care for us (6:26, 32-33). The expression, **the lure of riches,** has a range of meanings: the seductiveness of wealth, the deceptions of wealth, the pleasures of being wealthy. Seeking and serving wealth is incompatible with seeking and serving God (6:19-21, 24). Anxieties and the lure of wealth are like **thorns** that **choke** out the life of discipleship, smothering **the word** of Jesus so that **it bears no fruit**

in and through us. As before, **fruit** stands for deeds, for doing the will of God (7:16-21; 12:33).

For reflection: What anxieties and desires are obstacles to my bearing fruit?

23 But the seed sown on rich soil is the one who hears the word and understands it, who accepts and comprehends the word and shapes his or her life accordingly. Such a person is able to withstand hardships that come as a result of being a disciple of Jesus; such a person is not sidetracked by anxieties or by the attractions of wealth. Therefore she or he **indeed bears fruit and yields a hundred or sixty or thirtyfold.** The Greek for **yields** is the word for "produces" or "does"; **fruit** again stands for deeds. The one who hears the word and really **understands it** puts the word into action (7:24), doing the will of the heavenly Father (7:21). The test for hearing the message of Jesus with understanding is whether one bears fruit, whether what one *does* is in line with what one hears. The one who really grasps and accepts the message of Jesus **yields a hundred or sixty or thirtyfold.** All are good harvests; the different **yields** may simply indicate that some bear more fruit than others.

In the context of the ministry of Jesus, the parable applies to the mixed responses Jesus has received. Some have been unmoved by his words; some perhaps followed him for a while but have fallen away; some have persevered, growing in understanding, and are on their way to yielding a harvest.

In the context of Matthew's community, the parable speaks to the mixed response the gospel has received. Some have rejected it, including Jewish leaders in competition with Matthew's church for the allegiance of Jews. Some embraced the gospel with joy but have fallen away in the face of hardships and persecutions. Others have been distracted by worldly concerns and a desire for wealth. Still others have accepted and understood the gospel and put it into practice, yielding a rich harvest.

Jesus' explanation of the parable poses questions for readers today. What kind of soil am I? Does how I live indicate that I have grasped and accepted the gospel of Jesus? What fruit is my life yielding?

For reflection: What questions does this parable pose to me?

ORIENTATION: *Matthew resumes recounting the parables Jesus told to a crowd on the seashore.*

The Parable of the Weeds among the Wheat

24 He proposed another parable to them. "The kingdom of heaven may be likened to a man who sowed good seed in his field. **25** While everyone was asleep his enemy came and sowed weeds all through the wheat, and then went off. **26** When the crop grew and bore fruit, the weeds appeared as well. **27** The slaves of the householder came to him and said, 'Master, did you not sow good seed in your field? Where have the weeds come from?' **28** He answered, 'An enemy has done this.' His slaves said to him, 'Do you want us to go and pull them up?' **29** He replied, 'No, if you pull up the weeds you might uproot the wheat along with them. **30** Let them grow together until harvest; then at harvest time I will say to the harvesters, "First collect the weeds and tie them in bundles for burning; but gather the wheat into my barn.""

NT: Matt 13:36-43

24 **He proposed another parable to them:** Jesus is in a boat, speaking "at length in parables" to a crowd gathered on the shore of the Sea of Galilee (13:2-3). Matthew recounted the parable about seeds falling on different kinds of ground (13:3-9), but interrupted his account of what Jesus said to the crowd to relate what Jesus said to his disciples (13:10-23). Now Matthew returns to the parables that Jesus addresses to the crowd (see 13:34).

Parables: See page 262

The kingdom of heaven may be likened to a man who sowed good seed in his field. Jesus has announced that the **kingdom of heaven** is at hand (4:17) and is breaking into the world through his ministry (12:28), but Jesus has not explained what the kingdom of heaven is. Jesus does not offer a definition but employs parables or comparisons to convey what the kingdom of heaven is like. In this parable, the **kingdom of heaven** is being **likened** not simply to a **man** who sowed seed in a field but to the whole situation presented in the parable.

Kingdom of heaven: See page 266

25 **While everyone was asleep his enemy came** under the cover of darkness **and sowed weeds all through** the field that had just been sown with **wheat, and then went off.** The Greek word translated **weeds** refers to a noxious grasslike plant that resembles wheat in its early stages of growth.

26 **When the crop grew and bore fruit, the weeds appeared as well.** The wheat and the weeds sprout up mixed together.

27 Eventually someone detects the weeds and raises the alarm. **The slaves of the householder came to him and said, "Master, did you not sow good seed in your field?"** The word translated **Master** is translated "lord" in some contexts. Here it has the connotation of ownership: the **Master** owns **slaves** as well as farmland and a house. The question, **Master, did you not sow good seed in your field?** is rhetorical. Of course he sowed **good seed:** no farmer in his right mind would sow weeds. So **where have the weeds come from?**

Servant, slave: See page 429
Lord: See page 133

28 **He answered, "An enemy has done this."** The master does not name the enemy or explain why he acted so maliciously; he simply attributes the presence of weeds to **an enemy.** In response, **his slaves said to him, "Do you want us to go and pull them up?"** If the weeds were allowed to grow and were harvested with the wheat and milled together, the resulting flour would be toxic. The slaves seem to presume that they would be able to separate the weeds from the wheat, and they are looking for the go-ahead to do so.

29 **He replied, "No, if you pull up the weeds you might uproot the wheat along with them."** The **weeds** and **wheat** have grown together so that their roots are intertwined. Pulling out the weeds would **uproot the wheat** as well and destroy the crop.

30 The master instructs his slaves, **Let them grow together until harvest; then at harvest time I will say to the harvesters, "First collect the weeds."** In Jesus' parable, the master does not spell out every step in the harvesting process; everyone in Jesus' audience would have known how grain crops were harvested. Grain fields were cut down with a scythe, with

the stalks gathered by armfuls and carried to a barn or threshing floor. The master will instruct his harvesters, After you have scythed the field and sorted out the weed stalks from the wheat stalks, **collect the weeds and tie them in bundles for burning** in cooking fires, **but gather the wheat into my barn.** While the wheat was growing, the weeds could not be removed without uprooting the wheat. Only at harvest time, after the field has been cut, can the sorting out take place.

Like most of Jesus' parables, the parable of the weeds among the wheat has different applications and shades of meaning in different contexts. In the context of Jesus' ministry, the first stirrings of the kingdom of heaven are like a field with wheat and weeds mixed together. Jesus has sown good seed by his preaching and teaching, his healings and exorcisms, yet Jesus' efforts have not resulted in a weed-free crop. Those who gather around Jesus include sinners in need of divine healing (9:10-13). Some may think that Jesus needs to do a housecleaning and make a clear distinction between those who are completely with him and all others (12:30). Some Jewish groups of the time, such as Pharisees and Essenes, drew lines between themselves and outsiders. John the Baptist expected the one coming after him to "gather his wheat into his barn, but the chaff he will burn with unquenchable fire" (3:12), but Jesus has not done this. Jesus has welcomed everyone to himself (11:28), regardless of their condition. Jesus' parable conveys that sorting out the unrighteous from the righteous is not part of the coming of the kingdom of heaven at this point in his ministry. There will be a sorting out down the road, but for now the presence of weeds in the crop Jesus planted is to be tolerated.

For Matthew's first readers, the parable bore lessons about tolerance and patient forbearance within the church community. Some Christians might profess faith in Jesus as Lord and perform mighty works in his name, yet fall so short of obeying God's will that Jesus will label them "evildoers" (7:21-23). Trying to purge the community of all who might fall short of God's will would cause horrible turmoil in the church. Jesus commanded that his followers refrain from judging others (7:1); critical judgments should be directed against oneself (7:3-5). The church will be made up of sinners and saints until the final harvest.

For reflection: What lessons does this parable hold for me about tolerance and patient forbearance?

Mustard Seed and Leaven
31 He proposed another parable to them. "The kingdom of heaven is like a mustard seed that a person took and sowed in a field. **32** It is the smallest of all the seeds, yet when full-grown it is the largest of plants. It becomes a large bush, and the 'birds of the sky come and dwell in its branches.'"

33 He spoke to them another parable. "The kingdom of heaven is like yeast that a woman took and mixed with three measures of wheat flour until the whole batch was leavened."

Gospel parallels: Mark 4:30-32; Luke 13:18-21
OT: Ezek 31:6; Dan 4:9

31 He proposed another parable to them: Jesus has told two parables involving seeds (13:3-9, 24-30) and now he tells **another parable** featuring seeds. **The kingdom of heaven is like a mustard seed that a person took and sowed in a field.** While **mustard** plants were grown for the flavorful oil in their seeds, there is a something out of the ordinary in a person going to a field and planting a single **mustard seed.** Farmers normally sow many seeds, expecting that not all will produce a harvest (see 13:4-7). **The kingdom of heaven is** somehow **like** a person sowing **a mustard seed** with confidence that it will grow into a plant.

Parables: See page 262
Kingdom of heaven: See page 266

32 It is the smallest of all the seeds: in the world of Jesus, a mustard seed was invoked as the ultimate in tininess (see 17:20). **Yet when full-grown it is the largest of plants.** Mustard is an annual herb that usually grows to a height of two to six feet, but sometimes to eight feet or higher. **It becomes a large bush**—the Greek literally reads that it becomes a tree—**and the "birds of the sky come and dwell in its branches."** There is a great contrast between how small a mustard seed is and how large a plant it produces. It is an exaggeration to characterize a fully grown mustard plant as a tree, but doing so may be an allusion to the Old Testament's use of a tree as a symbol for a great kingdom (Ezek 17:22-24; 31:3-9; Dan 4:7-9). Saying that **Birds of the sky come and dwell in its branches** suggests the idea of a kingdom sheltering its people (Ezek 31:6; Dan 4:9).

If before telling this parable Jesus had taken an opinion survey of the crowd on the seashore and asked them, "What will it be like when God establishes his reign?" he might have gotten answers ranging from "It will be like a general leading an army to liberate us from Roman rule" to "It will be a like an angel with a fiery sword striking down evildoers and announcing the arrival of the age to come." It is very doubtful that anyone would have suggested, "It will be like a man planting a tiny seed that grows into a plant large enough to shelter birds in its branches." Yet Jesus says that this is what the kingdom of heaven is like.

For reflection: What does Jesus' parable convey to me about the kingdom of God?

The ministry of Jesus has been but a mustard seed in the field of the world. He has attracted attention wherever he has gone, but he has not traveled very far; he has healed the afflicted but not made much of a dent in the sufferings of the world; he has attracted a band of followers, but they are very few out of all the women and men on earth. Jesus' parable acknowledges that the first stirrings of the kingdom of heaven are quite modest. But this tiny seed will grow into a large plant; it will become a great kingdom offering shelter. Only one seed needed to be planted: Jesus' mission of establishing God's reign. This small seed will succeed.

The parable of the mustard seed carried a message of encouragement for Matthew's first readers. Although the church was growing, it was still quite insignificant in comparison to the Roman Empire. The modest scope of the church should not cause doubt or discouragement.

For reflection: Am I beset by doubts or discouragement over the coming of God's reign? What is the message of the parable of the mustard seed for me?

33 **He spoke to them another parable,** pairing it with the previous parable. The parable of the mustard seed was based on farming, men's work; Jesus' next parable is based on baking, women's work. **The kingdom of heaven is like yeast that a woman took and mixed with three measures of wheat flour until the whole batch was leavened.** At the time of Jesus, **yeast** (a better translation would be "leaven") was sourdough, that is, leavened dough kept unbaked from previous bread making. A little leavened dough could leaven a whole new batch of dough (see Gal 5:9). This woman prepares a huge batch, using **three measures of wheat flour—** about fifty pounds of wheat, enough to make bread for over one hundred

people. The woman **mixed** (literally, "hid") the leavening in the flour **until the whole batch was leavened.**

Jesus proclaims that **the kingdom of heaven is like** leaven that permeates and transforms a huge batch of dough. God is establishing his reign not through earthly or heavenly armies but through Jesus' walking from village to village in rural Galilee, quietly going about his mission (12:15-21). Despite such modest, almost hidden beginnings, there will be great results.

Matthew's first readers may have found encouragement in the notion that the reign of God is like leaven, quietly but surely transforming the world. They might have found leaven a good image for their own roles of service: even if they were not in a position to accomplish great things, they were able to do small things, leavening the lives of those around them.

For reflection: How am I to be a leaven in my own personal circumstances?

The Significance of Telling Parables

34 All these things Jesus spoke to the crowds in parables. He spoke to them only in parables, 35 to fulfill what had been said through the prophet:

> **"I will open my mouth in parables,**
> **I will announce what has lain hidden from the foundation**
> **[of the world]."**
> Gospel parallels: Mark 4:33-34
> OT: Psalm 78:1-2

34 **All these things Jesus spoke to the crowds in parables.** Jesus addressed a crowd gathered on the shore of the Sea of Galilee and "spoke to them at length in parables" (13:2-3); Matthew recounted four of the **parables** (13:3-9, 24-33). **He spoke to them only in parables:** Jesus adopted parables as his manner of speaking to crowds. He explains to his disciples that he does so because many in the crowds have little interest in his message (13:10-15): Jesus speaks to veiled minds in veiled speech. Matthew now adds another explanation for why Jesus speaks to the crowds **only in parables.**

Parables: See page 262

35 Jesus speaks in parables **to fulfill what had been said through the prophet:** although Matthew characterizes the words that follow as having been said by a **prophet,** they are from Psalm 78. We might best understand **what had been said through the prophet** as what had been said prophetically in Scripture. Matthew periodically points out how Jesus has fulfilled Scripture (1:22; 2:15, 17, 23; 4:14; 8:17; 12:17) and does so again here.

> *Attend, my people, to my teaching;*
>> *listen to the words of my mouth.*
> *I will open my mouth in story,*
>> *drawing lessons from of old.*
>> Psalm 78:1-2

Psalm 78 recites the history of God's people beginning with their exodus from Egypt; the opening verses of this psalm are an invitation to listen to and learn from this history. Matthew understands Jesus' telling parables as a fulfillment of the promise, **I will open my mouth in parables, / I will announce what has lain hidden from the foundation [of the world].** (Matthew uses a Greek version of the psalm that is somewhat different from the Hebrew text translated in the New American Bible.) While Psalm 78 looks back on the exodus from Egypt as the beginning of Israel's story, Jesus' **parables** deal with something that has much earlier roots: they **announce what has lain hidden from the foundation [of the world].** What has been **hidden** up until Jesus are "the mysteries of the kingdom of heaven" (13:11), God's plans to establish his reign. Jesus has told four parables to convey what God's reign is like (13:3-9, 24-33). Jesus' parables may be puzzling to those who are not receptive (3:13-15), but his parable-telling is a fulfillment of Scripture and part of his mission to make God known (11:25-27). The mysteries of God cannot be captured in simple definitions but must be announced in the elusive and evocative speech of parables.

> *For reflection: What does Jesus' using parables to speak about the hidden plans of God tell me about these plans?*

An Interpretation of the Parable of the Weeds

36 Then, dismissing the crowds, he went into the house. His disciples approached him and said, "Explain to us the parable of the weeds in the

field." [37] He said in reply, "He who sows good seed is the Son of Man, [38] the field is the world, the good seed the children of the kingdom. The weeds are the children of the evil one, [39] and the enemy who sows them is the devil. The harvest is the end of the age, and the harvesters are angels. [40] Just as weeds are collected and burned [up] with fire, so will it be at the end of the age. [41] The Son of Man will send his angels, and they will collect out of his kingdom all who cause others to sin and all evildoers. [42] They will throw them into the fiery furnace, where there will be wailing and grinding of teeth. [43] Then the righteous will shine like the sun in the kingdom of their Father. Whoever has ears ought to hear."

NT: Matt 13:24-30; 1 Cor 15:24-25

36 **Then, dismissing the crowds,** who had been standing on the seashore listening to his parables (13:2-9, 24-35), Jesus **went into the house.** Before telling parables to the crowds, Jesus had been in a house with his disciples (12:49–13:1). Now he goes back **into the house.** It might have been Peter's house in Capernaum (8:14), but whose house and where it is located are not of concern to Matthew. Matthew's interest lies in Jesus' sending the crowds away so that he is able to instruct **his disciples.**

They **approached him and said, "Explain to us the parable of the weeds in the field."** Jesus told a parable about a man sowing wheat in his field, an enemy sowing weeds among the wheat, and the owner of the field allowing them to grow together until harvest (13:24-30). The disciples want Jesus to explain the parable. They call it **the parable of the weeds in the field** even though wheat figures as prominently in the parable as **weeds.** Jesus' interpretation will deal largely with the weeds.

Disciple: See page 66

37 **He said in reply, "He who sows good seed is the Son of Man."** Jesus uses the expression, **the Son of Man,** as a way of referring to himself (8:20; 9:6; 10:23; 11:19; 12:8, 32, 40), and he identifies himself as the sower.

Son of Man: See page 151

38 Jesus sows not merely in Galilee; **the field** that Jesus sows **is the world.** Jesus' mission is universal and extends to the entire earth. The **good seed** that Jesus sows is **the children of the kingdom.** We might have expected Jesus to say that he sows the message of the kingdom, but he interprets what he sows as those who respond to his message. **The children of the**

kingdom are women and men who belong to the kingdom of heaven, who embrace the teachings of Jesus and do the will of God (7:21; 12:50). **The weeds are the children of the evil one.** The expression **the evil one** refers to Satan (5:37; 6:13; 13:19), who is also called the devil (verse 39); **the children of the evil one** are men and women under the sway of Satan. In Jesus' interpretation of the parable, the **world** seems made up of only two kinds of people: **children of the kingdom** and **children of the evil one.** A reason for this stark, either-or view will emerge shortly.

Satan: See page 55

39 The presence of children of the evil one in the world is due to Satan: **the enemy who sows them is the devil.** Jesus is overcoming Satan and establishing the reign of God, as is evident by his exorcisms (12:28-29). Yet Jesus' interpretation of the parable presents children of the kingdom and children of the evil one living together in the world, like wheat and weeds growing together in a field. Jesus does not speak of the children of the kingdom steadily overcoming or replacing the children of the evil one. In the parable, the wheat does not crowd out the weeds.

> *For reflection: What is my reaction to the picture Jesus paints of evil continuing in the world despite his mission?*

The harvest is the end of the age: like wheat and weeds growing together until **the harvest,** good and evil will coexist in the world until **the end of the age.** Jesus has spoken of two ages, "this age" in which we now live and "the age to come" when God's reign will be complete (12:32). Just as Jesus' mission extends to the entire world (verse 38), so his mission of raising up children of the kingdom will continue until **the end of the age.** Then there will be a **harvest:** prophets used a harvest as an image for judgment (Jer 51:33; Hosea 6:11; Joel 4:12-13). **The harvesters are angels,** serving as divine helpers, gathering men and women for judgment (see also 24:31).

The age to come: See page 250
Judgment: See page 557
Angels: See page 33

40 Jesus has interpreted seven elements of his parable (sower, field, good seed, weeds, enemy, harvest, harvesters) but has passed over other elements, such

as the impracticality of trying to uproot the weeds and the need for patient tolerance until harvest time. His interpretation focuses on certain elements of the parable in order to make an application. He now interprets an eighth element from the parable—burning in a fire—at some length; it is the focal point of his interpretation. **Just as weeds are collected and burned [up] with fire:** in the parable, the **weeds** are sorted out from the wheat after the field has been cut and are bundled for use as fuel in cooking fires (13:30). **So will it be at the end of the age:** something analogous to burning in fire will happen when God brings this age to an end.

41 **The Son of Man will send his angels:** angels are messengers and agents of God, but Jesus speaks of himself as **the Son of Man** being able to command and **send his angels.** In the context of Jesus' mission in Galilee, this is an exalted claim for Jesus to make about himself. For Matthew's church, however, "all power in heaven and on earth" had been given to the risen Jesus (28:18). Matthew's readers would have understood Jesus' speaking of himself here as **the Son of Man** as a way of referring to himself in his future position, seated at the right hand of God (26:64) and sharing God's authority. He will send his angels, **and they will collect out of his kingdom all who cause others to sin and all evildoers.** The Greek for **all who cause others to sin** means all stumbling blocks, all who trip up others and lead them astray. **All evildoers** is literally "the doers of lawlessness," all who do not do the will of God (see 7:21-23). We might expect Jesus to say that the angels will collect those who do evil out of the world—but Jesus says that they will collect them **out of his kingdom.** We might best understand Jesus to refer to his power and reign over the world after his resurrection (28:18), a reign that will be manifest at the end of this age (16:27). That **evildoers** will be found in **his kingdom** means that the world—and even the church (7:15, 21-23)—is a mixture of good and evil.

42 **They will throw them into the fiery furnace:** the cooking-fire fate of the weeds in the parable becomes an image for the eternal fate of evildoers who are excluded from the kingdom of God. Jesus has spoken of Gehenna as a place of fiery punishment (5:22), and he will use the image of fiery punishment again (13:50; 25:41); a **fiery furnace** echoes an expression found in the Book of Daniel (Dan 3:6). In the fiery furnace, **there will be wailing and grinding of teeth,** an idiom for being in great distress (8:12; 13:50; 22:13; 24:51; 25:30).

43 In his interpretation of the parable, Jesus has dwelt upon the fate of sinners at some length (verses 40-42); the fate of the children of the kingdom receives briefer mention: **Then the righteous will shine like the sun in the kingdom of their Father.** The righteous are those who do the will of God and enter into the kingdom of heaven (5:20; 7:21). To **shine like the sun** echoes the Book of Daniel's speaking of the just rising to "shine brightly / like the splendor of the firmament" (Dan 12:2-3). Shining like a brilliant light can also be an image for experiencing and sharing the glory of God, who "dwells in unapproachable light" (1 Tim 6:16; see also Rev 21:23). During his transfiguration Jesus will shine like the sun (17:2), as a foretaste of his risen glory and of the glory of those who rise with him.

> *For reflection: Is my life's primary goal to one day shine like the sun in the presence of my heavenly Father? What am I doing to achieve this goal?*

Jesus has spoken of sending his angels to collect evildoers out of "his kingdom" (verse 41); they will gather the righteous as well (24:31) and bring them into **the kingdom of their Father.** Jesus speaks of two kingdoms in his interpretation of the parable: a kingdom, or reign, of Jesus that lasts until the end of the age, and a kingdom of the Father in the age to come. Paul spoke similarly about the work of Jesus in relation to his Father when he wrote that Jesus "must reign until he has put all his enemies under his feet." Then "comes the end" when Jesus "hands over the kingdom to his God and Father" (1 Cor 15:24, 25). Usually, however, Jesus speaks of the kingdom in this age as the kingdom of God, not his (Jesus') kingdom (see 12:28, for example).

Jesus concludes his interpretation of the parable by saying, **Whoever has ears ought to hear,** an exhortation to his listeners to understand what he has just said (see 11:15; 13:9). What has Jesus said? He has spoken of the glorious fate of the righteous: they will shine like the sun in their Father's kingdom. Nevertheless, his interpretation of the parable focuses on the children of the evil one and their punishment: he has indeed made it into "the parable of the weeds in the field" (verse 36). While his parable about the wheat and weeds growing together taught the need for patient tolerance (13:24-30), his interpretation of this parable warns against being an evildoer who will end up in a fiery furnace. We are to be tolerant of the shortcomings of others, but it is dangerous to be tolerant of our own sins—eternally dangerous.

Jesus' interpretation of the parable divides the world into children of the kingdom and children of the evil one; there is no in-between category for those who fall short of doing God's will but are not so wicked as to be children of Satan. Yet most of us seem to ourselves to fall somewhere in the middle. We are not so holy that we will be hailed as saints after we die; we are not so evil that we deserve a death penalty in this life or the next. Ultimately, however, we will be either with God in eternity or in the tragic state Jesus symbolizes by a fiery furnace. Jesus' interpretation of the parable projects onto this life the reality of the next: we are now either on our way to God or we are not. **Whoever has ears ought to hear** and understand the eternal consequences of their decisions and actions.

For reflection: What have I heard in Jesus' interpretation of the parable of the weeds?

Why would Jesus deliver such a stark message to his disciples? Perhaps as a wake-up call, conveying, "Pay attention to what I will go on to say to you; do what is necessary to enter the kingdom."

Giving All to Gain All

⁴⁴ "The kingdom of heaven is like a treasure buried in a field, which a person finds and hides again, and out of joy goes and sells all that he has and buys that field. ⁴⁵ Again, the kingdom of heaven is like a merchant searching for fine pearls. ⁴⁶ When he finds a pearl of great price, he goes and sells all that he has and buys it."

NT: Matt 6:33; 10:39; Phil 3:7-11

44 Jesus, in a house with his disciples (13:36), continues to instruct them. He tells them **the kingdom of heaven is like a treasure buried in a field.** In an age before safe-deposit boxes, it was a common practice to bury valuables in the ground (25:18, 25) to hide them from burglars (6:19; 24:43). The **treasure** might have been a jug of valuable coins or jewelry. If the one who buried the valuables died without telling anyone what he or she had buried and where, it could lie undetected indefinitely. **A person finds** a treasure buried in a field. Since the Greek word for **field** primarily refers to land that was farmed, we might imagine a farmworker or day laborer plowing a field and unearthing the treasure. He **hides** the treasure **again,** reburying it. He does not make off with the treasure but takes steps that give him legal claim to the treasure: he **goes and sells all that he has and buys that field.** He is not a wealthy man—certainly not if he is a farmworker or day laborer—and he has to sell **all that he has** to be able to buy the field. This he does gladly, **out of joy:** he is obtaining something worth far more than it costs him.

The **kingdom of heaven is like** this **treasure** that a man discovered and acquired. He was not searching for treasure when he came across it; the good news of the kingdom of God sometimes breaks into our lives unexpectedly, filling us with joy. There is a cost to entering the kingdom, but the cost—even if it means giving up everything—is insignificant compared to what we receive.

Kingdom of heaven: See page 266

For reflection: How did I discover the treasure of the gospel?

45 **Again, the kingdom of heaven is like a merchant searching for fine pearls.** In the world of Jesus, **pearls** were valued more highly than they are now and were very expensive, perhaps comparable to diamonds today. The Greek word translated **merchant** means a wholesale dealer, not a shopkeeper; since pearls were very expensive, the merchant was presumably a person of means. Pearls were imported from India; this pearl **merchant** could have been an importer. He was traveling about **searching for fine pearls,** seeking the very best.

46 His search is successful, and **he finds a pearl of great price,** an extraordinarily valuable pearl, a pearl of a pearl. **He goes and sells all that he has and buys it.** He does not merely sell off his inventory of other pearls but **sells all that he has,** however considerable his holdings might be. His quest was for the finest of pearls, and he is willing to trade everything for this truly great pearl.

The **kingdom of heaven is like** the pearl that the merchant searched for and discovered and bought, selling all to do so. Some of us have found God and his reign at the end of a long search. We had some idea of what we were looking for, but were nevertheless awed by the greatness of what we discovered. Even if it means giving up everything else, attaining what we were searching for is a bargain.

For reflection: What have I longed for and searched for and found? What am I still searching for?

The man who discovered the hidden treasure was presumably an ordinary worker of modest means; the merchant who found the magnificent pearl was a man of some wealth. One found his treasure accidentally, the other at the end of a search. Despite their differences, there are important similarities between them. Both were willing to give all to gain greater; both end up with something of awesome value. The primary lesson of the two parables is found in their common elements.

The context of these parables in Matthew's gospel gives them particular significance. They follow a sobering warning against ending up in a fiery furnace in the age to come (13:36-42). The parables of the treasure and the pearl are an invitation to the disciples to joyfully seize the treasure of shining "like the sun in the kingdom of their Father" (13:43), even at the cost of giving up everything. The mysteries of the kingdom of heaven have been revealed to them (13:11; see also 11:25-27); what they have seen and heard makes them truly blessed (13:16-17). Now they have the opportunity to seek first the kingdom of God (6:33), counting everything else as loss for its sake.

Every subsequent disciple of Jesus is faced with the same opportunity. Every disciple must embrace losing her or his life in order to gain eternal life (10:39). Paul, for one, was willing to pay the price (Phil 3:7-11).

For reflection: Am I willing to give all to gain all? What is holding me back?

The Sorting Out
⁴⁷ "Again, the kingdom of heaven is like a net thrown into the sea, which collects fish of every kind. ⁴⁸ When it is full they haul it ashore and sit down to put what is good into buckets. What is bad they throw away. ⁴⁹ Thus it will be at the end of the age. The angels will go out and separate the wicked from the righteous ⁵⁰ and throw them into the fiery furnace, where there will be wailing and grinding of teeth."

OT:Lev 11:9-12; Deut 14:9-10
NT:Matt 4:19; 13:36-43; 22:10-14

47 Again, the kingdom of heaven is like a net thrown into the sea, which collects fish of every kind. Jesus often bases his parables on the experiences of his listeners. Some of his disciples had been commercial fishermen

(4:18-22); all of them would likely have seen fishermen at work. The Greek word for **net** means a dragnet, deployed between two boats. Lowered into the sea, the net **collects fish of every kind.** The New American Bible supplies the word **fish,** but Matthew's Greek is not so specific; the Greek literally reads that the net "collects from every kind" or species. All kinds of things end up in fishermen's nets: fish and eels and crabs and seaweed. Fishermen wish that their nets would snare only marketable fish, but that is not the way nets work.

Kingdom of heaven: See page 266

Fishing: See page 65

48 **When it is full they haul it ashore.** It is inefficient to row to shore dragging a half-filled net; fishermen keep a net deployed until it is **full** and then **haul it ashore and sit down to put what is good into buckets.** A **good** catch is something that can be eaten, and for commercial fishermen something that can be sold. The law of Moses distinguishes between clean and unclean sea creatures, limiting Jewish consumption to certain kinds of fish (Lev 11:9-12; Deut 14:9-10). Everything else snagged in a fishing net is a worthless nuisance for fishermen. **What is bad**—inedible or unclean—**they throw away.**

Jesus tells his disciples that the kingdom of heaven and its coming is like a fishing net collecting all kinds of things, which the fishermen then sort out, keeping what is usable and throwing away the rest. Jesus goes on to interpret one element of this comparison.

49 **Thus it will be at the end of the age,** when the age in which we live gives way to "the age to come" (12:32). There will be a final sorting out: **the angels will go out and separate the wicked from the righteous.** Just as fishermen sort their catch, separating what is inedible from the edible, so angels as divine helpers will **separate the wicked from the righteous.** The **righteous** are those who do the will of God (7:21; see also 5:20; 12:50); the **wicked** are those who do not. At the last judgment, the complexities and mixtures of good and evil that characterize us in this life will be reduced to our being among either the **wicked** or the **righteous.**

The age to come: See page 250

Angels: See page 33

Judgment: See page 557

50 Angels will **throw them**—the wicked—**into the fiery furnace, where there will be wailing and grinding of teeth.** The image of **fiery** punishment, as in Gehenna (5:22), is an image for being in torment and suffering eternal exclusion from the kingdom of God. The great distress of those who are excluded is conveyed by the idiom of **wailing and grinding of teeth** (see 8:12; 13:42).

The interpretation of the sorting out of what was collected in the fishing net (verses 49-50) repeats many elements of the interpretation of the parable of the wheat and weeds growing together until harvest (13:40-43). The sorting of the harvest and the sorting of the net are images for the last judgment. In the interpretation of the sorting of the net, however, nothing is said about what awaits the righteous; the accent is entirely on the destiny of the wicked. This negative accent conveys a somber warning: don't be counted among the wicked when the final sorting out takes place!

Jesus has been instructing his disciples in private (13:36), and has sandwiched an exhortation for them to give all to acquire the treasure of entering into the kingdom of God (13:44-46) between warnings against being excluded from the kingdom at the last judgment (13:39-42; 47-50). Jesus gives these instructions against the backdrop of many people rejecting him or being indifferent to him (11:19; 12:14, 24; 13:13-15) and thereby risking exclusion from the kingdom on the day of judgment (11:20-24). Jesus wants his disciples to enter through the narrow gate (7:13) and "shine like the sun in the kingdom of their Father" (13:43); he issues a stern warning in order to strengthen their resolve.

For reflection: What message does the parable of the net and its interpretation convey to me?

Matthew's church may have found another lesson as well in the parable of the net. Jesus' disciples were to be "fishers of men" (4:19). Their net will gather in "bad and good alike" (22:10), and the church must have some tolerance for its converts and members being a mixture of the righteous and the unrighteous. The ultimate sorting out will be done by God after the age for fishing has ended.

Treasures New and Old
51 "Do you understand all these things?" They answered, "Yes." 52 And he replied, "Then every scribe who has been instructed in the kingdom

of heaven is like the head of a household who brings from his store-room both the new and the old." **53** When Jesus finished these parables, he went away from there.

NT: Matt 23:34

51 Jesus has been instructing his disciples (13:36) and asks them, **Do you understand all these things?** While **all these things** includes the parables Jesus has just told and explained (13:37-50), it includes as well "all these things" that "Jesus spoke to the crowds in parables" (13:34, referring to 13:3-9, 24-33). The parables addressed to the crowds and to the disciples deal with the kingdom of heaven: its modest beginnings, the varied re-sponses to it, its great value, the judgment ushering in its fulfillment at the end of the age. These are aspects of "the mysteries of the kingdom of heaven" that have been made known to the disciples (13:11; see 11:25-27), and Jesus asks them whether they **understand all these things.** It is important to **understand** what Jesus is teaching because it is "the one who hears the word and understands it, who indeed bears fruit" and yields a rich harvest (13:23).

They answered, "Yes." The disciples think they understand what Jesus has been teaching them.

For reflection: How well do I understand "all these things" that Jesus has been teaching? What things do I find difficult to understand?

52 Jesus uses a parable to draw out a consequence of understanding his teachings. **And he replied, "Then every scribe who has been instructed in the kingdom of heaven is like the head of a household."** The Greek expression translated **then** has the sense of "because of this": something is made possible when one understands Jesus' teachings. Jesus speaks of **every scribe:** until now, all references in Matthew's gospel to scribes have been to those who study and teach the law of Moses (2:4; 5:20; 7:29) and who, with one exception (8:19) are critical of Jesus (9:3; 12:38). After the time of Jesus, Christians will study the law of Moses and the rest of the Scriptures, and in Matthew's church those who are learned in the Scrip-tures will be called scribes (see 23:34). While Jesus is speaking to his dis-ciples, his words also apply to future church leaders, especially those who interpret Scripture.

Scribes: See page 138

Jesus refers to every scribe **who has been instructed in the kingdom of heaven:** the Greek word translated **instructed** is a verb form of the word "disciple" and means to be trained as and become a disciple. Being **instructed in the kingdom of heaven** means understanding Jesus' teachings about God's plans and shaping one's life accordingly. The Christian **scribe** who has absorbed and lives out Jesus' teachings **is like the head of a household who brings from his storeroom both the new and the old.** The **head of a household** has authority over his household; a Christian scribe has authority to teach in the household of Jesus, the family formed around Jesus (12:48-50). The word translated **storeroom** means "treasure" or "treasury," and it has rich associations in Jesus' teachings (6:19-21; 13:44). "A good person brings forth good out of a store of goodness" (12:35—literally, out of a "good treasure"). Those who have **been instructed in the kingdom of heaven** have a treasure that they can share: they can bring forth **both the new and the old.** The **new** is the revelation brought by Jesus (11:25-27; 13:11, 16-17); the **old** is the revelation conveyed through Moses and the Scriptures. The **new** is mentioned before the **old:** the revelation brought by Jesus has priority and provides the key for interpreting previous revelation (5:17-48). Church leaders—including those called scribes in Matthew's church community—will carry on Jesus' mission, interpreting and applying the Scriptures in light of Jesus. Matthew himself was likely one of these scribes; his gospel highlights how Jesus is the fulfillment of Scripture (1:22-23; 2:15, 17-18, 23; 3:3; 4:13-16; 8:16-17; 12:17-21; 13:34-35; 21:4-5).

Kingdom of heaven: See page 266

While Jesus' parable is about scribes it has a message for every disciple. All of us have a **storeroom** that we can draw upon to help others, a treasury of what we have received from Jesus and are able to pass on.

For reflection: What am I able to bring forth from my storeroom? What is my call and service within the family of Jesus?

53 When Jesus finished these parables, he went away from there. Jesus is finished, for the moment, with his instructions to his disciples. Jesus **went away from there** and to his home town of Nazareth (13:54).

Parables: See page 262

Jesus Is Rejected in Nazareth

54 He came to his native place and taught the people in their synagogue. They were astonished and said, "Where did this man get such wisdom and mighty deeds? **55** Is he not the carpenter's son? Is not his mother named Mary and his brothers James, Joseph, Simon, and Judas? **56** Are not his sisters all with us? Where did this man get all this?" **57** And they took offense at him. But Jesus said to them, "A prophet is not without honor except in his native place and in his own house." **58** And he did not work many mighty deeds there because of their lack of faith.

Gospel parallels: Mark 6:1-6
NT: Matt 2:23; 11:5-6; Luke 4:16-30; John 4:44; 6:42

54 **He came to his native place,** his hometown. Joseph settled his family in Nazareth after their return from Egypt, when Jesus was a young child (2:23). Jesus grew up in Nazareth and was popularly thought of as Jesus from Nazareth or "Jesus the Nazorean" (26:71; see 2:23; 21:11). He "left Nazareth and went to live in Capernaum" (4:13) at the beginning of his public ministry; this is his first—and last—subsequent visit to Nazareth recounted by Matthew. Jesus **taught the people in their synagogue.** The word **synagogue** means "assembly" and came to designate the building Jews assembled in for Scripture reading and prayer, particularly on the Sabbath. Since Nazareth was a farming village of only a few hundred people, it may not have had a synagogue building; Sabbath gatherings might have taken place in the village square. During his public ministry, Jesus "went around all of Galilee, teaching in their synagogues, proclaiming the gospel of the kingdom" (4:23; see also 9:35; 12:9). Jesus followed his customary practice when he came to Nazareth: he **taught the people in their synagogue,** in their assembly.

Nazareth: See page 38
Synagogue: See page 104

Matthew does not describe the content of Jesus' teachings but reports the reaction of those who heard him: **they were astonished** by his words. At the conclusion of the Sermon on the Mount "the crowds were astonished at his teaching, for he taught them as one having authority" (7:28-29). What Jesus taught, and the authority with which he taught it, were astonishing.

For reflection: What about Jesus' teachings most astonishes me?

The reaction of the people of Nazareth, however, was not simple aston-ishment but skepticism and indignation. They **said, "Where did this man get such wisdom and mighty deeds?"** By Jesus' **wisdom** they refer to his preaching and teaching, which characteristically centered on the coming reign of God (4:17, 23; 9:35). His **mighty deeds** included the healings and exorcisms he performed (4:23; 9:35; 11:5). Matthew has not mentioned Je-sus performing any healings or exorcisms in Nazareth, but word of what he did elsewhere would have reached them. His healings were widely known (4:24-25; 9:26, 31; 11:2). Chorazin, Bethsaida, and Capernaum "where most of his mighty deeds had been done" (11:20-21, 23) were within a day's walk of Nazareth. The people of Nazareth want to know where **this man** got the authority to teach and the power to heal. Their question is phrased a little contemptuously: they literally refer to Jesus as *this one*: **Where did** this one, this guy, **get such wisdom and mighty deeds?**

55 The people of Nazareth think they know who Jesus is. He had grown up among them, and in a village of several hundred people everybody knew everybody. The people of Nazareth knew his father: **Is he not the carpen-ter's son?** The Greek word translated **carpenter** means an artisan who works not just with wood but with any hard material, including stone. Houses in Nazareth generally had walls of unworked stones; wood was used sparingly. Jesus is known as the **son** of the village artisan. (Mark tells us that Jesus was such an artisan himself—Mark 6:3.) The people of Naz-areth do not refer to Joseph by name, although Matthew's readers know that that was the name of Jesus' legal father (1:16, 18-21, 25). Joseph does not appear on the scene during Jesus' public ministry (see 12:46), leading to the presumption that Joseph had died.

The people of Nazareth know the rest of Jesus' family as well: **Is not his mother named Mary and his brothers James, Joseph, Simon, and Judas?** Jesus' **mother** and **brothers** bear traditional Jewish names—perhaps a sign that they were a devout Jewish family. **Mary** was named after Miriam, sister of Moses; **James** is a form of Jacob, the father of the twelve tribes of Israel. **Joseph, Simon, and Judas** were named after Joseph, Simeon, and Judah, sons of Jacob.

56 **Are not his sisters all with us?** The names of Jesus' **sisters** are not given, but he apparently has a number of them who **all** live in Nazareth. While mention of Jesus' brothers and sisters could imply that Joseph and Mary

293

had children after Jesus, from the early centuries the church understood these brothers and sisters to be either children of Joseph from a previous marriage or cousins of Jesus. Matthew does not address the degree of relationship between the brothers and sisters and Jesus; for his account it is sufficient that Jesus is known to have family ties in Nazareth.

The people of Nazareth are sure they know who Jesus is. They have known him most of his life; they know his whole family. They cannot reconcile the Jesus they think they know so well with the Jesus who is filled with wisdom and who performs mighty deeds. Jesus apparently did not teach with authority or heal the sick when he lived in Nazareth; how is he able to do so now? **Where did this man get all this?** This can be a legitimate question: does Jesus' authority and power come from God? But on the lips of the people of Nazareth the question conveys skepticism: Where did *this one* get all this? Who does he think he is—a carpenter's son speaking and acting on behalf of God?

BACKGROUND: BROTHERS AND SISTERS OF JESUS Brothers of Jesus are mentioned in the gospels as well as in Acts 1:14, 1 Corinthians 9:5, and Galatians 1:19. Four brothers are listed by name in Matthew 13:55 and Mark 6:3: James, Joses (or Joseph), Simon, and Judas; unnamed sisters are mentioned in Matthew 13:56 and Mark 6:3. While these references might be interpreted to mean that Mary and Joseph had children after Jesus' birth, other passages seem to indicate a different Mary as the mother of James and Joses (Matt 27:56; Mark 15:40), and the church from early times has held to the perpetual virginity of Mary. One explanation, circulated in the second-century writings Protoevangelium of James and Infancy Gospel of Thomas, is that the brothers and sisters of Jesus were children of Joseph from a previous marriage. St. Jerome (342–420) proposed that the brothers of Jesus were his cousins, since the Hebrew word for brother can also mean "cousin." Jerome's explanation became widely but not universally accepted (Greek has a word for cousin, used in Col 4:10: "Mark the cousin of Barnabas"). The gospels present the brothers of Jesus as having no faith in him during his public ministry (Mark 3:21, 31; John 7:3-7). But Paul lists a James, who was not one of the twelve apostles, as among those to whom Jesus appeared after his resurrection (1 Cor 15:5-7). "Mary the mother of Jesus, and his brothers," awaited Pentecost in the upper room (Acts 1:13-14). "James the brother of the Lord" (Gal 1:19) emerged as the leader of the Christian community in Jerusalem (Acts 12:17; 15:13-21; 21:18; Gal 2:9, 12).

57 And they took offense at him. They are scandalized by Jesus, tripped up by him. The people of Nazareth cannot reconcile the man of wisdom and mighty deeds who stands before them with the Jesus they thought they knew. When disciples of John the Baptist came to Jesus, he pointed out the mighty deeds he was working and said, "Blessed is the one who takes no offense at me" (11:4-6). The people of Nazareth acknowledged that Jesus did mighty deeds (verse 54) but they **took offense at him.**

For reflection: How well do I think I know Jesus? Does anything about Jesus or his teachings trip me up?

But Jesus said to them, "A prophet is not without honor except in his native place and in his own house." Jesus might be invoking a popular proverb. This is the only time in Matthew's gospel that Jesus refers to himself as a **prophet;** he will later be hailed as a prophet by the crowds (21:11, 46). The proverb does not match up exactly with Jesus' experience. Although some have embraced him, he has also met indifference or rejection (8:34; 9:3, 11, 34; 11:19-24; 12:2, 14, 24, 38). Perhaps Jesus invokes the proverb as a sad commentary on the people of Nazareth: he is dishonored more here than anywhere elsewhere.

58 And he did not work many mighty deeds there because of their lack of faith. The **mighty deeds** performed by Jesus were not displays of power for their own sake but were his freeing men and women from the grip of Satan and evil, enabling them to live under the reign of God (12:28). It took faith to perceive the significance of Jesus' healings and exorcisms; it took faith to welcome the power of Jesus into one's life. Jesus told the woman who was healed when she touched his garment, "Your faith has saved you" (9:22). The Greek term for the **lack of faith** of the people of Nazareth is literally their "unbelief"—not a neutral absence of faith but disbelief, a refusal to believe. In the face of such disbelief, Jesus **did not work many mighty deeds there.**

For reflection: Where do I need to grow in faith so that Jesus might do more for me?

Jesus moved to Capernaum and made it "his own town" (9:1); "most of his mighty deeds" were done in Capernaum and in nearby Chorazin and

Bethsaida—yet the people of those towns did not embrace his message (11:20-24). Now his "native place," where he had lived virtually all of his life, rejects him. Perhaps this was not a surprise to Jesus: his parables of the coming of the kingdom of God convey that there will be many failures (13:3-8, 18-30, 37-43; 47-49). But it is still very sad that Jesus is rejected by those who had known him for years.

For reflection: Have I known Jesus for many years—but still do not know him?

CHAPTER 14

The Death of the Forerunner

1 At that time Herod the tetrarch heard of the reputation of Jesus **2** and said to his servants, "This man is John the Baptist. He has been raised from the dead; that is why mighty powers are at work in him."

3 Now Herod had arrested John, bound [him], and put him in prison on account of Herodias, the wife of his brother Philip, **4** for John had said to him, "It is not lawful for you to have her." **5** Although he wanted to kill him, he feared the people, for they regarded him as a prophet. **6** But at a birthday celebration for Herod, the daughter of Herodias performed a dance before the guests and delighted Herod **7** so much that he swore to give her whatever she might ask for. **8** Prompted by her mother, she said, "Give me here on a platter the head of John the Baptist." **9** The king was distressed, but because of his oaths and the guests who were present, he ordered that it be given, **10** and he had John beheaded in the prison. **11** His head was brought in on a platter and given to the girl, who took it to her mother. **12** His disciples came and took away the corpse and buried him; and they went and told Jesus.

> Gospel parallels: Mark 6:14-29; Luke 3:19-20; 9:7-9
> OT:Lev 18:16; 20:21
> NT:Matt 4:12, 17; 11:2; 16:13-14; 17:12-13

1 At that time, around when Jesus met rejection in Nazareth (13:54-58), **Herod the tetrarch heard of the reputation of Jesus.** Jesus' public ministry has taken place in Galilee, which was ruled on behalf of Rome by **Herod** Antipas, a son of Herod the Great. His official title was **tetrarch,** which meant the ruler of a fourth of a kingdom; he was sometimes popularly referred to as a king (verse 9). Herod Antipas **heard of the reputation of Jesus.** Herod was the type of ruler who kept himself informed of what was happening, lest he be caught off guard by anything that would threaten his rule. As the next verse indicates, he heard of the healings and exorcisms performed by Jesus, reports of which were circulated widely (4:24-25).

2 Herod Antipas **said to his servants, "This man is John the Baptist. He has been raised from the dead; that is why mighty powers are at work in him."** Herod's identification of Jesus as a risen **John the Baptist** is puzzling, even bizarre. John was still alive when Jesus began exercising his **mighty powers** over sickness and evil (see 11:2-5); how could Jesus do so as John **raised from the dead** if John had not yet died? There was no first-century Jewish belief that coming back from the dead would give one extraordinary abilities, so why would a risen John—who did not exercise miraculous powers during his earthly life—have **mighty powers** after his return to life? Herod Antipas seems to have a superstitious fear that John has returned from the dead to plague him and has done so in the person of Jesus, equipped with worrisome **mighty powers.**

3 Matthew has not recounted how John the Baptist died, but he does so now in a flashback. **Now Herod had arrested John, bound [him], and put him in prison on account of Herodias, the wife of his brother Philip.** Members of the dynasty spawned by Herod the Great and his ten wives sometimes intermarried. **Herodias** was the daughter of one of Herod Antipas's half brothers and had been the wife of another half brother, whom Matthew calls **Philip** (the first-century Jewish historian Josephus calls Herodias's first husband Herod and says that it was their daughter Salome whom Philip married). Herod Antipas had divorced his first wife to marry Herodias, who was his sister-in-law and niece. Herodias thus was successively married to two of her uncles.

4 **for John had said to him** (the Greek could also be translated "kept saying to him"), **"It is not lawful for you to have her."** It was not against Jewish law for Herod Antipas to divorce his first wife, but the law of Moses prohibited a man from marrying his brother's wife (see Lev 18:16), branding it

BACKGROUND: HEROD ANTIPAS A son of Herod the Great, Herod Antipas ruled Galilee as Jesus was growing up and during his public ministry. Herod Antipas's mother, Malthace, one of his father's ten wives, was a Samaritan. After the death of Herod the Great in 4 B.C., Rome divided his kingdom among three of his sons. Herod Antipas was made tetrarch (ruler of a fourth of a kingdom) of Galilee and of a region east of the Jordan River called Perea; he is sometimes called Herod the Tetrarch in the gospels and sometimes simply Herod. Herod Antipas executed John the Baptist, but he was not as paranoid and ruthless as his father, and Galilee was generally tranquil during his more than forty years of rule. Herod Antipas was deposed by Rome and exiled in A.D. 39. *Related topic: Herod the Great (page 35).*

incest (Lev 20:21; there was an exception to this rule—see Deut 25:5-6). John the Baptist may also have criticized Herod Antipas for other things, for Antipas was not noted for obedience to the Mosaic law, and John was not reticent in his denunciations (3:7-10).

5 **Although he wanted to kill him, he feared the people, for they regarded him as a prophet.** Herod Antipas would have liked to do away with John the Baptist, but John had a sizeable popular following (3:5) who revered him as a **prophet** (11:9; 21:26). Rome expected its local rulers to pay taxes and preserve law and order; Herod survived as a ruler for over forty years by forgoing precipitous actions that would incite unrest. Holding John in prison kept him out of the spotlight; Herod **feared** that killing him might rouse **the people.**

6 **But at a birthday celebration for Herod, the daughter of Herodias performed a dance before the guests and delighted Herod.** Celebrating a **birthday** with a banquet was a pagan rather than a Jewish practice. **The daughter of Herodias** (unnamed by Matthew but called Salome by the historian Josephus) was from her first marriage. Hollywood has probably been right to portray her **dance** as lascivious. A member of a ruling family making such a display of herself at a banquet would have been highly extraordinary and scandalous, but the Herodian dynasty was no stranger to scandal.

7 Herod Antipas was delighted by her dance **so much that he swore to give her whatever she might ask for.** Herod made an ill-considered and extravagant promise, binding himself to it with an oath. Pagan banquets ordinarily included much drinking; had Herod drained too many goblets of wine?

8 Offered the ancient equivalent of a blank check, the daughter asked her mother how it should be filled in. Herodias apparently wanted John dead as much as Herod did and instructed her daughter accordingly. **Prompted by her mother, she said, "Give me here on a platter the head of John the Baptist."** Perhaps the banquet setting suggested that John's head be gruesomely paraded as one more dish; displaying his head on a platter in any case would provide incontrovertible evidence of his death.

9 **The king was distressed** by the girl's request. But the reason for his distress is not evident in Matthew's account. Herod Antipas wanted John dead (verse 5) and now had the girl's demand as an excuse for killing him. Perhaps, though, the gruesome request was too much for even Herod to stomach easily. And perhaps, too, Herod was distressed by the prospect of John's execution inflaming the crowds that revered John (verse 5). But to deny the girl's request would be reneging on a sworn promise he had made in front of others and would mean loss of face for Herod. Hence, **because of his oaths and the guests who were present, he ordered that** the head of John the Baptist **be given** to her.

10 **and he had John beheaded in the prison.** There was not even the pretence of a trial; John was executed on the whim of those in power. Rome would not hold Herod Antipas accountable unless Rome's interests were jeopardized; the arbitrary execution of a local religious figure was tolerable as long as it did not cause political unrest. According to the historian Josephus, the **prison** in which John was held and executed was Machaerus, a palace-fortress east of the Dead Sea in a territory ruled by Herod Antipas. In Matthew's account of events, Herod's birthday banquet could have taken place there. Josephus provides a somewhat different motive for Herod having John executed; there may have been several factors that led to his death. Matthew and Josephus agree on the fundamental fact: Herod Antipas had John the Baptist put to death.

11 **His head was brought in on a platter and given to the girl, who took it to her mother.** Matthew does not indicate the lapse of time between the girl's request and the delivery of John's head; his account can be read as if

---

BACKGROUND: JOSEPHUS ON THE DEATH OF JOHN THE BAPTIST The Jewish historian Josephus (who lived from A.D. 37 to roughly A.D. 100) attributed John's death to Herod Antipas's fear of his popularity: "When others crowded around John and were deeply moved by his preaching, Herod became afraid. John's ability to sway the people might lead to some kind of uprising, for they seemed willing to act on John's advice. So Herod thought it best to take action, not wanting to be caught by surprise and face problems that would make him regret his hesitation. Because of Herod's suspicions, then, John was taken in chains to the fortress called Machaerus and put to death" (*The Antiquities of the Jews,* XVIII, 5, 2).

events followed quickly upon one another, as they could have if all the action took place at Machaerus.

12 His disciples came and took away the corpse and buried him. John the Baptist had **disciples** (9:14; 11:2); they provide a proper burial for his body. Then **they went and told Jesus** about John's death. John the Baptist was the forerunner of Jesus (3:1-2, 11-12) and played this role even in his death. If Herod Antipas can do away with John, those who wield power can do away with Jesus. John and Jesus preached repentance in preparation for the coming of the kingdom of heaven (3:2; 4:17), and those who proclaim the reign of God can meet with violent opposition from those whose allegiance is to the reign of Rome or any other earthly power. John's arrest had led Jesus to begin his public ministry (4:12, 17); John's death will be a sign for Jesus to begin wrapping up his ministry (14:13), for John's death prefigures his own (17:12-13).

For reflection: What message does the death of John the Baptist have for me?

ORIENTATION: *Although Matthew told of the death of John the Baptist as a flashback (14:3-12), Matthew resumes his account of Jesus' ministry as if Jesus is just now hearing of John's death. The chronology of events seems less important to Matthew than Jesus' reaction to John's execution.*

Jesus Feeds a Vast Crowd
13 When Jesus heard of it, he withdrew in a boat to a deserted place by himself. The crowds heard of this and followed him on foot from their towns. **14** When he disembarked and saw the vast crowd, his heart was moved with pity for them, and he cured their sick. **15** When it was evening, the disciples approached him and said, "This is a deserted place and it is already late; dismiss the crowds so that they can go to the villages and buy food for themselves." **16** [Jesus] said to them, "There is no need for them to go away; give them some food yourselves." **17** But they said to him, "Five loaves and two fish are all we have here." **18** Then he said, "Bring them here to me," **19** and he ordered the crowds to sit down on the grass. Taking the five loaves and the two fish, and looking up to heaven, he said the blessing, broke the loaves, and gave them to

the disciples, who in turn gave them to the crowds. [20] They all ate and were satisfied, and they picked up the fragments left over—twelve wicker baskets full. [21] Those who ate were about five thousand men, not counting women and children.

Gospel parallels: Mark 6:32-44; Luke 9:10-17; John 6:1-15
NT: Matt 9:36; 14:10-12; 15:29-39; 26:26-29

13 **When Jesus heard of it**—when Jesus heard from John's disciples that John had been executed by Herod Antipas (14:10-12)—**he withdrew in a boat to a deserted place by himself.** Jesus had been in Nazareth (13:54-58) but was back at the Sea of Galilee when he received the report of John's death. **He withdrew:** Jesus previously withdrew from where Pharisees were plotting his death (12:14-15), and he goes off again when he learns of John's beheading. Did Jesus fear that he might be next on Herod's list? More likely Jesus took John's death as a foreshadowing of his own (see 17:12-13) and wanted to be **by himself** to reflect and pray about what lay ahead (see 14:22-23). Jesus went **in a boat to a deserted place.** Matthew does not specify the location of the **deserted place,** but if it was on the eastern shore of the Sea of Galilee (see 14:22, 34) it would have been outside the territory ruled by Herod Antipas.

Sea of Galilee: See page 153

The crowds heard of this and followed him on foot from their towns. Crowds constantly flocked to Jesus, bringing those who were sick for him to heal (4:24-25; 8:16; 9:2, 32-33; 12:22). **Their towns** may have been villages on or near the Sea of Galilee, such as Chorazin, Bethsaida, and Capernaum (11:20-24). Word got around that Jesus had set out in a boat, and **crowds** went **on foot** along the shore to his destination. Their doing so is an index of their hunger for what Jesus is able to do for them: heal their sicknesses and free them from the grip of evil.

For reflection: How hungry am I for what Jesus offers me?

14 It may have taken some hustle to reach Jesus' destination on foot faster than he did in a boat, but many people did so. **When he disembarked and saw the vast crowd, his heart was moved with pity for them.** Jesus would have had reason to be irritated by the presence of crowds if the point of his going off in a boat was to escape the crowds and have some privacy. The

crowds have generally not grasped his teachings (13:10-15); the towns "where most of his mighty deeds had been done" had not repented (11:20). Nevertheless, **when Jesus saw the crowds** waiting for him, **his heart was moved with pity for them.** The Greek word translated by the phrase **his heart was moved with pity** means to have a gut reaction of compassion: Jesus is profoundly moved by their needs, just as he had been previously overcome with compassion at the sight of those in need (9:36). **He cured their sick:** they had tracked him down so that their sick might be healed, and in his compassion he healed them.

For reflection: What does Jesus' compassion for this crowd tell me about Jesus? About his compassion for me?

15 Jesus continued to heal the sick for some time; **when it was evening, the disciples approached him and said, "This is a deserted place and it is already late; dismiss the crowds so that they can go to the villages and buy food for themselves."** Like Jesus, the disciples are concerned for the well-being of the crowds. The time for the evening meal had passed and people were hungry. Although they were in a **deserted place,** they were within walking distance of **villages** where they could **buy food for themselves.** The disciples make the commonsense suggestion that Jesus **dismiss the crowds** so that they can do so.

16 But **[Jesus] said to them, "There is no need for them to go away."** The crowds would **need** to **go away** from Jesus only if they had pressing needs that he could not meet. By saying that **there is no need for them to go away,** Jesus indicates that he can meet their needs—and by extension, all human needs.

How will Jesus take care of the hunger of the crowds? He tells his disciples, **give them some food yourselves.** The Greek of Matthew's gospel emphasizes **yourselves;** Jesus tells his disciples, "*You* give them something to eat." There is no need for anyone to go away from Jesus to have their needs met, but Jesus meets needs through his followers. The message for Matthew's readers is that Jesus wants to meet the needs of others through them.

For reflection: To what extent do I look upon myself as Jesus' instrument for meeting human needs?

17 The disciples are willing to do what Jesus asks them to do but do not think that they can do very much. **But they said to him, "Five loaves and two fish are all we have here."** Bread was the staple food in the diet of ordinary people; **loaves** were usually round, about an inch high and eight inches in diameter. The **fish** were likely dried or salted and were eaten to flavor bread rather than as a main dish. **Five loaves and two fish** would have sufficed for a sparse evening meal for the Jesus and a handful of his disciples, but they were hardly enough to feed a crowd.

18 **Then he said, "Bring them here to me."** Jesus asks his disciples to bring him what they have, however little it might be.

19 **and he ordered the crowds to sit down**—literally, to recline—**on the grass.** Jews had adopted the Greek custom of reclining at banquets; reclining **on the grass** is also be a comfortable way to have a picnic. **Taking the five loaves and the two fish, and looking up to heaven, he said the blessing.** Jesus acts as a host at a Jewish meal would, making the customary **blessing** that was offered before eating. **Looking up to heaven** is a gesture of prayer

---

BACKGROUND: DIET Bread was the basic food of ordinary people at the time of Jesus and provided a substantial part of their daily calorie intake. Most families baked their own bread daily in an outdoor oven and ate bread at every meal. Bread was usually made from wheat; barley bread was cheaper but less desirable. Bread made up so much of the diet that the word "bread" could be used to refer to food in general. Grain was also eaten parched ("roasted"—Ruth 2:14). Vegetables such as beans, lentils, cucumbers, and onions rounded out meals, along with fruits such as grapes, figs, dates, and pomegranates. Grapes could be processed into wine or raisins. Olives were crushed for oil, which was used in cooking as well as in oil lamps. Goats and sheep provided milk, yogurt, and cheese. Fish were usually dried or salted to preserve them and were eaten more often as a condiment for bread than as a main course. Herbs, spices, and salt added taste to even simple meals. Ordinary people ate meat only on special occasions, such as feasts. Meals were eaten with the fingers, with pieces of bread used as edible spoons to scoop up porridges and soak up sauces (Ruth 2:14; John 13:26), as is still the custom in some Middle Eastern cultures today. Members of the upper class ate much better than ordinary people: imported wines graced their tables, along with ample meat. *Related topic: Banquets (page 464).*

(see Psalm 123:1). The **blessing** said before Jewish meals is not a blessing of the food but a thanksgiving to God for providing the food. A traditional Jewish blessing over bread is "Blessed are you, O Lord our God, King of the universe, who bring forth bread from the earth."

After offering the blessing, Jesus **broke the loaves, and gave them to the disciples, who in turn gave them to the crowds.** Matthew has yet to recount anything extraordinary taking place. Jesus asked his disciples to give the crowds something to eat; they replied that they had only five loaves and two fish; Jesus asked that they be brought to him; he offered a blessing as would be done at any meal, broke the bread into portions, and gave them to his disciples, who gave them to the crowds. The only oddity is passing out such a small amount of food to a "vast crowd" (verse 14); it could not be expected to go very far.

For reflection: However little it may be, what am I able to put in the hands of Jesus for him to use?

20 Yet the result was extraordinary indeed: **They all ate and were satisfied.** The Greek word for **were satisfied** has the connotation that they ate their fill. Matthew provides no description of the mechanics whereby five loaves and two fish become sufficient to feed a vast crowd; he simply notes that **they all ate,** the entire crowd, eating enough to be completely **satisfied.** Nor does Matthew recount any amazement on the part of the crowd or exclamations of praise afterwards. Matthew's focus is on Jesus' taking the little the disciples could provide him and its becoming enough to satisfy a crowd. It became more than enough: **and they picked up the fragments left over—twelve wicker baskets full.** There was far more food at the end than at the beginning. **Wicker baskets** were used for carrying food and other items when traveling. **Twelve** is the number of apostles (10:1-2), corresponding to the twelve tribes of Israel (19:28). The fact that there are leftovers is significant: Jesus meets needs abundantly. Jesus can take the little we have and make it an abundance for others.

21 **Those who ate were about five thousand men, not counting women and children.** This incident is often referred to as the Feeding of the Five Thousand, but Matthew notes that **women and children** were fed, as well as the roughly **five thousand men.** Jesus is concerned for women and children no less than for men.

Mathew has told of two meals that were quite different from each other (14:6-11, 15-21). One was a birthday celebration for Herod Antipas; its menu undoubtedly included fine foods and imported wines. A decadent dance led to the death of John the Baptist. The second meal took place on grass and was hosted by Jesus; the food was working-class fare. This second meal did not lead to a death, but it foreshadowed another meal that would. At the Last Supper, Jesus will again take bread, say a blessing, break the bread, and give it to his disciples (26:26), doing so in anticipation of his death on the cross. Jesus' feeding of the crowd is an image for Jesus' nourishing of his followers in the Eucharist; both in turn foreshadow the eternal "banquet in the kingdom of heaven" (8:11; see also 26:29).

For reflection: What significance do I find in Jesus' feeding of the crowd?

Who Walks on Water?
22 Then he made the disciples get into the boat and precede him to the other side, while he dismissed the crowds. **23** After doing so, he went up on the mountain by himself to pray. When it was evening he was there alone. **24** Meanwhile the boat, already a few miles offshore, was being tossed about by the waves, for the wind was against it. **25** During the fourth watch of the night, he came toward them, walking on the sea. **26** When the disciples saw him walking on the sea they were terrified. "It is a ghost," they said, and they cried out in fear. **27** At once [Jesus] spoke to them, "Take courage, it is I; do not be afraid." **28** Peter said to him in reply, "Lord, if it is you, command me to come to you on the water." **29** He said, "Come." Peter got out of the boat and began to walk on the water toward Jesus. **30** But when he saw how [strong] the wind was he became frightened; and, beginning to sink, he cried out, "Lord, save me!" **31** Immediately Jesus stretched out his hand and caught him, and said to him, "O you of little faith, why did you doubt?" **32** After they got into the boat, the wind died down. **33** Those who were in the boat did him homage, saying, "Truly, you are the Son of God."

Gospel parallels: Mark 6:45-52; John 6:16-21
OT: Exod 3:13-14; Isaiah 43:10; 51:12
NT: Matt 8:23-27; 16:16; 27:54

22 When Jesus learned of the execution of John the Baptist, he went "in a boat to a deserted place by himself," but his desire for privacy was frustrated by a crowd who arrived on foot (14:13). Out of compassion he healed their sick and fed them (14:14-21); now, their needs met, he again seeks some time alone. Then—immediately after the crowd was fed and the leftovers were gathered up—he made the disciples get into the boat and precede him to the other side, while he dismissed the crowds. Jesus sent his disciples ahead of him to the other side of the Sea of Galilee; we will learn that they land at Gennesaret (14:34), on the northwestern shore. The disciples had earlier asked Jesus to "dismiss the crowds" so that the people could buy food (14:15), but Jesus dismissed them only after he fed them.

23 After doing so, he went up on the mountain by himself to pray. The Greek word translated mountain can also mean a "hill"; steep hills ring much of the Sea of Galilee. Jesus went by himself to pray, just as he taught his disciples to pray in private (6:6). The context suggests that Jesus wanted to pray in light of the execution of John the Baptist (14:9-13), which Jesus realized foreshadowed his own death (17:12-13). Jesus' prayer on the mountain may have had the same theme as his prayer in Gethsemane to his Father: "your will be done" (26:42)—a prayer he taught his followers to pray (6:10).

For reflection: What do I imagine Jesus prayed about after the death of John the Baptist?

When it was evening he was there alone. It was already evening when the disciples suggested that Jesus dismiss the crowds (14:15); when it was evening perhaps means later that same evening, as twilight faded and it became night. Jesus had gone up a hill by himself and is now there alone: Matthew emphasizes Jesus' solitude.

24 Meanwhile the boat, already a few miles offshore: the Sea of Galilee is about seven miles across at its widest. The disciples were in the middle of this lake but not making much progress because the boat was being tossed about by the waves, for the wind was against it. The Greek word translated being tossed about literally means "being tortured" and indicates a situation of extreme distress. The hills surrounding the Sea of Galilee

are cut by deep valleys that funnel winds onto the lake. The disciples were rowing into a strong **wind** that was blowing **against** them.

Sea of Galilee: See page 153

While we understand winds and storms at sea as meteorological phenomena, the disciples probably did not think of them in purely physical terms. In the Psalms, the perils of the sea are images for evil forces (Psalms 18:5; 32:6; 69:2-3, 15-16). The disciples may have thought they were contending not simply with wind and waves but with chaos and death in the darkness of night.

The wind-and-wave-battered boat bearing the disciples has long been taken as a symbol of the church (see also 8:23-27). Those in the boat have been sent forth by Jesus but face opposition and danger. Jesus is not bodily present; he is at prayer, at the right hand of his Father (26:64; Rom 8:34). The church might seem to be making little headway despite hard rowing, but it has been so for disciples of Jesus from the very first.

For reflection: What does the image of the disciples at sea convey to me about the church? About my own discipleship?

25 We must presume that Jesus, atop a hill by the lake, is aware of the strong wind and of the struggle his disciples are enduring. Yet he does not cut short his prayer to come to his disciples; it is only **during the fourth watch of the night** that **he came toward them, walking on the sea.** The Roman way of reckoning divided the period from 6:00 p.m. to 6:00 a.m. into four watches; **the fourth watch of the night** ran from 3:00 to 6:00 a.m. The disciples have been battling strong headwinds from evening until almost dawn. Jesus sent his disciples off to row into a headwind and let them contend with it through the night.

For reflection: Has my doing what Jesus asks me to do ever seemed like rowing into a headwind in darkness?

Jesus now comes to his disciples, **walking on the sea.** Jesus is doing something beyond human capability. Old Testament texts proclaim God's mastery over the chaos of the sea; a few texts use the image of God striding or making his way upon the waters (Job 9:8; Psalm 77:20; Isaiah

43:16). The next verse indicates that these texts did not pop into the disciples' minds when they saw Jesus walking toward them on the sea.

26 **When the disciples saw him walking on the sea they were terrified. "It is a ghost," they said, and they cried out in fear.** The disciples do not recognize the one who is **walking on the sea** as Jesus; they take it to be a **ghost** or apparition. The disciples think they are seeing something ominous: **They were terrified,** and **they cried out in fear.** A hard night's rowing into a headwind—and now a ghost has come to haunt them!

27 **At once [Jesus] spoke to them:** as soon as he hears the disciples' fearful cries, **at once** he speaks to them to reassure them. He tells them, **Take courage, it is I; do not be afraid.** The exhortations to **take courage** and **not be afraid** have much the same meaning. They are an invitation to have faith that Jesus can take care of them (see 9:2, 22). The disciples have reason to **be afraid:** some of them have fished the Sea of Galilee for years and know that they are in a precarious situation, out on rough waters at night and exhausted from rowing. Jesus does not calm the wind and waves; he tells his disciples to have **courage** and not be **afraid,** despite the wind and waves, because **it is I.** In its simplest meaning, **it is I** identifies the one walking on the water as Jesus: **it is I,** Jesus, who have come to you and tell you to have courage and not be afraid. Even if you are battered by wind and waves far from shore in darkness, you have nothing to fear, because **it is I.** I will take care of you.

> For reflection: *When has Jesus given me the faith and courage to overcome my fears?*

Readers of Matthew's gospel can find additional meaning in Jesus' words, **it is I.** The Greek words translated **it is I** can also be translated "I am" and are an echo of God's identification of himself to Moses: "Tell the Israelites: I AM sent me to you" (Exod 3:14). God also refers to himself as "I am" or "It is I" in prophecies of Isaiah that promise delivery from exile (Isaiah 43:10; 51:12). God's "I am" implies "I am here for you": "I am with you to save you, to rescue you" (Jer 42:11). Jesus is Emmanuel, "God is with us" (1:23). Who is it who walks on the sea as God strides on the waters? It is God-with-us, Jesus, who comes to rescue his disciples as God rescued his people from slavery in Egypt and from exile in Babylon.

"But," said Moses to God, "when I go to the Israelites and say to them, 'The God of your fathers has sent me to you,' if they ask me, 'What is his name?' what am I to tell them?" God replied, "I am who am." Then he added, "This is what you shall tell the Israelites: I AM sent me to you."

Exodus 3:13-14

For reflection: What glimpse into the identity of Jesus do I find in his walking on the sea and saying, "It is I"?

28 **Peter said to him in reply, "Lord, if it is you, command me to come to you on the water."** The word **Lord** ranges in meaning from a polite form of address to a title for God. On Peter's lips here it probably has the sense of master: Peter acknowledges Jesus as one who has authority. **If it is you** may betray uncertainty on Peter's part: is the one who comes walking on the sea really Jesus? More likely it expresses recognition: *Since* it is you, Jesus, **command me to come to you on the water.** We might expect Peter to ask, "If it is you, please calm the wind and waves!" Yet Peter's request, while surprising, makes sense in light of what it means to be a disciple of Jesus. Peter does not get out of the boat on his own initiative but asks Jesus to bid him: **command me.** Discipleship means awaiting and obeying Jesus' commands. Peter asks, command me **to come to you:** discipleship means being with Jesus. By asking Jesus to command that he come to him **on the water,** Peter asks to be able to walk on the water just as Jesus does. Jesus expelled demons and healed illnesses (4:23-24; 9:35) and gave Peter and the rest of the Twelve authority to do the same (10:1, 8). Peter asks to be able to do what Jesus does, even to walk on water.

Lord: See page 133

29 **He said, "Come."** The Greek word for **come** has the connotation "come here." **Peter got out of the boat and began to walk on the water toward Jesus.** Peter was listed as the first of the twelve apostles (10:2); this is the first time in Matthew's gospel that he steps forth in a distinctive way.

For reflection: What is the most implausible thing I have accomplished because Jesus invited and empowered me to do so?

30 **But when he saw how [strong] the wind was he became frightened.** The wind did not begin to blow more strongly as Peter walked toward Jesus; the change came in Peter. He **saw** how fiercely the wind was churning up waves and spray—which meant that he had taken his eyes off Jesus. Peter had reason to be **frightened** if his attention was on the wind and waves. There are things that dismay and alarm us if we dwell on them. It is only when our focus is on Jesus that we can view our concerns in proper perspective.

The Letter to the Hebrews exhorts us to "persevere in running the race that lies before us while keeping our eyes fixed on Jesus" (Heb 12:1-2). Peter took his eyes off Jesus and could not finish the course he had set out on. **Beginning to sink, he cried out, "Lord, save me!"** In a previous storm at sea the disciples cried out to Jesus, "Lord, save us!" (8:25); Peter echoes this cry. The word **save** can broadly refer to any rescue from danger and distress. Matthew's gospel also uses the word "save" to refer to rescue from everlasting death (19:25; 24:13), and Matthew's readers can adopt Peter's words as a plea for eternal salvation: **Lord, save me!** As our prayer for salvation, it acknowledges Jesus to be **Lord** as God is called Lord.

For reflection: Have I ever cried out in desperation, "Lord, save me"?

31 **Immediately Jesus stretched out his hand and caught him,** responding at once to Peter's plea. Jesus **stretched out his hand** to Peter as he had stretched out his hand to heal a leper (8:3). He **caught him,** taking hold of Peter, lifting him up out of the sea. Jesus' stretching out his hand to Peter to lift him up is an image for his stretching out his hand to us to lift us up from death and raise us to eternal life with him.

Jesus **said to him, "O you of little faith, why did you doubt?"** Peter had **faith**—but not enough. The Greek word for **doubt** means to be divided, to vacillate and waver, and thus not have complete trust. Peter had faith that Jesus could enable him to walk on the sea, but fright drowned out faith when he turned his attention from Jesus to the wind. Jesus notes the **little faith** of his disciples on a number of occasions (6:30; 8:26; 16:8; 17:20). They have faith, but not enough faith to remain steadfast in crises. Peter's faltering at sea foreshadows a later time when fear will scuttle his faith (26:69-75). Peter—and all disciples of Jesus—will always have need to cry out to Jesus, "Lord, save me!"

For reflection: How strong is my faith when it is put to the test?

32 **After they got into the boat, the wind died down.** A previous storm at sea ended when Jesus "rebuked the winds and the sea, and there was great calm" (8:26). Now it takes no word or gesture of Jesus to still the wind; his presence in the boat with his disciples brings calm. Realizing that the risen Jesus is present with us (see 28:20) calms the turmoil of our lives.

33 **Those who were in the boat did him homage.** To do **homage** means to prostrate oneself before another in reverence or worship (see 2:2, 8, 11; 8:2; 9:18). The disciples are awed by Jesus' walking on the water and calming the wind, and they bow down before him, **saying, "Truly, you are the Son of God."** When Jesus calmed an earlier storm, his disciples "were amazed and said, 'What sort of man is this, whom even the winds and the sea obey?'"(8:27). Now they recognize what sort of man he is: he is **the Son of God.** The Old Testament calls a variety of figures sons of God; Jesus however is in a unique sense **the Son of God,** proclaimed by God to be his beloved Son (3:17), able to reveal the Father as only the Son can (11:25-27), exercising God's authority over the seas and winds. The disciples are beginning to grasp that Jesus is **the Son of God,** and they bow down before him. Jesus has met with indifference and rejection from many quarters, but his disciples are growing in their recognition of who he is.

Son of God: See page 52

The disciples' exclamation, **Truly, you are the Son of God** anticipates Peter's profession of Jesus' identity, "You are the Messiah, the Son of the living God" (16:16), and anticipates as well the words of the soldiers on Golgotha after Jesus' death, "Truly, this was the Son of God!" (27:54). Matthew's gospel raises questions about Jesus: What sort of man is he that he can walk on water and calm storms? Who do his disciples think he is? Matthew's gospel answers the questions it raises, proclaiming that **truly** he is **the Son of God.**

For reflection: Who do I profess Jesus to be? What does it mean for my relationship with him, and my relationship with God, that Jesus is the Son of God?

Jesus Saves All Who Turn to Him

³⁴ After making the crossing, they came to land at Gennesaret. ³⁵ When the men of that place recognized him, they sent word to all the surrounding country. People brought to him all those who were sick ³⁶ and begged him that they might touch only the tassel on his cloak, and as many as touched it were healed.

> Gospel parallels: Mark 6:53-56
> OT:Num 15:37-40; Deut 22:12
> NT:Matt 4:23-25; 8:16; 9:20-22; 12:15; 14:30

34 Jesus sent the disciples in a boat ahead of him to the other side of the Sea of Galilee (14:22) and walked on the water to join them in the boat (14:25-33). **After making the crossing, they came to land at Gennesaret.** The region called **Gennesaret** lies on the northwest shore of the Sea of Galilee roughly three miles from Capernaum. **Gennesaret** is a fertile plain that stretches about three miles along the shore of the sea and a mile inland.

35 **When the men of that place recognized him:** Jesus had a widespread reputation as a healer (4:23-25), and those who lived within a few miles of Capernaum—his base of operations during his Galilean ministry (4:13)—easily **recognized him.** They **sent word to all the surrounding country** that Jesus had come to their region. Consequently **people brought to him all those who were sick** for him to heal, as happened throughout his public ministry (4:23-24; 8:16; 12:15). Matthew emphasizes that **all** who were sick from **all** of the surrounding area were brought to Jesus; Matthew's message may be that all who are in need should turn to Jesus.

36 Jesus often healed with a touch or a word (8:3, 15; 9:6, 25, 29; 12:13), but Matthew does not recount his doing so now. Perhaps so many had been brought to Jesus that they despaired of receiving his individual attention and so they **begged him that they might touch only the tassel on his cloak.** The law of Moses commanded Jewish men to wear tassels on the four corners of their cloaks as a reminder to keep God's commandments (Num 15:37-40; Deut 22:12). Jesus obeyed the Mosaic law, keeping even what we might think of as a ritualistic requirement—something to bear in mind when reading the next incidents that Matthew narrates (15:1-20).

Those who were sick **begged** to touch a tassel on Jesus' cloak so that they might be healed, as the woman with a hemorrhage had done, thinking, "If only I can touch his cloak, I shall be cured" (9:20-21). For them, as for the women, touching the tassel was an expression of faith in Jesus; Jesus told the woman, "Your faith has saved you" (9:22). **And as many as touched it were healed,** just as the woman with the hemorrhage was healed (9:22). The Greek word Matthew uses here for **healed** has the connotation of being completely healed or made whole. No matter how many reached out to Jesus for healing, **as many as** reached out to him were made completely whole.

The word used here for **healed** is based on a word that occurs six verses earlier in Matthew's gospel and is there translated "save": the sinking Peter cries out to Jesus, "Lord, save me" (14:30). Jesus saved, rescued, Peter from drowning and calmed the sea; now he saves people from sickness. Jesus' healing and saving power is not limited to Peter and the inner circle of his disciples; Jesus extends his healing and saving love to all who turn to him, symbolized by his healing of all the sick from all the region (verse 35).

For reflection: How am I most in need of Jesus' healing and rescue? What are the lessons for me of Jesus' healings at Gennesaret?

CHAPTER 15

The Tradition of the Elders

¹ Then Pharisees and scribes came to Jesus from Jerusalem and said, **²** "Why do your disciples break the tradition of the elders? They do not wash [their] hands when they eat a meal." **³** He said to them in reply, "And why do you break the commandment of God for the sake of your tradition? **⁴** For God said, 'Honor your father and your mother,' and 'Whoever curses father or mother shall die.' **⁵** But you say, 'Whoever says to father or mother, "Any support you might have had from me is dedicated to God," **⁶** need not honor his father.' You have nullified the word of God for the sake of your tradition. **⁷** Hypocrites, well did Isaiah prophesy about you when he said:

> **⁸** 'This people honors me with their lips,
>   but their hearts are far from me;
> **⁹** in vain do they worship me,
>   teaching as doctrines human precepts.'"

Gospel parallels: Mark 7:1-13
OT:Exod 20:12; 21:17; Lev 20:9; Deut 5:16; Isaiah 29:13
NT:Luke 11:37-38

1 **Then Pharisees and scribes came to Jesus from Jerusalem.** Jesus is at Gennesaret (14:34), a region on the northwest shore of the Sea of Galilee. Some **Pharisees** (a religious group) and **scribes** (religious scholars who in this incident are probably also Pharisees) come **from Jerusalem** to Jesus. Word of what Jesus was doing and teaching had reached Jerusalem (4:25), and a group of Pharisees and scribes travel to Galilee to confront him. They may not have had an official mandate to investigate Jesus, but their reports could have influence: **Jerusalem** was the center of Jewish religious life.

Pharisees: See page 231
Scribes: See page 138
Jerusalem: See page 440

2 They asked him, **"Why do your disciples break the tradition of the elders?"** By **the tradition of the elders** they mean regulations and customs developed by earlier generations of Pharisees to apply the law of Moses to

315

everyday life. Although the Pharisees were the most popular Jewish religious movement of the time, not every Jew accepted and followed the Pharisees' traditions for living according to the law. It is evident from the question put to Jesus that he did not require his **disciples** to follow **the tradition of the elders.** He is charged with allowing his disciples to **break** this tradition as one breaks or transgresses a law, and his questioners want to know **why** he allows them to do so.

Disciple: See page 66

The status of **the tradition of the elders** was at issue when Matthew wrote his gospel. Matthew's church had Jewish Christian roots, and its leaders were in competition with other Jewish leaders for the allegiance of Jews. These other Jewish leaders (who would come to be called rabbis) embraced and expanded the tradition of the elders as the proper way to

---

BACKGROUND: CLEAN AND UNCLEAN The Old Testament contains complex regulations regarding the clean and the unclean (e.g., chapters 11 through 15 of Leviticus). The clean could come in contact with the holy, and the unclean could not. An unclean person could not worship in the Temple. A person could become unclean either through sin or for a variety of reasons that had nothing to do with sin. Sexual intercourse, even if perfectly moral, rendered one unclean, as did certain diseases, contact with a corpse, or eating certain forbidden foods. Some types of uncleanness were contagious. In these cases, contact with an unclean person or object rendered a person unclean. An unclean person could be made clean through remedies that depended on the type of uncleanness. Washing with water and the passage of a certain amount of time were required, and, for more serious types of uncleanness, sacrifice in the Temple. Most Jews were probably ritually unclean much of the time but could remedy their condition in order to enter the Temple area. Maintaining or restoring cleanness was important for priests because they served in the Temple, and special rules pertained to them. Ritual cleanness was a particular concern for the Pharisees, and their program aimed at maintaining in everyday life the ritual purity, or cleanness, required for Temple worship. Archaeologists have found widespread evidence of concern for ritual cleanness in Galilee and Judea (baths for ritual washing; cups and bowls carved from stone, which made them impervious to uncleanness), but most Jews of Jesus' time did not observe the detailed traditions of the Pharisees. *Related topics: Pharisees (page 231), Social boundaries (page 324).*

observe the law of Moses. Jewish Christians obeyed the law of Moses but did not accept the tradition of the elders as an authentic interpretation and application of it. Jesus' attitude toward the tradition of the elders guided Jewish Christians in responding to those who wanted to know **why** they did not follow **the tradition of the elders.**

The Pharisees and scribes present an instance of Jesus' disciples not following the tradition of the elders: **They do not wash [their] hands when they eat a meal.** The hand washing in question was not for the sake of hygiene but to remove ritual impurity. The law of Moses did not require ordinary Jews to ritually purify their hands before eating, although it did indicate that hand washing could remove ritual impurity (Lev 15:11). The Mosaic law required priests to wash their hands and feet before offering sacrifice (Exod 30:17-21), and it required them to be ritually clean (which might entail ritual washing) before eating their share of the sacrifice (Lev 22:4-7). In order to sanctify the lives of Jews who were not priests, Pharisees tried to extend to everyday life the ritual purity required of priests serving in the Temple. Hence they adopted the practice of washing their hands before eating in order to remove any ritual uncleanness that might have been incurred by touching something or someone unclean.

3 Jesus does not immediately explain why he allows his disciples to eat without ritually washing their hands. He has been asked a question charging that he violates the tradition of the elders, and he responds with a counter-question that lodges a far more serious charge. **He said to them in reply, "And why do you break the commandment of God for the sake of your tradition?"** While Jesus' disciples "break the tradition of the elders" (verse 2), those questioning Jesus **break the commandment of God**—and do so **for the sake of** their **tradition.** The Pharisees considered their tradition to be the way one obeyed God's commands, but Jesus tells them that they are using their tradition as a pretext for disobeying God's commands—a very serious charge.

4 Just as the Pharisees and scribes put forth Jesus' disciples' failure to ritually wash their hands as an instance of breaking the tradition of the elders, so Jesus provides an example of the Pharisees' breaking a commandment of God. **For God said, "Honor your father and your mother."** Jesus quotes the fourth commandment (Exod 20:12; Deut 5:16). To **honor** one's **father and mother** means not only to respect them

but to care for them and provide for their needs. The commandment applies to adults, requiring them to support their elderly parents. To indicate the seriousness of the commandment to honor one's parents, Jesus quotes another prescription of the law: **Whoever curses father or mother shall die** (Exod 21:17; Lev 20:9). God commands that parents be honored; cursing one's father or mother dishonors them. The law of Moses was liberal in prescribing a death penalty; among the transgressions deemed worthy of death were adultery (Lev 20:10), working on the Sabbath (Exod 31:14-15; 35:2), striking a parent (Exod 21:15), and cursing a parent.

> *Honor your father and your mother, that you may have a long*
> *life in the land which the Lord, your God, is giving you.*
> *Exodus 20:12*

5 Jesus tells the Pharisees and scribes that in contrast to what "God said" (verse 4) is what they say: **But you say, "Whoever says to father or mother, 'Any support you might have had from me is dedicated to God,' need not honor his father."** Declaring something, such as money or property, **dedicated to God** meant pledging it to the Temple, perhaps as a deferred gift. Such pledges were made through a vow, and God commanded that vows be fulfilled (Num 30:2-3; Deut 23:22-24). But what if one's father or mother needed help, and one's resources have been dedicated—vowed—to God? Pharisees had a tradition that held that a vow dedicating property to God took precedence over the obligation to materially assist one's parents (in later times other Pharisees would disagree with this view).

6 Those who held that the vow of property to God took precedence over the obligation to support one's parents declared that the person who had made such a vow **need not honor his father:** he was excused from his obligation to materially assist his father. But this is contrary to the clear command of God to honor one's father and mother. Jesus charges, **You have nullified the word of God for the sake of your tradition.** Jesus earlier charged that they had broken God's commandment for the sake of their tradition (verse 3); now he charges that they have **nullified the word of God,** not simply breaking it but abolishing it **for the sake of** their tradition. Breaking a law at least acknowledges the law; nullifying a law pretends to do away with it and is a more serious affront to the lawgiver.

7 Jesus labels as **hypocrites** those who use interpretations of God's commands to subvert God's commands. The Greek word **hypocrite** means "actor, someone who pretends." It is a pretense of obedience to God when one uses traditions that purport to implement God's commands to nullify God's commands.

For reflection: Is there any pretense in my relationship with God?

Jesus applies a scathing prophecy of Isaiah (Isaiah 29:13) to those who substitute their traditions for God's commands: **Well did Isaiah prophesy about you when he said:**

8 **This people honors me with their lips, / but their hearts are far from me.** Isaiah addressed his prophecy to the people of Jerusalem and Judea, accusing them of giving only lip service to God. In the biblical view, the heart is the core of a person, the seat of thinking, feeling, and willing. Honoring God with our **lips** is empty if our **hearts,** our selves, **are far from** God.

> [T]his people draws near with words only
> and honors me with their lips alone,
> though their hearts are far from me,
> And their reverence for me has become
> routine observance of the precepts of men.
> Isaiah 29:13

For reflection: Am I wholeheartedly oriented toward God?

9 **In vain do they worship me, / teaching as doctrines human precepts.** God pays little attention to worship given him by those whose hearts are not in it and whose religious practices are based on what they want to do rather than on what God wants them to do. Matthew follows a Greek translation of Isaiah that speaks of **teaching as doctrines** of God **precepts** that are only **human.** Jesus charges that the Pharisees and their scribes are substituting their precepts and observances for what God wants.

For reflection: Do I substitute what I want to do for what God wants me to do, telling myself that this is God's will for me?

319

Jesus previously disagreed with Pharisees over the proper interpretation of God's law (see 12:1-14); he now confronts the basis on which Pharisees interpret God's law. Jesus rejects "the tradition of the elders" (verse 2), characterizing it as an obstacle to obeying God rather than an aid to obedience. In the time of Matthew, rejection or acceptance of the tradition of the elders was be a major point of contention between Jews who accepted Jesus as the Messiah and Jews who did not. Matthew presents Jesus as the one who fulfills and authentically interprets God's law (5:17-48); Jesus' interpretation should be followed rather than "the tradition of the elders."

What Defiles?

[10] He summoned the crowd and said to them, "Hear and understand. [11] It is not what enters one's mouth that defiles that person; but what comes out of the mouth is what defiles one." [12] Then his disciples approached and said to him, "Do you know that the Pharisees took offense when they heard what you said?" [13] He said in reply, "Every plant that my heavenly Father has not planted will be uprooted. [14] Let them alone; they are blind guides [of the blind]. If a blind person leads a blind person, both will fall into a pit." [15] Then Peter said to him in reply, "Explain [this] parable to us." [16] He said to them, "Are even you still without understanding? [17] Do you not realize that everything that enters the mouth passes into the stomach and is expelled into the latrine? [18] But the things that come out of the mouth come from the heart, and they defile. [19] For from the heart come evil thoughts, murder, adultery, unchastity, theft, false witness, blasphemy. [20] These are what defile a person, but to eat with unwashed hands does not defile."

Gospel parallels: Mark 7:14-23
OT:Exod 20:1-17; Lev 11
NT:Luke 6:39

10 He summoned the crowd: Jesus wants to say something that has importance not just for his disciples but for all Jews. Jesus has just had a sharp exchange with some Pharisees and scribes over "the tradition of the elders" (15:1-9), and he presumably wants to draw a lesson or issue a warning based on this exchange. Jesus **said to them, "Hear and understand."** Jesus has previously exhorted his listeners to **hear** what he is telling them (11:15; 13:9, 18, 43). This was implicitly an exhortation to understand the meaning of his words, as Jesus now makes explicit: **Hear and understand.**

11 It is not what enters one's mouth that defiles that person; but what comes out of the mouth is what defiles one. In Jewish usage, the word **defiles** means to make ritually unclean. Jesus was challenged for allowing his disciples to violate the tradition of the elders by eating without washing their hands to remove ritual uncleanness (15:1-2), and he responded by criticizing the tradition of the elders as an obstacle to obeying God's laws (15:3-9). Now Jesus shifts the focus from how one eats (with washed or unwashed hands) to what one eats—to **what enters one's mouth.** It is again a shift from matters of tradition (like hand washing) to the law itself, for the law of Moses divided living creatures into the clean and the unclean and forbade Israelites from eating those that were unclean (Lev 11). Jesus seems to say, however, that it does not matter what one eats; what matters is what one says: **It is not what enters one's mouth that defiles that person; but what comes out of the mouth is what defiles one.** To hold that it does not matter what one eats ignores or nullifies the food regulations of the law of Moses—but is this what Jesus intends? Jesus criticized the Pharisees for nullifying God's commands (15:6); he said that he did not come to abolish God's law and that "not the smallest letter or the smallest part of a letter will pass from the law" (5:17-18). Yet if Jesus declares that it does not matter what one eats, then he has seemingly dropped not merely letters but whole paragraphs from the law.

> This is the law for animals and birds and for all the creatures
> that move about in the water or swarm on the ground, that you
> may distinguish between the clean and the unclean, between
> creatures that may be eaten and those that may not be eaten.
> Leviticus 11:46-47

What is it that Jesus wishes the crowd to "hear and understand" (verse 10) when he says that **it is not what enters one's mouth that defiles** but **what comes out of the mouth?** The significance of Jesus' words is not immediately apparent, nor is it apparent how they can be reconciled with previous teachings of Jesus. At this point the crowd might be waiting for Jesus to amplify his declaration about what enters and comes out of one's mouth and explain what it is that he wants them to understand.

12 Then his disciples approached and said to him, "Do you know that the Pharisees took offense when they heard what you said?" The Pharisees would have been offended by Jesus' denunciation of them as hypocrites whose hearts were far from God and who substituted their traditions for God's commands (15:3-9). What person who considers himself or herself to be devout would not be offended at being called a hypocrite? They may also have taken offense at his saying that it was not what enters one's mouth that defiles but what comes out (verse 11), if they grasped the significance of these words.

13 **He said in reply, "Every plant that my heavenly Father has not planted will be uprooted."** Jesus invokes agricultural imagery. A farmer might plant a plot of beans and pull out any weeds that sprout up among them. So too God, whom Jesus refers to as **my heavenly Father,** will uproot whatever he has not planted. Jesus conveys that the Pharisees are not plants his Father has planted and that they will be uprooted. When will this happen? Jesus' declaration provides no timetable. We can note that the word **uprooted** is used only one other time in the Gospel of Matthew (13:29), in a parable about the need to tolerate weeds among the wheat until the harvest (13:24-30). Those whom Jesus' **heavenly Father has not planted will be uprooted**—but not necessarily right away.

For reflection: What are the implications of my being planted in this life by my heavenly Father?

14 **Let them alone; they are blind guides [of the blind].** Because of lack of effective medical treatments, blindness was more common in the ancient world than it is in the developed world today. Blindness deprived ordinary people of the ability to earn a living, reducing some to begging. Blindness was a devastating disability for **guides,** who had to be able to see where they were going in order to lead. To call others **blind guides** accuses them of being incompetent to do what they purport to do. **If a blind person leads a blind person, both will fall into a pit:** those who are blind and in need of a guide to help them get around would be better off staying home than entrusting themselves to another blind person to guide them. Jesus characterizes the Pharisees as **blind guides,** unable to see the ways of God and unable to lead others along the ways of God.

For reflection: Is my spiritual vision clear enough that I am able to guide others? How can I tell?

Jesus tells his disciples, **let them alone.** In the context of Jesus' ministry his words can mean "Just ignore the Pharisees and their taking offense at me." Jesus' words may have had a more pointed meaning for Matthew's church. The Greek words translated **let them alone** may also be translated "leave them" and thus may be an exhortation for Matthew's readers to reject the leadership of the successors of the Pharisees, the early rabbis. Matthew proclaimed that God intended the Jewish people to find salvation in Jesus the Messiah; the successors of the Pharisees did not accept Jesus as the Messiah and they proposed a path for Judaism based on "the tradition of the elders." Matthew's gospel exhorts Jews to *leave them,* to reject the way of the early rabbis and to embrace the way of Jesus.

This will not be the last time in Matthew's gospel that the Pharisees are called blind or blind guides (see 23:16, 17, 19, 24, 26). If our only information about the Pharisees came from Matthew's gospel, we would have a decidedly negative view of them. Yet from other sources we know that the Pharisees' aim was to help Jews live out God's law, which is a praiseworthy aim. This required interpreting God's commandments and applying them to daily life—a necessity for religious leaders in every era. Not all Pharisees lived up to the ideals they professed, but it is doubtful whether Pharisees were more hypocritical in their practice of religion than any other religious group—including Christians. There were conflicts between Jesus and the Pharisees during his public ministry, and there were conflicts between the church and the successors of the Pharisees in later years. The gospels present the Christian side of these conflicts and do not paint a complete picture of the Pharisees.

15 **Then Peter said to him in reply, "Explain [this] parable to us."** Peter does not have in mind what Jesus just said about the Pharisees (verses 13-14) but Jesus' earlier statement that "it is not what enters one's mouth that defiles that person; but what comes out of the mouth is what defiles one" (verse 11). A **parable** can be a cryptic saying, and Peter finds Jesus' words in need of explanation. Peter acts as the spokesman for the disciples, taking the initiative to ask that Jesus explain his saying **to us.**

Parables: See page 262

16 **He said to them, "Are even you still without understanding?"** Before Jesus made his pronouncement about what enters and leaves the mouth, he exhorted the crowd to "hear and understand" his words (verse 10). Matthew

gave no indication whether the crowd understood what Jesus said, but Peter and the disciples have not. Even though the disciples have been granted knowledge of the mysteries of the kingdom of heaven (13:11; see also 11:25; 13:51), there are matters about which **even** they are **still without understanding.**

Jesus' words about his disciples still being without understanding may have carried special meaning for Matthew's audience. The church was slow to understand the full significance of Jesus' words about what enters and leaves the mouth. The first disciples of Jesus were Jews who continued to obey the dietary regulations of the law of Moses. As Gentiles became Christians, questions arose over whether they too were bound by dietary regulations and whether those who followed such regulations could eat with—and celebrate the Eucharist with—those who did not (see Acts 10-11; 15; Gal 2). There was a period during which **even** the leaders of the church did not understand all the implications of Jesus' pronouncement regarding what defiles.

BACKGROUND: SOCIAL BOUNDARIES Religious practices done out of obedience to God can have social consequences. The law of Moses commanded circumcision, Sabbath observance, not eating certain foods, and avoiding anything considered unclean. By observing these commandments, Jews were set apart from those who did not observe them. Because of laws and traditions that specified what could be eaten, Jews could not dine at Gentiles' tables. When Gentile converts began to be added to an originally Jewish Christian church, it raised issues about how these ordinances should be observed. Some Jewish Christians were shocked by Peter's association with the Gentile convert Cornelius: "You entered the house of uncircumcised people and ate with them" (Acts 11:3). Later, when Peter was pressured into not eating with Gentile Christians, Paul scathingly criticized him (Gal 2:11-14). Since the Eucharist was celebrated as a meal, Jewish food laws—functioning as a barrier between those who adhered to such laws and those who did not—threatened to split the church in two. Hence there was intense debate over the bindingness of Jewish laws that created social boundaries (Acts 15:1-29). The Letter to the Ephesians proclaims that Christ broke down the barriers between Jew and Gentile: "For he is our peace, he who made both one and broke down the dividing wall of enmity, through his flesh, abolishing the law with its commandments and legal claims, that he might create in himself one new person in place of the two" (Eph 2:14-15; see also Eph 3:1-6). *Related topic: Clean and unclean (page 316).*

For reflection: What aspects of the gospel of Jesus Christ have I been slowest to understand? Where do I need greater insight?

17 Jesus previously explained parables to his disciples (13:18-23, 36-43), and he addresses his cryptic saying about what enters and leaves the mouth, beginning with what enters: **Do you not realize that everything that enters the mouth passes into the stomach and is expelled into the latrine?** Jesus rather graphically points out that whatever humans eat passes through them; clean and unclean foods alike end up in a latrine. Jesus does not explicitly say that because food passes through the body without entering the heart it cannot defile, but this implication can be drawn from his words.

18 **But the things that come out of the mouth come from the heart.** In the biblical view of the human person, the **heart** is the seat of thinking and willing; the heart represents the core of a person (note how the heart is spoken of in 5:8, 28; 6:21; 11:29; 13:15, 19). Jesus has said that "from the fullness of the heart the mouth speaks" (12:34): our words express our true condition—even our lies, for they testify that we are liars. **The things that come out of the mouth come from the heart,** and because of this they can **defile.**

19 **For from the heart come evil thoughts, murder, adultery, unchastity, theft, false witness, blasphemy.** Jesus earlier said that "an evil person brings forth evil out of a store of evil" (12:35); the image of a "store," or inner treasury, is an equivalent way of speaking of the heart, the core of a person (see 6:21). The **heart** is the font of **evil thoughts,** and from evil thoughts flow evil actions. Jesus provides examples of evil actions, generally following the order in which they are forbidden in the Ten Commandments: **murder** (Exod 20:13), **adultery** and **unchastity** (Exod 20:14), **theft** (Exod 20:15), and **false witness** (Exod 20:16). He does not mention sins against all of the Ten Commandments; he is just providing some examples to illustrate his point. He concludes his list with **blasphemy,** which might be understood as a violation of the second commandment (Exod 20:7; see also Lev 24:16).

20 **These are what defile a person:** evil intentions and actions like those Jesus lists, which come from the heart (verse 18), **are what defile.** Jesus has shifted attention from ritual defilement to moral defilement. A Jew would become ritually unclean by eating anything unclean, and one who was unclean could not worship in the Temple. Yet there were remedies for ritual impurity; it was not a fatal affliction. The defilement incurred by committing sins such as murder, adultery, and theft is a far more serious matter. Jesus is much more concerned about the defilement brought by sin than he is about ritual defilement.

Jesus can now answer the question about why his disciples do not wash their hands before they eat (15:2). If what is eaten does not bring moral defilement, then even less does how it is eaten: **To eat with unwashed hands does not defile.** Eating with ritually unclean hands is insignificant compared to incurring the defilement of sin. Sin, not dirty hands, separates us from God.

Did Jesus intend to nullify the food regulations of the law of Moses when he proclaimed that "it is not what enters one's mouth that defiles that person; but what comes out of the mouth is what defiles one" (verse 11)? All evidence indicates this was not his intention. Jesus obeyed all of the law of Moses, even what we consider ritual requirements like wearing tassels on his cloak (14:36). Had Jesus eaten any foods declared unclean by the Mosaic law, his critics would surely have charged him with it. Had Jesus explicitly taught that his followers were freed from the food regulations of the law of Moses, the matter would have been settled for the early church. Instead food remained a hotly debated issue (see Gal 2:11-14).

What then did Jesus mean when he said, "It is not what enters one's mouth that defiles that person; but what comes out of the mouth is what defiles one"? His words are best taken as a prophetic pronouncement akin to God's statement through Hosea, "It is love that I desire, not sacrifice" (Hosea 6:6)—words quoted twice by Jesus in Matthew's gospel (9:13; 12:7). God was not abolishing sacrificial offerings with this pronouncement; God was indicating that he valued love far more than animal sacrifices. So too Jesus taught that it is not so much what a person eats that defiles; the evil a person does is far more defiling. Jesus did not overturn food laws but taught that there were more important matters. Jesus wanted the crowd to "hear and understand" (verse 10) that the ritual cleanness that was of such concern to the Pharisees (15:2) was not God's greatest concern. Jesus will teach that God's priorities lie in "the weightier things of the law" (23:23), above all love of God and love of one another (22:36-40). Too much attention to less important matters can distract us from God's priorities.

For reflection: What are God's priorities for me? How have I made God's priorities my priorities?

In time the church will find a fuller meaning in Jesus' words (verse 11) and draw the implication that all foods are clean (see Mark 7:19; Rom 14:14-20). Gentile converts need not follow the food regulations of the law of Moses; all Christians could eat together and share the Eucharist.

A Canaanite Woman's Faith

21 Then Jesus went from that place and withdrew to the region of Tyre and Sidon. 22 And behold, a Canaanite woman of that district came and called out, "Have pity on me, Lord, Son of David! My daughter is tormented by a demon." 23 But he did not say a word in answer to her. His disciples came and asked him, "Send her away, for she keeps calling out after us." 24 He said in reply, "I was sent only to the lost sheep of the house of Israel." 25 But the woman came and did him homage, saying, "Lord, help me." 26 He said in reply, "It is not right to take the food of the children and throw it to the dogs." 27 She said, "Please, Lord, for even the dogs eat the scraps that fall from the table of their masters." 28 Then Jesus said to her in reply, "O woman, great is your faith! Let it be done for you as you wish." And her daughter was healed from that hour.

Gospel parallels: Mark 7:24-30
NT: Matt 8:5-13; 10:5-6

21 **Then Jesus went from that place:** the last **place** mentioned in Matthew's gospel was Gennesaret, a region on the northwest shore of the sea of Galilee (14:34). It was presumably in this region that Jesus spoke about the tradition of the elders and the source of defilement (15:1-20) before he **withdrew to the region of Tyre and Sidon.** On a previous occasion Jesus **withdrew** to avoid conflict with Pharisees (12:14-15), and this may again have been his motive (see 15:12). Jesus traveled **to the region of Tyre and Sidon:** Matthew's Greek might also be translated that Jesus traveled *toward* the region of Tyre and Sidon. It is unclear in Matthew's account whether Jesus left Galilee and entered the region of Tyre and Sidon or went to a part of Galilee that was adjacent to the region of Tyre and Sidon. **The region of Tyre and Sidon** lay along the Mediterranean coast and was predominantly Gentile.

22 **And behold, a Canaanite woman of that district came.** Those who lived around Tyre and Sidon were referred to in Greek as Phoenicians (see Mark 7:26), but Matthew calls this woman a **Canaanite.** Tyre and Sidon were part of Canaan in the Old Testament era (Gen 10:19), and Matthew invokes Old Testament associations when he refers to the woman as a **Canaanite:** Israelites and Canaanites were ancient enemies. The woman who approaches Jesus is not just a Gentile but a **Canaanite.**

A Canaanite woman of that district came: the word translated **came** means "came out," and Matthew's Greek could also be translated, "A Canaanite woman came out of that district." It remains ambiguous whether Jesus entered into the region of Tyre and Sidon and a woman came to him, or whether Jesus stayed in Galilee and a woman came out to him from the district of Tyre and Sidon.

The Canaanite woman **called out**—literally, "kept calling out"—**"Have pity on me, Lord, Son of David!"** The title **Lord** was used for those with authority; by calling Jesus **Lord** the woman acknowledges that Jesus has authority. She also calls Jesus **Son of David.** Jesus is a descendant of David through Joseph's legal paternity (1:1, 20-21), but this might not have been on the woman's mind (how would she have known of it?). Jesus has been hailed as **Son of David** in conjunction with his healings and exorcisms (9:27; 12:22-23), which the woman might have heard of because Jesus' reputation had spread throughout the region (4:24). She has come to him seeking an exorcism: she tells him, **My daughter is tormented by a demon**—literally, is severely demon-possessed. As a mother, she is deeply distressed by her daughter's affliction and wants her to be well. From Matthew's account we cannot tell whether she brought her daughter with her; Matthew does not always list everyone present in a scene.

BACKGROUND: TYRE AND SIDON were the largest cities in southern Phoenicia, the Mediterranean coastal region northwest of Galilee. Both cities, lying in what is today's Lebanon, were seaports and trading centers. Tyre was about 35 miles northwest of the Sea of Galilee; Sidon lay about 22 miles up the coast from Tyre. Lands under the control of Tyre and Sidon extended east and south toward Galilee. Galilee provided grain and other crops to Tyre and Sidon in both Old and New Testament times (see Ezek 27:17; Acts 12:20). The populations of Tyre and Sidon were predominantly Gentile with a Jewish minority. The church took root in Tyre and Sidon within a few decades of the resurrection of Jesus (see Acts 21:3-6; 27:3).

Lord: See page 133
Son of David: See page 16
Demons, unclean spirits: See page 177

The woman cried out to Jesus, **have pity on me,** asking that he free her daughter from the demon. Jesus has been moved with pity at the sight of those in need (9:36; 14:14), and he healed two blind men who cried out to him, "Son of David, have pity on us" (9:27-30). Surely Jesus will respond to this mother who cries out to him as **Lord** and **Son of David** and asks that he **have pity** on her.

23 **But he did not say a word in answer to her.** Jesus does not free her daughter from the demon or tell her why he is denying her request. We must wonder why Jesus is deaf to her appeal; Matthew has not recounted Jesus rejecting any other request for his mercy.

His disciples came and asked him, "Send her away, for she keeps calling out after us." The disciples are apparently walking along with Jesus, for they speak of the women **calling out after us,** as if she is tagging along behind them. The disciples are annoyed by the woman's pleas for mercy, **for she keeps calling out.** This mother's concern for her daughter is evident in her persistence, but she is a noisy nuisance to the disciples, and they want Jesus to **send her away.** Some scholars suggest that they are asking Jesus, "Free her daughter from the demon to shut her up." Other scholars think they just want Jesus to get rid of her. The disciples exhibit little compassion for the woman or her tormented daughter—and strangely, neither does Jesus.

For reflection: Have I treated the suffering of others as a nuisance and inconvenience?

24 Whether or not the disciples were implicitly asking Jesus to honor her request, he explains why he does not do so. **He said in reply, "I was sent only to the lost sheep of the house of Israel."** Jesus seems to direct his **reply** to his disciples, continuing to ignore the woman. **The house of Israel** is a biblical expression for the people of Israel (Ezek 34:30; Acts 2:36). The expression **the lost sheep of the house of Israel** conveys that the whole **house of Israel** is **lost sheep** in need of rescue. Jesus has been **sent** to rescue them; **sent** implies sent by God. God has sent Jesus **only** to

the people of Israel: Jesus' mission is specifically to the Jewish people. Jesus ignores the woman's pleas for pity because she is not Jewish. She is a Canaanite (verse 22), as estranged from the Jewish people as one can be.

Jesus chose twelve of his disciples to have a special share in his mission, giving them the authority to proclaim the message he proclaimed and to heal as he healed (10:1; 7). When Jesus sent them out on their first mission, he forbade them to enter pagan territory; they were to go only "to the lost sheep of the house of Israel" (10:5-6). Jesus restricted their mission to the limits of his mission. With few exceptions (8:5-13, 28-34), Jesus has traveled only in Jewish areas and only healed Jews.

25 Whether or not the woman overheard Jesus telling his disciples that he was sent only to Jews, she continues to entreat him. **But the woman came and did him homage, saying, "Lord, help me."** To do **homage** means to prostrate oneself before another, an act of humility and a position of supplication (8:2; 9:18; 18:26; 20:20) or worship (2:11; 4:9; 14:33). The woman again addresses Jesus as **Lord** and makes her plea: **Help me.** She does not need to spell out what kind of **help** she wants from Jesus; her daughter is tormented by a demon, and she has come to Jesus as one who has authority over demons.

Such a simple prayer—**Lord, help me**—but sometimes all that needs saying.

For reflection: When have I been most in need of Jesus' help? How did I go about asking for his help?

26 **He said in reply, "It is not right to take the food of the children and throw it to the dogs."** In the Old Testament **dogs** are primarily viewed as wild scavengers (Exod 22:30; 1 Kings 14:11; 21:23-24; 2 Kings 9:33-36) rather than as tame pets (Tobit 6:2; 11:4). The image of throwing food to dogs is that of tossing refuse out of the house, where wild dogs will dispose of it. Jesus says that **it is not right to take the food** meant to nourish **children and throw it** away as garbage to be eaten by **dogs.** Jesus' words are a parable that compares Jews to the children of a family and Gentiles to scavenging dogs; Jesus' healings and exorcisms are meant for the children. God selected the Israelites to be a people who were special to him (Exod 19:5; Deut 7:6; 14:2; 26:18), and he sent Jesus to the Israelite people (verse 24). This woman is not an Israelite; she is a Canaanite and

excluded from God's plans for his people. Jesus is justified in shooing her away as one shoos a strange dog from a picnic table.

For reflection: What is my reaction to Jesus' justification for not healing the woman's daughter?

27 Despite Jesus' rebuff the woman will not give up. **She said, "Please, Lord, for even the dogs eat the scraps that fall from the table of their masters."** For a third time the woman calls upon Jesus as **Lord.** She modifies Jesus' parable by substituting pet dogs for wild scavenging dogs (having pet dogs was more common among Gentiles than Jews). Pet **dogs eat the scraps that fall from the table of their masters.** The Greek word translated **masters** is a form of the word "lord": the woman acknowledges that Jews have a status superior to hers. Her words express humility, as had her prostrating herself before Jesus. Yet she is also relentlessly persistent; one has the impression that if Jesus came up with another reason for not healing her daughter, she would come up with another argument why he should.

For reflection: How persistent am I in praying for those whom I love? How do I respond if my prayers do not seem to be answered?

28 **Then Jesus said to her in reply, "O woman, great is your faith!"** Jesus has noted the little faith of his disciples (6:30; 8:26; 14:31); the only person in Matthew's gospel whose faith Jesus characterizes as **great** is this Canaanite woman. Many had come to Jesus with the expectation, the faith, that he could heal them (4:24; 8:16; 14:13, 35). What was so distinctive about this woman that Jesus praises her **great** faith? One element was certainly her persistence in asking Jesus to have pity on her, which indicated her confidence that he could and would. Another distinctive element is her calling repeatedly upon Jesus as Lord and doing homage to him. Matthew's readers call Jesus "Lord" as God is called "Lord," and they give homage to Jesus as they give homage to God. Even if this woman did not realize the full meaning of professing Jesus to be Lord, she sets an example of faith in Jesus.

Because of her faith Jesus tells her, **Let it be done for you as you wish.** Jesus reverses his previous denial of mercy to her, despite the fact that she is a Canaanite, not an Israelite. Matthew concludes his account by reporting that **her daughter was healed from that hour.** Matthew provides no further details; his spotlight is on what led to the healing, not the healing itself. Jesus had his mind changed by a woman; the limits of his mission were stretched by a Gentile's faith.

For reflection: What does it tell me about Jesus that he is able to change his mind, even about something so important as his mission?

The incident may have been a two-edged sword for the early church. Those who wanted the church to adhere to its Jewish origins could point to Jesus' saying that his mission was only to Israelites. Those who wanted the church to welcome Gentiles could point to his complying with the woman's request despite her being a Canaanite.

The woman's words and actions are a model for us. Even though Jesus seemed deaf to her pleas, even though he brushed her off, she was determined to have her daughter healed and was tenacious in seeking healing from the one who could heal. She is the embodiment of Jesus' teaching on persistence in prayer (7:7-11).

For reflection: What is the most meaningful element of this incident for me? What lesson does the Canaanite woman hold for me?

Jesus Heals Many

²⁹ Moving on from there Jesus walked by the Sea of Galilee, went up on the mountain, and sat down there. ³⁰ Great crowds came to him, having with them the lame, the blind, the deformed, the mute, and many others. They placed them at his feet, and he cured them. ³¹ The crowds were amazed when they saw the mute speaking, the deformed made whole, the lame walking, and the blind able to see, and they glorified the God of Israel.

OT:Isaiah 29:23; 35:4-6
NT:Matt 4:23–5:1; 11:5; 14:14, 35-36; Mark 7:31-37

29 Moving on from there Jesus walked by the Sea of Galilee. Jesus had been at the Sea of Galilee before traveling toward or into the region of Tyre and Sidon (14:34; 15:21) and now returns **from there** to **the Sea of Galilee.** He **went up on the mountain and sat down there.** The Sea of Galilee is ringed by hills; Jesus climbed one of them. Jesus previously **went up the**

mountain and **sat down** in order to teach (5:1-2), but Matthew does not does not present him teaching now—at least not with words.

Sea of Galilee: See page 153

30 **Great crowds came to him, having with them the lame, the blind, the deformed, the mute, and many others.** During Jesus' previous visit to the Sea of Galilee "people brought to him all those who were sick" (14:35). Now that he has returned, those in need of healing are again brought to him: the **lame** and the **blind,** the **deformed** (maimed or crippled) and the **mute** (the Greek word for "mute" can also mean "deaf"). Matthew notes that **many others** were brought to Jesus, meaning women and men suffering from many other disabilities and illnesses. **They placed them at his feet, and he cured them.** On a previous occasion Jesus' "heart was moved with pity" at the sight of a crowd "and he cured their sick" (14:14). Matthew does not mention Jesus' compassion now, but it was surely at work when Jesus **cured** the hurting people who were brought to him (see also 15:32).

Throughout his public ministry those who were in need of healing came or were carried to Jesus. Matthew has described a number of individual healings and exorcisms performed by Jesus; others he has presented only in summary (4:23-25; 8:16; 9:35; see also 11:5), as he does here. This will be the last summary in Matthew's gospel of Jesus' healings in Galilee, but that does not mean that Jesus brought his healing work to an end.

For reflection: Do I turn to Jesus for healing? Do I bring him in prayer those in need of healing?

31 **The crowds were amazed when they saw the mute speaking, the deformed made whole, the lame walking, and the blind able to see.** We might wonder why the **crowds were amazed** that Jesus healed the **mute** and **deformed,** the **lame** and **blind,** for the crowds had brought them to Jesus to be healed! Perhaps the amazement came from Jesus' exceeding even their greatest hopes for those they brought to him. In amazement and gratitude **they glorified the God of Israel,** recognizing that Jesus healed through the power of God. God is glorified as **the God of Israel** in psalm acclamations: "Blessed be the LORD, the God of Israel" (Psalms 41:14; 72:18; 106:48).

Matthew does not point out here that Jesus fulfilled prophecy, but he could have, for Isaiah spoke of God coming to save his people, healing the blind and deaf, the lame and the dumb (Isaiah 35:4-6). In another passage God says that his people will "be in awe of the God of Israel" when they see him at work in their midst (Isaiah 29:23). God has sent his Son Jesus to save and heal "the lost sheep of the house of Israel" (15:24); God is at work in Jesus, fulfilling Old Testament hopes.

> *Here is your God,*
> > *he comes with vindication;*
> *With divine recompense*
> > *he comes to save you.*
> *Then will the eyes of the blind be opened,*
> > *the ears of the deaf be cleared;*
> *Then will the lame leap like a stag,*
> > *then the tongue of the dumb will sing.*
> > > *Isaiah 35:4-6*

ORIENTATION: *Matthew twice recounts Jesus feeding a large crowd (14:13-21; 15:32-39). Because of similarities between the two accounts, scholars suspect that one event was remembered in two slightly different traditions, each of which was incorporated by Mark (Mark 6:34-44; 8:1-10) and by Matthew into their gospels and presented as two events (see Matt 16:9-10; Mark 8:18-20).*

Jesus Has Compassion on a Hungry Crowd

[32] Jesus summoned his disciples and said, "My heart is moved with pity for the crowd, for they have been with me now for three days and have nothing to eat. I do not want to send them away hungry, for fear they may collapse on the way." [33] The disciples said to him, "Where could we ever get enough bread in this deserted place to satisfy such a crowd?" [34] Jesus said to them, "How many loaves do you have?" "Seven," they replied, "and a few fish." [35] He ordered the crowd to sit down on the ground. [36] Then he took the seven loaves and the fish, gave thanks, broke the loaves, and gave them to the disciples, who in turn gave them to the crowds. [37] They all ate and were satisfied. They picked up the fragments left over—seven baskets full. [38] Those who ate were four thousand men, not counting women and children. [39] And when he had

dismissed the crowds, he got into the boat and came to the district of Magadan.

Gospel parallels: Mark 8:1-10
NT: Matt 14:13-21; 16:9-10; 26:26-28

32 Jesus summoned his disciples: Jesus has been on a hill near the Sea of Galilee, healing people (15:29-31), and this remains the setting. He tells his disciples, **My heart is moved with pity for the crowd, for they have been with me now for three days and have nothing to eat.** "Great crowds" came to Jesus, bringing the infirm for him to heal (15:30); they remained with Jesus **for three days.** Does this imply that the number of infirm was so large that it took Jesus three days to heal them?

Disciple: See page 66

For reflection: What does it convey to me about Jesus if he spent three days healing those who were brought to him?

During the **three days,** those who have come to Jesus have eaten whatever food they brought with them, and they now **have nothing to eat.** Jesus is sensitive to their condition, and their hunger arouses his compassion: **My heart is moved with pity for the crowd.** The expression **my heart is moved with pity** means to have a gut reaction of compassion. Jesus does not feel a little sad that they have nothing to eat; he is profoundly moved by their hunger, as he has previously been profoundly moved by human needs (9:36; 14:14).

Jesus puts his compassion into action, taking the initiative to do something about the hunger of the crowd. He **summoned** his disciples, pointed out that the crowd had nothing to eat, told his disciples of his compassion, and said **I do not want to send them away hungry, for fear they may collapse on the way.** Jesus realistically recognizes that those who have been with him for three days are so **hungry** that they are in no condition to walk any distance. Jesus is unwilling to send them away without first nourishing them.

For reflection: What do Jesus' words tell me about his compassion? About the compassion he asks me to have for others?

We may be able to perceive a deeper level of meaning in Jesus' words. He spoke of the crowd becoming weary and collapsing **on the way,** meaning on the way back to their homes. But **the way** will become an expression used by the early church for the way of discipleship (Acts 9:2; 18:25-26; 19:9, 23; 24:14, 22). We can take Jesus' words as an expression of his concern that those who follow the way of discipleship be nourished and sustained so that they might not grow weak on their journey.

33 **The disciples said to him, "Where could we ever get enough bread in this deserted place to satisfy such a crowd?"** The disciples realize that Jesus summoned them and pointed out the crowd's hunger because he wanted them to do something about it. They understand Jesus' expectations of them better than they did when previously faced with a crowd's hunger (14:15-16). Yet they are nonetheless puzzled over what they should do, and they respond to Jesus' expectations by making an excuse: **Where could we ever get enough bread in this deserted place to satisfy such a crowd?** How can **we** do anything? They are in a **deserted place,** an uninhabited area rather than a wilderness (there are no deserts in Galilee); they are not near villages where they might buy food. Their puzzlement shows that they have not learned the lesson of Jesus' previous feeding of a crowd: Jesus can provide for human needs.

34 With only minor variations, events unfold again as they did before (14:17-21). **Jesus said to them, "How many loaves do you have?"** Granted, there is not a bakery nearby, so what do you have on hand? What are you able to give? **"Seven," they replied, "and a few fish."** The word used here for **fish** means a small fish, used as a condiment for bread in the diet of ordinary people. The disciples have enough food to provide a sparse meal for themselves and Jesus.

Diet: See page 304

35 **He ordered the crowd to sit down**—literally, to recline, as at a banquet—**on the ground.**

36 **Then he took the seven loaves and the fish** and **gave thanks:** a host at a Jewish meal would offer a blessing in thanksgiving to God for the food. The Greek word for **gave thanks** gives us the word "Eucharist"; the same word will be used to describe Jesus' giving thanks over a cup of wine at

the Last Supper (26:27; see also 1 Cor 11:24). Jesus then **broke the loaves, and gave them to the disciples, who in turn gave them to the crowds.** The disciples put what they have at the disposal of Jesus, and he has them use it to meet the needs of the crowd.

For reflection: What have I put at the disposal of Jesus, for the sake of others?

37 **They all ate and were satisfied.** Not only was a large crowd fed until their stomachs were full and they were **satisfied** but there was food left over: **They picked up the fragments left over—seven baskets full.** As in the previous incident, Matthew does not describe the mechanics of how Jesus made a few loaves and fish satisfy the hunger of a large crowd; Matthew simply notes that it happened and that there were substantial leftovers. More food was left over than the disciples had to start with.

38 **Those who ate were four thousand men, not counting women and children.** The Greek word translated **not counting** means "apart from"; there were **women and children** in the crowd along with **four thousand men.** They all **ate** and were satisfied.

The differences between the two feedings recounted by Matthew lie mainly in numbers (how many loaves fed how many people with how many baskets of leftovers); these differences are unimportant incidentals. The important elements are the same: Jesus expects his disciples to feed the hungry; he provides for the needs of many by using the little the disciples put at his disposal; his feeding of the crowd foreshadows what will happen at the Last Supper, when he will take bread, say a blessing, break it, and give it to his disciples as his body (26:26). Those who follow "the way" of discipleship will have the Eucharist to nourish and sustain them on their journey to "the banquet in the kingdom of heaven" (8:11).

In his second account of Jesus' feeding a crowd, Matthew highlights Jesus' compassion. Jesus' heart is moved with pity for those who are hungry and weak; he will not send them off empty. Jesus' disciples must have the same compassion and not turn away those in need to fend for themselves.

For reflection: What can I learn from this second account of Jesus' feeding a crowd that I did not learn from the first account (14:13-21)?

39 **And when he had dismissed the crowds, he got into the boat and came to the district of Magadan.** Now that the crowds have been fed, they can return home without the risk of collapsing from hunger on the way. The event took place near the shore of the Sea of Galilee; after sending the crowd off, Jesus got into a **boat** and went **to the district of Magadan.** This is the only mention of **Magadan** in the Bible (or in any ancient writing), and its location is unknown, save that it is somewhere on the shore of the Sea of Galilee.

CHAPTER 16

Another Demand for a Sign
1 The Pharisees and Sadducees came and, to test him, asked him to show them a sign from heaven. **2** He said to them in reply, "[In the evening you say, 'Tomorrow will be fair, for the sky is red'; **3** and, in the morning, 'Today will be stormy, for the sky is red and threatening.' You know how to judge the appearance of the sky, but you cannot judge the signs of the times.] **4** An evil and unfaithful generation seeks a sign, but no sign will be given it except the sign of Jonah." Then he left them and went away.

> Gospel parallels: Mark 8:11-13; Luke 11:16, 29; 12:54-56
> OT:Jonah 3:4
> NT:Matt 12:38-40; John 6:30

1 **The Pharisees and Sadducees came and, to test him, asked him to show them a sign from heaven.** That **Pharisees** and **Sadducees** would form an alliance to test Jesus is a little odd, for there were pronounced differences between Pharisees and Sadducees. **Pharisees** were a grassroots renewal movement and primarily laymen; **Sadducees** were a small religious aristocracy in Jerusalem that included members of the high priestly families. Pharisees and Sadducees disagreed about some basic religious beliefs (see Acts 23:6-10). They may have formed a united front against Jesus because both groups, each in their own way, considered him a threat (obvious in the case of Pharisees—15:1-20). They **came** to Jesus: Jesus was last at Magadan, somewhere on the shore of the Sea of Galilee (15:39). **Sadducees** were centered in Jerusalem and **came** with some **Pharisees** to confront Jesus, as some Pharisees and scribes came from Jerusalem to Jesus on a previous occasion (15:1).

> Pharisees: See page 231
> Sadducees: See page 476

These Pharisees and Sadducees came to Jesus **to test him.** The Greek word for **test** can also be translated "tempt" and was used for Satan's tempting of Jesus (4:1, 3). They ask Jesus **to show them a sign from heaven.** A **sign from heaven** would be a sign from God in heaven, authenticating Jesus as God's agent. Jesus has just healed a great many people (15:29-31) and fed a crowd (15:32-38), but those who are hostile to Jesus do not accept these works as originating in the power of God. Those who wish to reject Jesus can explain away his acts of mercy and power (see 9:34; 12:24). In demanding a **sign from heaven,** those testing Jesus might be asking for a sign in the sky (the Hebrew, Aramaic, and Greek words for heaven also mean "sky"). They might want a voice from heaven (perhaps like at 3:17 and 17:5) or a cosmic display (perhaps like those mentioned at 24:29) to confirm Jesus' works on earth.

For reflection: What are the signs that tell me who Jesus is? What does Jesus do that most clearly reveals that he is God's agent?

Matthew has recounted much the same demand for a sign on a previous occasion (12:38). Even though the crowds glorified God for healing their disabled through Jesus (15:31), Jesus faces opposition, now not only from Pharisees but also from Sadducees, the Jewish power elite in Jerusalem. Matthew's gospel seems to be heading toward a showdown between Jesus and his adversaries.

2 **He said to them in reply:** some ancient manuscripts of Matthew's gospel present a longer version of Jesus' response; other manuscripts present a shorter version. The longer version is printed in brackets by the New American Bible: [**In the evening you say, "Tomorrow will be fair, for the sky is red."** In the longer version, Jesus first responds to the demand for a sign from heaven by invoking a popular bit of wisdom about signs in the sky (again, "heaven" and "sky" are the same word). In Palestine, as in most places, atmospheric conditions sometimes provide clues to what the weather will be like. A red sky in the evening means calm winds the next day.

3 **and, in the morning, "Today will be stormy, for the sky is red and threatening."** A red sky in the morning, however, means that storms are likely; fishermen should be cautious about venturing far out from shore. The English equivalent of the proverb is "Red sky at night, sailors' delight; red sky in morning, sailors take warning."

Jesus tells those confronting him that they know how to interpret the timing of redness in the sky correctly: **You know how to judge the appearance of the sky.** Yet there are other time-related signs whose meaning escapes them: **but you cannot judge the signs of the times.**] This marks the end of the longer version found in some manuscripts, and it is the only occurrence of the expression **the signs of the times** in Scripture. The Greek word used here for **times** is sometimes used for specific or decisive times, including the end-times (see 8:29). Jesus proclaimed that a decisive time had arrived: "The kingdom of heaven is at hand" (4:17); "The kingdom of God has come upon you" (12:28). Jesus healed the infirm (15:30-31), which perceptive observers should have understood as a sign that the prophetic expectations of the Scriptures were being fulfilled (see Isaiah 35:4-6). Those confronting Jesus are oblivious to signs that the kingdom of God is at hand. Yet how much more important it is to perceive what God is doing than whether it is going to rain!

For reflection: What are the signs of the times today? Where do I perceive God to be at work? What response am I making to what God is doing?

4 **An evil and unfaithful generation seeks a sign, but no sign will be given it except the sign of Jonah.** The word **unfaithful** is literally "adulterous" and signifies unfaithfulness to God. Those who are turned away from God may clamor for signs on demand; those who are committed to God have little need for such signs. Jesus made the same response on a previous occasion when pressed for a sign (12:39), and he went on to indicate that **the sign of Jonah** was a foreshadowing of his burial and resurrection (12:40). Now, however, Jesus simply says that **no sign will be given . . . except the sign of Jonah.** Without having heard Jesus' previous elaboration it is doubtful that the Pharisees and Sadducees would understand the **sign of Jonah** in terms of Jesus' conquest of death. Rather, in the present context the **sign of Jonah** is best understood as an allusion to the proclamation of Jonah that led the people of Nineveh to repent: "Forty days more and Nineveh shall be destroyed" (Jonah 3:4). Jesus called men and women to "repent, for the kingdom of heaven is at hand" (4:17); those who could read the signs of the times should realize that Jesus' proclamation of the kingdom and call to repentance was no less urgent than Jonah's message.

Then he left them and went away. Jesus has nothing more to say to those who came to test him; his message and deeds are public knowledge. It is up to them to respond to his message, just as it was up to the people of Nineveh to decide whether they would change their ways in light of Jonah's message.

The Leaven of the Pharisees and Sadducees

5 In coming to the other side of the sea, the disciples had forgotten to bring bread. **6** Jesus said to them, "Look out, and beware of the leaven of the Pharisees and Sadducees." **7** They concluded among themselves, saying, "It is because we have brought no bread." **8** When Jesus became aware of this he said, "You of little faith, why do you conclude among yourselves that it is because you have no bread? **9** Do you not yet understand, and do you not remember the five loaves for the five thousand, and how many wicker baskets you took up? **10** Or the seven loaves for the four thousand, and how many baskets you took up? **11** How do you not comprehend that I was not speaking to you about bread? Beware of the leaven of the Pharisees and Sadducees." **12** Then they understood that he was not telling them to beware of the leaven of bread, but of the teaching of the Pharisees and Sadducees.

Gospel parallels: Mark 8:14-21
NT: Matt 14:15-21; 15:32-38; Luke 12:1

5 **In coming to the other side of the sea, the disciples had forgotten to bring bread.** Matthew does not provide enough information for us to reconstruct the setting with certainty. One possibility: Jesus traveled alone by boat to Magadan, somewhere on the western shore of the Sea of Galilee (15:39), and then went to an undisclosed location (16:4) **on the other side of the sea,** perhaps along the northern or eastern shore. There his disciples catch up with him, but they **had forgotten to bring bread** with them. There were no restaurant chains in the first century; travelers usually carried food, at least enough for a meal (see 14:17; 15:34). This the disciples neglected to do, and it will be evident that their oversight weighed on them.

6 **Jesus said to them, "Look out, and beware of the leaven of the Pharisees and Sadducees."** By issuing the double warning, **Look out, and beware of,** Jesus indicates that it is important for his disciples to take note of what he is saying and be on their guard against **the leaven of the Pharisees and Sadducees.** But what is their **leaven?** Jesus' saying is cryptic and demands reflection. **Leaven** (translated "yeast" in 13:33) makes dough rise; a little leaven is enough for an entire batch of dough (Paul twice quotes a proverb to this effect—1 Cor 5:6; Gal 5:9). **Leaven** can symbolize a potent transforming agent or a pervading influence. Leaven is not bad (Jesus compares the kingdom of heaven to leaven—13:33), but there is something about **the leaven,** that is, the influence, **of the Pharisees and Sadducees** that the disciples must be very wary of. Jesus has just had a confrontation with some Pharisees and Sadducees who demanded a sign (16:1-4), and they are most likely still on his mind.

Pharisees: See page 231
Sadducees: See page 476

7 The minds of the disciples are elsewhere; they may not have been with Jesus during his confrontation with the Pharisees and Sadducees. The disciples are preoccupied with their next meal and their failure to bring along anything to eat. They seem to pick up on Jesus' mention of leaven, connect it with leavened bread, and suppose that Jesus' warning has something to do with their not bringing food: **They concluded among themselves, saying, "It is because we have brought no bread."** That Jesus was telling them to be on their guard against the Pharisees and Sadducees completely eludes them.

For reflection: What anxious thoughts preoccupy me, distracting me from hearing God's word to me?

8 **When Jesus became aware of this he said, "You of little faith, why do you conclude among yourselves that it is because you have no bread?"** The disciples have **little faith:** they are not without faith, for they have enough trust in Jesus to leave behind their former lives and follow him (4:18-22; 9:9). But they have insufficient faith that Jesus can take care of them. Jesus said they had "little faith" when they panicked during a storm at sea (8:23-26); Jesus said that Peter had "little faith" when he became frightened while walking on the water (14:28-31). Jesus taught that those who worry, "What are we to eat?" have "little faith" (6:30-31). Yet now the disciples are so concerned about having **no bread** that they miss what Jesus is saying to them. They are demonstrating **little faith** in him, not trusting that he can work things out.

For reflection: How strong is my faith that Jesus will take care of my needs? How have I experienced him doing so?

9 Their lack of faith in Jesus is particularly ironic in light of what Jesus has done recently. Jesus reminds them of it: **Do you not yet understand, and do you not remember the five loaves for the five thousand, and how many wicker baskets you took up?** There had been "twelve wicker baskets full" of leftovers from **the five loaves** that had fed more than **five thousand** people (14:15-21). Didn't the disciples **remember** this? Didn't they **understand** the implications of Jesus' feeding five thousand with five loaves and having *leftovers*? Didn't they **understand** that if Jesus could feed five thousand he could feed a handful of disciples?

10 On top of that, the lesson they should have learned from Jesus' feeding of the five thousand had been repeated (15:32-38). **Or the seven loaves for the four thousand, and how many baskets you took up?** Jesus again highlights that there were leftovers after he satisfied the hunger of a large crowd with a very small amount of food. If the disciples missed the significance of Jesus' first feeding of a crowd, surely they should have caught it the second time and been freed from anxieties over their next meal. They should have faith that Jesus can provide for them; they should have their attention on what Jesus is saying to them and not on bread.

11 Jesus asks them, **How do you not comprehend that I was not speaking to you about bread?** Jesus wants them to get their minds off bread and pay attention to his warning about the Pharisees and Sadducees, which he repeats: **Beware of the leaven of the Pharisees and Sadducees.**

12 This time the disciples get the point: **Then they understood that he was not telling them to beware of the leaven of bread, but of the teaching of the Pharisees and Sadducees.** The disciples understand that the "leaven of the Pharisees and Sadducees" (verses 6, 11) is their **teaching**. Teaching can have an effect on others, as leaven has on dough. Jesus tells his disciples to **beware** of their teaching and influence.

What is the significance of Jesus' warning during his public ministry, and for Matthew's church?

At the time of Jesus, Pharisees and Sadducees disagreed about many religious matters (see Acts 23:6-10); they did not propose a common body of **teaching**. They did, however, form the most significant elements of Jewish religious leadership at the time of Jesus. **Sadducees,** a small elite, held positions of power in Jerusalem; **Pharisees** were a grassroots movement respected by many Jews. For the disciples, Jesus' warning meant to be wary of the current Jewish religious leadership: they rejected Jesus (16:1), and his disciples needed to be on their guard against them.

Jewish religious diversity at the time of Jesus: See page 45

By the time Matthew wrote, **Sadducees** had disappeared as an identifiable group. Their power derived from their control of the Temple and Jewish affairs in Jerusalem; the Roman destruction of Jerusalem and the Temple in A.D. 70 meant their demise. **Pharisees,** whose status did not depend on the Temple, survived and formed an important element in the Jewish leadership that evolved after A.D. 70. The teachings of the Pharisees—"the tradition of the elders" (15:2)—became the basis of a Jewish religious practice and way of life that was not dependent on Temple sacrifice. For Matthew's church, Jesus' warning meant to be wary of the emerging Jewish leadership, the early rabbis, who were competing with the leaders of Matthew's church for the allegiance of Jews. At issue was whether God wanted the Jewish people to follow the teachings of Jesus or the tradition of the elders. Matthew's gospel proclaims that the teachings of Jesus are the authentic interpretation of the law of Moses (5:17-48; 7:24-27), and Matthew's readers must **beware of** competing interpretations.

Jewish religious diversity at the time of Matthew: See page 491

For reflection: What are the teachings or religious views that I need to be wary of today?

ORIENTATION: *In terms of its number of words, we have reached the midpoint of Matthew's gospel. The events that take place here are at its heart: Peter's profession of who Jesus is (16:13-19), Jesus' revelation that he must suffer, die, and be raised (16:20-23), and the requirements of discipleship (16:24-28).*

Peter Identifies Jesus; Jesus Identifies Peter

13 When Jesus went into the region of Caesarea Philippi he asked his disciples, "Who do people say that the Son of Man is?" **14** They replied, "Some say John the Baptist, others Elijah, still others Jeremiah or one of the prophets." **15** He said to them, "But who do you say that I am?" **16** Simon Peter said in reply, "You are the Messiah, the Son of the living

God." [17] Jesus said to him in reply, "Blessed are you, Simon son of Jonah. For flesh and blood has not revealed this to you, but my heavenly Father. [18] And so I say to you, you are Peter, and upon this rock I will build my church, and the gates of the netherworld shall not prevail against it. [19] I will give you the keys to the kingdom of heaven. Whatever you bind on earth shall be bound in heaven; and whatever you loose on earth shall be loosed in heaven."

> Gospel parallels: Mark 8:27-29; Luke 9:18-20
> OT: Isaiah 22:20-22
> NT: Matt 11:25-27; 14:33; 18:17-18; Mark 6:14-16; Luke 22:31-32; John 1:40-42, 49; 6:68-69; 11:27; 21:15-19

13 When Jesus went into the region of Caesarea Philippi: after coming to "the other side of the sea" of Galilee (16:4-5), Jesus and the disciples walked north to **the region of Caesarea Philippi.** Matthew does not describe Jesus entering the city of Caesarea Philippi but simply going to its **region** (the gospels do not portray Jesus going into any major town save Jerusalem). Relatively few Jews lived in Caesarea Philippi or the surrounding villages, leading to the surmise that Jesus took his disciples to this region so that they could have some time by themselves (Jesus was often mobbed in Jewish areas: 4:23–5:1; 8:1, 16-18; 14:13-14, 34-36; 15:29-32).

BACKGROUND: CAESAREA PHILIPPI (not to be confused with Caesarea, a city on the Mediterranean coast that is mentioned in Acts) lay about twenty-five miles north of the Sea of Galilee, in the northern portion of the territory ruled by Philip at the time of Jesus. (Today this region is called the Jaulan or Golan Heights.) The site of Caesarea Philippi had long been a place of pagan worship, centered on a powerful spring that poured forth from the mouth of a cave and was one of the sources of the Jordan River. In the centuries immediately before the time of Jesus the site was dedicated to the Greek nature god Pan and called Paneas. Herod the Great built a temple at Paneas dedicated to the Roman emperor Caesar Augustus. After the death of Herod the Great in 4 B.C., rule over the region northeast of the Sea of Galilee passed to his son Philip. Philip enlarged Paneas, renaming it Caesarea in honor of the Roman emperor. It came to be called "Philip's Caesarea" (Caesarea Philippi) to distinguish it from other cities named in honor of the emperor. At the time of Jesus, Caesarea Philippi was largely Gentile in population and pagan in religion; only a small minority of Jews lived in the city and nearby villages.

He asked his disciples, "Who do people say that the Son of Man is?"
Jesus uses the expression **the Son of Man** as a way of referring to himself
(8:20; 9:6; 11:19; 12:8, 32; 13:37). Jesus has devoted considerable effort
to teaching and healing people, and he asks how people perceive him.

Disciple: See page 66

Son of Man: See page 151

14 **They replied, "Some say John the Baptist."** Herod Antipas, the ruler of
Galilee, thought that Jesus was John the Baptist raised from the dead
(14:1-2); others also associated Jesus with John. While there were some
similarities between Jesus and John (compare 3:1-2 and 4:17), there were
also marked differences in their messages and manner (11:18-19). It is
perplexing that Jesus should be thought to be John, since Jesus' ministry
was well underway before John the Baptist was executed (11:2-6).

Others said that Jesus was **Elijah.** This was a more understandable
conjecture. **Elijah** had been taken up to heaven at the end of his life
(2 Kings 2:11), and he was expected to return before "the day of the
LORD" when God would come in judgment (Mal 3:23-24; Sirach 48:4,
9-10). Elijah had been a wonder-working prophet; Jesus worked wonders
and spoke authoritatively for God. But Jesus claimed an intimate relationship with God as his Father (11:27) that Elijah never claimed.

Still others thought that Jesus was **Jeremiah or one of the prophets.**
Jesus was viewed as a prophet (21:11, 46), which might be why he was
identified with John the Baptist (a prophet—11:9) or Elijah or Jeremiah.
Jesus implicitly characterized himself as a prophet when he invoked a
proverb about prophets and honor (13:57). **Jeremiah** was among the
most revered of the prophets, but it is unclear why some would identify
Jesus specifically with Jeremiah. Jeremiah prophesied the fall of Jerusalem
and suffered, and Jesus will foretell the fall of Jerusalem and suffer, but
he has not yet done so; consequently, this cannot account for some already identifying him with Jeremiah.

The crowds consider Jesus to be someone who speaks for God; they
have a favorable but inadequate view of him. The disciples do not report
anyone saying that Jesus is the Messiah.

*For reflection: What do I say to those today who have a favorable but in-
adequate view of Jesus?*

15 He said to them, "But who do you say that I am?" In the Greek of Matthew's gospel, **you** is emphatic and plural: Jesus asks his disciples, Who do *you yourselves* say that I am? When Jesus calmed a storm on the Sea of Galilee, his disciples wondered, "What sort of man is this, whom even the winds and the sea obey?" (8:27). John the Baptist sent messengers to Jesus, asking "Are you the one who is to come, or should we look for another?" (11:2-3). After Jesus healed a man, the crowds wondered, "Could this perhaps be the Son of David?" (12:23). Now Jesus asks his disciples, **Who do you say that I am?**

> For reflection: Who do I say that Jesus is? Who do I proclaim him to be with my words and with my life?

16 **Simon Peter said in reply:** On an earlier occasion, Peter asked Jesus to "explain [this] parable to us," acting as a spokesman for the disciples (15:15), but Peter is now speaking on his own behalf, as is clear from what follows. Just as Peter invited Jesus to command him to walk upon the water (14:28-29), so Peter now ventures out over the depths of mystery. He tells Jesus, **You are the Messiah, the Son of the living God.** This is the first time in Matthew's gospel that a disciple calls Jesus **the Messiah,** or Christ, although readers of Matthew's gospel have known that Jesus is the Messiah from its opening pages (1:1, 16-18). At the time of Jesus, different Jews had different expectations of who the **Messiah** would be and what he would do. The most common expectation was that he would be a descendant of David who would rule on behalf of God, restoring Jewish independence and vanquishing enemies. Some expected the coming of the Messiah would mean that God was bringing the present age to an end and inaugurating a new age. Peter professes his belief that Jesus is not, as most view him, simply a prophet but that he is **the Messiah**—a unique agent of God who brings God's plans for his people to fulfillment.

Peter also professes that Jesus is **the Son of the living God.** Scripture speaks of God as **the living God** to contrast God with lifeless idols (2 Kings 19:16-19; Dan 14:5; Acts 14:15) or to affirm God's power and majesty (Deut 5:26; Joshua 3:10; Jer 10:10; Dan 6:27; Heb 10:31). Jesus is the Son of this God. Just as there was no single, clearly defined understanding of the Messiah at the time of Jesus, so too the expression "son of God" could have a range of meanings. God could refer to an Israelite king as his son (2 Sam 7:14), and an upright man could be called a son of

God (Wisd 2:18). Matthew's readers know that Jesus is the Son of God in a unique sense. God proclaimed from heaven, "This is my beloved Son, with whom I am well pleased" (3:17). Jesus spoke of knowing God as his Father

---

BACKGROUND: MESSIAH, CHRIST   There is a temptation to define the meaning of the title "Messiah," or "Christ," in terms of who Jesus is, and to presume that this is the meaning that the word *messiah* had for Jews at the time of Jesus. The situation was more complex, however. The Hebrew word *messiah* is a noun meaning "anointed one," that is, a person anointed, or smeared, as with olive oil. Israelite kings were ceremonially anointed, as were high priests. Thus a king could be referred to as God's "anointed" (Psalm 2:2). Based partly on a prophecy of the prophet Nathan, an expectation developed that an anointed descendant of David would play a decisive role in God's plans for his people; Nathan had prophesied to David that his throne would "stand firm forever" (2 Sam 7:16). David's dynasty came to an end with the Babylonian conquest of 587 B.C., and Jews were under foreign rule for the next four centuries. In the two centuries before Jesus, there was a resurgence of hopes for rule by a descendant of David—a messiah. Alongside various expectations for a kingly messiah, Jewish writings from this period spoke of other messianic figures; there was no single clearly defined picture of a messiah. One Jewish group, the Essenes, expected God to send two messiahs: a kingly messiah descended from David and a priestly messiah descended from Aaron. Most messianic hopes had a political dimension: God would bring an end to Roman domination. Some expected God to bring the present age to an end and to usher in a new age. There was no expectation that a messiah would suffer: the "servant" of Isaiah 52:13–53:12 was not identified with the Messiah before the time of Jesus.

Jesus was ambivalent about being called the Messiah. On the one hand, he could accept it, because he *was* establishing the reign of God as God's agent. On the other hand, popular understandings of what a messiah would do usually included the overthrow of Roman rule, and that was not Jesus' mission. Jesus clarified what it meant for him to be called the Messiah through his teachings, death, and resurrection. The New Testament, written in Greek, uses the Greek word for "anointed," *christos,* which gives us the word "Christ." The early church embraced the word "Christ" as its most common title for Jesus, so much so that it evolved from being a title (Jesus the Christ) to being virtually a second name (Jesus Christ). *Related topics: The age to come (page 250), Essenes (page 238), Jewish expectations at the time of Jesus (page 515), Kingdom of heaven (page 266), Nonbiblical writings (page 198), Psalms of Solomon (page 354).*

in the way that only the Son can know him (11:27). Peter grasps the implications of this: Jesus is uniquely **the Son of the living God.**

Son of God: See page 52

After Jesus calmed a storm at sea, his disciples "did him homage"—an act of reverence or worship—and proclaimed, "Truly you are the Son of God" (14:33). Peter now has greater insight into Jesus' identity. Peter links Jesus' being **the Messiah** with his being **the Son of the living God.** No Old Testament prophecy refers to the Messiah as the Son of God, although there are hints in 2 Samuel 7:12-14 and Psalm 2:2, 6-7. Peter makes the connection: Jesus is not only God's agent but is in a special sense God's Son. Jesus is **the Messiah, the Son of the living God.**

For reflection: What does it mean for me that Jesus is the Messiah and Son of God?

17 **Jesus said to him in reply, "Blessed are you, Simon son of Jonah."** Jesus responds to Peter with a beatitude, proclaiming him fortunate. He addresses him as **Simon,** the name his father **Jonah** gave him. He tells Simon that he is blessed because **flesh and blood has not revealed this to you**—revealed that Jesus is the Messiah and Son of the living God. **Flesh and blood** is an idiom for that which is human. Jesus tells Simon that he did not recognize his identity by human reasoning or learn it from another human; rather, it was revealed to him by **my heavenly Father.** Jesus had burst out in praise to his Father for the revelations he gave to the childlike (11:25-26). Now Jesus proclaims Peter blessed because he has received such a revelation (see also 13:16-17).

Beatitudes: See page 73

18 **And so I say to you, you are Peter, and upon this rock I will build my church.** Simon has identified Jesus as the Messiah and Son of God, and now Jesus gives Simon a new identity. Jesus does so with a wordplay in Aramaic, the native language of Jesus and his disciples. Jesus tells him, "You are *kepha*," the Aramaic word for rock, "and upon this *kepha* I will build my church." Matthew does his best to reproduce the wordplay in Greek by writing, "You are *Petros*, and upon this *petra* I will build my church." *Petra* is the Greek word for rock; Greek grammar dictates that it take the form *Petros* when it designates a man.

There are no known instances of the Aramaic word *kepha* (or the Greek word *Petros*) being used as a name by Palestinian Jews during or before the time of Jesus. Jesus was not assigning Simon a recognized name; Jesus was calling Simon "rock"—naming him "rock"—and from this the name "Peter" was born (the Greek *Petros* gives us the English Peter). Simon thereafter became commonly known as Peter—so much so that Matthew has been referring to him as Peter (4:18; 8:14; 10:2; 14:28-29; 15:15; 16:16) because this was the name familiar to Matthew's readers.

Jesus tells Simon, You are rock, **and upon this rock I will build my church.** The word **church** means an assembly or congregation. In the Old Testament, it was used to refer to the people of Israel. By **my church** Jesus is first of all referring to the new family of his disciples, those who do the will of his Father (12:48-50). Jesus intends this family to endure after his death and resurrection and be an assembly, or congregation, of those who do his Father's will. In the past, God gave new names to those who played major roles at critical times in his plans for his people (Abram became Abraham—Gen 17:5; Sarai became Sarah—Gen 17:15; Jacob became Israel—Gen 35:10). Now Simon becomes Peter, the rock upon which Jesus will build his church.

What was the significance of Jesus telling Peter that he was the **rock** upon which he would **build** his church? The natural association for the disciples and for Matthew's readers would be Jesus' previous words about something being built on **rock**: those who listen to Jesus' teachings and act on them "will be like a wise man who built his house on rock" (7:24). Despite storms, the house endures, because "it had been set solidly on rock" (7:25). Jesus wants to build a **church** or community that will follow his teachings and endure all storms; he will build it upon Peter as its **rock.**

Jesus promises that **the gates of the netherworld shall not prevail against it**—against his church. In the Old Testament, the **netherworld** is the region beneath the earth where men and women go when they die (Num 16:31-33), good and evil alike (Eccl 9:2-6). **The gates of the netherworld** represent the realm and power of death (see Wisd 16:13; Isaiah 38:10). Jesus assures Peter that death **shall not prevail against** his church—that it will not die out.

There is another possible interpretation. Late in the Old Testament era the netherworld became thought of as a place of punishment for the wicked (see Luke 16:22-26) and an abode of evil spirits. In this understanding, **the gates of the netherworld** would represent evil forces like Satan, and Jesus would be assuring Peter that the powers of evil will never triumph over his church.

For reflection: What does Jesus' assurance that the church will prevail mean for me?

19 Jesus promises Peter, **I will give you the keys to the kingdom of heaven.** In a prophecy of Isaiah, God promises to make a certain Eliakim the master of the king's palace in Jerusalem, saying, "I will place the key of the House of David on his shoulder" (Isaiah 22:22). This will give Eliakim the authority to admit or turn away those seeking entrance to the palace. Peter will be given **the keys to the kingdom of heaven**—not to heaven itself but to **the kingdom of heaven,** to God's active rule over his people begun in the community gathered around Jesus. Peter will have the authority to admit or turn away those who seek to "enter into the kingdom of heaven" (5:20).

Kingdom of heaven: See page 266

Jesus also promises Peter, **Whatever you bind on earth shall be bound in heaven; and whatever you loose on earth shall be loosed in heaven.** In Jewish writings after the time of Jesus, the authority to bind and to loose variously meant to declare a commandment binding or not binding, to impose rules and sanctions, to admit or exclude from the community. It is difficult to know what shades of meaning **bind** and **loose** had at the time of Jesus. Broadly, though, the authority given to Peter to **bind on earth** and to **loose on earth** meant the authority to interpret and apply the teachings of Jesus. Jesus warned his disciples against "the teaching of the Pharisees and Sadducees" (16:12). He is now making provision for an authentic source of teaching for his community of disciples. To "bind" and to "loose" probably also means the authority to admit or to exclude from the community. Jesus promises that Peter's exercise of his authority will be ratified **in heaven.** Peter is to be the master of the household of Jesus on earth, with the authority from God necessary to manage this household.

For reflection: Where do I turn for an authentic interpretation of the message of Jesus?

Jesus uses imagery in his declarations to Peter—flesh and blood, rock, gates of the netherworld, keys, binding and loosing—and does not define

Peter's role or authority in the technical language of theologians and canon lawyers. Jesus says nothing about Peter's role being assumed by another person after Peter's death but leaves the matter—as he leaves many matters—to the guidance of the Holy Spirit (see John 16:12-13; Acts 15:28-29).

Jesus Reveals That He Must Suffer, Die, and Be Raised

20 Then he strictly ordered his disciples to tell no one that he was the Messiah.

21 From that time on, Jesus began to show his disciples that he must go to Jerusalem and suffer greatly from the elders, the chief priests, and the scribes, and be killed and on the third day be raised. 22 Then Peter took him aside and began to rebuke him, "God forbid, Lord! No such thing shall ever happen to you." 23 He turned and said to Peter, "Get behind me, Satan! You are an obstacle to me. You are thinking not as God does, but as human beings do."

Gospel parallels: Mark 8:30-33; Luke 9:21-22
NT: Matt 4:17; 17:22-23; 20:17-19; 26:2

20 Peter professed Jesus to be "the Messiah, the Son of the living God," and Jesus proclaimed that Peter's insight was a revelation given him by God (16:16-17). Yet **then he strictly ordered his disciples to tell no one that he was the Messiah.** Why would Jesus acclaim Peter's identification of him as the **Messiah** and then forbid his disciples to tell others about it? The answer lies in how the Messiah was thought of at the time of Jesus. While there were various expectations, most Jews thought that the Messiah would restore Jewish independence and initiate a golden age for God's people. A hymn written less than a century earlier hailed "the Lord Messiah" who would "cleanse Jerusalem from gentiles"—from its Roman rulers (Psalms of Solomon 17—not in the Bible). Jesus did not accept popular Jewish expectations as his job description; his mission was to do the will of his Father who sent him (10:40; 15:24; 26:39), and his Father had a different purpose for him. Jesus needs to show his disciples the kind of messiah he is before they can proclaim his identity to others.

Disciple: See page 66
Messiah, Christ: See page 349

For reflection: What do I have in mind when I proclaim that Jesus is the Messiah, the Christ?

21 **From that time on, Jesus began to show his disciples that he must go to Jerusalem and suffer greatly from the elders, the chief priests, and the scribes, and be killed and on the third day be raised.** Matthew began his account of Jesus' public ministry by writing that "from that time on, Jesus began to preach" (4:17). Now for a second time Matthew uses the phrase **from that time on** to signal a beginning. Many of Jesus' efforts have been directed at teaching and healing the crowds; now his focus will be on preparing his disciples for his death.

Jesus began to show his disciples what must happen in the days ahead. Jesus is God's revealer (11:27), and he now reveals to his disciples things about his identity and mission that cannot be fathomed simply by human reasoning (see 16:17).

Jesus began to show his disciples **that he must go to Jerusalem.** The key word is **must,** and here it means what must happen *as God's will.* Jesus

---

BACKGROUND: PSALMS OF SOLOMON Eighteen hymns called the Psalms of Solomon were written around 50 B.C., probably in Jerusalem. While not part of Scripture, they shed light on the messianic expectations of some Jews around the time of Jesus. One psalm speaks of a messiah who will deliver Jews from Roman rule and lead them into holiness: "See, Lord, and raise up for them their king, the son of David, to rule over your servant Israel in the time you have chosen, O God. Gird him with strength to shatter unrighteous rulers, to cleanse Jerusalem from gentiles who trample and destroy it, . . . to destroy their sinful pride like a clay pot, to smash their plan with an iron rod . . . He will have gentile nations serving under his yoke . . . and he will cleanse Jerusalem and make it holy as it was in the beginning. . . . For all shall be holy, and their king shall be the Lord Messiah. He will not trust in horse and rider and bow; he will not multiply gold and silver for war. . . . He himself will be free from sin so as to rule over a great people. He will put officials to shame and drive out sinners by the strength of a word. And he will not weaken during his days, because of his God, for God has made him powerful with a holy spirit. . . . This is the majesty of the king of Israel, whom God knew, to raise him over the house of Israel" (PsSol 17:21-24, 30, 32-33, 36-37, 42). The "Lord Messiah" of this psalm, while sinless, is a human being, and his rule takes place on this earth. *Related topics: Jewish expectations at the time of Jesus (page 515), Messiah, Christ (page 349), Nonbiblical writings (page 198), Son of David (page 16).*

is revealing to his disciples what he must do as the Messiah and Son of God to carry out God's will. Four things **must** happen. The first is that he **must go to Jerusalem,** the site of the Temple and the center of Jewish life. Matthew has not described Jesus previously visiting Jerusalem.

Jerusalem: See page 440

Second, Jesus must **suffer greatly from the elders, the chief priests, and the scribes.** The words translated **suffer greatly** could also be translated "suffer many things." There was no popular expectation that the Messiah would suffer (the "suffering servant" of Isaiah 52:13–53:12 was not identified with the Messiah before the time of Jesus), but Jesus reveals to his disciples that it is God's will that he **suffer greatly.** Jesus will suffer at the hands of **the elders, the chief priests, and the scribes,** the three categories of members in the Sanhedrin, the Jewish religious council in Jerusalem. Jewish people in general will not be the cause of Jesus' sufferings, only the Jewish religious leadership.

Elders: See page 451
High priest, chief priests: See page 566
Scribes: See page 138
Sanhedrin: See page 601

Third, Jesus must **be killed.** Jesus has previously given hints of his death—he will be taken away (9:15) and spend three days in the grave (12:40)—but this is his first explicit announcement that he must die. Being killed runs counter to expectations for the Messiah; the Messiah would triumph over enemies, not suffer death. Jesus does not immediately explain why it is God's will that he suffer and **be killed;** Jesus is just beginning to **show his disciples** what **must** happen.

Fourth, Jesus must **on the third day be raised.** The expression **on the third day** can be an idiom for a few days (see Hosea 6:2). The implication of **be raised** is be raised *by* God. Many Jews expected a resurrection of the dead at the end of this age; but Jesus speaks of God vindicating him shortly after his death, raising him up as part of what **must** happen.

If these things **must** happen to Jesus, no wonder he does not want his disciples telling people that he is the Messiah! God's plan for Jesus as the Messiah is so different from people's expectations, that calling Jesus the Messiah now would be an obstacle to their grasping the true nature of his messiahship.

Jesus has proclaimed what **must** happen as God's will, but it is not easy for us to understand why God decided that his beloved Son should suffer and die as the way of giving us eternal life.

For reflection: What is my reaction to Jesus' words about what must happen to him?

22 **Then Peter took him aside and began to rebuke him.** Peter takes Jesus aside to have a private word with him and begins to **rebuke** Jesus, as one might rebuke a willfully obtuse person. Peter tells Jesus, **God forbid, Lord! No such thing shall ever happen to you.** Peter couches his rebuke respectfully, calling Jesus **Lord,** but he flatly contradicts what Jesus said must happen: **no such thing shall ever happen to you.** Peter thinks he understands better than Jesus what it means for Jesus to be the Messiah and Son of God. How could the Messiah experience defeat? How could God allow his Son to suffer and be killed? Matthew's readers know that Jesus is the *beloved* Son of God (3:17): how could it be God's will that his beloved Son suffer greatly?

Lord: See page 133

For reflection: Have I ever rebuked God for the way he handles things? Have I been tempted to do so?

23 **He turned and said to Peter, "Get behind me, Satan! You are an obstacle to me. You are thinking not as God does, but as human beings do."** The Hebrew word *satan* means "adversary" or "accuser"; it eventually became a name for the chief of evil spirits. By denying that Jesus must suffer and die, Peter has made himself an **obstacle** to Jesus carrying out God's will. The Greek work for **obstacle** means "a stumbling block"; Peter the rock (16:18) has become a stone in Jesus' path. Peter's fault lies in **thinking not as God does, but as human beings do.** Jesus was trying to show his disciples what must happen as God's will; despite God's revelation to Peter (16:17), Peter persists in human ways of thinking.

Satan: See page 55

For reflection: To what extent does my thinking reflect God's values and priorities?

By clinging to human ways of thinking, Peter has aligned himself with Jesus' chief adversary, **Satan.** Satan tried to get Jesus to swerve from doing God's will by exempting himself from suffering: "If you are the Son of God, command that these stones become loaves of bread . . . if you are the Son of God, throw yourself down" (4:3, 6). Now Peter, though acknowledging that Jesus is the "Son of the living God" (16:16), would also deflect Jesus from the path he must follow.

While Jesus told Satan to "Get away" (4:10), Jesus tells Peter to **get behind me,** to resume his position as a follower, walking behind Jesus. Jesus will go on to tell Peter and all his disciples—including us—what is involved in following him (16:24-26).

For reflection: What is the lesson for me in Peter the rock becoming a stumbling block?

The Cost and Reward of Discipleship

24 Then Jesus said to his disciples, "Whoever wishes to come after me must deny himself, take up his cross, and follow me. **25** For whoever wishes to save his life will lose it, but whoever loses his life for my sake will find it. **26** What profit would there be for one to gain the whole world and forfeit his life? Or what can one give in exchange for his life? **27** For the Son of Man will come with his angels in his Father's glory, and then he will repay everyone according to his conduct. **28** Amen, I say to you, there are some standing here who will not taste death until they see the Son of Man coming in his kingdom."

Gospel parallels: Mark 8:34–9:1; Luke 9:23-27
NT: Matt 7:21; 10:23-25, 38-39; 13:40-43; John 12:25

24 Jesus revealed to his disciples that he must go to Jerusalem to suffer, be killed, and be raised (16:21). Disciples must become like their master (10:25); the disciples of Jesus must follow the path he takes. **Then Jesus said to his disciples, "Whoever wishes to come after me must deny himself, take up his cross, and follow me."** To **come after** (or behind) means to follow Jesus as a disciple; Jesus used the same expression when he told Peter to get "behind" him (16:23). **Wishes** has nuances of both "whoever *desires* to be his disciple" and "whoever *is resolved* to be his disciple."

Disciple: See page 66

Whoever wants to be Jesus' disciple **must deny himself** or herself. To **deny** someone means to renounce having any connection with that person (as Peter will deny Jesus—26:34, 69-75). To **deny** oneself means extinguishing self-centeredness, leaving one's old self behind, abandoning oneself to the will of God. To deny oneself is not giving up chocolates for Lent but having a heart transplant, allowing God to replace our hearts of stone with hearts of flesh (see Ezek 11:19). The verb **deny** is in a tense that indicates a single act rather than a continuing action.

Whoever wishes to be Jesus' disciple must **take up his** or her **cross.** Those who were to be crucified were made to carry the crossbeam to the place of their execution, where upright beams were already set in place. To carry a crossbeam meant to be on the way to a shameful and horrible death. When Jesus spoke of a **cross,** his disciples would have understood it as an image for an excruciating death (an image he previously used—10:38). Giving one's life to Jesus means being willing to give up one's life for him. Whoever wishes to be Jesus' disciple must **take up** his or her cross, not grudgingly enduring it but accepting and embracing it. The verb **take up** is in a tense that indicates a single act rather than a continuing action. To **deny** oneself and **take up** one's cross is a decisive, life-changing step.

Crucifixion: See page 635

Jesus tells those who desire to be his disciples **follow me:** they must walk after him along the path he takes, willingly sharing his fate. Disciples must so closely identify themselves with Jesus that they have no other identity. Paul expresses it: "I have been crucified with Christ; yet I live, no longer I, but Christ lives in me" (Gal 2:19-20). The verb **follow** is in a tense that can convey continuing action: being a disciple of Jesus is life-long endeavor.

For reflection: What does it mean for me to deny myself, take up my cross, and follow Jesus?

25 Why should anyone embrace self-denial to the point of death? Jesus provides three sets of considerations, each beginning with "for." **For whoever wishes to save his life will lose it.** The word **life** in this context could also be translated "self." **Whoever** draws back from denying himself, whoever tries to preserve her life by not following Jesus along the way of the cross, will **lose** his or her life. It is implied that the loss of life will occur at a final judgment (see verse 27). Jesus tells his followers that they cannot **save themselves, but whoever loses his life for my sake will find it.** Losing one's life for the **sake** of, on account of, Jesus means denying oneself in order to follow Jesus. Those who do so **will find** life at the final judgment—**find** in the sense of obtain or acquire. The cost of discipleship may be high, but the reward is immeasurably greater: eternal **life.**

For reflection: Where am I in the process of saving my life or losing my life?

26 **What profit would there be for one to gain the whole world and forfeit his life?** (The Greek text of Matthew's gospel reads, *For* **what profit would there be**). Suppose you were able to **gain the whole world:** your every whim would be satisfied as long as you live—but then what? If you **forfeit** your life at the final judgment, what **profit** do you have? **Or what can one give in exchange for his life?** What is the fair market value of your **life** or self; what would you be willing to take **in exchange** for ceasing to exist—or for being thrown into Gehenna (5:29-30)? Jesus' questions put self-seeking and self-denial in the perspective of eternity.

27 **For the Son of Man will come with his angels in his Father's glory, and then he will repay everyone according to his conduct.** Jesus has referred to himself as **the Son of Man** in conjunction with his public ministry (16:13); now he uses this expression to speak of himself after he has been raised from the dead (16:21). Then he will be **in his Father's glory** and will come with **his angels** to execute judgment. Jesus previously spoke of his role at the final judgment (7:21-23; 13:40-43) and will do so again (19:28; 25:31-46). He refers to angels as **his angels,** under his command (see also 13:41). The one who must go to Jerusalem to suffer and be killed will judge the human race after he has been raised—the ultimate in reversals of fortune. **He will repay everyone according to his conduct:** Jesus echoes words used in the Old Testament (Psalm 62:13; Prov 24:12; Sirach 35:22) but applies them to the last judgment. We will be judged according to our **conduct**—according to whether we have done the will of God (7:21), whether we have accepted and acted on the teachings of Jesus (7:24), whether we have put aside our old selves in order to follow Jesus as his disciples.

Son of Man: See page 151
Angels: See page 33
Judgment: See page 557

For reflection: Am I conducting my life in a manner that prepares me for judgment?

28 **Amen, I say to you, there are some standing here who will not taste death until they see the Son of Man coming in his kingdom.** Jesus is speaking to his disciples (verse 24), and he solemnly proclaims that some of them will live long enough to see him **coming in his kingdom.** He previously referred to the kingdom of the Son of Man in speaking about the judgment at the end of the age (13:40-43), and he again seems to be speaking of final judgment, when everyone will be repaid according to their conduct (verse 27). Yet when Matthew wrote his gospel over a half century later, virtually all if not all of the first disciples of Jesus had died, and Jesus had not yet come again. How did Matthew and his readers understand Jesus' solemn declaration? It is not the first time that Jesus has spoken of the end of this age as if it were right around the corner (see 10:23), and it will not be the last (see 24:34). We will defer consideration of this difficult issue until a later point in Matthew's gospel (see 24:32-36).

Peter strenuously rejected Jesus' words about his suffering and death (16:21-22). Matthew does not recount how Peter and the other disciples react to Jesus' demand that they deny themselves and take up crosses to follow him. Perhaps their response was stunned silence.

CHAPTER 17

A Vision of Jesus in His Father's Glory

1 After six days Jesus took Peter, James, and John his brother, and led them up a high mountain by themselves. **2** And he was transfigured before them; his face shone like the sun and his clothes became white as light. **3** And behold, Moses and Elijah appeared to them, conversing with him. **4** Then Peter said to Jesus in reply, "Lord, it is good that we are here. If you wish, I will make three tents here, one for you, one for Moses, and one for Elijah." **5** While he was still speaking, behold, a bright cloud cast a shadow over them, then from the cloud came a voice that said, "This is my beloved Son, with whom I am well pleased; listen to him." **6** When the disciples heard this, they fell prostrate and were very much afraid. **7** But Jesus came and touched them, saying, "Rise, and do not be afraid." **8** And when the disciples raised their eyes, they saw no one else but Jesus alone.

Gospel parallels: Mark 9:2-8; Luke 9:28-36
NT:Matt 3:17; 4:18-22; 12:17-21; 14:26-27; 2 Pet 1:16-18; Rev 1:13-18

1 **After six days:** Matthew usually does not say how much time passes between one incident and the next in his gospel, but he does so now. Jesus "began to show his disciples" that he must suffer, die, and be raised, and that they must deny themselves and take up their crosses to follow him (16:21, 24), and **six days** pass. Matthew may want his readers to presume that Jesus spent these days showing his disciples what was God's path for him and for them, a path through suffering and death into life. As Peter's reaction indicated (16:22), these are difficult truths for disciples of Jesus to face.

After these six days **Jesus took Peter, James, and John his brother, and led them up a high mountain by themselves.** Jesus selects three of the first four he called to be disciples (4:18-22) to accompany him **up a high mountain** where they can be **by themselves.** Jesus previously taught and healed crowds on mountains (5:1-7:29; 15:29-31); now he wants **Peter, James, and John** to witness something on a mountain away from the crowds. (Only one other time in Matthew's gospel will Jesus take Peter, James, and John apart to be with him—26:37-38.)

2 **And he was transfigured before them;** implied is that Jesus was transfigured by God. The word **transfigured** means a profound transformation:

361

Paul uses the same Greek word for our being transformed into the image of the risen Jesus (2 Cor 3:18). Matthew uses imagery to convey what the transfigured Jesus looked like: **his face shone like the sun and his clothes became white as light.** A face shining like the sun evokes notions of the light of God's face (Psalm 4:7) and of Moses' face, radiant after being in God's presence (Exod 34:29-35). Jesus spoke of himself coming "in his Father's glory" (16:27); his transfiguration is a foretaste of that glory. That his **clothes became white as light** likewise conveys his sharing in God's glory. Psalm 104 speaks of God "clothed with majesty and glory, / robed in light as with a cloak" (Psalm 104:1-2; see also Dan 7:9).

Jesus will call what Peter, James, and John experience a "vision" (17:9); they are being shown what the risen Jesus will be like. They are also shown what they will be like when they are raised to life to "shine like the sun in the kingdom of their Father" (13:43), sharing with Jesus in his Father's glory.

For reflection: What does the vision given to Peter, James, and John convey to me about who Jesus is? About my eternal destiny?

BACKGROUND: MOUNT OF TRANSFIGURATION The Gospels of Matthew and Mark tell of Jesus taking Peter, James, and John "up a high mountain" (Matt 17:1; Mark 9:2). Jesus and his disciples had been in the region of Caesarea Philippi (Matt 16:13; see Mark 8:27), which was on the southernmost slope of Mount Hermon, the highest peak in the area. Mount Hermon lies on the border between present-day Lebanon and Syria; it has an elevation of 9,232 feet and is covered with snow for most of the year. Since the gospels do not name the mountain on which Jesus was transfigured, we cannot be sure of its location. Mount Hermon certainly qualifies as a "high mountain." On the other hand, some days passed between Jesus' traveling to Caesarea Philippi and his ascending a mountain (Matt 17:1; Mark 9:2), allowing time for him to have gone to another region. Uncertainty over the site of the transfiguration led to speculation about various locations. Eusebius (a bishop, church historian, and geographer who died around A.D. 340) thought it was either Mount Hermon or Mount Tabor in Galilee. In A.D. 348, Bishop Cyril of Jerusalem advocated Tabor, and St. Jerome subsequently supported his choice. Tabor is a majestic rounded hill rising 1,485 feet above the Jezreel Valley. There was apparently a village on Tabor's summit at the time of Jesus, making it a less-private location than Mount Hermon. Cyril and Jerome might have had pilgrims in mind when they proposed Tabor, for it lay only six miles from Nazareth and was far more convenient for pilgrims to visit than the rugged heights of Hermon.

3 Their vision continues: **And behold, Moses and Elijah appeared to them, conversing with him.** What is the significance of **Moses** and **Elijah** appearing with Jesus rather than other Old Testament figures such as David and Isaiah? There are two considerations. First, the Old Testament describes only two individuals ever ascending Mount Sinai, where God made a covenant with his people: **Moses** (Exod 19:1-3, 20) and **Elijah** (1 Kings 19:8-13, which uses the name "Horeb" for Sinai). The appearance of these two men indicates that what happens on the mountain of Jesus' transfiguration is linked with what happened on Mount Sinai. Second, God gave his law through Moses, and Elijah was the first great prophet of the Old Testament era; Moses and Elijah can represent the law and the prophets. Jesus said, "Do not think that I have come to abolish the law or the prophets. I have come not to abolish but to fulfill" (5:17). The presence of **Moses and Elijah,** conversing with Jesus, testifies that Jesus is the fulfillment of the law and the prophets. Jesus brings to completion what God began on Mount Sinai.

4 **Then Peter said to Jesus in reply, "Lord, it is good that we are here."** Peter is not content to gaze on a transfigured Jesus speaking with Moses and Elijah; Peter involves himself in the scene. He addresses Jesus as **Lord,** or Master, a respectful title that is also used for God. Peter declares that **it is good that we are here.** What follows may indicate that Peter intends his **we** to include Jesus, Moses, and Elijah. If so, Peter's pronouncement is presumptuous: who is he to declare what is **good** for heavenly figures? In any case, Peter wants to prolong what is occurring and makes a proposal. He begins with a deferential **If you wish,** leaving the decision up to Jesus. But his proposal is fanciful, almost absurd: **I will make three tents here, one for you, one for Moses, and one for Elijah;** I will take care of your needs. But a transfigured Jesus and Moses and Elijah hardly need shelter from the elements or tents to sleep in at night. Perhaps Peter is trying to sidetrack Jesus from going to Jerusalem to suffer and die (see 16:22); perhaps Peter thinks Jesus will be safe if he can get him to remain on the mountain.

Lord: See page 133

5 Peter's proposal is smothered before his words are out of his mouth. **While he was still speaking, behold, a bright cloud cast a shadow over them.** In the Old Testament, God's presence was simultaneously manifested and concealed by a **cloud** (Exod 19:9, 16; 24:15-16; 34:5; 40:34-35; 1 Kings

8:10-12; 2 Macc 2:8). That the cloud is **bright** conveys the radiance of God's glory. The cloud **cast a shadow over them:** it overshadowed or enveloped Jesus, Moses, and Elijah, obscuring them from the disciples' view.

Then from the cloud came a voice that said, "This is my beloved Son, with whom I am well pleased; listen to him." Before Jesus began his public ministry, "a voice came from the heavens, saying, 'This is my beloved Son, with whom I am well pleased'"(3:17). Now, before Jesus sets out for Jerusalem and death (16:21), God speaks again, addressing Peter, James, and John. God again proclaims, **This is my beloved Son, with whom I am well pleased.** As before, the Greek word for **beloved** can convey the notion of "only beloved": Jesus is uniquely the **Son** of God and loved by him. God proclaims that he is **well pleased** with Jesus, echoing a prophecy of Isaiah in which God proclaims "here is my servant whom I uphold, / my chosen one with whom I am pleased" (Isaiah 42:1). Another prophecy in Isaiah speaks of God's servant accepting suffering and death for the sake of others (Isaiah 52:13–53:12). God the Father is pleased that his Son Jesus is set upon serving him, even at the cost of his life.

Son of God: See page 52

The voice from the cloud commands Peter, James, and John to **listen to him.** In Hebrew, to **listen** to someone sometimes means both to hear and to obey what is said. The disciples are to **listen** to all that Jesus teaches and are to live by his teachings. (The Sermon on the Mount concludes with Jesus saying, "Everyone who listens to these words of mine and acts on them . . ."—7:24.) The law was given through Moses, and God spoke to his people through prophets like Elijah, but Jesus is greater than Moses and Elijah: he is the beloved Son of God. His words are to be heeded even more than the words of Moses and the prophets.

God's command, **listen to him,** can have a more specific meaning. Jesus has told his disciples that he must go to Jerusalem, suffer greatly, be put to death, and rise; he has told them that they must deny themselves and take up their crosses if they wish to follow him (16:21, 24). These are hard realities to accept, but God commands Peter, James, and John to **listen** to what Jesus has been telling them. Disciples must embrace Jesus' words as the way to life (see 16:25-27).

For reflection: How carefully do I listen to the words of Jesus? How consistently do I try to live them out?

6 **When the disciples heard this, they fell prostrate**—literally, they "fell on their faces"—**and were very much afraid.** Hearing God speak is an awesome experience; the disciples are so terrified that they fall down. What God says to them is not in itself terrifying; that God speaks to them fills them with fearful awe. For a creature to be addressed by her or his creator is awesome indeed.

> *For reflection: When have I had a sense that God was in some manner speaking to me? What was my reaction?*

7 **But Jesus came and touched them, saying, "Rise, and do not be afraid."** When Jesus came walking on the sea to his disciples, he calmed their fears by saying, "Take courage, it is I; do not be afraid" (14:27). Now Jesus **came** to his terrified disciples, but they did not see him; their faces are to the ground. Jesus **touched them** to reassure them that he was with them. He tells them to **rise** so that they can see him. Because he is with them, they have nothing to fear; he tells them **do not be afraid.** They should not be afraid even if God speaks to them from a shining cloud, for Jesus is beside them. Furthermore, God is their Father, and as his children, they do not need to be afraid of his voice.

8 **And when the disciples raised their eyes, they saw no one else but Jesus alone.** After Jesus touched them they **raised their eyes** from the ground. Matthew writes that they saw **no one else but Jesus alone,** emphasizing that only Jesus remains with them. The cloud of God's presence has vanished, as have Moses and Elijah. The disciples' focus is to be on Jesus, listening to his words (verse 5), taking them to heart.

Jesus will continue to speak to his disciples about his coming suffering and death (17:12, 22-23). Peter, James, and John have now been given a vision of the outcome of his suffering and dying: Jesus will enter into glory, as will those who follow along his path.

> *For reflection: What is the significance and message of Jesus' transfiguration for me?*

The Coming of Elijah
[9] **As they were coming down from the mountain, Jesus charged them, "Do not tell the vision to anyone until the Son of Man has been raised**

from the dead." **¹⁰ Then the disciples asked him, "Why do the scribes say that Elijah must come first?"** ¹¹ He said in reply, "Elijah will indeed come and restore all things; ¹² but I tell you that Elijah has already come, and they did not recognize him but did to him whatever they pleased. So also will the Son of Man suffer at their hands." ¹³ Then the disciples understood that he was speaking to them of John the Baptist.

> Gospel parallels: Mark 9:9-13
> OT: 2 Kings 2:11; Sirach 48:4, 9-11; Mal 3:1, 23-24
> NT: Matt 11:7-15, 18; 14:3-12; 16:20-21

9 **As they were coming down from the mountain** where Jesus was transfigured (17:1-8), **Jesus charged them, "Do not tell the vision to anyone until the Son of Man has been raised from the dead."** Jesus characterizes what Peter, James, and John saw on the mountain as a **vision.** He commands them not to tell **anyone**—apparently including even the other disciples—what they had seen until he **has been raised from the dead.** In order to be raised from the dead, Jesus must die. Peter, James, and John have been given a vision of Jesus in his Father's glory (16:27), but to attain that glory he "must go to Jerusalem and suffer greatly . . . and be killed" (16:21). Jesus in his glory cannot be understood apart from Jesus in his suffering and death. The disciples must have the whole picture of who Jesus is before they can announce it to others. Hence they are to say nothing about their vision of a transfigured Jesus, just as they are "to tell no one that he was the Messiah" (16:20), until he **has been raised from the dead.**

Son of Man: See page 151

For reflection: Do I focus more on Jesus in his glory or in his suffering and death?

10 **Then the disciples asked him, "Why do the scribes say that Elijah must come first?"** Perhaps their seeing Elijah with Jesus (17:3) reminded them of Jewish expectations regarding Elijah, just as Jesus' mention of leaven had reminded them that they had no bread (16:6-7). **Elijah** at the end of his days on earth had been taken up to heaven in a fiery chariot (2 Kings 2:11). The book of Malachi ends with a prophecy that Elijah would return before "the day of the LORD" (Mal 3:23-24), and **scribes** (religious scholars) such as Sirach had echoed this belief (Sirach 48:4, 9-11). The

disciples might want to know how Elijah fits into what Jesus is doing. If the kingdom of heaven is at hand (4:17) and has come upon them through Jesus (12:28), does this mean that "the day of the LORD" was arriving without Elijah having **come first**?

Scribes: See page 138

The day of the Lord: See page 48

Lo, I will send you
  Elijah, the prophet,
Before the day of the LORD comes,
  the great and terrible day,
To turn the hearts of the fathers to their children,
  and the hearts of the children to their fathers.
                                        Malachi 3:23-24

How awesome are you, Elijah! . . .
You are destined, it is written, in time to come
  to put an end to wrath before the day of the LORD,
To turn back the hearts of fathers toward their sons,
  and to re-establish the tribes of Jacob.
                                        Sirach 48:4, 10

11 Jesus in any case addresses their question. **He said in reply, "Elijah will indeed come and restore all things."** Jesus agrees that **Elijah will indeed come** as part of God's plan. In Malachi's prophecy, **restore all things** has the sense of restoring family relationships (Mal 3:24).

12 In Jesus' view, expectations about Elijah have already been fulfilled, even though this has gone unnoticed: **but I tell you that Elijah has already come, and they did not recognize him.** Jesus has John the Baptist in mind; John carried out the role expected for Elijah, even if this was not popularly perceived (see 11:18). Jesus identified John with Elijah and applied a prophecy of Malachi to John: "This is the one about whom it is written: 'Behold, I am sending my messenger ahead of you; / he will prepare your way before you'"(11:10, quoting Mal 3:1). The book of Malachi goes on to identify this messenger as Elijah (Mal 3:23). John the Baptist prepared the way for Jesus; hence Jesus could maintain that **Elijah has already come** in the person of John. Yet **they did not recognize him but**

did to him whatever they pleased. Here, they stands for those in charge—Herod Antipas in particular, who had John beheaded (14:3-12).

John the Baptist was the forerunner of Jesus in death as well as life; Jesus proclaims, So also will the Son of Man suffer at their hands. At their hands means at the hands of the authorities; Jesus must "suffer greatly from the elders, the chief priests, and the scribes" (16:21). Jesus had his suffering and death on his mind before he went up the mountain where he was transfigured, and his suffering and death are still on his mind as he is "coming down from the mountain" (verse 9).

13 Then the disciples understood that he was speaking to them of John the Baptist. Jesus' words may have jogged their memories, and they now recall Jesus' previous identification of John the Baptist with Elijah (11:14).

To modern readers, John's carrying out the role expected of Elijah may seem a secondary matter. For Matthew's first Jewish Christian readers, however, it was one more assurance that the prophecies of the Old Testament were fulfilled in Jesus: Elijah came in the person of John to prepare for Jesus. Modern readers might note that Malachi's words about Elijah are the final words of the Old Testament in our Bibles (Mal 3:23-24, numbered in some translations as 4:5-6); the next words are those of Matthew. The layout of our Bibles proclaims Jesus to be the fulfillment of Old Testament expectations.

The Power of Faith

14 When they came to the crowd a man approached, knelt down before him, 15 and said, "Lord, have pity on my son, for he is a lunatic and suffers severely; often he falls into fire, and often into water. 16 I brought him to your disciples, but they could not cure him." 17 Jesus said in reply, "O faithless and perverse generation, how long will I be with you? How long will I endure you? Bring him here to me." 18 Jesus rebuked him and the demon came out of him, and from that hour the boy was cured. 19 Then the disciples approached Jesus in private and said, "Why could we not drive it out?" 20 He said to them, "Because of your little faith. Amen, I say to you, if you have faith the size of a mustard seed, you will say to this mountain, 'Move from here to there,' and it will move. Nothing will be impossible for you." [21]

Gospel parallels: Mark 9:14-29; Luke 9:37-43
NT:Matt 10:1, 8; 21:21-22; Luke 17:5-6; 1 Cor 13:2

14 **When they came to the crowd:** when Jesus, Peter, James, and John come down from the mountain where Jesus was transfigured (17:1-2, 9), they come **to the crowd.** Matthew's last mention of a crowd was some days ago, when Jesus dismissed a crowd and went off in a boat (15:39). Matthew does not explain how **the crowd** came to be there. He is less interested in the details of what happens after Jesus comes down from the mountain than in the significance of what happens. **A man approached** Jesus and **knelt down before him,** a gesture of supplication and homage.

15 He **said, "Lord, have pity on my son."** The man addresses Jesus as **Lord,** acknowledging that Jesus has authority—implicitly, the authority to do what this man asks of him. He pleads, **have pity on my son.** The plea of this man for his son parallels the plea of the Canaanite woman for her daughter; she also called Jesus Lord and asked for his pity (15:22). His son needs Jesus' healing mercy because **he is a lunatic and suffers severely; often he falls into fire, and often into water.** The Greek word translated **lunatic** means "moonstruck"; the English word **lunatic** is from the Latin word for moon, *luna.* The boy suffers periodic seizures, an affliction that in the ancient world was thought to be caused by the moon changing phases. Today the boy might be diagnosed as having a form of epilepsy. An epileptic seizure can strike in any location, including near a cooking fire or lake: **often he falls into fire, and often into water.** The boy **suffers severely** from his affliction, and his father wants him freed from his malady.

Lord: See page 133

16 **I brought him to your disciples, but they could not cure him.** Jesus had a well-established reputation as a healer (4:24; 9:35; 14:1-2, 35; 15:29-30). Disciples were expected to be like their masters (see 10:25); while Jesus was on the mountain, this man **brought** his son to Jesus' **disciples** in the hope that they could cure him. Jesus had given twelve specially chosen disciples "authority over unclean spirits to drive them out and to cure every disease and every illness" (10:1) and told them to "cure the sick, raise the dead, cleanse lepers, drive out demons" (10:8). Presumably some of the Twelve were at the foot of the mountain while Jesus was transfigured. They should have been able to free the boy of his affliction, **but they could not cure him.** They were not able to do what Jesus had empowered them to do.

Disciple: See page 66

We can note that while Matthew has told his readers that the Twelve were given authority by Jesus over illnesses and sent out to heal (10:1, 5-8), Matthew has not recounted instances of Jesus' disciples healing anyone. This is the first time Matthew describes an opportunity for them to exercise the healing power Jesus gave them—and they fail.

For reflection: What has Jesus called and enabled me to do that I am not doing?

17 **Jesus said in reply, "O faithless and perverse generation, how long will I be with you? How long will I endure you?"** Jesus' words are a cry of exasperation, even frustration. Most of those who have heard Jesus' preaching and teaching have not accepted his message (11:16-24; 12:41-42; 13:13-15, 54-58). Jesus has referred to them as "this generation" (11:16; 12:41-42), "this evil generation" (12:45), "an evil and unfaithful generation" (12:39; 16:4), and now as a **faithless and perverse generation.** Jesus seems to be exasperated by his disciples as well; their failure to heal the boy triggered his outburst. Jesus' cries, **How long will I be with you? How long will I endure you?** echo Old Testament cries that ask **how long** an unfortunate situation will continue (Num 14:11, 27; 1 Kings 18:21; Psalm 4:3; Prov 1:22-23; Jer 4:14; 13:27; 31:22). How long must Jesus endure misunderstanding and rejection? Jesus' cry, **How long will I be with you?** has particular significance: Jesus is about to set out for Jerusalem, where he will suffer and die (16:21; 17:12, 22-23). There is not much time left for his disciples to begin behaving like his disciples.

For reflection: Does my image of Jesus allow for him to be exasperated? Frustrated?

Jesus' exasperation seems to pass, and he turns his attention to the boy with seizures. He tells the father, **Bring him here to me.**

18 **Jesus rebuked him**—the Greek could also be translated "rebuked *it*," referring to the demon—**and the demon came out of him, and from that hour the boy was cured.** As in some previous healings (9:32-33; 12:22) Jesus restores physical wholeness by expelling a demon. The words **from that hour** signify "at once"; the boy was instantly healed of his affliction. Matthew recounts the healing in few words; his interest lies in what happens next.

Demons, unclean spirits: See page 177
Demons and sickness: See page 244

19 **Then the disciples approached Jesus in private,** as if they were embarrassed by their performance and did not want to discuss it in front of a crowd. They ask Jesus, **Why could we not drive it out?** Their question indicates that they tried to drive out the demon and are baffled about why they were unable to do so. What went wrong?

20 **He said to them, "Because of your little faith."** Jesus characterized his disciples as having **little faith** when they panicked during a storm on the Sea of Galilee (8:25-26), when Peter began to sink while walking on the water (14:30-31), and when the disciples were worried about their next meal (16:8; see also 6:30). The disciples are not completely without faith (even if Jesus in his outburst may have included them in the "faithless and perverse" generation—verse 17), but their faith is not up to surmounting challenges; it falters when put to the test. When faced with a boy who suffered from seizures, they were unable to draw on the power of Jesus, a power that could only be exercised through faith in the one who had given it to them.

Jesus solemnly assures them, **Amen, I say to you, if you have faith the size of a mustard seed, you will say to this mountain, 'Move from here to there,' and it will move.** Moving a mountain may have been a proverbial expression at the time of Jesus, used to express great difficulty or impossibility. If so, Jesus builds on it. Jesus speaks of a **mustard seed** and a **mountain.** A mustard seed was considered "the smallest of all the seeds" (13:32) and may have been the smallest thing in a Galilean's experience. In contrast, a **mountain** was likely the largest thing a Galilean ever beheld (stars don't count: they look small). **Faith the size of a mustard seed** is a very tiny bit of faith. Jesus tells his disciples, if you have even a tiny bit of faith you can say to **this** mountain—the "high mountain" where Jesus was transfigured (17:1)—**"Move from here to there," and it will move.** Faith, even the smallest amount of faith, can accomplish what is very difficult, even impossible: **nothing will be impossible for you.** If the disciples had had sufficient faith they would have been able to cure the boy. There are no limits to what can be accomplished through faith; **nothing will be impossible** for followers of Jesus who have even a mustard seed of faith.

For reflection: How do I understand Jesus' promise that a mustard seed of faith can move a mountain? That nothing is impossible for one who has faith? What is the measure of my faith?

We may puzzle over two aspects of Jesus' solemn proclamation. First, Jesus said that his disciples had **little faith.** If **faith the size of a mustard seed** can move a mountain, should not their faith, however **little,** have been sufficient to free the boy of his affliction? Second, Jesus seems to promise more than we experience. Despite our faith, mountains remain firmly rooted, difficulties persist, some things remain impossible for us.

For reflection: Am I puzzled by Jesus' words?

Jesus' first disciples should have taken his words as an exhortation to have greater faith, greater trust, greater confidence in him; we should take them as his exhortation to us. Yet faith is not a magic button we can push to accomplish our will and make our troubles go away. Faith is our realizing that what is impossible for us is possible for God (see 19:26) and our entrusting ourselves into his hands. Faith leads us into the realm of the impossible, just as faith led Peter out of the boat to walk on the water. Sometimes we, like Peter, find ourselves sinking and must cry out to the one who can do the impossible, "Lord, save me!" (14:30).

21 (Some manuscripts of Matthew's gospel include at this point the verse, "But this kind does not come out except by prayer and fasting." These words are not found in the most reliable manuscripts and were probably inserted by a scribe who added a variant of Mark 9:29 to Matthew's account. The New American Bible omits this verse.)

Jesus Again Speaks of His Dying and Being Raised
²² **As they were gathering in Galilee, Jesus said to them, "The Son of Man is to be handed over to men, ²³ and they will kill him, and he will be raised on the third day." And they were overwhelmed with grief.**
> Gospel parallels: Mark 9:30-32; Luke 9:44-45
> NT: Matt 9:15; 12:40; 16:21; 17:9, 12

22 **As they were gathering in Galilee:** the last geographical marker in Matthew's gospel was Jesus going "into the region of Caesarea Philippi" (16:13)

which lay outside of Galilee. Now **they**—Jesus and his disciples—are back in **Galilee.** The meaning of Matthew's writing that they **were gathering in** Galilee is uncertain; perhaps it conveys that they were getting ready to travel together to Jerusalem (see 16:21). What will happen in Jerusalem is certainly on Jesus' mind; he **said to them, "The Son of Man is to be handed over to men."** Jesus uses the expression **the Son of Man** as a way of referring to himself, as he has before (for example, 8:20; 9:6; 11:19; 12:8). The Greek might be translated more literally as "the Son of Man is *about* to be handed over." Jesus had cried out, "How long will I be with you" (17:17); the answer is, Not long. In some contexts the Greek word translated **be handed over** means "be betrayed"; Matthew uses the word when he characterizes Judas Iscariot as the one who betrayed Jesus (10:4). There are two levels of meaning in Jesus' being **handed over.** He will be handed over by Judas to those who will arrange his death. Yet this will be the working out of God's will (see 16:21); Jesus will be handed over *by* God to death.

Galilee: See page 68
Son of Man: See page 151

23 After Jesus is handed over to men, **they will kill him.** Jesus states this as a fact but does not go into how it will happen. After he has been killed, **he will be raised on the third day;** the Greek implies be raised *by* God. God will not allow death to prevail over his Son.

Bibles usually portray Jesus' words as his second prediction of his passion (with 16:21 the first), but in Matthew's gospel Jesus has alluded to his death a number of other times (9:15; 12:40; 17:9, 12). Jesus knows what lies ahead and accepts the prospect of death as God's will for him. But Jesus has yet to say anything about why it is God's will or what it will accomplish. These are matters that probably puzzled the disciples: why was Jesus, the Messiah and Son of God (16:16), to die?

The prospect of Jesus' death was more than the disciples could bear; **they were overwhelmed with grief.** The realization that he is going to die has sunk in, but they do not have a corresponding grasp of what it means that **he will be raised on the third day.** Death is easier for humans to comprehend than resurrection.

For reflection: How would I have reacted to Jesus' words if I had been one of his first disciples? Do I ponder why it was God's will that Jesus die?

Taxes and Giving Scandal

24 When they came to Capernaum, the collectors of the temple tax approached Peter and said, "Doesn't your teacher pay the temple tax?"
25 "Yes," he said. When he came into the house, before he had time to speak, Jesus asked him, "What is your opinion, Simon? From whom do the kings of the earth take tolls or census tax? From their subjects or from foreigners?" **26** When he said, "From foreigners," Jesus said to him, "Then the subjects are exempt. **27** But that we may not offend them, go to the sea, drop in a hook, and take the first fish that comes up. Open its mouth and you will find a coin worth twice the temple tax. Give that to them for me and for you."

OT:Exod 30:11-16
NT:Matt 22:15-22; Rom 13:6-7

24 Jesus and his disciples gathered in Galilee (17:22). **When they came to Capernaum, the collectors of the temple tax approached Peter.** Jesus moved to **Capernaum** at the beginning of his public ministry (4:13) and made it his base of operations in Galilee (see 9:1). **The temple tax** was an annual half-shekel assessment on every Jewish male twenty years or older for the support of the temple (see Exod 30:11-16). For Jews living outside of Jerusalem, it was normally collected at their place of residence about four weeks before Passover. **Collectors** of this tax approach Peter and ask him, **Doesn't your teacher pay the temple tax?** Those who were not Jesus' disciples sometimes refer to him as a **teacher** (9:11; 12:38), indicating how they perceive him. In Greek, the question, **Doesn't your teacher pay the temple tax?** is phrased in a way that invites a yes response, that is, Yes, he pays it.

Capernaum: See page 61
Temple: See page 442

25 Peter gives them the answer they invited: **"Yes," he said.** Peter could have said, "I will have to ask him" but takes it upon himself to speak for Jesus. Peter has spoken up before, sometimes impetuously (14:28; 15:15; 16:16, 22; 17:4). **When he came into the house:** presumably this is Peter's house in Capernaum (8:5, 14), where Jesus lodged as his guest (see 9:28; 13:1, 36). **Before he had time to speak, Jesus asked him:** Jesus has exhibited great perceptiveness on other occasions (9:4; 12:25); now he knows what is on Peter's mind before Peter tells him. Jesus asks him, **What is your opinion, Simon?** What do you think? **From whom do the kings of the earth take tolls or census tax? From their subjects or from foreigners?** Jesus proposes a parable in the form of a question. **Tolls** (customs) and **census tax** are two forms of taxation and may stand for all taxes. The word translated **subjects** is literally "sons"; the word translated **foreigners** can mean those who are not one's own. **Kings** don't collect taxes from their own children but from those who are not members of the royal family. By translating Jesus' question in terms of **subjects** and **foreigners,** the New American Bible gives his words a broader application: kings are more likely to impose taxes on conquered nations than on their own people. In either interpretation, the answer to Jesus' question is obvious.

Peter's house: See page 148

26 **When he said, "From foreigners," Jesus said to him, "Then the subjects are exempt."** Jesus is addressing the question of whether he—and by implication, his disciples—should pay the temple tax. His answer is that he and they are **exempt** because they are **subjects** whose king does not tax them. The word translated **subjects** is again literally "sons." Jesus is the Son of God (3:17; 17:5); his disciples are his brothers and sisters (12:50), and God is their Father (5:45; 6:9). The Father does not impose taxes on his children; hence they are **exempt** from the temple tax.

For reflection: What are the greatest benefits I receive as a child of God?

27 The fact that Jesus and his disciples are exempt from paying the temple tax does not mean that they should not pay it. Jesus indicates that such tax should be paid so **that we may not offend them.** The word **offend** means to scandalize; **them** are narrowly the tax collectors (verse 24) and broadly all Jews. If exercising one's rights scandalizes others, then it is better to forgo one's rights than to give scandal. (Paul will apply this principle to what one eats—1 Cor 8:8-13). Rather than **offend** anyone, Jesus tells Peter to pay the temple tax for both of them. Jesus gives elaborate and perplexing instructions for how Peter is to do so: **go to the sea, drop in a hook, and take the first fish that comes up. Open its mouth and you will find a coin worth twice the temple tax. Give that to them for me and for you.** Peter's paying their taxes together may be another indication that Jesus lives in Peter's house.

Jesus could have simply told Peter to pay the temple tax; it was a very modest amount compared with other taxes Peter paid. We might also be puzzled by Jesus' performance of what seems to be a gratuitous wonder: surely there were ordinary ways in which Jesus could have provided Peter with a coin.

Perhaps we can take Jesus' instruction as a way of dramatizing God's provision for the needs of his children (6:25-33), even supplying payment for a tax he does not impose. The main point of the incident, however, does not lie in how Peter obtains the tax money; Matthew does not bother to recount Peter's catching of the fish. The main point is that disciples of Jesus must avoid giving scandal, even if it means forgoing their rights.

For reflection: How willing am I to forgo my rights for the sake of others? How careful am I about not giving scandal?

Matthew wrote his gospel after the Temple was destroyed in 70 A.D. Rome continued to impose a temple tax on Jews, but now for a temple of Jupiter in Jerusalem. This incident may have guided Matthew's Jewish Christian readers: even though they should not have to pay taxes for a pagan temple, it is better that they do so to avoid upsetting the authorities. (Paul will advocate paying whatever taxes Rome imposes—Rom 13:6-7.)

CHAPTER 18

True Greatness

¹ At that time the disciples approached Jesus and said, "Who is the greatest in the kingdom of heaven?" **²** He called a child over, placed it in their midst, **³** and said, "Amen, I say to you, unless you turn and become like children, you will not enter the kingdom of heaven. **⁴** Whoever humbles himself like this child is the greatest in the kingdom of heaven. **⁵** And whoever receives one child such as this in my name receives me."

> Gospel parallels: Mark 9:33-37; Luke 9:46-48
> NT: Matt 5:3; 11:29; Mark 10:15; Luke 18:17

1 **At that time the disciples approached Jesus:** Jesus and his disciples are in Capernaum; Jesus has been talking with Peter about their obligation to pay the temple tax (17:24-27). The other **disciples approached** and asked Jesus, **Who is the greatest in the kingdom of heaven?** It is not apparent why this question should be on their minds. The last time Jesus addressed his disciples as a group he spoke of his being handed over to death, and they were overwhelmed with grief (17:22-23). Why wonder now **who is greatest?** Furthermore, Jesus has already provided one criterion of greatness—obeying and teaching God's commandments: the one who does so "will be called greatest in the kingdom of heaven" (5:19). Have the disciples forgotten? Perhaps we can conclude that the disciples are set on achieving status and this preoccupation has bubbled to the surface. The Greek word for **greatest** in some contexts means "biggest"; who is the biggest man, not on campus, but in God's entire kingdom? The **kingdom of heaven** is God's ultimate rule over everyone and everything at the end of this age and, as its preliminary stage, God's rule over those whom Jesus has gathered to himself. Those who do the will of God are brothers and sisters of Jesus (12:50) on their way into the kingdom of heaven (7:21).

> Disciple: See page 66
> Kingdom of heaven: See page 266

2 Jesus dramatizes his response: **He called a child over** and **placed it in their midst.** The Greek word used here for **child** usually means a young child, in some contexts an infant. This child is old enough to walk and to

377

respond to Jesus' call. **Midst** means "middle" or "center"; by placing the child **in their midst,** Jesus make the child the center of attention.

3 Exhibit in place, Jesus solemnly proclaims, **Amen, I say to you, unless you turn and become like children, you will not enter the kingdom of heaven.** We might understand that to **become like children** means to become childlike in innocence, simplicity, openness, affection, spontaneity, and the like. In the culture in which Jesus lived, however, becoming like a child had a different meaning. Children had little in the way of rights, power, or social status. Children were dependent on others to supply their needs. For grown men and women, the prospect of becoming **like children** was not very appealing. Nonetheless, that is what Jesus solemnly demands of his disciples: he tells them, **unless you turn and become like children, you will not enter the kingdom of heaven.** The word **turn** means to turn around, change direction: the disciples must not make merely an adjustment in their thinking and behavior but a reversal. They are concerned with greatness in the kingdom of heaven; their aim should instead be littleness, being as insignificant and powerless and dependent as a child. **Unless** they do so, they **will not** even **enter the kingdom of heaven,** much less be the greatest in it.

4 Jesus now answers his disciples' question. **Whoever humbles himself like this child is the greatest in the kingdom of heaven.** Children did not need to humble themselves; they already were nobodies. Adults, however, have to humble themselves, setting aside whatever status they enjoy, making themselves little. Downsizing one's self-assertiveness and pride makes one a bigger person; freely chosen lowliness is greatness in the eyes of God.

Humbling oneself to be like a child resonates with Jesus' earlier teachings. He proclaimed the blessedness of the "poor in spirit"—those who become like children—"for theirs is the kingdom of heaven" (5:1). He told his disciples to depend on their heavenly Father for what they need to survive (6:25-34), just as children depend on their parents. He sent the Twelve out on mission carrying no money or provisions but relying on God's caring for them through the hospitality of others (10:9-11). He referred to his disciples as "little ones" (10:42) and praised his Father for revealing to the childlike what was hidden from the learned (11:25). Jesus is "meek and humble of heart" (11:29) and calls his disciples to be the same.

They must shed all pretensions of greatness, of power, of self-reliance; they must entrust themselves as children into the hands of their heavenly Father.

For reflection: What does it mean for me to turn and become like a child? What effect would this have on my relationship with God? My relationships with others?

5 Jesus used a child as a model for what the disciples are to become, and he continues to speak of a child, but now as receiving care: **And whoever receives one child such as this in my name receives me.** To receive a child means to accept, welcome, care for a child. To receive a child in the **name** of Jesus means because of Jesus or on behalf of Jesus. Jesus tells his disciples that whoever **receives** a **child such as** the one standing before them **receives me.** Jesus identifies himself with this child—and by extension with all the powerless people of the world. Jesus will go on to speak of his disciples as "little ones" (18:6, 10, 14); he has promised that "whoever gives only a cup of cold water to one of these little ones" because he is a disciple will be rewarded (10:42). In his description of the last judgment, Jesus will identify himself with the hungry and poor and imprisoned and say, "Whatever you did for one of these least brothers of mine, you did for me" (25:35-40). The disciples asked Jesus who was the greatest; Jesus has told them that they must turn around their thinking so that their concern is to become nobodies who serve nobodies, for in doing so they serve him.

For reflection: Do I treat the nobodies I encounter as I would like to treat Jesus?

ORIENTATION: *Having answered the disciples' question about greatness (18:1-5), Jesus instructs them about their relationships with one another (18:6-35). His teachings provide guidelines for life within the church.*

Lead No One into Sin!
6 **"Whoever causes one of these little ones who believe in me to sin, it would be better for him to have a great millstone hung around his neck and to be drowned in the depths of the sea.** 7 **Woe to the world because**

of things that cause sin! Such things must come, but woe to the one through whom they come! **8** If your hand or foot causes you to sin, cut it off and throw it away. It is better for you to enter into life maimed or crippled than with two hands or two feet to be thrown into eternal fire. **9** And if your eye causes you to sin, tear it out and throw it away. It is better for you to enter into life with one eye than with two eyes to be thrown into fiery Gehenna."

Gospel parallels: Mark 9:42-48; Luke 17:1-2
NT: Matt 5:22, 29-30; 10:28; 13:41-42, 49-50

6 **Whoever causes one of these little ones who believe in me to sin:** Jesus is speaking to his disciples, and **whoever** refers to whoever among them. The Greek word translated **causes . . . to sin** means to put a stumbling block in the path of someone to trip them up. In some contexts it can mean to give offense (see 17:27); here it means to cause someone to fall into sin or to lose their faith in Jesus. In a broad sense, the **little ones who believe in me** are disciples of Jesus, those who have made themselves little, becoming like children (18:3-4). In a narrower sense, the **little ones** are the weakest and most vulnerable members of the community of Jesus' followers. Should any disciple cause another **to sin, it would be better for him**—the one leading another into sin—**to have a great millstone hung around his neck and to be drowned in the depths of the sea.** Grain was milled between a lower stone set in place and an upper stone that turned; a **great millstone** is literally a "donkey" millstone, an upper grinding stone so heavy that it took a donkey to turn it. Being thrown into the sea with **a great millstone hung around** one's neck would insure speedy descent to **the depths of the sea.** It would be **better** for a follower of Jesus **to be drowned** than incur what will happen to whoever **causes one of these little ones who believe in me to sin.** On another occasion Jesus said that "all who cause others to sin" will be thrown "into the fiery furnace, where there will be wailing and grinding of teeth" (13:41-42), an image for punishment in the age to come.

7 Jesus adds two woes. Just as a beatitude congratulates someone for being fortunate, a woe laments their misfortune. **Woe to the world because of things that cause sin!** Jesus' first **woe** is over the general state of affairs in this **world.** His disciples face many obstacles, many temptations, many opportunities to fall. **Such things must come:** temptations and stumbling blocks are inevitable in a world marred by sin. **But woe to the one through**

whom they come! Jesus' second woe proclaims the unfortunate situation of those who cause others to sin. They are on a path that leads to fiery destruction (13:41-42). These woes reinforce Jesus' warning to his disciples: Lead no one into sin!

Woes: See page 499

For reflection: Am I in any way the cause of someone sinning or losing faith in Jesus? What can I do to repair the damage I have done?

8 Disciples of Jesus must be wary not only of causing others to sin; they must be equally wary of causing themselves to stumble. **If your hand or foot causes you to sin, cut it off and throw it away.** The Greek word for **causes . . . to sin** again means to place a stumbling block in someone's path—in this case, one's own path. A **hand** or **foot** cannot be the cause of sin; Jesus' graphic language means, Whatever is leading you into sin, get rid of it! No matter how difficult you may find it to forgo sin, you will be far better off: **it is better for you to enter into life maimed or crippled than with two hands or two feet to be thrown into eternal fire.** To **enter into life** means to attain eternal life (see 7:14; 19:16-17; 25:46). Nonbiblical writings from around the time of Jesus used **fire** as an image for punishment after death. To **be thrown** into eternal fire implies, be thrown by God. One should be willing to do anything to escape such a fate; **throw** away a hand or foot if need be, lest your entire body **be thrown** into eternal fire. Jesus used similar language on another occasion to make the point that sin has horrible consequences (5:30).

Nonbiblical writings: See page 198

9 Jesus adds a second "it is better" warning to drive home his point. **And if your eye causes you to sin, tear it out and throw it away. It is better for you to enter into life with one eye than with two eyes to be thrown into fiery Gehenna.** Some nonbiblical writings used the valley of **Gehenna**, adjacent to Jerusalem, as a place for the **fiery** punishment of sinners after death (see 5:22). Again, to **be thrown** into fiery Gehenna implies, be thrown by God (see 10:28). Loss of an eye pales in comparison with ending up in Gehenna; **throw** away an eye rather than **be thrown** into fiery torment. Again, Jesus used similar language on another occasion to warn of the dreadful consequences of sin (5:29).

Gehenna: See page 88

For reflection: What causes me to stumble? What do I need to remove from my life in order to preserve my life?

Jesus' warnings are sobering. Those who lead others into sin—particularly the "little ones," the vulnerable members of the community—and those who lead themselves into sin jeopardize their eternal life.

God's Concern for His Little Ones
10 **"See that you do not despise one of these little ones, for I say to you that their angels in heaven always look upon the face of my heavenly Father. [11] 12 What is your opinion? If a man has a hundred sheep and one of them goes astray, will he not leave the ninety-nine in the hills and go in search of the stray? 13 And if he finds it, amen, I say to you, he rejoices more over it than over the ninety-nine that did not stray. 14 In just the same way, it is not the will of your heavenly Father that one of these little ones be lost."**

Gospel parallels: Luke 15:3-7
OT:Ezek 34:11-16

10 Jesus warned his disciples not to imperil "little ones" by causing them to fall into sin or disbelief (18:6-7). Nor are the disciples to disdain them: **See that you do not despise one of these little ones.** The **you** whom Jesus is addressing are his first disciples, but his admonition applies to the later church and especially to its leaders. To **despise** includes ignoring as well as scorning. The **little ones** are those who believe in Jesus (18:6), particularly those who are weak and vulnerable. Jesus admonishes his followers, **see that** you do not look down your noses on those whom you think are beneath you.

Jesus proclaims that **little ones** have an exalted status before God, **for I say to you that their angels in heaven always look upon the face of my heavenly Father.** Angels protected God's people (Psalms 34:8; 91:11-12), either the nation as a whole (Dan 10:13, 21; 12:1) or an individual (Tobit 5:22; 12:12-15; see also Heb 1:14). Angels assigned to individuals will become referred to as "guardian angels." Jesus speaks of the little ones having **angels in heaven** as if his disciples were already familiar with this notion and it is not something he has to explain to them. However, Jesus may be telling the disciples something new when he says that that these angels **always look upon the face of my heavenly Father.** Some Jews believed that only the highest angels had direct access to God. Jesus would be saying that the lowliness of the **little ones** is misleading: **their angels in heaven** are among the most exalted of angels, indicating that **little ones** are great in the eyes of God (indeed, the greatest—18:4). Jesus' main point is not about angels but that his followers must never despise or disregard those who seem weak and lowly.

Angels: See page 33

For reflection: Do I disregard or disdain anyone? How do I react when someone treats me as a nonentity?

11 (Some manuscripts of Matthew's gospel include at this point the verse, "For the Son of Man has come to save what was lost." These words are not found in the most reliable manuscripts and were probably inserted by a scribe who added a variant of Luke 19:10 to Matthew's account. The New American Bible omits this verse.)

12 Jesus tells a parable to reinforce his message, framing it in a way that invites his listeners to take a stand (see 17:25 for a similar instance of this tactic). **What is your opinion?** What do think? **A man has a hundred sheep**—a good-sized flock, more than the average Galilean would own. Perhaps though Jesus uses **a hundred** simply as a fairly large round number; not every detail in a parable must have significance. If **one of them goes astray, will he not leave the ninety-nine in the hills and go in search of the stray?** The answer might not be clear-cut to us. If we owned a hundred sheep, would we abandon ninety-nine of them to search for one that had wandered off? Or would we decide that it was better to guard the ninety-nine and write off the one as an unfortunate loss? That is not the answer Jesus expects. Jesus asks a leading question, framed in a way that invites a yes answer: **will he not . . . ?** Yes, the man will leave the ninety-nine and search for the one that went astray. What might happen to the ninety-nine is not an issue in Jesus' parable—again, not every element in a parable necessarily has significance. The focus is on what the man will do: if one of his sheep wanders away, he will **go in search** of it. Sheep that stray away make easy prey for predators; the man would want to find it before wolves do.

13 **And if he finds it, amen, I say to you, he rejoices more over it than over the ninety-nine that did not stray.** He rejoices over it, happy for the sheep that has been found and is now safe. He **rejoices more over** this sheep than **over the ninety-nine that did not stray** and were not in danger of perishing.

14 Jesus' parable is a comparison for how God looks upon those who stray: **In just the same way, it is not the will of your heavenly Father that one of these little ones be lost.** It is the "gracious will" of the Father that the childlike receive his revelation (11:25-26); his kingdom is made up of those who become like children (18:3)—and it is **not** his **will** that even a single **one of these little ones be lost.** To **be lost** means to perish: the **heavenly Father** does not want any of his little ones who stray to perish. He is like the man with the stray sheep; he goes in search of his little ones who stray, and he rejoices over them when they are found.

    Jesus' parable and interpretation echo a prophecy of Ezekiel in which God promises to shepherd the flock of his people: "I will rescue them from every place where they were scattered. . . . The lost I will seek out, the strayed I will bring back" (Ezek 34:12, 16).

    Jesus told this parable after warning his disciples against despising any of the little ones (verse 10). Not only must followers of Jesus avoid disdain for the weak and no-accounts in their midst; they must go out of their way to help them if they stray. Jesus' parable speaks of a sheep that "goes astray" (verse 12); applied to humans, the Greek word can mean "is deceived or misled." Some who stray from the flock of Jesus' followers may do so on their own, others because they are deceived by false teaching or misled by false leaders or tripped up by fellow Christians (see 18:6-7). The cause of their straying does not matter; followers of Jesus must seek out the stray before they perish. The church cannot remain content with the ninety-nine and write off the one who wanders; the church must act in accordance with the **will** of the heavenly Father (see 7:21), which is that not **one** of the **little ones be lost.**

    For reflection: What does Jesus' interpretation of the parable tell me about my heavenly Father? What hope does it offer me when I stray? How does it ask me to act toward the straying?

Jesus' Presence in His Church

15 "If your brother sins [against you], go and tell him his fault between you and him alone. If he listens to you, you have won over your brother. **16** If he does not listen, take one or two others along with you, so that 'every fact may be established on the testimony of two or three witnesses.' **17** If he refuses to listen to them, tell the church. If he refuses to listen even to the church, then treat him as you would a Gentile or a tax collector. **18** Amen, I say to you, whatever you bind on earth shall be bound in heaven, and whatever you loose on earth shall be loosed in heaven. **19** Again, [amen,] I say to you, if two of you agree on earth about anything for which they are to pray, it shall be granted to them by my heavenly Father. **20** For where two or three are gathered together in my name, there am I in the midst of them."

Gospel parallels: Luke 17:3
OT: Deut 19:15
NT: Matt 1:23; 7:7-11; 16:19; 21:22; 28:20; John 20:23

15 Jesus continues to provide guidelines for how his followers are to behave toward one another. **If your brother sins [against you]:** a **brother** or sister is a fellow member of the family of Jesus (12:50). The New American Bible prints the words **against you** in brackets because they are found in some manuscripts of Matthew's gospel but not others. **Go** to him, or her, like a shepherd seeking out a straying sheep in order to rescue it. **Tell him his fault:** point out what he has done and convince him that he is at fault. Do this **between you and him alone,** preserving his dignity and reputation. **If he listens to you,** acknowledging he is in the wrong and promising to change, **you have won over your brother.** The Greek for **won over** is literally "gained": you have gained—*regained*—a brother.

Jesus' directive is quite simple, but many of us do otherwise. We avoid difficult confrontations. We talk about the faults of others to everyone but them. We go over the head of someone who displeases us.

For reflection: If I believe someone is at fault, how do I try to work it out with the person?

16 **If he does not listen**—if you can't persuade him—**take one or two others along with you** to support your efforts. The aim is still to win back the one who has strayed. Jesus invokes Scripture as a reason for involving others:

so that **"every fact may be established on the testimony of two or three witnesses."** Deuteronomy required the testimony of two or more witnesses to establish a fact in a court setting (Deut 19:15), but in Jesus' application the setting is private. **Take one or two others along with you** as you strive to work things out, not ganging up on the other person but showing that you are not alone in being troubled by his or her behavior. Perhaps those you take with you will be able to motivate the person to change.

> One witness alone shall not take the stand against a man in regard to any crime or any offense of which he may be guilty; a judicial fact shall be established only on the testimony of two or three witnesses.
>
> Deuteronomy 19:15

For reflection: What has been my experience in enlisting others to help me work out a difficulty with another person?

17 **If he refuses to listen to them, tell the church.** The Greek word translated **church** means an assembly or congregation. In the present context, it refers to the local church congregation of the one who sinned and of those trying to rescue him from sin. If the person who sinned **refuses to listen** to those you bring with you, then enlist the support of the community. At the time Matthew wrote his gospel, Christians gathered in private homes to celebrate the Eucharist (Rom 16:3-5; 1 Cor 16:19; Col 4:15; Phlm 2); there may have been a number of such house churches in a city. A wealthy Christian might have a house large enough to accommodate a gathering of thirty to forty people; rarely was an individual church community much larger. Enlisting **the church** in the effort to rescue a member who went astray may have meant involving only a dozen or two people, all of whom would be well acquainted with the one who sinned.

If he refuses to listen even to the church—if the community effort fails—**then treat him as you would a Gentile or a tax collector.** For Jews, a **Gentile** was an outsider, and a **tax collector** was a sinner. For Matthew's church with its Jewish roots, to **treat** someone **as you would a Gentile or a tax collector** meant having nothing to do with the person. If all attempts to rescue a straying member fail, then that person is to be excluded from the local church community in the hope that this drastic action will bring repentance. (Paul instructed the church in Corinth to exclude a man who was having sexual relations with his stepmother, so that the man would ultimately be saved: 1 Cor 5:1-5.)

Tax collectors: See page 163

Even if treating someone **as you would a Gentile or a tax collector** can mean excluding them from the community, that is not all it can mean. Jesus enlarged the scope of his mission in response to a Gentile woman (15:21-28); he praised the faith of the Gentile centurion and indicated that Gentiles would enter the kingdom of heaven (8:5-13). Jesus confounded some Jews by sharing table fellowship with tax collectors and sinners (9:10-11; 11:19). If Jesus' example is imitated, then treating others **as you would a Gentile or a tax collector** means being merciful to them (9:12-13). Jesus said that his Father wanted his disciples to rescue the straying (18:12-14), and he will go on to say that his disciples must forgive without limit (18:21-35). Even if Jesus makes provision for a church community to exclude a wayward member, that is not his last word about dealing with those who fall into sin.

For reflection: How do I deal with those I consider guilty of serious sin?

18 Jesus assures his community of followers that they have the authority to exclude those who must be excluded: **Amen, I say to you, whatever you bind on earth shall be bound in heaven, and whatever you loose on earth shall be loosed in heaven.** In the previous verses, Jesus has used "you" in the singular, telling an individual disciple what to do if a brother or sister sins. Now Jesus switches to a plural **you** and addresses his words to the community of his followers. The expressions **bind on earth** and **loose on earth** can have a variety of meanings. Jesus used these expressions to give Peter the authority to teach (16:19). In the present context, to **bind on earth** and **loose on earth** mean to exclude from or admit into the church community. Decisions his followers make **on earth** about exclusion from the community will be ratified **in heaven**. The community has the authority to regulate its membership.

19 Jesus explains why the community of his followers has such authority. **Again, [amen,] I say to you, if two of you agree on earth about anything**

for which they are to pray, it shall be granted to them by my heavenly Father. Even if a local church is made up of only two members, it is nonetheless a community. When a community of Jesus' followers unites in prayer, his heavenly Father hears and honors their prayer. The Greek for anything can mean "every legal matter"; the context may imply that the community is praying over the matter of excluding someone. If the community reaches a consensus after prayer, it shall be granted to them by God: he will ratify their decision to exclude or not.

These words of Jesus can have a broader meaning if they are read independent of their context in Matthew's gospel. If two of Jesus' followers agree on earth about anything for which they are to pray, it shall be granted to them by his heavenly Father. This is a great assurance that our prayers are heard. Yet if Jesus' words are taken as an absolute assurance, he seems to promise more than we experience. There are families that prayed fervently that a stricken family member get well, only to have their loved one die. As with other assurances that Jesus gives that our prayers will be answered (see 7:7-11; 21:22), we must ponder the meaning of Jesus' words.

> For reflection: How do I understand Jesus' promise that the prayer of two of his followers will be granted? What has been my experience of praying with others for something we wanted God to grant?

20 Jesus gives the reason why God will grant what the community of his followers asks in prayer: For where two or three are gathered together in my name, there am I in the midst of them. A local church may be only two or three; numbers do not matter. When Jesus speaks of gathering together in my name he means coming together because of him, particularly in prayer. He proclaims that when his followers gather together, there am I in the midst of them. Jesus refers to his presence to his followers after his death and resurrection. He doesn't explain the manner of his presence but assures his followers that he will be with them. God grants the prayers of a church community because Jesus is in the midst of them, joined with them in prayer.

Jesus' promise that he will be in the midst of his followers is made in the context of explaining why church communities have authority from God to regulate membership. However, Jesus' words have broader application. Jesus came to us as Emmanuel, God-with-us (1:23). After his resurrection he will tell his disciples, "I am with you always, until the end of the age" (28:20). He will not be bodily present as he was to his first disciples, but he will be present nonetheless in every church gathering as long as this age will endure.

> *For reflection: What does Jesus' promise to be in the midst of his followers mean to me? How have I experienced Jesus' presence in his followers gathered together?*

Mercy Without Measure

21 Then Peter approaching asked him, "Lord, if my brother sins against me, how often must I forgive him? As many as seven times?" **22** Jesus answered, "I say to you, not seven times but seventy-seven times. **23** That is why the kingdom of heaven may be likened to a king who decided to settle accounts with his servants. **24** When he began the accounting, a debtor was brought before him who owed him a huge amount. **25** Since he had no way of paying it back, his master ordered him to be sold, along with his wife, his children, and all his property, in payment of the debt. **26** At that, the servant fell down, did him homage, and said, 'Be patient with me, and I will pay you back in full.' **27** Moved with compassion the master of that servant let him go and forgave him the loan. **28** When that servant had left, he found one of his fellow servants who owed him a much smaller amount. He seized him and started to choke him, demanding, 'Pay back what you owe.' **29** Falling to his knees, his fellow servant begged him, 'Be patient with me, and I will pay you back.' **30** But he refused. Instead, he had him put in prison until he paid back the debt. **31** Now when his fellow servants saw what had happened, they were deeply disturbed, and went to their master and reported the whole affair. **32** His master summoned him and said to him, 'You wicked servant! I forgave you your entire debt because you begged me to. **33** Should you not have had pity on your fellow servant, as I had pity on you?' **34** Then in anger his master handed him over to the torturers until he should pay back the whole debt. **35** So will my heavenly Father do to you, unless each of you forgives his brother from his heart."

Gospel parallels: Luke 17:4
OT:Gen 4:23-24; Sirach 28:1-5
NT:Matt 6:12, 14-15; Mark 11:25; James 2:13

21 Then Peter approaching asked him, "Lord, if my brother sins against me, how often must I forgive him? As many as seven times?" Peter sometimes acts as a spokesman for the disciples (15:15; 17:4); at other times he speaks on his own behalf (14:28; 16:16), as is the case here: "If **my** brother sins against **me,** how often must I forgive him?" Peter may have in mind Jesus' instruction to go to a brother who "sins [against you] . . . and tell him his fault" (18:15). What if he acknowledges he is in the wrong and promises to change, but then continues in his wayward ways: **how often must I forgive him?** Peter proposes a generous measure of forgiveness for a repeat offender: **as many as seven times?** In biblical idiom, **seven** stands for fullness or completeness (see 12:45). Peter is asking whether he must always forgive. Even if we understand Peter to mean literally **seven times,** he is expressing a high expectation. To forgive someone **seven times** is more forgiveness than many of us can muster. After the third or fourth offense we may decide that the offender is not going to change and does not deserve more forgiveness.

Lord: See page 133

For reflection: Has anyone repeatedly harmed me? Have I repeatedly forgiven?

22 Jesus answered, "I say to you, not seven times but seventy-seven times." The Greek words translated **seventy-seven times** can also be translated "seventy *times* seven times," and translators from ancient until modern times have vacillated between interpretations. Which translation is chosen does not matter; seventy-seven times and seventy times seven times both represent utter fullness of forgiveness, limitless forgiveness, forgiving as many times as there is occasion to do so. How often must followers of Jesus be willing to forgive? As often as a wayward brother or sister is willing to make a fresh start (18:15), as often as one is injured (verse 21).

For reflection: Have I given up forgiving anyone? What is keeping me from forgiving?

In Genesis, God promised Cain that he would be avenged sevenfold if anyone killed him (Gen 4:15). Cain's descendant Lamech boasted that he exacted greater vengeance: "I have killed a man for wounding me, / a boy for bruising me. / If Cain is avenged sevenfold, / then Lamech seventy-sevenfold" (Gen 4:23-24). The way of Lamech is massive retaliation; the way of Jesus is accepting injury (5:38-39) and forgiving without limit. Jesus teaches how to live under the reign of God now in order to be part of the kingdom of God when it is established in its fullness. This is the perspective of the Sermon on the Mount (Matt 5-7), and this is the perspective in which forgiving **seventy-seven times** is required.

23 **That is why the kingdom of heaven may be likened to a king who decided to settle accounts with his servants.** Jesus tells a parable about the reign of God to show **why** it is necessary for his disciples to forgive without limit. The parable likens **the kingdom of heaven** to a series of events. They begin with **a king who decided to settle accounts with his servants.** The mention of a **king** in a parable about **the kingdom of heaven** plants the notion that this parable is about God and God's ways. The king decides to settle accounts with his **servants:** the Greek word translated **servants** literally means "slaves." In the first century, some slaves held high positions; these slaves may have been the king's chief administrators, managing his estates and tax system. The king wishes to **settle accounts** with them, collecting what is due him.

Parables: See page 262
Kingdom of heaven: See page 266
Servant, slave: See page 429

24 **When he began the accounting, a debtor was brought before him who owed him a huge amount.** The Greek words translated **a huge amount** are literally "tens of thousands" of talents. Ten thousand was the largest number used in counting and therefore the number invoked to indicate a huge amount (see 1 Cor 14:19); the best counterpart for us might be a trillion. Since the Greek word here is plural, we may think of trillions. A talent was the largest monetary unit; in first-century Palestine a talent was equivalent to six thousand denarii (one denarius was "the usual daily wage" for an ordinary worker—20:2). The **debtor** thus **owed** the king what it would take an ordinary worker more than sixty million days—more than two hundred thousand years—to earn. How this **debtor** came to owe such a staggering amount is left unexplained; that is not at issue in the parable. Jesus uses the largest number and largest monetary unit familiar to his listeners to convey that the man owed an immensely **huge debt.**

25 **Since he had no way of paying it back, his master ordered him to be sold, along with his wife, his children, and all his property, in payment of the debt.** The Greek word for **master** is the same word that is translated "Lord" in verse 21; here it connotes ownership—the master owns the slave. **Since** the slave **had no way of paying** back a debt of tens of thousand of talents, his owner **ordered him to be sold,** along with all that was his: **his wife, his children, and all his property.** This would not bring in much **in payment of the debt** compared with the size of the debt, but it would be all that the master could salvage. Today we might think of a bankruptcy sale in which everything is auctioned to raise as much money as possible, even though it is less than what is owed.

26 **At that, the servant fell down** and **did him homage,** prostrating himself in abject supplication, **and said, "Be patient with me, and I will pay you back in full."** He asks for time to pay back what he owes: **be patient with me.** His promise, **I will pay you back in full** is ridiculous: his debt is so huge that there is no way that he can ever repay it, no matter how much time his master might give him. He could just as well have said, "Be patient with me, and I will fly to the moon and discover gold to pay off my debt."

27 The master knows that this slave will never be able to repay a significant portion of the debt, much less pay it back in full. The slave is in a hopeless situation, yet his utter hopelessness moves his master to be merciful to him. **Moved with compassion the master of that servant let him go and forgave him the loan.** What he owed is termed a **loan,** but this word seems to be simply a synonym for debt and does not necessarily imply that the slave borrowed the immense sum from his master. The Greek word translated **moved with compassion** has the connotation of being profoundly moved by a gut reaction of compassion; it is used elsewhere in Matthew's gospel to describe Jesus' compassion (9:36; 14:14; 15:32; 20:34). Out of compassion for the slave, the master **forgave** his debt: while the slave only asked for time to pay off his debt, his master cancels it entirely. He gives his slave a chance to make a new start on life.

28 **When that servant had left, he found one of his fellow servants who owed him a much smaller amount.** The **fellow servants** are literally fellow "slaves." The Greek words translated **a much smaller amount** are literally

"a hundred denarii"—one hundred days' wages for an ordinary worker (see 20:2). Even though the debtor was one of his fellow slaves and the debt modest, **he seized him and started to choke him**—a demeaning physical assault—demanding, **"Pay back what you owe."**

29 **Falling to his knees, his fellow servant begged him, "Be patient with me, and I will pay you back."** The words **falling to his knees** translate the same Greek word that is translated "fell down" in verse 26: the second slave prostrates himself before the first slave just as the first slave had prostrated himself before his master. The second slave makes virtually the same appeal as the first had made, pleading with him to **be patient with me** and promising, **I will pay you back.** Unlike the first slave's promise (verse 26), his promise is reasonable. He does not have the money on hand, but it would take less than four months' work to earn the amount, even at first-century minimum wages.

30 **But he refused. Instead, he had him put in prison until he paid back the debt.** In the Roman Empire, debtors could be imprisoned until family or friends paid off what they owed (see 5:26).

31 **Now when his fellow servants saw what had happened, they were deeply disturbed, and went to their master and reported the whole affair.** They were extremely upset by the way one of their fellow slaves was treating another and thought that their master ought to know about it.

32 **His master summoned him and said to him, "You wicked servant!"** The slave is called **wicked** not because he had a debt he could not repay but because of how he behaved after his debt was forgiven. His master tells him, **I forgave you your entire debt because you begged me to.** The slave had **begged** only for time to pay off the debt, but in his compassion the master had forgiven his **entire debt,** as huge as it was.

33 **Should you not have had pity on your fellow servant, as I had pity on you?** The mercy the servant received from his master set the pattern for what he was to do. Comparatively little was expected of him: he had been forgiven a debt more than six hundred thousand times greater than the one he should have forgiven. The mercy he had been shown would always far outstrip any mercy that he practiced.

34 **Then in anger his master handed him over to the torturers until he should pay back the whole debt.** The connotation of **torturers** is jailers. Imprisoned debtors could be tortured as an incentive for their family and friends to pay off their debts as quickly as possible. For this slave to be imprisoned and tortured **until** his **whole debt** was repaid meant there would be no end to his suffering: his debt was too large ever to be repaid. Jesus' parable concludes on a very stark note.

35 Jesus makes the lesson of his parable for his disciples explicit: **So will my heavenly Father do to you, unless each of you forgives his brother from his heart.** Forgiving **from the heart** means complete forgiveness, not grudgingly mumbled forgiveness. Unless the disciples of Jesus forgive unreservedly, they face a fate comparable to that of the unforgiving slave who was handed over to the torturers. This seems a shocking punishment for the **heavenly Father** to inflict on his children, and we will consider it again shortly.

For reflection: What does Jesus' warning mean for me?

Jesus' parables implies that his disciples have received forgiveness of an immense debt. In Aramaic, the word for debt is also used for sin; this is its meaning when disciples of Jesus pray to their Father in heaven, "forgive us our debts" (6:12). Sin as an offense against the God who created us and holds us in existence is a debt utterly beyond our ability to repay; God's forgiveness is of its nature a ten-thousand-talent forgiveness. God's forgiveness wipes the slate clean and gives us a new start; his forgiveness makes it possible for us to have eternal life.

For reflection: What has God forgiven me? What has God given me?

After Jesus taught his followers to pray, "Forgive us our debts, as we forgive our debtors" (6:12), he commented: "If you forgive others their transgressions, your heavenly Father will forgive you. But if you do not forgive others, neither will your Father forgive your transgressions" (6:14-15; see also Sirach 28:1-5). The measure we use in our dealing with others will be the measure used for us (7:2). The merciful will be shown mercy by God (5:7); conversely, as James will express, God's "judgment is merciless to the one who has not shown mercy" (James 2:13).

Jesus' parable puts receiving and granting forgiveness in perspective: God's forgiveness always far outstrips our own. We are to forgive each other seventy-seven times—without limit—because there are no limits to God's forgiveness of us. We are to forgive the debts of others—the harm they do us—because God has forgiven us the immensely greater debt of our sins against him. Our heavenly Father's mercy is without measure; we must be merciful in turn (see 5:43-48).

For reflection: How has the mercy I have received from God moved me to be merciful?

Jesus assured his disciples that their heavenly Father cares for them (6:25-34; 7:11; 10:29-31) and invites them "to shine like the sun" in his kingdom (13:43); he does not want a single one of them to be lost (18:14). How then could the heavenly Father consign any of his children to unending torment? We should note that this is not the only time that Jesus issues a dire warning about the eternal consequences of our actions (see 5:22; 13:41-42, 49-50; 18:6-9). Jesus proclaims both that God's mercy is without measure (verses 23-27) and that we will be held accountable for what we do (verses 34-35). How the two fit together is a mystery that must be pondered. Clearly, though, our refusing to forgive others jeopardizes the forgiveness we receive from God.

For reflection: How do I reconcile the possibility of eternal punishment with God's mercy?

CHAPTER 19

ORIENTATION: *Jesus concludes his public ministry in Galilee and leaves for Jerusalem, where he will suffer, die, and be raised (16:21).*

Living for the Kingdom
1 When Jesus finished these words, he left Galilee and went to the district of Judea across the Jordan. **2** Great crowds followed him, and he cured them there. **3** Some Pharisees approached him, and tested him, saying, "Is it lawful for a man to divorce his wife for any cause whatever?" **4** He said in reply, "Have you not read that from the beginning the Creator 'made them male and female' **5** and said, 'For this reason a man shall leave his father and mother and be joined to his wife, and the two shall become one flesh'? **6** So they are no longer two, but one flesh. Therefore, what God has joined together, no human being must separate." **7** They said to him, "Then why did Moses command that the man give the woman a bill of divorce and dismiss [her]?" **8** He said to them, "Because of the hardness of your hearts Moses allowed you to divorce your wives, but from the beginning it was not so. **9** I say to you, whoever divorces his wife (unless the marriage is unlawful) and marries another commits adultery." **10** [His] disciples said to him, "If that is the case of a man with his wife, it is better not to marry." **11** He answered, "Not all can accept [this] word, but only those to whom that is granted. **12** Some are incapable of marriage because they were born so; some, because they were made so by others; some, because they have renounced marriage for the sake of the kingdom of heaven. Whoever can accept this ought to accept it."

Gospel parallels: Mark 10:1-12; Luke 16:18
OT:Gen 1:27; 2:23-24; Lev 18:6-18; Deut 24:1-4
NT:Matt 5:31-32; 1 Cor 7:7-11, 25-35

1 **When Jesus finished these words:** Matthew uses this expression to signal the end of a block of Jesus' teachings (see also 7:28; 11:1; 13:53), but Jesus will continue to teach as the occasion arises. After Jesus finished giving guidelines for life within the community of his followers (18:3-35) **he left Galilee.** Jesus had come to **Galilee** after John the Baptist was arrested (4:12); he made Capernaum his base (4:13) and began to proclaim the arrival of the kingdom of heaven (4:17). Save for brief excursions to regions

adjacent to Galilee (8:28; 16:13; perhaps 15:21), Jesus' entire ministry has been carried out in rural Galilee. Now he "must go to Jerusalem" to suffer, die, and be raised (16:21). Together with his disciples (see 17:22), **he left Galilee and went to the district of Judea across the Jordan.** The words **across the Jordan** mean east of the Jordan River, but the **district of Judea** lay west of the Jordan. The most likely meaning of Jesus going **to the district of Judea across the Jordan** is that he traveled south along the eastern side of the Jordan River, a route used by Jews traveling from Galilee to Jerusalem to avoid passing through Samaritan territory (Samaritans could be hostile to Jewish pilgrims on their way to Jerusalem—Luke 9:51-53). Pilgrims taking the route on the east side of the Jordan would cross the river to the eastern side just south of the Sea of Galilee and would cross back to the western side of the river just north of the Dead Sea. From there they would travel through Jericho (see 20:29) on their way into **Judea** and Jerusalem.

Galilee: See page 68

2 **Great crowds followed him:** Jesus will arrive in Jerusalem sometime before Passover (26:2); these **crowds** may be Galileans traveling to Jerusalem to celebrate the feast, taking the same route as Jesus and his disciples. **He cured them there:** Jesus healed the sick among them along the route to Jerusalem. Whenever Jesus sees those who are infirm, he is moved with compassion and heals them (9:35-36; 14:13-14; 15:30-32; see also 4:23-24; 8:16; 12:15). Jesus' ministry in Galilee may have reached its end, but there is no end to his compassion and healing.

3 **Some Pharisees approached him, and tested him,** hoping to trip him up. They asked, **Is it lawful for a man to divorce his wife for any cause whatever?** Jews accepted that a husband could **divorce his wife;** a Jewish wife could not divorce her husband. **Divorce** implied the right to remarry. Pharisees debated what constituted sufficient grounds for divorce. Some held that a man could divorce his wife **for any cause whatever;** others

---

BACKGROUND: JUDEA was the region of Palestine around and to the south of Jerusalem. It was originally the territory of the tribe of Judah, which gave it its name. Israelites from this region who had been in exile in Babylon returned to Judea after 538 B.C. Thereafter they began to be called Judeans, which passed through Greek and Latin into English as the word "Jews."

---

maintained that there must be a weighty cause like infidelity. On the surface, the Pharisees who approach Jesus might be asking him where he stands in the debate. But these Pharisees are asking about what is **lawful** to test him, and their question can be interpreted, "Is there *any reason at all* that justifies divorce?" They presumably know that Jesus forbids divorce (5:32), and they want to lure him into contradicting the law of Moses.

Pharisees: See page 231

4 He said in reply, "**Have you not read** in the book of Genesis **that from the beginning the Creator 'made them male and female.'"** Jesus appeals to what God did in **the beginning,** at creation, before sin entered the world. The **Creator** fashioned humans to be **male and female** and attracted to each other.

> God created man in his image;
> > in the divine image he created him;
> > male and female he created them.
> > > > > Genesis 1:27

5 Jesus continues to invoke the words of Genesis: **For this reason**—because of their sexual differentiation and mutual attraction—**a man shall leave his father and mother and be joined to his wife, and the two shall become one flesh.** It was God's purpose in creating humans as male and female that they would marry and **the two shall become one flesh** (the New American Bible translation of Gen 2:24 reads "become one body," translating the Hebrew word for flesh as "body"). The Hebrew notion of a human's **flesh** encompassed the whole person as a physical being. Becoming **one flesh** means that a woman and a man are intimately united—two lives joined in a common life.

> That is why a man leaves his father and mother and clings to his
> wife, and the two of them become one body.
> > > > > Genesis 2:24

6 Jesus emphasizes the unity of a man and a woman in marriage: **So they are no longer two, but one flesh.** Their intimate union is part of God's purpose in creating the human race the way he did. **Therefore, what God has joined together, no human being must separate.** Since it is God's

intention that a woman and a man become one in marriage, **God has joined** them **together.** And what God has joined together, **no human being must separate.** In context, **no human being** means no *husband*: because wives and husbands have been joined together by God, husbands may not divorce their wives. Divorce is counter to God's intent.

> *For reflection: If I am married, how has my marriage matched up with God's intentions? If I am single, what married couple is the best model for me of what marriage should be?*

7 On hearing this, those seeking to entrap Jesus probably thought, "Gotcha!" (or its first-century equivalent), confident that they had lured Jesus into contradicting the law of Moses. **They said to him, "Then why did Moses command that the man give the woman a bill of divorce and dismiss [her]?"** How can you claim that God prohibits divorce when there is a **command** of Moses requiring that a man who is dismissing his wife give her **a bill of divorce?** The law in question—Deut 24:1-4—addresses the situation in which a husband divorces his wife, she remarries, and her second husband then divorces her. In such a case, can her first husband take her as his wife again? (The answer is no.) In dealing with this situation, the law refers to the first husband's handing her "a bill of divorce" (Deut 24:1), which serves as written proof that he is relinquishing his rights to her and that another man is free to take her as his wife. This text in Deuteronomy is the only passage in the law of Moses that explicitly addresses the practice of divorce, although two passages forbid divorce in certain situations (Deut 22:13-19, 28-29) and other passages presume that there are women who have been divorced by their husbands (Lev 21:7, 13-14; 22:13; Num 30:10).

> *When a man, after marrying a woman and having relations*
> *with her, is later displeased with her because he finds in her*
> *something indecent, and therefore he writes out a bill of divorce*
> *and hands it to her, thus dismissing her from his house. . . .*
> *Deuteronomy 24:1*

8 He said to them, **"Because of the hardness of your hearts Moses allowed you to divorce your wives."** While the Pharisees spoke in terms of a command (verse 7), as if the law commanded divorce, Jesus more accurately

characterizes divorce as something that the law **allowed.** The law of Moses made allowance for men divorcing their wives, and Jesus attributes this allowance to **hardness** of **hearts,** meaning resistance to God's ways. There are other examples in Deuteronomy of allowance being made for humans falling short of what God intended. It was God's intent in giving his people a land that none of them should be in need, but God knew that there would be poverty and commanded generosity to the poor (Deut 15:4, 11). It was God's intent that he rule over his people as their king, but if they insisted on having a human king, Deuteronomy prescribed how he was to rule (1 Sam 8:7; Deut 17:14-20). The law of Moses does not endorse poverty or kingship but makes provision for them. Similarly, the law makes provision for husbands divorcing their wives, but this hardly commends, much less commands, divorce.

The law of Moses made allowance for divorce **but from the beginning it was not so,** and God's original intent in creating humans is more significant than later concessions. Jesus' mission is to announce and inaugurate the reign of God (4:17; 12:28), God's rule over his creation. God's will for his creation was thwarted almost from the start (Gen 3–11), but the coming of God's kingdom means his will being done "on earth as in heaven" (6:10).

9 Jesus authoritatively interpreted the law of Moses in his Sermon on the Mount (5:17-48), describing how one must live to enter the kingdom of heaven (5:20; 7:21). Jesus prohibited divorce (5:31-32), and he reaffirms his teaching: **I say to you, whoever divorces his wife (unless the marriage is unlawful) and marries another commits adultery.** In the law of Moses, **adultery** is an offense a wife commits with another man when she is unfaithful to her husband, a violation of his rights to her (Exod 20:14; Lev 20:10; Deut 22:22). A husband did not commit adultery against his wife by having intercourse with another woman (though it was adultery against her husband if the other woman was married). This somewhat one-sided view of adultery perhaps stemmed from viewing a wife as in some sense the property of her husband (see Exod 20:17) and from a concern that any children she bore be her husband's.

Jesus, however, says that **whoever divorces his wife** and **marries another commits adultery,** that is, violates the rights of his first wife. Jesus proclaims that husbands can commit adultery against their wives just as wives can against their husbands. Jesus implicitly teaches that there is a basic equality between men and women in marriage. Husbands "lording it over" their wives is a consequence of sin (Gen 3:16), not God's original intent in two becoming one flesh.

> For reflection: What do Jesus' words about marriage mean to me in my situation?

As in the Sermon on the Mount (5:32) there seems to be an exception to the prohibition of divorce: (unless the marriage is unlawful). These words are, as before, best understood as a comment inserted by Matthew to apply Jesus' teaching to the situation of his church. Some Gentile converts were apparently married to close relatives, a practice tolerated in the Greek and Roman world but not by Jews (Lev 18:6-18) or by the church (Acts 15:20, 29; 21:25). By adding the comment (unless the marriage is unlawful), Matthew indicated that dissolving such unlawful marriages is not a violation of Jesus' prohibition of divorce.

Matthew's gospel situates Jesus' first prohibition of divorce within the context of the righteousness required to enter the kingdom of heaven (5:20, 32), which is also the context for his prohibitions of anger (5:22), lust (5:28), taking oaths (5:34), and retaliation (5:39), and his command to love one's enemies (5:44). Jesus upholds the permanence of marriage as

BACKGROUND: UNLAWFUL MARRIAGES In Matthew's gospel, Jesus twice forbids divorce but each time with a qualification. The New American Bible translates the qualification, "unless the marriage is unlawful" (Matt 5:32; 19:9). Some translations interpret the qualification differently; the Revised Standard Version has "except on the ground of unchastity." The Greek word in question, *porneia*, can cover a range of immoral sexual behaviors. Paul uses *porneia* to describe a man living with his father's wife (i.e., having sexual relations with his stepmother—1 Cor 5:1). *Porneia* most likely also refers to incestuous marriage between close relatives in some passages in Acts. The early church required Gentile converts "to abstain from meat sacrificed to idols, from blood, from meats of strangled animals, and from unlawful marriage [*porneias*]" (Acts 15:29; see also Acts 15:20; 21:25). These prohibitions reflect ordinances that the law of Moses imposed on non-Israelite resident aliens as well as on Israelites, including the prohibition of marriage between close relatives (Lev 17:7-15; 18:6-18, 26). *Porneia* most likely carries the same meaning in Matthew 5:32 and 19:19: a married couple may not divorce unless they were close relatives who should not have married; such incestuous marriages should be dissolved.

part of God's intent in creating humans to be male and female; by inaugurating God's kingdom on earth, Jesus is bringing God's creation in line with God's will. Yet we fall short of carrying out God's will; we do not submit to God's reign as we should. Some who are in or have been in difficult marriages may long for a concession like that in the law of Moses, allowing divorce and remarriage. Applying and living up to Jesus' teaching about marriage is a challenge for individuals and for the church today—as is living up to all his teachings.

For reflection: How has God made allowances for my hardness of heart? What teachings of Jesus do I find to be particularly difficult to follow?

10 **[His] disciples said to him, "If that is the case of a man with his wife, it is better not to marry."** Did they say this tongue in cheek? Was it a petulant reaction to Jesus' demand, akin to saying "If I have to keep honest books, I won't start a business"? Or did they really find marriage appealing only if divorce was possible? It is uncertain precisely how we should take their words.

11 However their response might be interpreted, Jesus uses it as the occasion to complement his teaching on marriage with a teaching on remaining unmarried. **He answered, "Not all can accept [this] word, but only those to whom that is granted."** The **word** Jesus refers to is not his prohibition of divorce but the disciples' saying "it is better not to marry." The implication of **is granted** is granted by God. **Not all** can embrace a life of celibacy **but only those to whom** it is granted as a gift from God. Jesus upholds marriage as God's intent for men and women but adds that some will not marry because remaining unmarried is their calling and gift from God.

12 Jesus uses a graphic comparison to explain why some do not marry. **Some are incapable of marriage because they were born so:** the Greek word translated **incapable of marriage** is literally "eunuchs." Some are eunuchs because that is the way they were born. **Some, because they were made so by others:** the Greek literally reads, "There are eunuchs who were made eunuchs by humans." Jesus refers to castration, perhaps as an act of violence, perhaps as a requirement for serving in a royal court (Acts tells of a eunuch who was a high official for the queen of Ethiopia—Acts 8:27). **Some, because they have renounced marriage for the sake of the kingdom**

402

of heaven: literally, "There are eunuchs who make eunuchs of themselves for the sake of the kingdom of heaven." Some are born eunuchs and some are made eunuchs, and some, figuratively, become eunuchs by living celibately and forsaking marriage **for the sake of the kingdom of heaven.** (Jesus' imagery is decidedly male, but his message applies equally to women and men.) The Greek word translated **for the sake of** could also be translated "on account of." Remaining single on account of the kingdom of heaven might mean forgoing marriage in the expectation that the end of the age is at hand and it is not the time to start a family (see Paul's reasoning in 1 Cor 7:25-31). More likely, **for the sake of** the kingdom of heaven means *for the service of* the kingdom. While most Jews married, some remained single in order to carry out God's call to them—Jeremiah, for example (Jer 16:1-2), and most notably Jesus himself (speculations that he was married are without merit). John the Baptist likely remained single, as did Paul (1 Cor 7:7-8; a few speculate that Paul was a widower). Some Essenes, a Jewish group at the time of Jesus, forsook marriage.

Kingdom of heaven: See page 266
Essenes: See page 238

Jesus adds, **Whoever can accept this ought to accept it.** Whoever is called by God to remain single in order to serve the kingdom **ought to accept it.** Not all receive this call, but those who do should embrace it as God's gift to them.

For reflection: What is my fundamental call and gift from God?

Children of the Kingdom
¹³ Then children were brought to him that he might lay his hands on them and pray. The disciples rebuked them, ¹⁴ but Jesus said, "Let the children come to me, and do not prevent them; for the kingdom of heaven belongs to such as these." ¹⁵ After he placed his hands on them, he went away.

Gospel parallels: Mark 10:13-16; Luke 18:15-17
OT: Gen 48:14-16
NT: Matt 5:3, 10; 18:1-5

13 **Then children were brought to him:** the Greek word for **children** is used for young children. Their being young is also indicated by their being

brought or carried to Jesus. They are brought to Jesus so **that he might lay his hands on them and pray** for them. Laying hands on someone's head while blessing him or her was an ancient practice (Gen 48:14-16). The crowds, apparently accompanying Jesus as he travels from Galilee to Jerusalem (19:1; 20:17), view him as someone whose blessing might carry special weight. **The disciples rebuked them:** Jesus' disciples tried to stop those who were seeking Jesus' blessing for the children. Matthew does not explain the disciples' motive. Since children had little social standing, did the disciples think that Jesus was too important to waste his time on no-bodies? Did they want Jesus' attention for themselves? Whatever their thinking, they missed the implication of Jesus' telling them that whoever receives a child receives him (18:5): would Jesus himself then turn children away? Whenever Jesus has spoken of children or little ones, he has indicated their importance in the eyes of God (see 11:25; 18:4, 10, 14).

For reflection: Have I in any way impeded anyone from coming to Jesus?

14 **Jesus said** to his disciples, issuing a double command to make his desires perfectly clear, **Let the children come to me, and do not prevent them.** Jesus invites the weary to come to him (11:28), and he welcomes children as well. No one is to keep children from coming to Jesus; they are part of his new family (12:49-50). Indeed, they are an important part of his family: **for the kingdom of heaven belongs to such as these.** Another way of translating Jesus' words would be, "Of such as these is the kingdom of heaven." Jesus proclaimed that the poor in spirit and the persecuted are blessed, "for theirs is the kingdom of heaven" (Matt 5:3, 10); Jesus makes the same pronouncement about **such as these**—about children and those who are like children. Children in their dependence and receptivity are able to receive **the kingdom of heaven** as a gift, which is the only way it can be received. The dependence and receptivity of children is the model for how everyone, whatever their age, must welcome and accept God's reign. Jesus told his disciples, "Unless you turn and become like children, you will not enter the kingdom of heaven" (18:3). God is establishing his reign on earth through Jesus (12:28); the nobodies gathered around Jesus, including children and outcasts (9:9-11), the poor and persecuted (5:3, 10), are entering **the kingdom of heaven.** Jesus does not want anyone turned away.

Kingdom of heaven: See page 266

15 **After he placed his hands on them** and blessed them **he went away,** continuing his journey toward Jerusalem.

> *For reflection: What does Jesus' welcoming children and blessing them tell me about his attitude toward me? About how he expects me to treat the children and nobodies I encounter?*

Wealth and the Kingdom

16 Now someone approached him and said, "Teacher, what good must I do to gain eternal life?" 17 He answered him, "Why do you ask me about the good? There is only One who is good. If you wish to enter into life, keep the commandments." 18 He asked him, "Which ones?" And Jesus replied, "'You shall not kill; you shall not commit adultery; you shall not steal; you shall not bear false witness; 19 honor your father and your mother'; and 'you shall love your neighbor as yourself.'" 20 The young man said to him, "All of these I have observed. What do I still lack?" 21 Jesus said to him, "If you wish to be perfect, go, sell what you have and give to [the] poor, and you will have treasure in heaven. Then come, follow me." 22 When the young man heard this statement, he went away sad, for he had many possessions. 23 Then Jesus said to his disciples, "Amen, I say to you, it will be hard for one who is rich to enter the kingdom of heaven. 24 Again I say to you, it is easier for a camel to pass through the eye of a needle than for one who is rich to enter the kingdom of God."

> Gospel parallels: Mark 10:17-25; Luke 18:18-25
> OT: Exod 20:12-16; Lev 18:5; 19:18; Deut 5:16-20; 30:15-20; Tobit
> 4:7-11; Sirach 29:8-12
> NT: Matt 5:17-19, 48; 6:19-21, 24; 7:21; 13:44-46; 22:34-40; Rom 13:9

16 **Now someone approached him and said, "Teacher, what good must I do to gain eternal life?"** Jesus is commonly viewed as a **teacher** (8:19; 9:11; 12:38; 17:24), as one who instructs about God and God's ways. This person wants to **gain eternal life** and asks Jesus **what good** thing or deed **must I do** to have it. Asking Jesus this question acknowledges that he is able to teach how one can achieve eternal life.

While Jesus has referred to eternal life in his teachings (7:14; 18:8-9), this is the first time that the expression **eternal life** appears in Matthew's gospel. It is found in some late Old Testament books (Dan 12:2 literally

405

speaks of awakening to "eternal life"; see also 2 Macc 7:9). **Eternal life** is a life of happiness in the age to come. The idea that a person could enjoy a life after death was a relatively recent development in Jewish thinking, and not all Jews accepted it. The one who comes to Jesus believes in the possibility of eternal life and wants to know how to attain it.

17 Jesus **answered him, "Why do you ask me about the good? There is only One who is good."** Jesus' response seems odd. The man has not asked about **the good** in general but about what good he needed to do to gain eternal life. And while God is supremely good, in the Old Testament he is not the **only One who is** called **good;** God's creation, for example, is repeatedly termed good (Gen 1:4, 10, 12, 18, 21, 25, 31). The man asked how he might attain eternal life; Jesus' response seems unresponsive.

We have been reading Matthew's gospel without bringing in material from the other gospels. However, this passage is an instance where comparing Matthew's account with Mark's may shed light. In Mark's account of this incident, the man addresses Jesus as "Good teacher," and Jesus responds, "Why do you call me good? No one is good but God alone" (Mark 10:17-18). Matthew most likely had a copy of Mark's gospel in front of him

---

BACKGROUND: LIFE AFTER DEATH For the ancient Israelites, a human being was living flesh, and meaningful life apart from the flesh was inconceivable. There was no belief in an immortal soul; the Hebrew word that is sometimes translated as "soul" can mean the livingness of a body but not something that can enjoy existence apart from a body. What survived death was at best a shadow or a ghost of one's former self, consigned to a netherworld beneath the surface of the earth (Num 16:31-33). The netherworld was a place of darkness and silence; those in the netherworld were cut off from the living and from God (Job 14:20-22; Sirach 17:22-23). Good and bad alike languished in the netherworld, sharing the same fate (Eccl 9:2-6). It was only near the end of the Old Testament era that hopes arose that there would be meaningful life after death. These hopes were often expressed in terms of bodily resurrection from the dead (2 Macc 7; Dan 12:2). However, the book of Wisdom, written around the time of Jesus, drew on Greek thinking and taught that after death, "the souls of the just are in the hand of God" (Wisd 3:1). Greek philosophers thought of souls as immortal and as temporarily imprisoned in bodies (see Wisd 9:15); death meant the release of the soul from this imprisonment. Some nonbiblical writings presumed that there would be life in the age to come but were vague about its nature. *Related topics: The age to come (page 250), Nonbiblical writings (page 198), Resurrection (page 478).*

---

when he wrote, and he apparently edited Mark's account to remove any suggestion that Jesus was not good, but his reworking left puzzling elements. We might best pass over the puzzles and continue on with Matthew's account.

Jesus responds to the man's question: **If you wish to enter into life, keep the commandments.** The law of Moses presents itself as the way to life (Lev 18:5; Deut 30:15-20), by which is meant long life on this earth. In Jesus' perspective, however, obedience to God's will, expressed in **the commandments,** is the way to **enter into** eternal **life.**

> *Keep, then, my statutes and decrees, for the man who carries*
> *them out will find life through them.*
> *Leviticus 18:5*

Jesus' words apply to all who want to have eternal life: **If you wish to enter into life, keep the commandments.** It is those who do the will of God who will enter the kingdom of heaven (7:21).

> *For reflection: What does Jesus' insistence on obedience to God's commands tell me about Jesus? What does it tell me I must do to enter eternal life?*

18 **He asked him, "Which ones?"** We again might be puzzled by the course the conversation takes. To ask which of God's commands must be obeyed invites the answer, "All of them, of course!" Jesus had solemnly proclaimed, "Amen, I say to you, until heaven and earth pass away, not the smallest letter or the smallest part of a letter will pass from the law" and that not even the least of God's commands could be ignored (5:18-19). However, Jesus will not invoke his earlier teaching in his reply to the man. Perhaps we should therefore take the question **Which ones?** to have the sense, Which of God's commands are the most important? There are many commands in the law of Moses (613 by a later count), and some of them are weightier than others.

Jesus responds by reminding the man of some of God's basic commands: **Jesus replied, "You shall not kill; you shall not commit adultery; you shall not steal; you shall not bear false witness."** These are four of the Ten Commandments given on Mount Sinai (Exod 20:13-16; Deut 5:17-20). Each is a prohibition, telling what not to do.

407

19 To these four prohibitions Jesus adds two commands telling what must be done. The first, **honor your father and your mother,** is also one of the Ten Commandments (Exod 20:12; Deut 5:16), occurring before the four prohibitions Jesus singled out. Perhaps Jesus quotes it afterwards to pair it with another positive command: **you shall love your neighbor as yourself.** This is not one of the Ten Commandments but is found elsewhere in the law (Lev 19:18). By quoting this last command with some of the Ten Commandments, Jesus indicates that it is no less important than the commands God issued when he made a covenant with his people. Where the four "you shall not" commands prohibit injuries to other people, the command **you shall love your neighbor as yourself** demands that we do good to others, as well as not harming them. We must be just as caring for others as we are for ourselves, just as concerned for their good as we are for our own (see also 7:12; 22:39).

For reflection: How well do I keep God's basic commands? In practice, do I love others as I love myself?

It is striking that Jesus highlights commandments dealing with how we treat one another and does not quote commandments that have to do with our relationship with God. Jesus does not deny that we should love and serve God (see 22:36-40) nor does he teach that loving others means that we can disregard any of God's laws (see 5:18-19). But in Matthew's gospel, Jesus' emphasis is on our treatment of others as the basis upon which we will be judged (see 25:31-46) and rewarded for the good we do (10:41-42).

For reflection: On what basis do I expect God to judge me? What will he point out that I have done? That I have failed to do?

20 **The young man said to him:** we learn that the man who came to Jesus is **young.** The Greek word used here for **young** could mean that he is in his twenties. He tells Jesus, **All of these** commandments **I have observed.** How should we take his claim? Perhaps he has observed God's commandments, at least those that Jesus quoted. Jews did not consider it impossible to keep God's law. Two centuries earlier Sirach taught, "If you choose you can keep the commandments" (Sirach 15:15); Paul boasted that he was blameless in observing the law (Phil 3:6). On the other hand,

perhaps there is an element of self-delusion in the **young man**'s claiming **all of these I have observed:** had he truly loved his neighbor as himself? The reader is left knowing that the young man considers himself obedient to God's commands but not knowing whether God would agree with his self-assessment.

The young man's next words are also open to more than one interpretation: **What do I still lack?** Asked as an honest question, his words would be an acknowledgement that to gain eternal life he needed to do more than keep God's commandments. But asked as a rhetorical question, his words would convey the opposite: "So I'm not lacking anything, right?" Biblical scholars commonly treat his words as an honest question, but I lean toward the second interpretation. Jesus told him, "If you wish to enter into life, keep the commandments" (verse 17) and he had kept them. Why should the young man think that more was required of him?

21 Whether or not the young man perceived that he was lacking anything, Jesus judged that he was. **Jesus said to him, "If you wish to be perfect":** our idea of **perfect** is being without imperfections and defects, like a flawless diamond. But the Greek word for **perfect** has a different connotation; it means to be whole and complete, to achieve one's goal or end. In its only other occurrence in Matthew's gospel, "be perfect" means to love as God loves (5:48). Jesus tells the young man, if you want to attain what you are lacking, if you want to completely follow God's will for you, if you want to achieve your goal of eternal life, **go, sell what you have and give to [the] poor, and you will have treasure in heaven. Then come, follow me.** In this string of imperatives (**go, sell, give, come, follow**) the most fundamental is the last: **follow me.** Jesus invites the young man to become his disciple, just as he invited Peter and Andrew, James and John (4:18-22), Matthew (9:9), and others (see 8:21-22; 10:1-4). God's reign is being established on earth in those whom Jesus gathers to himself (12:28, 49-50). If he is to **be perfect** and complete, the young man who has kept God's law needs to join himself with the one who brings God's law to fulfillment (5:17).

For reflection: How have I joined myself to Jesus?

Following Jesus means setting aside anything that is an impediment to discipleship (8:21-22; 10:37-38). The first four disciples left behind their fishing gear to follow Jesus as he traveled around Galilee (4:20, 22); Matthew left his job as a tax collector (9:9). Now this young man also must leave things behind. Jesus tells him, **go, sell what you have:** get rid of what you cannot carry with you as you follow me (see 4:19-22). **Give the** proceeds to the **poor,** who are dependent on the generosity of others for their survival. In helping the poor the young man **will have treasure in heaven,** in the eternal life he seeks. Jesus urges his followers to "store up treasures in heaven" (6:20). Some Old Testament writings held that one stored up treasure by helping those in need (Tobit 4:7-11; Sirach 29:8-12). We do not love our neighbor as ourselves unless we use our resources to meet their needs. The young man claimed he loved his neighbor (verses 19-20); Jesus invites him to do so completely.

Matthew has not yet indicated whether the young man has many or few possessions, but the requirements of discipleship make no distinction. Jesus calls everyone, rich or poor, who would be his disciple to leave behind whatever keeps them from walking in his footsteps.

For reflection: Is there anything that Jesus is asking me to leave behind so that I can follow him?

22 **When the young man heard this statement, he went away sad, for he had many possessions.** We learn that the man is rich: to follow Jesus he would have to divest himself of **many possessions.** The Greek word for **possessions** can mean "lands"; the young man may have owned estates— the primary form of wealth in a farming economy. He enjoyed a life of comfort and security; to become a disciple of Jesus would mean being dependent on the hospitality of others (see 8:20; 10:9-13). This radical change was more than the young man could accept, and **he went away sad.** The kingdom of heaven is like a treasure in a field or a pearl of great price, and he was not willing to sell all that he had to obtain it (see 13:44-46).

23 **Then Jesus said to his disciples, "Amen, I say to you, it will be hard for one who is rich to enter the kingdom of heaven."** Jesus solemnly tells his disciples that it will be difficult for one who is wealthy to enter into eternal life in **the kingdom of heaven.** Jesus taught that it is impossible to serve both God and wealth; one's allegiance will be to one or the other (6:24). He included "the lure of riches" among the obstacles that choke

out the "word of the kingdom" (13:19, 22). He warned that there is no profit in gaining the whole world at the cost of one's eternal life (16:26). The rich young man is an illustration of the snare of wealth. Even though he obeyed God's commands, he could not bring himself to forsake his wealth in order to follow Jesus on the path to eternal life. How **hard** it is for those with wealth to let go of what they have in order to gain what they lack!

Kingdom of heaven: See page 266

24 **Again I say to you:** Jesus repeats his warning for emphasis, framing it as a comparison. **It is easier for a camel to pass through the eye of a needle than for one who is rich to enter the kingdom of God.** Jesus uses striking images, like having a log in one's eye (7:3), to make a point. A **camel** was the largest animal in the region (Jesus will use a camel in another vivid comparison—23:24). The **eye of a needle** was the tiniest opening familiar to his listeners. Jesus invokes the largest and the smallest to convey the great difficulty those with wealth have in entering God's kingdom: it would be **easier** for a **camel** to go through **the eye of a needle.** Some have tried to weaken Jesus' pronouncement by claiming that he was talking about a rope, not a camel, or that the eye of a needle was a small gate in the wall of Jerusalem. Such suggestions are not only baseless but miss the point: Jesus intends his comparison to be outlandish to convey how outlandishly hard it is **for one who is rich to enter the kingdom of God.**

Today there are readers of Matthew's gospel who do not consider themselves wealthy, but nevertheless enjoy comforts, securities, and luxuries that only the very wealthy enjoyed at the time of Jesus. We do not have to be wealthy by the standards of our society for Jesus' words about the dangers of wealth to be a warning for us.

For reflection: How are comforts or security or wealth—or my desires for them—impeding me from wholeheartedly following Jesus?

How Are We Saved?
25 When the disciples heard this, they were greatly astonished and said, "Who then can be saved?" **26** Jesus looked at them and said, "For human beings this is impossible, but for God all things are possible." **27** Then Peter said to him in reply, "We have given up everything and

followed you. What will there be for us?" [28] Jesus said to them, "Amen, I say to you that you who have followed me, in the new age, when the Son of Man is seated on his throne of glory, will yourselves sit on twelve thrones, judging the twelve tribes of Israel. [29] And everyone who has given up houses or brothers or sisters or father or mother or children or lands for the sake of my name will receive a hundred times more, and will inherit eternal life. [30] But many who are first will be last, and the last will be first.

> Gospel parallels: Mark 10:26-31; Luke 18:26-30
> OT: Dan 7:9-10, 13-14
> NT: Matt 4:18-22; 9:9; 10:1-8; 18:4; Luke 22:28-30

25 **When the disciples heard** Jesus say "it will be hard for one who is rich to enter the kingdom of heaven" and "it is easier for a camel to pass through the eye of a needle than for one who is rich to enter the kingdom of God" (19:23-24) **they were greatly astonished.** The disciples apparently shared a view, based on Scripture (Deut 28:1-14; Job 1:9-10; 42:10; Sirach 11:21-22), that wealth is a sign of God's favor. Those who are wealthy should then find it easiest to enter the kingdom of heaven. But Jesus proclaims wealth to be an obstacle to entering God's kingdom, and this leaves the disciples **greatly astonished.** If those who enjoy God's favor will find it hard to enter God's kingdom, **who then can be saved?** The word **saved** can mean saved from sickness (9:22) or death (see 8:25; 14:30) but here means being given life after death (10:22). A young man came to Jesus seeking eternal life (19:16), which Jesus spoke of as entering God's kingdom (19:23-24); the disciples refer to the same reality as being **saved.** If those who are wealthy and apparently enjoy God's favor will have an exceedingly difficult time entering God's kingdom, **who then can be saved?**

26 **Jesus looked at them,** perhaps to make sure he had their full attention, **and said, "For human beings this is impossible, but for God all things are possible."** Being saved—attaining eternal life—is **impossible** for **human beings** to achieve on their own. Eternal life does not mean waking up in another place after death and resuming the life one lived on earth. Those who attain eternal life will "shine like the sun in the kingdom of their Father" (13:43)—an image for their being radically transformed (see also 22:30; 1 John 3:2). There will be a continuity between who we are in

this life and who we will be in the next life: we will still be ourselves. But our life in eternity will be unimaginably different from our life on this earth (see 1 Cor 2:9). It is **impossible** for us to effect the transformation that will take place when we enter eternal life, **but for God all things are possible.** God can give us life in eternity just as he gave us life on earth (see 2 Macc 7:20-23, 28-29).

For reflection: How strong is my faith that God can give me life after death just as he has given me life on earth?

27 **Then Peter said to him in reply:** Peter acts as a spokesman for the disciples. He points out to Jesus, **We have given up everything and followed you.** Perhaps Peter has in mind the young man who did not give up his wealth to follow Jesus (19:21-22); in contrast to him, the disciples **have given up everything** and have **followed** Jesus (4:20, 22; 9:9). Peter wants to know what reward they will receive for doing so: **What will there be for us?** Peter may be reacting to Jesus' statement that it is impossible for human beings to save themselves and attain eternal life. Does that make human effort pointless? Does that mean that the disciples **have given up everything** for nothing—that they are no better off than they would be if they were still fishing and collecting taxes?

For reflection: What have I given up to follow Jesus? What have I not given up?

28 Jesus disabuses them of any notion that their commitment to him is in vain. **Jesus said to them, "Amen, I say to you that you who have followed me, in the new age, when the Son of Man is seated on his throne of glory, will yourselves sit on twelve thrones, judging the twelve tribes of Israel."** Jesus addresses the twelve disciples he selected to have a special role (10:1-4). Jesus speaks of what will happen in **the new age,** which is elsewhere called "the age to come" (12:32). Jesus, **the Son of Man,** will be **seated on his throne of glory,** sharing God's power and glory (see Dan 7:9-10, 13-14). Jesus has elsewhere referred to his exalted role when this age ends, when he will judge men and women (7:21-23; 13:40-43; 16:27; see also 25:31-32; 26:64).

Son of Man: See page 151
The age to come: See page 250

When Jesus is seated on his throne in the age to come, his twelve specially chosen disciples will also be enthroned: they will **sit on twelve thrones, judging the twelve tribes of Israel.** Jesus chose twelve disciples to match up with **the twelve tribes of Israel.** That in the new age the twelve disciples will be **judging** these tribes could mean passing judgment on them. However, those who sit on **thrones** have broad authority; kings exercise executive and legislative as well as judicial functions. **Judging** here means "presiding over." Most of the **twelve tribes of Israel** vanished after Assyrian invasions and deportations eight centuries before the time of Jesus, but there were popular hopes, based on prophecies (Isaiah 49:6; Jer 31:1-14; Ezek 37:15-28; 47:13), that God would restore the tribes when he established his rule (Tobit 13:3-5; 14:3-7; Sirach 36:10). Jesus sent out the Twelve to the house of Israel (10:6), as he himself had been sent (15:24). **In the new age** the Twelve will preside over **the twelve tribes of Israel.** Although the Twelve will form the nucleus of the early church, Jesus here promises them a role in the age to come.

29 After having told Peter what the Twelve will specifically receive, Jesus speaks of what all disciples will receive for what they have given up. **And everyone who has given up houses or brothers or sisters or father or mother or children or lands for the sake of my name:** Jesus provides some examples of what his disciples might have **given up** in order to follow him. He lists seven examples, perhaps to symbolize everything that might have to be given up, the number seven representing fullness in biblical idiom. His examples fall into two groups: family members (brothers, sisters, father, mother, children) and property (houses, lands). Any or all of these might have to be given up **for the sake of my name,** an expression that means for the sake of Jesus. Some relinquishing might be involuntary, as disciples are rejected by their families because of Jesus (see 10:21, 34-36).

For reflection: What losses have I accepted in order to be a disciple of Jesus?

Those who have endured the loss of family and property for the sake of Jesus **will receive a hundred times more:** what they have given up will be like a seed that yields a hundredfold harvest (see 13:8). Their losses will be made up many times over, and they **will inherit eternal life.** They will attain what the rich young man sought (19:16), for they have responded to Jesus' call to leave things behind in order to follow him. What is impossible for humans to achieve on their own will be given to them by the God for whom all things are possible (verses 25-26).

Jesus proclaims that it is impossible for us to achieve eternal life on our own (verses 25-26); we must receive it as a gift from God just as children receive what they lack from their parents (see 18:3; 19:14). Jesus also proclaims that we must keep God's commandments in order to enter eternal life (19:16-17); we will be rewarded for the good we do (6:3-4; 10:41-42; see also 25:31-40). We must live by both truths, accepting eternal life as God's gift to us even as we try to obey God's commands, loving and serving others, denying ourselves, and taking up our crosses to follow Jesus (16:24).

For reflection: How well am I able to accept the truth that eternal life is God's gift to me even though I will be rewarded or punished on the basis of my behavior?

30 Jesus adds an observation that he may have made many times in the course of his ministry (see 20:16). **But many who are first will be last, and the last will be first.** In the "new age" (verse 28), **many who are first** in the present world **will be last,** and those who are **last** now **will be first.** Those who are **first** now are those who have power, status, and wealth, which are obstacles to entering the kingdom of heaven. Unless a person turns away from them, she or he will not enter God's kingdom (see 18:3; 19:23-24). Those who are **last** now are those who have made themselves nobodies for the sake of Jesus, leaving everything behind; they shall be **first** (see also 18:4). Our instincts, however, are to be first here and now; teams enthusiastically chant "We're number 1!" but rarely "We're in last place!" Jesus calls for us to reverse our values and usual way of thinking, in anticipation of the day when the **first will be last, and the last will be first.**

For reflection: What do I do to make myself last?

CHAPTER 20

ORIENTATION: *Although Bibles introduce a chapter break, Jesus' words are a*
continuation of his teachings to his disciples about being saved
(19:25-30).

The Parable of the Generous Vineyard Owner
¹ "The kingdom of heaven is like a landowner who went out at dawn to
hire laborers for his vineyard. **²** After agreeing with them for the usual
daily wage, he sent them into his vineyard. **³** Going out about nine
o'clock, he saw others standing idle in the marketplace, **⁴** and he said to
them, 'You too go into my vineyard, and I will give you what is just.'
⁵ So they went off. [And] he went out again around noon, and around
three o'clock, and did likewise. **⁶** Going out about five o'clock, he
found others standing around, and said to them, 'Why do you stand
here idle all day?' **⁷** They answered, 'Because no one has hired us.' He
said to them, 'You too go into my vineyard.' **⁸** When it was evening the
owner of the vineyard said to his foreman, 'Summon the laborers and
give them their pay, beginning with the last and ending with the first.'
⁹ When those who had started about five o'clock came, each received
the usual daily wage. **¹⁰** So when the first came, they thought that they
would receive more, but each of them also got the usual wage. **¹¹** And
on receiving it they grumbled against the landowner, **¹²** saying, 'These
last ones worked only one hour, and you have made them equal to us,
who bore the day's burden and the heat.' **¹³** He said to one of them in
reply, 'My friend, I am not cheating you. Did you not agree with me for
the usual daily wage? **¹⁴** Take what is yours and go. What if I wish to
give this last one the same as you? **¹⁵** [Or] am I not free to do as I wish
with my own money? Are you envious because I am generous?' **¹⁶** Thus,
the last will be first, and the first will be last."

OT:Lev 19:13; Deut 24:14-15; Isaiah 5:1-7

1   **The kingdom of heaven is like:** Matthew's Greek text reads, *For* **the**
kingdom of heaven is like, connecting what Jesus says now with his just
having told his disciples, "But many who are first will be last, and the last
will be first" (19:30). Jesus tells a parable to compare the reign of God to
a series of events, beginning with **a landowner who went out at dawn to**
hire laborers for his vineyard. The disciples would have had no difficulty

imagining the scene. A **vineyard** required relatively few year-round workers, but extra help was needed to harvest the grapes when they were at their proper ripeness. The **laborers** available for hire would have been without regular employment and may have included subsistence farmers who had lost their land because of drought, indebtedness, and taxes. Day laborers were at the bottom of the economic ladder, akin to migrant farmworkers today. The workday for farmworkers was from sunrise to sunset (see Psalm 104:22-23); the vineyard owner **went out at dawn to hire** day laborers for his vineyard. Verse 3 indicates that he went to the village marketplace, where the unemployed gathered hoping someone would hire them.

Parables: See page 262
Kingdom of heaven: See page 266

Although Jesus' parable begins with what was a common scene in a farming economy, his disciples and some of Matthew's first readers might have suspected that he had something else in mind. A vineyard is used as a symbol for Israel in the Old Testament, with the vineyard owner being God (Psalm 80:9-16; Isaiah 5:1-7; Jer 12:10). Jesus' parable seems to be set at harvest time, and in another parable, Jesus used a harvest as an image for the end of the age (13:39). Jesus will have to finish his parable for its full meaning to emerge, but its opening words already trigger associations.

The vineyard of the LORD of hosts is the house of Israel.
Isaiah 5:7

2 The vineyard owner found men looking for work, and **after agreeing with them for the usual daily wage, he sent them into his vineyard.** The Greek words translated **the usual daily wage** mean literally "a denarius for the day." A denarius was a coin that was the common wage for manual laborers for a day's work. In terms of purchasing power, a denarius would have been roughly equivalent to a modern minimum wage, barely sufficient for survival.

3 **Going out about nine o'clock, he saw others standing idle in the marketplace.** We might wonder, "Why didn't he hire enough workers the first time?" But some elements of parables must be accepted as part of the story and not pushed for further meaning. The Greek word translated **idle** means "unemployed" and does not necessarily imply laziness. A **marketplace**

was an open area where vendors could set up stalls; it also functioned as a public area (see 11:16; 23:7) in villages where houses usually crowded upon one another. Here the unemployed gathered, available for hire.

4 The vineyard owner said to those looking for work, **You too go into my vineyard, and I will give you what is just.** He does not specify how much he will pay them but assures them that it will be **just.** The workers would assume (as would readers of Matthew's gospel) that it would be proportionate to how many hours they work but less than a denarius, since they will not be giving the vineyard owner a full day's work.

5 **So they went off. [And] he went out again around noon, and around three o'clock, and did likewise.** Again, we might wonder why the vineyard owner did not hire these workers earlier or whether they did not show up in the marketplace until midday, but such matters are beyond the scope of the parable. The picture Jesus paints is of a vineyard owner repeatedly seeking out and hiring workers for his vineyard, as if he wants to employ as many as possible, even if it means not getting a full day's work from all of them. That he did **likewise** with the noon and three o'clock workers as he had with the nine o'clock workers implies that he promised each group a just wage without specifying what it would be.

6 **Going out about five o'clock, he found others standing around.** The Greek word translated **five o'clock** literally means "eleventh." Daylight was divided into twelve hours; the vineyard owner goes to the marketplace about an hour before sunset. This is very late in the workday to go in search of laborers, but the vineyard owner did so anyway and **found** some men **standing around** in the marketplace. He asked them, **Why do you stand here idle all day?** The word **idle** again can simply mean "unemployed." The vineyard owner asks them why they have been without work **all day,** seemingly implying that they have been available for hire since dawn. We must not speculate why the vineyard owner didn't find them earlier. Jesus' parable simply presents the vineyard owner searching out workers even at the eleventh hour and finding some who had been unemployed all day.

For reflection: What significance do I see in the vineyard owner searching for laborers even as the day draws to a close?

7 **They answered, "Because no one has hired us."** They wanted work—that is why they stood around the marketplace all day—but no one had **hired** them. In any pool of manual laborers, the hardiest get hired first. Perhaps no one had hired these workers because they appeared weak or infirm or were old, and not likely to produce as much work for a denarius as stronger or younger workers. Nevertheless, the vineyard owner **said to them, "You too go into my vineyard."** He hires them but does not tell them what he will pay them. For them, the prospect of being paid for an hour's work was better than no pay at all that day.

8 **When it was evening** and the work day was over, **the owner of the vineyard said to his foreman:** the Greek word translated **owner** is the same word that is translated as "lord" in other contexts. Matthew's first readers used the word as a title for God. This would reinforce the notion, present from the beginning of the parable, that the vineyard owner represents God. The vineyard owner tells **his foreman** who supervised the workers, **Summon the laborers and give them their pay, beginning with the last and ending with the first.** Since day laborers usually had no savings, the law of Moses required that they be paid each day for their work (Lev 19:13; Deut 24:14-15). However, there is nothing in the law or in first-century Jewish culture that suggests that the first laborers to be paid should be those who were **last** to be hired, with the **first** hired being paid last. This seems to be a quirk on the part of the vineyard owner—yet the disciples and Matthew's readers can recall that Jesus proclaimed that "many who are first will be last, and the last will be first" (19:30) before telling this parable. Even if Jesus is not done with the parable, the disciples and Matthew's readers can suspect that the point of the parable might have something to do with the last being first.

Lord: See page 133

> *You shall pay him each day's wages before sundown on the day itself, since he is poor and looks forward to them.*
> *Deuteronomy 24:15*

9 **When those who had started about five o'clock came, each received the usual daily wage**—literally, each received a denarius. Jesus does not explain why the vineyard owner chose to give them a full day's pay even though they had only worked about an hour. We might speculate that he realized that an hour's wage would not be enough for them to buy a day's food for themselves and their families, and he paid them in light of their needs. It is hard enough for those who earn minimum wage to support themselves and their families; it is impossible if the only work available is part-time.

10 Jesus skips over payment of the workers hired at three, noon, and nine as not relevant to his parable. **So when the first came, they thought that they would receive more:** they had seen how much those hired last were paid, and they quite naturally assumed that they would be paid more. Everyone knows that more work should mean more pay. **But each of them also got the usual wage**—each also received a denarius, the same amount paid to those hired last.

11 **And on receiving it they grumbled against the landowner,** complaining about how he was treating them.

12 They said to him, **These last ones worked only one hour, and you have made them equal to us, who bore the day's burden and the heat.** They had worked from sunrise to sunset, bearing the full **day's burden.** They had sweated in **the heat** of the day. They had given the vineyard owner his denarius's worth of labor, but **these last ones,** who **worked only one hour,** certainly had not. Yet, they complain, **you have made them equal to us.** They are not necessarily asking that the vineyard owner take back some of his payment to those hired last; they are protesting what they see as the injustice of their not being paid more. Perhaps we sympathize with them and would have felt the same if we had been in their sandals. If so, Jesus' parable will have a particular message for us.

> For reflection: At this point in the parable, what is my attitude toward the vineyard owner's actions?

13 **He said to one of them in reply, "My friend, I am not cheating you. Did you not agree with me for the usual daily wage?"** The vineyard owner addresses one of the complainers as **my friend,** an expression that indicates that the vineyard owner is speaking to him in a confrontational tone of voice (see its other two occurrences in Matthew—22:11-12; 26:49-50). The vineyard owner tells him **I am not cheating you**—literally, "I am not doing you an injustice." The vineyard owner promised a just wage

to workers hired in the middle of the day (verse 4), and he has paid a just wage as well to those hired first: they were promised and received a denarius for their work (verses 1-2, 10). They accepted this pay rate when they were hired: **Did you not agree with me for the usual daily wage?** Justice is giving a person his or her due, and these workers have received what they agreed was due them.

14 **Take what is yours and go:** accept the amount you agreed to and get on with your life. Don't grumble about not being paid more; don't be envious of anyone who receives a bonus. **What if I wish to give this last one the same as you?** What if I desire that he be as well off at the end of the day as you, as able to provide for his family as you can for yours?

15 **[Or] am I not free to do as I wish with my own money?** This is the real issue. The vineyard owner has done all that justice demands, but justice does not bar him from doing more. The vineyard owner is **free** to do what he wishes with his **own money.** He can throw it in the sea and it would be no injustice to those hired first. He can use it to pay those hired last more than they deserve. He asks the worker, **Are you envious because I am generous?** The Greek word translated **generous** is literally "good": the vineyard owner has been good to workers no one else would hire. He asks, Do you resent my being good? **Are you envious** of those who benefit from my generosity? The vineyard owner is not at fault for being **generous;** the worker is at fault for being **envious.** Hence the confrontational tone in which the vineyard owner speaks to him, conveying, "You are in the wrong, not I."

Jesus' parable is a challenge to readers of Matthew's gospel who find themselves siding with the daylong workers against the vineyard owner. Those who feel that his generosity toward some workers is an injustice toward others are invited to examine their own attitudes about justice and generosity. Perhaps putting ourselves in the place of the one-hour workers who received the full day's pay needed to support their families will change our perspective on the vineyard owner—and perhaps our perspective on the justice and mercy of God.

For reflection: Who do I most naturally identify with when I read this parable: those hired first or those hired last? What might this tell me about myself? Am I more inclined to be envious of others or grateful for the generosity shown me?

16 **Thus, the last will be first, and the first will be last.** Jesus again invokes the maxim that was the point of departure for his parable (19:30) but reverses its order to emphasize that **the last will be first.** Jesus is not simply referring to the last hired being paid first. He told the parable to convey a message to his first disciples. Peter asked Jesus what reward they would receive for giving up everything to follow him, and Jesus spoke of a special role for the Twelve (19:27-28). But Jesus also said that every disciple would receive eternal life (19:29)—God's minimum wage, as it were, for those he brings into the vineyard of his kingdom. At the harvest of the last judgment (13:39, 43), those who are **last** among Jesus' followers will be rewarded as are the **first.** Some whom Jesus welcomed to himself were sinners (9:10-13; 11:19), yet their reward will still be eternal life (see 21:31). Should Jesus' inner circle of disciples be envious of them? Should those who forsake marriage to serve the kingdom of God (19:12) be jealous of those who enjoy marriage and yet attain eternal life? Should any disciple of Jesus grumble against God for being generous in giving eternal life?

Jesus' parable may have had particular meaning for Matthew's church. In its origins it was made up of Jews who accepted Jesus as the Messiah and Son of God, and who followed his interpretation of the law of Moses. But increasing numbers of Gentiles were joining the church. These eleventh-hour additions had not borne the heat and toil of the centuries, as had the Jewish people, but they were receiving the same reward of eternal life. Was this unjust on God's part? Should Jewish Christians be envious of Gentile Christians who did not obey all the prescriptions of the law of Moses but were nonetheless on an equal footing with them in attaining eternal life?

Jesus' parable may have a message to those today who have been life-long Christians and have made sacrifices because of their allegiance to God. God will give them their due, but God is free to give others more than their due. God asks those who question his ways, "Are you envious because I am generous?"

For reflection: What is the message of Jesus' parable for me? When have I been resentful because God seems to favor others more than he favors me? Does such resentment reveal ingratitude for what God has given me?

On the Way to Jerusalem, Crucifixion, and Resurrection

17 As Jesus was going up to Jerusalem, he took the twelve [disciples] aside by themselves, and said to them on the way, **18** "Behold, we are going up to Jerusalem, and the Son of Man will be handed over to the chief priests and the scribes, and they will condemn him to death, **19** and hand him over to the Gentiles to be mocked and scourged and crucified, and he will be raised on the third day."

> Gospel parallels: Mark 10:32-34; Luke 18:31-34
> NT: Matt 9:15; 12:40; 16:21; 17:9, 22-23; 26:2

17 **As Jesus was going up to Jerusalem:** Jesus is on his way from Galilee (19:1) to **Jerusalem** (21:10) shortly before Passover (26:2). Jerusalem is about twenty-five hundred feet above sea level and people spoke of **going up** to Jerusalem. **He took the twelve [disciples] aside by themselves, and said to them on the way:** great crowds (19:2) are traveling the same route as Jesus and his disciples—presumably Galileans on their way to Jerusalem for Passover. Jesus takes his disciples **aside by themselves** to talk with them. That Jesus speaks to his disciples **on the way** can simply mean that he speaks to them on the way to Jerusalem. But **the way** was an expression used in the early church for the way of discipleship (Acts 9:2; 18:25-26; 19:9, 23; 22:4; 24:14, 22), and it may have had this connotation for some of Matthew's first readers. What Jesus says to his twelve disciples on the way to Jerusalem has implications for everyone who follows Jesus along the way of discipleship.

> Jerusalem: See page 440
> Disciple: See page 66

18 **Behold, we are going up to Jerusalem.** The word **Behold** functions like an exclamation point in front of a sentence; Jesus wants his disciples to pay close attention to his words. He tells them **we are going up to Jerusalem** not because the disciples have forgotten their destination but because he earlier told them that he must go to Jerusalem to suffer and be killed (16:21), and now he is making this journey. His death might have seemed like a distant prospect when he previously spoke of it (9:15; 12:40; 16:21; 17:9, 22-23), but now every footstep brings him closer to suffering and dying. Jesus includes his disciples in his journey: **we are going up to Jerusalem**. His disciples must share in his fate (see 16:24).

Jesus tells his disciples that in Jerusalem **the Son of Man**—an expression Jesus uses to refer to himself—**will be handed over to the chief priests and the scribes.** The **chief priests** included the high priest and other members of the priestly elite in Jerusalem; **scribes** refers here to influential religious scholars. Together they represent the Jewish religious leadership in Jerusalem. Jesus will be **handed over** to them, which can have two levels of meaning (see 17:22). On one level it means that someone—Judas—will hand Jesus over to the authorities (the Greek word for "hand over" can also mean "betray"—10:4). On another level it means that Jesus will be handed over by God; Jesus' death will be the working out of God's will (see 16:21). After Jesus has been handed over to the religious authorities, **they will condemn him to death.** The word **condemn** is a legal term and conveys that some sort of legal proceedings will result in Jesus' receiving the sentence of **death.**

Son of Man: See page 151
High priest, chief priests: See page 566
Scribes: See page 138

19 After condemning Jesus to death, the chief priests and scribes will **hand him over to the Gentiles:** by **Gentiles** Jesus refers to Romans, who had ruled Palestine for almost a century. Jesus will be handed over to the Romans **to be mocked and scourged and crucified:** he will be transferred to Roman authorities so that they will put him to death. This is the first mention in Matthew's gospel of Jesus being **crucified,** although Jesus has spoken of taking up one's cross to follow him (10:38; 16:24). Romans inflicted crucifixion on non-Roman undesirables; if Jesus is handed over to the Romans to be put to death, he can anticipate being **crucified.** Romans **scourged** those to be crucified to weaken them and increase their suffering.

Death will not triumph over Jesus; he tells his disciples that **he will be raised on the third day.** That he **will be raised** implies he will be raised by God, just as he will be handed over by God (verse 18). Many Jews accepted that there would be a resurrection of the dead at the end of this age, but Jesus speaks of his being raised **on the third day,** not long after he is put to death.

While Jesus gives his disciples a preview of what will happen after he reaches Jerusalem, he does not explain why it will happen. Why is it God's will that he suffer and be put to death? What will his death accomplish?

There may be a hint in Jesus' having just said that "the last will be first" (20:16). Jesus will accept crucifixion, a death imposed on those who are last in this world, but he will be raised to be enthroned as first in God's kingdom (see 19:28).

Peter reacted with horrified disbelief when Jesus previously spoke of his death (16:22), but Matthew does not indicate the disciples' reaction now. The next event that Matthew recounts (20:20-28) will indicate that they do not grasp the implications of Jesus' death.

For reflection: What is my response to Jesus' words?

Jesus As a Ransom

20 Then the mother of the sons of Zebedee approached him with her sons and did him homage, wishing to ask him for something. **21** He said to her, "What do you wish?" She answered him, "Command that these two sons of mine sit, one at your right and the other at your left, in your kingdom." **22** Jesus said in reply, "You do not know what you are asking. Can you drink the cup that I am going to drink?" They said to him, "We can." **23** He replied, "My cup you will indeed drink, but to sit at my right and at my left [, this] is not mine to give but is for those for whom it has been prepared by my Father." **24** When the ten heard this, they became indignant at the two brothers. **25** But Jesus summoned them and said, "You know that the rulers of the Gentiles lord it over them, and the great ones make their authority over them felt. **26** But it shall not be so among you. Rather, whoever wishes to be great among you shall be your servant; **27** whoever wishes to be first among you shall be your slave. **28** Just so, the Son of Man did not come to be served but to serve and to give his life as a ransom for many."

Gospel parallels: Mark 10:35-45; Luke 22:24-26
OT:Isaiah 52:13–53:12
NT:Matt 10:24-25; 18:1-4; 23:11; 27:55-56; John 13:4-5, 12-17;
    1 Tim 2:5-6

20 **Then the mother of the sons of Zebedee approached him.** Jesus tells his disciples that he will be crucified in Jerusalem (20:17-19), and **then the mother of the sons of Zebedee** approaches him. She appears on the scene abruptly; Matthew will later tell his readers that she was one of the women who followed Jesus to Jerusalem and ministered to him (27:55-56).

Matthew does not provide her name but uses the rather awkward phrase, **the mother of the sons of Zebedee,** to identify her. She approaches Jesus **with her sons.** Matthew does not name her sons either, but his readers know that **the sons of Zebedee** are James and John (4:21-22), chosen by Jesus to be among the Twelve (10:1-2) and privileged to see Jesus in transfigured glory (17:1-2). Nor will Matthew call James and John by name in what follows. By not naming them or their mother, Matthew makes it easier for his readers to identify with them. We are to put ourselves in their place and listen to Jesus' words to them as his words to us.

This mother came with her two sons to Jesus **and did him homage, wishing to ask him for something.** She kneels or prostrates herself before Jesus, indicating that she has a request to make of him (see 8:2; 15:25).

21 Jesus knows she wants to ask something of him, and **he said to her, "What do you wish?" She answered him, "Command that these two sons of mine sit, one at your right and the other at your left, in your kingdom."** It is not entirely clear what she has in mind when she refers to Jesus' **kingdom.** Jesus has spoken frequently about God's kingdom, that is, the kingdom of heaven, but rarely of his own kingdom and then only in terms of what will happen at the end of this age (13:40-41; 16:28; see also 19:28). There were popular expectations that the Messiah would establish a here-and-now rule on this earth, and his disciples may have shared these expectations (Acts 1:6). Whatever notion this woman has of Jesus' **kingdom,** she expects that Jesus will rule over it, and she wants her **two sons** to sit on the **right** and **left** sides of Jesus' throne. These were positions of prestige and power in a king's court. She asks Jesus to **command** that her sons be the top two after him in his kingdom.

For reflection: If I were able to be face-to-face with Jesus, what would I request from him?

22 **Jesus said in reply, "You do not know what you are asking. Can you drink the cup that I am going to drink?"** In the Greek, each **you** is plural; Jesus addresses his response not to the mother but to her two sons (had they put her up to asking on their behalf?). He tells them that they do not realize what they are asking for; their idea of his kingship is off target. He asks them whether they are able to **drink the cup** that he is going to drink. In the psalms, a **cup** represents one's fortune or destiny, whether

good (Psalms 16:5; 23:5) or bad (Psalms 11:6; 75:9). Prophets spoke of the cup of God's wrath (Isaiah 51:17; see Jer 25:15; 49:12; Ezek 23:31-34), meaning suffering as punishment for sin. When Jesus asks the two sons whether they can **drink the cup** that he is **going to drink,** he is asking whether they are able to share in his destiny and suffering. He has told them that he will be mocked, scourged, and crucified before being raised (20:19) to reign (19:28); are they able to endure what he is about to endure in order to enter into his reign? **They said to him, "We can."** They respond with confident self-assurance—unwarranted assurance, as it will turn out (see 26:56).

> *For reflection: How confident am I in my ability to endure suffering as a disciple of Jesus?*

23 He replied, **"My cup you will indeed drink,"** even if they do not now understand what it entails. Acts recounts the apostles being flogged (Acts 5:40) and James being put to death (Acts 12:2); disciples of Jesus will share in his sufferings. However, it does not follow that the more pain one endures now, the higher a place one will have earned in the hereafter. He tells the two sons, **but to sit at my right and at my left, [this] is not mine to give but is for those for whom it has been prepared by my Father.** God is like the vineyard owner who is free to do as he wishes (20:15); it is up to God to decide if some should receive special honors in the kingdom of heaven.

24 **When the ten heard this, they became indignant at the two brothers.** The other **ten** were upset by the possibility that they had been upstaged by the **two brothers;** each wanted a top spot for himself. They miss the implications of drinking Jesus' cup of suffering; their hearts are set on attaining honor and power for themselves.

> *For reflection: Do I see something of myself in the disciples' wanting the best for themselves?*

25 **But Jesus summoned them,** presumably all twelve because they all needed to hear the same message. He **said, "You know that the rulers of the Gentiles lord it over them, and the great ones make their authority over them felt."** The disciples' experience of **the rulers of the Gentiles** would have been of Romans governing Palestine, either through kings such

as Herod the Great and his sons or through governors such as Pontius Pilate. Jesus tells his disciples, **you know** how they govern. Those in authority **lord it over** those under them; those with power over others **make their authority over them felt.** Power breeds arrogance, domination, exploitation. That is all too often the way the world operates, from petty officials who abuse those under them to dictators who enrich themselves and impoverish their people.

26 **But it shall not be so among you.** The way of the world is not the way of Jesus, and it is not to be the way of his followers, as they should already realize (see 18:1-4). Jesus tells them, **Rather** than wanting positions of power where you can dominate others, **whoever wishes to be great among you shall be your servant.** A **servant** by definition serves others, performing tasks like waiting on table (see 8:15). **Whoever wishes to be great** in the family of Jesus (12:49-50) must make himself or herself the **servant** of the other members of the family. This is a directive for every disciple of Jesus and especially for those in leadership within the community of his followers. If she wanted her sons to be great, the mother of the sons of Zebedee should have asked that they be assigned to wash dishes at the banquet in the kingdom of heaven (see 8:11).

For reflection: In my exercise of whatever authority I have, do I follow the way of the world or the way of Jesus? To what extent is my heart set on serving others?

27 By equating greatness with service, Jesus turns the way of the world on its head; he goes on to make the reversal absolute. He tells the Twelve and all his followers, **whoever wishes to be first among you shall be your slave.** Slaves did the will of their masters without having a say in the matter; slaves lived for the sake of others. Those who wish to be great in the family of Jesus must be its servants; **whoever wishes to be** not only great but **first** in this family must be its **slave,** at the complete disposal of the other members of the family. Jesus has twice spoken of the last being first (19:30; 20:16); slaves were the **last** and least within a regular household, but the first in the household of Jesus.

For reflection: Do I resent having to do the bidding of others? How willing am I to put myself at the disposal of the church?

28 **Just so, the Son of Man did not come to be served but to serve and to give his life as a ransom for many.** The words **just so** connect the disciples' service with Jesus' service: Jesus is the model for what his disciples are to do (see 10:24-25). Jesus **did not come to be served but to serve.** While the Greek word here for **serve** is sometimes used for waiting on table, its basic meaning is to act as a go-between, perform a task for someone, act on someone's behalf. Jesus has **come** to serve his Father; he is God's agent in establishing the reign of God. Jesus has at the same time come to serve women and men, freeing them from the grip of evil, drawing them into the reign of God (see 12:28): that is what God sent Jesus to do. **Just so,** his disciples must do the same. They must serve their Father in heaven by serving others, easing their afflictions, inviting them into the reign of God.

Son of Man: See page 151

For reflection: How does Jesus' example of service guide me in serving?

BACKGROUND: SERVANT, SLAVE Both servants and slaves did the bidding of others, and may even have done identical work, but with a major difference: servants were hired, slaves were owned. A servant was free to decide whom to work for and could quit; a slave had no choice but to work for his or her owner. At the time of Jesus, one became a slave by being born to a woman slave, by being taken as a prisoner of war, by incurring a debt one could not pay off, by voluntarily becoming a slave, or by being kidnapped. Slaves made up around a fifth of the population in the Roman Empire. There are important differences between slavery in the first-century Roman Empire and slavery in the Americas in the seventeenth to nineteenth centuries, and further differences between slavery in Palestine and slavery in other parts of the Roman Empire. In the world of Jesus, slavery was not based on race: the slaves referred to in Jesus' parables are usually Jews owned by other Jews. Owners could treat slaves badly, but slaves could own property (including other slaves!) and hold important positions; some slaves were better educated than their owners. Slaves served as managers, doctors, and bankers as well as farmworkers and domestic servants. Some freely chose slavery because it offered them guaranteed employment: slaves were sometimes better off than day laborers. Slaves could be freed after a certain period of service; a slave of a Roman citizen was generally given citizenship upon being freed. There are different Greek words for servant and slave, but the New American Bible often translates the Greek word for slave as "servant" (e.g., Matt 18:23; 21:34; 22:3; 24:45; 25:14), apparently to avoid confusing the ancient practice of slavery with slavery in the American experience.

Jesus' ultimate act of service will be **to give his life as a ransom for many.** Jesus will **give his life;** he will be "mocked and scourged and crucified" (20:19). The word **many** here means "a great number" of people; it does not imply "not all." The word **for** can mean "in place of" as well as "on behalf of," and may hint that Jesus will suffer death in place of others. He will give his life **as a ransom.** A **ransom** was the payment made to buy freedom for a slave or to liberate a captive (Lev 25:47-52; 1 Macc 10:33). Ransom was paid to the one owning the slave or holding the captive. If Jesus literally gives his life as a **ransom,** then we might ask who receives the payment of his life. There is no good answer to this question, which indicates that Jesus is using the word **ransom** metaphorically, rather than literally. The Old Testament uses "ransom" as a metaphor for God's freeing the Israelites from Egypt (Deut 7:8; 9:26; 13:6; 15:15; 21:8; 24:18) and from exile in Babylon (Isaiah 51:11; Jer 31:11). God did not make a payment to the Egyptians or the Babylonians to ransom his people. In the same way, Jesus' giving his life as a **ransom for many** means that Jesus wins their freedom, without implying that his life is a payment made to anyone.

Jesus has spoken of what must happen to him (16:21); he will be "handed over" by his Father to suffer and die (17:22; 20:18-19). This is the first time Jesus indicates what his death will accomplish: he will give his life **as a ransom for many,** releasing them from bondage. Jesus does not explain what kind of bondage they are in. However, Matthew's readers can recall that an angel told Joseph that Mary would bear a son "and you are to name him Jesus, because he will save his people from their sins" (1:21). During the Last Supper, Jesus will speak of shedding his blood "on behalf of many for the forgiveness of sins" (26:28). Jesus gives his life to ransom us from the bondage of our sins.

For reflection: Do I look upon Jesus as one who has ransomed and freed me? As one who has given his life in place of mine?

ORIENTATION: *Jesus and his disciples are traveling from Galilee to Jerusalem. After taking a route along the east side of the Jordan River (19:1), they have crossed the Jordan and have traveled west to Jericho. Now they are about to begin the ascent to Jerusalem.*

Those Who Are Blind Receive Sight

29 As they left Jericho, a great crowd followed him. 30 Two blind men were sitting by the roadside, and when they heard that Jesus was passing by, they cried out, "[Lord,] Son of David, have pity on us!" 31 The crowd warned them to be silent, but they called out all the more, "Lord, Son of David, have pity on us!" 32 Jesus stopped and called them and said, "What do you want me to do for you?" 33 They answered him, "Lord, let our eyes be opened." 34 Moved with pity, Jesus touched their eyes. Immediately they received their sight, and followed him.

Gospel parallels: Mark 10:46-52; Luke 18:35-43

29 **As they left Jericho, a great crowd followed him.** The town of **Jericho** lies about fifteen miles from Jerusalem. Jesus is on the last leg of his journey to Jerusalem to suffer and die and be raised. A **great crowd** has been following Jesus since he left Galilee (see 19:2). Many in this crowd are likely on their way to Jerusalem to celebrate Passover (see 26:2). Even if they are not disciples of Jesus, they view Jesus favorably because he has been healing the sick among them (19:2).

30 **Two blind men were sitting by the roadside**—a favored location for beggars who relied on the generosity of pilgrims on their way to Jerusalem. **They heard that Jesus was passing by:** they presumably heard some in the crowd talking about Jesus. Hearing that Jesus was near **they cried out, "[Lord,] Son of David, have pity on us!"** The New American Bible prints **Lord** in brackets because not all manuscripts of Matthew's gospel

---

BACKGROUND: JERICHO can lay claim to being both the lowest and the oldest city on earth. Jericho lies in the Jordan Valley, ten miles from where the Jordan River empties into the Dead Sea. The city is about 850 feet below sea level (for comparison, Death Valley in the United States is about 280 feet below sea level). Jericho was built at the site of a powerful spring that flows to this day. In ancient Jericho, archaeologists have discovered a thirty-foot-high tower and city walls dating from around 8,000 B.C.—almost seven thousand years before Joshua came along. At the time of Jesus, the tower and the wall had long been buried in a pile of rubble. Jericho lay along one of the most commonly used routes for travel between Galilee and Jerusalem. The road from Jericho to Jerusalem went by a palace that Herod the Great had built to enjoy Jericho's warm winter weather; Jerusalem, only fifteen miles away but twenty-five hundred feet above sea level, is cold and damp in the winter.

---

include this word. For these two men to address Jesus as **Lord** acknowledges his authority and power, but Matthew's readers would have found fuller meaning in the word. Jews used **Lord** as a title or name for God, and the early church began to call Jesus **Lord,** just as God is called **Lord** (see Phil 2:11; 1 Thess 1:1). The two men who are blind also call Jesus **Son of David.** Here too there can be different shades of meaning. For Matthew's readers, Jesus is the **Son of David** who is the Messiah (1:1, 6-16; see also 22:41-45). During his public ministry, Jesus is hailed as **Son of David** in conjunction with his healings (9:27; 12:22-23; 15:22), possibly because in Jewish tradition Solomon, the son of David, was thought to have had healing powers. Jesus had a widespread reputation as a healer (4:24-25), and these two men may be appealing to him as the healing **Son of David.** They call out to him, **have pity—mercy—on us!** The Canaanite woman whose daughter was tormented by a demon called out to Jesus, "Have pity on me, Lord, Son of David!" (15:22); these men make the same cry for Jesus' mercy.

Lord: See page 133
Son of David: See page 16

31 **The crowd warned them to be silent:** the crowd accompanying Jesus rebukes the two men, trying to silence them. Matthew does not explain the crowd's reason for doing so; perhaps they consider blind beggars a nuisance, not worth Jesus' notice. Had they known Jesus better, they would have realized that he welcomes outcasts and nobodies to himself (9:10; 11:19; 18:1-5; 19:13-15). **But they called out all the more, "Lord, Son of David, have pity on us!"** The two men persist in their pleas, crying out all the louder. They have little to lose but a lot they might gain from Jesus. One motive for persistence in prayer can be our realization that we have no good alternative. Their cry to Jesus as **Lord,** asking that he **have pity,** is, in the Greek of Matthew's gospel, *Kyrie, eleison*—Greek words traditionally used in the liturgy. We echo the plea of the two men whenever we pray, Lord, have mercy.

For reflection: Where am I in greatest need of the Lord's mercy? How persistently do I cry out for his mercy?

32 **Jesus stopped:** Jesus came to serve (20:28), and he stops to do so even as he is on his way to Jerusalem and the climax of his life on earth. He **called**

them, indicating his responsiveness to them. He asks, **What do you want me to do for you?** He leaves it to them to say what they want him to do for them.

33 **They answered him, "Lord, let our eyes be opened."** They continue to address Jesus as **Lord;** they want him to give them sight.

34 **Moved with pity, Jesus touched their eyes.** The expression **moved with pity** conveys that Jesus is moved in his inner depths with profound compassion, as he has been moved with compassion for others in need (9:36; 14:14; 15:32). Although Jesus can heal with a word of command (9:6; 12:13; 15:28; 17:18; see also 8:8), he sometimes heals with a touch (8:3, 15; 9:29), perhaps to physically convey his compassion. He does so now: **Jesus touched their eyes,** and **immediately they received their sight.** Matthew concludes his account by noting that after being given sight by Jesus, they **followed him.** To follow Jesus is the definition of discipleship. These two men begin to follow Jesus as he nears the end of his journey to Jerusalem; they are like the workers hired by the vineyard owner at the eleventh hour (20:6-7).

The healing of two who were blind can have symbolic meaning. Jesus has repeatedly spoken of his coming death (16:21; 17:22-23; 20:17-19), and his disciples have repeatedly failed to comprehend the implications of his words (16:22; 18:1; 20:20-21, 24). The disciples need spiritual sight no less than the two men in Jericho needed physical sight. Jesus is moved with compassion for his disciples as he was for the two men by the roadside; he is willing to give them spiritual sight even at the eleventh hour so that they can follow him along the way of the cross. The disciples' prayer—and ours as well—should be the prayer of the two by the roadside: Lord, have mercy on us. Lord, let our eyes be opened.

For reflection: What message does this incident have for me?

CHAPTER 21

ORIENTATION: *As Jesus enters Jerusalem, he acts out a prophecy in order to dramatize the kind of messiah he is.*

Not a Warrior King

[1] When they drew near Jerusalem and came to Bethphage on the Mount of Olives, Jesus sent two disciples, [2] saying to them, "Go into the village opposite you, and immediately you will find an ass tethered, and a colt with her. Untie them and bring them here to me. [3] And if anyone should say anything to you, reply, 'The master has need of them.' Then he will send them at once." [4] This happened so that what had been spoken through the prophet might be fulfilled:

[5] "Say to daughter Zion,
    'Behold, your king comes to you,
    meek and riding on an ass,
    and on a colt, the foal of a beast of burden.'"

[6] The disciples went and did as Jesus had ordered them. [7] They brought the ass and the colt and laid their cloaks over them, and he sat upon them. [8] The very large crowd spread their cloaks on the road, while others cut branches from the trees and strewed them on the road. [9] The crowds preceding him and those following kept
crying out and saying:

"Hosanna to the Son of David;
    blessed is he who comes in the name of the Lord;
    hosanna in the highest."

[10] And when he entered Jerusalem the whole city was shaken and asked, "Who is this?" [11] And the crowds replied, "This is Jesus the prophet, from Nazareth in Galilee."
Gospel parallels: Mark 11:1-11; Luke 19:28-40; John 12:12-16
OT:Psalm 118:25-26; Isaiah 62:11; Zech 9:9-10
NT:Matt 11:29; 12:19-20

1 **When they drew near Jerusalem and came to Bethphage on the Mount of Olives:** Jesus and his disciples have traveled from Jericho (20:29) to the eastern outskirts of **Jerusalem.** The **Mount of Olives** is a ridge of hills just east of Jerusalem. **Bethphage** was a village on an eastern slope of the Mount of Olives; its location is not known with certainty today, but it would have been about a mile from Jerusalem. The road from Jericho ran past Bethany (21:17) and Bethphage before coming over the crest of the Mount of Olives. On reaching Bethphage, **Jesus sent two disciples** to carry out a task.

Jerusalem: See page 440

2 He told them, **Go into the village opposite you, and immediately you will find an ass tethered, and a colt with her. Untie them and bring them here to me.** The **village opposite** the disciples was apparently Bethphage, off to the side of the road. An **ass,** or donkey, was a common beast of burden; a **colt** here means a young donkey. Jesus speaks with assurance about what the disciples will find in the village. Is Jesus demonstrating superhuman knowledge, or has someone told him where the animals are tethered?

We might note that Jesus does not explain to his disciples why he wants them to fetch the ass and the colt. Sometimes disciples need to carry out Jesus' instructions without immediately knowing what their obedience will accomplish.

For reflection: When have I obeyed Jesus without knowing where it would lead?

3 **And if anyone should say anything to you, reply, "The master has need of them." Then he will send them at once.** Jesus continues to speak with assurance about what will happen in the village, but who is he referring to when he speaks of **the master** who needs the animals? The Greek word translated here as **master** (and in some other contexts as "lord") means someone with authority, and it can refer to ownership. **The master** is literally *their* master—the master of the ass and the colt—and would seem to refer to the owner of the animals. Has he told Jesus about his ass and colt and put them at Jesus' disposal? It is less likely that Jesus is referring to himself as **the master** of the animals. Jesus knows that his disciples' mission will be successful and the ass and colt will be sent **at once.**

Lord: See page 133

4 Matthew notes, **This happened so that what had been spoken through the prophet might be fulfilled.** In sending his disciples to fetch an ass and a colt, Jesus is making arrangements to enter Jerusalem in a manner described in prophecy.

5 Matthews quotes the prophetic texts that Jesus will fulfill: **Say to daughter Zion, / "Behold, your king comes to you, / meek and riding on an ass, / and on a colt, the foal of a beast of burden."** The first words are from Isaiah: **Say to daughter Zion** (Isaiah 62:11). **Zion** was originally a name for the fortified hill that made up Jerusalem when David conquered it (2 Sam 5:7). **Daughter Zion** became a poetic way to refer to the city of Jerusalem and, by extension, to its citizens.

> Say to daughter Zion,
>> your savior comes!
>> Isaiah 62:11

The remainder of the prophecy Matthew quotes is from Zechariah, who spoke of a king riding a donkey into Jerusalem (Zech 9:9). Kings did ride donkeys or mules (1 Kings 1:32-40) but not into battle; in wars, kings rode on horses or in chariots. The **king** who would come to Jerusalem would demonstrate that he was **meek** and not a warrior king by **riding on an ass, / and on a colt, the foal of a beast of burden.** Zechariah's prophecy goes on to speak of the king banishing the implements of war and proclaiming peace to the nations (Zech 9:10).

> Rejoice heartily, O daughter Zion,
>> shout for joy, O daughter Jerusalem!
> See, your king shall come to you;
>> a just savior is he,
> Meek, and riding on an ass,
>> on a colt, the foal of an ass.
> He shall banish the chariot from Ephraim,
>> and the horse from Jerusalem;
> The warrior's bow shall be banished,
>> and he shall proclaim peace to the nations.
>> Zechariah 9:9-10

Pilgrims normally entered Jerusalem on foot, but Jesus will ride into Jerusalem like the king in Zechariah's prophecy to indicate that he is not a warrior messiah bent on establishing an earthly kingdom. Jesus is "meek and humble of heart" (11:29), not a man of violence (12:19-20); he forbids his disciples from following the way of violence (5:38-39; 26:51-52).

For reflection: What does the example and teaching of Jesus about violence require of me?

6 **The disciples went and did as Jesus had ordered them.** They carry out Jesus' instructions. Being a disciple of Jesus is not simply a matter of learning from him but of doing what he asks.

Disciple: See page 66

7 **They brought the ass and the colt and laid their cloaks over them, and he sat upon them.** Their **cloaks** (outer garments) provided improvised saddlecloths on which Jesus could sit. But how are we to visualize two animals being brought to Jesus and his sitting **upon them** for his ride into Jerusalem? It would take a circus acrobat to ride two donkeys at the same time, and scholars have long noted the improbability of Jesus doing so. (The other three gospels have Jesus riding a single animal: Mark 11:7; Luke 19:35; John 12:14.) One explanation is that while Zechariah's prophecy employs the Hebrew poetic practice of using two parallel expressions to speak of the same thing—here riding on one animal: "riding on an ass, / on a colt, the foal of an ass" (Zech 9:9)—Matthew quotes a Greek translation of this prophecy that contains an *and*, making it seem like the prophecy is speaking of two animals: "riding on an ass, and on a

---

BACKGROUND: ZION, DAUGHTER ZION The name "Zion" has multiple associations in the Old Testament. It was originally a name for Jerusalem when it was a Jebusite fortress; David captured "the stronghold of Zion" and made it "the City of David" (2 Sam 5:7). After Solomon built his Temple north of the City of David, Zion became a name for the hill on which the Temple stood; Psalm 74:2 asks God to "Remember Mount Zion where you dwell" (see also Isaiah 8:18). Zion also came to mean the entire city of Jerusalem (Isaiah 40:9) and its inhabitants (Isaiah 51:16). "Daughter Zion" is a poetic expression for the city of Jerusalem (Psalm 9:15) and those who live in it (Micah 4:10). There are scattered references in the New Testament to Zion, Mount Zion, and Daughter Zion.

colt, the foal of a beast of burden" (verse 5). Matthew presents Jesus fulfilling Zechariah's prophecy with literal exactness, even if it requires Jesus to ride two animals. The important point is not whether Jesus rode one donkey or two but the message he sends by riding into Jerusalem in a manner that recalls Zechariah's prophecy.

Cloaks: see Clothing, page 95

8 **The very large crowd spread their cloaks on the road, while others cut branches from the trees and strewed them on the road.** Matthew indicates that there is a **very large crowd** on the road; they are presumably on their way to Jerusalem to celebrate Passover (see 19:1-2; 20:29; 26:2). Pilgrims more than tripled Jerusalem's population during the major feasts. They carpet the road for Jesus with **their cloaks** and with **branches** they have cut. They treat Jesus royally (see 2 Kings 9:13), providing him the counterpart of a red carpet.

For reflection: What do I do to honor Jesus?

9 **The crowds preceding him and those following kept crying out:** Jesus is in a procession of pilgrims coming into Jerusalem, filling the road before and after him. The Mount of Olives is a ridge a few hundred feet higher than Jerusalem. Pilgrims caught their first sight of Jerusalem and of the Temple from the crest of the Mount of Olives—and what a sight it was! Herod the Great had sheathed the exterior of the Temple with gold. The first-century Jewish historian Josephus describes it shining so brightly in the sun that one had to turn one's eyes away. Pilgrims must have experienced a surge of joy on seeing it, erasing the fatigue of the climb from Jericho to the summit of the Mount of Olives. It would be natural for them to keep cry **crying out** in their exuberance.

Temple: See page 442

This crowd kept **saying: "Hosanna to the Son of David."** The Hebrew words represented by **hosanna** literally mean "save, please" or "help, please"; Psalm 118 uses the words to ask God to "grant salvation" (Psalm 118:25). In popular usage, however, **hosanna** came to be an acclamation or cry of praise, and that is probably its sense here: "Praise to the Son of David." (The *Didache*, a very early Christian writing that describes the celebration of the Eucharist, has "Hosanna to the God of David" as one of the prayers.) The crowd hails Jesus as **the Son of David,** a title that can have different nuances. The crowd may view Jesus as **the Son of David** because he heals those who are afflicted (9:27; 12:22-23; 15:22; 20:30-31); Jesus healed some in the crowd on the way to Jerusalem (19:1-2). For Matthew's readers, Jesus is **the Son of David** who is the Messiah (1:1, 6-16; see also 22:41-45). Some in the crowd who hailed Jesus as **the Son of David** may also have had a messianic meaning in mind. Although the Messiah is never called the Son of David in the Old Testament, the Psalms of Solomon identified "the Lord Messiah" with "the son of David." This nonbiblical writing speaks of the Messiah expelling Gentiles from Jerusalem and smashing sinners with an iron rod—an understanding of the Messiah that Jesus is trying to counter by riding a donkey into Jerusalem.

The *Didache*: See page 129
Son of David: See page 16
Psalms of Solomon: See page 354

The crowd also cries out, **blessed is he who comes in the name of the Lord,** words taken from Psalm 118:26. This psalm was prayed at Passover and used to greet pilgrims entering Jerusalem. As a pilgrimage greeting, the crowd's words have the sense, "Blessed in the name of the Lord is he who comes to Jerusalem on pilgrimage." However, Jesus has spoken of himself as having "come" to accomplish certain things (5:17; 9:13; 10:34-35; 20:28); Matthew's readers can understand the crowd's cry as having the sense, Blessed is he who comes to Jerusalem to carry out God's will (see also 3:11; 11:3). The crowd's final cry is **hosanna in the highest.** The literal sense would be, May God in highest heaven save—save Jesus. The popular meaning may have been, Praise to God in the highest heaven. Jesus is given the ancient equivalent of a ticker-tape parade as he enters Jerusalem.

> LORD, *grant salvation!*
>   LORD, *grant good fortune!*
>
> *Blessed is he*
>   *who comes in the name of the* LORD.
> *We bless you from the* LORD's *house.*
>   Psalm 118:25-26

10 **And when he entered Jerusalem the whole city was shaken and asked, "Who is this?"** The people of **Jerusalem** were used to crowds of exuberant pilgrims arriving before feasts, but Jesus' entry was extraordinary. **The whole city was shaken,** as if by an earthquake. Decades earlier "all Jerusalem" was "greatly troubled" by news of the birth of a "newborn king of the Jews" (2:2-3); Jerusalem is now shaken by his arrival in town. The people of Jerusalem ask, **Who is this?** They do not seem to know who Jesus is, and they wonder who comes into their midst accompanied by the clamor of crowds.

Matthew's gospel confronts its readers with the same question: Who is this? What message does Jesus' riding into Jerusalem as a meek king have for me?

11 **And the crowds replied, "This is Jesus the prophet, from Nazareth in Galilee."** The **crowds** are those who accompanied Jesus into Jerusalem (verses 8-9), including pilgrims from Galilee (see 19:1-2). They tell the people of Jerusalem, **This is Jesus the prophet.** Jesus was commonly viewed as a **prophet** (16:13-14), someone who speaks for God. Jesus does not seem to be thought of as the Messiah except by his disciples (16:16-17), and the significance of his riding a donkey into Jerusalem seems lost

---

BACKGROUND: JERUSALEM lies on rocky hills about twenty-five hundred feet above sea level; hence the Bible speaks of "going up" to Jerusalem and "going down" from Jerusalem. Jerusalem's importance was political and religious rather than geographic or economic. It did not lie on any trade routes, nor is the region a lush agricultural area: the eastern outskirts of Jerusalem border on the Judean wilderness. However, David had chosen Jerusalem to be his capital, and Solomon had built the first Israelite Temple in Jerusalem. Jerusalem remained the religious center even after Israelite political independence was lost. Jerusalem's population at the time of Jesus is estimated to have been around forty thousand. Well over one hundred thousand more people would crowd into the city during pilgrimage feasts (Passover, Weeks, Booths). The Temple was the mainstay of Jerusalem's economy, by one estimate accounting for 20 percent of the city's income. The massive revamping of the Temple complex that Herod the Great began in 20 B.C. continued almost until the time of the Jewish revolt in A.D. 66—a major public-works project. Offerings brought to the Temple and the sale of animals for sacrifice brought income to Jerusalem and to those who controlled the Temple. Jerusalem was a company town, and that company was the Temple. *Related topic: Temple (page 442).*

on the crowds. **Jesus**—a form of the name "Joshua"—was a common name for Jewish men of the time. This Jesus is identified as the Jesus who is **from Nazareth**. Perhaps **Nazareth** was so insignificant a village that it was necessary to add that it was **in Galilee**. Even though Jesus has lived in Capernaum since the beginning of his public ministry (4:13) he is still associated with the village in which he grew up (2:23; 13:54-58).

Nazareth: See page 38

Galilee: See page 68

Jesus Disrupts Temple Commerce

12 Jesus entered the temple area and drove out all those engaged in selling and buying there. He overturned the tables of the money changers and the seats of those who were selling doves. **13** And he said to them, "It is written:

'My house shall be a house of prayer,'
  but you are making it a den of thieves."

14 The blind and the lame approached him in the temple area, and he cured them. **15** When the chief priests and the scribes saw the wondrous things he was doing, and the children crying out in the temple area, "Hosanna to the Son of David," they were indignant **16** and said to him, "Do you hear what they are saying?" Jesus said to them, "Yes; and have you never read the text, 'Out of the mouths of infants and nurslings you have brought forth praise'?" **17** And leaving them, he went out of the city to Bethany, and there he spent the night.

Gospel parallels: Mark 11:15-19; Luke 19:45-48; John 2:13-22

OT: Psalm 8:2-3; Isaiah 56:7; Jer 7:1-15

NT: Matt 24:1-2

12 After his dramatic entry into Jerusalem (21:7-11), **Jesus entered the temple area.** The **temple** was near the center of a thirty-five-acre rectangular **area** enclosed by colonnaded halls. Sacrifices were offered on an altar in front of the Temple; a variety of other activities took place in the outermost courtyard and halls, including the selling of animals to be sacrificed. It was more convenient for pilgrims to buy animals in Jerusalem than to bring animals with them. There were markets for sacrificial animals on the Mount of Olives, but it seems that the high priest, Caiaphas, had recently opened a market in the Temple area. Upon entering the **temple area,** Jesus **drove out all those engaged in selling and buying there.** Matthew writes that Jesus expelled **all** who were selling and buying, but that is hard to visualize. The Court of the Gentiles, where the commerce was taking place, covered about twenty-five acres. If Jesus was so disruptive that all commerce came to a halt, the Temple police or the Roman soldiers keeping watch from the adjacent Antonia Fortress would have stepped in. But no one intervenes to stop Jesus, leading to the surmise that his action was a limited and symbolic disruption of commerce rather than a complete purging of all selling and buying from the entire Temple area.

Jesus' actions, however limited they might have been, were certainly disruptive: **He overturned the tables of the money changers,** sending coins flying. Payment of the Temple tax (17:24-27; Exod 30:11-16) could

---

BACKGROUND: TEMPLE In the ancient Near East, a temple was thought of as the "house" or "palace" of God. Solomon (who ruled from about 970 to 931 B.C.) built the first Israelite Temple in Jerusalem. From the time of King Josiah (who ruled from about 640 to 609 B.C.), this Jerusalem Temple was the only site where Jews could offer animal sacrifices. Solomon's Temple was destroyed by the Babylonians in 587 B.C. A second Temple was built after the Exile and dedicated in 515 B.C. Herod the Great rebuilt and refurbished this second Temple, enlarging the surrounding courtyard to more than thirty-five acres. Around the perimeter of the courtyard, Herod erected magnificent colonnaded halls similar to structures found in the Greek and Roman world. The Temple itself was not a huge building; the precedent established by Solomon's Temple limited its interior floor plan to about 30 by 90 feet (see 1 Kings 6:2). Herod added auxiliary rooms and a grand entrance, substantially increased the height of the structure, and plated its exterior with gold. Worshipers gathered outside the Temple rather than within it. An altar for offering burnt sacrifices stood in a courtyard reserved for priests that was in front of—east of—the Temple. East of the Court of Priests was a small Court of Israel, which ritually clean Jewish men could enter, and to its east was a Court of the Women for ritually clean Jews of any age or sex. The remaining, and by far the largest, portion of the Temple area was a Court of the Gentiles, available to both Jews and non-Jews. The open spaces and colonnaded halls in the Court of the Gentiles provided places for meetings, instruction, the selling of animals for sacrifice, and the changing of coins for Temple taxes and offerings. The Temple also served as a national religious treasury and depository for savings (see 2 Macc 3:5-12). Rome destroyed the Temple in A.D. 70 while putting down a Jewish revolt. It was never rebuilt.

be made only in certain currencies. Many coins in circulation in the Roman Empire bore pagan inscriptions (see 22:19-21) and had to be exchanged for approved coins—a service provided by **money changers.** Jesus also upset **the seats of those who were selling doves.** Doves were offered in connection with ritual purification (Lev 15:13-15; 28-30), and were also the sacrificial offerings of the poor in place of more expensive animals (Lev 5:7; 12:8; 14:21-22).

13 **He said to them, "It is written: 'My house shall be a house of prayer,' / but you are making it a den of thieves."** Jesus quotes a prophecy of Isaiah in which God speaks of the Temple as **my house** and proclaims that it is to be **a house of prayer** (Isaiah 56:7). Jesus tells the vendors and money changers that instead of the Temple being a house of prayer they **are making it a den of thieves.** Does Jesus mean that the vendors and money changers were defrauding their customers? Possibly, but there is no ancient evidence that Temple vendors were dishonest. There is evidence that those who controlled the Temple—the high priest and chief priests—derived wealth from Temple income and commerce. Excavations in Jerusalem discovered a neighborhood of palatial houses occupied by the priestly aristocracy. Ancient writings describe the high-priestly families as corrupt, exploitative, and self-enriching. It is likely that Jesus' charge that the Temple had become **a den of thieves** was aimed more at those who controlled the Temple than simply at low-level vendors and money changers. A religious aristocracy was using God's house as their private profit center.

> For my house shall be called
> a house of prayer for all peoples.
> Isaiah 56:7

There may be an ominous implication in Jesus' charge that the Temple was being made into **a den of thieves.** This expression occurs in a prophecy in which Jeremiah foretells the destruction of the Temple (Jer 7:1-15). Jeremiah reminds his listeners that God allowed his shrine at Shiloh to be destroyed and warns that the same fate awaits the Jerusalem Temple because God's people will not abandon their sinful ways. By disrupting the commerce connected with sacrificial worship in the Temple, Jesus may be foreshadowing the end of that worship. Jesus will later foretell the destruction of the Temple (24:1-2).

*Are you to steal and murder, commit adultery and perjury, burn
incense to Baal, go after strange gods that you know not, and yet
come to stand before me in this house which bears my name, and
say: "We are safe; we can commit all these abominations again"?
Has this house which bears my name become in your eyes a den
of thieves? . . . You may go to Shiloh, which I made the dwelling
place of my name in the beginning. See what I did to it because
of the wickedness of my people Israel. . . . I will do to this house
named after me, in which you trust, and to this place which I
gave to you and your fathers, just as I did to Shiloh.*

Jeremiah 7:9-12, 14

*For reflection: What meaning do I see in Jesus' actions and words in the
Temple area? What message do they have for me?*

14 **The blind and the lame approached him in the temple area, and he
cured them.** Even though he will suffer and be put to death in Jerusalem,
Jesus heals the afflicted of the city, just as he earlier had compassion on
others in need (9:36; 14:14; 15:32; 20:34). Some scholars suggest that
there is significance in Jesus healing those who are **blind** and **lame** in **the
temple area.** The blind and lame may not have been allowed into the inner courts of the Temple because of an interpretation of 2 Sam 5:8 ("The
blind and the lame shall not enter the palace"). If this prohibition was in
place, then by healing those who were blind or lame Jesus not only restores them physically but allows them fuller access to God.

*For reflection: What does it tell me about Jesus that he continues to heal
even as his death draws near?*

15 **When the chief priests and the scribes saw the wondrous things he was
doing, and the children crying out in the temple area, "Hosanna to the
Son of David," they were indignant.** Jesus told his disciples that he
"must go to Jerusalem and suffer greatly from the elders, the chief priests,
and the scribes" (16:21; see also 20:18). This is his first encounter with
the chief priests and the scribes, the religious leadership in Jerusalem.
They are not **indignant** because Jesus interfered with Temple commerce.
(Had it been such a minor incident that they had not yet heard about it?)
They are **indignant** because they **saw** Jesus doing the **wondrous things** of

healing the blind and lame, resulting in **children crying out in the temple area, "Hosanna to the Son of David."** The children echo the cry of those who accompanied Jesus into Jerusalem (21:9); once again Jesus is hailed as **the Son of David** in conjunction with his healing (9:27; 12:22-23; 15:22; 20:30-31). The chief priests and scribes might have interpreted **the Son of David** in a messianic sense and been indignant that Jesus received such acclaim. To them Jesus may have seemed a Galilean villager intruding on their religious turf.

High priest, chief priests: See page 566
Scribes: See page 138
Son of David: See page 16

16 They **said to him, "Do you hear what they are saying?"** The implication is that it is improper for Jesus to be hailed as the Son of David and he should have silenced the children. **Jesus said to them, "Yes; and have you never read the text, 'Out of the mouths of infants and nurslings you have brought forth praise'?"** Jesus invokes words from a psalm as justification for the children's cries (Psalm 8:3). In Psalm 8, the children's praise of God silences those opposed to God. Matthew quotes a Greek translation of Psalm 8 that makes their **praise** more explicit than in the Hebrew text of the psalm. By invoking this text, Jesus conveys that the children's cries of praise for him are just as appropriate as the children's cries of praise in Psalm 8. What is hidden from the wise and learned—chief priests and scribes—has been revealed to children (see 11:25).

> O LORD, our Lord,
> > how awesome is your name through all the earth!
> > You have set your majesty above the heavens!
> Out of the mouths of babes and infants
> > you have drawn a defense against your foes,
> > to silence enemy and avenger.
> > > Psalm 8:2-3

17 And leaving them, he went out of the city to Bethany: Jesus breaks off the confrontation with the religious leaders and leaves Jerusalem. He goes to **Bethany** on the Mount of Olives; **there he spent the night.** Far more pilgrims came to Jerusalem for Passover than could be accommodated in the city itself. Some stayed at night in nearby villages such as Bethany, lodging with relatives or friends or camping out.

A Fig Tree and Faith
[18] When he was going back to the city in the morning, he was hungry. [19] Seeing a fig tree by the road, he went over to it, but found nothing on it except leaves. And he said to it, "May no fruit ever come from you again." And immediately the fig tree withered. [20] When the disciples saw this, they were amazed and said, "How was it that the fig tree withered immediately?" [21] Jesus said to them in reply, "Amen, I say to you, if you have faith and do not waver, not only will you do what has been done to the fig tree, but even if you say to this mountain, 'Be lifted up and thrown into the sea,' it will be done. [22] Whatever you ask for in prayer with faith, you will receive."

    Gospel parallels: Mark 11:12-14, 20-24
    NT: Matt 7:7-11; 17:19-20; 18:19; Luke 17:5-6; John 14:13-14; 15:7; 16:23-24; James 1:6-8; 1 John 5:14-15

18 Jesus spent the night in Bethany (21:17), about two miles east of Jerusalem. **When he was going back to the city** of Jerusalem **in the morning, he was hungry.** If Jesus had stayed with someone in Bethany, they likely would have provided him breakfast or food to carry with him: the demands of hospitality were taken very seriously (see Luke 11:5-6). That Jesus is **hungry** as he walks back to Jerusalem may indicate that he and his disciples were camping out in Bethany. More pilgrims came to Jerusalem

---

BACKGROUND: BETHANY was a village on a southeastern slope of the Mount of Olives, about two miles from Jerusalem (John 11:18). Because during major feasts Jerusalem was crowded with pilgrims and accommodations were scarce, Jesus spent his nights in Bethany when he came to Jerusalem for Passover (Matt 21:17; Mark 11:11-12; see Luke 21:37). The gospels do not make it clear whether Jesus stayed with friends in Bethany or simply camped out. The Gospel of John presents Mary, Martha, and Lazarus as residents of Bethany (11:1) but is the only gospel to do so. Luke seems to situate Mary and Martha in a village near Galilee (Luke 10:38-42); Matthew and Mark do not mention the two sisters or Lazarus. Matthew and Mark describe Jesus eating at the home of Simon the Leper in Bethany (Matt 26:6-13; Mark 14:3-9); John describes a similar meal in Bethany with Martha, Mary, and Lazarus (John 12:1-8).

for the major feasts than could find accommodations, and many, especially the poor, spent the nights in the open. The Greek word translated **in the morning** literally means "early": Matthew will recount Jesus' having a very full day.

19 **Seeing a fig tree by the road, he went over to it, but found nothing on it except leaves.** Matthew's readers might assume that there should have been edible fruit on the tree; otherwise why would a hungry Jesus go to it? **And he said to it, "May no fruit ever come from you again." And immediately the fig tree withered.** It might seem that Jesus is out of sorts and petulantly withers a fig tree that did not provide him breakfast, but this would be out of character for the Jesus we have met in the pages of Matthew's gospel. A Jesus who would not turn stones to bread to satisfy his hunger (4:2-4) would hardly wither a fig tree simply because he was hungry. We need to consider other factors.

One factor: the fig harvest in Palestine is in the fall, but it is now near Passover (see 26:2), a springtime feast. No Palestinian Jew—Jesus included—would expect to find ripe figs on a tree during Passover. Another factor: prophets used the devastation of fig trees as a symbol for God's punishment (Hosea 2:14; Amos 4:9). A third factor: prophets sometimes delivered messages through their actions, as when Jeremiah smashed a pottery flask to symbolize the destruction of Jerusalem (Jer 19:1-13; see also Isaiah 20:1-4; Jer 13:1-11; 27:1-8; Ezek 4:1-15; 5:1-15). A final factor: Jesus performed symbolic acts by entering Jerusalem on a donkey (21:7-10) and disrupting Temple commerce 21:12-13). These factors suggest that Jesus knew that the fig tree would be barren, but went to the tree to perform an act symbolizing divine judgment. Jesus proclaimed that "every tree that does not bear good fruit will be cut down and thrown into the fire" (7:19; see also 3:10); Jesus used the fig tree as a visual aid. It is not immediately clear who will be judged and punished by God for not bearing fruit. One candidate, however, must be those whom Jesus accused of turning the Temple into a den of thieves (21:13).

For reflection: How do I understand Jesus' withering of the fig tree? What message does it have for me?

20 **When the disciples saw this, they were amazed and said, "How was it that the fig tree withered immediately?"** The disciples are **amazed** that the fig

tree withered at Jesus' word—but after having seen Jesus expel demons, calm storms, and raise the dead, should anything he does amaze them? If Jesus intended to dramatize a message of divine judgment by withering the tree, they didn't get it. Instead they ask him, "How did you do that?"

21 Jesus does not try to explain the significance of the fig tree's withering but uses his disciples' question as an opportunity to teach them about praying with faith. **Jesus said to them in reply, "Amen, I say to you, if you have faith and do not waver":** Jesus prefaces his teaching with **Amen, I say to you** to stress its importance. His disciples are to **have faith** and **not waver** or doubt: faith and doubt are contraries. When Peter became frightened while walking on the water and began to sink, Jesus said to him, "O you of little faith, why did you doubt?" (14:31). Jesus' disciples sometimes demonstrate "little faith" (8:26; 16:8), limiting what they are able to accomplish (17:19-20). Jesus tells them, **if you have faith and do not waver, not only will you do what has been done to the fig tree, but even if you say to this mountain, "Be lifted up and thrown into the sea," it will be done.** With faith, Jesus' disciples will be able to do what Jesus did to the fig tree and **even** more. Taken literally, **this mountain** would be the Mount of Olives, which lay between Bethany and Jerusalem (21:17-18), and **the sea** could be the Dead Sea, visible from some places on the Mount of Olives. But Jesus probably does not intend his words to be taken so literally; he previously invoked the idea of moving a mountain to stand for what is impossible (17:20), and he makes use of the idea again. As before, his message is that "nothing will be impossible" (17:20) for those who **have faith and do not waver.**

22 Jesus makes it clear that he is talking about prayer, not performing side-show wonders: **Whatever you ask for in prayer with faith, you will receive.** Jesus assured his disciples that their Father in heaven knows what they need before they ask (6:8); he urged them to ask with the confidence of a child seeking what it needs from its parents (7:7-11); he promised that when his followers joined together in prayer, their prayer would be answered (18:19). His disciples should not be startled that he promises that **whatever** they **ask for in prayer with faith,** they **will receive.** Praying **with faith** means praying with confidence and not wavering or doubting (verse 21).

Does Jesus require too much? Wavering and doubting seem part of the human condition. Does Jesus promise too much? Is it our experience that we receive whatever we pray for? Later New Testament writers will echo Jesus' teaching about praying without doubting (James 1:6-8) but also introduce a nuance: "We have this confidence in him, that if we ask anything *according to his will*, he hears us" (1 John 5:14; emphasis added). How are we to balance asking God for what we want and praying "your will be done" (6:10)? Prayer is not like going to an ATM machine to receive cash; prayer is our entering into the mystery of God.

For reflection: How do I understand Jesus' teaching about praying with faith? When have I prayed with greatest faith? How was my prayer answered?

ORIENTATION: *Jesus rose early (21:18) and will spend the day teaching in the Temple area (21:23–23:39) and on the Mount of Olives (24:1–26:2). Conflicts between Jesus and Jewish authorities will lead to their seeking his death (26:3-5).*

John and Jesus, Chief Priests and Elders
23 When he had come into the temple area, the chief priests and the elders of the people approached him as he was teaching and said, "By what authority are you doing these things? And who gave you this authority?" 24 Jesus said to them in reply, "I shall ask you one question, and if you answer it for me, then I shall tell you by what authority I do these things. 25 Where was John's baptism from? Was it of heavenly or of human origin?" They discussed this among themselves and said, "If we say 'Of heavenly origin,' he will say to us, 'Then why did you not believe him?' 26 But if we say, 'Of human origin,' we fear the crowd, for they all regard John as a prophet." 27 So they said to Jesus in reply, "We do not know." He himself said to them, "Neither shall I tell you by what authority I do these things.
28 "What is your opinion? A man had two sons. He came to the first and said, 'Son, go out and work in the vineyard today.' 29 He said in reply, 'I will not,' but afterwards he changed his mind and went. 30 The man came to the other son and gave the same order. He said in reply, 'Yes, sir,' but did not go. 31 Which of the two did his father's will?" They answered, "The first." Jesus said to them, "Amen, I say to

you, tax collectors and prostitutes are entering the kingdom of God before you. [32] When John came to you in the way of righteousness, you did not believe him; but tax collectors and prostitutes did. Yet even when you saw that, you did not later change your minds and believe him."

Gospel parallels: Mark 11:27-33; Luke 20:1-8
NT: Matt 3:1-17; 7:21-23; 11:7-19; 14:5; Luke 3:12-13; 7:29-30

23 Early in the morning Jesus comes from Bethany, where he had spent the night, into Jerusalem (21:17-18). **When he had come into the temple area, the chief priests and the elders of the people approached him as he was teaching.** There would have been nothing out of the ordinary in Jesus **teaching** in **the temple area:** teachers commonly met with students in the Court of the Gentiles or in the colonnaded halls around the edge of the Temple enclosure. Matthew does not tell his readers what Jesus was teaching; Jesus could have taught about the kingdom of heaven (4:17) and what one must do to enter it (see chapters 5 to 7). **Chief priests** included the current and former high priests and other high-ranking priests. **The elders of the people** were influential lay leaders. Chief priests and elders, along with some scribes, made up the Sanhedrin, the Jewish ruling council in Jerusalem (see 26:59). They are not happy with what Jesus has been doing and ask him, **By what authority are you doing these things? And who gave you this authority?** By **these things** they might mean Jesus' dramatic entry into Jerusalem (21:7-11), his disruption of Temple commerce (21:12-13), his healing in the Temple area to the acclaim of children (which bothered the chief priests: 21:14-16), and now his teaching in the Temple area—presumably teaching with authority, as he has done in the past (7:29). What is Jesus' **authority** for doing these things, and **who gave** him such authority? Matthew's readers know the source of Jesus' authority: he is the Son of God, sent to reveal God and inaugurate his reign (3:17; 11:25-27; 12:28; 17:5). But these Jewish leaders do not perceive who Jesus is, and their questions are a challenge: Who do you think you are?

Temple: See page 442
High priest, chief priests: See page 566
Sanhedrin: See page 601

24 Jesus said to them in reply, **"I shall ask you one question, and if you answer it for me, then I shall tell you by what authority I do these things."** Responding to a question with a counter question was a common debating tactic of the time. If Jesus is to tell the chief priests and elders **by what authority** he does **these things,** he will first ask a question to lay the groundwork for his response.

25 **Where was John's baptism from?** Jesus may include John's entire ministry under the heading of John's **baptism,** which was its most distinctive feature. **Was it of heavenly or of human origin?** Was John's mission from God, or was it a human initiative? John was either authorized by God to do what he did or he acted without God's authorization. The chief priests and elders **discussed this among themselves and said, "If we say 'Of heavenly origin,' he will say to us, 'Then why did you not believe him?'"** If John had been sent by God, then the chief priests and elders should have been the first to embrace his message: leaders should lead. But, as Jesus knows (verse 32), they had not believed John or heeded his call to repentance.

26 **But if we say, "Of human origin," we fear the crowd, for they all regard John as a prophet.** John had a large popular following (3:5-6) who viewed him as a prophet (11:7-9; 14:5). Chief priests and elders were not very popular despite the power they wielded, and they consequently had to be concerned with how their words and actions would be received by the people (see 21:46; 26:5). Claiming that John was deluded about his mission would upset those who revered him.

27 Faced with unpalatable alternatives, the chief priests and elders decide to feign ignorance: **So they said to Jesus in reply, "We do not know."** There

---

BACKGROUND: ELDERS The word "elder" (*presbyteros* in Greek) literally means someone who is *older* (Luke 15:25), and it was used to refer to someone with authority within a family or a clan or within a group such as a synagogue (Luke 7:3). Religious scholars of the past could also be called elders (Mark 7:3). In the gospels, the word "elders" usually refers to wealthy and influential Jewish laymen, particularly those who are part of the Sanhedrin in Jerusalem (Mark 15:1). In the early church, the word "elders," or "presbyters," was used for local church leaders (Acts 14:23), and the Greek word came through Latin into English as the word "priest." *Related topic: Sanhedrin (page 601).*

---

is a sense in which their claim is true: they do not perceive that God sent John to prepare the way for Jesus (3:3); they do not know what God has been about in John and Jesus.

For reflection: When faced with difficult choices, do I look for the easiest way out?

Jesus **said to them, "Neither shall I tell you by what authority I do these things."** If they will not answer Jesus' question, **neither** will he answer theirs. Had they acknowledged that John's authority came from God, Jesus could have proclaimed that his authority also came from God. He could have reminded them that John foretold one who would come after him (3:11-12) and that John recognized him as the coming one (3:13-15). However, those who refuse to acknowledge that John's authority was from God are not likely to accept that Jesus' authority is from God.

28 Jesus follows up by addressing a parable to the chief priests and elders: **What is your opinion? A man had two sons. He came to the first and said, "Son, go out and work in the vineyard today."** Jesus' parable has a family setting, with a son old enough to work in the family vineyard being asked to help out that day. The request to **work in the vineyard today** is unexceptional: family members were expected to help out with household and farming chores. Yet mention of a **vineyard** may have triggered an association for Jesus' audience and Matthew's first readers: in a memorable prophecy, Isaiah used a vineyard to represent God's people (Isaiah 5:1-7), suggesting that the father in the parable represents God.

29 **He said in reply, "I will not."** The son tells his father that he does not want to work in the vineyard—a response that could have earned a rebuke, but this father seems to tolerate his son's refusal. The son told his father he would not go and work in the vineyard, **but afterwards he changed his mind and went.** The Greek word translated **he changed his mind** has connotations of "regret" and "remorse": the son later had a change of heart and **went** to work in the vineyard as he had been asked.

30 **The man came to the other son and gave the same order:** the father made the same request of both his sons. The second son **said in reply, "Yes, sir."** The Greek word translated **sir** can also be translated "lord"; the

second son seems to speak respectfully to his father. This son agreed to work **but did not go.** There is no mention of the second son's changing his mind after agreeing to work. Was his **Yes, sir** hollow and deceptive, or did he have good intentions but fail to act on them? In any case, the second son told the father what he wanted to hear but did not do what the father asked.

Lord: See page 133

Jesus' parable might bring to mind his words, "not everyone who says to me, 'Lord, Lord,' will enter the kingdom of heaven, but only the one who does the will of my Father in heaven" (7:21). The second son called his father "sir," lord, but did not do his will; the first son had a change of heart and did carry out his father's will. Jesus' parable, like his earlier teaching, puts the focus on behavior, on doing God's will (see also 12:50).

For reflection: Which son am I most like? When have I had a change of heart and undertaken to do what God asked of me?

31 Jesus puts the chief priests and elders on the spot, demanding their opinion (verse 28): **Which of the two did his father's will?** It would be hard for them to feign ignorance again (verse 27), for it is obvious which of the two sons did what the father asked. **They answered, "The first."** This allows Jesus to apply the parable to them. **Jesus said to them, "Amen, I say to you, tax collectors and prostitutes are entering the kingdom of God before you."** Chief priests and elders would have viewed **tax collectors** and **prostitutes** as sinful men and women, religious outcasts. **Tax collectors** were spoken of in the same breath as sinners (9:10-11; 11:19) and scorned for extorting taxes on behalf of Roman occupiers. **Prostitutes** were likewise engaged in a sinful occupation, with their clientele likely including foreign soldiers stationed by Rome. If chief priests and elders were asked to rank Jews according to their obedience to the law of Moses, they would probably put themselves near the top of the list and put tax collectors and prostitutes at the bottom. Yet Jesus proclaims to these chief priests and elders that **tax collectors and prostitutes are entering the kingdom of God before you.** The **kingdom of God** means the same as the kingdom of heaven: God's reign over men and women and all creation. Scholars suggest that the words **entering . . . before you** may mean entering *instead of* you. The words at least mean that those who are last in the eyes of the religious establishment are well on their way into the kingdom of God, while religious leaders are lagging behind. It is a shocking pronouncement in either interpretation, and Jesus goes on to explain why he makes it.

Tax collectors: See page 163
Kingdom of heaven: See page 266

For reflection: Whom might we view as the counterparts of tax collectors and prostitutes in our society today?

32 **When John came to you in the way of righteousness, you did not believe him.** The **way of righteousness** means God's way (see 3:15); John proclaimed what God wanted, demanding repentance and changed lives because God's kingdom was at hand (3:1-10). These chief priests and elders **did not believe him** or acknowledge that his authority came from God (see verse 25); they felt no need to repent. That is why they are at the end of the line of those entering the kingdom of God, if they are in line at all (verse 31). In contrast to them, **tax collectors and prostitutes did** believe John and heed his message. Matthew has not described John's encounters with tax collectors and prostitutes, but Jesus' words presume they occurred. The sight of sinners being brought to repentance by John should have given pause to religious leaders who rejected John: surely God must have been working through him. **Yet,** Jesus tells the chief priests and elders, **even when you saw that, you did not later change your minds and believe him.** The Greek word translated **change your minds** again has the connotation of "regret" and "remorse" (see verse 29). These leaders had written off John, and nothing was going to change their hearts.

Through his parable, Jesus compares tax collectors and prostitutes to the son who first said no but then did the father's will; the chief priests and elders are like the son who professed obedience but did not live out what he professed. The preaching of John expressed the Father's will; one's response to John's message was an index of one's response to God. By this index, the chief priests and elders fared badly.

Matthew's first readers might have taken the tax collectors and prostitutes as representing Gentiles—those who had not obeyed the law of Moses but who had now responded to God's message and were entering the church. For us today, Jesus' parable is a reminder that God does not want lip service but active obedience (see 7:21; 15:8; Rom 2:13; James 1:22). It is also a warning that God may look with favor upon some whom we scorn.

For reflection: What is the particular message of Jesus' parable for me?

The Vineyard Tenants and the Owner's Son

33 "Hear another parable. There was a landowner who planted a vineyard, put a hedge around it, dug a wine press in it, and built a tower. Then he leased it to tenants and went on a journey. **34** When vintage time drew near, he sent his servants to the tenants to obtain his produce. **35** But the tenants seized the servants and one they beat, another they killed, and a third they stoned. **36** Again he sent other servants, more numerous than the first ones, but they treated them in the same way. **37** Finally, he sent his son to them, thinking, 'They will respect my son.' **38** But when the tenants saw the son, they said to one another, 'This is the heir. Come, let us kill him and acquire his inheritance.' **39** They seized him, threw him out of the vineyard, and killed him. **40** What will the owner of the vineyard do to those tenants when he comes?" **41** They answered him, "He will put those wretched men to a wretched death and lease his vineyard to other tenants who will give him the produce at the proper times." **42** Jesus said to them, "Did you never read in the scriptures:

'The stone that the builders rejected
has become the cornerstone;
by the Lord has this been done,
and it is wonderful in our eyes'?

43 Therefore, I say to you, the kingdom of God will be taken away from you and given to a people that will produce its fruit. [**44** The one who falls on this stone will be dashed to pieces; and it will crush anyone on whom it falls.]" **45** When the chief priests and the Pharisees heard his parables, they knew that he was speaking about them. **46** And although they were attempting to arrest him, they feared the crowds, for they regarded him as a prophet.

Gospel parallels: Mark 12:1-12; Luke 20:9-19
OT:Psalm 118:22-23; Isaiah 5:1-7

33 Jesus told a parable about two sons, addressing it to chief priests and elders (21:23-32). He continues with a second parable directed at them, telling them, **Hear another parable.** By announcing that it is a **parable,** Jesus conveys that he will tell a story that will provide a comparison or comparisons. **There was a landowner who planted a vineyard, put a hedge around it, dug a wine press in it, and built a tower.** This is the third time in Matthew's gospel that Jesus uses a **vineyard** as the setting for a parable (see 20:1-16; 21:28-32). Hillsides too steep to grow grain could be terraced and grapevines **planted;** someone starting a **vineyard** might **put a hedge around it** to protect it. A **wine press** could be **dug** in an outcropping of limestone bedrock, with an upper basin for pressing grapes and a lower basin for collecting the juice (archaeologists have found remains of such winepresses, including one on a Nazareth hillside). A **tower** was used to keep watch over the ripened crop until it was harvested.

Parables: See page 262

The beginning of Jesus' parable echoes a prophecy in which Isaiah uses a vineyard to represent the inhabitants of Jerusalem and Judah (Isaiah 5:1-7). God, who created the vineyard, expected it to bear good fruit for him, but it did not; therefore it will become a ruin (Isaiah 5:4-6). By echoing Isaiah's prophecy, Jesus conveys that the **landowner** in his parable stands for God and the **vineyard** for God's people.

> My friend had a vineyard
>   on a fertile hillside;
> He spaded it, cleared it of stones,
>   and planted the choicest vines;
> Within it he built a watchtower,
>   and hewed out a wine press. . . .
> The vineyard of the LORD of hosts
>   is the house of Israel,
> and the men of Judah are his
>   cherished plant.
>   Isaiah 5:1-2, 7

After the **landowner** established his vineyard, **he leased it to tenants and went on a journey.** Jesus' parable has a different plot than Isaiah's prophecy, which did not involve **tenants.** It was not uncommon in Galilee

456

for absentee landowners to entrust their vineyards or farms to **tenants** who would work them in return for a share of the harvest. Those listening to Jesus' parable would interpret the **tenants** given charge of God's vineyard as representing the leaders of God's people.

For reflection: What responsibilities in his vineyard has God entrusted to me?

34 **When vintage time drew near, he sent his servants to the tenants to obtain his produce.** At harvest time a landowner would expect to receive his share of the crop; this landowner sends **his servants,** literally, his "slaves," to collect it. Those interpreting the parable as being about God's dealings with his people would understand the **servants** to represent prophets, who are called God's servants, or slaves, in the Old Testament (2 Kings 9:7; 17:13; Ezra 9:11; Isaiah 20:3; Jer 7:25; 25:4; Ezek 38:17; Amos 3:7; Zech 1:6). God sent prophets so that he might obtain from his people what was due him: allegiance, obedience, justice.

Servant, slave: See page 429

35 **But the tenants seized the servants and one they beat, another they killed, and a third they stoned.** Tenants normally paid landowners what was due; to withhold the landowner's portion of the harvest invited eviction. These **tenants,** however, behave very brutishly—so brutishly that those listening to Jesus' parable must have shaken their heads in disbelief. Tenants would have to be deranged to beat and kill the landowner's servants. Yet if the **servants** represent prophets sent by God to his people, then the brutish behavior reflects the historical record. Prophets were often rejected and even killed (1 Kings 19:10; 2 Chron 36:15-16; Neh 9:26; Jer 2:30; 26:20-24)—at least one by stoning (2 Chron 24:20-21).

For reflection: How do I treat those who bring God's message to me?

36 **Again he sent other servants, more numerous than the first ones.** The vineyard owner continues to try to collect what is due him, sending even **more numerous** servants. But the tenants **treated them in the same way** as they treated the first servants, beating and killing them. As a comparison for God's dealing with his people, sending even **more numerous** prophets after the first are rejected reveals God's persistent concern for his people. If his efforts are rebuffed, God tries harder.

37 **Finally, he sent his son to them, thinking, "They will respect my son."** This might seem foolhardy: knowing that the tenants kill those sent to them, should the vineyard owner put his son's life at risk? Perhaps he reasoned that it was one thing to kill mere slaves but quite another thing to kill his very own son: **they will respect my son.** God, however, would be under no illusions about what would happen if he sent his **son.** Yet God sent him anyway (see 10:40; 15:24), sent him **finally,** as the culmination of his efforts (see Heb 1:1-2). The application of the parable is clear: Jesus is the **son** sent by the Father to his people.

> *For reflection: What does it tell me about God that he would send his Son, knowing how those he sends are treated?*

38 **But when the tenants saw the son, they said to one another, "This is the heir. Come, let us kill him and acquire his inheritance."** Although our knowledge of first-century legal practices is limited, it seems that if a property owner died without leaving a heir, then tenants on the property might have first claim to it. The tenants interpret the son's showing up as an indication that his father has died and he has come to claim the property as **the heir.** They think that killing him will allow them to **acquire his inheritance.**

39 **They seized him, threw him out of the vineyard, and killed him.** The tenants continue on their murderous course. The parable foreshadows what will happen to Jesus the Son at the hands of those entrusted with the vineyard of God's people: chief priests and other leaders will hand him over to be put to death (16:21; 20:18-19). Jesus will be led **out** of Jerusalem to be **killed** (27:31-32; see Heb 13:12).

40 Jesus has been addressing the parable to chief priests and elders, and he asks them to supply an ending for the parable: **What will the owner of the vineyard do to those tenants when he comes?** Surely he would not ignore the murder of his son. There is a second level of meaning in Jesus' question: the Greek word translated **owner** is the word that is also translated "lord," reinforcing that the vineyard owner stands for the Lord God. What will God do to those who reject and kill his Son? Will God do the same as humans would do?

Lord: See page 133

41 They answered him, "He will put those wretched men to a wretched death." Matthew's gospel uses a Greek play on words to formulate their response (wretched men . . . wretched death). The law of Moses allowed strict retribution: "life for life, eye for eye, tooth for tooth" (Deut 19:21). Those who murdered the servants and son of the vineyard owner would themselves be put to death. The vineyard owner would then lease his vineyard to other tenants who will give him the produce at the proper times. The owner created the vineyard to have its produce, and he will engage new tenants who will give him his share. In the parable's application, God will replace those who are not leading his people properly with those who will. The Greek word translated produce is literally "fruits," an image for deeds (3:8, 10; 7:16-20; 12:33); the new leaders will provide God with a harvest of upright behavior from his people.

42 Jesus will apply the lesson of the parable to religious leaders, but he first addresses something that the parable did not resolve. In the parable, the owner's son is killed, and that is the end of him. This is unsatisfactory if the son is to stand for Jesus. Jesus switches from agricultural to architectural imagery to speak of what will become of him. Jesus said to them, "Did you never read in the scriptures: 'The stone that the builders rejected / has become the cornerstone; / by the Lord has this been done, / and it is wonderful in our eyes'?" Jesus invokes Scripture, as he has done in previous confrontations (12:3, 5; 19:4-5; 21:13, 16). He quotes verses 22 and 23 from Psalm 118, the psalm used to hail him as he entered Jerusalem (21:9; Psalm 118:25-26). A stone that was rejected as unsuitable by builders has become the cornerstone of a new building. A cornerstone is a foundation block linking two walls at a corner; the positioning of the cornerstone determines the placement of the building and the alignment of its walls. A stone cast aside as unusable ends up being the most significant stone in the structure—a complete reversal of its fortunes. Jesus will be taken out and killed (verse 39), but he will be made the foundational stone of something new. By the Lord has this been done: God will vindicate Jesus, raising him from the dead (16:21; 17:23; 20:19). It is wonderful in our eyes: God's raising of Jesus will be a cause for marvel and amazement. Jesus does not explicitly foretell his being raised from the dead to the chief priests and elders, but by invoking words from Psalm 118 he indicates that God will intervene to make him the foundation of something new despite his having been rejected.

> The stone the builders rejected
> has become the cornerstone.
> By the LORD has this been done;
> it is wonderful in our eyes.
>   Psalm 118:22-23

43 Jesus returns to the parable and draws a lesson from it. Just as the vine-yard owner would replace the bad tenants with new tenants who would give him the vineyard's produce (verse 41), **therefore, I say to you,** Jesus tells the chief priests and elders, **the kingdom of God will be taken away from you and given to a people that will produce its fruit.** The **kingdom of God,** in Matthew's gospel usually referred to as the kingdom of heaven, means God's active reign. To tell the chief priests and elders that **the kingdom of God will be taken away from you** means that they will be relieved of the roles that God had assigned them in his reign. These roles will be **given to a people that will produce its fruit.** Who these **people** are is left unspecified; the only thing that identifies them is that they will **produce** the **fruit** of God's reign, that is, they will help women and men to live under God's reign. Jesus is not saying that God's king-dom will be taken away from Jews and given to Gentiles; the context in-dicates that Jesus means that God's people will be given new leadership. Jews (and ultimately Gentiles—28:19) who accept Jesus as the Son of God and follow his teachings will be a community built on the rock of Peter (16:18). Peter and the other disciples will be **given** leadership over those who are entering into the kingdom of God. They will be expected to **pro-duce** fruit for the one who entrusts them with leadership responsibilities.

Kingdom of heaven: See page 266

For reflection: What fruit am I bearing for God?

44 **[The one who falls on this stone will be dashed to pieces; and it will crush anyone on whom it falls.]** Not all ancient manuscripts of Mat-thew's gospel contain this verse, which is why the New American Bible encloses it in brackets. Biblical scholars are divided over whether Mat-thew's gospel originally included these words or whether a copyist added them, borrowing from Luke 20:18. **The one who falls on this stone will be dashed to pieces** may be drawn from Isaiah 8:14-15; the image is one of falling from a height and smashing on a rock. **It will crush anyone on**

whom it falls is an opposite image, that of a boulder falling upon and crushing someone, faintly reflecting imagery used in Daniel 2:34, 44-45. Jesus spoke of himself as the stone rejected by the builders (verse 42); this stone will crush those who reject it. This is a harsh image, but so is the image of being thrown into a fiery furnace (13:42). Throughout Matthew's gospel, Jesus warns that those who do evil will be punished (5:22; 13:41-42, 49-50; 18:6-9, 34-35). Jesus' words are a warning to those who will have him put to death: he knows what "must" happen (16:21) but he gives those who will be responsible for his death every chance to have a change of heart (see also 26:20-25).

45 **When the chief priests and the Pharisees heard his parables, they knew that he was speaking about them.** While **chief priests** have been present since Jesus came into the Temple area (21:23), this is the first indication that there were **Pharisees** among those to whom Jesus was speaking. For Matthew's first readers, "the chief priests and the elders of the people" (21:23) would have represented Jewish leaders at the time of Jesus, while **Pharisees** would have represented some Jewish leaders at the time of Matthew—specifically, those Jewish leaders who did not accept Jesus as the Messiah but who taught that Jews should follow "the tradition of the elders" (15:2). The **parables** were about two sons (21:28-32) and about vineyard tenants and the owner's son (verses 33 to 41). **They knew that he was speaking about them:** they realized Jesus was comparing them to a son who professed obedience but did not obey, and to vineyard tenants who kill the owner's son. They should take Jesus' words as a warning and call to repentance, but they will not heed them.

High priest, chief priests: See page 566
Pharisees: See page 231

For reflection: Has Jesus directed any warnings to me? Have I heeded them?

46 **And although they were attempting to arrest him, they feared the crowds, for they regarded him as a prophet.** From now on, Jewish leaders in Jerusalem will seek to eliminate Jesus. However, they must proceed cautiously. Jesus is held in high esteem by many, including the crowds who accompanied him into Jerusalem and shouted, "Hosanna to the Son of David; / blessed is he who comes in the name of the Lord" (21:9).

461

They regarded him as a prophet: when these crowds were asked, "Who is this?" they replied, "This is Jesus the prophet, from Nazareth in Galilee" (21:10-11). Jesus was popularly thought of as a prophet, a messenger from God (16:13-14). Chief priests and elders had been reluctant to say anything negative about John the Baptist out of fear of the crowds who regarded John as a prophet (21:26), and the same fear prevents them from arresting Jesus. Jerusalem was bursting with pilgrims who had come to celebrate Passover; arresting someone whom they revered as a prophet might start a riot. Rome expected Jewish leaders to keep order, not stir up trouble.

CHAPTER 22

ORIENTATION: *Jesus continues to address parables to religious leaders in the Temple precincts (see 21:28-46).*

The Parables of the Wedding Feast

¹ Jesus again in reply spoke to them in parables, saying, ² "The kingdom of heaven may be likened to a king who gave a wedding feast for his son. ³ He dispatched his servants to summon the invited guests to the feast, but they refused to come. ⁴ A second time he sent other servants, saying, 'Tell those invited: "Behold, I have prepared my banquet, my calves and fattened cattle are killed, and everything is ready; come to the feast."' ⁵ Some ignored the invitation and went away, one to his farm, another to his business. ⁶ The rest laid hold of his servants, mistreated them, and killed them. ⁷ The king was enraged and sent his troops, destroyed those murderers, and burned their city. ⁸ Then he said to his servants, 'The feast is ready, but those who were invited were not worthy to come. ⁹ Go out, therefore, into the main roads and invite to the feast whomever you find.' ¹⁰ The servants went out into the streets and gathered all they found, bad and good alike, and the hall was filled with guests. ¹¹ But when the king came in to meet the guests he saw a man there not dressed in a wedding garment. ¹² He said to him, 'My friend, how is it that you came in here without a wedding garment?' But he was reduced to silence. ¹³ Then the king said to his attendants, 'Bind his hands and feet, and cast him into the darkness outside, where there will be wailing and grinding of teeth.' ¹⁴ Many are invited, but few are chosen."

        Gospel parallels: Luke 14:15-24
        OT: Isaiah 25:6
        NT: Matt 7:13-14; 8:11-12; 13:24-30, 36-43, 47-50; 28:19

1 **Jesus again in reply spoke to them in parables:** the sense is, Jesus spoke again in parables to some chief priests and Pharisees (see 21:45). That Jesus tells them **parables** may hint that the following story is not one parable but two.

        Parables: See page 262

2 **The kingdom of heaven may be likened to** the situation of **a king who gave a wedding feast for his son.** Weddings were celebrated with banquets; a **king** could be expected to throw a great **feast** for the **wedding** of **his son.** Since Jesus is telling this parable to provide a comparison for the **kingdom of heaven,** his listeners can assume that the **king** stands for God. The **feast** might remind them of "the banquet in the kingdom of heaven" (mentioned at 8:11; see Isaiah 25:6). It might also be assumed that if the king stands for God, then **his son** will represent Jesus, who has referred to himself as a bridegroom (9:15). However, the king's son will play no role in the parable. Not every element of a parable must be assigned significance.

Kingdom of heaven: See page 266

Marriage practices: See page 479

3 **He dispatched his servants to summon the invited guests to the feast.** The **guests** had been notified in advance of the **feast** and **invited** to attend; they had presumably accepted the invitation. On the day of the feast, when the food is ready, the king sends **his servants,** literally, his "slaves," to **summon the invited guests** to come. The king's **servants** represent God's messengers or prophets, as in the parable about the vineyard tenants (21:34-36). **But those who were invited refused to come.** No reason is given why they are now unwilling to attend, and their refusal would

---

BACKGROUND: BANQUETS or feasts played important social and religious roles at the time of Jesus. Banquets were not only a chance for ordinary people to enjoy ample food and wine, which they otherwise rarely did, but also a form of entertainment in a world that offered few diversions compared with the modern world. Banquets marked special occasions, such as weddings (Matt 22:2; John 2:1-3) or the homecoming of a wayward son (Luke 15:23). Those who were wealthy could feast every day (Luke 16:19). Banquets were also used to celebrate religious feasts, such as Passover (Exod 12:1-28). It was the custom at Greek banquets for diners to recline on their left side on cushions or couches arranged in a U-shape. Servants served the food on low tables inside the U. Jews adopted the custom of reclining during banquets, as John portrays in his account of the Last Supper (John 13:12, 23-25). The prophets spoke of God providing a banquet for his people (Isaiah 25:6), and Jesus used a feast as an image for the reign of God (Matt 8:11; 22:1-14; Luke 13:28-29; 14:15-24). Having plenty of good food to eat would have sounded heavenly to Jesus' listeners. *Related topic: Diet (page 304).*

---

be inexplicable in real life. Why would they pass up a sumptuous feast and risk the king's displeasure? While Jesus' parables are usually based on imaginable situations, in some instances the intended message of a parable shapes the story line. This seems to be happening here. Since Jesus has been telling parables that apply to religious leaders (21:45), these leaders might rightly suspect that they are being compared to **invited guests** who refuse to come to a king's feast. It would be inexplicable for them to turn down an invitation to the banquet in the kingdom of God, but Jesus' parable conveys that they are doing so by not heeding the summons of God's messengers.

Servant, slave: See page 429

For reflection: How eager am I to attend God's eternal banquet? How am I responding to God's invitation?

4 The king tries again: **a second time he sent other servants** to summon the invited guests. The king instructs his servants to entice them: **Tell those invited: "Behold, I have prepared my banquet, my calves and fattened cattle are killed, and everything is ready."** The servants are to trumpet the menu: **calves and fattened cattle,** the choicest of meats. **Everything** is cooked and **ready** to be eaten; those invited should **come to the feast.** God is concerned that those invited to the banquet in the kingdom of heaven **come to the feast.**

5 The king's messengers are no more successful the second time. **Some** on the guest list **ignored the invitation and went away, one to his farm, another to his business.** They pay no attention to the king's invitation and go about business as usual. There is no indication that there is anything pressing about their work that day, nothing that could not be postponed. Their refusal to attend the feast continues to be inexplicable. Going on with our lives as usual and ignoring God's invitations to us is also inexplicable.

For reflection: Has the routine of my life made me indifferent to God's invitation?

6 Even more inexplicable is the response of some who were invited. **The rest laid hold of his servants, mistreated them, and killed them.** This would

be preposterous in real life: I kill your servants because they asked me to come to your banquet? The story is being driven by its application rather than by plausibility. As in the previous parable (21:34-36), the **servants** represent prophets who are rejected and killed (see 1 Kings 19:10; 2 Chron 24:20-21; 36:15-16; Neh 9:26). By pointing this parable at religious leaders, Jesus is identifying them with those who not only turn down God's invitation but mistreat and kill those bearing the invitation. Jesus foresees that the Jerusalem religious establishment will hand him over to suffer and die (16:21; 20:18-19).

7 The parable reaches its peak of implausibility: **The king was enraged and sent his troops, destroyed those murderers, and burned their city.** While the banquet is on the table, the king deploys his army, finds and kills those who murdered his servants, burns the city in which they live (where presumably others live as well)—all before the food gets cold (see verse 8). And done on a festive wedding day, as if it could not wait until tomorrow! If the story is shaped by its application, then we must look for the application to make sense of it.

Jesus is issuing a warning to those who will be responsible for his death. The king destroying murderers and burning their city can be taken as a vivid way of conveying that God will punish those who do evil. The Old Testament speaks of captured cities being burned and their inhabitants killed (Joshua 6:21, 24; Judges 1:8; 18:27; 20:48; 1 Macc 5:28, 35); Jesus might be using this as an image for punishment without intending it to be interpreted literally and applied to a specific city. Similarly, Jesus spoke of evildoers being thrown into "the fiery furnace" (13:42) without intending to teach that God maintains a blast furnace in eternity.

Some of Matthew's first readers, however, might have understood Jesus' words in light of the destruction of Jerusalem by Rome in A.D. 70 and interpreted this destruction as God's punishment. Some Christians have given it this interpretation, although doing so creates serious problems for our understanding of God and of how God punishes sin. See the Comment "Did God destroy Jerusalem to avenge Jesus?"

For reflection: What do I understand to be the meaning of the king destroying murderers and burning their city? What message does it bear for me?

8 The parable continues as if the king had not taken a time-out to burn a city. **Then he said to his servants, "The feast is ready, but those who were invited were not worthy to come."** By refusing to attend, those who had been **invited** demonstrated that they were not **worthy to come** to the feast; some demonstrated even greater unworthiness by mistreating and killing the king's servants. Yet **the feast is** still **ready** and waiting.

9 **Go out, therefore, into the main roads and invite to the feast whomever you find.** The first guest list had presumably been selective, just as we invite family and friends to a wedding reception. Now, however, the guest list is **whomever** the king's slaves can find when they go out onto the **main roads.** The Greek expression translated **main roads** means roads leading out of a city: all from far and wide are to be invited to the **feast.** Matthew's first readers would have found the words **invite . . . whomever you can find** reflected in the church's mission to "make disciples of all nations" (28:19).

For reflection: What does the king's inviting whomever can be found to his feast tell me about God?

COMMENT: DID GOD DESTROY JERUSALEM TO AVENGE JESUS? The Old Testament presents the destruction of Jerusalem by Babylon in 586 B.C. as God's punishment (see Deut 28:45-57 and chapters 6, 21, and 22 of Jeremiah). Some Christians have given a similar interpretation to the destruction of Jerusalem by Rome in A.D. 70: it was God's punishment for crucifying Jesus. Bishop Eusebius, a fourth-century historian, in recounting the destruction of Jerusalem and loss of Jewish life, wrote, "The judgment of God at last overtook them for their abominable crimes against Christ and his apostles . . . their crime against the Christ of God a very little time later brought on them God's vengeance" (*History of the Church,* III:5). It is difficult, however, to reconcile this interpretation of what happened in A.D. 70 with the teachings of Jesus. Those who suffer and die in calamities are not necessarily greater sinners than those who are spared (Luke 13:1-5). Would the God who wants us to love our enemies in imitation of his love (Matt 5:43-48) turn a deaf ear to Jesus' prayer from the cross, "Father, forgive them, they know not what they do" (Luke 23:34)? Were God to exact retribution for the death of his Son, justice would require that he punish those responsible for his death, not those who were in Jerusalem forty years later. Jesus foresaw and lamented that Jerusalem was on a path to destruction (see Matt 23:37–24:2; Mark 13:1-2, 14-19; Luke 19:41-44), but that does not mean that its destruction was God's vengeance on the city.

10 **The servants went out into the streets and gathered all they found, bad and good alike.** Mentioning the **bad** before the **good** emphasizes that it is not a matter of the newly invited guests deserving to be invited (see 5:45, where both bad and good receive God's life-sustaining sunshine). The king's slaves gather **all** they can, whatever their condition. The king's wishes are fulfilled, and **the hall was filled with guests.** The kingdom of heaven is like a banquet that God wants completely filled; he invites everyone to it, even those who do not deserve to come.

> For reflection: What are the implications for me of God gathering the unworthy to himself?

The hall being filled with guests may mark the end of a parable about a wedding feast; what follows may be a second parable. The message of the first parable has to do with guests originally invited to a banquet being replaced by new guests. As addressed to chief priests and Pharisees (21:45), the parable characterizes them as those who have been invited to "the banquet in the kingdom of heaven" but who are ignoring the invitation and mistreating the messengers. The parable warns them that they face God's judgment, a warning also found in the previous parable about the vineyard tenants and the owner's son (see 21:41). Their places in the banquet will be filled by others (see 8:11-12; 21:43), just as others will be given leadership in the vineyard of God's people in place of them (21:41).

Matthew's first readers would have interpreted the **all** who were brought into the banquet to include Gentiles as well as Jews. Matthew's readers can also understand the parable as another instance in which Jesus teaches that the community of his followers will include both the **bad** and the **good,** like a field with both weeds and wheat (13:24-30, 36-43) or like a fishing net that hauls all sorts of things out of the sea (13:47-50). Good and bad will be mixed together until the final judgment.

11 Jesus continues with what is best read as a second wedding feast parable appended to the first. **But when the king came in to meet the guests he saw a man there not dressed in a wedding garment.** Contrary to some speculations, there was no distinctive **wedding garment** that guests were expected to wear at the time of Jesus. Wedding feasts, like any formal occasion, simply called for one's best attire—at least clean clothing. But a **man**

shows up in dingy, dirty clothing. If this is a continuation of the previous parable, then his attire is understandable: he has been hauled in off the street by the king's servants, wearing what he was wearing. If this verse marks a new parable, then the parable begins with a man showing up at a wedding feast dressed in clothing so inappropriate as to be an insult to the host.

12 The king treats the man's clothing as insulting. **He said to him, "My friend, how is it that you came in here without a wedding garment?"** Addressing him as **my friend** is confrontational (see 20:13; 26:50). How is it that you are dressed in shabby, dirty clothing at a wedding feast? The king gives the man an opportunity to defend his behavior, **but he was reduced to silence.** He knows his attire is unacceptable, and he has no excuse for not putting on clean clothing.

13 Those who will not make even a minimal effort to make themselves presentable do not belong at a wedding feast. **Then the king said to his attendants, "Bind his hands and feet, and cast him into the darkness outside, where there will be wailing and grinding of teeth."** Binding his **hands and feet** would prevent him from coming back into the feast, but the rest of the king's words indicate that this is a parable about the final judgment (see 8:12; 13:42, 50; 24:51; 25:30, where similar language is used to characterize a final desolate state). While the previous parable spoke of both "bad and good alike" being gathered into the feast (verse 10), those who remain willfully bad will be cast out from it. The wedding garment—clean clothing—represents the repentance and righteousness necessary to partake in the banquet of the kingdom of heaven (see 5:20). The community of Jesus' followers includes all who have responded to Jesus' invitation, "bad and good alike," but those who do not do the will of God will not enter the kingdom of heaven (7:21). Exiled to the outer darkness, they will weep and grind their teeth over their loss.

For reflection: What am I doing to make myself presentable for the heavenly banquet?

14 Jesus concludes with a cryptic saying: **Many are invited, but few are chosen.** The word **many** does not imply "not all"; it only conveys that a great number **are invited** (verses 9 and 10 indicate that all are invited). The word

few has a relative sense: not all who are invited will end up being **chosen**. Those **chosen** (elsewhere called the elect—24:22, 24, 31) are those who accept God's invitation to his banquet and live upright lives in order to be part of it. **Many are invited, but few are chosen** is not a statistical observation but an exhortation: you have been **invited;** strive to be among the **chosen**. This saying makes much the same point as Jesus' earlier words about entering the kingdom through the narrow gate, avoiding the broad road that leads to destruction (7:13-14). Complacency is dangerous; doing God's will is all-important (7:21; 12:50).

For reflection: What does this saying of Jesus mean for me?

Who Is Due What?

[15] **Then the Pharisees went off and plotted how they might entrap him in speech.** **[16]** **They sent their disciples to him, with the Herodians, saying, "Teacher, we know that you are a truthful man and that you teach the way of God in accordance with the truth. And you are not concerned with anyone's opinion, for you do not regard a person's status.** **[17]** **Tell us, then, what is your opinion: Is it lawful to pay the census tax to Caesar or not?"** **[18]** **Knowing their malice, Jesus said, "Why are you testing me, you hypocrites?** **[19]** **Show me the coin that pays the census tax."** **Then they handed him the Roman coin.** **[20]** **He said to them, "Whose image is this and whose inscription?"** **[21]** **They replied, "Caesar's."** **At that he said to them, "Then repay to Caesar what belongs to Caesar and to God what belongs to God."** **[22]** **When they heard this they were amazed, and leaving him they went away.**

> Gospel parallels: Mark 12:13-17; Luke 20:20-26
> OT:Psalm 24:1
> NT:Matt 12:14; 21:33-46; Rom 13:1-7

15 While in the Temple area (21:23), Jesus addressed parables to some chief priests and Pharisees, warning that they would face God's judgment for rejecting God's messengers (21:41; 22:7). They got the point: "they knew that he was speaking about them" (21:45). **Then the Pharisees went off and plotted** against Jesus (Matthew has recounted their plotting on another occasion: 12:14). They would like to see Jesus arrested but are held back because of his popularity with the crowds (21:46), so they look for a way to **entrap him in speech.** The Greek word for **entrap** is used for the snaring of animals. They want to snare Jesus into saying something that will either be grounds for arrest or will undercut his popularity with the crowds.

Pharisees: See page 231

16 **They sent their disciples to him, with the Herodians.** Matthew's account reads as if the plotting was done quickly and a party is sent to Jesus while he is still in the Temple area (Matthew will not mention Jesus leaving the Temple area until 24:1). On the other hand, Jesus will later claim that "day after day I sat teaching in the Temple area" (26:55), providing ample time for plots to be hatched and carried out. Perhaps in 21:23 to 23:39 Matthew gathers together what happened on a number of days and presents it as if it took place on one day, just as in the Sermon on the Mount (chapters 5–7) Matthew compiles what Jesus taught on different occasions and presents it as one sermon. In any case, some Pharisees send **their disciples** to Jesus along with some **Herodians.** The **disciples** of the Pharisees are presumably those who are studying under teachers who are Pharisees. Matthew's first readers might associate the disciples of the Pharisees with those in their day who were advocating that Jews follow the "tradition of the elders" (see 15:2) rather than accepting Jesus as the Messiah and following his interpretation of the law of Moses. The **Herodians** are presumably supporters of the dynasty of rulers founded by Herod the Great. Pharisees and Herodians make strange bedfellows, but they have a reason for approaching Jesus together.

BACKGROUND: HERODIANS Little is known of the Herodians other than what their name probably implies: they were supporters of the dynasty founded by Herod the Great. One of his sons, Herod Antipas, ruled Galilee and an area east of the Jordan River during Jesus' public ministry; another son, Philip, ruled the region northeast of the Sea of Galilee (see Luke 3:1). The Herodians likely included men whom Herod Antipas or Philip had entrusted with royal estates, who served as their officials, or who were in other ways dependent on them for their wealth and position. The Herodians' interests would have lain in keeping Herod Antipas and Philip in power and friendly to them. Since Herod Antipas and Philip ruled on behalf of Rome, their supporters would also have been loyal to Rome and would have favored payment of taxes. The Herodians may have hoped Rome would again place Judea under the rule of a descendant of Herod (which Rome will do during A.D. 41–44). *Related topics: Herod the Great (page 35), Herod Antipas (page 298).*

Those who come to Jesus try to lure him into their trap with flattery. They say to him, **Teacher, we know that you are a truthful man and that you teach the way of God in accordance with the truth.** Jesus has been teaching in the Temple area (21:23), which might be why they address him as **Teacher.** In Matthew's gospel, only those who are not Jesus' disciples call him a teacher (9:11; 12:38; 17:24; 19:16; 22:24, 36); Jesus' disciples recognize that he is more than a teacher. Jesus teaches **the way of God,** meaning the way of living that God requires (the "way of righteousness"—21:32). They tell Jesus that he is **a truthful man** and teaches what God wants **in accordance with the truth.** What they say is correct: Jesus truly teaches what God wants. But their words ring hollow: if Jesus truly teaches the way of God, why do they not accept his teachings? Why are they out to entrap him? They continue, **And you are not concerned with anyone's opinion, for you do not regard a person's status.** Again, what they say is correct: Jesus does not tailor his message or use flattery to gain acceptance; Jesus is as concerned for outcasts as for those with high status (see 9:10). There is again irony: they are flattering Jesus by saying he does not use flattery; they are tailoring their words to lure him into speaking boldly.

For reflection: What does it mean for me that Jesus teaches the way of God? That Jesus is concerned for me whatever my status?

17 **Tell us, then, what is your opinion: Is it lawful to pay the census tax to Caesar or not?** Asking, **is it lawful?** means asking whether it is permitted by the law of Moses and is acceptable to God (see 12:10; 19:3). **Caesar** was the family name of the Roman emperor Julius Caesar (who ruled from 49 to 44 B.C.) and became a title for the emperors who succeeded him. The **census tax** was a Roman tax collected in areas ruled by Roman governors. Rome imposed a governor on Judea in A.D. 6 and assessed an annual tax on every adult; a census was taken to establish the list of those who had to pay the tax (hence it is called a **census tax**). Some Jews rebelled against paying this tax (see Acts 5:37). The first-century Jewish historian Josephus wrote that the rebellion was incited by a man who called Jews "cowards for consenting to pay tribute to the Romans and tolerating mortal masters, after they had God for their Lord." The rebellion was put down, and the census tax remained unpopular: it was not only one more tax but a symbol of submission to Rome.

Those seeking to entrap Jesus try to force him to take a stand either for or against paying the census tax; either option will get him into trouble. The many Jews who thought that God's people should not be ruled by foreigners resented the census tax and would be upset if Jesus upheld it. His popularity with the crowds, which was holding his adversaries in check (21:46), might plummet. But if he taught that Jews should not pay the census tax, he could be denounced to the Roman authorities as a rebel (the leader of the A.D. 6 tax revolt was apparently executed). The otherwise odd pairing of Pharisees and Herodians makes sense: Pharisees were widely respected and could try to sway the crowds against Jesus, while Herodians had standing with Roman authorities and could lodge charges against him.

18 **Knowing their malice,** that they were out to entrap him, **Jesus said, "Why are you testing me, you hypocrites?"** This is not the first time Jesus' adversaries tested him (16:1; 19:3); the Greek word for **testing** was also used for Satan's tempting (4:1). Hypocrisy is at root a disconnect between appearance and reality; Jesus calls those testing him **hypocrites** because their flattery is a smoke screen. They do not ask their question because they are uncertain whether they should pay the tax but to trap Jesus into taking a stand that would jeopardize him.

BACKGROUND: ROMAN EMPIRE At the time of Jesus, the Roman Empire included all the lands bordering the Mediterranean Sea and extended through western Europe as far as Britain. The Roman general Pompey had intervened in a Jewish civil war in 63 B.C., conquering Jerusalem and pushing aside the ruling Jewish Hasmonean dynasty, thus bringing Palestine under Roman domination. This was a time of transition within the Roman government, as power became consolidated in an emperor and conquered lands gradually came under direct Roman rule. In this transitional period, Rome sometimes ruled through client kings, such as Herod the Great and his sons. The Roman government was content to have the Herods rule on its behalf as long as they did so competently, were loyal to Rome, and paid taxes. Other regions were ruled as Roman provinces by governors sent from Rome. Judea became a Roman province in A.D. 6 after Rome deposed Herod's son Archelaus for incompetence. During Jesus' public ministry, Pontius Pilate was the Roman governor of Judea and some adjacent areas. In A.D. 66, many Jews in Palestine rebelled against Roman rule, with disastrous consequences. Rome put down the revolt, destroying Jerusalem in AD. 70. *Related topics: Herod the Great (page 35), Herod Antipas (page 298), Pilate (page 619).*

---

19 Jesus says to them, **Show me the coin that pays the census tax.** His response requires a visual aid. Roman taxes had to be paid in Roman currency. Jesus apparently does not have such a coin (perhaps he never carried money—see 10:9), but those testing him could produce one, and **they handed him the Roman coin,** literally, a denarius, equivalent to a day's wage for an ordinary worker (see 20:2).

20 **He said to them, "Whose image is this and whose inscription?"** Like modern coins, ancient coins bore images and inscriptions. The most widely used Roman denarius of the time of Jesus carried an image of the emperor Tiberius (who ruled from A.D. 14 to 37). He had been adopted by the previous emperor, Augustus, and his denarius had the inscription "Tiberias Caesar Augustus, son of the divine Augustus." Calling the emperor divine was part of a growing cult of the emperor in Roman civil religion. The other side of this denarius had the inscription, "Supreme pontiff," meaning that Tiberias was the highest priest mediating between the people and the gods. Hailing a Roman emperor as divine or as the highest priest ran counter to Jewish beliefs, but Jesus does not address the issue of Jews using such coins. He simply asks, **Whose image is this and whose inscription?**

21 **They replied, "Caesar's." At that he said to them, "Then repay to Caesar what belongs to Caesar."** Jesus' words are a bit cryptic; he does not directly say, "Pay the census tax." The word translated **repay** can mean "give back" (it is translated "paying it back" in 18:25) and also, simply, "give" (it is translated "give"—meaning "pay"—in 20:8 and 21:41). The Greek for **what belongs to Caesar** is literally "the things of Caesar." Coins bearing the emperor's image and inscription are things of Caesar; give Caesar what is his. Jesus implies, "Those who use Roman coins are enmeshed in the economic system of the Roman empire. Paying taxes is part of the package."

If Jesus had stopped here, he would have made sufficient response to those trying to entrap him. His words were neither seditious nor a ringing endorsement of Roman rule; he said nothing his opponents could use again him.

But Jesus does not let matters rest with what may be owed the emperor. Jesus goes on to say, **and repay to God what belongs to God**—literally, give to God the things of God. And what **belongs to God?** Everything! "The earth is the LORD'S and all it holds, / the world and those who live there" (Psalm 24:1). Jesus uses a question about paying a specific tax as an opportunity to address the far more important issue of what is owed God. We are to render to God all that is his due as the one who created the universe and brought us into being. Jesus does not spell out what God is due, but he has told a parable about producing fruit as God's due (21:33-43), and he will shortly teach that the greatest commandment is "You shall love the Lord, your God, with all your heart, with all your soul, and with all your mind" (22:37). God's demands are all-encompassing. A government may be due our taxes (see Rom 13:7), but God is due our entire being, everything we are or can do.

For reflection: What do I owe God? What payment am I making him?

22 **When they heard this they were amazed** at how skillfully Jesus avoided their trap and changed the topic to what God is due. **Leaving him they went away,** defeated. Since the Pharisees are temporarily silenced, others will come forward to test Jesus.

Resurrection

23 **On that day Sadducees approached him, saying that there is no resurrection. They put this question to him,** **24** **saying, "Teacher, Moses said, 'If a man dies without children, his brother shall marry his wife and raise up descendants for his brother.'** **25** **Now there were seven brothers among us. The first married and died and, having no descendants, left his wife to his brother.** **26** **The same happened with the second and the third, through all seven.** **27** **Finally the woman died.** **28** **Now at the resurrection, of the seven, whose wife will she be? For they all had been married to her."** **29** **Jesus said to them in reply, "You are misled because you do not know the scriptures or the power of God.** **30** **At the resurrection they neither marry nor are given in marriage but are like the angels in heaven.** **31** **And concerning the resurrection of the dead, have you not read what was said to you by God,** **32** **'I am the God of Abraham, the God of Isaac, and the God of Jacob'? He is not the God of the dead but of the living."** **33** **When the crowds heard this, they were astonished at his teaching.**

> Gospel parallels: Mark 12:18-27; Luke 20:27-40
> OT:Exod 3:5-6; Deut 25:5-10; 2 Macc 7:20-29
> NT:Acts 23:6-8; 1 Cor 15:35-57

23 **On that day,** the day Jesus came to the Temple to teach (21:23), **Sadducees approached him.** The **Sadducees** were a Jerusalem elite that included influential priests; some of the chief priests who had been the target of Jesus' parables (21:28–22:14) likely were Sadducees. Although belief in the resurrection of the dead was fairly widespread among Jews in the first century, Sadducees rejected the notion (see Acts 23:6-8). They seem to be aware that Jesus teaches that there will be a resurrection (see 12:41), and they come to him **saying that there is no resurrection.** To challenge the possibility that the dead will rise, **they put** a **question to him.**

Resurrection: See page 478

24 Sadducees did not accept the resurrection of the dead because they did not find it taught in the law of Moses and the books they accepted as Scripture. They begin their challenge by invoking the law: **Teacher, Moses said, "If a man dies without children, his brother shall marry his wife and raise up descendants for his brother."** If Jesus is a religious **teacher,** he can be expected to understand and uphold what **Moses said.** Included in the law are provisions that preserve family heritage. One provision deals with a husband dying without leaving a son as his heir; to preserve the husband's family name and keep his land within his family, the deceased man's brother is to marry his widow and beget a son to carry on his dead brother's name and inherit his land. This provision lies behind several incidents in the Old Testament (Gen 38:6-11, 26), but the practice may have fallen into disuse by the time of Jesus. Yet the law was on the books, and it provided a basis for the Sadducees to propose a "what if" situation to Jesus.

BACKGROUND: SADDUCEES were an aristocratic group or party centered in Jerusalem and largely made up of high-priestly families and members of the upper class. They were an elite and hence a rather small group within Jewish society. Sadducees were religiously conservative, upholding their own interpretation of the law of Moses and rejecting traditions developed by Pharisees. The Sadducees also rejected beliefs in a resurrection of the dead and new beliefs about angels that had arisen in the second century B.C. (see Acts 23:6-8). Sadducees cooperated with Roman rule in order to maintain their privileged status. Sadducees as an identifiable group did not survive the Roman destruction of Jerusalem in A.D. 70.

When brothers live together and one of them dies without a son,
the widow of the deceased shall not marry anyone outside the
family; but her husband's brother shall go to her and perform the
duty of a brother-in-law by marrying her. The first-born son she
bears shall continue the line of the deceased brother, that his
name may not be blotted out from Israel.

Deuteronomy 25:5-6

25 **Now there were seven brothers among us.** In biblical idiom, the number **seven** represents completeness; the Sadducees are setting up an extreme situation. The say that the seven **brothers** were **among us,** but they are proposing a hypothetical situation rather than reporting an actual case. **The first married and died and, having no descendants, left his wife to his brother.** They speak of the **wife** as if she were something that the deceased man **left** as an inheritance **to his brother,** but they are referring to the brother's marrying the widow to fulfill the law.

26 **The same happened with the second** brother: he died without leaving a male heir; **and the third** brother married her and died heirless, **through all seven.** The situation is highly improbable, but even one man dying and his brother marrying his widow would provide a test case.

27 **Finally the woman died.** Her death completes the scenario that sets up the question (verse 23) they want to put to Jesus.

28 **Now at the resurrection, of the seven, whose wife will she be?** Their question rests on several presuppositions. One presupposition is that although a man may have more than one wife (Solomon reportedly had seven hundred—1 Kings 11:3), a wife cannot have more than one husband. A second presupposition is that if there is resurrected life, it will be basically a continuation of this life in a more pleasant setting. Hence what is impossible in this life—a woman having more than one husband—will be impossible in the next life. Since in the example the Sadducees set up, **all** seven brothers **had been married to her,** each of them had a claim on her as his wife. If there is a resurrection of the dead, how are their competing claims to be handled? The point the Sadducees wish to make is that there cannot be a resurrection because if there were, then impossible situations like this would arise.

29 Jesus said to them in reply, "You are misled because you do not know the scriptures or the power of God." Jesus does not mince words. The Sadducees are mistaken about the resurrection because they do not understand **the scriptures,** God's written word. Nor do they understand **the power of God,** what God is able to do. These are serious charges to make against those who view themselves as paragons of orthodoxy, and Jesus goes on to substantiate each charge.

30 Jesus first addresses what God is able to do. **At the resurrection they neither marry nor are given in marriage but are like the angels in heaven.** Contrary to the view of the Sadducees, resurrected life is not simply a continuation of this life. **At the resurrection,** women and men will be transformed and enter into a new mode of existence; they will be **like the angels in heaven.** First-century Jews did not think of angels as disembodied spirits; angels were envisioned as having the appearance of young men (Mark 16:5), sometimes shining radiantly (28:2-3), sometimes passing for ordinary humans (Tobit 5:4-5). To be like the angels means that one will have a transformed body (Paul will call it "a spiritual body": 1 Cor 15:44). Like angels, resurrected humans will not need to eat or drink (Tobit 12:19).

BACKGROUND: RESURRECTION While there was apparently no belief in an afterlife worth living during most of the Old Testament era, various hopes for the resurrection of the dead arose in the two centuries before Jesus. These hopes were associated with expectations that God would transform the world, ending the present age and inaugurating an age to come. One of the first hopes was that martyrs who had given up their lives for their faith would be raised to new life so that they could be part of God's new creation (2 Macc 6-7). The book of Daniel went a step further: not only would the righteous be raised to be part of God's reign, but the wicked would be raised as well, to be punished (Dan 12:2). How Jews conceived of resurrected bodies depended on how they conceived of God's reign in the age to come. If the age to come would be like the present age except that God would be in charge, then a person's body in the age to come would be like that person's present body (2 Macc 14:46). Some conceived of the age to come in less-earthly terms and thought that resurrected bodies would be heavenly bodies, making humans like angels. At the time of Jesus, some Jews, including Pharisees, believed in the resurrection of the dead, but other Jews, including Sadducees, did not (Acts 23:7-8). *Related topics: The age to come (page 250), Jewish expectations at the time of Jesus (page 515), Judgment (page 557), Life after death (page 406).*

Nor will they need to beget a new generation of children to replace older generations as they die: there is no death in life after death. Consequently the resurrected **neither marry nor are given in marriage.** The expression refers to what men and women do when they enter into marriage: men **marry** their wives and women **are given in marriage** by their fathers to their husbands (see 24:38). In context, Jesus is not saying that new marriages will not take place in heaven but that marriage as it is on earth will not continue after the resurrection. Because of the power of God to transform us through resurrection—a power that the Sadducees do not understand—the problem they pose in the example of a woman married to seven husbands will not occur.

Angels: See page 37

Other than saying that those who are resurrected will be like angels and "will shine like the sun in the kingdom of their Father" (13:43), Jesus does not describe what resurrected life will be like. We will be ourselves, but transformed through "the power of God" (verse 29). Paul will struggle

---

BACKGROUND: MARRIAGE PRACTICES The love of wife and husband for each other could be just as heartfelt in ancient as in modern times and sexual attraction just as passionate (see Song of Songs). Yet the understanding and practice of marriage in the Old Testament has its differences from marriage in the modern Western world. The primary purpose of marriage was to beget children, specifically sons who could continue the father's family name and inherit the father's family lands. Hence shame befell a barren wife, however much her husband might love her (1 Sam 1:1-8). If a husband died without leaving a son, his brother was to marry his widow and beget an heir for him (Deut 25:5-6). A man could have more than one wife (Deut 21:15-17), but a wife could not have more than one husband, for that would create family heritage tangles. Inheritance passed to sons, with a double share to the oldest (Deut 21:17). Only by exception could daughters inherit (Num 27:8), and then with restrictions to keep the inheritance within the father's clan (Num 36:6-9). Marriages were arrangements between families as well as between husband and wife. Particularly when those getting married were young (as early as puberty for a girl and a few years older for a boy), their fathers arranged their betrothal, sometimes drawing up a contract (see Tobit 7:13). A betrothed woman might continue to live with her family for a period of time (Matt 1:18). There was no wedding ceremony as such but a party or feast to celebrate a wife moving into the home of her husband (Matt 22:2-10; 25:1-13; Mark 2:19; John 2:1-10).

---

to convey what resurrected life will be like (1 Cor 15:35-57); it is beyond out imagining (see 1 Cor 2:9). Our hope for eternal life does not rest on our understanding it; our hope is based on our faith that God is able to give us life in eternity as he has given us life on this earth (see 2 Macc 7:20-23, 28-29): "for God all things are possible" (19:26).

> For reflection: How firm is my hope that God will sustain me in existence after I die? How do I envision the life I will have with God in eternity?

Some (I am among them) who have enjoyed a long and happy married life may be disappointed by the prospect of their marriages being dissolved when they reach heaven. However, Jesus' words in this passage apply most directly to the procreative aspect of marriage: in heaven there will be no need to beget heirs. Perhaps the companionship dimension of marriage will endure in a transformed manner in eternity, so that those whom God has joined together (see 19:4-6) may in some way remain together, just as we hope that our relationships with all whom we love will continue in eternity. How God will work this out is, like resurrected life itself, beyond our imagining—but nevertheless possible for God.

31 After speaking of the power of God to give resurrected life, Jesus turns to the Scriptures that the Sadducees fail to understand (verse 29). **And concerning the resurrection of the dead, have you not read what was said to you by God:** Jesus treats the Scriptures as what has been **said to you by God.** There is a passage **concerning the resurrection of the dead** that the Sadducees need to consider:

> For reflection: In what ways do I experience the words of Scripture as spoken by God to me?

32 **I am the God of Abraham, the God of Isaac, and the God of Jacob.** Jesus quotes from the book of Exodus, which the Sadducees accept as authoritative Scripture (they do not accept later Old Testament writings, such as Daniel, that speak clearly of the resurrection of the dead—Dan 12:2). God, speaking from a burning bush, identified himself to Moses as **the God of Abraham, the God of Isaac, and the God of Jacob.** Abraham, Isaac, and Jacob had died centuries before Moses was born, but God does not tell Moses that he *was* their God back when they were alive. God speaks

in the present tense and says **I am** their God, as if they are still alive. Jesus proclaims, **He is not the God of the dead but of the living.** Abraham, Isaac, and Jacob must in some way be **living,** even though they have died, for God is still their God. The personal relationship that God began with them continues after their death, which means that they survive as individuals after death. Their manner of survival after death is left unspecified (on another occasion, Jesus spoke of their being "at the banquet in the kingdom of heaven"—8:11). The fact of their survival must give pause to those who say that there is no resurrection (verse 23) or who claim that they can find no evidence for resurrection in Scripture: God's words to Moses in Exodus imply that death does not terminate God's relationship with those who die.

> God said, "Come no nearer! Remove the sandals from your feet, for the place where you stand is holy ground. I am the God of your father," he continued, "the God of Abraham, the God of Isaac, the God of Jacob."
>
> Exodus 3:5-6

33 Jesus' reply to the Sadducees silences them (see 22:34) even if it does not win them over. His teaching about resurrection impresses those who overhear it: **When the crowds heard this, they were astonished at his teaching.** It is near Passover (26:2), when the Temple courtyards would be filled with pilgrims. **Crowds** have witnessed Jesus' encounter with the Sadducees, and they are **astonished at his teaching**—the usual reaction of those who hear Jesus' teaching (7:28-29; 13:54; 19:25). Jesus exhibits a command of Scripture and speaks authoritatively, even about what awaits us after death. The crowds accept Jesus as a prophet (21:11, 46), as one who speaks for God.

> For reflection: What astonishes me about Jesus' teaching about resurrection? What hope does it give me?

The Great Commandments
34 When the Pharisees heard that he had silenced the Sadducees, they gathered together, **35** and one of them [a scholar of the law] tested him by asking, **36** "Teacher, which commandment in the law is the greatest?" **37** He said to him, "You shall love the Lord, your God, with all your

heart, with all your soul, and with all your mind. ³⁸ This is the greatest and the first commandment. ³⁹ The second is like it: You shall love your neighbor as yourself. ⁴⁰ The whole law and the prophets depend on these two commandments."

> Gospel parallels: Mark 12:28-34; Luke 10:25-28
> OT:Lev 19:18; Deut 6:5
> NT:Matt 5:43-48; 7:12; 19:19; Rom 13:8-10; Gal 5:14; 1 John 3:17;
>   4:7-11, 19-21

34 Jesus bested some Sadducees in a debate over the resurrection of the dead (22:23-33). **When the Pharisees heard that he had silenced the Sadducees, they gathered together.** Since **Pharisees** accepted the resurrection of the dead (see Acts 23:8), they would not have been unhappy that Jesus **silenced the Sadducees** who were denying the resurrection (22:23). Nevertheless, these Pharisees are set against Jesus, and **they gathered together** to conspire against him. What follows (22:41) indicates that we might imagine them huddling together in a Temple courtyard near where Jesus is teaching. They select one of their own to try again to entrap Jesus in his speech (see 22:15-16).

> Pharisees: See page 231
> Sadducees: See page 476

35 **One of them [a scholar of the law] tested him by asking:** not all manuscripts of Matthew's gospel include **a scholar of the law,** but the test is about the law of Moses, and it makes sense for the Pharisee to pick someone who is learned in the law (Matthew's gospel elsewhere uses the term "scribe" for such religions scholars—2:4; 5:20; 7:29; 9:3, etc.). This scholar **tested** Jesus **by asking** him a question. As in previous situations in which Pharisees tested Jesus (16:1; 19:3; 22:18), the intent is to trip him up.

36 The scholar's question is, **Teacher, which commandment in the law is the greatest?** The **law** of Moses contained many commandments; rabbis will later tally them as 248 commanding what to do and 365 commanding what not to do, for a total of 613 commandments. Some of these commandments are less weighty than others (Deut 22:6-7 prescribes what to do if one finds a bird on a nest with chicks or eggs in it). Even if all God's commands are to be obeyed, **which commandment in the law is the greatest?** The scholar calls Jesus a **teacher**—that is, someone who teaches

how the law of Moses is to be interpreted and obeyed, as Jesus did in the Sermon on the Mount. Someone who teaches about the law should know which of its commandments is the **greatest**. The scholar asks which is the greatest commandment to test Jesus (verse 35), presumably hoping that Jesus will give an inadequate answer and discredit himself as a teacher.

37 **He said to him, "You shall love the Lord, your God, with all your heart, with all your soul, and with all your mind."** Jesus quotes a command that was well known by every Jew. It occurs in a passage in Deuteronomy that became the opening words of a prayer recited morning and evening by devout Jews (Deut 6:4-5; the prayer is called the Shema, after its first word in Hebrew). God commands his people to **love** him as their God. Preceding this command in Deuteronomy are Moses' words, "These then are the commandments, the statutes and decrees which the LORD, your God, has ordered that you be taught to observe" (Deut 6:1; see also Deut 10:12-13; 30:10). **Love** of God is expressed in allegiance and obedience.

For reflection: How do I love God?

> *Hear, O Israel! The LORD is our God, the LORD alone! There-*
> *fore, you shall love the LORD, your God, with all your heart, and*
> *with all your soul, and with all your strength.*
> *Deuteronomy 6:4-5*

God commands his people to love him **with all your heart, with all your soul, and with all your mind.** In biblical idiom, the **heart** is the core of the human person, the seat of thinking, willing, and feeling. To love God with **all** of one's heart is to love him with one's whole being. The word translated **soul** is in some other contexts translated "life" (2:20; 6:25; 10:39; 16:25-26; 20:28); it means "one's livingness." To love God with **all** one's soul is to love him with one's entire life and energy. One's **mind** is one's thinking and understanding; to love God with **all** one's mind is to live completely focused on God. **Heart, soul,** and **mind** are not three different components of the human person but three ways of expressing the whole person: we are to love God with all we are. We are to give to God what belongs to God (22:21), which is our entire selves.

For reflection: How completely do I love God?

38 Jesus proclaims, **This is the greatest and the first commandment.** Our **greatest** obligation, our **first** priority, is to love God with all our heart, with all our soul, with all our mind.

> *For reflection: Is loving God the greatest goal of my life? What can I do to make it my top daily priority?*

39 The scholar asked Jesus which commandment was greatest, and Jesus has answered his question. The scholar would be hard pressed to say that Jesus had answered incorrectly: no commandment can take precedence over loving God. But Jesus expands on his answer, just as he did when asked whether it was lawful to pay the census tax (22:21). Jesus associates a **second** commandment with the first. **The second is like it:** the Greek word for **like** has the connotation of sameness: the second commandment is of the same nature as the first and of comparable importance. Jesus again quotes from the law of Moses: **You shall love your neighbor as yourself** (Lev 19:18). God commands that we treat our **neighbor** as well as we treat ourselves, that we not exploit our neighbor for our own advantage, that we be as concerned for our neighbor's well-being as we are for our own. Jesus made the same demand when he taught, "Do to others whatever you would have them do to you" (7:12). As with love of God, love of neighbor is a matter of behavior and not just attitude.

> *For reflection: Do I treat others as well as I treat myself? Do I help those in need as I would want to be helped if I were in their shoes?*

> *Take no revenge and cherish no grudge against your fellow countrymen. You shall love your neighbor as yourself. I am the LORD.*
> *Leviticus 19:18*

For the ancient Israelites, one's **neighbor** meant a fellow Israelite; the boundaries of love were the borders of Israel. Jesus abolishes limits on love. When he taught, "Do to others whatever you would have them do to you" (7:12) he included all others. The first time Jesus quoted the commandment to love one's neighbor he went on, "I say to you, love your enemies, and pray for those who persecute you" (5:43-44). We cannot love just those who love us (see 5:46); we must love everyone, treating them as we would like to be treated, treating them as well as we treat ourselves.

For reflection: What are the limits of my love? Of my compassion for those in need?

By adding a second commandment to the first and saying that it is **like** it, Jesus connects love of neighbor with love of God. Jesus does not identify love of God with love of neighbor but indicates that the two are inseparable. Loving God includes imitating his loving by extending our love to all whom God loves (see 5:44-48). The love we practice toward others is an index of our love for God ("If anyone says, 'I love God,' but hates his brother, he is a liar; for whoever does not love a brother whom he has seen cannot love God whom he has not seen"—1 John 4:20). When we encounter unlovableness in others, we find the strength to love them in God's love for us and our love for God.

For reflection: What linkage have I experienced between loving God and loving my neighbor?

40 The whole law and the prophets depend on these two commandments. The **law and the prophets** represent the Scriptures and God's revelation through these Scripture (see 5:17; 7:12). The commandments to love God and love our neighbor are not only the **two** great **commandments;** they are the basis and purpose of all of God's other commandments. Jesus upholds God's laws and teaches how they are to be fulfilled (see 5:17); love is the guiding principle for interpreting and applying the law. Paul will proclaim that love of neighbor fulfills the whole law (Rom 13:8-10; Gal 5:14). God wants love.

For reflection: Have I made love my guiding principle for living according to God's law?

Although the command to love God is the greatest commandment, this is the only passage in Matthew's gospel in which Jesus explicitly teaches that we are to love God. Yet this is the third time in Matthew's gospel that we hear the commandment to love our neighbor as ourselves (5:43; 19:19; 22:39), in addition to Jesus' injunction to treat others as we would like to be treated (7:12). Perhaps this command bears repeating. It is easy for us to not love our neighbors as ourselves: we simply need not lift a finger on their behalf.

Whose Son Is the Messiah?

41 While the Pharisees were gathered together, Jesus questioned them, **42** saying, "What is your opinion about the Messiah? Whose son is he?" They replied, "David's." **43** He said to them, "How, then, does David, inspired by the Spirit, call him 'lord,' saying:

> **44** 'The Lord said to my lord,
> "Sit at my right hand
> until I place your enemies under
> your feet"'?

45 If David calls him 'lord,' how can he be his son?" **46** No one was able to answer him a word, nor from that day on did anyone dare to ask him any more questions.

> Gospel parallels: Mark 12:35-37; Luke 20:41-44
> OT:Psalm 110:1
> NT:Matt 1:1, 6-16; 3:17; 11:2, 25-27; 14:33; 16:16, 20-21; 17:5

41 While the Pharisees were gathered together: they had **gathered together,** apparently near where Jesus was teaching within the Temple precincts, and one of them had questioned Jesus about the greatest commandment (22:34-36). After answering the question posed to him (22:37-40), **Jesus questioned them.** He has been repeatedly questioned by those who challenge his authority (21:23) and want to trip him up (22:15-17, 23-28, 35-36); now he has his own questions for the **Pharisees.**

Pharisees: See page 231

42 Jesus asked them, **What is your opinion about the Messiah?** Different Jews had different views **about the Messiah;** there was no single understanding of the Messiah shared by everyone at the time of Jesus. There would have been nothing extraordinary in asking the Pharisees about their views of the Messiah. But there is a second level of meaning in Jesus' question. Jesus knows—and Matthew's readers know—that he is the Messiah, or Christ (1:1, 16, 18; 2:4; 11:2; 16:16, 20). Since the Pharisees do not perceive that Jesus is the Messiah, they do not realize that he is asking a question about himself.

Messiah, Christ: See page 349

To ask for someone's views of the Messiah was to invite a long lec-
ture; there were many speculations about what he would be like and what
he would accomplish. Jesus narrows his inquiry to a more manageable
question: **Whose son is he?** Whose descendant will the Messiah be? This
was a legitimate question to raise. While most Jews who expected God to
send a messiah believed that he would be a descendant of David, the
Essenes expected two messiahs, a kingly messiah descended from David
and a priestly messiah descended from Aaron, with the priestly messiah
having precedence over the kingly one. Pharisees did not expect a priestly
messiah, and **they replied** that the Messiah would be **David's son.**
Prophecies spoke of a descendant of David reigning (Isaiah 9:5-6; 11:1-9;
Jer 23:5; Ezek 34:23-24; 37:24-25) in fulfillment of God's promises to
David (2 Sam 7:11-16; Psalm 89:4-5, 30-38). The Pharisees probably
thought that they were on solid ground in saying that the Messiah would
be a descendant of David. Matthew's readers would agree: they know that
David is one of Jesus' ancestors (1:1, 6-16).

Essenes: See page 238

43 After Peter proclaimed Jesus to be the Messiah, Jesus "strictly ordered his
disciples to tell no one that he was the Messiah" (16:20), because popular understandings of the Messiah did not do justice to his identity and
mission. Jesus now wants to show the Pharisees that their understanding
of the Messiah is inadequate. He does so by posing more questions. **He
said to them, "How, then, does David, inspired by the Spirit, call him
'lord' . . . ?"** Jesus will go on to quote words from Psalm 110. Jewish tradition ascribed this psalm to **David;** this is reflected in the heading
added to Psalm 110, "A psalm of David" (Psalm 110:1). Jesus accepts the
tradition that David wrote Psalm 110 and says that he did so **inspired by
the Spirit,** literally, "*in* the Spirit." Just as the Spirit of God inspired
prophets (Num 11:25-29; 1 Sam 10:6, 10; Ezek 11:4-5; Joel 3:1), so the
Spirit inspired David. David proclaimed of himself, "The spirit of the
LORD spoke through me; / his word was on my tongue" (2 Sam 23:2).
Since David's words in Psalm 110 are inspired by the Spirit, they are
trustworthy. Jesus interprets Psalm 110 as referring to the Messiah,
whom David, as the author of the psalm, calls **lord.**

The Spirit: See page 21
Lord: See page 133

44 Jesus quotes the relevant verse: **The Lord said to my lord, / "Sit at my right hand / until I place your enemies under your feet"** (Psalm 110:1). The first **Lord** in this verse is the Lord God. Psalm 110 uses the Hebrew word *YHWH* as the personal name for God. Out of reverence, Jews did not speak God's name but pronounced a Hebrew word for "Lord" when they came to *YHWH* in their reading of Scripture. Jesus interprets the second **lord** to be the Messiah. Jesus understands Psalm 110 as David saying, **The Lord** God **said to my lord** the Messiah, **"Sit at my right hand until I place your enemies under your feet."** God invites the Messiah to sit at his right hand, the position of power and honor (see 20:21), until God defeats the Messiah's enemies and places them under the Messiah's feet.

A psalm of David.

The LORD *says to you, my lord:*
"Take your throne at my right hand,
while I make your enemies your footstool."
Psalm 110:1

45 The Pharisees said that the Messiah was David's son (verse 42), but **if David calls him "lord," how can he be his son?** A son might address his father as **lord** (or "sir"—see 21:30), but a father would never call his son his lord. If David calls the Messiah **lord,** then the Messiah is superior to David, and it is inadequate to think of the Messiah as simply David's son.

BACKGROUND: GOD'S NAME The word "God" is the generic name for the Supreme Being. In addition to the generic Hebrew word for God, the Old Testament also uses the personal name for God, which in Hebrew is written with letters that correspond to the English letters *YHWH*. Biblical Hebrew was written largely without vowels, and thus it is impossible to be certain how this name was pronounced; it may have been pronounced "Yahweh." The Old Testament presents God revealing his name, *YHWH*, to Moses at the burning bush (Exod 3:15). Out of reverence, Jews in the time of Jesus (as still today) avoided saying the name of God; when they read Scripture aloud and came to the name *YHWH*, they substituted a Hebrew word for "Lord." When the Hebrew Scriptures were translated into Greek, the Greek word for Lord was used to translate *YHWH*. The Old Testament of the New American Bible uses the word "LORD" (printed with large and small capitals), and on rare occasions "GOD," to stand for the Hebrew *YHWH*.

The Pharisees have no answer to Jesus' question, **How can he be his son?** Nor did they have an adequate answer to Jesus' earlier question about the Messiah, "Whose son is he?" (verse 42). Matthew's readers, however, know the answer: Jesus the Messiah is the son of David (1:1) and, much more importantly, he is the Son of God (3:17; 11:25-27; 14:33; 16:16; 17:5).

Jesus' exchange with the Pharisees is more than a matter of wordplay on a psalm; it exposes their ignorance about the Messiah. One reason the Pharisees do not recognize Jesus as the Messiah is because they are looking for the wrong kind of messiah.

When Matthew wrote his gospel, the early rabbis who followed the teachings of the Pharisees also failed to recognize Jesus as the Messiah. This incident helped Matthew's church understand why: those who do not acknowledge Jesus as the Messiah do not understand the kind of messiah God sent. They do not grasp that the Messiah is the Son of God who suffers, dies, and is raised (16:21) and who is now, as Psalm 110 foreshadows, seated at the right hand of God (26:64; Acts 2:32-36; Rom 8:34; Eph 1:20; Col 3:1; Heb 1:3, 13; 8:1; 10:12; 1 Pet 3:22).

For reflection: What does it mean for me that Jesus, the Son of God, suffered and died to fulfill his role as the Messiah? That he is now seated at the right hand of God?

46 Jesus' question—"If David calls him 'lord,' how can he be his son?"— stumps the Pharisees, and **no one was able to answer him a word:** none of them had even a single **word** to say in response. **Nor from that day on did anyone dare to ask him any more questions.** Those who have questioned Jesus to entrap him have seen him repeatedly escape their snares (22:15-40); now he is coming up with questions they cannot answer. The time for verbal sparring with Jesus is over. The next time Jesus' opponents make an appearance in Matthew's gospel they will be consulting how best to have him arrested and put to death (26:3-5). First, though, Jesus still has much to teach during the very full day that began in Matthew's gospel at 21:18 and extends to 26:2.

CHAPTER 23

ORIENTATION: *Jesus has had a series of exchanges with religious leaders intent on entrapping him (22:15-46). Now he addresses the shortcomings of these leaders, telling his disciples not to imitate them. Matthew presents Jesus' message with an eye to the situation of his church.*

Humble Service, Not Honors

[1] Then Jesus spoke to the crowds and to his disciples, [2] saying, "The scribes and the Pharisees have taken their seat on the chair of Moses. [3] Therefore, do and observe all things whatsoever they tell you, but do not follow their example. For they preach but they do not practice. [4] They tie up heavy burdens [hard to carry] and lay them on people's shoulders, but they will not lift a finger to move them. [5] All their works are performed to be seen. They widen their phylacteries and lengthen their tassels. [6] They love places of honor at banquets, seats of honor in synagogues, [7] greetings in marketplaces, and the salutation 'Rabbi.' [8] As for you, do not be called 'Rabbi.' You have but one teacher, and you are all brothers. [9] Call no one on earth your father; you have but one Father in heaven. [10] Do not be called 'Master'; you have but one master, the Messiah. [11] The greatest among you must be your servant. [12] Whoever exalts himself will be humbled; but whoever humbles himself will be exalted."

Gospel parallels: Mark 12:38-39; Luke 11:43, 46; 14:11; 18:14; 20:45-46
NT: Matt 6:1-6, 16-18; 7:21; 12:49-50; 20:25-28

1 **Then,** after Jesus' disputes with religious leaders (21:23–22:46), **Jesus spoke to the crowds and to his disciples.** The setting continues to be the Temple courtyard; **the crowds,** along with Jesus' **disciples,** have witnessed the disputes. Matthew's first readers might have understood the **disciples** to stand for themselves and the **crowds** for Jews who had not yet become disciples of Jesus.

Disciple: See page 66

2 Jesus acknowledges that **the scribes and the Pharisees have taken their seat on the chair of Moses.** Jewish teachers normally sat while teaching (see 5:1). In later centuries, synagogues will have a prominent seat for rabbis

490

to use while instructing in the law of Moses. In the first century, however, **the chair of Moses** seems to have been a figurative expression for the authority to teach the law of Moses. **Scribes** and **Pharisees** have laid claim to this authority.

Scribes: See page 138
Pharisees: See page 231

For Matthew's first readers, **the scribes and the Pharisees** would have stood for the early rabbis who were urging Jews to follow "the tradition of the elders" (15:2) as the way to observe the law of Moses. They had become the leaders in some synagogues in the region in which Matthew wrote his gospel. Some Jewish Christians in Matthew's church continued, or wanted to continue, to be part of synagogue life: accepting Jesus as the Messiah did not mean turning their backs on their Jewish heritage. They were caught in the middle as the gap widened between synagogue and church.

BACKGROUND: JEWISH RELIGIOUS DIVERSITY AT THE TIME OF MATTHEW

Jews in Palestine rebelled against Roman rule in A.D. 66. In putting down the revolt, Rome swept away mainstays of Jewish life, including the Temple with its sacrifices, which were the basis of the leadership of the priestly elite. Many Jews were utterly demoralized. A few harbored hopes that revolt might yet win independence from Rome, and another revolt, also unsuccessful, broke out in A.D. 132. Some Jews put their hopes in God vindicating his people by bringing this age to an end—a view reflected in the nonbiblical writings 4 Ezra and 2 Baruch. Jewish Christians believed that Jesus was the fulfillment of what God had been doing with his people; Jews should accept Jesus as the Messiah and his teachings as the authoritative interpretation of the law of Moses. Pharisees, joined by some scribes, priests, and others, continued their development of a Judaism focused on obedience to the law of Moses in the circumstances of everyday life. Their program proved increasingly influential and gave rise to what is called rabbinic Judaism. The leaders of this emerging rabbinic Judaism did not embrace Jesus or his interpretation of the law, and synagogues they led became increasingly inhospitable to Jewish Christians. Matthew's Jewish Christian community was in competition with emerging rabbinic Judaism for the allegiance of Jews, with rabbinic Judaism prevailing. *Related topics: Nonbiblical writings (page 198), Pharisees (page 231), Scribes (page 138).*

---

3 **Therefore, do and observe all things whatsoever they tell you:** this is the most puzzling statement in Matthew's gospel. Jesus has repeatedly taken issue with the Pharisees (5:20; 9:10-13; 12:1-14; 15:1-20), calling them "blind guides" (15:14) and warning his disciples to "beware of the leaven of the Pharisees and Sadducees," their teachings (16:6, 12). How then could Jesus say **do and observe all things whatsoever they tell you?** Scholars have made many suggestions for how Jesus' words are to be understood. Perhaps Jesus' words are a tacit acknowledgement of the influence of scribes and Pharisees rather than an endorsement of it. If Jewish Christians are to continue to be part of synagogue life, they will have to reach an accommodation with synagogue leaders. To do otherwise would mean breaking ties with the synagogue. These ties will eventually snap, but it is doubtful that all Jewish Christians had completely broken away or been expelled from synagogues when Matthew wrote his gospel.

However Jesus' puzzling words are to be understood, his emphasis is on what follows: **but do not follow their example. For they preach but they do not practice.** Literally, do not do according to their works, for they say but do not do. There is a discrepancy between the words and the deeds of these religious leaders. Jesus puts the priority on doing over saying: "Not everyone who says to me, 'Lord, Lord,' will enter the kingdom of heaven, but only the one who does the will of my Father in heaven" (7:21). Jesus will shortly accuse his opponents of hypocrisy (23:13), of not living out what they profess. They consequently cannot be models for others.

Do not follow their example is the message for followers of Jesus in this and the following sections of Matthew's gospel. Jesus will highlight and condemn failures of religious leaders and in doing so convey that his disciples are to behave differently.

For reflection: In what areas of my life do I fail to put into practice what I profess?

4 Jesus provides examples of behavior that is not to be imitated. **They tie up heavy burdens [hard to carry] and lay them on people's shoulders, but they will not lift a finger to move them.** Pharisees interpreted the law of Moses and applied it to everyday life, particularly regarding Sabbath observance, tithing, and ritual purity. Matthew's gospel portrays them as holding that plucking grain and healing are works forbidden on

the Sabbath (12:1-2, 10) and that ritual washing of hands is necessary before eating (15:2). While their intent is to help people observe the law, Jesus judges that their applications of the law are a **heavy burden** that is **hard to carry**. Pharisees **lay** this burden **on people's shoulders, but they will not lift a finger to move them:** they make no effort to lighten the load or to help people carry the burden. They are insensitive to the impact of their edicts—a lack of compassion that Jesus' followers are not to imitate. Jesus teaches how the law of Moses is to be observed (for example, 5:17-48) but the burden he places on his disciples is light and easy to bear (see 11:30).

For reflection: Do I burden others with loads that I do not help them carry?

5 Jesus provides a second example of behavior not to be imitated: **All their works are performed to be seen.** Deeds **performed to be seen** are performances to gain admiration. Jesus warned against such performances (6:1): no trumpet blasts to announce donations (6:2-4), no ostentatious prayer in synagogue or on the street corner (6:5-6), no wan appearance while fasting (6:16-18).

Jesus mentions religious practices that his opponents perform to gain admiration. **They widen their phylacteries**—small boxes containing Scripture passages, worn on the forehead and left arm by devout Jews while praying. Jesus does not challenge the practice of wearing phylacteries (he may have worn them himself) but ostentation in doing do. To **widen** phylacteries may mean wearing phylacteries noticeably larger than usual or binding them on with extra wide straps, in either case to proclaim one's piety. Were Jesus to make a parallel criticism of Christians today he might say, "They go about with foot-long crosses dangling from their necks."

BACKGROUND: PHYLACTERIES are small leather boxes containing Scripture passages on pieces of parchment, bound with straps to the forehead and left arm. In Deuteronomy God enjoins his people to "take to heart these words which I enjoin on you today. . . . Bind them at your wrist as a sign and let them be as a pendant on your forehead" (Deut 6:6, 8; see also Exod 13:9, 16; Deut 11:18). Devout Jews began to wear phylacteries several centuries before the time of Jesus as an observance of this command. The Scripture passages placed in phylacteries are Exod 13:1-16 and Deut 6:4-9; 11:13-21; some first-century phylacteries also contained a copy of the Ten Commandments. Phylacteries are not mentioned in the Old Testament, and in the New Testament only at Matthew 23:5.

Similarly, those who wish to display their piety **lengthen their tassels.** Jewish men wore **tassels** on the lower hem of their cloaks as a reminder of God's commandments (Num 15:38-39; see also Deut 22:12). Again, Jesus does not disapprove of the practice (he wore such tassels himself—9:20; 14:36) but only of ostentation designed to attract admiration. Wearing tassels to proclaim one's piety is a distraction from rather than a reminder of God's commands.

For reflection: When have I consciously or unconsciously behaved in ways meant to impress others with my piety?

6 The goal of making public displays of piety is to gain the honor of others, and those whom Jesus criticizes love being honored. Jesus mentions examples of honors **they love.** They love **places of honor at banquets,** seats beside or near the host. Seating at formal banquets was not random but reflected the relative importance of the guests (see Luke 14:7-10). Jesus portrays the scribes and Pharisees as wanting the most prestigious seats at banquets. They similarly love **seats of honor in synagogues,** perhaps on a high bench where everyone can see them.

Banquets: See page 464
Synagogue: See page 104

While Jesus criticizes scribes and Pharisees for loving seats of honor, his own disciples have exhibited a similar lust. The sons of Zebedee wanted to sit at the right and left of Jesus in his kingdom (20:21), and the rest of the disciples reacted as if they wanted such places of honor for themselves (20:24). Lusting for honors is a temptation that can beset all followers of Jesus and in all spheres of life. Those who have public roles in the church or in society face the occupational hazard of being honored. Jesus' words are a warning against loving honors, even if they are unavoidable.

For reflection: What is my reaction if I am honored or praised? What do I do to win the honor and praise of others?

7 Those whom Jesus criticizes love **greetings in marketplaces:** what is at issue are not hellos exchanged between friends but respects paid by those of lower status to those of higher status. Jesus criticizes those who love to be

shown deference as they go about in public; they want their religious credentials to give them celebrity status. They love being hailed with **the salutation "Rabbi."** To call someone **rabbi** (Hebrew for "my great one") was an honorific address—perhaps more deferential than "sir" today and virtually "your excellency."

8 Jesus is using the behavior of scribes and Pharisees as examples of what not to do (verse 3), as he now makes explicit. **As for you, do not be called "Rabbi."** Jesus' disciples are not to seek or accept the honor of being deferentially greeted as **rabbi.** By the time Matthew writes his gospel, **rabbi** was becoming a title for Jewish teachers; Matthew's first readers associated the term with those who had teaching authority in synagogues. Jesus tells his disciples, **You have but one teacher,** referring to himself. Jesus uniquely teaches who God is (11:27) and how one enters into the reign of God; he is the **one teacher** who is able to speak authoritatively for God (see 7:28-29). There will always be need for teaching within the church (see 28:20), but those who teach are passing on the message of Jesus the **one teacher.** Teachers will inevitably have some title reflecting their function, but Christians teachers will not be known as rabbis (in Matthew's church they were apparently called scribes—see 13:52; 23:34). Because they have one teacher, Jesus tells his disciples **you are all brothers.** Jesus' disciples are his family, brothers and sisters with one another (12:49-50).

9 Jesus continues to teach that his followers should shun honorific titles. **Call no one on earth your father:** calling someone **father** was an expression of respect (see Acts 7:2; 22:1). It may have had the overtone of spiritual father when addressed to a religious leader. Jesus' disciples are to reserve the word for God: **you have but one Father in heaven.** Jesus has

---

BACKGROUND: RABBI The Hebrew word *rab* means "big" or "great"; with a first-person possessive ending it becomes *rabbi*, "my great one." The word "rabbi" is not found in the Old Testament but had become a deferential form of address by the time of Jesus. Eventually this respectful form of address came to be used as a title for those with teaching authority within Judaism, which is the meaning that the title "rabbi" has today. Some of this shift from being simply a deferential form of address to being also a title for a teacher is reflected in the gospels. Sometimes Jesus is called "rabbi" in settings in which he is not teaching (Mark 9:5; 11:21). Yet the later meaning is reflected in some passages, where "rabbi" is equated with "teacher" (Matt 23:8; John 1:38; 3:2).

spoken repeatedly to his disciples about their heavenly Father (5:43-48; 6:1-18, 25-34; 7:7-11; 10:19-20, 29; 18:10-14) and does not want the word "father" used in a way that obscures the fatherhood of God.

Despite this admonition, there is a long tradition of addressing priests as father. Paul's example is sometimes invoked: he spoke of himself as the father of those he brought to faith ("I became your father in Christ Jesus through the gospel"—1 Cor 4:15; see also 1 Thess 2:11; Phlm 10). Yet Paul also compared himself to a woman in labor (Gal 4:19) and to a nursing mother (1 Thess 2:7) with respect to his converts. Paul was quite clear that God is *the* Father (Rom 8:15; 1 Cor 8:6; Gal 4:6).

10 Do not be called "Master": the Greek word translated **Master** can mean "teacher," in the sense of "guide." **You have but one master, the Messiah.** Jesus' disciples should look to him as their **master** and teacher. Verse 10 conveys the same message as verse 8 but in different words: don't accept honors for passing on the message of salvation.

Messiah, Christ: See page 349

This is the only verse in the gospels in which Jesus directly refers to himself as **the Messiah.** Jesus did not allow his disciples to speak of him as the Messiah (16:20), because it would have caused misunderstanding: he did not match up with popular views of the Messiah. We might have expected Jesus to simply say, **You have but one master** without referring to himself as **the Messiah,** just as in verse 8 he said, "You have but one teacher." After his death and resurrection the church quickly began to speak of him as "the Messiah, the Christ," making it virtually his second name (Paul refers to him as "the Lord Jesus Christ" in what is probably the first verse of the New Testament to be written—1 Thess 1:1). Matthew speaks of Jesus as "Christ" (1:1, 18), translated here as "Messiah," and has Jesus using the term for himself. Matthew does not present a stenographic record of Jesus' words but uses language his church will understand.

Jesus condemns love of honors, which can be expressed through different titles in different settings. The three titles used as examples—rabbi, father, master—reflect a first-century Jewish setting. Today charities recognize donors by publishing their names, assigning major donors to a "Benefactor's Council" or some other exalted category. Jesus would prefer that our listing read "Anonymous" (see 6:3-4).

11 Jesus has told his followers to avoid imitating those who love honors and titles; now he tells his followers what they are to do instead. **The greatest among you must be your servant.** All his disciples are brothers and sisters of one another (verse 8) and cannot lord it over one another. To the contrary, the one who is **greatest** in the family of Jesus is the **servant** of the other members of the family. Jesus has already told his disciples that greatness means service in imitation of his example (20:25-28), but it is a message that bears repeating. A servant does not burden others but bears their burdens (see verse 4). A servant does not make a show of serving (see verse 5), for a servant's attention is on the needs of others rather than on his or her reputation. A servant is not concerned about status and honors (see verses 6 to 10), because a servant claims no status. A servant simply serves—and in Jesus' family that is true greatness.

> *For reflection: Do I think of myself as a servant? Do I behave like a servant in my interactions with others?*

12 Those who pursue status and honors in this life forfeit them in eternity: **Whoever exalts himself will be humbled**—humbled by God at the final judgment. Those who spurn status and honors in order to serve will have their greatness recognized in eternity: **but whoever humbles himself will be exalted** by God. Jesus again echoes earlier teaching: "Whoever humbles himself like this child is the greatest in the kingdom of heaven" (18:4).

Jesus confers authority on the church (16:18-19; 18:18), and he also proclaims how authority is to be exercised: "You know that the rulers of the Gentiles lord it over them, and the great ones make their authority over them felt. But it shall not be so among you. Rather, whoever wishes to be great among you shall be your servant; whoever wishes to be first among you shall be your slave" (20:25-27). The disciples of Jesus are brothers and sisters who are to be servants of one another, disregarding honors and titles, humbling themselves in imitation of the humble Jesus (11:29), who did not come to be served but to give his life in service (20:28).

ORIENTATION: *Jesus pronounces seven "woes" on scribes and Pharisees, in a manner reminiscent of the way in which Old Testament prophets denounced the conduct of God's people. These woes are a counterpart to the beatitudes in the Sermon on the Mount (5:3-10).*

1: Woe to Those Who Are Obstacles
13 **"Woe to you, scribes and Pharisees, you hypocrites. You lock the kingdom of heaven before human beings. You do not enter yourselves, nor do you allow entrance to those trying to enter." [14]**
Gospel parallels: Luke 11:52

13 Woe to you, scribes and Pharisees, you hypocrites. Jesus has lamented woeful behavior on other occasions (11:21; 18:7) and now directs his woes at the **scribes and Pharisees** he has been criticizing (23:1-7). Matthew's first readers would understand them to represent the early rabbis. A **woe** deplores someone's unfortunate condition; Jesus laments religious leaders who are **hypocrites.** Jesus has repeatedly condemned hypocrisy (6:2, 5, 16; 7:5; 15:7; 22:18), a disconnect between appearance and reality. Jesus' first woe laments the disconnect between appearing to lead people to God while actually being an obstacle blocking people from God. **You lock the kingdom of heaven before human beings.** Jesus has spoken of entering the kingdom of heaven (5:20; 7:21; 18:3; 19:23-24) and has used the image of a gate leading into it (7:13-14); here the image is of a door that is closed in the face of others and locked. Those locking the door are locked out themselves: **You do not enter yourselves, nor do you allow entrance to those trying to enter.** Jesus' mission is to bring women and men into the reign of God; those who oppose him do not enter God's reign and impede others from entering. Those who block entrance into God's reign for themselves and others are in a woeful state (see 18:6-7).

Scribes: See page 138
Pharisees: See page 231
Kingdom of heaven: See page 266

For reflection: What obstacles have I put in the way of others drawing closer to God? What obstacles have I put on my own path to God?

[14](Some manuscripts of Matthew's gospel include at this point the verse, "Woe to you, scribes and Pharisees, you hypocrites. You devour the houses of widows and, as a pretext, recite lengthy prayers. Because of this, you will receive a very severe condemnation." These words are not found in the most reliable manuscripts and were probably inserted by a scribe who added an adaptation of Mark 12:40 to Matthew's woes. The New American Bible omits this verse.)

2: Woe to Those Who Misshape Others

15 "**Woe to you, scribes and Pharisees, you hypocrites. You traverse sea and land to make one convert, and when that happens you make him a child of Gehenna twice as much as yourselves.**"

15 Woe to you, scribes and Pharisees, you hypocrites. You traverse sea and land to make one convert. A convert is a Gentile who embraces Judaism, becoming obedient to the law of Moses and accepting circumcision if male. There is little ancient evidence that Jews generally sought to convert Gentiles but Acts indicates that there were converts (Acts 2:11; 6:5; 13:43). Jesus describes the **scribes and Pharisees** as zealously seeking to make converts, even if they have to **traverse sea and land to make one** single **convert.** The expression **sea and land** represents the whole earth and might also remind ancient readers of the hazards of travel (see 2 Cor 11:25-26). Jesus says that scribes and Pharisees are in a woeful state because **when that happens**—when they convert someone—**you make him a child of Gehenna twice as much as yourselves.** A **child of Gehenna** is one who is destined for the punishment symbolized by **Gehenna.** How do the scribes and Pharisees produce converts who are **twice** as bad as themselves? Pharisees presumably taught their converts to follow "the tradition of the elders" (15:2), which they proposed as the proper way to

---

BACKGROUND: WOES A woe is the opposite of a beatitude. While a beatitude congratulates someone as fortunate, a woe laments and reproaches someone for his or her unfortunate condition. Just as a beatitude encourages the behavior that is being praised, a woe warns against the behavior that is being lamented. There are about fifty woes in the Old Testament, mostly as prophetic denunciations of those who do evil. Chapter 5 of Isaiah pronounces six woes: "Woe to those who call evil good, and good evil" (Isaiah 5:20; see also 5:8, 11, 18, 21-22). The New Testament has thirty-seven woes. Luke's gospel pairs four beatitudes with four woes (Luke 6:20-26). A woe is a cry of grief and alarm over a course of action that will bring God's punishment (see Matt 11:20-24). Woes are warnings and expressions of sorrow, not curses.

observe the law of Moses. Jesus has rejected these traditions as subverting rather than implementing God's law (15:3-9). Converts are often very zealous; if the converts made by Pharisees are **twice** as zealous as their converters for traditions that Jesus rejects, then we can understand Jesus pronouncing a woe upon those who make such converts. The broader lesson might be a warning against letting our flaws take root in and blossom in others.

Gehenna: See page 88

For reflection: Have I handed on any of my faults to others? What might I do to repair the damage?

3: Woe to Those Who Split Hairs

16 "Woe to you, blind guides, who say, 'If one swears by the temple, it means nothing, but if one swears by the gold of the temple, one is obligated.' **17** Blind fools, which is greater, the gold, or the temple that made the gold sacred? **18** And you say, 'If one swears by the altar, it means nothing, but if one swears by the gift on the altar, one is obligated.' **19** You blind ones, which is greater, the gift, or the altar that makes the gift sacred? **20** One who swears by the altar swears by it and all that is upon it; **21** one who swears by the temple swears by it and by him who dwells in it; **22** one who swears by heaven swears by the throne of God and by him who is seated on it."

NT: Matt 5:33-37; 15:14

16 Woe to you, blind guides: Jesus does not name the scribes and Pharisees in this woe, but he has previously called Pharisees **blind guides** (15:14), incapable of seeing God's ways and of leading others along these ways. Jesus provides examples of spiritual blindness. Some say that **if one swears by the temple, it means nothing, but if one swears by the gold of the temple, one is obligated.** Swearing an oath invokes God as a witness to the truth of what one is saying. Oaths were much more part of everyday life in the first century than they are today. Oaths were not limited to grave matters; we might imagine a marketplace vendor swearing to a customer that he could not possibly take less than a quarter denarius for a bushel of vegetables. Out of reverence, Jews avoided speaking God's name in oaths and swore instead by something associated with God. But what were acceptable substitutes for God's name? Were some oath formulas binding and others not? Those whom Jesus laments as **blind guides** had rules for determining the validity of oaths. One rule was that **If one swears by the temple, it means nothing, but if one swears by the gold of the temple, one is obligated.** The **gold** of the Temple may have been offerings, or perhaps its gold utensils or exterior plating. Swearing either by **the temple** or by its **gold** were ways of invoking God in an oath without naming him directly; one was judged a valid substitute for God's name and the other not.

17 Jesus finds the rule ridiculous. **Blind fools, which is greater, the gold, or the temple that made the gold sacred?** Gold has no sacredness in itself but only becomes **sacred** through its association with the Temple. How then could gold serve as a valid substitute for God's name in an oath, but not the Temple itself?

18 Another rule was, **If one swears by the altar, it means nothing, but if one swears by the gift on the altar, one is obligated.**

19 Jesus again finds the rule ridiculous. **You blind ones, which is greater, the gift, or the altar that makes the gift sacred?** Offerings such as animals and crops became **sacred** through their being placed on the **altar** (see Exod 29:37). Jesus' reasoning with respect to **the gift** and **the altar** is the same as his reasoning about gold and the Temple: if the altar makes the gift sacred, how can an oath invoking a gift be binding, but not an oath invoking the altar?

20 Jesus rejects distinctions between valid and invalid substitutes for God's name in oaths. **One who swears by the altar swears by it and all that is upon it;**

21 **one who swears by the temple swears by it and by him who dwells in it.** The emphasis in Jesus' statement falls on **him who dwells in** the Temple—God. Whatever substitutes are used in oaths for God's name, the point of taking an oath is to invoke God as one's witness. It is invoking God, rather than the fine print of the wording, that makes an oath an oath.

22 Jesus alludes to what was apparently a rule regarding use of the terms **heaven** and **the throne of God** in oaths. He does not quote the rule but

pronounces it to be as pointless as the other rules: **one who swears by heaven swears by the throne of God and by him who is seated on it.** It does not matter what words one uses to invoke God in an oath; an oath is an oath.

Jesus derides these hairsplitting rules about oaths in order to show that those who propose such rules are blind guides (see verses 16, 17, 19). Woe to such guides—and by implication woe to those who follow them, for they will end up falling into a pit (see 15:14). Jesus uses rules about oaths as examples of spiritual blindness, not to instruct his followers in the proper form to use in oaths. Jesus has told them that oaths are unnecessary and to be avoided (5:33-37).

Jesus also told his followers that whoever says to his brother, "You fool" risks ending up in Gehenna (5:22). Yet now Jesus calls those who split hairs about oaths "blind fools" (verse 17). Does Jesus violate his own teaching? Or is Matthew responsible for using the word "fool" in expressing Jesus' message? Relations between Christian leaders and the early rabbis were tense, and it is easy to imagine that there was name calling.

4: Woe to Those with Misplaced Priorities

23 **"Woe to you, scribes and Pharisees, you hypocrites. You pay tithes of mint and dill and cummin, and have neglected the weightier things of the law: judgment and mercy and fidelity. [But] these you should have done, without neglecting the others. 24 Blind guides, who strain out the gnat and swallow the camel!"**

> Gospel parallels: Luke 11:42
> OT:Micah 6:8

23 **Woe to you, scribes and Pharisees, you hypocrites. You pay tithes of mint and dill and cummin.** The law of Moses required farmers to give **tithes,** that is, one-tenth, of their harvests for the support of Levites and priests (Num 18:21-32); grain and wine are mentioned (Num 18:26-27). Pharisees, who stressed tithing (see Luke 18:11-12), applied the law to herbs grown as seasonings: **mint and dill and cummin.** In contrast to such scrupulosity about observing the law in minute matters, Jesus accuses the scribes and Pharisees of having **neglected the weightier things of the law: judgment and mercy and fidelity.** The word for **judgment** can mean "justice," which is its connotation here. Jesus has twice quoted Hosea to proclaim that God wants **mercy** (9:13; 12:7; Hosea 6:6), so it is no surprise that Jesus highlights the need for mercy. **Fidelity** has broad application but here seems to mean fidelity to God. Justice, heartfelt mercy, and loyalty to God are **the weightier things of the law,** the most important of its demands. Jesus echoes a prophecy of Micah in which God requires "only to do the right and to love goodness, / and to walk humbly with your God" (Micah 6:8; the word translated "goodness" in Micah's prophecy can also be translated "mercy"). **These you should have done, without neglecting the others.** Jesus does not say that tithing garden herbs is wrong but condemns concern about small matters while ignoring what is more important. Jesus emphasizes the basics: love of God and neighbor (22:37-40), justice, mercy, faithfulness. To tithe herbs but neglect **the weightier things of the law** is playacting at religion. Jesus calls those who do so **hypocrites.**

For reflection: Have I made love, justice, mercy, and fidelity to God my top priorities?

24 Jesus uses a vivid image to drive home his point, **Blind guides, who strain out the gnat and swallow the camel!** Storage jars for wine and other liquids did not have lids secure enough to keep out insects. The contents of a jar could be poured through a cloth to **strain out** bugs that had gotten into the jar. Most flying and crawling insects were unclean, and consuming them was forbidden (Lev 11:20-23, 41; Deut 14:19-20). Those whom Jesus laments **strain out the gnat** but **swallow the camel.** Camels were the largest animals in Palestine, classified by the law as unclean and not to be eaten (Lev 11:4; Deut 14:7). While the law had camel steaks in mind, Jesus' image is of swallowing a whole camel after filtering out a single tiny gnat. It is a striking image for ignoring what is important while focusing on trivia.

For reflection: What trivial concerns distract me from doing what is truly important?

5: Woe to Those Concerned Only With Appearances
25 **"Woe to you, scribes and Pharisees, you hypocrites. You cleanse the outside of cup and dish, but inside they are full of plunder and self-indulgence.** 26 **Blind Pharisee, cleanse first the inside of the cup, so that the outside also may be clean."**
Gospel parallels: Luke 11:39-41
NT: Matt 15:7-8, 18-20

25 **Woe to you, scribes and Pharisees, you hypocrites. You cleanse the outside of cup and dish** and by implication not the inside. Jesus' audience might have wondered whether he was speaking about dishwashing in general or about the Pharisees' traditions for ritually purifying dishes (see Mark 7:4). In either case, cleansing only the exterior is unsatisfactory. **But inside they are full of plunder and self-indulgence:** we could understand dishes and cups being dirty inside but how can they be **full of plunder and self-indulgence?** Jesus' statement is cryptic; he has a fondness for cryptic sayings (15:11; 16:4, 6; 22:14, 21) and vivid comparisons (19:24; 23:24). Jesus uses a **cup** and a **dish** washed only on the outside as a comparison for the scribes and Pharisees. They may appear clean but are filthy inside, **full of plunder and self-indulgence.** The word **plunder** refers to stolen goods and by extension means "greed"; **self-indulgence** is the opposite of self-control. Jesus accuses the scribes and Pharisees of indulging themselves at the expense of others, even though they take pains to appear to be upright. Jesus provides no specifics or evidence for his charge, but it is in line with his earlier calling scribes and Pharisees **hypocrites** because, while they honor God with their lips, their hearts are far from him (15:1, 7-8). It is what is in one's heart that counts (see 15:18-20), not the show one puts on for others. Jesus has used almsgiving, prayer, and fasting as examples of religious practices that can be done for show (6:1-2, 5, 16).

26 **Blind Pharisee, cleanse first the inside of the cup, so that the outside also may be clean.** In context, cleansing **the inside of the cup** means purging oneself of greed and self-indulgence. If one is clean on the inside, one will be entirely clean—the likely meaning of Jesus' saying, **so that the outside also may be clean.** Those who are truly good do not need to put on a show; their goodness will show through.

> *For reflection: Do I need to clean out any greed or self-indulgence from within myself?*

6: Woe to Those Who Are Lawless

27 "**Woe to you, scribes and Pharisees, you hypocrites. You are like whitewashed tombs, which appear beautiful on the outside, but inside are full of dead men's bones and every kind of filth.** 28 Even so, on the

outside you appear righteous, but inside you are filled with hypocrisy and evildoing."

> Gospel parallels: Luke 11:44
> OT:Num 19:11-16
> NT:Matt 7:21-23; 15:1-9

27 Jesus' sixth woe addresses the same condition condemned in the fifth woe but with more jarring imagery. **Woe to you, scribes and Pharisees, you hypocrites. You are like whitewashed tombs.** Touching a corpse or human bones made one ritually unclean, as did touching a grave (Num 19:11-13, 16). Those without the means to afford elaborate tombs were buried in simple graves dug in the ground. Anyone inadvertently walking on such a grave would be made ritually impure. Maintaining ritual purity in order to take part in Passover celebrations was especially important, so in the spring, **tombs** or graves were **whitewashed** to provide a visual warning, Don't touch! Whitewash, made from lime, was also used to paint walls (see Acts 23:3) to beautify them. Graves whitewashed as a warning may **appear beautiful on the outside, but inside are full of dead men's**

COMMENT: INTERPRETING MATTHEW 23 Chapter 23 of Matthew's gospel contains harsh charges seemingly out of keeping with a noncontentious Jesus who said he was meek and humble of heart, who forbade abusive speech, and who taught love of enemies (5:22, 44; 11:29; 12:19-20). Some factors to keep in mind: (1) Pharisees were a renewal movement whose goal was implementing God's laws in daily life—a laudable aim. Jesus had serious disagreements with Pharisees but was closer in his views to the Pharisees than he was to any other first-century Jewish group that we know of. (2) In first-century Mediterranean cultures, disagreements were often expressed in terms that we find harsh today. Charges such as hypocrisy were hurled at opponents to discredit them (see Rom 2:21-24). (3) Matthew wrote chapter 23 of his gospel not simply to recount conflicts at the time of Jesus but to address conflicts of his own day. This chapter reflects a heated debate going on among Jews, with Jewish Christians on one side and the early rabbis on the other. Chapter 23 reassures Jewish Christians they have chosen the right side. It also instructs them how they are not to behave. (4) Hypocrisy is a human rather than a specifically religious failing. Despite "pharisaical" becoming an adjective for hypocrisy, there is nothing in the teachings of the Pharisees and early rabbis that made them more susceptible to hypocrisy than anyone else, including disciples of Jesus. One best reads chapter 23 with an eye on one's own failings rather than on the failings of others, ancient or modern.

bones and every kind of filth. Tombs, however decorated they might be, are still tombs, **full of dead men's bones** and a source of ritual impurity. That tombs contain **every kind of filth** can refer to decaying corpses: "When a man dies, he inherits corruption; / worms and gnats and maggots" (Sirach 10:11). **Filth** also has the connotation of ritual uncleanness. Jesus' denunciation of the scribes and Pharisees is harsh: **You are like whitewashed tombs,** full of filth.

Burial practices: See page 652

28 **On the outside you appear righteous** to people, **but inside you are filled with hypocrisy and evildoing.** Being **righteous** means doing God's will. The word translated **evildoing** literally means "lawlessness." Scribes and Pharisees may claim they are following the law of Moses, but their traditions subvert the law (15:1-9). The disconnect between appearing to be **righteous** and law-abiding while really being lawless is **hypocrisy.**

Matthew's first readers would apply Jesus' words to the early rabbis; but the word **evildoing** is a barb that hooks both Matthew's first readers and his readers today. At the judgment, Jesus will say to those who call upon him as Lord but did not do his Father's will, "Depart from me, you evildoers" (7:21-23; see 13:41). Those who profess to be Jesus' disciples but do not live according to his teachings are no less guilty of **hypocrisy** than those whom Jesus lamented as whitewashed tombs.

For reflection: Do I whitewash any of my own conduct?

7: Woe to Those Who Persecute God's Messengers

²⁹ "Woe to you, scribes and Pharisees, you hypocrites. You build the tombs of the prophets and adorn the memorials of the righteous, ³⁰ and you say, 'If we had lived in the days of our ancestors, we would not have joined them in shedding the prophets' blood.' ³¹ Thus you bear witness against yourselves that you are the children of those who murdered the prophets; ³² now fill up what your ancestors measured out! ³³ You serpents, you brood of vipers, how can you flee from the judgment of Gehenna? ³⁴ Therefore, behold, I send to you prophets and wise men and scribes; some of them you will kill and crucify, some of them you will scourge in your synagogues and pursue from town to town, ³⁵ so that there may come upon you all the righteous blood shed upon earth, from the righteous blood of Abel to the blood of Zechariah,

the son of Barachiah, whom you murdered between the sanctuary and the altar. ³⁶ Amen, I say to you, all these things will come upon this generation."

> Gospel parallels: Luke 11:47-51
> OT: Gen 4:8-10; 2 Chron 24:19-22
> NT: John 16:2; Acts 7:58–8:3; 12:1-3; 22:3-5, 19-20; 26:9-11; 2 Cor 11:24; Phil 3:5-6

29 Woe to you, scribes and Pharisees, you hypocrites. You build the tombs of the prophets and adorn the memorials of the righteous. Building elaborate monuments over or at the entrance of **tombs** was a Greek custom adopted by wealthy Jews shortly before the time of Jesus. The Hasmonean dynasty of Jewish rulers built memorial tombs for themselves (1 Macc 13:27-30); remains of other tomb monuments can be seen today in the Kidron Valley opposite Jerusalem. Building memorial tombs for **prophets** and notable **righteous** figures was a way of honoring them. There is no historical record of **scribes and Pharisees** playing a significant role in erecting memorial tombs. Perhaps Jesus associates them with the practice in order to make a point that will apply to a broader group.

30 You say, "If we had lived in the days of our ancestors, we would not have joined them in shedding the prophets' blood." Old Testament texts speak of prophets being killed (1 Kings 19:10; 2 Chron 24:19-21; Jer 2:30); Jewish tradition held that Isaiah was sawn in half and Jeremiah stoned (these traditions are alluded to in Heb 11:37). Jesus addresses those who tell themselves that **if we had lived in the days of our ancestors** (literally, our "fathers"), **we would not have joined them in shedding the prophets' blood.** It is easy to distance oneself from sins committed by others and to tell oneself, "I would never do such awful things." This can be self-serving self-deception.

31 Thus you bear witness against yourselves that you are the children (literally, the "sons") **of those who murdered the prophets.** Jesus uses their claim that they would never have murdered prophets as evidence to the contrary. Jesus' argument rests on the double meaning of "son of" in Hebrew and Aramaic. "Son of" can indicate physical descent, as in James being "the son of Zebedee" (4:21). But "son of" is also an idiom for sharing the characteristics of someone or something and for belonging to a certain group. Jesus called James and John "sons of thunder," indicating that they had stormy dispositions (Mark 3:17); those who will rise on the last days are, literally, "sons of the resurrection" (Luke 20:36). The double meaning of being a "son of" is paralleled in the saying, "like father, like son." Those who say that they would never have murdered prophets acknowledge that they are sons of those who did, and Jesus takes this as an acknowledgment that they are like their fathers: **thus you bear witness against yourselves.**

32 Jesus next words are ironic, even sarcastic: **now fill up what your ancestors measured out!** The sense seems to be, finish what your fathers began, complete their work of murdering God's messengers. Old Testament prophets issued taunts that seemed to urge people along the wrong path but meant the opposite: "Come to Bethel and sin" (Amos 4:4). Jesus' words are likewise a taunt, seemingly urging murder but in reality decrying it.

33 **You serpents, you brood of vipers:** calling others the offspring of venomous snakes is the language of insult (3:7; 12:34). **How can you flee from the judgment of Gehenna?** That is, how can you escape God's **judgment** that will consign you to **Gehenna,** a place of punishment? It is a rhetorical question, for no one can avoid God's judgment. The sense of this and the previous verse is, "Go ahead and sin so that you will be punished by God." Yet is that really Jesus' message? Is the Jesus who came as a merciful physician (9:12-13) now like a doctor who advises his patients to take up smoking? We can only imagine a physician urging smoking as last-resort sarcasm to wake up a patient who is in denial about a serious health issue. Jesus' words are directed at those whose present course of action will lead to **the judgment of Gehenna** and can be interpreted as a last-resort effort to wake them up by insult and sarcasm.

Gehenna: See page 88

34 **Therefore,** so that you can finish the work of murdering God's messengers that your fathers began, **behold, I send to you prophets and wise men and scribes.** Jesus did not send **prophets** to anyone during his public ministry, but there were prophets in the early church (Acts 11:27-28; 13:1; 15:32; 21:10; 1 Cor 12:10, 28-29; 14:1, 29-33; Eph 4:11). Likewise, Jesus' disciples were not called **wise men** or **scribes** during his public ministry,

but these titles may have been designations for teachers in Matthew's church (for "scribe" see 13:52). Jewish Christian **prophets and wise men and scribes** who try to bring the message of Jesus to other Jews will meet opposition: **some of them you will kill and crucify, some of them you will scourge in your synagogues and pursue from town to town.** Acts records two followers of Jesus being killed by fellow Jews: Stephen (Acts 7:58-60) and James the son of Zebedee (Acts 12:1-3). Jews did not have the authority to **crucify**—Rome reserved that form of execution for itself (see John 18:31-32)—but they could denounce someone to Roman authorities to be crucified, as will happen to Jesus. The law of Moses permitted scourging but limited it to forty lashes (Deut 25:1-3); the practice was to administer only thirty-nine to be on the safe side. For **prophets and wise men and scribes** to be scourged in **synagogues** (see also 10:17) implies that they were Jews subject to synagogue authorities. Jesus has already warned his followers that they will be persecuted and have to flee **from town to town** (10:23).

Synagogue: See page 104

There is no historical evidence of large-scale Jewish persecution of Christians—certainly nothing like the sporadic persecutions by Roman emperors. There was rancor and sometimes violent opposition in some towns, apparently including where Matthew wrote his gospel. The best known Pharisee to persecute followers of Jesus was Paul (see Phil 3:5-6). Acts recounts Paul's saying that he persecuted Christians "to death" (Acts 22:4), that he used to "imprison and beat" them (Acts 22:19), that he voted that they be put to death (Acts 26:10). Paul was complicit in the martyrdom of Stephen (Acts 7:58-8:1). After he became a follower of Jesus, Paul suffered what he had once inflicted: "five times at the hands of the Jews I received forty lashes minus one" (2 Cor 11:24).

35 Jesus will send prophets, wise men, and scribes who will be persecuted **so that there may come upon you**—the persecutors—**all the righteous blood shed upon earth, from the righteous blood of Abel to the blood of Zechariah, the son of Barachiah, whom you murdered between the sanctuary and the altar.** The expression **righteous blood** means *innocent* blood, the blood of someone who did not deserve to die. Such blood cries out for God's vengeance (Gen 4:10; Isaiah 26:21; Ezek 24: 7-8). To speak of shed blood being **upon** or on a person means that the

person is responsible for the death of the one whose blood was shed (see Jer 26:15; 51:35; Acts 5:28). **Abel** was the first innocent person to be slain in the first book of Scripture (Gen 4:8). In the Jewish ordering of the books of Scripture, 2 Chronicles is the final book. The last death of an innocent person recounted in 2 Chronicles is that of **Zechariah,** who was stoned to death "in the court of the LORD'S temple" (2 Chron 24:21) **between the sanctuary and the altar.** Chronicles names Jehoiada as the father of this Zechariah (2 Chron 24:20, 22); the Zechariah who was **the son of Barachiah** was a different prophet (Zech 1:1, 7). There are over thirty Zechariahs in the Old Testament; Jewish tradition sometimes confused them, as seems to be the case here. Jesus' intent is to speak of **all the righteous blood shed upon earth** from the first death in the first book of Scripture to the last death in the last book. Those who fill up the measure of what their fathers began (verse 32) by persecuting God's messengers (verse 34) join in this stream of murder and take its punishment upon themselves.

36 **Amen, I say to you, all these things will come upon this generation.** By **this generation** Jesus refers to his contemporaries (11:16; 12:41-42, 45; 17:17); whatever will happen will affect more than just scribes and Pharisees. It is not clear what Jesus refers to by **all these things.** Is he referring to the persecution of those who bring God's message? Is he referring to the punishment of those who persecute them? Whatever it is, it will happen soon. Jesus has spoken on several occasions as if time is running out (10:23; 16:28), and he will go on to speak about what lies ahead (23:37–25:46). We will return to this verse later.

Jesus' final woe is the most disturbing of the seven. Jesus seems to urge his adversaries to bring God's punishment on themselves by persecuting God's messengers. Yet it is important to remember that woes function as warnings. We have interpreted Jesus' words as sarcasm meant to get through to those who were on a path to destruction. Perhaps his tactic had an effect. Some Pharisees did become followers of Jesus; Paul is the most notable but not the only example (see Acts 15:5). Some scribes likely joined the early church (see 13:52), as did a number of priests (Acts 6:7).

For reflection: What is the most sobering word Jesus has addressed to me?

ORIENTATION: *Jesus concludes his woes with a lament for those who are a path to destruction.*

Jesus' Lament over Jerusalem
37 "**Jerusalem, Jerusalem, you who kill the prophets and stone those sent to you, how many times I yearned to gather your children together, as a hen gathers her young under her wings, but you were unwilling!** **38** **Behold, your house will be abandoned, desolate.** **39** **I tell you, you will not see me again until you say, 'Blessed is he who comes in the name of the Lord.'**"

> Gospel parallels: Luke 13:34-35
> OT:Psalm 118:26; Ezek 10
> NT:Matt 10:23; 16:28; 21:9

37 Jerusalem, Jerusalem, you who kill the prophets and stone those sent to you. We can imagine Jesus speaking in a sad tone of voice, calling out, **Jerusalem, Jerusalem,** much as we might twice speak the name of a dear friend who is in dire straits: "Kathy, Kathy, how could this happen to you?" Jesus has just referred to the murder of **prophets** (23:31) and to Zechariah (23:35), whom people did **stone** (2 Chron 24:21). Those who kill God's messengers are liable to "the judgment of Gehenna" (23:33), a punishment that Jesus does not want them to bring on themselves. He tells Jerusalem, **How many times I yearned to gather your children together, as a hen gathers her young under her wings.** The **children** of a city are its inhabitants (Isaiah 66:8; Baruch 5:5; Joel 2:23). A **hen gathers her young under her wings** to protect them. Jesus uses this maternal image to express his compassion and concern for the people of Jerusalem: he **yearned** to **gather** them to himself so that he could shelter them. He says that he yearned to do so **many times.** In Matthew's gospel this is Jesus' first visit to Jerusalem, and he has been in town only two days (see 21:10, 17-18). Matthew's gospel, like each gospel, presents an abbreviated account of Jesus' public ministry (John's gospel recounts Jesus visiting Jerusalem several times).

Jerusalem: See page 440

For reflection: What message do I hear in Jesus' comparison of himself to a hen wanting to shelter her young?

But you were unwilling! The people of Jerusalem have not allowed Jesus to gather them to himself. Jesus is popular with the crowds, particularly with those who have come to Jerusalem to celebrate Passover (21:8-11, 15-16, 46; 22:33). But esteem is not the same as allegiance; many come to Jesus for healing but do not model their lives on his teachings. The religious leadership of Jerusalem rejects Jesus, and this leadership will determine the course of events.

For reflection: Am I in any way putting Jesus off and not letting him shelter me?

38 Jerusalem is on a course to destruction: **Behold, your house will be abandoned, desolate.** Jesus can be speaking of Jerusalem as the **house** of its citizens and saying that it will become **abandoned** and **desolate.** But **house** also has a more specific connotation: the Temple was the **house** of God (the Hebrew words translated as "temple" mean literally "house" and "palace"), and Jesus is now in a temple courtyard (see 21:23; 24:1). **Your house will be abandoned** implies abandoned by God. Ezekiel spoke of the presence of God leaving the Temple at the time of the Babylonian conquest of Jerusalem (Ezek 10). Jesus' words are cryptic but seem to convey that God will again abandon his Temple and leave it **desolate.** Jesus does not say how or when this will happen, but he has just referred to something happening within a generation (23:36). Jesus will go on to say explicitly that the Temple will be destroyed (24:1-2).

39 **I tell you, you will not see me again until you say, "Blessed is he who comes in the name of the Lord."** This is Jesus' last public appearance before his arrest; the remainder of his teachings will be for his disciples in private. The crowds who accompanied him into Jerusalem hailed him with the words of Psalm 118, **Blessed is he who comes in the name of the Lord** (21:9; Psalm 118:26). They **will not see** him **again** until some future time, when they will again hail his coming. Jesus has made references to his future coming (10:23; 16:28) and will speak of it shortly (24:27, 30, 37, 39, 42, 44).

Lord: See page 133

How is it that those who are unwilling to accept Jesus (verse 37) will at some future time hail his coming? One possibility: his future coming will be so awe inspiring that even those now indifferent or hostile to him will be swept up into his praise (Paul will speak of every knee bending before Jesus in his exaltation and every tongue acknowledging him—Phil 2:9-11).

We can imagine that Jesus' disciples, perplexed by his words about Jerusalem's desolation and about his coming, would want to ask him questions. They will have a chance to do so (24:3).

CHAPTER 24

When Will This Happen?
¹ Jesus left the temple area and was going away, when his disciples approached him to point out the temple buildings. ² He said to them in reply, "You see all these things, do you not? Amen, I say to you, there will not be left here a stone upon another stone that will not be thrown down."
³ As he was sitting on the Mount of Olives, the disciples approached him privately and said, "Tell us, when will this happen, and what sign will there be of your coming, and of the end of the age?"
Gospel parallels: Mark 13:14; Luke 21:5-7
NT: Matt 10:23; 12:32; 13:39-40, 49; 16:27-28; 19:28; 23:39

1 **Jesus left the temple area:** Jesus has been in the Temple precincts, engaged in disputes with religious leaders (21:23–23:39). Now he leaves, apparently making his way back toward Bethany, where he will stay the night (see 21:17; 26:6). The road from Jerusalem to Bethany goes over the Mount of Olives. He **was going away when his disciples approached him to point out the temple buildings.** The western slope of the Mount of Olives provides a panoramic view of Jerusalem and the Temple lying below. Herod the Great had expanded the Temple complex and ringed it with colonnaded halls, making it worthy of being listed as a wonder of the ancient world. The **disciples** apparently found the sight very impressive and wanted to **point out the temple buildings** to Jesus, much as tourists visiting the Grand Canyon might point out the view to one another.

Temple: See page 442
Disciple: See page 66

2 When Jesus looks at the Temple buildings, he sees not only what they are but what they will become. **He said to them in reply, "You see all these things, do you not? Amen, I say to you, there will not be left here a stone upon another stone that will not be thrown down."** Jesus solemnly assures his disciples—Amen, I say to you—that the Temple buildings will be so completely demolished that there **will not be left here a stone upon another stone.** Jesus foreshadowed the destruction of the Temple and the end of its sacrificial worship by his disruption of commerce

in the Temple courtyards (21:12-13), and he alluded to the Temple as a house that would be abandoned and desolate (23:38). Now he clearly states that the Temple will be destroyed. His prediction is shocking. The Temple was not simply Herod's architectural marvel but the place of God's special presence on earth and the only place where Jews could offer sacrificial worship. The destruction of the first Temple and of Jerusalem in 586 B.C. had been a shattering trauma for God's people (see the book of Lamentations). It is to happen again.

3 **As he was sitting on the Mount of Olives, the disciples approached him privately.** Matthew's account echoes his earlier account of Jesus going up another mountain and sitting down to instruct his disciples and the crowds (5:1-2). Jesus will again teach (24:4–25:46), but this time his teaching will be to his disciples, **privately.** The time for his public teaching and healing is over (see 23:39); in a few days he will be put to death (26:1-2). His last teachings will be for his disciples, instructing them in how to behave in the years ahead.

BACKGROUND: JEWISH EXPECTATIONS AT THE TIME OF JESUS Jews were ruled by Rome or by Rome's client kings, and their taxes were burdensome. The high priest served at the pleasure of Roman authority. Devout Jews revered the Temple, but many had low regard for those who controlled it. The situation Jews found themselves in fell far short of what God had seemingly promised his people through prophecy: rule by a descendant of David, an era of peace and prosperity, God manifestly dwelling in his Temple in Jerusalem, Gentiles either turning to the God of Israel or being subject to the rule of Israel, and God's Spirit being poured out. Any Jew who took these prophecies seriously had to be struck by the disparity between how things were and how prophecies promised they would be. Hopes and expectations were fanned by various nonbiblical writings in the two centuries before Jesus. These writings spoke of God acting soon to set things right. Different Jewish groups envisioned different scenarios for what God would do. Some expected God to act directly; some expected God to act through one or more messiahs. Some foresaw the conversion of Gentiles to allegiance to the God of Israel; others foresaw their destruction. Some thought the end of the present age was near and that God's final triumph over evil was not far off. While there was no agreement over how God would bring an end to the unsatisfactory situation in which God's people found themselves, many shared the expectation that God would do something about it. *Related topics: The age to come (page 250), Kingdom of heaven (page 266), Messiah, Christ (page 349), Nonbiblical writings (page 198).*

After hearing Jesus' prediction of the destruction of the Temple, his disciples have some questions. They ask, **Tell us, when will this**—the destruction of the Temple—**happen?** They do not ask how or why the Temple will be demolished but only **when.** They ask, **What sign will there be of your coming, and of the end of the age?** Jesus has referred to his future **coming** (10:23; 16:27-28; 23:39); he has spoken of **the end of the age** (13:39-40, 49) and of the age to come or the new age (12:32; 19:28). The disciples associate Jesus' coming with the end of the age and want to know **what sign will there be** of its happening. They ask their question against a backdrop of Jewish expectations that God was going to do something to rescue his people from their sorry condition, perhaps by bringing this age to an end. They want to be able to recognize the **sign** that it is about to happen.

The age to come: See page 250

For reflection: How strong is my curiosity about God's timetables?

ORIENTATION: *Although the disciples want to know when the Temple will be destroyed and what sign will announce Jesus' coming at the end of the age (24:3), Jesus' lengthy response indicates that it is more important for them to know what their attitudes and actions should be as they await these events (24:4–25:46).*

Do Not Be Deceived or Alarmed; Just Persevere
4 Jesus said to them in reply, "See that no one deceives you. **5** For many will come in my name, saying, 'I am the Messiah,' and they will deceive many. **6** You will hear of wars and reports of wars; see that you are not alarmed, for these things must happen, but it will not yet be the end. **7** Nation will rise against nation, and kingdom against kingdom; there will be famines and earthquakes from place to place. **8** All these are the beginning of the labor pains. **9** Then they will hand you over to persecution, and they will kill you. You will be hated by all nations because of my name. **10** And then many will be led into sin; they will betray and hate one another. **11** Many false prophets will arise and deceive many; **12** and because of the increase of evildoing, the love of many will grow cold. **13** But the one who perseveres to the end will be saved. **14** And this gospel of the kingdom will be preached throughout the world as a witness to all nations, and then the end will come."

Gospel parallels: Mark 13:5-8, 10, 13; Luke 21:8-11, 17, 19
NT: Matt 5:10-12, 44; 7:15, 21-23; 10:21-22; 13:20-21, 24-30, 36-43,
47-50; John 15:18-21

4 **Jesus said to them in reply, "See that no one deceives you."** Every human is susceptible to deception, perhaps especially those who are eager to know what lies in the future. Jesus exhorts his disciples to be on their guard lest they be deceived.

5 **For many will come in my name, saying, "I am the Messiah."** There was no single understanding of who the **Messiah** would be or what he would do, and Jesus may be referring to those who will claim some sort of messianic credentials (several such figures might be mentioned in Acts 5:36-37 and 21:38). Coming **in my name** could mean purporting to fulfill his role. Such pretenders **will deceive many.** Those who are eager to rally behind leaders claiming divine credentials make themselves vulnerable to deception. Jesus' disciples are to take care that they are not deceived by such claims.

Messiah, Christ: See page 349

6 **You will hear of wars and reports of wars,** of actual wars and of rumored wars; **see that you are not alarmed** by what you hear. **For these things must happen, but it will not yet be the end.** That wars **must happen** can mean that wars are inevitable as long as humans harbor hatred and greed (see James 4:1-2). But it probably carries the deeper meaning that all human history, even including wars, is in God's hands (the book of Revelation uses the same expression for what **must happen**—Rev 1:1; 4:1; 22:6—to refer to the unfolding of God's plans). Despite wars, **it will not yet be the end** of the age. There were popular Jewish expectations, based on prophecies (Dan 7:21-22; Zech 14:3-5), that there will be wars as this age comes to an end. The disciples want to know what sign will indicate the end of this age (24:3); Jesus tells them that wars will occur but are not a sign of the end.

The age to come: See page 250

7 Jesus repeats that wars are to be expected and expands the list of non-signs: **Nation will rise against nation, and kingdom against kingdom; there will be famines and earthquakes from place to place.** Writings from the time of Jesus that claimed to be revelations of what lay ahead viewed disasters such as wars, famines, and earthquakes as signs of the end. Matthew's first readers would have experienced or heard of such disasters. There was a Jewish rebellion against Roman rule in A.D. 66-70, a severe famine in A.D. 46-48 (see Acts 11:28), and earthquakes rocked Antioch in A.D. 37 and 42. But were these signs that the end was at hand?

8 **All these are the beginning of the labor pains.** Wars, famines, and earthquakes belong to a period of suffering before the end of the age. That **all these** disasters are but **the beginning of the labor pains** means that more pains will follow. No disaster or set of disasters can be taken as a sign of the end; they are simply part of life in this age. Even though writings that claim to be revelations of the end consider them signs, Jesus' disciples should not be deceived into thinking they are signs.

Despite Jesus' admonition not to be alarmed by wars (verse 6), we find wars and natural disasters deeply disturbing. For us they are not signs of the end but puzzles of the present: we cannot understand how a loving God allows the suffering and death inflicted by a genocidal war or a massive earthquake or a catastrophic hurricane. We believe that everything is

---

BACKGROUND: REVELATIONS OF THE END A number of books written in the centuries around the time of Jesus employed a distinctive type of writing to convey a vision of God triumphing over evil. Two of these books are Daniel in the Old Testament and Revelation in the New Testament; there were similar writings that were not accepted as inspired Scripture. The Book of Revelation's Greek title is *Apokalypsis,* a word that means "an uncovering" or "a revelation." These writings, often called apocalyptic, unveil what is hidden, characteristically employing symbols and imagery to do so. This type of writing grew out of Old Testament prophecies that described a future that would be quite different from the present (Isaiah 24–27; 34–35; 56–66; Ezek 38–39; Joel 3–4; Zech 9–14; Mal 3). Apocalyptic writings often contain an account of a revelation given to a human being by an angel, telling what is going to happen in the future by means of symbolic accounts of events on earth and in heaven. This type of writing flowered in difficult times, when evil seemed to be winning out and the only hope was for God's intervention. Different books described different futures, but they commonly spoke of God judging and destroying the wicked, transforming this world, and beginning a new age. Those who remained faithful to God would be rewarded in an afterlife. *Related topics: The age to come (page 250), Jewish expectations at the time of Jesus (page 515), Nonbiblical writings (page 198).*

in the hands of God and wonder why these disasters occur. Jesus does not answer our "Why?" but he does provide a note of hope: if the sufferings of the present time are labor pains, then we can look forward to the birth of something that will more than make up for the pain (see John 16:21). Paul writes, "I consider that the sufferings of the present time are as nothing compared with the glory to be revealed for us" (Rom 8:18).

For reflection: What meaning and mystery do I find in human suffering? How does my hope for life in eternity sustain me through present trials?

9 **Then,** while all this is going on, **they will hand you over to persecution, and they will kill you.** It is left unspecified who **they** are who will hand over Jesus' disciples to persecution. The word translated **persecution** can mean "tribulation" or "affliction." Jewish writings about the end of this age characterized it as a time of tribulation (see Dan 12:1). Disciples of Jesus will suffer tribulation—will be persecuted—because they are his disciples.

For reflection: What affliction or difficulty have I endured because I am a disciple of Jesus? Have I gotten off light or had more than my share?

They will kill you: Jesus has warned that some would lose their lives because they were his disciples (10:21; 23:34). Matthew's first readers were probably aware of the martyrdoms of Stephen (Acts 7:58-60) and James the son of Zebedee (Acts 12:1-2), and almost certainly had heard that many Christians had died in Rome during Nero's persecution that began in A.D. 64. **You will be hated by all nations because of my name.** To be hated **because of my name** means to be hated because one is Jesus' disciple and is identified with him. Jesus issued the same warning previously (10:22; see also John 15:18-21). Tacitus, a late first-century Roman historian, portrayed Christians as being so widely despised that they made an easy target for Nero's persecution.

Jesus taught how his followers should respond to persecution. They were to consider themselves fortunate and blessed: "Blessed are you when they insult you and persecute you and utter every kind of evil against you [falsely] because of me. Rejoice and be glad, for your reward will be great in heaven" (5:11-12). He told his disciples, "Love your enemies, and pray for those who persecute you" (5:44). Persecution should elicit rejoicing; persecutors must be loved.

For reflection: What is my response to affliction? To those who afflict me?

10 **And then many will be led into sin.** The pressure that persecution and hatred will put on the community of Jesus' followers will take its toll. **Many**—an indeterminate number—**will be led into sin:** the Greek word means to be scandalized or tripped up; they will fall away because of persecution. Jesus warned that some who embrace his message with joy will fall away when they have to endure affliction and persecution (13:20-21). Not only will some of his followers fall away, **they will betray and hate one another.** Christians will **betray** fellow Christians to the authorities during times of persecution, bringing suffering onto others so that they can escape suffering themselves. Love endures suffering to preserve others from suffering; **hate** passes on suffering to others. This will happen even within families, tearing them apart: "Brother will hand over brother to death, and the father his child; children will rise up against parents and have them put to death" (10:21).

11 Compounding the persecutions and betrayals will be Christian leaders who lead astray: **Many false prophets will arise and deceive many.** There will be **prophets** in the early church, speaking on behalf of Jesus (23:34). Some who claim to speak on his behalf will be **false prophets** whose message is not from him. Jesus warned, "Beware of false prophets, who come to you in sheep's clothing, but underneath are ravenous wolves" (7:15). On the day of judgment Jesus will tell some who prophesied in his name, "I never knew you. Depart from me, you evildoers" (7:23). Jesus' earlier warning about false messiahs applies as well to false prophets: "See that no one deceives you" (verse 4). Despite Jesus' warning, false prophets will **deceive many,** leading them away from the truth and away from doing God's will.

12 **And because of the increase of evildoing**—literally, of "lawlessness"—**the love of many will grow cold.** Jesus might be referring to **evildoing** in the surrounding society, but he is more likely speaking of evildoing, or lawlessness, within the community of his followers. As a result of defections, betrayal, and false prophecy, there will be an increase of lawlessness, of revolting against God's will, and **the love of many will grow cold.** Jesus links love of God and love of neighbor (22:37-39) and includes both here when he speaks of **love.** Love is the fulfillment of God's law (22:40); lawlessness extinguishes love.

Jesus' description of what lies ahead for his followers is sobering. The world around them will be in turmoil (verses 6-8); they will be hated, persecuted, even killed (verse 9). Even more disheartening, the community of his followers will be racked by desertion, betrayal, hatred, deception, lawlessness, and love-gone-cold (verses 10-12). Jesus has alluded to the mixed condition that will persist in the community of his followers, telling parables that compared the reign of God on earth to a field with weeds as well as wheat (13:24-30, 36-43) and to a fishing net that collects the bad as well as the good (13:47-50). His disciples want to know what sign will announce the end of the age; Jesus' focus is on their coming to grips with the difficulties of this age. He does not want them to be scandalized and fall away.

For reflection: Have I been scandalized by the failings of fellow Christians? How do I respond to their failings?

13 **But the one who perseveres to the end will be saved.** The expression **to the end** means to the end of the age but can have the secondary meaning of to the end of one's life. **Will be saved** means saved by God—brought into his kingdom and given eternal life (see 19:16-17, 23-25). The one who **perseveres** in following the way of Jesus despite turmoil and affliction and betrayal will be given eternal life. Those who endure through the labor pains of the present (verse 8) will "shine like the sun in the kingdom of their Father" (13:43).

For reflection: What hope and encouragement does Jesus' promise give me?

14 Even though Jesus' focus is on what his disciples are to do in the present age rather than on when it will end, he does give them one assurance about the end. **And this gospel of the kingdom will be preached throughout the world as a witness to all nations, and then the end will come.** The **gospel** of the kingdom is the good news that God is establishing his reign through Jesus (see 4:17; 12:28). Jesus' final charge to his disciples will be to "make disciples of all nations, . . . teaching them to observe all that I have commanded you" (28:19-20). In fulfillment of this command, the message of Jesus **will be preached throughout the world as a witness to all nations.** This will take some time—Jesus does not say how long—and only **then the end will come.** God will not bring this age

521

to an end until people throughout the world have had a chance to hear and respond to the **gospel.**

Gospel: See page 211
Kingdom of heaven: See page 266

For reflection: What is my role in making known the good news of the kingdom? How am I fulfilling my role?

The Time to Flee
15 "When you see the desolating abomination spoken of through Daniel the prophet standing in the holy place (let the reader understand), **16** then those in Judea must flee to the mountains, **17** a person on the housetop must not go down to get things out of his house, **18** a person in the field must not return to get his cloak. **19** Woe to pregnant women and nursing mothers in those days. **20** Pray that your flight not be in winter or on the sabbath, **21** for at that time there will be great tribulation, such as has not been since the beginning of the world until now, nor ever will be. **22** And if those days had not been shortened, no one would be saved; but for the sake of the elect they will be shortened."

Gospel parallels: Mark 13:14-20; Luke 21:20-23
OT:1 Macc 1:54-61; Dan 9:27; 11:31; 12:1, 11; Joel 2:2
NT:Matt 24:1-3

15 The disciples asked Jesus when the Temple would be destroyed (24:1-3). Jesus does not give them a date but speaks cryptically about something happening in or to the Temple. **When you see the desolating abomination spoken of through Daniel the prophet standing in the holy place:** a **desolating abomination** is something loathsome and appalling. The expression comes from the book of **Daniel the prophet** (Dan 9:27; 11:31; 12:11), where it refers to a pagan altar that the Syrian ruler Antiochus IV Epiphanes erected over the altar of sacrifice in the Temple as part of his program to suppress Jewish religious practices in 168–167 B.C. (see 1 Macc 1:54-61). Jesus borrows the expression to convey that something horrifying will occur **in the holy place,** a term for the Temple (2 Macc 8:17; Acts 6:13; see also 21:28). Jesus does not say what **the desolating abomination** will be. Jesus' disciples may have understood it as something awful that would happen to the Temple, comparable to its desecration by Antiochus IV Epiphanes. Matthew has an aside for his audience:

(Let the reader understand). Matthew's readers would have interpreted **the desolating abomination** to be the destruction of the Temple during the Roman conquest of Jerusalem in A.D. 70.

> *Armed forces shall move at his command and defile the sanctu-*
> *ary stronghold, abolishing the daily sacrifice and setting up the*
> *horrible abomination.*
>
> *Daniel 11:31*

16 While Jesus does not say what the desolating abomination will be, he speaks as if it will be obvious when it happens. When it does happen, **then those in Judea must flee to the mountains.** In times of war, **mountains** or hills provided places of refuge (1 Sam 26:1; 1 Macc 2:28); during the second Jewish revolt against Rome (A.D. 132–135), Jewish fighters took refuge in hillside caves near the Dead Sea. When a horrifying abomination occurs, then those in Jerusalem and in the surrounding region of **Judea** should **flee.** Several ancient sources speak of Christians who lived in Jerusalem at the time of the Jewish revolt of A.D. 66–70 leaving the city to take refuge in Pella, one of the cities of the Decapolis east of the Jordan River.

Judea: See page 397

17 Flight must be without delay: **a person on the housetop must not go down to get things out of his house.** Houses had flat roofs that were used for sleeping on hot nights, for drying crops, and other activities (Joshua 2:6; 1 Sam 9:25-26; Acts 10:9). Roofs were accessible by a ladder or outside stairway. Those who are on a roof when the horrifying event occurs should get down quickly and run for their lives, not taking time **to get things out of the house.** There will be no time to grab belongings.

18 **A person in the field must not return to get his cloak.** A cloak was an outer garment that was also used as a cover at night (see Exod 22:25-26). A cloak was an encumbrance during manual labor, so a farm worker would take off his cloak or leave it at home. **A person** working in a **field** when the horrible event occurs **must not return to get his cloak** from wherever he had left it. It will be urgent to flee immediately, with no side trips.

Clothing: See page 95

For reflection: How easy do I find it to act quickly and decisively?

523

19 **Woe to pregnant women and nursing mothers in those days.** Jesus'
woe laments those who will find it difficult to flee quickly. Jesus could
have mentioned the lame and arthritic as examples of those who cannot
sprint away from danger. Perhaps he chose **pregnant women and nursing mothers** because each of them will be bearing not one life but two
as they flee.

Woes: See page 499

20 **Pray that your flight not be in winter or on the sabbath.** In Palestine,
winter is the rainy season as well as the coldest time of the year. Travel
during winter can be difficult because of muddy roads and swollen
creeks. Sleeping outdoors in the hills through cold, rainy nights is bone
chilling, especially if there is no time to retrieve one's cloak before fleeing. The law of Moses restricted travel **on the sabbath** (Exod 16:29); the
allowable "sabbath day's journey" (Acts 1:12) was about a thousand yards
(using Num 35:5 to interpret Exod 16:29). While some Jews held that
life-threatening situations suspended Sabbath regulations (1 Macc 2:32-
41), other Jews did not allow this exception (see 2 Macc 6:11). Jesus considered human need more important than restrictive interpretations of
Sabbath rest (12:1-13). There would be some Jewish Christians in the
early church who strictly adhered to the law of Moses (Acts 15:1, 5), perhaps invoking Jesus' statement that "not the smallest letter or the smallest part of a letter will pass from the law" and his upholding even the
least of the commandments (5:18-19; 23:23-24). Such Jewish Christians
might have a crisis of conscience when faced with the necessity of fleeing
on the Sabbath.

Jesus tells his followers, **Pray that your flight** will not be in winter or
on the Sabbath; pray that you will be able to flee without extra physical or
spiritual hardship. Since Jesus' followers are to flee at the first sight of the
horrifying abomination in the Temple, such prayer asks God to arrange
the timing of the abomination so that they will be able to get away more
easily. This implies that the timing of the abomination is in God's hands.
It also implies that Jesus does not know exactly when it will occur: he
foresees that something horrifying will happen, but he does not know
whether it will be in the winter or on what day of the week. His followers
are to **pray** for their heavenly Father's provident care for them in what
will be a critical and difficult time.

*For reflection: What lesson can I learn from Jesus' instructing his follow-
ers to pray that a trial will not come upon them at a bad time? Why
might he not instead instruct them to pray that the trial would never
happen?*

21 **For at that time there will be great tribulation:** the appearance of some
horrifying abomination will signal a time of terrible suffering. The suffering will be so severe that there will have been nothing comparable to it
since the beginning of the world until now, nor ever will there be such
suffering again. Jesus echoes phrases from Daniel and Joel that predict
times of unparalleled distress. Daniel spoke of "a time unsurpassed in distress / since nations began until that time" (Dan 12:1). Joel spoke of rav-
ages whose "like has not been from of old, / nor will it be after them, /
even to the years of distant generations" (Joel 2:2). It is unclear whether
Jesus literally means that the tribulation associated with the horrible
abomination will be the greatest suffering in all of human history or
whether Jesus is simply using traditional phrases to convey that there will
be great suffering. Ancient siege warfare starved cities into submission
(see Deut 28:49-57 for the horrors of sieges). The first-century Jewish historian Josephus describes the people within Jerusalem suffering appall-
ingly from starvation, infighting, and anarchy during the Roman siege in
A.D. 70. Criminals broke into houses to steal food and tortured men and
women to make them turn over hidden provisions. Josephus characterizes
their suffering as the greatest ever endured.

22 **And if those days had not been shortened, no one would be saved; but
for the sake of the elect they will be shortened.** The **elect** are those chosen by God (22:14; see also Deut 7:6-8; Psalm 105:6; Isaiah 43:20; 65:9).
No one would be saved has the sense, no human being would survive
alive. The timetable for the great tribulation is in the hands of God, and
if the length of the tribulation **had not been shortened** by God, no one
would survive it. God will shorten the tribulation **for the sake of the
elect.** If Jesus is referring to events connected with the destruction of
Jerusalem in A.D. 70, then his words might mean that some of God's chosen will be trapped in the city during the siege, and that God will shorten
the siege so that they might survive. However, Jesus' words might better
apply to the time of tribulation expected at the end of this age. Jesus goes
on to speak of what will happen before the end (24:23-31).

ORIENTATION: *Jesus again warns against being misled by false claims (24:23-26;*
see also 24:4-5, 11) before speaking about his coming (24:27-31).

The Coming of the Son of Man

[23] "If anyone says to you then, 'Look, here is the Messiah!' or, 'There he is!' do not believe it. [24] False messiahs and false prophets will arise, and they will perform signs and wonders so great as to deceive, if that were possible, even the elect. [25] Behold, I have told it to you before-hand. [26] So if they say to you, 'He is in the desert,' do not go out there; if they say, 'He is in the inner rooms,' do not believe it. [27] For just as lightning comes from the east and is seen as far as the west, so will the coming of the Son of Man be. [28] Wherever the corpse is, there the vultures will gather.

[29] "Immediately after the tribulation of those days,

the sun will be darkened,
    and the moon will not give its light,
and the stars will fall from the sky,
    and the powers of the heavens will
      be shaken.

[30] And then the sign of the Son of Man will appear in heaven, and all the tribes of the earth will mourn, and they will see the Son of Man coming upon the clouds of heaven with power and great glory. [31] And he will send out his angels with a trumpet blast, and they will gather his elect from the four winds, from one end of the heavens to the other."

    Gospel parallels: Mark 13:21-27; Luke 17:23-24, 37
    OT:Isaiah 13:9-10; Dan 7:13-14
    NT:Matt 7:15, 22-23; 13:40-43, 49; 16:27

23 **If anyone says to you then:** Jesus returns to what his disciples may expect during the time when the gospel of the kingdom is preached throughout the world (24:14). Jesus tells his disciples that when anyone claims, **"Look, here is the Messiah!"** or, **"There he is!"** they should **not believe it.**

    Messiah, Christ: See page 349

24 **False messiahs and false prophets will arise:** Jesus has warned his disci-ples that **false messiahs** (24:5) and **false prophets** will appear (24:11; see

also 7:15), and he repeats his warning. Since Jesus has spoken about false indicators of the end of the age (24:4-8), we might surmise that the **false prophets** will claim that the end has arrived or that a false messiah is Jesus. Those making false claims may mislead many, for **they will perform signs and wonders so great as to deceive, if that were possible, even the elect.** Jesus does not explain how the false messiahs and prophets will be able to perform great signs and wonders but acknowledges that they will be able to do so (see also 7:22-23). Jesus told his disciples, "See that no one deceives you" (24:4), and his warning bears repeating, because many will be deceived (24:5), possibly even **the elect,** God's chosen ones.

We can note that Jesus refused to perform signs and wonders on demand (4:3-7; 12:38-39; 16:1-4) and tried to minimize reports of his extraordinary powers (8:4; 9:30). False messiahs and prophets will do the opposite, using whatever powers they have as credentials authenticating their claims. However, their ability to perform wonders is no guarantee of the truthfulness of what they say (see Deut 13:2-4). Jesus urges his disciples to be skeptical when wonders are used as proofs of extravagant claims.

For reflection: How do I decide if someone's teachings or claims are trustworthy?

25 Behold, I have told it to you beforehand. Jesus is warning his disciples about the tribulations and snares that lie ahead for them. They are not to be surprised when false prophets arise in the community of Jesus' followers, just as they should not be surprised when they encounter hatred and persecution, and even when some of their number defect or grow unloving (24:9-12). All these things will happen, but they are not to be taken as signs that the end is at hand. Nor are they to scandalize Jesus' followers and cause them to fall away: Jesus foresees these challenges and exhorts his followers to endure through them. "The one who perseveres to the end will be saved" (24:13).

For reflection: Do I imagine that Jesus would be surprised by anything happening in the church today?

26 So if they say to you, "He is in the desert," do not go out there; if they say, "He is in the inner rooms," do not believe it. There may have been some popular expectations, perhaps based on Hosea 2:16-17, that the

Messiah would begin his mission in the **desert** (Acts 21:38 refers to a messianic figure who led his followers into the desert). However, the **desert** might simply serve here as an image for a wide-open space in contrast to hidden **inner rooms**. Jesus' words would then have the sense, No matter where they claim the Messiah is, whether in the most public or the most private of places, **do not believe it.** Any claimed sightings of the Messiah are wrong.

27 The reason why all claims about the Messiah's whereabouts will be wrong is that his coming will be so unmistakable that there will be no opportunity for rumors. **For just as lightning comes from the east and is seen as far as the west, so will the coming of the Son of Man be.** Just as a lightning bolt arches across the sky and is visible from east to west, so the **coming of the Son of Man** will be visible to all. Jesus speaks of himself as **the Son of Man** in reference to his **coming** at the end of the age (see also 10:23; 16:27-28). The disciples asked Jesus, "What sign will there be of your coming?" (24:3) and Jesus tells them that his coming will be obvious. He will come in a manner that leaves no doubts or uncertainties, no question in anyone's mind of whether this is really Jesus or not.

Son of Man: See page 151

28 Jesus adds another comparison for his coming, this one cryptic: **Wherever the corpse is, there the vultures will gather.** Scholars have proposed different interpretations of these words; the most satisfactory is that Jesus' coming will be as evident as a **corpse** marked by the gathering of **vultures.** When his disciples saw vultures circling in the sky they knew that there was a dead or dying human or animal somewhere below. The coming of Jesus will be just as evident.

29 **Immediately after the tribulation of those days:** Jesus has been speaking about what will happen at the end of this age and the difficulties that will precede it. **Those days** echoes the way in which the Old Testament speaks of a "day of the Lord," when God will vanquish evil (see, for example, Joel 3:4-5). Some Jews interpreted Dan 12:1 ("It shall be a time unsurpassed in distress") to be an indication that the end of this age would be a time of great **tribulation.** When the difficulties of the last days have run their course, then **the sun will be darkened, / and the moon will not give its light, / and the stars will fall from the sky, / and the powers of**

the heavens will be shaken. Jesus invokes images and phrases from the prophets to convey that something momentous will take place (Isaiah 13:9-10; Joel 2:10-11; 3:3-4). Prophets used images of heavenly upheaval to indicate that when God acted on the "day of the Lord" to set things right, his actions would have cosmic consequences. **The sun will be darkened** as during a solar eclipse; **the moon will not give its light** as during a lunar eclipse; **the stars will fall from the sky** as they appear to do during a meteor shower. **The powers of the heavens will be shaken** may simply be a summary of what will happen to the sun, moon, and stars. However, **the powers of the heavens** might refer to the angels, who were popularly thought to control stars. Heavenly bodies **will be shaken** as by a cosmic earthquake, signifying that something of cosmic importance is happening.

> Lo, the day of the LORD comes,
> > cruel, with wrath and burning anger;
> To lay waste the land
> > and destroy the sinners within it!
> The stars and constellations of the heavens
> > send forth no light;
> The sun is dark when it rises,
> > and the light of the moon does not shine.
> > > > Isaiah 13:9-10

30 **And then the sign of the Son of Man will appear in heaven.** The event whose importance is so great that it must be conveyed by images of cosmic upheaval is the coming of **the Son of Man.** The **sign of** the Son of Man is sometimes interpreted to mean some sign of his coming that will appear in the heavens, perhaps a cross. But the Greek expression translated the **sign of** the Son of Man is best understood to mean the "sign that is" the Son of Man (just as "the sign of Jonah" is Jonah himself rather than a sign announcing Jonah—16:4). Accompanied by cosmic fanfare, Jesus will appear, like lightning flashing across the sky.

Jesus' disciples asked, "What sign will there be of your coming?" (24:3). The answer is that there will be no sign save his coming itself. The shaking of the heavens, even if interpreted literally, accompanies the coming of Jesus rather than preceding it as a sign. Jesus response to the disciples' question is, "You will know it when it happens."

At the appearance of the Son of Man **all the tribes of the earth will mourn.** This is open to several interpretations. **The tribes of the earth** are presumably those who are not disciples of Jesus. Will they **mourn** out of fear for themselves at his coming? Out of repentance? Out of remorse for not having been his followers? The reason for their mourning is uncertain, but it is clear that Jesus' coming will have an impact on **all the tribes of the earth,** the entire human race.

For reflection: What would be my first reaction if Jesus were to suddenly appear?

Jesus continues to speak of his coming, echoing what is written in the book of Daniel: **and they will see the Son of Man coming upon the clouds of heaven with power and great glory.** Daniel in a vision sees a heavenly figure who is "like a son of man," meaning like a human being. This heavenly figure comes on the clouds of heaven into the presence of God and is given everlasting dominion and glory. Jesus speaks of himself coming as **the Son of Man,** endowed with **power and great glory.** While in Daniel's vision, the one like a son of man comes into the presence of God, Jesus speaks of his coming to earth, where his presence will be experienced

---

BACKGROUND: COSMIC SIGNS For us, the sun turning dark and stars colliding with the earth would mean the end of our world. These cosmic events had a different significance at the time of Jesus. The universe was thought of as the earth and the dome of the sky above it (Gen 1:6-8), with sun, moon, and stars set in this dome (Gen 1:14-18). God's dwelling was imagined to be in the uppermost part of the sky (Gen 28:12; Deut 26:15; 1 Kings 8:30; 2 Macc 3:39—the Hebrew and Greek words for sky also mean "heaven"), although the heavens could not contain him (1 Kings 8:27). Stars looked small—small enough to fall from the sky as meteorites. Eclipses of the sun were known to occur. Eclipses of the moon can give it a deep red or copper hue, due to the refraction of its light by the earth's atmosphere; Joel spoke of the sun being "turned to darkness, / and the moon to blood" (Joel 3:4). Since these events happened in God's heavenly domain, they were taken as signs of God's action. When the prophets announced that God was going to act, as on a "day of the LORD," they sometimes invoked cosmic events as signs of God's acting (Isaiah 13:9-10; Joel 2:10-11; 3:3-4). By the time of Jesus, these cosmic signs had become a standard way of indicating that God was acting in some very significant way without meaning that the physical universe was coming to an end. *Related topic: The day of the Lord (page 48).*

by all tribes and peoples. In Daniel the heavenly figure is given dominion over all nations and peoples; Jesus does not explicitly say that he will have such dominion, but it is implied (see also 28:18). If the heavens quake at his coming in **great glory,** nothing on earth can withstand his **power.**

> As the visions during the night continued,
> I saw
>> One like a son of man coming,
>> on the clouds of heaven;
>> When he reached the Ancient One
>> and was presented before him,
>> He received dominion, glory, and kingship;
>> nations and peoples of every language
>> serve him.
>> His dominion is an everlasting dominion
>> that shall not be taken away,
>> his kingship shall not be destroyed.
>> Daniel 7:13-14

31 **And he will send out his angels with a trumpet blast:** Jesus has previously spoken of **his angels** playing a role at the end of the age, implying that he will have the authority to command angels (13:41; 16:27). A **trumpet blast** summons a gathering (Isaiah 27:13) or announces that something important is about to happen; the "day of the Lord," when God executed judgment, would be heralded by trumpet blasts (Joel 2:1; Zeph 1:14, 16). Jesus in his power and glory will **send out** his angels, **and they will gather his elect from the four winds, from one end of the heavens to the other.** Jesus' **elect** are his chosen ones, those who answered his call to discipleship and became members of his new family (12:49-50). They will be found everywhere in the whole earth because of the preaching of the gospel throughout the world (24:14). Jesus' angels will **gather** them **from the four winds,** from all directions. Gathering them **from one end of the heavens to the other** means from one horizon to the other. Jesus does not say here what will happen after his family is gathered; previously he promised that "the righteous will shine like the sun in the kingdom of their Father" (13:43).

Angels: See page 33

531

In the creed, we profess of Jesus, "He will come in glory to judge the living and the dead, and his kingdom will have no end." Jesus uses imagery like the sun being darkened and his coming on a cloud to convey what is beyond our imagining: the risen and glorified Jesus will manifest his presence and inaugurate the new age of God's complete reign. Words cannot express its full reality; we must make do with images for "what eye has not seen, and ear has not heard, / and what has not entered the human heart, / what God has prepared for those who love him" (1 Cor 2:9).

For reflection: What does Jesus' portrayal of his coming convey to me? What hope does it give me?

ORIENTATION: *Jesus tells a series of parables pertaining to the time before his coming (24:32–25:30).*

The Parable of the Fig Tree

32 "Learn a lesson from the fig tree. When its branch becomes tender and sprouts leaves, you know that summer is near. **33** In the same way, when you see all these things, know that he is near, at the gates. **34** Amen, I say to you, this generation will not pass away until all these things have taken place. **35** Heaven and earth will pass away, but my words will not pass away.

36 "But of that day and hour no one knows, neither the angels of heaven, nor the Son, but the Father alone."

Gospel parallels: Mark 13:28-32; Luke 21:29-33
NT: Matt 10:23; 16:28

32 **Learn a lesson from the fig tree.** The word translated **lesson** is literally "parable"; Jesus uses a **fig tree** as a comparison. Fig trees are common in Palestine; there were likely some on the Mount of Olives near where Jesus was instructing his disciples (24:3). Unlike most trees that grow in Palestine, fig trees drop their leaves during the winter. Jesus reminds his disciples that **when its branch becomes tender and sprouts leaves,** which happens in late springtime, **you know that summer is near.** A fig tree leafing out is a sign of the times (see 16:3), indicating that summer is just around the corner.

Parables: See page 262

33 **In the same way** that fig trees leafing out is a sign that summer is near, **when you see all these things, know that he is near, at the gates.** Since Jesus has been speaking of events that will occur before his coming, it is natural to interpret **all these things** as the preliminary events (24:4-26) and to understand **he is near** to refer to Jesus' coming (24:27-31). **At the gates** alludes to the gates of a city: Jesus will have reached the city limits, as it were. He tells his disciples, **when you see all these things,** as if these events will happen within their lifetimes.

34 **Amen, I say to you, this generation will not pass away** until all **these things have taken place.** This **generation** means those alive at the time of Jesus (see 11:16; 12:39, 41-42, 45; 16:4; 17:17; 23:36). Jesus solemnly assures his disciples that before this generation dies out, **all these things** that Jesus has spoken of will **have taken place.** Apparently included in **all these things** would be the destruction of the Temple (24:2) and the preaching of the gospel throughout the world (24:14), as well the various difficulties that followers of Jesus will endure.

35 Jesus' next words are a parenthetical comment that adds weight to what he has just said: **Heaven and earth will pass away, but my words will not pass away.** The heavens and the earth will wear out (Psalm 102:26-27; Isaiah 51:6; see also Matt 5:18), but Jesus' words will endure. God's word stands forever (Psalm 119:89; Isaiah 40:8); as the Son, Jesus is able to reveal the Father (11:27) and Jesus' words are the word of God.

> For reflection: Do I accept Jesus' words as God's word to me? What impact do his words have on the way I live?

36 After what Jesus has just said, his next statement comes as a shock: **But of that day and hour no one knows, neither the angels of heaven, nor the Son, but the Father alone.** The **day and hour** are the time of Jesus' coming at the end of the age. **No one knows** when that will be—not Jesus' disciples after listening to what he has just said about what lies ahead, not readers of Matthew's gospel who have taken in these words. Nor do **the angels of heaven** know when the end will be, although their heavenly status presumably gives them privileged insight into God's plans. Not even **the Son,** Jesus, knows when he will come and this age will end. Despite Jesus' knowing the Father as only **the Son** can (11:27), despite Jesus' foreseeing things that lie ahead, Jesus does not know when his Father will wrap everything up. No one knows **but the Father** and the Father **alone.** Human efforts to deduce the time of Jesus' coming are futile; the timing is known only by God.

Angels: See page 33
Son of God: See page 52

If Jesus does not know when the end will come, what are we to make of his statements that indicate that it will happen within the lifetime of some of his listeners? He said to those he was sending on mission, "Amen, I say to you, you will not finish the towns of Israel before the Son of Man comes" (10:23). He said to his disciples, "Amen, I say to you, there are some standing here who will not taste death until they see the Son of Man coming in his kingdom" (16:28). He has just spoken of the present generation not passing away "until all these things have taken place" (verse 34), and he has asserted that their taking place will indicate that "he is near, at the gates" (verse 33).

The best solution I can suggest is as follows. Jesus proclaimed that God's plan was reaching its fulfillment: "the kingdom of heaven is at hand" (4:17). He foresaw that he would be put to death and raised from the dead and would come in power and glory to establish God's reign in its fullness. It was urgent that men and women embrace what God was doing through him. He made statements about his coming that conveyed the urgency of the times. He admitted that he did not know the timetable for his coming but sometimes spoke of it as if it would occur soon.

Save for his coming, the events he spoke of happened within a generation: wars and famines, persecution and defections, false prophets and messiahs, the destruction of the Temple and the preaching of the gospel far beyond Palestine. Some New Testament writings reflect a belief that Jesus will come rather soon (Rom 13:11-12; 1 Cor 1:7-8; 4:5; 7:29, 31; Phil 1:6, 10; 4:5; Heb 10:25; James 5:8-9; 1 Pet 4:7; 1 John 2:18; Rev 22:10, 12, 20). Paul at one point apparently expected that it would be within his lifetime (1 Thess 4:15). Other New Testament writings try to temper such expectations (John 21:20-23; 2 Pet 3:3-10). It is easiest to understand the early church's expectation that Jesus would come soon if Jesus sometimes spoke of his coming soon, even though he also said that he did not know when it would happen.

Jesus' confessed ignorance of the timing of the end must be taken into account as we ponder the union of the divine and the human in him. Conceived through the Holy Spirit (1:18, 20), he is the Son of God (3:17; 17:5) and enjoys a unique relationship with God as his Father (11:27). He is empowered by the Holy Spirit (12:28) to vanquish evil, heal the sick, and raise the dead. He has foresight greater than that enjoyed by any prophet but does not know everything that is in the mind of God. He is Emmanuel, God-with-us (1:23), but in coming to be with us he "emptied himself" (Phil 2:7) and accepted the limitations of our human condition, including limited knowledge and a limited span of life on this earth. The ultimate manifestation of the humanity of Jesus is not his ignorance of when the end will be but his death on a cross. For more on the human knowledge of Jesus, see *Catechism of the Catholic Church* #472–474.

For reflection: What does Jesus' ignorance of the timing of the end reveal to me about Jesus?

Parables of the Unforeseen

37 "For as it was in the days of Noah, so it will be at the coming of the Son of Man. **38** In [those] days before the flood, they were eating and drinking, marrying and giving in marriage, up to the day that Noah entered the ark. **39** They did not know until the flood came and carried them all away. So will it be [also] at the coming of the Son of Man. **40** Two men will be out in the field; one will be taken, and one will be left. **41** Two women will be grinding at the mill; one will be taken, and one will be left. **42** Therefore, stay awake! For you do not know on which day your Lord will come. **43** Be sure of this: if the master of the house had known the hour of night when the thief was coming, he would have stayed awake and not let his house be broken into. **44** So too, you also must be prepared, for at an hour you do not expect, the Son of Man will come."

Gospel parallels: Luke 12:39-40; 17:26-27, 34-35
OT:Gen 6:11–7:23
NT:Matt 24:36

37 Jesus has just told his disciples that no one knows the time of his coming at the end of the age; he does not even know himself (24:36). He follows up with parables about the unforeseen timing of his coming. In the first, he compares his coming to what happened at the time of Noah: **For as it was in the days of Noah, so it will be at the coming of the Son of Man.**

Son of Man: See page 151

38 **In [those] days before the flood, they were eating and drinking, marrying and giving in marriage, up to the day that Noah entered the ark.** Noah was the only one to receive a weather forecast from God and instructions to build an ark (Gen 6:14-17). Everyone else went on with their lives as usual, **eating and drinking** and doing their normal activities. **Marrying and giving in marriage** describe weddings from a male point of view: men marry women and fathers give their daughters in marriage. Jesus does not portray those living at the time of Noah as engaged in sinful activities; his attention is on their going about their lives, oblivious to what was about to happen.

39 **They did not know** there was going to be a flood **until the flood came and carried them all away** without warning. **So will it be [also] at the coming of the Son of Man.** Women and men will be going about their lives as usual when Jesus comes like lightning flashing across the sky (24:27). Just as those at the time of Noah **did not know** there was a flood coming, so Jesus' coming will catch everyone unaware.

40 Jesus' next parable is very compressed and must be filled out. **Two men will be out in the field; one will be taken, and one will be left.** Two men are going about their farmwork when Jesus comes. **One will be taken** into the kingdom of God (see 13:43; 24:31). The other **one will be left** out of the kingdom, cast "into the darkness outside, where there will wailing and grinding of teeth" (22:13). The parable presumes that one deserves entry into the kingdom and the other does not. The focus of the parable is on the unforeseen coming of Jesus: two men will go to work that day, not realizing that they will not return home that night.

41 Jesus balances his parable about men at work with a parable about women at work: **Two women will be grinding at the mill; one will be taken, and one will be left.** Grinding grain and baking bread were done by women. Archaeological finds of ancient millstones indicate that we should envision the **two women** kneeling, facing each other with a large flat stone between them, pushing a second smaller stone back and forth,

536

grinding grain between the two stones. (Back then, most bread could have been labeled, "Stone-Ground Whole Wheat Bread.") **One** of the women grinding grain **will be taken** into the kingdom when Jesus comes, **and one will be left** out. Women will be going about daily chores when the end of the age arrives unannounced.

42 These parables of the unexpectedness of Jesus' coming carry a lesson: **Therefore, stay awake! For you do not know on which day your Lord will come.** To **stay awake** means to be vigilant and prepared for his coming. Jesus tells his disciples that vigilance is necessary because **you do not know on which day your Lord will come.** Jesus refers to himself coming as **your Lord:** Jesus will be called Lord as God is called Lord (see 7:21-22).

Lord: See page 133

43 Jesus adds yet another parable about something happening when it is not expected. **Be sure of this: if the master of the house had known the hour of night when the thief was coming, he would have stayed awake and not let his house be broken into.** Because the homeowner did not know that a thief was coming that night, he did not stay awake to guard his house; consequently it was burglarized. Thieves do not schedule appointments or send reminder cards ahead of their visits. Because one cannot know when a burglar will come, constant vigilance is necessary.

44 **So too, you also must be prepared, for at an hour you do not expect, the Son of Man will come.** Jesus tells his disciples that he will come **at an hour you do not expect,** conveying once again that they cannot know the time of his coming (see 24:36, 42). **So too,** like a homeowner awake and alert lest he be burglarized, disciples **also must be prepared** for the coming of Jesus at a time that cannot be predicted. **Be prepared** means the same as "stay awake" (verse 42); Jesus will go on to tell parables that deal with what is involved in being prepared and watchful (24:45–25:30).

If Jesus' disciples cannot know the time of his coming, then what did Jesus mean when he told them to "learn a lesson from the fig tree" and said that when "all these things" happened, he would be "near, at the gates" (24:32-33)? Despite the preliminary events occurring within a generation (24:34) and Jesus' being near, the time of his coming is unknowable. Perhaps the lesson of the fig tree has to do less with timing than with preparedness: all the conditions for Jesus' coming are already in place, so his disciples must now be constantly ready for him to come.

For reflection: Do I think that because Jesus could come at any time, the odds are he will not come in my lifetime?

New Testament writings echo Jesus' comparison of his coming to the unexpectedness of burglary and his call for readiness. Paul writes that "the day of the Lord will come like a thief at night" (1 Thess 5:2; see also 2 Pet 3:10). In the book of Revelation, Jesus says, "If you are not watchful, I will come like a thief, and you will never know at what hour I will come upon you" (Rev 3:3; see also Rev 16:15). Hence the repeated exhortations to be on guard (1 Cor 16:13), to stay awake (1 Thess 5:6), to be vigilant (1 Pet 5:8), to be watchful (Rev 3:2).

For reflection: How watchful and prepared am I for the coming of Jesus? Have my daily activities and routine dulled me to his nearness?

ORIENTATION: *After parables that convey that he will come at an unforeseen time (24:36-44), Jesus tells parables that instruct his disciples about what their attitudes and actions should be as they await his coming (24:45–25:30).*

Faithful or Unfaithful Service

[45] "Who, then, is the faithful and prudent servant, whom the master has put in charge of his household to distribute to them their food at the proper time? [46] Blessed is that servant whom his master on his arrival finds doing so. [47] Amen, I say to you, he will put him in charge of all his property. [48] But if that wicked servant says to himself, 'My master is long delayed,' [49] and begins to beat his fellow servants, and eat and drink with drunkards, [50] the servant's master will come on an unexpected day and at an unknown hour [51] and will punish him severely and assign him a place with the hypocrites, where there will be wailing and grinding of teeth."

Gospel parallels: Luke 12:41-46
NT: Matt 24:36, 42, 44

45 **Who, then, is the faithful and prudent servant:** Jesus begins a parable with a question that invites his listeners to identify themselves with a **servant** who is **faithful** and **prudent.** To be **faithful** means to be trustworthy and reliable; to be **prudent** (the Greek word could also be translated as "wise") is to behave sensibly, even shrewdly (see 10:16). The word translated **servant** is literally "slave"; the slave's **master** or owner gives him a task. He is to be **in charge of his household to distribute to them their food at the proper time.** The word translated **household** means *the slaves of a household.* The first slave is not given absolute authority over the other slaves but is made responsible for providing them with **food** from the household stores. **At the proper time** means when they are hungry, not at the convenience of the slave in charge of food distribution.

Servant, slave: See page 429

The word translated **master** can also be translated "lord"; he stands for Jesus as the master or Lord (24:42). Jesus entrusts responsibilities to his disciples, whom he has called to be servants, even slaves, of one another (20:26-27). While the parable has special application to those with leadership roles in the community of his followers, the parable has a message for all of his disciples. Every disciple is entrusted with responsibilities by Jesus and is to carry them out faithfully and wisely.

Lord: See page 133

For reflection: What has Jesus charged me to do for him? How faithfully am I carrying out the responsibilities he has given me?

46 The story line of the parable implies that after making one of his slaves responsible for caring for his other slaves, the master goes off and at some later time returns. **Blessed is that servant whom his master on his arrival finds doing so**—finds carrying out his responsibilities. It is implied that the master arrives unexpectedly and **finds** the slave hard at work. The slave's faithfulness is not last-minute playacting; he had no way of knowing when his master would return. Jesus pronounces the slave **blessed** and fortunate—a beatitude. The slave is praised for **doing** the will of his master: Jesus has repeatedly emphasized the importance of **doing** (7:21, 24; 12:50; 21:28-31).

Beatitudes: See page 73

47 A faithful slave receives a reward appropriate for a slave: **Amen, I say to you, he will put him in charge of all his property.** Before, the slave had only been in charge of food distribution, but now he will be **in charge of all** of his master's **property.**

48 **But if that wicked servant says to himself, "My master is long delayed."** Jesus may seem to introduce a second **servant,** or slave, at this point in the parable, one who is **wicked** in contrast to the first slave who is faithful. However, Jesus can just as well be talking about two different paths that one slave could take. The first half of his parable (verses 45-47) would then have the sense, "If a slave put in charge of food distribution is faithfully carrying out his responsibilities when his master returns, he will be rewarded." The second half of the parable addresses contrasting behavior. If the slave is **wicked** instead of faithful, he may tell himself, **My master is long delayed,** so I don't need to be on my best behavior.

Matthew wrote his gospel a half century after the death and resurrection of Jesus. Despite some expectations that Jesus would come in glory within the lifetime of his first disciples (see 10:23; 16:28; 24:33-34), Jesus had not come. Feeling that his coming was **long delayed,** some in Matthew's church may have become dispirited and have been tempted to grow lax in awaiting his coming. Jesus' parable acknowledges that his coming may be delayed and instructs his disciples how they should deal with this delay.

For reflection: What impact does Jesus' two-thousand-year delay have on my faith and behavior?

49 In his wickedness, the servant **begins to beat his fellow servants**—those he should have been caring for. He begins to **eat and drink with drunkards,** presumably using the household food supply for his orgies. He uses the position his master has given him to tyrannize his fellow servants and indulge himself—irresponsible behavior that is the opposite of faithful service.

50 **The servant's master will come on an unexpected day and at an unknown hour.** There will be no warning of his coming; the slave will be caught off guard in his wicked conduct. The **unexpected day** and **unknown hour** echo Jesus' earlier words about his coming at an unknown day

and hour (24:36, 42, 44). Even if some think that his coming is "long delayed" (verse 48), he will surely come, and at his coming he will see whether his disciples are behaving faithfully or wickedly.

51 If the master comes and finds the slave behaving wickedly, he **will punish him severely,** literally, he will cut him in two—we might say, tear him to pieces. The master will **assign him a place with the hypocrites, where there will be wailing and grinding of teeth.** Jesus has pronounced woes upon **hypocrites** (23:13, 15, 23, 25, 27, 29) and warned that they are on a path to Gehenna, a symbol for punishment in the age to come (23:33). **Wailing and grinding of teeth** are associated with exclusion from the kingdom of God (8:11-12; 13:41-42, 49-50; 22:13).

Jesus' parable about two ways of behaving while a master's return is delayed is directed at those who await Jesus' coming. To be watchful and prepared for his coming (24:42, 44) means to be faithful in carrying out the responsibilities he has given us: watchfulness entails service. Even if his coming seems long delayed, he will come, and there will be a sorting out. Disciples who faithfully do what Jesus asks of them will be rewarded; those who use the delay in Jesus' coming as a time for self-indulgence will be punished.

> *For reflection: If Jesus were to come today, would I be prepared for his coming? What is the lesson of this parable for me?*

CHAPTER 25

ORIENTATION: *Jesus continues to instruct his followers about what their attitudes and behavior should be as they await his coming. He balances a parable about wise and wicked men (24:45-51) with a parable about wise and foolish women (25:1-13).*

Waiting Wisely or Foolishly

[1] "Then the kingdom of heaven will be like ten virgins who took their lamps and went out to meet the bridegroom. [2] Five of them were foolish and five were wise. [3] The foolish ones, when taking their lamps, brought no oil with them, [4] but the wise brought flasks of oil with their lamps. [5] Since the bridegroom was long delayed, they all became drowsy and fell asleep. [6] At midnight, there was a cry, 'Behold, the bridegroom! Come out to meet him!' [7] Then all those virgins got up and trimmed their lamps. [8] The foolish ones said to the wise, 'Give us some of your oil, for our lamps are going out.' [9] But the wise ones replied, 'No, for there may not be enough for us and you. Go instead to the merchants and buy some for yourselves.' [10] While they went off to buy it, the bridegroom came and those who were ready went into the wedding feast with him. Then the door was locked. [11] Afterwards the other virgins came and said, 'Lord, Lord, open the door for us!' [12] But he said in reply, 'Amen, I say to you, I do not know you.' [13] Therefore, stay awake, for you know neither the day nor the hour."

OT: 1 Macc 9:37, 39
NT: Matt 7:21-27; 8:11; 9:15; 22:1-4; 24:36, 42, 44-51

1 **Then the kingdom of heaven will be like:** the time frame continues to be the period before the coming of Jesus in glory (24:37-44). At his coming **the kingdom of heaven**—God's reign—will be established in its fullness. The situation of those awaiting Jesus' coming is **like** that of **ten virgins who took their lamps and went out to meet the bridegroom.** The setting for Jesus' parable is a wedding feast. A man and a woman entered into marriage in two stages: betrothal and beginning to live together. There was apparently no wedding ceremony as such but a feast to celebrate the bride moving into the home of her husband. Jesus does not need to describe all the particulars because his disciples are familiar with wedding customs. His parable begins at the point where a **bridegroom** is on his way

to his house, presumably with his bride; when they arrive, the wedding feast will begin. Jesus has compared himself to a **bridegroom** (9:15); the coming of the bridegroom in the parable will represent Jesus' coming at the end of the age to inaugurate "the banquet in the kingdom of heaven" (8:11).

Kingdom of heaven: See page 266
Marriage practices: See page 479

The last leg of bridegroom's journey to the wedding feast will be turned into a joyful procession (see the wedding procession in 1 Macc 9:37, 39). **Ten virgins** will go **out to meet** the bridegroom and join the procession. That they are **virgins** indicates that they are young and unmarried; their virginity does not play a role in the parable. **Ten** symbolizes fullness and completeness; the ten young women can stand for all followers of Jesus. They take **lamps** to meet the bridegroom: the wedding procession is at night. The Greek word translated **lamps** ordinarily refers to torches—perhaps sticks with rags wound on the end, soaked in olive oil and set aflame. Such torches would not only provide light for the procession but would add a festive touch.

2 Jesus provides the punch line of the parable at the start: **Five of them were foolish and five were wise.** Jesus' disciples don't need to focus on every detail of what happens when ten young women go out to meet the bridegroom; the disciples only need to be alert to how five of the women were **foolish** and how five were **wise,** and then draw lessons for themselves.

3 **The foolish ones, when taking their lamps, brought no oil with them.** They brought torches with rags soaked with oil, or lamps filled with oil, but did not bring any additional oil with them. They presumed that their torches or lamps would burn long enough to greet the bridegroom and would not need replenishing. This will turn out to be a **foolish** assumption.

4 **but the wise brought flasks of oil with their lamps.** Half of the women brought a backup supply of oil in case it was needed. The parable will present these women doing various things, but it is solely because of their foresight in bringing extra oil that they are called **wise,** or "prudent," as the Greek word is translated in 24:45.

5 **Since the bridegroom was long delayed, they all became drowsy and fell asleep.** The **bridegroom** does not arrive as expected; his coming is **delayed.** Jesus does not give a reason for the delay; it is not important for the parable. (What wedding ever starts on time?) The bridegroom is **long delayed,** just as in the previous parable the master's return was long delayed (24:48). The young women **all** became drowsy and **fell asleep,** the wise as well as the foolish. They are not criticized for falling asleep; the bridegroom's long delay means it is past their bedtime.

6 **At midnight, there was a cry, "Behold, the bridegroom! Come out to meet him!"** Someone spots the bridegroom coming and rouses everyone who is to take part in the procession. **Come out** to where the procession forms **to meet him** and provide a festive welcome.

7 **Then all those virgins got up and trimmed their lamps.** The next verse indicates that the **lamps,** or torches, had been burning while the young women slept. They do whatever adjusting is now necessary.

8 **The foolish ones said to the wise, "Give us some of your oil, for our lamps are going out."** Their lamps, or torches, after burning during the bridegroom's long delay are now so low on oil that they are **going out.** They ask the women who brought extra oil to share it with them.

9 **But the wise ones replied, "No, for there may not be enough for us and you."** The Greek words translated **there may not be enough** probably have the stronger meaning, "there *certainly* would not be enough." The five of the young women who brought extra oil for their own torches do not have enough to replenish ten torches. Sharing their oil would mean that all the torches would sputter out during the procession. The parable does not portray the five wise women as heartless and selfish but as realistic and practical: better to have five flaming torches than none at all. They tell the other women, **Go instead to the merchants and buy some for yourselves.** Would there be olive oil stores open in the middle of the night? Perhaps not, but the word **merchants** conveys the notion of selling; surely on the night of a wedding feast someone will be awake who will be able to supply some oil.

10 The five whose torches are going out accept the suggestion. **While they went off to buy it, the bridegroom came and those who were ready went into the wedding feast with him.** The bridegroom finally arrives and the procession takes place without the five who are off buying oil. The procession makes its way into the house where the **wedding feast** is being held; the five women **who were ready** for the bridegroom's coming go into the feast **with him.** Jesus does not need to describe the wedding feast; his disciples knew that they were lavish affairs. Jesus has previously compared the kingdom of God to a wedding feast (22:1-4).

> *For reflection: Does entering a feast with Jesus provide me with an image for heaven?*

After the wedding procession entered the house, **then the door was locked.** At this point the story line of the parable is shaped by its application. There would be little reason to secure a wedding feast by locking the door. Such feasts were lengthy affairs and in rural villages there was probably a lot of coming and going while the feast was in progress. It was not the end of the world if someone showed up late: had not the bridegroom himself been long delayed in his arrival? However, if the wedding feast represents the banquet in the kingdom of heaven, then there indeed will be a point at which the door will be locked and entrance will no longer be possible: the final judgment will be final.

11 **Afterwards the other virgins came and said, "Lord, Lord, open the door for us!"** Whether or not they were able to obtain oil is now irrelevant: the wedding procession is over. Their cry, **Lord, Lord,** might have the sense of "Sir, sir, let us in!" But the parable's application to the end of the age is in the fore: the cry is to Jesus as Lord, solemnly imploring him as **Lord, Lord** and asking entrance into the kingdom of heaven (see 7:21 for the same cry).

Lord: See page 133

12 **But he said in reply, "Amen, I say to you, I do not know you."** A bridegroom would be heartless to turn away young women who were to have been part of the wedding party; the story line of the parable is being determined by the finality of the final judgment. Jesus earlier warned that at the judgment he would say, "I never knew you," to some who cried out to him, "Lord, Lord" (7:21-23), and his parable ends with the same solemn

disclaimer: **I do not know you.** All ten women had been invited to the feast, but like the women grinding grain, some "will be taken" into the feast and some "will be left" out (24:41). Whether we will enter the banquet of the kingdom of heaven will depend on whether we behave wisely or foolishly as we await Jesus the bridegroom.

13 **Therefore, stay awake, for you know neither the day nor the hour.** Jesus repeats the lesson he has been trying to get across to his disciples. No one knows the **day** and **hour** of Jesus' coming at the end of the age (24:36); **therefore** his disciples must **stay awake** (24:42), prepared for his coming at an hour they do not expect (24:44, 50). To **stay awake** does not mean to go without sleep: the five wise women in the parable fell asleep but nonetheless were admitted to the feast. To stay awake means to be prepared for Jesus' coming being delayed, even long delayed. It is foolish to live as if he will come soon and no provision need be made for an extended time of waiting.

For reflection: What is the lesson of this parable for me?

The parable of the wise, or prudent, and foolish women is a counterpart to the parable of the prudent and wicked slaves (24:45-51). One slave counted on his master's being delayed and was caught in his wickedness when the master returned earlier than expected. The foolish women counted on the bridegroom coming soon and made no provision for a delay. The prudent slave and the prudent women stand for those who are ready for Jesus to come at any time.

The parable of the wise or foolish women also has a counterpart in the parable of the wise and foolish house builders (7:24-27). In that parable, to be wise meant to listen to Jesus' words and act on them; to be foolish meant to fail to act on Jesus' words. Taking these two parables in conjunction with one another can convey that we are to await Jesus' coming by living according to his teachings.

Yet how can we take to heart Jesus' admonition to be prepared for his coming after it has been delayed for two thousand years? Perhaps the delay has its own message. Perhaps God's timetable for his creation (24:36) is as prolonged as the universe he created is vast. Perhaps we should behave as if it is God's intent that the human race populate the earth indefinitely. This might mean conserving natural resources and preserving the environment: we cannot count on Jesus coming soon to take us to a new dwelling if we make our present dwelling uninhabitable.

For reflection: What lessons do I draw from the delay in Jesus' coming?

The Parable of the Talents

14 "It will be as when a man who was going on a journey called in his servants and entrusted his possessions to them. **15** To one he gave five talents; to another, two; to a third, one—to each according to his ability. Then he went away. Immediately **16** the one who received five talents went and traded with them, and made another five. **17** Likewise, the one who received two made another two. **18** But the man who received one went off and dug a hole in the ground and buried his master's money. **19** After a long time the master of those servants came back and settled accounts with them. **20** The one who had received five talents came forward bringing the additional five. He said, 'Master, you gave me five talents. See, I have made five more.' **21** His master said to him, 'Well done, my good and faithful servant. Since you were faithful in small matters, I will give you great responsibilities. Come, share your master's joy.' **22** [Then] the one who had received two talents also came forward and said, 'Master, you gave me two talents. See, I have made two more.' **23** His master said to him, 'Well done, my good and faithful servant. Since you were faithful in small matters, I will give you great responsibilities. Come, share your master's joy.' **24** Then the one who had received the one talent came forward and said, 'Master, I knew you were a demanding person, harvesting where you did not plant and gathering where you did not scatter; **25** so out of fear I went off and buried your talent in the ground. Here it is back.' **26** His master said to him in reply, 'You wicked, lazy servant! So you knew that I harvest where I did not plant and gather where I did not scatter? **27** Should you not then have put my money in the bank so that I could have got it back with interest on my return? **28** Now then! Take the talent from him and give it to the one with ten. **29** For to everyone who has, more will be given and he will grow rich; but from the one who has not, even what he has will be taken away. **30** And throw this useless servant into the darkness outside, where there will be wailing and grinding of teeth.'"

Gospel parallels: Luke 19:11-27
NT: Matt 13:12; 24:42, 44; 25:13; 1 Cor 12:4-31

547

14 Jesus has just told his disciples to stay awake, for they do not know when he will come (25:13). **It**—his coming—**will be** like the events that unfold **when a man who was going on a journey called in his servants,** literally, his "slaves," **and entrusted his possessions to them.** As the next verse makes clear, **possessions** refers to money. Like a landowner entrusting his vineyard to tenants (21:33-41), a wealthy person might entrust his or her money to slaves for management (see 24:45 for an example of a slave holding a management position). This man **who was going on a journey** relied on his slaves to be honest and competent; it was better to have them manage his investment funds while he was away than to have his money sit idle and unproductive.

Servant, slave: See page 429

15 **To one he gave five talents.** A talent was originally a unit of weight, somewhere over fifty pounds (the "large hailstones like huge weights" of Rev 16:21 are hailstones literally weighing a talent). Eventually the word "talent" came to designate that weight of precious metal or coins; that is its meaning here. A talent was the largest monetary unit, equivalent in first-century Palestine to six thousand denarii (a denarius was "the usual daily wage" for an ordinary worker—20:2). The man who is about to leave on a journey **gave**—entrusted—sums of money to his slaves. To one he entrusted **five talents,** an amount it would take an ordinary worker a century to earn. **To another** of his slaves he entrusted **two** talents; **to a third, one** talent. Even the slave receiving a single talent is given a considerable amount, equivalent to what an ordinary worker would earn in twenty years. The man entrusts talents **to each according to his ability:** he divides up his money among his slaves based on each one's **ability** to manage his funds. The man does not expect more from a slave than the slave is able to deliver. Similarly, Jesus does not ask us to bear a burden (11:30) or accomplish a task beyond our capability.

Then he went away. Jesus does not recount the man's giving any detailed instructions to his slaves about what they are to do with the funds entrusted to them. The funds are at their disposal to manage, and they must decide how to make best use of them. God likewise allows us a lot of leeway in how we use what has been entrusted to us. God's plan for us generally requires us to fill in the fine print.

This verse ends awkwardly with the word **immediately,** a word that should have been considered the first word of the following verse when

Matthew's gospel was divided into verses by a printer, Robert Estienne, in his 1551 edition of the New Testament.

16 Immediately **the one who received five talents went and traded with them.** He starts right away to make use of what has been entrusted to him, treating it as a matter of urgency. The word translated **traded** literally means "worked" and covers a broader range of business activities than trading. The one who received five talents works **with** them: he actively involves himself in managing his master's money. He undertakes business ventures, using the talents to fund them. His ventures are successful, and he makes **another five** talents in profits.

17 **Likewise, the one who received two made another two.** The second slave is also successful in doubling what has been entrusted to him.

18 **But the man who received one went off and dug a hole in the ground and buried his master's money.** Burying valuables was a common way of safeguarding them, reflected also in the parable of the treasure buried in a field (13:44). Thieves might break into a house and steal what was inside (6:19; 24:43); money or jewelry buried in the ground was virtually theft-proof. The third slave takes a safe course of action—but one that has no prospect of turning a profit.

19 **After a long time the master of those servants came back and settled accounts with them.** Since he has been away **a long time,** his slaves have had ample opportunity to make use of the funds entrusted to them. On his return, he **settled accounts** with his slaves: he wants back the funds he has put at their disposal, along with whatever profit they have made for him.

At the beginning of the parable, Jesus indicated that it would deal with his coming (verses 13-14), and applications begin to emerge. The man's return **after a long time** calls to mind the long-delayed return of the master of the faithful and wicked slaves (24:48) and the long-delayed coming of the bridegroom to the wedding feast (25:5). Both of those parables taught what one should do if Jesus' coming is delayed; the present parable does as well. The man who had been on a journey is referred to as the **master** of the slaves, using the Greek word that can also be translated "lord." Jesus told his disciples that they must be constantly prepared for his coming, "for you do not know on which day your Lord will come"

(24:42). The coming of the master after a long time represents the coming of the Lord Jesus at the end of the age. When the master ccomes back, he settles accounts with his slaves; Jesus' coming will mean settling accounts at a final judgment (see 7:21-23; 13:40-43, 49-50; 16:27).

Lord: See page 133

20 **The one who had received five talents came forward bringing the additional five.** He returns the original five talents to his master along with the **additional five** he made in profits. **He said, "Master, you gave me—entrusted me with—five talents. See, I have made five more."** It is taken for granted that the slave will return the funds entrusted to him; the accent is on what he has been able to earn with the funds: **See, I have made five more.**

21 The master is very pleased with what his slave has accomplished and commends him: **His master said to him, "Well done, my good and faithful servant."** His slave has been **faithful** in carrying out his responsibilities; he is a **good** administrator. The master not only commends him but rewards him: **Since you were faithful in small matters, I will give you great responsibilities**—more literally, "You were faithful over a few things; I will appoint you over many things." Those listening to the parable might question whether five talents—an immense sum—should be considered a small matter. It is small only in comparison with the reward that the slave receives. God is also generous in his reward, a hundredfold generous (19:29). As with a faithful slave in a previous parable (24:45-47), the reward for good service is greater responsibilities. But that is not the end of it. The master invites his slave, **Come, share your master's joy.** He treats the slave as he would a friend, sharing his joy with him.

    Share is literally "enter into," and those listening to this story as a parable about Jesus' coming to inaugurate God's kingdom in its fullness might recall that Jesus has spoken many times of entering the kingdom of heaven or entering eternal life (5:20; 7:13-14, 21; 18:3, 8-9; 19:16-17, 23-24; 23:13). The faithful slave entering into his master's joy is an image for entering God's eternal kingdom and sharing God's joy.

For reflection: Do I think of heaven as my sharing God's joy?

22 [Then] the one who had received two talents also came forward and said, "Master, you gave me two talents. See, I have made two more." The second slave had been entrusted with less than the first slave because he had less ability (verse 15). Nonetheless, the second slave did a good job with what was entrusted to him and doubled it. He did not make as much profit for his master as had the first slave, but he was not expected to. He was only expected to do a good job with the talents given him.

23 The master commends and rewards the second slave exactly as he had the first. His master said to him, 'Well done, my good and faithful servant. Since you were faithful in small matters, I will give you great responsibilities. Come, share your master's joy." Even though the second slave gave him only two talents in profits, he receives the same praise and reward as the slave who made five talents. Both doubled what was entrusted to them. The parable conveys that God judges us on how well we make use of our gifts, not on how many gifts we are given.

24 Then the one who had received the one talent came forward and said, "Master, I knew you were a demanding person, harvesting where you did not plant and gathering where you did not scatter." The slave who was entrusted with one talent thinks his master is a demanding person, literally, a "hard" person. Gathering where you did not scatter means gathering crops where you did not scatter seeds—the same meaning as harvesting where you did not plant. Perhaps the slave literally means that his master reaps crops that others planted, or perhaps the expressions are simply a way of conveying that his master takes advantage of situations. In either case, the slave considers his owner to be tough-minded and opportunistic.

25 so out of fear I went off and buried your talent in the ground. Out of fear the slave does what seems to him to be safest. Fear is the opposite of faith (see 8:26; 14:30-31); the slave had no faith in his master's fairness or compassion. Consequently he is unable to take risks: what would his master do to him if he failed? The slave was more interested in safeguarding himself than in earning a profit for his master.

> For reflection: Does my view of God enable me to act with faith and take risks in serving him?

In one sense, the slave's strategy worked: no one discovered the buried talent. The slave was able to dig it up and return it. He tells his master, **Here it is back.**

26 **His master said to him in reply, "You wicked, lazy servant!"** Although the master has his talent back, he is very displeased with his slave. He calls him **wicked** and **lazy.** What has the slave done to make him **wicked?** A wicked slave in a previous parable may have used household provisions for drunken parties (24:48-49), but this slave did not spend the talent on himself. However, burying the talent was **lazy,** and the master will go on to call him a useless slave (verse 30). The slave's wickedness lies in his being lazy and useless. God's standard for us is not merely that we never do anything wrong but that we do good.

The master glosses over the slave's characterization of him as a demanding, or hard, person (verse 24) but repeats the rest of the slave's words about him: **So you knew that I harvest where I did not plant and gather where I did not scatter?** The word **knew** might have the connotation of "thought": So you thought that I harvest where I did not plant? The master is not necessarily acknowledging that he takes what belongs to others; he is simply reminding the slave that he, the slave, views his master as someone who takes advantage of situations.

27 He tells the slave, **Should you not then,** since you view me as one who is after gain, **have put my money in the bank so that I could have got it back with interest on my return?** The word **bank** means "moneylenders." Jews were forbidden to charge **interest** on loans to one another (Exod 22:24; Lev 25:36-37; Deut 23:20) but could collect interest from non-Jews (Deut 23:21). If the slave was too fearful or lazy to manage the talent himself, he should have deposited it with moneylenders so that his master would receive interest. Instead the slave did nothing with it, burying it in the ground, despite knowing that his master wanted his money to earn a profit.

28 **Now then! Take the talent from him and give it to the one with ten.** The slave who made a five-talent profit demonstrated that he was able to do a good job investing his master's money. The master takes the talent from the hapless slave and entrusts it to the slave with the greatest ability to manage it.

29 **For to everyone who has, more will be given and he will grow rich; but from the one who has not, even what he has will be taken away.** The modern counterpart to this saying is, The rich get richer and the poor get poorer. Jesus used this line of reasoning on another occasion, in connection with understanding his message (13:12): those with understanding grow in understanding, while those who do not understand grow more unknowing. Here the saying generalizes one of the lessons of the parable: **everyone who has** been entrusted with talents and uses them properly **will be given** more, **and he will grow rich.** On the other hand, **the one who has not** properly used what was entrusted to her or him will have even that **taken away.** The lesson seems to be that God's gifts are like athletic skills: use them or lose them.

30 **And throw this useless servant into the darkness outside, where there will be wailing and grinding of teeth.** Jesus concludes the parable with language that reflects his coming at the end of the age. Being thrown into the **darkness outside** is an image for exclusion from the kingdom of God (8:11-12; 22:13). **Wailing and grinding of teeth** expresses the anguish of those who are excluded from the kingdom and are punished in the age to come (8:12; 13:42, 50; 22:13; 24:51). Not making proper use of what God entrusts to us and being **useless** to him means we risk ending up in the outer darkness.

> *For reflection: Do I consider not using my gifts to be sinful? How useful have I been for God?*

Jesus told this parable in the course of teaching his disciples how they are to be awake and prepared for his coming (24:42, 44; 25:13). They are to make use of the resources that have been entrusted to them and carry out their responsibilities. Being awake and prepared for Jesus' coming does not mean going sleepless and watching the skies; it means being hard at work, making the best use we can of the talents entrusted to us— giving Jesus his money's worth. We will be judged on our use of our talents; God will bring us into his joy if we have made good use of our gifts.

With Jesus' parable in mind, writers in the Middle Ages began to use the word "talent" as a poetic expression for the endowments and abilities one had been given. Their figurative use became the meaning we attach to the word today. "Talented" has overtones both of proficiency and of giftedness. These notions help us apply the parable of the talents to ourselves. What gifts and proficiencies have been entrusted to me? How can I best make use of them for Jesus?

For reflection: What talents has God entrusted to me?

The letters of the New Testament do not use the word "talent" but speak of followers of Jesus receiving gifts. Some gifts, like prophecy and healing (1 Cor 12:9-10), are manifestly extraordinary. Other gifts of service seem rather ordinary, almost prosaic: almsgiving and works of mercy (Rom 12:6-8), assistance and administration (1 Cor 12:28), hospitality (1 Pet 4:9-10). Paul insists that every disciple is gifted by God for the sake of others, that there is a variety of gifts, that even seemingly minor roles of service are important (1 Cor 12:4-31). Jesus' parable of the talents teaches that we are to use our gifts and resources, whatever they might be, as diligently as we can—using them to help others, as Jesus will make clear (25:31-46). "As each one has received a gift, use it to serve one another as good stewards of God's varied grace" (1 Pet 4:10).

For reflection: What has Jesus called me to do to serve him? How have I been equipped to carry out my call? How well am I making use of my gifts?

ORIENTATION: *Jesus spoke of his coming (24:29-31) and went on to teach how his disciples should await it (24:32–25:30). Now he tells them how they will be judged when he comes.*

The Judgment

[31] "When the Son of Man comes in his glory, and all the angels with him, he will sit upon his glorious throne, [32] and all the nations will be assembled before him. And he will separate them one from another, as a shepherd separates the sheep from the goats. [33] He will place the sheep on his right and the goats on his left. [34] Then the king will say to those on his right, 'Come, you who are blessed by my Father. Inherit the kingdom prepared for you from the foundation of the world. [35] For I was hungry and you gave me food, I was thirsty and you gave me drink, a stranger and you welcomed me, [36] naked and you clothed me, ill and you cared for me, in prison and you visited me.' [37] Then the righteous will answer him and say, 'Lord, when did we see you hungry

and feed you, or thirsty and give you drink? ³⁸ When did we see you a stranger and welcome you, or naked and clothe you? ³⁹ When did we see you ill or in prison, and visit you?' ⁴⁰ And the king will say to them in reply, 'Amen, I say to you, whatever you did for one of these least brothers of mine, you did for me.' ⁴¹ Then he will say to those on his left, 'Depart from me, you accursed, into the eternal fire prepared for the devil and his angels. ⁴² For I was hungry and you gave me no food, I was thirsty and you gave me no drink, ⁴³ a stranger and you gave me no welcome, naked and you gave me no clothing, ill and in prison, and you did not care for me.' ⁴⁴ Then they will answer and say, 'Lord, when did we see you hungry or thirsty or a stranger or naked or ill or in prison, and not minister to your needs?' ⁴⁵ He will answer them, 'Amen, I say to you, what you did not do for one of these least ones, you did not do for me.' ⁴⁶ And these will go off to eternal punishment, but the righteous to eternal life."

OT:Dan 7:13-14; 12:2
NT:Matt 5:7; 13:41-43, 49-50; 16:27; 24:29-31; John 5:27-29

31 Jesus used cosmic imagery to convey what it will be like when he comes at the end of the age (24:29-31); now he talks about what his coming will mean for the human race. **When the Son of Man comes in his glory, and all the angels with him:** Jesus refers to himself as **the Son of Man** and echoes his earlier statements about his coming "with his angels in his Father's glory" (16:27) and "coming upon the clouds of heaven with power and great glory" (24:30). **He will sit upon his glorious throne** echoes his saying that in the new age he will be "seated on his throne of glory" (19:28). Those who sit on a **throne** have authority.

Son of Man: See page 151
Angels: See page 33

32 Jesus said that when he came in glory with his angels he would "repay everyone according to his conduct" (16:27). That is the scene he now describes. **All the nations will be assembled before him:** although some scholars suggest **all the nations** refers to Gentiles only, **all the nations** is best interpreted as every human being, Gentile and Jew alike. All who have died will have risen to face judgment (see 12:41-42; Dan 12:2). **And he will separate them one from another, as a shepherd separates the sheep from the goats.** Jesus' point in comparing the separation to a

555

shepherd sorting out **the sheep from the goats** may simply be that it will be as easy for Jesus to sort out individuals at the judgment as it is for a shepherd to sort out sheep from goats in his flock. Goats were not considered bad and sheep good; both were useful and valued. (Otherwise, why raise goats?) Nor was it normally necessary to segregate them. But if a shepherd needed to separate his sheep from his goats, it was easy to do so. Likewise, Jesus will have no trouble sorting out the human race when he comes in judgment.

33 **He will place the sheep on his right and the goats on his left.** James and John had wanted to sit at the right and left of Jesus in his kingdom (20:21), which were the places of highest honor. Here, however, **right** and **left** have a different significance. Because most people are right-handed, **right** had ancient connotations of being good and **left** of being bad (the latter is reflected in the word "sinister," which comes from the Latin word for "left"). However, the essential note is that at the judgment, human beings will be sorted into two groups so that they can be dealt with differently. Jesus could just as well put the groups in front of and behind him.

At this point Jesus' listeners—and Matthew's readers—might wonder to themselves, Which group will I be in?

34 **Then the king will say to those on his right:** Jesus identifies himself at his coming as **the king,** sitting on a throne (verse 31). The book of Daniel speaks of one like a son of man coming on the clouds of heaven to receive dominion, glory, and kingship from God (Dan 7:13-14). Jesus has spoken often of the kingdom of God, or kingdom of heaven, which implies that God is king (see also 5:35; 18:23; 22:2). Jesus has also spoken of the kingdom of the Son of Man (13:41; 16:28) which implies a kingly role for himself. Jesus is not trying to explain the relationship between himself as king and his Father as king; Jesus is conveying that at his coming he will exercise authority as a king exercises authority, which is to say absolutely, as far as the king's subjects are concerned. He will say to those he has put on his right, **Come, you who are blessed by my Father.** Jesus invited Peter and Andrew to "come after me" (4:19); he invited all who labor and are burden to "come to me" (11:28). At the judgment, Jesus will issue his final call to **come,** addressed to those who are **blessed by my Father.** It is unclear whether Jesus placed on his right those whom his Father has already declared blessed, or whether the Father blesses those

whom Jesus places on his right. In either case Jesus proclaims the blessedness and good fortune of those he invites to **come**. He tells them, **Inherit the kingdom prepared for you from the foundation of the world.** To **inherit the kingdom** means to "inherit eternal life" (19:29)—to enter the kingdom of God and gain eternal life (19:16, 23-24). This life has been **prepared for you from the foundation of the world.** The **foundation of the world** means its creation (see 13:35). The state of eternal blessedness that those on Jesus' right inherit is something that God had in mind from the beginning. God brought the universe into being so that women and men may live on this earth and enter into eternal life. That is the ultimate meaning and purpose of the universe. The stars will eventually flicker out—our sun will exhaust its fuel in another five billion years or so—but we who live on this earth will endure for eternity. The immensity and complexity of the universe is an indication of the grandeur of God's plan for us.

Kingdom of heaven: See page 266

For reflection: What do Jesus' words convey to me about the purpose of my life on earth? What hope do his words give me?

35 Jesus has put some men and women on his right, but he has not explained why they were selected to inherit eternal life. This he now does, telling them,

---

BACKGROUND: JUDGMENT For much of the Old Testament era, Israelites did not expect a meaningful life after death but only a shadowy existence in the netherworld for good and bad alike. As expectations arose that there would be life after death, so also arose the expectation that God would judge individuals after death, rewarding those who had led good lives and punishing those who had done evil. God's judgment is implicit in the book of Daniel, written about 164 B.C.: "Many of those who sleep / in the dust of the earth shall awake; / Some shall live forever, / others shall be an everlasting horror and disgrace" (Dan 12:2). The book of Judith, written after Daniel, speaks of judgment: "The LORD Almighty will requite them; / in the day of judgment he will punish them: / He will send fire and worms into their flesh, / and they shall burn and suffer forever" (Judith 16:17). In some nonbiblical writings of the era, God's judgment marks the transition between this age and the age to come; some of these writings portray Gehenna as the place of fiery punishment. *Related topics: The age to come (page 250), Gehenna (page 88), Life after death (page 406), Nonbiblical writings (page 198), Resurrection (page 478).*

For I was hungry and you gave me food, I was thirsty and you gave me drink. Jesus doesn't explain how he came to be **hungry** and **thirsty;** he simply states that he was and that those on his right gave him **food** and **drink.** He tells them that he was **a stranger and you welcomed me.** The word translated **stranger** might also be translated "foreigner" or "alien." **You welcomed me**—invited me in—means you gave me a place to stay and something to eat (see Gen 18:1-8 and 19:1-3 for examples of hospitality). During his public ministry, Jesus was dependent on the hospitality of others (8:20), but this judgment scene includes all women and men of all time and not just those who were alive at the time of Jesus. How they extended hospitality to Jesus remains to be explained.

Hospitality: See page 188

36 Jesus says I was **naked and you clothed me.** Again there is no explanation of the circumstances but only a statement of what happened. Jesus continues, I was **ill and you cared for me:** the Greek for **cared for** can mean "visit." Visiting those who are sick should include meeting their needs, for example, preparing meals for them. I was **in prison and you visited me:** visiting those **in prison** usually meant bringing them food. Jails at the time of Jesus did not supply meals; relatives or friends of those being detained had to provide for their needs.

Jesus' listing of six ways in which he received assistance should be taken as examples and not an exhaustive listing of all acts of mercy. The common thread running through them is providing for someone who, for whatever reason (poverty, alien status, illness, imprisonment) is in need. Jesus' examples cover basic human necessities—food, clothing, shelter.

For reflection: Who are those who are most in need in my world? In the world at large today? How am I able to help them?

37 Those on Jesus' right are puzzled by his words. **Then the righteous will answer him and say, "Lord, when did we see you hungry and feed you, or thirsty and give you drink?"** They apparently can remember feeding those who were hungry and providing drink to the thirsty, but they do not recall doing so for Jesus. They address him as **Lord** and ask him, **When did we see you** hungry or thirsty? **When** did we **feed you** or **give you drink?**

Lord: See page 133

558

Jesus refers to those who cared for his needs as **the righteous.** He has taught that righteousness is necessary to enter the kingdom of heaven (5:20) and has spoken of angels separating the wicked from the righteous at the end of the age (13:49); "the righteous will shine like the sun in the kingdom of their Father" (13:43). Jesus has not offered a definition of righteousness, although it involves keeping God's commandments (5:17- 19) and doing God's will (7:21). Calling those who assisted him **the righteous** fills in what it means to be righteous: righteousness is caring for those in need. This view of righteousness should not be a surprise to the disciples or the readers of Matthew's gospel. Jesus proclaimed that God desires mercy (9:13; 12:7; 23:23) and that those who extend mercy will be judged mercifully (5:7). God wants love (22:36-39)—even of enemies (5:43- 48)—expressed through deeds (7:21); that is the basis of the law and the prophets (7:12; 22:40). Jesus here provides examples of mercy and love in action: feeding those who are hungry, caring for those who are ill, provid- ing clothing and shelter to those in need.

> For reflection: Is my idea of righteousness not doing anything wrong, or is it doing good for others?

38 The righteous continue their questions. **When did we see you a stranger and welcome you, or naked and clothe you?** They do not remember see- ing Jesus among those whom they provided with hospitality and clothing.

39 Nor do they recall seeing Jesus among the ill or imprisoned that they vis- ited, bringing aid: **When did we see you ill or in prison, and visit you?** This is the third time they ask Jesus **when did we see you** (see verses 37- 38): they do not believe they have ever seen Jesus.

40 **And the king will say to them in reply, "Amen, I say to you, whatever you did for one of these least brothers of mine, you did for me."** In context, **these least brothers of mine** are those who are hungry, thirsty, foreigners, naked, ill, or imprisoned. Jesus calls them his **brothers,** or as- suredly, his sisters, just as he calls his disciples his brothers and sisters (12:50). Yet Jesus has not said that those who have been helped by the righteous are his disciples. Even if they are not disciples, even if they are the **least** brothers and sisters of Jesus, Jesus nevertheless tells the righteous that **whatever you did** to assist them **you did for me.** Jesus' words could

also be translated, "you did it *to* me." When you fed the hungry, you fed me; when you sheltered a homeless person, you sheltered me; when you visited a prisoner, you visited me.

Jesus does not explain how he is present in or identified with those in need, but he solemnly proclaims—**Amen, I say to you**—that helping them is helping him. If our assistance to the hungry and the alien and the afflicted is done to Jesus, then it is all the more urgent for us to act mercifully. Whatever we would want to do for Jesus if he was standing before us we must do for those in need.

For reflection: What are the implications for me of Jesus' assurance that in helping those in need I am helping him?

Saints such as Mother Teresa have been able to see Jesus in the poor and dying, but most of us see only the man or woman in front of us. We help others out of compassion for them, knowing that Jesus wants us to be compassionate. We may have little or no sense that we are giving a meal to Jesus, or visiting Jesus in a nursing home, or helping Jesus have a roof over his head. We will be among those who find out at the judgment that what we did we did to Jesus. Even reading Jesus' portrayal of the judgment scene will not ruin our surprise!

For reflection: Am I able to see Jesus in the needy, or do I simply help them because it is the right thing to do?

Some biblical scholars interpret the least brothers of Jesus to be disciples of Jesus and "all the nations" (verse 32) to represent those who are not disciples. In this interpretation, those who are not Jesus' disciples are judged according to how they treated Jesus' disciples. Other scholars hold the interpretation presented here: all nations means all *people*, and the least brothers of Jesus are those in need, whether disciples or not. In favor of this interpretation is the place of this judgment scene in Matthew's gospel: it is the climax of Jesus' instructions about how his disciples are to behave as they await his return (24:42–25:46). The judgment scene is meant to convey a message to them about what they should do until he comes. They are to extend mercy, feeding the hungry, sheltering the homeless, caring for those in need.

Jesus told his disciples that "where two or three are gathered together in my name, there am I in the midst of them" (18:20) and "whoever receives you receives me" (10:40). Jesus is also present in the hungry and thirsty, the alien and the imprisoned. Jesus is truly God-with-us (see 1:23), with all of us. The manner of his presence is something for theologians to wrestle with; the rest of us must wrestle with how we respond to Jesus' presence in every woman and man.

41 **Then he will say to those on his left, "Depart from me, you accursed, into the eternal fire prepared for the devil and his angels."** The Old Testament does not speak of an **eternal fire prepared for the devil and his angels,** but belief in such punishment developed shortly before the time of Jesus. The book of *Enoch* (a nonbiblical writing) speaks of angels who had intercourse with women (an interpretation of Gen 6:1-2, 4) and were being kept in chains until the day of judgment, when they would be cast into fire. This is reflected in the letter of Jude: "The angels too, who did not keep to their own domain but deserted their proper dwelling, he has kept in eternal chains, in gloom, for the judgment of the great day" (Jude 6; see also 2 Pet 2:4). Jesus was invoking an idea familiar to his listeners when he spoke of an eternal fire prepared for the devil. At the judgment, some humans will not be called blessed and invited to come into eternal life; rather they will be called **accursed** and told to **depart** to a place of torment.

Devil: See Satan, page 55
Nonbiblical writings: See page 198

Devil: See Satan, page 55
Nonbiblical writings: See page 198

42 Jesus explains to them why he is sending them away. **For I was hungry and you gave me no food, I was thirsty and you gave me no drink.**

43 He tells them that he had been **a stranger and you gave me no welcome, naked and you gave me no clothing, ill and in prison, and you did not care for me.**

44 Those being banished to a place of punishment are just as puzzled by Jesus' words as were those who were told to come into the kingdom. **Then they will answer and say, "Lord, when did we see you hungry or thirsty or a stranger or naked or ill or in prison, and not minister to your needs?"** They do not deny that they turned their back on those who were hungry or thirsty or a stranger or naked or ill or in prison. But they protest that they never refused to **minister to** Jesus' **needs.** The word translated **minister to** means "serve" or "help." They claim that they have never seen Jesus in need and refused to help him.

This is the fourth mention of those who are **hungry or thirsty or a stranger or naked or ill or in prison** (see verses 35-36, 37-39, 42-43). Repetition imprints these people in need in the mind of the listener or reader. No one pondering Jesus' account of the judgment can have any doubts whether Jesus wants us to help those in need.

45 He will answer them, "Amen, I say to you, what you did not do for one of these least ones, you did not do for me." Failure to help those in need is failure to help Jesus. It is not enough to avoid harming or oppressing others; positive assistance is required. To do nothing—to bury one's talent (25:18, 25)—leaves others in their misery.

46 And these will go off to eternal punishment: this is not the first time that Jesus has warned of a dire fate in the age to come (5:22, 29-30; 10:28; 13:40-42, 49-50; 18:8-9; 23:33). Jesus' warnings convey the message, See that you are not among those who will suffer **eternal punishment.** Jesus is speaking to his disciples in private (24:3). He is not talking in the abstract about some portion of the human race suffering eternal punishment; rather, he is instructing his followers how they are to behave. What they do or fail to do will have eternal consequences. They must live in a manner that will allow Jesus to place them among **the righteous** who go into **eternal life.** They must act with compassion toward those in need, feeding those who are hungry, caring for those who are ill, providing for basic human needs.

As the climax of Jesus' teachings to his followers about what they should do as they await his coming (24:32–25:46), the last judgment scene has rich meaning. His disciples must be like the faithful and prudent slave who distributed food to members of the household (24:45-47). Jesus' household is worldwide; his disciples must provide food to all who are hungry. They must be like the five wise virgins who were prepared for a delay in the bridegroom's return (25:1-10); disciples of Jesus must be prepared for the long haul, serving the needy until Jesus comes. His disciples must be like the slaves who made good use of the talents entrusted to them (25:14-23); they must use what they have to meet the needs of others. Jesus does not demand more of his disciples than they are equipped to do; he does ask that they make full use of their talents and resources to help those in need. Doing so is what it means to be awake and prepared for the coming of Jesus (24:42, 44; 25:13). Jesus "will repay everyone according to his conduct" (16:27), and he has made it clear what kind of conduct he expects.

Jesus' long discourse to his followers (24:4–25:46) ends on the note of the **righteous** entering **eternal life.** This is Jesus' goal for his first disciples and for all later disciples.

For reflection: In light of Jesus' portrayal of how I will be judged, what do I need to do that I am not doing?

CHAPTER 26

ORIENTATION: *We are at a turning point in Matthew's gospel. Jesus has completed his extended teachings; the time has come for him to die.*

Jesus Again Foretells His Death

¹ When Jesus finished all these words, he said to his disciples, ² "You know that in two days' time it will be Passover, and the Son of Man will be handed over to be crucified." ³ Then the chief priests and the elders of the people assembled in the palace of the high priest, who was called Caiaphas, ⁴ and they consulted together to arrest Jesus by treachery and put him to death. ⁵ But they said, "Not during the festival, that there may not be a riot among the people."

Gospel parallels: Mark 14:1-2; Luke 22:1-2
NT: Matt 9:15; 16:21; 17:12, 22-23; 20:18-19; 21:46; John 11:47-53

1 **When Jesus finished all these words:** Jesus has been instructing his disciples about his coming at the end of the age and what they should do to be prepared for his coming (24:4–25:46). Now Jesus has **finished** his teaching for the day. There is a second level of meaning in Matthew's words. Matthew usually marks the end of a block of teachings by writing, that "When Jesus finished these words" (or these instructions or these parables: 7:28; 11:1; 13:53; 19:1). Here, however, he writes that Jesus finished **all these words,** and **all** can include all of Jesus' teachings in the Gospel of Matthew. Jesus has **finished** his lectures; henceforth Jesus will teach more by example than by word. He does, however, want to warn his disciples about what lies ahead: **he said to his disciples,**

Disciple: See page 66

2 **You know that in two days' time it will be Passover.** Jesus and his disciples are in Jerusalem for **Passover.** The law of Moses required that Passover be celebrated in Jerusalem, the site of the Temple (Exod 12:14; Deut 16:5-6). Jesus' disciples **know** that Passover will begin in two days, but there is something else they should also know: in two days **the Son of Man will be handed over to be crucified.** Jesus has spoken about his death before, telling his disciples that he must go to Jerusalem and suffer greatly and be killed (16:21); he has spoken of his being handed over to those who would kill him (17:22-23), crucifying him (20:18-19). Jesus, **the**

Son of Man who will come in power and glory to judge the human race
(24:29-31; 25:31-46), will be **crucified.** Crucifixion was a horrible death
that Rome inflicted on rebels and the dregs of society. The contrast between Jesus in his glory and Jesus in his suffering could not be greater.
Jesus will be **handed over:** he will be betrayed into the hands of those
who will put him to death. The expression **handed over** also has the
connotation of being handed over by God: Jesus' death, even if the result
of betrayal, is part of God's plan. Jesus knows what must happen to him
(16:21); he has come to Jerusalem to carry out his Father's will.

Matthew does not recount the reaction of the disciples to Jesus'
words. We can wonder how well they grasp that Jesus has come to Jerusalem to die. Peter rejected the idea that Jesus would suffer and be killed
(16:22). After the royal welcome Jesus received when he entered Jerusalem (21:8-9), how could he be **crucified?**

Son of Man: See page 151
Feast of Passover and Unleavened Bread: See page 575
Crucifixion: See page 635

*For reflection: Had I been one of Jesus' first disciples, what would my re-
action have been to his saying that he would be crucified in two days?*

3 **Then the chief priests and the elders of the people assembled in the palace of the high priest, who was called Caiaphas.** The **chief priests** were
the most influential priests and included **Caiaphas,** who was the **high
priest** from A.D. 18 to 36. The **elders of the people** were the lay leadership and aristocracy of Jerusalem. Chief priests and elders made up the
bulk of the Sanhedrin (see 26:59), the Jewish ruling council in Jerusalem,
but Matthew does not present their assembly as a formal session of the
Sanhedrin. Their gathering is a caucus of influential leaders to make
plans. In the wake of Jesus' foretelling his death, some are plotting how to
bring it about:

Elders: See page 451
Caiaphas: See page 600

4 **and they consulted together to arrest Jesus by treachery and put him
to death.** That they would use **treachery** to arrest Jesus indicates evil intent
and also has the connotation of cunning. They **consulted together** to come
up with a way of getting rid of Jesus. Jesus disrupted Temple commerce the

565

previous day (21:12); he spoke to his disciples about the Temple being destroyed (24:1-2), and word of this may have reached the chief priests and elders (see 26:61). The Temple was the chief source of income for those who controlled it; a threat to the Temple was a threat to them. The chief priests and elders had confronted Jesus earlier that day about his actions in the Temple (21:23), and he had addressed parables to them that characterized them as corrupt leaders who would be replaced (21:28-45). They had wanted to arrest him then, but were held back by his popularity with the crowds (21:46). Now they deliberate how he might be arrested and put to death.

5 **But they said, "Not during the festival, that there may not be a riot among the people."** They are still leery of doing anything while Jerusalem is crowded with pilgrims for the **festival** of Passover. Jerusalem had a population of forty thousand or so; a hundred thousand or more came for Passover. Pilgrims had shouted out praise for Jesus as he entered Jerusalem (21:9); it would be safer to arrest him after they returned home and he was left with just his small band of followers.

BACKGROUND: HIGH PRIEST, CHIEF PRIESTS The office of high priest is traced back to Aaron in the Old Testament. Over the course of time, high priesthood became restricted to descendants of Zadok, the high priest at the time of Solomon. This succession was broken by Maccabean rulers in the second century B.C. when they usurped the office of high priest. Thereafter the high priest was a political appointee. Some Jews, especially the Essenes, considered these latter high priests illegitimate, since they were not descendants of Zadok. The high priest had religious functions, and only the high priest could enter the Holy of Holies of the Temple, once a year, on the Day of Atonement. The importance of the high priest extended beyond religious matters. The high priest had authority over the Temple and its income, which was the mainstay of the economy in Jerusalem. Because the high priest was the highest-ranking Jewish authority, he served as an intermediary between Rome and the Jewish people. Rome expected the high priest to help keep the nation in line and to insure payment of tribute, or taxes, to Rome, and the high priest remained in office at the pleasure of Rome. The gospels refer to "chief priests," a group that would have included the current high priest, former high priests, other high-ranking priests, and members of high-priestly families. The chief priests were a wealthy aristocracy within the priesthood; ordinary priests carried out their assigned duties in the Temple but had little say over how it was run.

Another factor probably entered into their thinking. Passover celebrated God's liberation of the Israelite people from slavery in Egypt (Exod 12:1-17; Deut 16:1-8). The feast was an occasion for nationalistic fervor, fanning desires to be independent of Roman rule. The first-century historian Josephus noted that Jewish rebellions usually started during religious festivals. The Roman governor Pontius Pilate lived in Caesarea on the Mediterranean coast but came to Jerusalem with his troops during feasts to extinguish any sparks of rebellion before they could flame into full revolt. Rome expected the chief priests and the elders to maintain law and order; it would be a mark against them if they did something that started a **riot**. They decide to let the pilgrims return home before moving against Jesus.

Events will prove that Jesus is right: he will be "handed over to be crucified" during Passover. Something will happen that will induce the chief priests and elders to arrest Jesus earlier than they planned.

We can note that the chief opponents of Jesus are now the aristocrats of Jerusalem—the chief priests and elders—and not the Pharisees and scribes who contended with Jesus during his public ministry. Save for a few incidents, Pharisees will not play a role in what happens in the days ahead.

A Memorable Act of Love

⁶ Now when Jesus was in Bethany in the house of Simon the leper, ⁷ a woman came up to him with an alabaster jar of costly perfumed oil, and poured it on his head while he was reclining at table. ⁸ When the disciples saw this, they were indignant and said, "Why this waste? ⁹ It could have been sold for much, and the money given to the poor." ¹⁰ Since Jesus knew this, he said to them, "Why do you make trouble for the woman? She has done a good thing for me. ¹¹ The poor you will always have with you; but you will not always have me. ¹² In pouring this perfumed oil upon my body, she did it to prepare me for burial. ¹³ Amen, I say to you, wherever this gospel is proclaimed in the whole world, what she has done will be spoken of, in memory of her."

Gospel parallels: Mark 14:3-9; John 12:1-8
OT: Deut 15:11
NT: Luke 7:36-50

6 **Now when Jesus was in Bethany:** after arriving in Jerusalem the previous day, Jesus spent the night in **Bethany** (21:17), a village on a southeastern

slope of the Mount of Olives. More pilgrims came to Jerusalem for Passover than could find accommodations in the city. Jesus and his disciples may have camped out (no one provided him with breakfast that morning, as a host should have done–21:18). Now, after a long day in Jerusalem (21:23–26:2) he is **in the house of Simon the leper.** The following verses indicate that his disciples are with him and they are having dinner. **Simon the leper** has invited them for a meal, which would be much appreciated if Jesus and his disciples were camping out. **Simon** is known as **the leper.** This indicates that he had leprosy but is presumably free of it now: if he still had an active case of leprosy, any who came in physical contact with him would have been made ritually unclean and unable to enter the Temple at Passover. Even if his leprosy was in the past he might still be called **Simon the leper** to distinguish him from other men named Simon, such as Simon the Cananean (10:4) and Simon the Cyrenian (27:32). Had Jesus healed Simon, as he healed other lepers (8:1-4; 11:5)? Matthew has not described any earlier encounters between Jesus and Simon, but Matthew does not recount all Jesus did during his years on earth. If Jesus had healed Simon, it would be natural for Simon to provide a dinner for Jesus and his disciples to express his gratitude.

Bethany: See page 446

Leprosy: See page 140

7 **A woman came up to him with an alabaster jar of costly perfumed oil.** Expensive perfumes were often kept in a jar or flask carved from **alabaster,** a translucent stone imported from Egypt. Olive **oil** could be **perfumed** with various fragrant substances and, depending on the fragrances, could be quite **costly.** An unnamed **woman** came to Jesus with an alabaster jar of expensive **perfumed oil and poured it on his head while he was reclining at table.** Jews had adopted the Greek custom of **reclining** at banquets–lying on one's left side on cushions arranged around a U-shaped arrangement of low tables. Waiters worked from inside the U. If this was the arrangement in Simon's house, then it provided a way for the woman to approach Jesus: she could place herself among those serving him. She came to him to pour oil **on his head.** Anointing one's head with oil was refreshing (6:17; see also Psalm 104:15; Amos 6:6); we might compare it to using body lotion today. Hosts might anoint the heads of their guests (Psalm 23:5; Luke 7:46). The woman **poured**–literally, "poured *out*"–her jar of **costly** oil on Jesus; the

disciples' reaction (verses 8-9) indicates that she used the whole jar. We are not told whether she was a wealthy woman or of modest means, but it was nevertheless an extravagant gesture.

Banquets: See page 464

At this point we have learned what she did but not why; we can pause to consider what might have been her motives. She is doing something nice for Jesus, but even more she is expressing affection and love, touching him, performing a personal act for him. It is unlikely that this is her first encounter with Jesus; it is more probable that he has touched her with his healing or teaching and had a profound impact on her. Out of gratitude and love she anoints his head. She does so wordlessly: there is no need to explain her action to him. She does so extravagantly, using the entire jar of costly oil to express the immensity of her gratitude and love.

For reflection: What do I imagine her motives to be? When have I felt the most gratitude and love for Jesus? What did I do to express it?

8 **When the disciples saw this, they were indignant and said, "Why this waste?"** The disciples are unconcerned about her motives; they view what she does as a **waste** of perfumed oil and are **indignant** over the waste. But how is anointing Jesus' head a **waste** of the oil? That was a proper use for perfumed oil. Their indignation must be over her using an entire jar of costly oil when a little would have sufficed. They view her act in purely utilitarian terms—a head anointing doesn't require a whole jar of oil—and miss the point of her extravagance.

Disciple: See page 66

9 The disciples comment that the jar of oil **could have been sold for much, and the money given to the poor.** Jesus has a special concern for those who are **poor** (11:5; 19:21), and he has just taught that he will judge everyone according to whether they helped those in need (25:31-46). Giving **money** to **the poor** (almsgiving: see 6:2-4) is the proper way to use one's money (see 6:19-21, 24). Since the woman's perfumed oil was costly, it **could have been sold for much** and provided a great deal of help for those in need. All that the disciples say is correct. However, it is also misguided; they miss the significance of the woman's act.

10 **Since Jesus knew this**—knew what his disciples were saying among themselves. Was this an instance of Jesus having extraordinary knowledge, or did Jesus overhear their mutterings and observe their scowls? Jesus knew his disciples and their ways of thinking. **He said to them, "Why do you make trouble for the woman? She has done a good thing for me."** The word translated **good** also means "beautiful." Rather than complain about what she did, the disciples should have applauded her doing something good and beautiful for Jesus. While Jesus has helped many people in the course of his ministry, healing and freeing and feeding them, Matthew's gospel recounts very few things being done for Jesus. Fellow pilgrims gave him a royal welcome into Jerusalem (21:8-9)—and various people extended hospitality to him (8:15; 9:9-10; 26:6)—but this woman's act is the most personal and magnanimous thing that anyone has done for Jesus. He will not let her loving deed be diminished by the disciples' complaints, nor will he allow them to **make trouble** for her.

For reflection: Do I complain about or make trouble for those who do things for Jesus but not the way that I would do them?

11 Jesus' disciples are right to be concerned about those who are in need. He tells them that **the poor you will always have with you.** Jesus does not put a stamp of approval on poverty but echoes an Old Testament verse that acknowledges that there will be people in need and commands that they be helped: "The needy will never be lacking in the land; that is why I command you to open your hand to your poor and needy kinsman in your country" (Deut 15:11). Jesus' disciples will **always** have opportunities to help those in need, and they must make use of such opportunities. Jesus tells them, though, **you will not always have me.** Jesus' death in two days continues to be on his mind (see 26:2). The bridegroom will be taken away, and the time for feasting will be over (9:15). Now, though, Simon the leper can provide a banquet for Jesus; now the woman can pour out her perfumed oil on his head. There is very little time left for such acts.

12 Jesus interprets her act in light of his coming death: **In pouring this perfumed oil upon my body, she did it to prepare me for burial.** Corpses were anointed with oils or buried with spices (2 Chron 16:14; John 19:39-40). Did the woman intend her act to be a burial anointing? Probably not, even if she knew that Jesus would die in two days. Bodies were anointed after death, not before, and she anointed only his head, not his entire body. Jesus' words reflect what is on his mind rather than what was on hers. His remaining time on earth is so short that everything that happens is refracted through the prism of his death.

Burial practices: See page 652

13 Jesus solemnly assures his disciples, **Amen, I say to you, wherever this gospel is proclaimed in the whole world, what she has done will be spoken of, in memory of her.** The **gospel** is the good news of what God is accomplishing through Jesus. During Jesus' public ministry, the good news is that the reign of God is at hand (4:17, 23; 9:35). After his resurrection, the gospel message will include his death and rising, and **this** gospel will be **proclaimed** to the **whole world** (see 24:14; 28:19). **Wherever** it is proclaimed it will include an account of what this woman did for Jesus. Her loving act must never be forgotten; it is a model for what every woman and man should want to do for Jesus.

Gospel: See page 211

While **memory of her** will endure, her name will be forgotten. Matthew tells us that her anointing took place in the house of Simon the leper but does not identify the woman who did the anointing! Why should Simon be named but not her? It seems—and is—unfair. Yet perhaps there is a silver lining in this cloud of forgetfulness. By consigning her to anonymity she can stand for every man and woman who is stirred with gratitude and love for Jesus. She represents every disciple who takes her or his place among those serving Jesus and does something beautiful for him. She stands for every disciple who does not count the cost of discipleship, who does not hold back from giving extravagantly. Jesus will preserve memory of them, as of her, where it counts most: in eternity.

For reflection: What lesson does this woman hold for me?

Judas Offers to Betray Jesus
14 Then one of the Twelve, who was called **Judas Iscariot,** went to the chief priests 15 and said, "What are you willing to give me if I hand him over to you?" They paid him thirty pieces of silver, 16 and from that time on he looked for an opportunity to hand him over.

Gospel parallels: Mark 14:10-11; Luke 22:3-6
OT: Exod 21:32; Zech 11:12-13
NT: Matt 10:1-7; 26:1-5

14 **Then one of the Twelve, who was called Judas Iscariot, went to the chief priests.** Jesus selected **twelve** disciples, gave them authority, and sent them on mission (10:1-7). In the new age they would sit on twelve thrones and judge the twelve tribes of Israel (19:28). The **Twelve** were the inner circle of Jesus' followers and presumably his closest friends. One of the Twelve **was called Judas Iscariot,** perhaps indicating that he is from the village of Kerioth. When Matthew first introduced Judas, he noted that he would betray Jesus (10:4); betrayal is indeed now on Judas' mind. He **went to the chief priests:** Judas takes the initiative and acts on his own accord. He seems to be aware that the chief priests want to arrest Jesus but are held back by his popularity with the crowds (21:46; 26:3-5).

High priest, chief priests: See page 566

15 **He said, "What are you willing to give me if I hand him over to you?"** Judas proposes to **hand** Jesus **over** to the chief priests at a time and place when he can be arrested quietly, without crowds interfering. Judas must have realized the enormity of what he was offering to do. He had just heard Jesus say that he would "be handed over to be crucified" (26:2), echoing his earlier warnings that he would be "handed over" to those who would put him to death (17:22-23; 20:18-19). Judas proposes that he be the one to **hand** Jesus **over.** He asks the chief priests, **what are you willing to give me?** While he wants payment for delivering Jesus to them, it is not clear that he is betraying Jesus simply for the sake of money. We have no reason to believe that Judas did not start out as a sincerely committed disciple of Jesus. He had accepted Jesus' invitation to follow him, leaving behind everything to do so (19:27). That Jesus selected him to be one of the Twelve indicates that Jesus considered him a true disciple, worthy to judge a tribe of Israel (19:28). How did Judas the committed disciple become Judas the betrayer? Matthew does not explain his change of heart but portrays Judas as wanting to profit from it. Judas is looking for severance pay, as it were, but the reason for his resigning from the company of Jesus remains unexplained.

For reflection: Is there anything in my own experience that gives me a notion of how Judas the disciple could become Judas the betrayer?

The chief priests welcome the possibility of being able to arrest Jesus earlier than they planned and **they paid him thirty pieces of silver.** Judas receives his pay in advance, as if the chief priests are so eager to do away with Jesus that they are willing to make payment up front. It is hard to pin down the worth of **thirty pieces of silver** because silver coins were minted in various monetary values. Thirty silver coins would probably have amounted to a few month's wages for an ordinary worker—not a large sum. The Old Testament background also suggests that Judas' pay was modest. The owner of a slave who had been gored by a bull was to receive thirty shekels of silver as recompense (Exod 21:32); Jesus' life is valued as that of a slave. In a prophecy of Zechariah, a shepherd receives thirty pieces of silver as wages but is instructed by God to throw them into the Temple treasury because they are an insultingly small payment for his work (Zech 11:12-13).

For reflection: In my following of Jesus, have I ever forsaken something valuable for a paltry payoff?

16 **From that time on he looked for an opportunity to hand him over.** Matthew has used the expression **from that time on** to signal the beginning of new stages in Jesus' life—first his public ministry (4:17) and then his orientation toward his coming death (16:21). Now it is the final stage, with Judas on the lookout for an **opportunity** when Jesus can be arrested without risking a riot.

In the space of a few verses (26:6-16) Matthew has presented a woman whose love for Jesus is so great that she pours out a jar of expensive oil on his head and a man whose heart is so closed to Jesus that he accepts a paltry sum for handing him over to death. The woman's oil cost considerably more than Judas received. Sin pays poorly; love does not count the cost.

Preparations for the Passover
17 On the first day of the Feast of Unleavened Bread, the disciples approached Jesus and said, "Where do you want us to prepare for you to eat the Passover?" 18 He said, "Go into the city to a certain man and tell him, 'The teacher says, "My appointed time draws near; in your house I

shall celebrate the Passover with my disciples."'" **19** The disciples then did as Jesus had ordered, and prepared the Passover.

> Gospel parallels: Mark 14:12-16; Luke 22:7-13
> OT:Exod 12:1-28; 13:3-10; Lev 23:4-14; Deut 16:1-8, 16
> NT:Matt 26:2, 12

17 **On the first day of the Feast of Unleavened Bread:** the **Feast of Unleavened Bread** lasted seven days, during which no leavened bread was eaten (Exod 23:15; 34:18; Lev 23:6; see also Exod 12:15-20; 13:3-7). The feast of Unleavened Bread began with the Passover meal, eaten after sunset (Jews reckon days from sunset to sunset). During the day leading up to the Passover meal, all leavened bread and starter dough were disposed of (Deut 26:4); in popular usage, some spoke of this as **the first day of the Feast of Unleavened Bread.** On this day **the disciples approached Jesus and said, "Where do you want us to prepare for you to eat the Passover?"** The feast of **Passover** and **Unleavened Bread** were celebrated by pilgrimage to Jerusalem (Exod 23:14-15; Deut 16:16), and the Passover meal had to be eaten within Jerusalem (Deut 16:5-7). Jesus has been staying in Bethany (21:17; 26:6), and his disciples want to know **where** in Jerusalem he will eat the Passover meal. Residents of Jerusalem made their extra rooms available to pilgrims for the Passover meal. The disciples will **prepare** a Passover meal for Jesus. This involved procuring a lamb, sacrificing it in the Temple, roasting it, baking unleavened bread, and preparing the other foods eaten during a Passover meal (Exod 12:8-9).

> Disciple: See page 66

18 **He said, "Go into the city to a certain man."** Jesus knows someone who will provide a room where he and his disciples can eat the Passover meal. Matthew has Jesus refer to him as **a certain man,** perhaps because his name had been forgotten by the time Matthew wrote his gospel. Jesus directs his disciples to **go into the city** to a man who has a house within the city **and tell him, "The teacher says, 'My appointed time draws near; in your house I shall celebrate the Passover with my disciples.'"** Jesus tells his disciples to refer to him as **the teacher** (see 23:8): the homeowner apparently recognizes Jesus as the teacher of God's ways even though he has not left everything to follow Jesus. The disciples are to relay to him Jesus' words, **In your house I shall celebrate the Passover with my disciples.** Jesus is confident that the homeowner will make a room available for him.

He says that he will celebrate Passover **with my disciples.** Passover meals were a family affair (Exod 12:3-40); the **disciples** are the new family of Jesus (12:48-50). He says, **My appointed time draws near.** Jesus knows that he will be handed over to be crucified at Passover (26:2, 12). The **appointed time** is the time appointed by God for Jesus to die in order to fulfill what must happen (16:21). The culmination of Jesus' mission **draws near.**

There are hints of another level of meaning in the **appointed time** drawing **near.** Matthew's gospel has used the Greek word translated **appointed time** to refer to the time when this age will end (8:29; 13:30, 39). The word translated **near** has been used for the kingdom of God or the end of the age drawing near or being at hand (3:2; 4:17; 10:7; 24:33). Jesus' death and rising will be a turning point in God's relationship with the human race, ushering in a new age.

19 **The disciples then did as Jesus had ordered, and prepared the Passover.** The homeowner does provide a place for Jesus to have a Passover meal with his disciples. Matthew does not go into the details of their preparation

BACKGROUND: FEAST OF PASSOVER AND UNLEAVENED BREAD Passover commemorated God's freeing the Israelites from captivity in Egypt; a description of the Passover meal and the command to celebrate it are found in chapter 12 of Exodus. The feast of Passover incorporated several ancient elements. One element was the annual sacrifice of a young lamb as an offering for the fertility and safety of the flock; shepherds made the offering in the spring before moving to new pastures. Another ancient element was a "feast of Unleavened Bread" (Exod 23:15; 34:18; Lev 23:6), an agricultural festival celebrating the beginning of the grain harvest. In Palestine during biblical times, grain crops grew during the winter, which is the only rainy season. Barley was the first grain to ripen in the spring. To celebrate the barley harvest, bread made from only newly harvested grain was eaten for seven days. This bread was unleavened because leaven was kept in the form of starter dough, and no grain or starter dough from previous harvests could be used during this feast (Exod 12:18-20). Passover thus incorporated traditions of nomadic shepherds and settled farmers but gave them greater meaning as part of a celebration of liberation from Egypt. Originally Passover was celebrated in one's home, wherever one lived; after sacrificial worship was restricted to the Temple in Jerusalem by King Josiah in 622 B.C., Passover became a pilgrimage feast celebrated in Jerusalem, since the sacrificing of lambs could then be done only at the Temple.

of the Passover meal. His sparse account puts the spotlight on the **disciples** doing **as Jesus had ordered**—a model for discipleship. The disciples asked Jesus what they were to do (verse 17); he told them (verse 18), and they did it (verse 19). Discipleship means doing the will of God taught by Jesus (7:21-25; 12:49-50); discipleship means doing what Jesus asks, even in mundane matters.

For reflection: How completely do I do what Jesus asks me to do? Is there anything he has asked me to do that I have not done?

Jesus Confronts His Betrayer

20 When it was evening, he reclined at table with the Twelve. **21** And while they were eating, he said, "Amen, I say to you, one of you will betray me." **22** Deeply distressed at this, they began to say to him one after another, "Surely it is not I, Lord?" **23** He said in reply, "He who has dipped his hand into the dish with me is the one who will betray me. **24** The Son of Man indeed goes, as it is written of him, but woe to that man by whom the Son of Man is betrayed. It would be better for that man if he had never been born." **25** Then Judas, his betrayer, said in reply, "Surely it is not I, Rabbi?" He answered, "You have said so."

Gospel parallels: Mark 14:17-21; Luke 22:14, 21-23; John 13:21-30
NT: Matt 17:22-23; 20:18-19; 26:2, 14-16

20 **When it was evening, he reclined at table with the Twelve.** The Passover meal was eaten in the **evening,** after sunset (see Exod 12:8). Jesus and his disciples **reclined at table.** The Passover meal may originally have been eaten while standing (see Exod 12:11), but Jews had adopted the Greek custom of reclining at banquets—lying on one's left side on cushions or couches. Reclining during the Passover meal became a sign of liberation from slavery in Egypt, since slaves did not banquet. (After the Middle Ages, most artistic depictions of the Last Supper portray Jesus and his disciples sitting, probably because reclining was not in fashion when the artists lived. We envision biblical events through the lens of our own experience.)

Banquets: See page 464

21 **And while they were eating, he said, "Amen, I say to you, one of you will betray me."** Passover meals are joyful occasions, a sharing of table fellowship in remembrance of God delivering his people from bondage in Egypt. Yet **while they were eating** Jesus interrupts their celebration with a shocking statement. He prefaces his pronouncement with a solemn **Amen, I say to you** to underline the gravity of what he is saying. **One of you,** one of the specially chosen Twelve, **will betray me.** The Greek word translated **betray** is sometimes translated "hand over." Jesus has warned his disciples that he will be handed over to those who will put him to death (17:22-23; 20:18-19), with the most recent warning coming little more than a day ago (26:2). Now he tells them that it will be **one of you** who hands me over. Matthew's readers know that the betrayer is Judas (26:14-16; see also 10:4), but this is the first time that Jesus' disciples hear that one of them will betray him. Judas, of course, knows what he has set in motion (26:14-16). Jesus' words are not simply a general announcement to the disciples but are pointed at Judas, letting him know that Jesus knows what he is about.

22 The disciples are quite naturally **deeply distressed at** hearing **this.** The Greek for **deeply distressed** can also be translated "overwhelmed with grief"—the disciples' reaction the first time Jesus spoke of his being handed over to those who will kill him (17:23). Now their distress is even greater, for they have learned that *one of them* will hand Jesus over to death. **They began to say to him one after another, "Surely it is not I, Lord?"** Their question is phrased in a way that invites a reassuring response from Jesus: "No, you are not the one." They address him as their **Lord,** acknowledging his authority. Yet their asking this question seems to betray an uneasiness, as if each of them thinks that he could betray Jesus. They do not issue a flat denial—"I would never do that!"—but seek Jesus' reassurance that they will not fail and betray him.

Lord: See page 133

For reflection: How sure am I that I will never turn away from or against Jesus? When have I come closest to doing so?

23 Jesus does not give them the reassurance they seek; perhaps their being unsure of their future faithfulness is a proper self-assessment. Instead **he said in reply, "He who has dipped his hand into the dish with me is the one who will betray me."** Pieces of bread were used as edible spoons to scoop up sauces from a **dish** (see Ruth 2:14). It became the custom to dip the bitter herbs eaten during the Passover meal (Exod 12:8) in a fruit sauce. **The one who will betray** Jesus has been eating from the same **dish** with him. This accentuates the enormity of his betrayal, but how much help is it in identifying the betrayer? Bowls of sauce were shared by several diners. Jesus' words only narrow down his betrayer to someone who is reclining near him. Judas, however, would have known that he had **dipped his hand into the dish with** Jesus and that Jesus is talking about him.

24 Jesus continues, **The Son of Man indeed goes, as it is written of him.** The word **goes** implies goes to his death; **written of him** means written about him in Scripture. There is no passage in the Old Testament that explicitly speaks of **the Son of Man** being put to death. Jesus may be applying a Scripture passage such as Isaiah 52:13–53:12 to himself as **the Son of Man.** Isaiah's prophecy speaks of a servant of God who is "cut off from the land of the living and smitten for the sin of his people" (Isaiah 53:8). Jesus **goes** willingly to his death; he embraces God's will for him (see 16:21). **But woe to that man by whom the Son of Man is betrayed.** While Jesus' death is God's will, the one who hands Jesus over to death is accountable for his betrayal. Jesus laments the betrayer's deplorable condition with a **woe.** The betrayer is bringing on himself a fate worse than death: **It would be better for that man if he had never been born.** Job's sufferings weighed on him so heavily that he would have preferred dying at birth or being stillborn (Job 3:11, 16). It would likewise **be better** for Jesus' betrayer to have **never been born.** Jesus does not spell out what fate awaits him but indicates that it will be horrible.

Son of Man: See page 151
Woes: See page 499

Judas must have taken Jesus' words as addressed to him. Jesus previously spoke of punishment awaiting evildoers in order to warn his listeners to avoid sin (5:29-30; 10:28; 18:8-9); Jesus is now giving Judas a last-minute warning. Even though Jesus knows what will happen, Judas is nevertheless free to change his mind and take a different course.

For reflection: What warnings has Jesus given me? How well have I heeded his warnings?

25 **Then Judas, his betrayer, said in reply, "Surely it is not I, Rabbi?"** Judas apparently kept silent when the other disciples asked for Jesus' reassurance, but now he speaks up. He asks Jesus the same question the others asked—**Surely it is not I?**—but he addresses Jesus as **Rabbi** rather than as Lord (see verse 22). While **Rabbi** is a respectful title it does not acknowledge Jesus' authority as does calling him Lord: Judas no longer accepts Jesus as his Lord. Even the seeming respect in calling Jesus **Rabbi** may be hypocritical. Judas says, **Surely it is not I,** when he knows that surely **it is.** His question seems desperate. Jesus **answered, "You have said so."** Jesus does not answer with a yes or no but uses an expression that indirectly affirms that Judas is indeed the betrayer. Jesus lets Judas know that he knows of Judas' betrayal, but Jesus does not provoke an open confrontation with Judas during his final meal with his disciples.

Rabbi: See page 495

If the other disciples overheard this exchange they apparently missed its significance. Had Jesus explicitly named Judas as the one who would hand him over, the other disciples might have beaten him and tied him up. By not naming him Jesus allows Judas to go ahead with his plot. Jesus knows that he will die because of Judas' betrayal; Jesus gives Judas an opportunity to change his course but does not otherwise try to halt the train of events that will culminate in his death.

Jesus Gives His Body and Blood

26 While they were eating, Jesus took bread, said the blessing, broke it, and giving it to his disciples said, "Take and eat; this is my body." 27 Then he took a cup, gave thanks, and gave it to them, saying, "Drink from it, all of you, 28 for this is my blood of the covenant, which will be shed on behalf of many for the forgiveness of sins. 29 I tell you, from now on I shall not drink this fruit of the vine until the day when I drink it with you new in the kingdom of my Father." 30 Then, after singing a hymn, they went out to the Mount of Olives.

Gospel parallels: Mark 14:22-26; Luke 22:14-20
OT:Exod 24:3-8; Isaiah 25:6-9; 52:13–53:12; Jer 31:31-34
NT:Matt 1:21; 14:13-21; 15:32-38; 20:28; John 6:51-58; 1 Cor
10:16-17; 11:23-27

26 **While they were eating:** the disciples had prepared a Passover meal (26:17-20), but Matthew provides no details about Passover foods or ritual. Instead he focuses on certain words and actions of Jesus. **Jesus took bread, said the blessing, broke it, and giving it to his disciples said, "Take and eat."** Jesus does what any father of a family or host presiding over a Jewish meal would do. He takes a loaf of **bread** and offers a **blessing** in thanksgiving to God for the bread (see 14:19). A traditional Jewish blessing over bread is, "Blessed are you, O Lord our God, King of the universe, who brings forth bread from the earth." Then Jesus **broke** the bread into pieces and gave it to **his disciples.** Sharing a loaf of bread is a sign of fellowship and shared lives. While telling his disciples to **take and eat** would have been unsurprising, Jesus' next words are unprecedented: **this is my body.** In the Hebrew way of thinking, the **body** was not just one's flesh but one's whole person as a physical being. Jesus gives bread to his disciples to **take and eat** and tells them that the bread they are to eat is his **body,** his person, his self. Bread nourishes physically; Jesus gives himself to his disciples as spiritual nourishment. The broken bread foreshadows the body of Jesus being broken in death. Jesus had compassion on the hungry crowds (14:14; 15:32); out of compassion he gives himself for and to his disciples.

Jesus' stunning words must be pondered as well as obeyed. What does it mean for bread to be the body of Jesus? What are the consequences of eating bread that is the body of Jesus? What fellowship with Jesus and with one another is created by sharing this bread?

For reflection: How do I understand Jesus' words, "This is my body"? What have been the consequences of my eating bread that is the body of Jesus?

27 **Then he took a cup** of wine, **gave thanks, and gave it to them, saying, "Drink from it, all of you."** Wine was drunk on festive occasions, such as Passover. Later Jewish practice calls for four cups of wine during the Passover meal, but it is uncertain whether this was the custom at the time of Jesus. Jesus **gave thanks** to God for the wine (see also 15:36). A traditional Jewish thanksgiving for wine is, "Blessed are you, O Lord our God, king of the universe, creator of the fruit of the vine." The Greek word translated **gave thanks** gives us the word "Eucharist." Jesus **gave the cup**

to his disciples: just as sharing a loaf of bread is a sign of fellowship, so is sharing a cup of wine. Jesus told the disciples, **Drink from it, all of you.** During a Passover meal there would have been nothing out of the ordinary in Jesus taking a cup of wine, thanking God for it, and passing it around to be shared.

28 Jesus' next words are unprecedented, just as were his words about the bread. He tells his disciples that they are to "drink from it, all of you," **for this is my blood of the covenant, which will be shed on behalf of many for the forgiveness of sins.** The Hebrew notion of **blood** was that it was the life of a human or an animal (Gen 9:4; Lev 17:11, 14; Deut 12:23). For Jesus to give his blood is to share his life. A **covenant** is an agreement or pact that establishes a relationship between two parties. The phrase **blood of the covenant** echoes words Moses uttered at Mount Sinai as he mediated the covenant between God and the Israelites. Bulls were offered in sacrifice to God, and their blood was divided into two portions. One portion was poured on the altar as an offering to God, and Moses sprinkled the other portion on the people as "the blood of the covenant" (Exod 24:8)–the blood that sealed their participation in the covenant that God was establishing with them.

> Then he took the blood and sprinkled it on the people, saying, "This is the blood of the covenant which the LORD has made with you in accordance with all these words of his."
> Exodus 24:8

Jesus' blood **will be shed** or poured out. Pouring out one's blood means pouring out one's life. Jesus' coming death will be a sacrificial offering to God; his shed blood will be **blood of the covenant,** sealing a new relationship between God and humans. Jesus' blood will be shed **on behalf of many:** the word **many** has the Hebrew sense of "all, as opposed to a few." Jesus will shed his blood on behalf of many **for the forgiveness of sins.** Before Jesus' birth, an angel told Joseph to name him Jesus "because he will save his people from their sins" (1:21). Jesus will "give his life as a ransom for many" (20:28), freeing them from slavery to sin. Jesus' offering of his life to God will create a covenant relationship with God characterized by the forgiveness of sins (see Jer 31:31-34).

For reflection: How do I understand Jesus' words about the wine that is his blood? How have I experienced the Eucharist as a sharing in the life of Jesus? What are the implications for me of Jesus' giving his life for the forgiveness of sins?

The expression **on behalf of many** and the notion of giving up one's life so that sins might be forgiven echoes a prophecy of Isaiah that speaks of a servant of God who suffers and dies on behalf of others, winning pardon for their sins (Isaiah 52:13–53:12).

> *Through his suffering, my servant shall justify many,*
> *and their guilt he shall bear . . .*
> *Because he surrendered himself to death*
> *and was counted among the wicked;*
> *And he shall take away the sins of many,*
> *and win pardon for their offenses.*
> *Isaiah 53:11-12*

29 The time for Jesus to shed his blood is so imminent that this is the last meal Jesus will have with his disciples before he dies. He says to them, **I tell you, from now on I shall not drink this fruit of the vine** (an idiom for wine) **until the day when I drink it with you new in the kingdom of my**

COMMENT: THE EUCHARIST Matthew's first readers would have known about Jesus' final meal with his followers even before they read Matthew's gospel. Proclaiming what Jesus did and said on the night before he died was part of the gospel message, as Paul makes clear (1 Cor 11:23-26). The church from its earliest days celebrated "the breaking of the bread" (Acts 2:42), or "the Lord's supper" (1 Cor 11:20). Matthew's audience would have understood his account of what Jesus did during the Last Supper in light of their own celebration of the Eucharist. The same is true for us today. Our understanding of the Eucharist rests not only on what we read in Matthew but also on what we read in the other gospels and writings of the New Testament. We are also the heirs of two millennia of theological reflection on the meaning of the Eucharist. St. Thomas Aquinas in the thirteenth century employed concepts from the Greek philosopher Aristotle in characterizing bread and wine becoming the body and blood of Christ as "transubstantiation"—a change of their underlying reality. The Roman Catholic Church embraces this term, even as it acknowledges that bread and wine being the body and blood of Christ surpasses our understanding.

Father. Jesus has referred to "the banquet in the kingdom of heaven" (8:11; see also 22:2; 25:10): being part of God's eternal reign will be like enjoying an unending "feast of rich foods and choice wines, / juicy, rich food and pure, choice wines" (Isaiah 25:6). Jesus will pour out his blood and die, but he will be raised (16:21; 17:9, 23; 20:19) and enthroned (19:28; 25:31) in **the kingdom of** his **Father.** Jesus tells his disciples that he will drink no more wine of this earth but will drink the **new** wine of the heavenly banquet—and drink it **with you:** they will participate in the eternal banquet of his Father's kingdom. The bread and wine that Jesus gives his disciples as his body and blood are a foretaste and foreshadowing of the banquet of eternity.

Kingdom of heaven: See page 266

For reflection: What hopes are conveyed to me by Jesus' speaking of drinking new wine with his followers in his Father's kingdom?

30 **Then, after singing a hymn, they went out to the Mount of Olives.** Later Jewish writings call for singing Psalms 114 (or 115) through 118 at the conclusion of a Passover meal; this may have been the custom at the time of Jesus and have been the **hymn** they sung. Jesus and his disciples leave the house in Jerusalem where they ate the Passover meal (26:17-19) and go **out to the Mount of Olives,** across the Kidron Valley from Jerusalem. Jesus and his disciples have been spending their nights in Bethany, two miles from Jerusalem (21:17; see also 26:6). The law requiring the Passover meal to be eaten in Jerusalem (Deut 16:5-7) was interpreted to mean that the entire night should be spent in Jerusalem. As a way of accommodating the pilgrims who flooded Jerusalem, the western slope of the **Mount of Olives,** which faces Jerusalem, was considered within the city limits. This may be why Jesus and his disciples go to the Mount of Olives instead of continuing on to Bethany.

Failure and Restoration
31 **Then Jesus said to them, "This night all of you will have your faith in me shaken, for it is written:**

'I will strike the shepherd,
and the sheep of the flock will be dispersed';

³² but after I have been raised up, I shall go before you to Galilee." ³³ Peter said to him in reply, "Though all may have their faith in you shaken, mine will never be." ³⁴ Jesus said to him, "Amen, I say to you, this very night before the cock crows, you will deny me three times." ³⁵ Peter said to him, "Even though I should have to die with you, I will not deny you." And all the disciples spoke likewise.

> Gospel parallels: Mark 14:27-31; Luke 22:31-34; John 13:36-38
> OT:Zech 13:7
> NT:Matt 16:21-25

31 **Then Jesus said to them:** it is nighttime, after the Passover meal (26:19-29). Jesus and his disciples have gone from Jerusalem to the Mount of Olives (26:30). While they are on their way to a place on the Mount of Olives called Gethsemane (26:36), Jesus tells his disciples that during **this night all of you will have your faith in me shaken.** The Greek word translated **have your faith . . . shaken** means to be tripped up by an obstacle, to take offense. **In me** might better be translated *"because of* me": Jesus will be the obstacle that trips up the disciples. Jesus proclaimed "blessed is the one who takes no offense at me" (11:6); the people of Nazareth had taken offense at Jesus (13:57), as had some Pharisees (15:12). Something will happen **this night** that will trip up the disciples, leading them to take offense at Jesus. Jesus has just given his disciples bread and wine as his body and blood (26:26-28), but nevertheless **all** of them will fail him before the night is out.

> *For reflection: What might I learn from the disciples failing Jesus so soon after receiving his body and blood?*

Jesus applies a prophecy of Zechariah to what will happen to him and to his disciples: **for it is written: "I will strike the shepherd, / and the sheep of the flock will be dispersed"** (see Zech 13:7). Jesus identifies himself as **the shepherd** (see 9:36). He will be struck down—crucified (26:2). While in Zechariah's prophecy God says, "Strike the shepherd," Jesus rephrases it so that God says, **I will strike the shepherd:** Jesus' death is part of God's will (see 16:21; 26:24, 54, 56) even though the humans involved are responsible for their actions (26:24). When Jesus is struck down, **the sheep of the flock will be dispersed.** Jesus adds **of the flock** to Zechariah's prophecy so that it applies more pointedly to the **flock** of Jesus' followers.

They will be **dispersed.** Following Jesus and being with him is at the heart of discipleship (4:18-22; 8:22; 9:9; 16:24; 19:21) but in the coming crisis his disciples will abandon him and be scattered.

> Strike the shepherd
> > that the sheep may be dispersed.
> > > Zechariah 13:7

32 Neither Jesus' death nor the disciples' scattering will be the end for them, however. Jesus tells them, **But after I have been raised up, I shall go before you to Galilee.** Jesus has repeatedly spoken of his being **raised**—raised by God—from death (16:21; 17:9, 23; 20:19). If it is God's will that the shepherd be struck down, it is also God's will that he be **raised up.** Jesus tells his disciples that after being raised **I will go before you to Galilee.** Most of the disciples are from **Galilee** (4:18-22; 9:9), and virtually all of Jesus' ministry took place in Galilee. Jesus will **go before** his disciples to Galilee. This does not mean that he will arrive in Galilee first but that he will lead his disciples in Galilee like a shepherd leading his flock. The scattered disciples will be gathered together by the risen Jesus; there will be a new beginning for them in the region where they began to follow him. They will abandon Jesus that night, but he will restore them after he is raised.

Galilee: See page 68

For reflection: What hope does Jesus' promise of restoration for failed disciples hold for me?

33 Peter hears Jesus say that all the disciples will be tripped up, but he seems to have then stopped listening to Jesus. He misses (or ignores) Jesus' promise of restoration but takes issue with Jesus' forecast of failure. **Peter said to him in reply, "Though all may have their faith in you shaken, mine will never be."** Peter allows that Jesus might be right about the rest of the disciples: **all** of them may have their faith shaken. But Peter denies that he will ever fail Jesus, claiming that his faith will **never** be shaken—he will never be tripped up. Peter contradicted Jesus when Jesus foretold his suffering and death (16:21-22), and Peter contradicts Jesus again when he foretells Peter's falling away. Peter considers himself to be better than the other disciples; he is certain that his commitment to Jesus is strong enough to overcome all obstacles.

34 Jesus knows that Peter's self-assurance is woefully misguided. **Jesus said to him, "Amen, I say to you, this very night before the cock crows, you will deny me three times."** Will Peter *never* fail Jesus? Jesus solemnly assures him that **this very night** he will stumble. **Before the cock crows,** before daybreak, Peter **will deny** Jesus. To **deny** means to disavow, disown, renounce, repudiate. Will Peter *never* fail Jesus? He will do so **three times.**

35 Despite Jesus' solemn assurance of what will happen, Peter contradicts him again. **Peter said to him, "Even though I should have to die with you, I will not deny you."** Peter now seems to accept that Jesus will die and proclaims that he is willing to die **with** him rather than deny him. Peter's words express the high commitment required of disciples. Jesus said, "Whoever wishes to come after me must deny himself, take up his cross, and follow me . . . whoever loses his life for my sake will find it" (16:24-25). But while Peter professes that he is willing to lose his life for the sake of Jesus, Jesus knows that Peter is in denial about who he will deny when the chips are down. Peter is not the only one in denial: **And all the disciples spoke likewise.**

All of Jesus' words will prove true. But should the disciples' professions that they will be faithful to Jesus even to the point of death be dismissed as simply empty bluster? Perhaps their misplaced confidence holds a lesson for all disciples of Jesus. We can be utterly sincere when we tell Jesus that we are willing to die for him, but we should not mistake our resolve for the strength to carry it out. It is better to place our trust in Jesus, who restores those who fail, than to trust ourselves to never fail.

For reflection: What warnings and lessons do Peter's claims have for me?

Matthew's account surrounds Jesus' giving of his body and blood to his disciples with betrayal, failure, and denial (26:20-35). One of the specially chosen Twelve will hand Jesus over to those who will put him to death (26:21-25). Peter, the rock upon whom Jesus will build his church (16:18), will repeatedly repudiate Jesus before the night is out. And despite their protestations of loyalty, all of the disciples will abandon Jesus. He nonetheless gives them bread and wine as his body and blood; Jesus' body will be broken and his blood shed so that their sins may be forgiven (26:26-28). Jesus promises to gather them together again after he is raised, and to bring them with him into the banquet of his Father's kingdom

(26:29). So too, Jesus died for us despite and because of our sins; Jesus gives himself to us in the Eucharist despite and because of our frailty.

Jesus Embraces His Father's Will

³⁶ Then Jesus came with them to a place called Gethsemane, and he said to his disciples, "Sit here while I go over there and pray." ³⁷ He took along Peter and the two sons of Zebedee, and began to feel sorrow and distress. ³⁸ Then he said to them, "My soul is sorrowful even to death. Remain here and keep watch with me." ³⁹ He advanced a little and fell prostrate in prayer, saying, "My Father, if it is possible, let this cup pass from me; yet, not as I will, but as you will." ⁴⁰ When he returned to his disciples he found them asleep. He said to Peter, "So you could not keep watch with me for one hour? ⁴¹ Watch and pray that you may not undergo the test. The spirit is willing, but the flesh is weak." ⁴² Withdrawing a second time, he prayed again, "My Father, if it is not possible that this cup pass without my drinking it, your will be done!" ⁴³ Then he returned once more and found them asleep, for they could not keep their eyes open. ⁴⁴ He left them and withdrew again and prayed a third time, saying the same thing again. ⁴⁵ Then he returned to his disciples and said to them, "Are you still sleeping and taking your rest? Behold, the hour is at hand when the Son of Man is to be handed over to sinners. ⁴⁶ Get up, let us go. Look, my betrayer is at hand."

Gospel parallels: Mark 14:32-42; Luke 22:39-46
NT: Matt 6:9-13; John 12:27; Heb 4:15; 5:7-9

36 **Then Jesus came with them to a place called Gethsemane.** Jesus and his disciples are on the Mount of Olives (26:30) where, as its name indicates, olive trees grow. The word **Gethsemane** in Aramaic means "oil press"; the **place called Gethsemane** was apparently a grove of olive trees near a press for extracting olive oil. A tradition dating back to at least the fourth century locates **Gethsemane** near the foot of the Mount of Olives, across the Kidron Valley from the Temple. Jesus **said to his disciples, "Sit here while I go over there and pray."** Jesus knows that before the night is over, he will be arrested and his disciples will scatter (26:21, 31); his arrest will lead to his crucifixion (26:2). Jesus wants to **pray** about what is at hand. He taught his followers, "When you pray, go to your inner room, close the door, and pray to your Father in secret" (6:6). There is no inner room available to Jesus, but he can ask his disciples to **sit here** while he goes off to pray.

587

37 **He took along Peter and the two sons of Zebedee,** James and John. They were (with Peter's brother Andrew) the first disciples Jesus called (4:18-22) and the first listed among the Twelve (10:2). Peter, James, and John witnessed Jesus' transfiguration (17:1-8), and he again wants them with him. James and John assured Jesus that they could drink the cup that he would drink (20:22), and Peter said that he was willing to die with Jesus (26:35). Their good intentions will soon be put to the test.

Jesus **began to feel sorrow and distress.** Jesus spoke many times about being put to death (9:15; 16:21; 17:22-23; 20:18-19; 26:2), accepting that it must happen (16:21) and that he will be giving his life as a ransom (20:28). He had just given a cup of wine to his disciples, telling them "this is my blood of the covenant, which will be shed on behalf of many for the forgiveness of sins" (26:28). Yet now Jesus experiences **sorrow and distress,** grief and anxiety, as the time for him to suffer and die draws near. Why would Jesus be grieved and troubled by what he has up until now accepted? Is Jesus recoiling from the horror of crucifixion now that it is at hand? Or is there some other cause for his sorrow and distress? Matthew's gospel does not explain why Jesus is troubled and sad. We are given a glimpse of the humanity of Jesus, yet we must ponder the significance of his sorrow and distress.

For reflection: How do I understand Jesus' sorrow and distress?

38 **Then he said to them, "My soul is sorrowful even to death."** Jesus lets Peter, James, and John know that he is profoundly grieved. The Hebrew notion of **soul** was that it was one's livingness; Psalms 42 and 43 use **my soul** as an expression for one's inner self (Psalm 42:6; 43:5). The Greek word used here for **sorrowful** means "extremely sad" or "greatly grieved." **Sorrowful even to death** is an idiom for intense sorrow, sorrow so painful one could die from it (see Sirach 37:2). (Save for Jesus' being moved with pity—9:36; 14:14; 15:32; 20:34—Matthew's gospel rarely speaks of Jesus' emotions, making his profound sorrow in Gethsemane all the more noteworthy.) Jesus asks Peter, James, and John to **remain here and keep watch with me.** To **keep watch**—literally, "stay awake"—means to be prepared for what lies ahead (see 24:42-44; 25:13). Jesus asks them to keep watch **with me:** he wants them to be near him and to follow his example. It is important for them to be prepared for what will happen, as he will now prepare himself.

39 **He advanced a little and fell prostrate in prayer.** To fall **prostrate** (literally, "upon one's face") on the ground is an act of homage (Gen 17:3; Ruth 2:10; 1 Sam 20:41; 2 Sam 9:6; 1 Kings 18:39). To fall **prostrate in prayer** could also indicate supplication or submission. Jesus prays, **My Father, if it is possible, let this cup pass from me; yet, not as I will, but as you will.** Jesus probably prayed out loud, as was customary Jewish practice. He addresses God as **my Father.** Jesus characteristically referred to God as **my Father** (7:21; 11:27; 20:23; 25:34; 26:29) and prayed to him as his **Father** (11:25-26). Jesus in his sorrow comes as the Son to his Father and asks that **if it is possible, let this cup pass from me.** A **cup** is a biblical image for one's fate or destiny, often of suffering (see Jer 49:12; Ezek 23:31-34). Jesus referred to his suffering and death as a cup that he would drink (20:22), but he now asks his Father to excuse him from drinking it: **let this cup pass from me.** We can again note that Jesus repeatedly spoke of his suffering and death without giving the least indication that he did not accept them as God's will (16:21; 17:12, 22-23; 20:18-19, 28; 26:2, 24, 28)—yet now he asks his Father to spare him. Jesus asks his Father to spare him **if it is possible,** if there is some way for God to accomplish his purposes other than through Jesus' suffering and death. God can change his mind, especially in response to prayer or repentance (2 Kings 20:1-6; Jer 18:5-10; Jonah 3:4-10). Jesus asks his Father to change his will regarding him.

To this prayer of supplication Jesus adds a prayer of submission: **yet, not as I will, but as you will.** Jesus subordinates his will to his Father's will. Jesus has always done his Father's will and taught the importance of doing his Father's will (see 3:15; 4:1-10; 7:21; 12:49-50). Despite Jesus' sorrow and distress over what awaits him, despite his desire to be excused from suffering and death, Jesus chooses his Father's will over his own.

For reflection: What have been my most heartfelt prayers of supplication and submission?

Matthew's gospel does not recount a voice from heaven answering Jesus' prayer. The God who proclaimed Jesus to be his beloved Son after his baptism (3:17) and during his transfiguration (17:5) is silent in Gethsemane. God's silence is God's answer: Jesus is not excused from the cup of suffering and death.

So too God can speak to followers of Jesus through silence. When God gives no new directions or permissions, when God seems silent and even absent, then disciples of Jesus must stay the course that God previously set them on.

40 Jesus interrupts his prayer to check on Peter, James, and John, whom he had asked to keep watch with him. **When he returned to his disciples he found them asleep. He said to Peter, "So you could not keep watch with me for one hour?"** Although Jesus addresses **Peter,** he refers to all three disciples: the Greek word **you** is plural. **One hour** is an indication of how long Jesus has been praying to his Father, asking that he be excused from the cup of suffering and death but nonetheless submitting himself to his Father's will. His disciples are not praying; they have fallen **asleep.** The Greek for **could not keep watch** is literally "were not strong enough to be awake." They who claimed that they could suffer and die with Jesus (20:22; 26:35) do not have the strength to stay awake for **one hour.** How will they fare when they are faced with more difficult challenges?

41 Jesus tells them, **Watch**—stay awake—**and pray that you may not undergo the test.** The Greek for **that you may not undergo the test** could also be translated "lest you enter into temptation." The disciples will shortly be tempted to abandon Jesus; their commitment to him will be put to the **test.** Jesus tells them to pray that they will be spared this **test,** just as he prayed that his Father spare him from suffering and death. Jesus could have told them to pray that they would be strong enough to overcome temptation and endure through testing, but he instead tells them to pray that they are not tested. Jesus has a realistic assessment of their ability to withstand testing and temptation: **The spirit is willing, but the flesh is weak.** In this context, **the spirit** represents desires and aspirations, while **the flesh** represents human frailty and weakness. The disciples may be **willing** to suffer with and for Jesus, but they will prove to be **weak** and fail when they are tested. Jesus might also be thinking of his own distress at the prospect of suffering and death as his Father's will for him: he knows firsthand the human struggle between spirit and flesh, between aspirations and weakness (see Heb 4:15). But Jesus primarily has his disciples in mind: he knows their willingness, but he also knows their weakness.

For reflection: How have I experienced my spirit being willing but my flesh weak?

42 Jesus had interrupted his prayer to check on his disciples but had not completed his prayer. **Withdrawing a second time, he prayed again, "My Father, if it is not possible that this cup pass without my drinking it, your will be done!"** While Jesus' prayer is very similar to what he prayed earlier, it is not identical. Previously Jesus asked that "if it is possible, let this cup pass from me" (verse 39). Now Jesus accepts the prospect that **it is not possible that this cup pass without** his **drinking it.** And if that is so, then he tells his Father, **your will be done!** There are two dimensions of meaning in saying to God, **your will be done.** The first accent is on what God does: **your will be done** asks God to accomplish his will. These words also express submission to God's will; here the accent is on the one praying. Jesus asks God to accomplish his will, and he expresses his complete submission to God's will, even though he would like to be spared the cup of suffering and death.

There are obvious parallels between Jesus' prayer in Gethsemane and how he taught his followers to pray. He prays to God as "My Father" (verse 39); they are to call upon God as "Our Father" (6:9). Jesus tells his Father, **your will be done;** they are to pray the same words (6:10). Jesus told Peter, James, and John to pray that they "not undergo the test" (verse 41); the petition, "do not subject us to the final test" (6:13) is similar. On the eve of his death Jesus demonstrates the profound meaning of the prayer he taught his followers.

For reflection: What insights does Jesus' prayer in Gethsemane give me into the meaning of the Our Father? When have I found it hardest to pray, "Thy will be done"?

43 Jesus interrupts his prayer to check on his disciples again. **Then he returned once more and found them asleep, for they could not keep their eyes open.** Peter, James, and John might have been able to make excuses for their not staying awake and praying, despite Jesus' repeated admonitions to keep watch (verses 38, 41). They had eaten a full meal with wine after sunset, and it is now the middle of the night. They are drowsy and unable to **keep their eyes open** despite good intentions. However, Matthew does not recount Jesus waking them to hear their excuses or to exhort them to stay awake. Jesus seems to have let them sleep on—perhaps in acknowledgment that the flesh is indeed weak.

44 **He left them and withdrew again.** Jesus expressed complete submission to his Father's will in his previous prayer (verse 42) but nonetheless **prayed a third time, saying the same thing again.** Biblically, doing something three times signals resolve (see 2 Kings 1:9-15); Paul prayed three times for relief from a thorn in the flesh (2 Cor 12:7-8). Jesus' **saying the same thing again** indicates his continued submission to his Father's will. Accepting God's will is not a one-time event but a continual process of submission.

The circumstances indicate that Jesus expressed his submission in act as well as word. As will soon be evident, Judas has gone off under the cover of darkness to inform the chief priests and elders that they have an opportunity to arrest Jesus in Gethsemane (26:47; see also 26:3-5, 14-15). Jesus knows what Judas is about (26:21-25). Jesus has been at prayer in Gethsemane for some time; his first session of prayer alone lasted about an hour (verse 40). Jesus had plenty of time to escape before an arresting party arrived. From Gethsemane it is only about a twenty-minute walk over the Mount of Olives to the beginning of the Judean wilderness, a desolate region extending east all the way to Jericho. The wilderness would have provided ample places for Jesus to hide. By remaining in Gethsemane in prayer, Jesus allows Judas to find him and for God's will to be done.

45 **Then he returned to his disciples and said to them, "Are you still sleeping and taking your rest?"** They obviously are sleeping; Jesus' words are ironic. **Behold, the hour is at hand when the Son of Man is to be handed over to sinners.** Jesus' time of waiting is over. The **hour** has arrived when he will **be handed over**—handed over to death by God through being handing over by Judas. Jesus will be handed over **to sinners.** Jesus has spoken of being handed over to men (17:22) and handed over to chief priests and scribes who will hand him over to Gentiles (20:18-19), but this is the first time he says that he will be handed over to **sinners.** Jesus will die at the hands of sinners—but also for them. He ate with sinners because he is a physician sent to the sick (9:10-13); he will shed his blood so that sins might be forgiven (26:28); he will save his people from their sins (1:21). The **hour is at hand** for the events that will bring forgiveness.

Son of Man: See page 151

46 Jesus tells his disciples—perhaps all of them and not just Peter, James, and John—Get up, let us go. Look, my betrayer is at hand. Jesus speaks with determination, embracing God's will as it unfolds. He does not wait for the betrayer to arrive with an arresting party but tells his disciples, Let us go to meet him. Perhaps Jesus has caught sight of "a large crowd, with swords and clubs" (26:47) making its way across the Kidron Valley to Gethsemane; Passover is celebrated at full moon. Jesus began his time of prayer in sorrow and distress (verses 37-38) but is now resolute in living out his words to his Father, "Your will be done!" (verse 42).

For reflection: When has prayer enabled me to embrace God's will?

Jesus Is Arrested in Fulfillment of Scripture

[47] While he was still speaking, Judas, one of the Twelve, arrived, accompanied by a large crowd, with swords and clubs, who had come from the chief priests and the elders of the people. [48] His betrayer had arranged a sign with them, saying, "The man I shall kiss is the one; arrest him." [49] Immediately he went over to Jesus and said, "Hail, Rabbi!" and he kissed him. [50] Jesus answered him, "Friend, do what you have come for." Then stepping forward they laid hands on Jesus and arrested him. [51] And behold, one of those who accompanied Jesus put his hand to his sword, drew it, and struck the high priest's servant, cutting off his ear. [52] Then Jesus said to him, "Put your sword back into its sheath, for all who take the sword will perish by the sword. [53] Do you think that I cannot call upon my Father and he will not provide me at this moment with more than twelve legions of angels? [54] But then how would the scriptures be fulfilled which say that it must come to pass in this way?" [55] At that hour Jesus said to the crowds, "Have you come out as against a robber, with swords and clubs to seize me? Day after day I sat teaching in the temple area, yet you did not arrest me. [56] But all this has come to pass that the writings of the prophets may be fulfilled." Then all the disciples left him and fled.

Gospel parallels: Mark 14:43-50; Luke 22:47-53; John 18:1-12
NT: Matt 5:17, 38-39, 43-44; 16:21; 26:3-5, 14-16, 21-25, 31-35, 45-46

47 Jesus told his disciples that the hour was at hand for him to be handed over to sinners, and that his betrayer was at hand (26:45-46), and while he was still speaking, Judas, one of the Twelve, arrived. That Judas is one

of the Twelve magnifies his betrayal. Jesus will die not because some by-stander turns him in to the authorities but because one of his closest as-sociates, someone he had selected for a special role (10:1-4), betrays him. Judas has been looking for an opportunity when Jesus could be arrested without triggering a riot (26:3-5, 14-16), and Jesus' relative isolation in Gethsemane at night is such an opportunity. Nothing has been said of Judas' whereabouts since the Passover meal (26:19-25). Presumably Judas went with the other disciples to the Mount of Olives with Jesus (26:30) and saw where Jesus was praying (26:36-39). While other disciples were sleeping (26:40, 43, 45), Judas went to the chief priests to tell them that Jesus was in Gethsemane. There would have been ample time for him to do so: Jesus prayed for more than an hour (26:40), while it was less than a twenty-minute walk from Gethsemane to the house of Caiaphas the high priest (see 26:57-58).

Now **Judas** arrives in Gethsemane **accompanied by a large crowd, with swords and clubs, who had come from the chief priests and the elders of the people.** The **large crowd** probably included Temple police, who were under the command of one of the **chief priests.** That the authorities would send **a large crowd** armed **with swords and clubs** to ar-rest Jesus indicates that they thought they might encounter resistance from Jesus' disciples or from pilgrims using the Mount of Olives as a campground during Passover (see 26:3-5).

High priest, chief priests: See page 566
Elders: See page 451

48 **His betrayer had arranged a sign with them, saying, "The man I shall kiss is the one; arrest him."** Apparently the arresting party cannot recog-nize Jesus by sight, especially at night. Jesus looks much like any other man; those who do not know him might pass him by on the street with-out taking notice. Judas makes arrangements to single Jesus out so that he can be seized.

49 **Immediately he went over to Jesus and said, "Hail, Rabbi!" and he kissed him.** On the surface, Judas' words and kiss are the normal way a disciple might greet his teacher. The word **hail** (literally, "rejoice") was a customary greeting; in the Greek of Matthew's gospel it is the counterpart to the Hebrew greeting of "peace." **Rabbi** was a respectful way of addressing an-other person and came to be used for teachers. Kissing another person on

the head or hand was a sign of friendship and respect (Paul will tell his readers to greet one another with a holy kiss: Rom 16:16; 1 Cor 16:20; 2 Cor 13:12; 1 Thess 5:26). In any other context Judas' greeting and kiss would have been unexceptional; in Gethsemane they are filled with deadly irony. Judas has hardly come to bring Jesus joy or peace, the connotations of **hail**. While calling Jesus **rabbi** is on the surface respectful, it is in contrast to calling him Lord, as do the other disciples (see 26:22, 25); Judas no longer accepts Jesus as his Lord. Judas addresses him as a rabbi or teacher, which is how those who are not disciples speak of Jesus (see 9:11; 12:38; 17:24; 22:16, 24, 36). Judas' kiss is as hypocritical as his greeting. It is not a sign of friendship or respect but a way of marking Jesus as the one to arrest.

Rabbi: See page 495

50 **Jesus answered him, "Friend, do what you have come for."** Jesus calls Judas his **friend** but with irony (see 20:13; 22:12). Judas should have been a faithful friend of Jesus but is acting like an enemy. Jesus did not break off his friendship with Judas; it is Judas who has turned away from him. By saying **do what you have come for** Jesus indicates that he knows Judas is betraying him and tells Judas to get on with it. In prayer, Jesus accepted being handed over to suffering and death as his Father's will (26:39, 42, 44) and continues to accept it as it is happening. **Then stepping forward they laid hands on Jesus and arrested him.** Judas' kiss has identified Jesus, and the arresting party seizes him.

For reflection: Have I betrayed or broken bonds of friendship?

51 **And behold, one of those who accompanied Jesus put his hand to his sword, drew it, and struck the high priest's servant, cutting off his ear.** One of Jesus' disciples is carrying a **sword**: the Greek word means a short sword—perhaps what we might consider a gigantic hunting knife. It was customary for travelers, even pilgrims, to carry swords as a protection against robbers, but in light of Jesus' condemnation of violent resistance (5:38-39) we are surprised that one of his disciples is armed. This disciple acts bravely but foolishly. To defend Jesus, he tries to single-handedly take on a large crowd armed with swords and clubs. He strikes out at **the high priest's servant** (literally, "slave")—perhaps the leader of the arresting party. The disciple's blow is not very skillful and only cuts off an **ear**—painful and disfiguring but far from fatal.

52 Jesus calls a halt to the violence: **Then Jesus said to him, "Put your sword back into its sheath."** Jesus goes on to give three reasons why resistance is misguided. The first reason is that **all who take the sword will perish by the sword** (see Gen 9:6). Violence begets violence; violence is self-destructive. Jesus' disciples must renounce violence and retaliation (5:38-39); Jesus' disciples must love enemies and pray for persecutors (5:43-44). Striking out with a sword is not what Jesus wants, even if it is done to defend him.

> For reflection: Am I doing anything for Jesus that he prefers I not do?
> How do I understand—and live by—his teachings about violence?

53 Jesus gives a second reason why the disciple's swordplay is misguided: **Do you think that I cannot call upon my Father and he will not provide me at this moment with more than twelve legions of angels?** A Roman legion normally had around six thousand soldiers. Rather than depending on twelve (or eleven) disciples to protect him, Jesus can call for **more than twelve legions of angels**—over seventy-two thousand. If a single angel could strike down one hundred and eighty-five thousand Assyrian soldiers at the time of Hezekiah (2 Kings 19:35; 2 Macc 15:22), twelve legions of angels would have no difficulty dealing with those who are arresting Jesus. The disciple's sword is utterly insignificant compared with the angelic might available to Jesus.

Angels: See page 33

Jesus' assertion that he could **call upon** his **Father** and his Father would **provide** him **at this moment with more than twelve legions of angels** throws light upon Jesus' prayer to his Father, "your will be done" (26:42). Jesus was free to say no to his Father's will, and he is free now to change his mind: he can ask his Father to send angels to prevent his arrest and his Father will do so. Jesus must freely embrace his Father's will every step of the way, to the very end.

54 Jesus could call upon an army of angels; **but** were he to do so, **then how would the scriptures be fulfilled which say that it must come to pass in this way?** Before Jesus began his public ministry, Satan tempted him to rely on angels to protect him from harm; Jesus cited Scripture in rejecting this temptation (4:5-7). Jesus upheld Scripture throughout his ministry

(5:17-19; 8:4; 15:3-6; 19:3-6; 22:37-40). The third and most important reason why Jesus rejects efforts (whether human or angelic) to prevent his arrest is that **the scriptures** must **be fulfilled.** These Scriptures **say that it must come to pass in this way.** In a narrow sense, what **must come to pass** is Jesus' arrest. In a broader sense, what **must come to pass** is the suffering and death that will follow upon Jesus' arrest: Jesus "must" suffer greatly and be killed (16:21). Jesus does not explain which **scriptures** he has in mind; he seems to be speaking of the Scriptures in general as a revelation of God's will. Jesus is committed to carrying out God's will, and his suffering and death will be a fulfillment of what is foretold and foreshadowed in the **scriptures**—the books we read as the Old Testament.

> *For reflection: What does it tell me about Jesus that he is able to call upon legions of angels? What does it tell me about Jesus that he chooses not to do so?*

55 Jesus turns from the sword-wielding disciple to those who have come to arrest him. **At that hour**—the hour for Jesus to be handed over (26:45)—**Jesus said to the crowds, "Have you come out as against a robber, with swords and clubs to seize me?"** The word translated **robber** has the connotation of a violent criminal; it came to also designate revolutionaries (the word is translated "revolutionaries" when it is used to describe the two men who are crucified with Jesus—27:38). Jesus is neither an armed criminal nor a violent revolutionary; it is ironic that it is thought necessary to use **swords and clubs** to arrest him who forbids violence. The arresting party came under the cover of night to seize Jesus, but he tells them **day after day I sat teaching in the temple area.** Matthew has simplified events by recounting only one day on which Jesus taught in the Temple area (21:23-24:1); Jesus says that he had done so **day after day.** He had been in a public place, **the temple area,** not in hiding. He **sat teaching:** Jewish teachers normally sat (see 5:1-2; 13:2-3; 23:2), but there might also be the connotation that Jesus was in one place, not moving around to elude anyone. There have been ample opportunities for Jesus' arrest. He tells the crowd, **Yet you did not arrest me.**

Temple: See page 442

56 The failure to arrest him earlier may have been due to a fear of the crowds who admired Jesus (21:46; 26:4-5), but it is part of a larger picture: **all this has come to pass that the writings of the prophets may be fulfilled.** By **all this** Jesus refers to the whole process that will culminate in his death and being raised, and not just to the circumstances of his arrest. Jesus again proclaims that events are taking place so that God's will as revealed in Scripture **may be fulfilled** (see verse 54). In the Greek of Matthew's gospel, the words **all this has come to pass that . . . may be fulfilled** echo Matthew's words about the conception of Jesus, "All this took place to fulfill" (1:22). From beginning to end Matthew's gospel proclaims Jesus as the fulfillment of Scripture (2:4-6, 23; 4:13-16; 8:16-17; 12:15-21; 13:34-35; 21:4-5; 26:31). Jesus came to fulfill the law and the prophets (5:17); he will go to his death so **that the writings of the prophets may be fulfilled.** Jesus does not single out specific prophets, but Matthew's readers who are familiar with the Hebrew Scriptures might think of Isaiah 52:13–53:12 as a prophecy fulfilled in the suffering, death, and vindication of Jesus.

Even as Jesus finishes speaking, a prophecy is fulfilled: **Then all the disciples left him and fled.** Earlier that night Jesus told his disciples, "This night all of you will have your faith in me shaken, for it is written: 'I will strike the shepherd, / and the sheep of the flock will be dispersed'" (26:31, invoking Zech 13:7). Although the disciples had protested that they would remain faithful to Jesus (26:33-35), now they **left him and fled.** What caused them to abandon Jesus? It was likely to escape arrest, although the armed crowd seems to have only been intent on seizing Jesus. On a deeper level the disciples could not bring themselves to follow Jesus' example of complete submission to God's will. The disciples are unwilling to pay the price of discipleship (see 10:38-39; 16:24-25). Rather than abandon themselves for the sake of Jesus, the disciples abandon Jesus. Jesus told Peter, James, and John to "watch and pray that you may not undergo the test" (26:41); they slept, and now they and the rest of the disciples fail the test.

Disciple: See page 66

For reflection: Does my knowledge of myself give me any insight into why the disciples fled when Jesus was arrested?

What lessons can we learn from the example of Jesus' first disciples? One betrays him, another resorts to violence, all of them flee. Their failures are a warning for us to watch and pray, to be prepared to be tested—and not to be too surprised when we fail. There is a second and more important lesson. Jesus foretold their scattering (26:31), but he also promised to gather them together again after he was raised from the dead (26:32). Matthew's readers know that Jesus kept his promise: had he not, there would be no church, no Matthew, no gospel. While the flesh is weak (26:41), Jesus is able to forgive and rehabilitate and grant fresh beginnings.

Jesus Testifies About Himself

57 Those who had arrested Jesus led him away to Caiaphas the high priest, where the scribes and the elders were assembled. **58** Peter was following him at a distance as far as the high priest's courtyard, and going inside he sat down with the servants to see the outcome. **59** The chief priests and the entire Sanhedrin kept trying to obtain false testimony against Jesus in order to put him to death, **60** but they found none, though many false witnesses came forward. Finally two came forward **61** who stated, "This man said, 'I can destroy the temple of God and within three days rebuild it.'" **62** The high priest rose and addressed him, "Have you no answer? What are these men testifying against you?" **63** But Jesus was silent. Then the high priest said to him, "I order you to tell us under oath before the living God whether you are the Messiah, the Son of God." **64** Jesus said to him in reply, "You have said so. But I tell you:

> From now on you will see 'the Son of Man
>   seated at the right hand of the Power'
>   and 'coming on the clouds of heaven.'"

65 Then the high priest tore his robes and said, "He has blasphemed! What further need have we of witnesses? You have now heard the blasphemy; **66** what is your opinion?" They said in reply, "He deserves to die!" **67** Then they spat in his face and struck him, while some slapped him, **68** saying, "Prophesy for us, Messiah: who is it that struck you?"

Gospel parallels: Mark 14:53-65; Luke 22:54, 63-71
OT: Psalm 110:1; Isaiah 50:6; 53:7; Dan 7:9, 13-14
NT: Matt 5:39; 9:2-3; 21:12-13; 24:1-2; 26:3-4; John 18:19-24

57 **Those who had arrested Jesus led him away to Caiaphas the high priest, where the scribes and the elders were assembled.** As the next verse indicates, Jesus is taken to the house of Caiaphas. **Caiaphas was the high priest** during Jesus' public ministry. Some **scribes** and **elders,** along with some chief priests (verse 59), have assembled in Caiaphas's house. Since it is the middle of the night at the beginning of Passover, such a gathering is highly unusual. Presumably after Judas reported that Jesus was in Gethsemane and could be arrested, a meeting of those who were intent on getting rid of Jesus was hastily convened.

High priest, chief priests: See page 566
Scribes: See page 138
Elders: See page 451

58 **Peter was following him at a distance:** although when Jesus was arrested "all the disciples left him and fled" (26:56), Peter did not run away completely. As Jesus was taken from Gethsemane to the house of Caiaphas, Peter was **following** after Jesus but from **a distance.** To follow Jesus is at the heart of discipleship (see 4:19, 22; 8:22; 9:9), but Jesus wants his disciples near him and sharing his life, not standing a distance off observing. Still, Peter demonstrates more faithfulness than the disciples who simply disappeared when their commitment to Jesus was tested by his arrest. Peter went **as far as the high priest's courtyard, and going inside he sat**

BACKGROUND: CAIAPHAS was high priest from A.D. 18 to 36—a long time for one man to hold this office. Caiaphas had good connections: his father-in-law was Annas, who served as high priest from A.D. 6 to 15, and who used his influence to obtain the high priesthood for five of his sons as well as for Caiaphas. More important, Caiaphas maintained a good relationship with the Roman procurators who governed Judea. These Roman governors appointed the high priest and could remove him from office at any time. In particular, Caiaphas seems to have cooperated with Pilate (who governed Judea from A.D. 26 to 35) despite Pilate's lack of sensitivity to Jewish religious concerns. Caiaphas may have been responsible for moving the sale of sacrificial animals into the Temple precincts; in any case, he profited from these commercial activities. Jesus' disruption of this commerce and talk of the Temple's destruction would have been reasons for Caiaphas to ask Pilate to get rid of Jesus. What are apparently the grave and bones of Caiaphas were discovered by archaeologists in 1990. *Related topics: Burial practices (page 652), High priest, chief priests (page 566).*

down with the servants to see the outcome. Houses usually had a court-yard; the homes of the upperclass often had several stories and a large courtyard. Jesus is taken into the house of Caiaphas, and Peter remains outside in the courtyard, where he sat down with the servants—probably servants of Caiaphas and of the chief priests, elders, and scribes who are at the meeting. Peter might have thought that he would remain undetected since it was night. Peter waited to see the outcome, to see what they would do with Jesus. Matthew may intend a deeper meaning by his choice of words. The word translated outcome means "end" or "goal." Jesus' life on earth is reaching its end and goal: he will give his life as a ransom (20:28).

For reflection: Have I ever distanced myself from Jesus to avoid hardship or suffering?

59 The chief priests and the entire Sanhedrin kept trying to obtain false testimony against Jesus in order to put him to death. Although Matthew writes as if the entire Sanhedrin—the Jewish ruling council—has convened, it is likely that this hastily called meeting is not a formal session of the whole council. The meeting is taking place in the house of Caiaphas, not in the Sanhedrin's normal meeting hall. Some members of the Sanhedrin had gathered a few days earlier in the house of Caiaphas and "consulted together to arrest Jesus by treachery and put him to death" (26:3-4), and they

---

BACKGROUND: SANHEDRIN At the time of Jesus, it was common for cities to have some form of city council, with what we think of as legislative, judicial, and executive responsibilities. In Jerusalem this council was called the Sanhedrin (from the Greek for "sitting together"). Its members were drawn from the aristocracy of high-priestly families and wealthy or influential citizens (elders) and included some religious scholars (scribes): see Mark 15:1. The high priest presided over the council's deliberations. Since A.D. 6, Judea and Jerusalem had been under direct Roman rule, exercised through governors such as Pontius Pilate. Rome normally allowed subject peoples to manage their own affairs, as long as public order was maintained and taxes paid. The Sanhedrin was the chief Jewish ruling body in Jerusalem under the umbrella of Roman authority. It dealt primarily with religious matters, but since religion pervaded all of Jewish life, authority in religious matters covered a wide range of concerns. The Sanhedrin's religious authority extended beyond Jerusalem, because of its makeup and the importance of the Jerusalem Temple in Jewish life. *Related topics: Elders (page 451), High priest, chief priests (page 566), Scribes (page 138).*

---

have come together again now that Jesus has been arrested. They decided at their previous meeting that Jesus should be put to death; now they look for a pretext for his execution. Jesus' death will upset those who revere him (see 21:46; 26:5), and these leaders may have to explain their actions. They **kept trying to obtain false testimony against Jesus:** it is unlikely that they were intent on obtaining **false** testimony as such; it is more likely that they were looking for any testimony that would enable them to **put him to death** and that they were not too concerned about the reliability of the testimony.

60 Even though they had lax standards for evidence justifying Jesus' execution, **they found none, though many false witnesses came forward.** Jesus has done nothing that warrants him being put to death, not even anything that **false witnesses** could twist into a death warrant. **Finally two came forward** and gave their testimony. The law of Moses required evidence from at least two witnesses in judicial proceedings (Deut 19:15), particularly in cases involving the death penalty (Num 35:30; Deut 17:6).

61 The two witnesses **stated, "This man said, 'I can destroy the temple of God and within three days rebuild it.'"** The expression **this man** has a slightly contemptuous ring (see 9:3; 12:24; 13:54). Did Jesus ever say what they allege he said? Jesus said that the Temple would be destroyed (24:1-2) and alluded to its destruction (23:38). When Jesus disrupted commerce in the Temple precincts, he quoted words from a prophecy of Jeremiah that foretold the Temple's destruction (21:12-13; Jer 7:9-14). Yet Jesus has given no indication that *he* would **destroy the temple of God** nor that *he* would **rebuild it.** Whenever Jesus spoke of something happening in **three days** or on the third day, he was speaking of his being raised from the dead (12:40; 16:21; 17:23; 20:19). The claim that Jesus **said, "I can destroy the temple of God and within three days rebuild it,"** may be based on things Jesus said but is garbled.

Temple: See page 442

Although Jesus never made the statement attributed to him, it contains truth. Jesus has extraordinary powers; he is able to heal the sick, forgive sins, expel demons, quiet storms, raise the dead, and call upon legions of angels. Destroying the Temple would be within his power if God wanted the Temple destroyed.

Whatever the other charges made against Jesus might have been, the allegation that he spoke of destroying the Temple would have been taken very seriously by the chief priests and wealthy aristocracy of elders. Not only was the Temple at the heart of Jewish worship; it was the basis of Jerusalem's economy and the source of the power and wealth of the chief priests. They had challenged Jesus' authority to disrupt commerce in the Temple precincts, for it was an assault on their own authority (21:23). When Jesus is crucified, he will be mocked for claiming that he would destroy the Temple (27:39-40). Clearly his actions in and words about the Temple hit a nerve.

62 **The high priest rose and addressed him, "Have you no answer?"** The high priest's question indicates that Jesus has not made any response to the charges being made against him. Caiaphas asks him, **What are these men testifying against you?** What about this charge? Do you claim you are able to destroy the Temple and rebuild it in three days?

63 **But Jesus was silent.** There is little point to his defending himself against false or garbled charges when his examiners have reached a guilty verdict before hearing any evidence (see 26:3-4, 59). More significant, any defense Jesus would mount for himself would impede the working out of God's will. Jesus must drink the cup of suffering and death (26:42); he must die in fulfillment of Scripture (26:54, 56). Jesus' silence signals his acceptance of God's will. Matthew's readers who are familiar with the Hebrew Scriptures might be reminded of a passage in Isaiah that speaks of a servant of God silently accepting death (Isaiah 53:7).

> Though he was harshly treated, he submitted
>   and opened not his mouth;
> Like a lamb led to the slaughter
>   or a sheep before the shearers,
>   he was silent and opened not his mouth.
>   Isaiah 53:7

Since Caiaphas cannot get Jesus to respond to the charges being made against him, Caiaphas changes tactics. Jesus created a stir by his dramatic entry into Jerusalem (21:8-11), by his disruption of Temple commerce (21:12-13), and by his confrontations with religious leaders

(21:23-46). He allegedly claimed that he could destroy and rebuild the Temple. Caiaphas demands to know who Jesus thinks he is that he can do such things: **the high priest said to him, "I order you to tell us under oath before the living God whether you are the Messiah, the Son of God."** Matthew's readers know that Jesus indeed is **the Messiah** (see 1:1, 17, 18; 2:4; 16:16) and **the Son of God** (see 3:17; 8:29; 11:25-27; 14:33; 16:16; 17:5)–but what meaning did these titles have for Caiaphas? When Caiaphas speaks of **the Messiah,** Caiaphas likely has in mind the popular understanding of the Messiah: a descendant of David who would restore Jewish independence and usher in a golden age. By **the Son of God** Caiaphas may only mean someone who has a special relationship with God (**the Son of God** did not yet have the specific meaning it would come to have for Christians). Caiaphas is asking Jesus, Do you pretend to be the Messiah, someone with a mandate from God? Is that why you have been so disruptive? Is that why you claim to have the power to destroy and rebuild the Temple?

Messiah, Christ: See page 349
Son of God: See page 52

After Peter professed Jesus to be the Messiah, the Son of the living God, Jesus "strictly ordered his disciples to tell no one that he was the Messiah" (16:16, 20) because popular understandings of the Messiah did not do justice to who Jesus is (see 22:41-46). But now Caiaphas orders Jesus **to tell us under oath before the living God whether you are the Messiah, the Son of God.** What response can Jesus give that will be true to his identity? If he swears that he is the Messiah and the Son of God, Caiaphas will consider Jesus a messianic pretender, someone who wants to displace the chief priests and elders and lead a rebellion against Roman rule. Yet Jesus cannot deny his identity: he is **the Messiah,** God's agent establishing God's reign; he is uniquely **the Son of God.**

64 **Jesus said to him in reply, "You have said so."** The sense of Jesus' response is, So you say. Jesus avoids taking an oath (he forbids oaths—5:33-37) and does not give a yes or no answer (see also 26:25). He does not deny that he is the Messiah and the Son of God, but neither does he endorse Caiaphas's understanding of what it means to be the Messiah and the Son of God. Jesus immediately goes on to say, **But I tell you: From now on you will see "the Son of Man / seated at the right hand of the**

Power" / and "coming on the clouds of heaven." Jesus refers to himself
as **the Son of Man** and applies two Scripture passages to himself that he
has previously invoked (22:44; 24:30). The book of Daniel portrays
thrones being set up in heaven and "one like a son of man coming, / on
the clouds of heaven" to receive glory and dominion (Dan 7:9, 13-14). In
Psalm 110, God speaks to the psalmist's Lord and tells him, "Take your
throne at my right hand" (Psalm 110:1). The image of the psalmist's Lord
sitting on a throne to the right of God's heavenly throne provides a link
with Daniel's vision of thrones being set up in heaven (Dan 7:9).

Son of Man: See page 151

As I watched,
> Thrones were set up
> and the Ancient One took his throne . . .

As the visions during the night continued,
I saw
> One like a son of man coming,
> on the clouds of heaven;
> When he reached the Ancient One
> and was presented before him,
> He received dominion, glory, and kingship;
> nations and peoples of every language serve him.
> His dominion is an everlasting dominion
> that shall not be taken away.

Daniel 7:9, 13-14

The LORD says to you, my lord:
> "Take your throne at my right hand,
> while I make your enemies your footstool."

Psalm 110:1

Jesus combines these Scripture passages so that **the Son of Man** is
first **seated at the right hand of the Power,** that is, at the right hand of
God, and then is **coming on the clouds of heaven.** When Peter professed
Jesus to be the Messiah and the Son of God, Jesus went on to speak of
his suffering and death (16:16,21). In response to Caiaphas's question
whether he is the Messiah and the Son of God, Jesus speaks of his exaltation.

Although Jesus faces death, God will raise him and enthrone him at his **right hand** (see 19:28; 25:31). Jesus is now held captive, but he will come **on the clouds of heaven.** Matthew's readers know that his coming on the clouds means his coming as judge at the end of this age (see 13:40-41; 16:27; 24:30-31; 25:31-32). Jesus tells Caiaphas and those with him, **From now on you will see** me enthroned by God and coming in glory. **From now on** means that Jesus' death and resurrection usher in a new era (see 23:39; 26:29). Those bent on Jesus' death **will see** Jesus in glory.

For reflection: Do I look forward to seeing Jesus in his glory, or do I fear facing him as my judge?

The chief priests and elders were not successful in obtaining testimony against Jesus; Jesus testifies on his own behalf and proclaims that God will vindicate and glorify him. Jesus has spoken to his disciples about his being raised and glorified (16:21, 27; 17:23; 19:28; 20:19; 24:30; 25:31), but this is his first proclamation of his exalted destiny to those who are not disciples.

65 **Then the high priest tore his robes and said, "He has blasphemed!"** Tearing one's garments was a traditional expression of grief, as upon hearing of someone's death (Gen 37:33-34; 2 Sam 1:4, 11-12; Judith 14:18-19; Job 1:18-20). It became a gesture expressing great distress or dismay (2 Kings 19:1; Acts 14:11-14). Caiaphas dramatically, even theatrically, demonstrates his shock at Jesus' words and proclaims, **He has blasphemed!** In a narrow sense, blasphemy is abuse of God's name; but a claim to divine prerogatives can be considered a blasphemous insult to God (Jesus' forgiving sins was judged blasphemy—9:2-3). Caiaphas takes Jesus' statement that he will be seated at God's right hand and come on the clouds of heaven as a blasphemous claim. Caiaphas asks, **What further need have we of witnesses? You have now heard the blasphemy.** No more **witnesses** need be brought in; all of those present **heard** what Jesus said and can testify to it. While Jesus' claims are labeled **blasphemy,** Matthew's readers know that they are true.

66 Caiaphas continues, **What is your opinion? They said in reply, "He deserves to die!"** They had gathered to get evidence that would justify putting Jesus to death (verse 59), and they now have evidence that **he deserves to die:** the penalty for blasphemy was death (Lev 24:16).

67 **Then they spat in his face and struck him, while some slapped him.** They demonstrate their contempt for Jesus, spitting **in his face** and physically abusing him. Someone who "deserves" to die "deserves" whatever other mistreatment can be inflicted on him. That religious leaders would take part in this degrading physical abuse is shocking. Their rationale might have been that Jesus blasphemously insulted God and they are upholding God's honor by dishonoring Jesus. Their example is a warning for us to take care in how we treat others under the pretext of defending God and God's ways.

Jesus taught that "when someone strikes you on [your] right cheek, turn the other one to him as well" (5:39), and Jesus lives out his teaching. Matthew's readers who are familiar with Isaiah might be reminded of a prophecy about a servant of God who did not shield his face from buffets and spitting (Isaiah 50:6), and understand this to be a Scripture fulfilled by Jesus (see 26:54, 56).

> I gave my back to those who beat me,
> my cheeks to those who plucked my beard;
> My face I did not shield
> from buffets and spitting.
>
> Isaiah 50:6

68 They taunted him, **Prophesy for us, Messiah: who is it that struck you?** Jesus has not denied that he is the **Messiah,** providing a pretext for their mockery. Asking him to **prophesy** and say **who is it that struck you** may demand that he name each of the people striking him as a demonstration of his prophetic powers (see 21:11, 46). Possibly (although Matthew does not mention it) Jesus has been blindfolded and they are playing a "Guess who hit you" game of the time similar to blindman's bluff. The aim in any case is to mock Jesus' supposed prophetic powers. "So you prophesy that you will be seated at God's right hand and come on the clouds? You can't even prophesy who is hitting you!" Yet there is ironic truth in their mockery: Jesus is the **Messiah,** and he is fulfilling his role as the Messiah by accepting abuse, suffering, and death.

For reflection: What does the image of Jesus being struck, spit upon, and mocked convey to me about him? About my following of him?

Peter Denies Jesus

69 Now Peter was sitting outside in the courtyard. One of the maids came over to him and said, "You too were with Jesus the Galilean." **70** But he denied it in front of everyone, saying, "I do not know what you are talking about!" **71** As he went out to the gate, another girl saw him and said to those who were there, "This man was with Jesus the Nazorean." **72** Again he denied it with an oath, "I do not know the man!" **73** A little later the bystanders came over and said to Peter, "Surely you too are one of them; even your speech gives you away." **74** At that he began to curse and to swear, "I do not know the man." And immediately a cock crowed. **75** Then Peter remembered the word that Jesus had spoken: "Before the cock crows you will deny me three times." He went out and began to weep bitterly.

Gospel parallels: Mark 14:66-72; Luke 22:55-62; John 18:15-18, 25-27
NT: Matt 5:33-37; 10:32-33; 26:31-35, 57-58

69 **Now Peter was sitting outside in the courtyard.** After Jesus was arrested and taken to the house of Caiaphas, Peter followed at a distance and waited with servants **in the courtyard** to see what would happen to Jesus (26:57-58). While Jesus is being confronted inside, Peter is confronted outside. **One of the maids** (a female servant or slave) **came over to him and said** to him, **"You too were with Jesus the Galilean."** She identifies Jesus as **the Galilean:** Jesus grew up in Galilee and carried out virtually all of his ministry in Galilee. She knows that Jesus is inside the house of Caiaphas, and she notices Peter in the courtyard (although it is night, there is a full moon at Passover). She tells Peter, **You too were with Jesus,** identifying Peter as one of Jesus' disciples. Had she seen Peter with Jesus as he was teaching in a Temple courtyard (see 26:55)? Her words are an observation rather than an accusation. She is probably not privy to the plans to do away with Jesus; there is no reason for her to think that Peter is wanted by the authorities. She simply remarks that Peter had been **with** Jesus.

Galilee: See page 68

How risky would it be for Peter to admit that he is a disciple of Jesus? The maid has no authority, but she could send word into the house that a disciple of Jesus is in the courtyard. However, the chief priests and elders have not exhibited any interest in Jesus' disciples. Those who arrested

Jesus apparently made no attempt to arrest the disciples: a large armed crowd (26:47) would have had no trouble taking them into custody if that was their mission. Still, Peter cannot be sure of the intentions of the chief priests and elders. Perhaps something is transpiring inside the house that will lead to an arrest warrant for the disciples. The worst-case scenario would be that Peter would be put to death along with Jesus—but Peter has professed that he is willing to die with Jesus rather than deny him (26:35).

70 Matthew does not tell us what went through Peter's mind but recounts his response: **But he denied it in front of everyone, saying, "I do not know what you are talking about!"** Peter addresses not only the maid but also **everyone** who was near enough to overhear her say that Peter was with Jesus. Peter evades the issue of whether he is a disciple of Jesus by feigning ignorance: **I do not know what you are talking about!** He clearly does know what she is talking about; avoiding an acknowledgment that he is a disciple of Jesus means he has in effect **denied** his association with Jesus. Even as Jesus is being mocked as a false prophet (26:68) his words foretelling Peter's denials are proving true (26:34).

For reflection: Have I ever been afraid to admit that I was a disciple of Jesus? What was the source of my fears?

71 **As he went out to the gate:** Peter walks toward the **gate** between the courtyard and the street to avoid further discussion—distancing himself not only from those in the courtyard but also from Jesus. **As he is going another girl saw him and said to those who were there, "This man was with Jesus the Nazorean."** She identifies **Jesus** as being from Nazareth (see 2:23). She recognizes Peter as having been **with Jesus** as one of his disciples and announces it to **those who were there,** bystanders in the courtyard.

Nazareth: See page 38

72 **Again he denied it with an oath, "I do not know the man!"** Peter no longer tries to evade the issue. He resorts to lying and compounds it **with an oath** despite Jesus' prohibition of oaths (5:33-37). For any disciple to say, **I do not know the man,** would be a terrible denial of Jesus; but these words are especially horrible on the lips of Peter. Peter was the first to be called by Jesus (4:18) and the first among the Twelve (10:2). Jesus apparently

stayed in Peter's house when in Capernaum (see 8:14-16; 9:28; 13:1, 36; 17:24-25); Peter has seen Jesus' transfigured glory (17:1-2). Peter professed Jesus to be the Messiah and Son of God (16:16); Peter is to be the rock on which Jesus builds his church, entrusted with the keys to the kingdom of heaven (16:18-19). But now Peter swears, **I do not know the man!** Peter refers to Jesus as **the man** and does not even use his name.

Jesus said, "Everyone who acknowledges me before others I will acknowledge before my heavenly Father. But whoever denies me before others, I will deny before my heavenly Father" (10:32-33). Has Peter forgotten Jesus' words? What will become of Peter?

73 Peter lingers at the courtyard gate. **A little later the bystanders came over and said to Peter, "Surely you too are one of them."** The **bystanders** who had been told by the girl that Peter was with Jesus (verse 71) believe her. They tell Peter, **Surely you too are one of** Jesus' disciples; **even your speech gives you away.** Just as there are regional accents in the United States, so natives of Galilee and of Jerusalem spoke Aramaic with different accents. A Galilean accent does not in itself mean one is a disciple of Jesus: there are many Galileans in Jerusalem for Passover, but only a handful of them are his disciples. However, there is apparently only one person with a Galilean accent in the courtyard of Caiaphas while Jesus the Galilean is being interrogated inside, and that seems to be no coincidence. **Surely** Peter is a disciple of Jesus; why else would a Galilean be there in the middle of the night?

74 **At that he began to curse and to swear, "I do not know the man."** Peter denies as vehemently as he can that he is associated with Jesus. To **curse** might mean to call down God's wrath on himself if he is lying; to **swear** might mean to deny under oath that he knows Jesus (whom Peter continues to refer to only as **the man**). It is possible, however, that Peter curses Jesus (see 1 Cor 12:3) to demonstrate that he is not a disciple of Jesus. (In later times, Roman persecutors will demand that Christians curse Christ to disavow any connection with him in order to avoid execution.) Peter has gone from evasion to perjury to cursing in order to disassociate himself from Jesus. **And immediately a cock crowed,** heralding dawn.

75 **Then Peter remembered the word that Jesus had spoken** the previous evening, **Before the cock crows you will deny me three times** (26:34). Peter

went out and began to weep bitterly. Matthew's account ends with Peter leaving the courtyard, leaving behind Jesus in the house of Caiaphas, and beginning to **weep bitterly.** We are left to speculate what thoughts and emotions gave rise to Peter's bitter tears. Remorse that he had let Jesus down? Sorrow over his own wretched weakness? Momentary despair because he had repudiated the one he had acknowledged to be the Son of God? Perhaps there is a clue in his tears being triggered by his remembering that Jesus had foretold his denials: perhaps Peter was overcome by the realization that Jesus knew he would deny him but loved him anyway.

For reflection: How do I understand Peter's bitter tears?

Peter's denials were not only a disavowal of Jesus but also of what Jesus invited him to be. Peter behaved fearfully, and fear is the opposite of faith (see 8:26; 9:22; 14:30-31); disciples were to be people of faith (17:20; 21:21). Peter acted out of self-preservation, but Jesus taught that "whoever wishes to save his life will lose it, but whoever loses his life for my sake will find it" (16:25).

Yet even as Jesus foretold that his disciples would abandon him and Peter would deny him, Jesus promised to gather them to himself again after he was raised from the dead (26:32). Many of Matthew's first readers probably had heard that Peter died a martyr, fulfilling his willingness to die for Jesus (26:35). Peter's abject failure conveys a message of hope: no matter how badly we have let Jesus down, he wants to gather us to him again. Jesus shed his blood for the forgiveness of sins (26:28) and offers us forgiveness, no matter how grievous our sins may be.

For reflection: What is the lesson of Peter's denials for me?

CHAPTER 27

ORIENTATION: *Matthew interrupted his account of Jesus' hearing before the chief priests and elders (26:59-68) to recount Peter's denials (26:69-75). After saying how the hearing concluded (verses 1-2), Matthew tells what happened to Judas and the money he received (verses 3-10).*

The Price of Innocent Blood

¹ When it was morning, all the chief priests and the elders of the people took counsel against Jesus to put him to death. ² They bound him, led him away, and handed him over to Pilate, the governor.

³ Then Judas, his betrayer, seeing that Jesus had been condemned, deeply regretted what he had done. He returned the thirty pieces of silver to the chief priests and elders, ⁴ saying, "I have sinned in betraying innocent blood." They said, "What is that to us? Look to it yourself." ⁵ Flinging the money into the temple, he departed and went off and hanged himself. ⁶ The chief priests gathered up the money, but said, "It is not lawful to deposit this in the temple treasury, for it is the price of blood." ⁷ After consultation, they used it to buy the potter's field as a burial place for foreigners. ⁸ That is why that field even today is called the Field of Blood. ⁹ Then was fulfilled what had been said through Jeremiah the prophet, "And they took the thirty pieces of silver, the value of a man with a price on his head, a price set by some of the Israelites, ¹⁰ and they paid it out for the potter's field just as the Lord had commanded me."

Gospel parallels: Mark 15:1; Luke 23:1; John 18:28
OT: Zech 11:13
NT: Matt 20:18-19; 26:14-16, 24-25; Acts 1:15-20

1 **When it was morning, all the chief priests and the elders of the people took counsel against Jesus to put him to death.** These leaders have been meeting in the house of Caiaphas since Jesus' arrest (26:57-58), building a case that would justify his death (26:59). It is now **morning;** they have been at it through the night. They have declared Jesus guilty of blasphemy and deserving to die (26:65-66). Their now taking **counsel against Jesus** might mean coming up with charges that could be made against him to Roman authorities so that those authorities would **put him to death.** Rome

generally reserved for itself the authority to execute anyone (see John 18:31). Blasphemy was not against Roman law. If Roman authorities were to execute Jesus, **the chief priests and the elders** would have to accuse him of a civil crime that carried a death penalty.

High priest, chief priests: See page 566

Elders: See page 451

2 **They bound him, led him away, and handed him over to Pilate, the governor.** Pontius **Pilate** had been the Roman **governor** of Judea and some adjacent regions since A.D. 26. He was both a military commander and civil administrator. His headquarters were at Caesarea on the Mediterranean coast, but he came with troops to Jerusalem during Jewish religious festivals to keep order. Those who seek Jesus' death **led him away** and **handed him over to Pilate,** intent on convincing Pilate that he should die. Before taking Jesus away **they bound him,** treating him like a violent criminal who had to be physically restrained. That is how they would like Pilate to perceive him.

Pilate: See page 619

Jesus said that he, the Son of Man, "will be handed over to the chief priests and the scribes, and they will condemn him to death, and hand him over to the Gentiles" (20:18-19). His words are being fulfilled.

3 Instead of immediately recounting Jesus' hearing before Pilate, Matthew tells what became of Judas and the money he received for betraying Jesus. The events Matthew describes may have unfolded over the course of several days. **Then Judas, his betrayer, seeing that Jesus had been condemned, deeply regretted what he had done.** After **Judas** led the arresting party to Jesus in Gethsemane (26:47), he presumably returned with them to the house of Caiaphas and, like Peter (26:58), waited to see the outcome. When Judas observed **that Jesus had been condemned** to die, he **deeply regretted what he had done.** Matthew does not explain why Judas has a change of mind, just as he did not explain how Judas the disciple became Judas the betrayer. That Jesus was **condemned** to die should have been no surprise to Judas: Jesus had said that his being handed over to the chief priests would result in his death (20:18-19; see also 16:21; 17:22-23; 26:2). When Judas offered to assist with Jesus' arrest (26:14-16), he surely knew that the chief priests wanted to get rid of Jesus.

Yet after Jesus is **condemned,** Judas **deeply regretted what he had done.** Perhaps the enormity of his betrayal hit home. The Greek word translated **deeply regretted** could also be translated "changed his mind" (see 21:29, 32) or "repented" (see Heb 7:21). This word is not the Greek word usually used for "repented" in the New Testament, but the two words have basically the same meaning and are used interchangeably in the Greek translation of the Old Testament. Judas seems overcome by remorse and repentance.

Repentance: See page 42

For reflection: Have I ever profoundly repented of something that I had done? Does my experience give me any insights into why Judas might have had a change of mind and repented?

John the Baptist told those who came to him, "Produce good fruit as evidence of your repentance" (3:8). If Judas sincerely repented, it should be evident in his actions. **He returned the thirty pieces of silver to the chief priests and elders.** Judas tries to rid himself of his ill-gotten gains (see 26:14-15); he no longer wants to profit from the death of Jesus.

4 Judas tells the chief priests and elders, **I have sinned in betraying innocent blood.** Judas does not try to evade responsibility for his deed but confesses, **I have sinned.** No beating around the bush, no evasive "mistakes were made," just the blunt admission **I have sinned.**

For reflection: How easy do I find it to admit to God or others that I have sinned?

Judas says that he **sinned in betraying innocent blood.** The expression **innocent blood** means the blood of an innocent person and has the connotation of the innocent person being killed (see Deut 19:11-13; 1 Sam 19:5; 2 Kings 21:16; Psalm 106:38; Jer 26:15). Deuteronomy states, "Cursed be he who accepts payment for slaying an innocent man!"—or more literally, for slaying "innocent blood" (Deut 27:25). Judas recognizes that Jesus is **innocent** and does not deserve death; Judas proclaims that he **sinned** in **betraying** Jesus to those who are intent on his death. Judas' repentance appears sincere.

If Judas thinks he can dissuade the chief priests and elders from carrying out their plot to eliminate Jesus, he is mistaken. **They said, "What is** that to us? Look to it yourself." They rebuff Judas, telling him that his betrayal is his problem, not theirs. They do not seem concerned that Jesus is **innocent.** They have determined their course of action and will not be deflected from it. The next verse implies that they refuse to accept the money Judas wanted to return. Judas cannot undo what he has done.

We too are not always able to undo what we have done. Sometimes the hurt or harm we have inflicted on others is beyond our ability to repair. We must pray for God's restoration for our victims and his forgiveness for ourselves.

5 **Flinging the money into the temple, he departed.** Matthew's words seemingly imply that Judas' encounter with the chief priests and elders took place in or near the **temple** and therefore sometime after their gathering in the house of Caiaphas. Since those who paid Judas will not take the money back, he throws **the money into the temple,** perhaps into an inner courtyard or toward the building that housed the Temple treasury (see verse 6). Judas returns the money to its direct or indirect source—Temple funds under the control of the chief priests. He rids himself of what he gained by betraying Jesus, continuing to demonstrate evidence of repentance.

Then Judas **went off and hanged himself.** His taking of his life is usually interpreted as an act of despair and not in any sense an act of repentance. However, we should try to understand what Judas might have thought he was doing and why. Augustine (who lived from A.D. 354 to 430) was not the first to teach that suicide is wrong, but his view that the commandment "You shall not kill" (Exod 20:13) applied to killing oneself was decisive in formulating the teaching of the church. The wrongness of taking one's own life was not as clearly perceived in the first century, however. The Old Testament recounts about half a dozen instances of individuals' taking their lives or hastening their deaths but never condemns their doing so (see Judges 9:52-54; 16:26-30; 1 Sam 31: 3-5; 2 Sam 17:23; 1 Kings 16:18-19; 2 Macc 14:41-46). The prevailing view in the ancient Mediterranean world was that while taking one's life was generally wrong, in certain circumstances it was the proper and even noble thing to do. 2 Maccabees tells how the Jewish leader "Razis, now caught on all sides, turned his sword against himself, preferring to die nobly rather than fall into the hands of vile men and suffer outrages unworthy of his noble birth" (2 Macc 14:41-42).

We cannot take the silence of the Old Testament or the views of the first century as a justification of suicide, but these views may have influenced Judas' attitude toward suicide. The law of Moses states that "whoever takes the life of any human being shall be put to death . . . A life for a life!" (Lev 24:17-18). Judas might have thought that he was acting as his own executioner and doing the proper thing to atone for betraying Jesus to death. In the Old Testament, Ahithophel was King David's advisor (2 Sam 15:12) but betrayed him (2 Sam 15:31); Ahithophel later hung himself (2 Sam 17:23). Judas the betrayer might have imitated the example of Ahithophel the betrayer.

Speculations about Judas' reasoning in taking his life remain speculations; Matthew only tells us that Judas hanged himself. We do not know why Judas betrayed Jesus; we do not know why Judas later regretted what he had done; we do not know what was going through his mind when he killed himself. Nor do we know how God judged him. Jesus warned that it would have been better for the one who betrayed him never to have been born (26:24). Yet Jesus also told his followers that they were to love their enemies in order to be like their heavenly Father, who is merciful to the bad as well as the good (5:43-48). Jesus gave his life for the forgiveness of sins (26:28), even the sins of Judas. We must leave the fate of Judas in the hands of God.

For reflection: Why do I think Judas took his life?

While we have considered the death of Judas at some length, Matthew does not do so. Matthew's account devotes more attention to what happened to the money paid Judas than to what happened to Judas.

6 **The chief priests gathered up the money, but said, "It is not lawful to deposit this in the temple treasury, for it is the price of blood."** The **temple treasury** held donations made to the Temple, as well as funds deposited there for safekeeping (see 2 Macc 3:5-12). **The price of blood** means that the money had been paid to procure someone's death. The **chief priests** decide that it would not be **lawful** for the Temple to accept Judas' money as a donation because of how it was earned (see Deut 23:19 for a prohibition of accepting tainted offerings). They do not seem troubled by the fact that they were the ones who had paid Judas **the price of blood.**

Temple: See page 442

7 **After consultation, they used it to buy the potter's field as a burial place for foreigners.** Even though the money cannot be accepted as a donation to the Temple, it can be used for a public purpose. A **potter's field** is a field owned by a potter, perhaps as a source of clay. Here **foreigners** means visitors to Jerusalem. It is Jewish practice to bury the dead on the day of death. If a visitor died while in Jerusalem, it was not practical to ship his or her corpse home. Visitors would generally not own a tomb in Jerusalem; hence the need for a **field** that could serve **as a burial place** for those who died while visiting Jerusalem. The chief priests seem rather scrupulous in making sure that the thirty pieces of silver—not a huge sum—are put to proper use, even though they were unscrupulous in their dealings with Jesus. They have strained out a gnat but swallowed a camel (see 23:23-24).

8 **That is why that field even today is called the Field of Blood.** Matthew indicates that the burial site is called **the Field of Blood** because it was purchased with money that was "the price of blood" (verse 6). **Even today** refers to when Matthew is writing his gospel. Anyone visiting Jerusalem could be shown a site **called the Field of Blood.**

The church historian Bishop Eusebius (who lived from about A.D. 260 to 340) wrote that the Field of Blood was adjacent to and southeast of Jerusalem, in the Hinnom Valley just before it joins the Kidron Valley. There are numerous first-century tombs in this area, many of them of the upper class.

9 Matthew has a reason for following the trail of the money paid Judas. **Then was fulfilled what had been said through Jeremiah the prophet, "And they took the thirty pieces of silver, the value of a man with a price on his head, a price set by some of the Israelites,**

10 **and they paid it out for the potter's field just as the Lord had commanded me."** Matthew has repeatedly shown how Jesus and events surrounding him have fulfilled the Scriptures (1:22-23; 2:4-6, 15, 17-18, 23; 4:13-16; 8:16-17; 11:10; 12:15-21; 13:14-15, 34-35; 21:4-5). The events of Jesus' arrest, suffering, and death continue to fulfill Scripture (26:54, 56), even down to the disposition made of the money Judas received.

Yet Matthew's use of Scripture in these verses leaves us scratching our heads. The book of **Jeremiah** does contain references to a potter (Jer 18:

1-6), to buying a field (Jer 32:6-9), and to a Potsherd Gate leading to a burial place in the Hinnom Valley (19:2, 6, 11). But the words that Matthew attributes to Jeremiah cannot be found in the book of Jeremiah. There is, however, a similarity to a prophecy of Zechariah: "But the LORD said to me, 'Throw it in the treasury, the handsome price at which they valued me.' So I took the thirty pieces of silver and threw them into the treasury in the house of the LORD" (Zech 11:13). The Hebrew text of Zechariah literally reads, "Throw it to the potter . . . and I threw it into the house of the LORD to the potter," which does not make sense. There seems to be a typographical error. The Hebrew words for treasury and potter differ by a single letter, and translations correct the text to read "treasury." Nevertheless, the Hebrew text as it stands provides a link with Jeremiah's passage about a potter, and this seems to have provided a basis for Matthew to rework and expand Zechariah's prophecy with material from Jeremiah and to attribute it to Jeremiah.

Even if there are perplexing elements in Matthew's use of Scripture here, the point he wishes to make is clear. Jesus will suffer and die in fulfillment of Scripture. Even seemingly minor details—what became of the money paid to Judas—are within the scope of God's designs.

Jesus Amazes Pilate

11 Now Jesus stood before the governor, and he questioned him, "Are you the king of the Jews?" Jesus said, "You say so." **12** And when he was accused by the chief priests and elders, he made no answer. **13** Then Pilate said to him, "Do you not hear how many things they are testifying against you?" **14** But he did not answer him one word, so that the governor was greatly amazed.

> Gospel parallels: Mark 15:2-5; Luke 23:2-3; John 18:29-38
> OT: Isaiah 52:14-15; 53:7
> NT: Matt 27:2

11 Jesus has been bound like a criminal and sent by the chief priests and elders to Pilate (27:2). When Pilate was in Jerusalem, he likely stayed in the grand palace built by Herod the Great near the main western gate of Jerusalem; this palace will later be referred to as the praetorium (27:27). As governor, Pilate was the supreme judge in regions under his jurisdiction and had the authority to impose the death penalty. **Now Jesus stood before the governor, and he questioned him, "Are you the king of the**

Jews?" Since the aim in bringing Jesus to Pilate is to have him executed,
the chief priests and elders had to lodge charges against Jesus that justified the death penalty. Pilate's question—**Are you the king of the Jews?**—
reflects the charges they made. They apparently said that Jesus claimed to
be or was hailed as the Messiah (see 27:17, 22), and they portrayed him as
a messiah bent on winning Jewish independence from Roman rule. Since
a Roman governor might not grasp the significance of a Jewish concept
like messiah, those who brought Jesus to Pilate translated it into words Pilate would understand: they said that Jesus claimed to be **king of the
Jews.** Rome had appointed Herod the Great to be **king of the Jews,** but
after his death in 4 B.C. Rome would not let other Jewish rulers use the
title. If Jesus was claiming this title for himself, then he was setting himself up against Rome, and Rome crucified rebels. Hence Pilate asks Jesus,
Are you the king of the Jews? In response **Jesus said, "You say so."** Jesus
avoids giving a yes or no answer (see 26:25, 64). Jesus is not **the king of
the Jews** in the sense that Pilate understands it: Jesus is not a revolutionary

---

BACKGROUND: PILATE Pontius Pilate was the Roman governor of Judea and the
adjacent regions of Samaria and Idumea from about A.D. 26 to 36. His official title was
prefect (military commander), but he also carried out the duties of a procurator (civil
administrator), keeping order and collecting taxes. Pilate was a member of the lower
Roman nobility that Rome drew on for governors of unimportant but sometimes trou-
blesome provinces like Judea. Pilate lived in Caesarea, on the Mediterranean coast,
using a seaside palace built by Herod the Great as his headquarters, or praetorium
(Paul was later held captive here: Acts 23:35). Pilate commanded about twenty-five
hundred to three thousand soldiers, most of whom were stationed in Caesarea but
some of whom manned the Antonia Fortress, adjacent to the Temple in Jerusalem.
During Jewish pilgrimage feasts, when Jerusalem was crowded with pilgrims, Pilate
and his Caesarea troops went to Jerusalem to keep order. Pilate could be quite heedless of Jewish sensitivities, and he aroused anger by bringing images of the Roman
emperor into Jerusalem and by taking money from the Temple treasury to pay for an
aqueduct. The gospels portray Pilate as weak and indecisive. Philo, a first-century
Jewish writer living in Egypt, might have been exaggerating when he characterized
Pilate as arrogant, corrupt, cruel, and given to executing people without trial. Pilate
seems to have been a man who made ill-considered decisions but backed down under pressure. He was removed as governor after his troops killed some Samaritans.
The fact that Pilate kept Caiaphas as high priest during his whole term as governor
indicates that the two men established a working relationship.

out to overthrow Roman rule. But he is God's agent establishing the reign of God; he is the Messiah and Son of God (16:16). Jesus cannot deny that his mission is to establish the kingdom of God, but neither can he affirm Pilate's understanding of this kingdom. His response, **You say so** has the sense, "That may be how you would think of me, but that is not how I think of myself."

For reflection: How do I think of Jesus as king?

12 **And when he was accused by the chief priests and elders, he made no answer.** Matthew does not tell his readers what Jesus was **accused** of, but the charges likely would have reinforced the notion that Jesus was a dangerous revolutionary. The chief priests and elders could have pointed out that Jesus had a large popular following (see 21:46; 26:5); they might have charged Jesus with planning to destroy the Temple (26:61), an act that would trigger rioting. Pilate would have taken seriously any charges that Jesus was a threat to public order: Pilate was in Jerusalem at Passover time to extinguish sparks of riot or revolt before they got out of hand. Whatever the accusations lodged against Jesus, **he made no answer,** just as he stood silent a few hours earlier when charges were made against him in the house of Caiaphas (26:63).

High priest, chief priests: See page 566
Elders: See page 451

13 Pilate is baffled by Jesus' silence. **Then Pilate said to him, "Do you not hear how many things they are testifying against you?"** Jesus is being accused of **many things** that are sufficiently serious to justify his execution. Those whose lives are at stake normally defend themselves against accusations; otherwise the judge might conclude that the charges are true.

14 **But he did not answer him one word, so that the governor was greatly amazed.** Jesus has accepted the prospect of suffering and death as his Father's will (26:42); there is little point in his contesting the charade that will provide a legal veneer for his execution. Pilate, however, is **greatly amazed.** Prisoners brought before him usually cringed in fear or pleaded for their lives or shouted defiance. Pilate had never encountered an accused man with the dignity and demeanor of Jesus, calmly forgoing any defense of himself.

Jesus' silence may again (see 26:63) remind Matthew's readers of Isaiah's prophecy of a servant of God who silently accepts death: "Like a lamb led to the slaughter / or a sheep before the shearers, / he was silent and opened not his mouth" (Isaiah 53:7). This prophecy begins by speaking of many being "amazed at him . . . because of him kings shall stand speechless" (Isaiah 52:14-15). Pilate is truly **amazed** by the man brought before him.

For reflection: What does the image of Jesus standing silent before Pilate convey to me about Jesus?

Responsibility for Jesus' Death

15 Now on the occasion of the feast the governor was accustomed to release to the crowd one prisoner whom they wished. **16** And at that time they had a notorious prisoner called [Jesus] Barabbas. **17** So when they had assembled, Pilate said to them, "Which one do you want me to release to you, [Jesus] Barabbas, or Jesus called Messiah?" **18** For he knew that it was out of envy that they had handed him over. **19** While he was still seated on the bench, his wife sent him a message, "Have nothing to do with that righteous man. I suffered much in a dream today because of him." **20** The chief priests and the elders persuaded the crowds to ask for Barabbas but to destroy Jesus. **21** The governor said to them in reply, "Which of the two do you want me to release to you?" They answered, "Barabbas!" **22** Pilate said to them, "Then what shall I do with Jesus called Messiah?" They all said, "Let him be crucified!" **23** But he said, "Why? What evil has he done?" They only shouted the louder, "Let him be crucified!" **24** When Pilate saw that he was not succeeding at all, but that a riot was breaking out instead, he took water and washed his hands in the sight of the crowd, saying, "I am innocent of this man's blood. Look to it yourselves." **25** And the whole people said in reply, "His blood be upon us and upon our children." **26** Then he released Barabbas to them, but after he had Jesus scourged, he handed him over to be crucified.

> Gospel parallels: Mark 15:6-15; Luke 23:13-25; John 18:38-40; 19:1-16
> OT: Isaiah 53:5

15 Jesus' silence amazes Pilate (27:14), and he decides to draw another prisoner into the proceedings against Jesus. Matthew breaks off his account of

Pilate's interrogation of Jesus to provide some background information. **Now on the occasion of the feast the governor was accustomed to release to the crowd one prisoner whom they wished.** This custom is not mentioned outside the gospels, but in the Greek and Roman world prisoners were sometime released at festivals as a goodwill gesture. Passover celebrates the liberation of Israelites from Egypt; liberating a prisoner during this **feast** would be fitting. A **prisoner** would most likely be someone awaiting trial; long-term imprisonment was not common in the ancient world.

16 As another bit of background information Matthew notes that **at that time they had a notorious prisoner called [Jesus] Barabbas.** A number of prisoners were apparently being held for Pilate to judge when he came to Jerusalem; only the most serious cases would be reserved for him. Among those in custody is **[Jesus] Barabbas.** The New American Bible prints [Jesus] in brackets because this name is found in only some ancient manuscripts of Matthew's gospel. Scholars reason that it is more likely that Matthew named him as "Jesus Barabbas" and some copyists deleted "Jesus" out of reverence for Jesus Christ, and less likely that Matthew called him "Barabbas" and some copyists added the name "Jesus." **Jesus** was a common Jewish name, a form of the name "Joshua." **Barabbas** in Aramaic means "son of Abba;" this particular **Jesus** is called the "son of Abba" to distinguish him from other men named Jesus. There are ancient examples of a man being called Abba or Barabbas. The Aramaic word *abba* means "father," so **Barabbas** is literally "son of the father." He is being held as a **prisoner** for Pilate to judge, which implies that he is charged with a serious crime. Matthew does not tell us the crime he is accused of but characterizes him as being **notorious.**

To Matthew's background information we can add some reasonable conjectures about the setting. When Pilate came to Jerusalem, he presumably used as his headquarters (see 27:27) the finest accommodations available, which would have been a palace-fortress complex Herod the Great built on high ground near the main western gate of Jerusalem. The palace portion of this complex would have had a large courtyard. Ancient legal proceedings were sometimes held outdoors, in a marketplace or courtyard. The person acting as judge would be seated on a platform—the "bench" of verse 19 (see also John 19:13). Roman legal proceedings began at dawn (see 27:1-2).

17 So when they had assembled—those seeking the release of a prisoner and those who had brought Jesus to Pilate—**Pilate said to them, "Which one do you want me to release to you, [Jesus] Barabbas, or Jesus called Messiah?"** On Pilate's lips, **Jesus called Messiah** has the ring of "Jesus the so-called Messiah." Pilate gives the crowd the option of releasing one **Jesus** or the other. There were apparently other prisoners being held in custody: two "revolutionaries" will be crucified with Jesus (27:38). Yet Pilate limits the crowd's choice to either **[Jesus] Barabbas** or **Jesus called Messiah.**

Pilate: See page 619

Messiah, Christ: See page 349

18 Matthew provides Pilate's motive for limiting the crowd's choice to these two men. **For he knew that it was out of envy that they had handed him over.** Pilate realizes that the chief priests and elders have handed Jesus over to him **out of envy** and not because Jesus deserves to be executed. They are presumably envious of Jesus' popularity with the crowds (21:8-11, 15, 46; 26:4-5), which is a threat to their own influence. In a broader sense **envy** can mean malicious intent ("By the envy of the devil, death entered the world"—Wisd 2:24). Pilate seems reluctant to condemn Jesus to death on the say-so of Jewish leaders, but also reluctant to alienate these leaders, because he needs their cooperation in maintaining tranquil Roman rule. Pilate tries to wiggle out of taking a stand by presenting the crowd with a choice: free either one Jesus or the other. Pilate seems to be banking on the crowd wanting to free the Jesus who is called the Messiah rather than the "notorious" Jesus called Barabbas. This will take Jesus' fate out of Pilate's hands and get him off the hook with the chief priests and elders.

19 **While he was still seated on the bench, his wife sent him a message, "Have nothing to do with that righteous man. I suffered much in a dream today because of him."** We might envision a messenger whispering in Pilate's ear after Pilate asks the crowd which Jesus they want released. His wife, who is with him in Jerusalem, had a dream **today**—that is, during the night that just ended. She does not describe the contents of the dream but says that she **suffered much** in the dream because of Jesus. Her message to her husband is clear: **Have nothing to do with that righteous man.** She characterizes Jesus as not merely innocent but **righteous.** Matthew's readers know that Jesus lived righteously, carrying out

623

God's will (3:15). Matthew's readers also know that God can communicate through dreams (1:20; 2:13, 19, 22), even to Gentiles: the magi were warned in a dream to avoid reporting Jesus' whereabouts to Herod (2:12), safeguarding Jesus' life. Now Pilate's wife, another Gentile, has a dream that might also preserve Jesus' life. Her message to Pilate is to **have nothing to do with** Jesus. Will he heed her advice?

Although Jesus knew what "must" happen as God's will (16:21), including his being handed over by Judas (17:22; 20:18), he gave Judas an opportunity to change his mind (26:20-25). Now through a dream God tries to stop Pilate from carrying out what "must" happen. The interplay between God's plans and human freedom is beyond our comprehension. Nonetheless, God's plans for our good will prevail (see Rom 8:28).

For reflection: How do I understand the significance of Pilate's wife's dream?

20 While Pilate pondered his wife's message, **the chief priests and the elders persuaded the crowds to ask for Barabbas but to destroy Jesus.** We should not imagine that all of Jerusalem was crowded into the courtyard with Pilate; those who were there had reasons for being there that morning. The **crowds** would have included members of the arresting party who took Jesus into custody and brought him to Pilate (see 26:47), the servants of the chief priests and elders who accompanied them that night (see 27:58), and any other supporters the chief priests and elders had rounded up. They needed little persuading to ask Pilate to free Barabbas and destroy Jesus. Others who were there probably came to ask for the release of Barabbas. Some may have come to ask for the release of other prisoners, but after Pilate limited the choice to Jesus or Barabbas, **the chief priests and the elders persuaded** them to ask for Barabbas. Their main goal, however, is not that Barabbas be released; those who handed Jesus over to Pilate want Pilate **to destroy Jesus,** and they persuade those present to clamor for Jesus' death.

21 **The governor said to them in reply, "Which of the two do you want me to release to you?"** Pilate has already asked this question (verse 17) but was interrupted by the message from his wife. The sense of **said to them in reply** is best taken to be, said to them again. Pilate goes ahead with his plan to have the crowd choose between Jesus and Barabbas. Perhaps he

reasons that the best way to have nothing to do with Jesus is to let the crowd ask for Jesus' release. If that is his intent, the crowd does not cooperate: **They answered, "Barabbas!"** Pilate has painted himself into a corner. He left it to the crowd to choose between Jesus and Barabbas and he cannot override their choice without losing face (Herod Antipas faced a similar quandary: 14:6-10).

22 The crowd's choice of Barabbas seems to leave Pilate at a loss. **Pilate said to them, "Then what shall I do with Jesus called Messiah?"** As governor, Pilate has the authority to do what he wants with Jesus. He can free Jesus along with Barabbas; he can punish Jesus or have him executed. There is no need for Pilate to consult others or to take their views into account. Yet Pilate seems to leave Jesus' fate up to those present that morning. Is Pilate trying to evade responsibility for what happens to Jesus?

    They all said, "Let him be crucified!" Crucifixion was the most painful and degrading form of execution employed by Rome, a horrible death inflicted on rebels, slaves, and those viewed as the dregs of society. The crowd wants Jesus destroyed (verse 21), **crucified.**

Crucifixion: See page 635

    Interpreters sometimes identify the crowd calling for Jesus' crucifixion with the crowd that gave Jesus a rousing welcome into Jerusalem (21:8-11). I believe it is a misreading of Matthew's gospel to think that those who shouted, "Blessed is he who comes in the name of the Lord," (21:9) are shouting, "Let him be crucified," a few days later. These are two different groups of people. Jesus has broad popularity, especially with those who came from Galilee to Jerusalem for Passover (19:1-2; 20:29; 21:8-11). The chief priests have not behaved as if they could turn these people against Jesus (21:46; 26:4-5), and there is no reason to believe they would have been able to do so now. Those who are assembled before Pilate and who can be persuaded to ask for Jesus' crucifixion are people who have had no attachment to Jesus. Their cry, **Let him be crucified,** is nevertheless chilling. Some may barely know who Jesus is, yet they wish a horrible death upon him.

For reflection: Am I indifferent to the suffering and death of those I do not know? Of those I consider enemies?

23 **But he said, "Why? What evil has he done?"** Pilate asks the crowd **why** should Jesus be crucified; what is their reason for wanting him dead? **What evil has he done?** is a rhetorical question: Pilate does not believe that Jesus has done anything **evil** (see verse 18), certainly nothing to merit crucifixion. **They only shouted the louder, "Let him be crucified!"** The crowd can give no justification for crucifying Jesus; they can only shout their demand **louder,** making up in volume what it lacks in merit.

24 **When Pilate saw that he was not succeeding at all:** Pilate is unsuccessful in convincing the crowd that Jesus does not deserve crucifixion. Instead, **a riot was breaking out.** Pilate came to Jerusalem to prevent civil disturbances during Passover, and he would have one on his hands if the **riot** spread beyond those in his courtyard. To quiet the crowd, Pilate gives in. **He took water and washed his hands in the sight of the crowd, saying, "I am innocent of this man's blood. Look to it yourselves."** The act of **washing** one's **hands** is used in the Old Testament to indicate one's innocence or noninvolvement (Deut 21:6-7), and this gesture could have much the same meaning in the Greek and Roman world. Pilate washes his hands of his involvement in the fate of Jesus. **I am innocent of this man's blood** means, I take no responsibility for his death (Paul uses a similar expression in Acts 20:26). **Look to it yourselves** does not mean that Pilate tells the crowd to crucify Jesus; it means, "The responsibility is yours." The chief priests and elders employed the same expression to tell Judas that he, not they, was responsible for betraying Jesus (27:4.) Pilate's wife urged him to have nothing to do with Jesus, and Pilate conveys in word and action that those who clamor for Jesus' death will bear the responsibility for it.

Pilate's disclaimers are meaningless; he will order Jesus' death (verse 26). No amount of hand washing can change the fact that Jesus was crucified by Pontius Pilate.

For reflection: Do I try to evade responsibility for my actions?

25 Those demanding that Jesus be crucified do not try to avoid responsibility. **And the whole people said in reply, "His blood be upon us and upon our children."** The notion of **blood** being **upon** someone is a biblical idiom for being responsible for someone's death (23:35; see also Jer 26:15; 51:35; Acts 5:28). By saying **His blood be upon us,** those in the

courtyard accept responsibility for the death of Jesus. By adding **and upon our children,** they acknowledge that they are putting their families on the line as well as themselves: what parents do affects their children. Their words do not mean that responsibility for Jesus' death will be passed on to their children and distant descendants like a genetic defect. The notion of parents spending their children's inheritance would be nearer the mark.

His blood be upon us and upon our children are words that have had a troubling history of interpretation. As the cry of **the whole people** they have been taken as a self-curse on the whole people of Israel. Some Christians understood the destruction of Jerusalem in A.D. 70 as the consequence of the blood of Jesus being upon the **children** of those who called for Jesus' execution. Jews will be persecuted as Christ-killers, forever responsible for crucifying Jesus.

COMMENT: WHO WAS RESPONSIBLE FOR JESUS' DEATH? Along with the four gospels, two other ancient writings help determine responsibility for Jesus' death. The Roman historian Tacitus (who lived from about A.D. 56 to 118) wrote that Christ "had been put to death by the procurator Pontius Pilate during the reign of Tiberius" (*Annals,* 15.44). The notice posted on the cross charged Jesus with being "The King of the Jews" (Matt 27:37; Mark 15:26; Luke 23:38; John 19:19)—an insurrectionist. Jesus was executed in the manner that Rome used to get rid of insurrectionists: crucifixion. At the time of Jesus, only Romans, not Jews, could crucify. Jesus died at Passover, when Jerusalem was filled with pilgrims. A city seething with religious and nationalistic fervor could generate sparks of revolt, and Pilate apparently treated Jesus as such a spark, crucifying him. The Jewish historian Josephus (who lived from about A.D. 37 to 100) wrote that Pilate, "upon hearing him accused by the men of the highest standing among us," condemned Jesus to be crucified (*Jewish Antiquities,* 18.3.3). Pilate acted at the urging of the high priest and his associates. They controlled the Temple, which was the source of their power and income. Jesus disrupted commerce in the Temple precincts, upsetting those in charge (Mark 11:15-18). More ominously, Jesus spoke about the Temple being destroyed (Mark 13:1-2). Religious disagreements certainly led some people to oppose Jesus. But those who were personally responsible for his death were a Roman governor bent on maintaining order and religious leaders whose status depended on the Temple. The Second Vatican Council stated, "Even though the Jewish authorities and those who followed their lead pressed for the death of Christ (cf. John 19:6), neither all Jews indiscriminately, nor Jews today, can be charged with crimes committed during his passion" (*Nostra Aetate,* 4).

Matthew hardly understood the crowd's cry as an eternal curse upon the Jewish people; Matthew proclaims the way of Jesus as the future of this people. Matthew's discontent is not with the Jews as a people but with those who are leading Jews in the wrong direction. I argued earlier that the destruction of Jerusalem in A.D. 70 should not be interpreted as God taking vengeance for the death of his Son (see "Did God destroy Jerusalem to avenge Jesus?" page 505). Jeremiah and Ezekiel proclaim that children are not punished for the sins of their parents (Jer 31:29-30; Ezek 18:1-20). Each of those who was involved in the death of Jesus bore individual responsibility for it, and their responsibility does not pass on to other Romans, Jews, or generations.

His blood be upon us and upon our children can carry a fuller meaning than intended by those in the courtyard or even by Matthew. Jesus said that his blood would be shed for the forgiveness of sins (26:28). The first letter of John proclaims that "the blood of his Son Jesus cleanses us from all sin" (1 John 1:7). The blood of Jesus allows forgiveness even for those responsible for his blood being shed (see also Luke 23:34).

For reflection: What do I understand to be the implications of the cry, "His blood be upon us and upon our children"?

26 **Then he released Barabbas to them, but after he had Jesus scourged, he handed him over to be crucified.** Jesus Barabbas who is "son of the father" is **released**; Jesus who is Son of the Father is sent off to an excruciating death. The freeing of Barabbas, whatever his crimes, serves as an image for our being freed from the consequences of our sins by the death of Jesus.

For reflection: Am I able to see myself in Barabbas?

Pilate **had Jesus scourged.** Romans used whips made of leather thongs braided with pieces of bone or metal; scourging flayed through flesh and muscle down to bone. Romans scourged as a punishment, but also **scourged** those who were going to be crucified to weaken them and increase their agony. Matthew does not dwell on the details of Jesus' scourging; his readers were familiar with Roman scourging and did not need to be told how horrible it was. Nor does Matthew apply to Jesus the prophecy, "Upon him was the chastisement that makes us whole, / by his stripes we were healed" (Isaiah 53:5). Although what happens to Jesus is in fulfillment of Scripture (26:54, 56), Matthew will not point out every passage.

After Jesus had been scourged, Pilate **handed him over** to soldiers **to be crucified.** Jesus' sentence of death is what Jesus said "must" happen to him (16:21); he foretold that the chief priests would "condemn him to death, and hand him over to the Gentiles to be mocked and scourged and crucified" (20:18-19). Jesus also foretold his being raised (16:21; 17:23; 20:19), but his path to risen life runs through an exceedingly dark valley. Jesus has stood silent during the exchanges between Pilate and the crowd; his next words will be spoken from the cross (27:46).

Jesus Is Mocked and Abused
27 Then the soldiers of the governor took Jesus inside the praetorium and gathered the whole cohort around him. **28** They stripped off his clothes and threw a scarlet military cloak about him. **29** Weaving a crown out of thorns, they placed it on his head, and a reed in his right hand. And kneeling before him, they mocked him, saying, "Hail, King of the Jews!" **30** They spat upon him and took the reed and kept striking him on the head. **31** And when they had mocked him, they stripped him of the cloak, dressed him in his own clothes, and led him off to crucify him.
32 As they were going out, they met a Cyrenian named Simon; this man they pressed into service to carry his cross.

Gospel parallels: Mark 15:16-21; Luke 23:26; John 19:2-3, 17
OT: Isaiah 50:6
NT: Matt 5:39, 41; 20:19; 27:26, 37

27 **Then the soldiers of the governor took Jesus inside the praetorium and gathered the whole cohort around him.** The **soldiers** under Pilate's command would have been for the most part Gentiles recruited in Syria and Palestine rather than ethnic Romans. **Praetorium** is a Latin term for a governor's official residence. Pilate's main praetorium was a palace Herod the Great built in Caesarea on the Mediterranean coast (see Acts 23:35); Pilate used Herod's Jerusalem palace when he came to town. This palace-fortress complex would have had multiple courtyards, and we should probably envision Jesus being taken into a courtyard where a **whole cohort** of soldiers gathered **around him.** A Roman **cohort** was about six hundred soldiers, but Matthew may simply mean that all the soldiers available converged around Jesus. Pilate is apparently not finished with the cases he is hearing that day, and the soldiers have some time to kill before they can execute the condemned as a batch. They use the time to amuse themselves at Jesus' expense.

28 The manner in which they mock Jesus indicates that they know he will be executed as "the King of the Jews" (see 27:37). How could this sorry figure, scourged and on the way to crucifixion, be a king? The soldiers mock such pretense. **They stripped off his clothes and threw a scarlet military cloak about him.** Kings wore robes of purple, but the soldiers do not have any purple garments available (purple dye was extremely expensive). The standard Roman **military cloak** was **scarlet** or red, close enough to purple to serve as mock royal clothing for Jesus.

29 **Weaving a crown out of thorns, they placed it on his head.** Crowns of the era were wreaths woven of laurel or ivy. Some ancient coins depict emperors wearing crowns with spikes representing rays of light, as if the emperor was a divinity radiating light (the crown atop the Statue of Liberty is spiked). Several species of thorned plants or bushes grow in Palestine (see 7:16; 13:7); the soldiers use one of them to fashion a spiked crown as a parody of an emperor's crown. The point is not so much to torture Jesus as to mock him as a pretend king. His kingly trappings are completed by placing **a reed in his right hand.** Kings held scepters; Jesus' mock scepter is a flimsy reed. **And kneeling before him,** as subjects kneel before a king, **they mocked him.** Roman emperors were greeted with the cry, "Hail, Caesar"; the soldiers **mocked** Jesus by crying out, **Hail, King of the Jews!**

The soldiers' mockery contains ironic truth. Just as Jesus is not the kind of messiah Caiaphas expected (26:63-64), so his kingship is not the kind of kingship the soldiers understand. For the soldiers, being a king means having power and lording it over others (see 20:25). They mock Jesus as powerless, as someone who is at the bottom of society and not, like an earthly king, at the top. In God's kingdom, however, the last will be first (19:30; 20:16). Jesus entered Jerusalem as a meek and nonviolent king (21:4-5) who will give his life as a ransom (20:28); at the end of the age he will be enthroned in kingly glory (25:31, 34).

30 **They spat upon him,** expressing contempt, **and took the reed and kept striking him on the head.** The soldiers' abuse becomes physical as well as verbal. Wearing a crown of thorns and having it battered with a reed would be painful, but not nearly as agonizing as the scourging Jesus endured.

Throughout this episode Matthew describes what the soldiers do and say but gives no indication that Jesus does or says anything to shield himself from abuse. Jesus said that he would be handed over to "Gentiles to be mocked and scourged and crucified" (20:19), and he turns the other cheek to those who abuse him (see 5:39). Matthew's readers might again recall (see 26:67) Isaiah's prophecy of a servant of God: "I gave my back to those who beat me, / my cheeks to those who plucked my beard; / My face I did not shield / from buffets and spitting" (Isaiah 50:6).

For reflection: What does the image of Jesus silently accepting mocking and abuse convey to me about him?

31 **And when they had mocked him, they stripped him of the cloak, dressed him in his own clothes, and led him off to crucify him.** Pilate has apparently finished his court docket now; two others will be executed along with Jesus (27:38). It is time for the soldiers to lead the condemned to the place of execution. Those to be crucified were made to carry the crossbeam from which they would hang; upright beams, perhaps about seven feet high, would already be set in the ground at the place of execution.

32 **As they were going out:** crucifixions were done outside of cities. Those leading Jesus to where he will be crucified **met a Cyrenian named Simon; this man they pressed into service to carry his cross.** Jesus is unable to **carry his cross,** that is, the crossbeam, by himself. Carrying a crossbeam would normally not have been difficult for Jesus; as "the carpenter's son" (13:55), Jesus presumably did carpentry himself (see also Mark 6:3) and would have carried many beams and stone blocks in the course of his work. The fact that he cannot do so now is probably an indication of how severely he has been torn and weakened by scourging (27:26). Soldiers in the Roman army had the authority to press Jews into service as temporary burden bearers, carrying baggage or other items for up to a mile (see 5:41). Because Jesus cannot carry his cross, the soldiers pick someone to do so, **a Cyrenian named Simon.** This **Simon** was from Cyrene, a city near the north coast of Africa with a sizeable Jewish population (the site is present-

day Libya). Simon may have come to Jerusalem for Passover, or he may have moved from Cyrene to Jerusalem. There is no indication that Simon had any previous involvement with Jesus; he is simply someone who is out on the street that day and available when the soldiers need someone to carry Jesus' cross.

Because Simon is **pressed into service,** he becomes the first person to take up a cross for Jesus (10:38; 16:24) and provides us with an image of discipleship. He is an image as well for our crosses sometimes seeming to be randomly assigned to us, not burdens we volunteered to carry. The fact that Matthew includes Simon's name perhaps indicates that Matthew's readers had already heard of him; Simon's encounter with Jesus that day may have led him to became a follower of Jesus. Jews from Cyrene were among the early leaders of the church in Antioch (Acts 11:19-20; 13:1), where Matthew likely wrote his gospel.

For reflection: What can I learn from Simon about my own discipleship? About my cross-bearing for Jesus? How have I been "pressed into service"?

Jesus Is Crucified

[33] And when they came to a place called Golgotha (which means Place of the Skull), [34] they gave Jesus wine to drink mixed with gall. But when he had tasted it, he refused to drink. [35] After they had crucified him, they divided his garments by casting lots; [36] then they sat down and kept watch over him there. [37] And they placed over his head the written charge against him: This is Jesus, the King of the Jews. [38] Two revolutionaries were crucified with him, one on his right and the other on his left.

Gospel parallels: Mark 15:22-27; Luke 23:32-34, 38; John 19:17-24
OT:Psalms 22:19; 69:21-22; Isaiah 53:12

33 **And when they came to a place called Golgotha (which means Place of the Skull):** at the time of Jesus, **Golgotha** was a hump of rock outside the western wall of Jerusalem, not far from a road leading from a city gate. **Golgotha** is an Aramaic word that Matthew translates for his readers as **Skull;** perhaps the rock reminded people of a skull. Romans used the site for crucifixions because those dying atop Golgotha would be in plain view of those entering and leaving Jerusalem (see 27:39). Rome imposed crucifixion not only to punish criminals but as a warning to others to avoid their fate by avoiding their crimes.

34 they gave Jesus wine to drink mixed with gall. It may have been customary to give **wine to drink** to those being crucified to dull the pain, although this would provide only minimal and temporary relief. Jesus is
given wine **mixed with gall,** a bitter substance. Offering Jesus bitter wine
is not an act of compassion but of spite. **But when he had tasted it, he
refused to drink.** Jesus recognizes the mockery in offering him wine
spiked with gall and does not drink it.

Matthew's account of Jesus being given wine mixed with gall echoes
Psalm 69:22. Matthew uses phrases from Scripture to recount Jesus'
death in order to convey that his death is in fulfillment of Scripture (see
26:54, 56).

> I looked for compassion, but there was none,
>> for comforters, but found none.
> Instead they put gall in my food;
>> for my thirst they gave me vinegar.
>> Psalm 69:21-22

35 After they had crucified him: Matthew mentions Jesus' crucifixion in
passing and provides no details. Like virtually everyone in the Roman
empire, Matthew's first readers were sufficiently acquainted with the horrors of crucifixion and needed no description of what was involved. Ancient writers considered it such a hideous form of death that it was best
not to talk about it.

Modern readers, however, should not pass over Jesus' crucifixion too
quickly. Paul wrote that he proclaimed "Christ crucified, a stumbling block

BACKGROUND: GOLGOTHA During the Old Testament era, the limestone hillside
west of Jerusalem was quarried for building blocks. Seams of quality limestone were
dug out; poor stone was left unquarried. Eventually the good stone played out, and
the quarry was abandoned. At the time of Jesus, the old quarry lay just outside the
western wall of Jerusalem. A hump of unquarried rock jutted up twenty to thirty feet
from the quarry floor. Romans used this mound of rock as a place to crucify criminals,
since it made a public display of their deaths. The site was called Golgotha, from the
Aramaic word for skull, perhaps because the unquarried hump of rock was shaped
like the top of a skull. The Latin word for skull gives us the name "Calvary." Today the
site of Golgotha is within the Church of the Holy Sepulchre in Jerusalem. *Related
topic: Tomb of Jesus (page 659).*

to Jews and foolishness to Gentiles" (1 Cor 1:23). If we do not find it scandalous and absurd that the Son of God was crucified, then perhaps we are taking crucifixion too lightly or not dwelling sufficiently on just who it is that died in this manner. Paul went on to write that the crucified Christ is "the power of God and the wisdom of God" (1 Cor 1:24), but we cannot grasp how Jesus' crucifixion is a demonstration of God's power and wisdom without confronting its scandalous absurdity.

For reflection: What does it mean to me that Jesus was crucified?

After passing quickly over Jesus' crucifixion, Matthew notes that **they divided his garments by casting lots.** Romans stripped their victims before affixing them to crosses; the shame of public nakedness was added to the agony of crucifixion (see Heb 12:2). The soldiers carrying out crucifixions apparently had the right to the minor possessions of those they executed, including their clothes. Matthew again echoes words from Scripture (Psalm 22:19) in describing how the soldiers divided Jesus' clothing, continuing to convey that what happens is in fulfillment of Scripture.

> [T]hey divide my garments among them;
> for my clothing they cast lots.
> Psalm 22:19

36 **then they sat down and kept watch over him there.** Those carrying out crucifixions would guard their victims to prevent others from rescuing them. In addition to his disciples, Jesus had a following among pilgrims who were in Jerusalem for Passover (see 21:8-11, 46; 26:4-5); might some of them be bold enough to try to free him? The soldiers take no chances and **kept watch over him;** they **sat down** to wait out his death throes.

37 **And they placed over his head the written charge against him.** Romans sometimes hung a **written charge** around the neck of a person being led off to be crucified, giving the reason why he was being put to death. In the case of Jesus they posted this charge **over his head** on the upright beam of the cross. The **charge** against Jesus read, **This is Jesus, the King of the Jews.** Pilate had asked Jesus, "Are you the king of the Jews?" and Jesus had not denied it (27:11). For Pilate, anyone pretending to be the king of the Jews was a rival to Rome's rule, someone who might stir up a

rebellion. Rome executed insurrectionists by crucifying them; Jesus was crucified as an insurrectionist **King of the Jews.** The **written charge** posted over his head served as a warning that the same manner of death awaited anyone else who challenged Roman rule. The charge was also posted in mockery (see the soldiers' earlier mockery of Jesus as a king—27:27-31). How could this sorry wretch, dying in agony, be a king?

The **written charge** against Jesus has more profound meaning than those who posted it realized. At his birth, he was given the name **Jesus** to signify that "he will save his people from their sins" (1:21); now he is shedding his lifeblood "for the forgiveness of sins" (26:28). He is a **King** who will sit enthroned over all nations and judge them at the end of the age (25:31-34). Jesus' kingship is established through his enduring the abasement of death on a cross and being raised by God.

For reflection: What does Jesus' crucifixion tell me about the significance of his being named Jesus? About his kingship?

BACKGROUND: CRUCIFIXION was an exceedingly cruel form of execution used by a number of ancient peoples. Rome adopted crucifixion as its way of executing slaves, rebels, and lower-class violent criminals. The Romans crucified many both before and after Jesus, including thousands when Rome put down the Jewish revolt of A.D. 66–70. Crucifixions were done in a variety of ways using different styles of crosses. Common Roman practice was to first scourge the one to be crucified, to increase suffering. Then the condemned was forced to carry a crossbeam to the place of execution, where an upright beam would already be in place. Roman crucifixions were done at public sites, such as along a busy road, in order to make them a public display. The one to be crucified was stripped of his clothing, and his arms were tied or nailed to the crossbeam. The crossbeam was then lifted up and fixed to the upright beam at a notch cut either in its top or in its side. Sometimes the person's feet were nailed or tied to the upright beam. Romans posted a sign indicating the crime for which the person was being crucified. Despite their suffering, those who were crucified could survive for several days, tormented by pain, thirst, insects, and the shame of dying naked before others. Death usually resulted from shock or suffocation when chest muscles gave out. A body was sometimes left on the cross until it disintegrated, eaten by rats and vultures. Crucifixion was designed to be as painful and degrading a death as possible. Rome used crucifixion not merely as a punishment but also as a warning of what would happen to those who challenged Roman authority.

38 **Two revolutionaries were crucified with him, one on his right and the other on his left.** The word translated **revolutionaries** means "bandits" but in the course of the first century came to be used for rebels. Rome usually did not crucify ordinary robbers; the two men crucified with Jesus were presumably found guilty of violent crimes. Jesus associated with outcasts and sinners throughout his life (9:10-11; 11:19) and is found in their company to the end.

Matthew's readers who were familiar with Isaiah might have been reminded of a prophecy about a servant of God who is vindicated by God because he "surrendered himself to death / and was counted among the wicked," thereby winning pardon for sins (Isaiah 53:12).

> *Therefore I will give him his portion among the great,*
> *and he shall divide the spoils with the mighty,*
> *Because he surrendered himself to death*
> *and was counted among the wicked;*
> *And he shall take away the sins of many,*
> *and win pardon for their offenses.*
> Isaiah 53:12

James and John wanted what they thought were positions of honor and power to the right and left of Jesus; Jesus warned them that this meant sharing in his sufferings (20:20-22). The two who are **crucified with him, one on his right and the other on his left,** unwittingly provide an image for discipleship. The road leads to Golgotha for those who take up their crosses and follow Jesus (see 10:38-39; 16:24-25).

For reflection: What might Jesus' being crucified between two criminals tell me about him? About being his disciple?

ORIENTATION: *In recounting how the crucified Jesus is mocked, Matthew probes the mystery of the Son of God dying to save others.*

Can This Be the Son of God?
39 **Those passing by reviled him, shaking their heads** 40 **and saying, "You who would destroy the temple and rebuild it in three days, save yourself, if you are the Son of God, [and] come down from the cross!"** 41 **Likewise the chief priests with the scribes and elders mocked him and**

said, **⁴²** "He saved others; he cannot save himself. So he is the king of Israel! Let him come down from the cross now, and we will believe in him. **⁴³** He trusted in God; let him deliver him now if he wants him. For he said, 'I am the Son of God.'" **⁴⁴** The revolutionaries who were crucified with him also kept abusing him in the same way.

> Gospel parallels: Mark 15:29-32; Luke 23:35-43
> OT: Psalm 22:8-9; Wisd 2:12-20
> NT: Matt 4:1-11; 26:60-64

39 **Those passing by reviled him:** Romans liked to stage crucifixions near busy roads so that those **passing by** would see what happened to those who ran afoul of Roman authority. Those who pass by Jesus on the cross **reviled him, shaking their heads.** Shaking one's head is a gesture of scorn, deriding someone for their sorry fate (2 Kings 19:21; Psalm 109:25; Lam 2:15). Matthew's account of the mockery echoes Psalm 22, a prayer of someone in dire straits: "All who see me mock me; / . . . they shake their heads at me" (Psalm 22:8).

> All who see me mock me;
>> they curl their lips and jeer;
>> they shake their heads at me:
> "You relied on the LORD—let him deliver you;
>> if he loves you, let him rescue you."
>
>   *Psalm 22:8-9*

40 The passersby who are reviling Jesus seem to be aware of what happened during Jesus' hearing before the religious authorities only hours earlier (26:57-68). We might speculate that some of them were allied with the religious authorities, but Matthew does not tell us who they are or how they learned of the charges made against Jesus. Matthew's interest is in what they say. They reviled Jesus, **saying, "You who would destroy the temple and rebuild it in three days, save yourself, if you are the Son of God, [and] come down from the cross!"** During his hearing, Jesus had been accused of saying, "I can destroy the temple of God and within three days rebuild it" (26:61). This is now flung in his face: if you are able to **destroy the temple and rebuild it in three days,** then you should be able to **save yourself** from crucifixion. If Jesus cannot escape from the cross, how could he destroy and rebuild the Temple? During his hearing, Jesus was asked whether he was the Messiah and the Son of God, and he did not deny it (26:63-64). Now he is taunted: **Save yourself, if you are the Son of God, [and] come down from the cross!** If Jesus cannot save himself, how could he be the Son of God? Someone who is the Son of God would certainly never end up on a cross! Jesus' crucifixion demonstrates that he is an impostor, and he is reviled for his pretensions.

Temple: See page 442
Son of God: See page 52

Before Jesus began his public ministry, Satan tempted him, "If you are the Son of God, command that these stones become loaves of bread" (4:3); "If you are the Son of God, throw yourself down" from the parapet of the Temple (4:6). Satan tried to sidetrack Jesus from his mission by getting him to use his status as the Son of God for his own advantage. At the climax of his mission, Jesus is similarly tempted: **if you are the Son of God,** then come down from the cross. But Jesus will not use his status as Son to evade his mission as Son. From beginning to end, Jesus faithfully carries out his Father's will, in fulfillment of Scripture (4:4, 7, 10; 26:42, 54, 56).

For reflection: What can I learn from Jesus' temptations? From his faithfulness despite temptation?

41 **Likewise the chief priests with the scribes and elders mocked him.** Chief priests, scribes, and elders had assembled in the middle of the night to build a case against Jesus that would justify his death (26:57, 59). Their quest has been successful: Jesus has been crucified. They **mocked him,** as victors mock those whom they have vanquished.

High priest, chief priests: See page 566
Scribes: See page 138
Elders: See page 451

42 Their mockery has several themes. They jeer, **He saved others; he cannot save himself.** The word **saved** means "rescued" and can be used for different kinds of rescue. When Jesus' disciples were in danger of drowning, they cried out for him to save them (8:25; 14:30). The woman with a hemorrhage believed that if she touched Jesus' cloak she would be cured, literally, be "saved" (see 9:21), rescued from her affliction. Jesus was widely known as

someone who healed those who were ill or demon possessed (4:23-25; 9:35; 11:2-5), and the religious authorities grant that Jesus **saved others.** But, they mock, **he cannot save himself;** he cannot rescue himself from the cross. What an irony: a savior of others who **cannot save himself.**

Jesus saves in a far more profound sense than his mockers realize. Being saved means not only rescue from danger or disease but being given eternal life in the kingdom of God (see 10:22; 16:25; 24:13). Jesus will save others eternally by not saving, or rescuing, himself. He will give his life as a ransom (20:28), shedding his blood for the forgiveness of sins (26:28); "he will save his people from their sins" (1:21). What an irony: a savior who saves others by not saving himself!

In a next bit of mockery the religious authorities exclaim, **So he is the king of Israel!** The charge on the cross calls Jesus the "King of the Jews" (27:37), but the religious authorities use the more familiar expression **king of Israel,** a title that occurs frequently in the Old Testament. The king of Israel ruled Israel and enjoyed the power and luxuries that came with being king. How could this wretch dying on a cross be a king? How could someone being executed by the Romans have any claim to be the ruler of God's people? **So he is the king of Israel!** Hah!

Those passing by challenged Jesus to come down from the cross (verse 40) and the religious leaders echo their cry: **Let him come down from the cross now.** They specify that Jesus should come down **now,** and if he does so, they say **we will believe in him.** Skeptics earlier demanded that Jesus produce a sign to authenticate himself as God's agent (12:38; 16:1). Jesus refused to provide such a sign, knowing that any sign could be explained away by those who did not want to believe (see 12:24). Jesus instead spoke cryptically of "the sign of Jonah" (12:39; 16:4) and used Jonah being in the belly of a fish as a comparison for the Son of Man being "in the heart of the earth three days and three nights" (12:40). The sign authenticating Jesus as God's agent will not be his coming down from the cross but his death and resurrection. Those who will come to **believe in him** must believe in him crucified and risen.

For reflection: Why do I believe in Jesus? What signs support my faith?

43 The religious leaders continue their mockery: **He trusted in God; let him deliver him now if he wants him.** If God does not **deliver him now,** then God must not want to preserve him; Jesus' trust in God has been

639

wishful thinking. Matthew formulates the mockery in words that echo Psalm 22: "You relied on the LORD—let him deliver you; / if he loves you, let him rescue you" (Psalm 22:9). The mockers add, **For he said, "I am the Son of God,"** apparently referring to his response to Caiaphas during his hearing (26:63-64). How could Jesus be **the Son of God** if God lets him die on a cross? The manner of Jesus' death surely refutes his claim to enjoy a special relationship with God.

Son of God: See page 52

In expressing the mockery hurled at Jesus, Matthew seems to echo not only Psalm 22 but also the book of Wisdom. In Wisdom, mockers say that a just man "boasts that God is his Father" (Wisd 2:16). They continue, "If the just one be the son of God, he will defend him. . . . / Let us condemn him to a shameful death; / for according to his own words, God will take care of him" (Wisd 2:18, 20).

44 **The revolutionaries who were crucified with him also kept abusing him in the same way.** Even those who are being **crucified with him** join in the mockery. That they abused him **in the same way** conveys that they too understood Jesus' crucifixion as utter defeat for him, shattering his pretensions to enjoy a special relationship with God.

The mockery hurled at the crucified Jesus was likely echoed in Matthew's time by Jewish leaders who did not accept Jesus as the Messiah. How could someone who was crucified be the Messiah and the Son of God? Matthew proclaims that Jesus accepted death as his Father's will and in fulfillment of Scripture, in order to save God's people from their sins. How Jesus died is only understandable in light of why he died.

We too must confront the challenge posed by Jesus' crucifixion. Is the manner in which Jesus died evidence that he was a deluded, false messiah, or is it evidence of a self-sacrificing love that brings us forgiveness and salvation? Is the crucifixion of Jesus foolishness and a stumbling block (see 1 Cor 1:23)—or a demonstration of the wisdom and power of God (see 1 Cor 1:24)?

For reflection: How often have I meditated on Jesus' crucifixion? What does his crucifixion reveal about God's ways?

Jesus Dies, Apparently Forsaken
45 From noon onward, darkness came over the whole land until three in the afternoon. **46** And about three o'clock Jesus cried out in a loud voice, *"Eli, Eli, lema sabachthani?"* which means, "My God, my God, why have you forsaken me?" **47** Some of the bystanders who heard it said, "This one is calling for Elijah." **48** Immediately one of them ran to get a sponge; he soaked it in wine, and putting it on a reed, gave it to him to drink. **49** But the rest said, "Wait, let us see if Elijah comes to save him." **50** But Jesus cried out again in a loud voice, and gave up his spirit.

> Gospel parallels: Mark 15:33-37; Luke 23:44-46; John 19:28-30
> OT:Psalms 22:2; 69:22; Amos 8:9

45 Matthew did not tell his readers the hour when Jesus was crucified (27:33-35), but it was before noon. **From noon onward, darkness came over the whole land until three in the afternoon.** The word translated **land** can also be translated "earth." It is unclear whether Matthew means that darkness came over the land of Judea or over the whole earth. Matthew provides no natural explanation for the **darkness.** It is not a solar eclipse, which cannot occur at full moon, when Passover is celebrated. For Matthew the darkness is an act of God. But what is the significance of God's covering the land with darkness? Matthew's Jewish Christian readers may have associated **darkness** coming over the land with the darkness expected on a "day of the Lord" when God would come in judgment. "On that day, says the Lord GOD, / I will make the sun set at midday / and cover the earth with darkness in broad daylight" (Amos 8:9; see also Isaiah 13:9-10; Joel 2:1-2, 10; 3:4; Zeph 1:14-15).

The day of the Lord: See page 48

The darkness lasted from **noon** until **three in the afternoon.** Matthew says nothing about what happened during these three hours, although he described what happened before (27:33-44) and will tell what happens afterwards. It is as if a cosmic silence as well as blackout envelopes the earth as Jesus hangs on the cross (see Rev 8:1 for a silent pause during momentous events).

For reflection: What significance do I see in the darkness?

46 Matthew has not recounted Jesus saying anything during his mockings and crucifixion (27:27-44); his last words were spoken to Pilate (27:11). After it has been dark for around three hours, Jesus breaks his silence: **And about three o'clock Jesus cried out in a loud voice, "Eli, Eli, lema sabach-thani?"** The words **cried out in a loud voice** have the sense, screamed with a loud cry. It is not an inarticulate scream; Jesus says in his native Aramaic, *Eli, Eli, lema sabachthani?* Matthew translates Jesus' cry as **My God, my God, why have you forsaken me?** These are the opening words of Psalm 22, a prayer of a person experiencing apparent abandonment by God.

> My God, my God, why have you abandoned me?
> Why so far from my call for help,
> from my cries of anguish?
>
> *Psalm 22:2*

How should we interpret Jesus' cry from the cross? Some note that the concluding sections of Psalm 22 express confidence in God (Psalm 22:23-32) and interpret Jesus' cry as an indication of his ultimate confidence in God, even in suffering crucifixion.

However, Jesus did not select a verse of Psalm 22 that expressed confidence to be his prayer from the cross; he used Psalm 22's bleakest verse as his scream: **My God, my God, why have you forsaken me?** Jesus does not address God as his Father, as he earlier did during his distress in Gethsemane (26:39, 42). Nevertheless, he cries out to God as **my God.** Jesus has not abandoned God or his mission from God, but in carrying out God's will he feels abandoned by God.

In the Psalms, to be abandoned, or forsaken, by God means not being helped by God in time of need or distress, not being rescued by him from harm, defeat, or death (Psalms 27:9, 12; 31:9; 38:20-22; 71:9-11; 78:62; 119:121). In this sense, Jesus has been forsaken by God. Jesus heard the taunt, "He trusted in God; let him deliver him now if he wants him" (27:43). If his Father looks on him as his beloved Son (3:17; 17:5), why doesn't his Father deliver him? Jesus' **why** is an implied plea for God to act. Jesus' anguished **why** is the cry of all who do not understand God's ways and God's seeming indifference to their suffering.

For reflection: When have I cried out, "Why?" to God? What answer did I receive?

No voice answers Jesus' cry. The heavens that opened after Jesus' baptism (3:16) remain closed; instead of a bright cloud enveloping him, as at his transfiguration (17:5), Jesus is now in darkness. To all appearances, God has abandoned his Son.

Throughout the centuries, some Christians have found it hard to accept that the Son of God could experience abandonment by God. Mystics have had the greatest insights into the desolation Jesus experienced, for they knew firsthand that one could be very near to God and yet experience God as utter absence and darkness.

For reflection: How do I understand Jesus' cry from the cross? What does it tell me about Jesus? What is my own experience of God's presence or absence?

47 **Some of the bystanders who heard it said, "This one is calling for Elijah."** Matthew does not say whether the **bystanders** are soldiers keeping watch over the executions (27:36) or others who happen to be there. They know who **Elijah** is, and they misunderstand Jesus' call, "Eli, Eli" (verse 46), as a

---

COMMENT: MYSTICS AND JESUS' CRY OF ABANDONMENT St. John of the Cross (1542–1591) considered Jesus' experience of abandonment on the cross a model for those who wished to enter into union with God: "Because I have said that Christ is the way and that this way is a death to our natural selves in the sensory and spiritual parts of the soul, I would like to demonstrate how this death is patterned on Christ's. For He is our model and light. . . . At the moment of His death He was certainly annihilated in His soul, without any consolation or relief, since the Father left Him that way in innermost aridity in the lower part. He was thereby compelled to cry out: *My God, my God, why have you forsaken me?* This was the most extreme abandonment, sensitively, that He had suffered in His life. And by it He accomplished the most marvelous work of His whole life. . . . He brought about the reconciliation and union of the human race with God through grace. The Lord achieved this, as I say, at the moment in which He was most annihilated in all things. . . . for He was forsaken by His Father at that time so as to pay the debt fully and bring man to union with God" (*The Ascent of Mount Carmel*, pages 124–125). St. Edith Stein (Sr. Teresa Benedicta of the Cross, 1891–1942) wrote in a study of St. John of the Cross, "Just as Jesus in the extreme abandonment at his death surrendered himself into the hands of the invisible and incomprehensible God, so will the soul yield herself to the midnight darkness of faith which is the only way to the incomprehensible God" (*The Science of the Cross*, page 121).

call to Elijah. Whether they know that Elijah was taken into heaven (2 Kings 2:11) and was expected to return before the "day of the LORD" (Mal 3:23-24; see also Sirach 48:9-12) is unclear. Matthew presents Jesus' cry being misunderstood without spelling out what was going through the minds of those who misunderstood it.

48 Immediately one of them ran to get a sponge; he soaked it in wine, and putting it on a reed, gave it to him to drink. Giving a crucified man a drink of **wine** would normally be an act of mercy, but if this is the intention it is the first bit of mercy shown Jesus during his ordeal. The Greek word Matthew uses here for **wine** refers to sour wine or vinegar; soldiers drank it as a cheap thirst quencher. Perhaps the one who gave Jesus such wine meant to revive him. Matthew likely sees it as a fulfillment of the Scripture, "for my thirst they gave me vinegar" (Psalm 69:22).

49 But the rest said, "Wait, let us see if Elijah comes to save him." The others at the cross tell the one offering wine to Jesus to leave him alone. Jesus could not save himself (27:40, 42); let's see if Elijah comes and saves him. Their words are banter. They have no interest in Jesus being rescued; they are passing the time until those who have been crucified die and they can go home.

50 But Jesus cried out again in a loud voice. The first time Jesus cried out in a loud voice he screamed, "My God, my God, why have you forsaken me?" (verse 46). Perhaps when he **cried out again in a loud voice** he repeated these words, or perhaps his cry was an inarticulate scream. After his final cry he **gave up his spirit.** The Hebrew and Greek words for **spirit** have a range of meaning. They can be translated as "breath"; by writing that Jesus **gave up his spirit,** Matthew could simply indicate that Jesus let out his last breath. There is a richer meaning of **spirit,** however. One's breath is the breath of life: God "formed man out of the clay of the ground and blew into his nostrils the breath of life, and so man became a living being" (Gen 2:7). At death, "the life breath returns to God who gave it" (Eccl 12:7; see also Psalm 104:29). Based on the notion of spirit as the breath of life, **spirit** can mean one's life, one's self (the Hebrew word for "soul" has much the same meaning). By writing that Jesus **gave up his spirit,** Matthew conveys that Jesus surrendered his life—not passively dying but entrusting himself through death into the hands of God.

For reflection: How do I understand the significance of Jesus giving up his spirit? What might it indicate about the attitude I should take toward my own death?

Even though Jesus' death carries out God's will (26:39, 42) in fulfillment of Scripture (26:54, 56) and brings forgiveness of sins (26:28), it leaves us with much to ponder. Why was it necessary that Jesus die for sins to be forgiven? Could not a merciful God grant forgiveness without requiring the suffering and death of his beloved Son? That Jesus died on a cross is an index of God's love for us (see Rom 5:8) but also a great mystery. In Matthew's account, Jesus embraces this mystery without apparently fully comprehending it, feeling forsaken as he is dying. The more we ponder the mystery of Jesus' death, the more we are led into the mystery of God.

For reflection: What impact does the crucifixion of Jesus have on my understanding of God?

To all appearances, Jesus' death represents utter defeat for him and the death knell for his mission. Who would want to commit their lives to a crucified man? Who would want to forsake themselves for one who was forsaken by God?

ORIENTATION: *Matthew recounts consequences of Jesus' death in a long sentence strung together with "ands" (verses 51-53)—a chain reaction of events. The New American Bible breaks up Matthew's sentence into shorter sentences, omitting some "ands."*

God's Response to Jesus' Death
⁵¹ And behold, the veil of the sanctuary was torn in two from top to bottom. The earth quaked, rocks were split, ⁵² tombs were opened, and the bodies of many saints who had fallen asleep were raised. ⁵³ And coming forth from their tombs after his resurrection, they entered the holy city and appeared to many. ⁵⁴ The centurion and the men with him who were keeping watch over Jesus feared greatly when they saw the earthquake and all that was happening, and they said, "Truly, this was the Son of God!"

Gospel parallels: Mark 15:38-39; Luke 23:47-48
OT:Ezek 37:12; Dan 12:2-3; Nahum 1:5-6

51 **And behold,** immediately upon the death of Jesus (27:50), **the veil of the sanctuary was torn in two from top to bottom.** The **veil of the sanctuary** likely refers to the veil covering the doorway to the innermost room of the Temple, the Holy of Holies (Exod 26:31-33; 40:21). The Holy of Holies was the place of God's special presence; only the high priest could enter it, and only once a year, on the Day of Atonement (Lev 16:1-19). That this veil **was torn** implies that it was torn by God. Its being **torn in two** can have different symbolic meanings. It can mean that the death of Jesus gave everyone access to God; entering into God's presence is no longer restricted to a single person or a single day of the year. The tearing of the veil in the heart of the Temple could also foreshadow the destruction of the entire Temple, a destruction Jesus foretold (24:1-2). God's presence will no longer be restricted to a special place; God will be present to his people through the enduring presence of the risen Jesus (see 18:20; 28:20). The veil of the sanctuary was torn in two **from top to bottom**— literally, "from above to below."

The veil was torn in two downward, and **the earth quaked**—literally, the earth "was shaken," implying that it was shaken *by* God. I imagine a shock wave from heaven tearing through the sanctuary veil and striking the earth, causing an earthquake. In the Old Testament, earthquakes manifest the presence of God (Exod 19:18; Judges 5:4-5; Psalm 68:8-9; Isaiah 63:19) and are among the upheavals of the "day of the Lord," when God will come in judgment (Isaiah 24:18-21; Joel 4:14-16; Nahum 1:5).

The day of the Lord: See page 48

The earth was shaken, and **rocks were split**—split by God. The earthquake fractures the limestone bedrock that lies under Jerusalem. Although the New American Bible translation reads that the sanctuary veil **was torn** and rocks **were split,** Matthew uses the same Greek verb in both instances; we are reading about a series of connected events. Rocks being split may be an allusion to the upheavals that will accompany God's coming in judgment: "Before his wrath, who can stand firm, / and who can face his blazing anger? / His fury is poured out like fire, / and the rocks are rent asunder before him" (Nahum 1:6).

52 Rocks were split, and **tombs were opened.** The passive construction **were opened** again implies God's action, and there is again a connection with what has gone before. Jewish burials in the Jerusalem area were in tombs

hewn in the limestone bedrock and hillsides (see 27:60). An earthquake split apart the bedrock, and **tombs** cut into this bedrock **were opened.**

Burial practices: See page 652

The chain reaction to the death of Jesus reaches its climax as tombs were opened **and the bodies of many saints who had fallen asleep were raised.** The **saints,** literally, "holy ones," are the righteous from before the time of Jesus (see 13:17; 23:29, 35). **Fallen asleep** is an idiom for having died (see 1 Cor 15:20; 1 Thess 4:13; 2 Pet 3:4). The **bodies** of **many** of the righteous who had died **were raised** by God. Many Jews expected that at the end of this age God would raise the dead to some kind of bodily life (2 Macc 7:10-11; 14:46; Isaiah 26:19; Dan 12:2). If God, in response to the death of Jesus, is raising the dead, then Jesus' death marks the beginning of the end of this age. The raising of some anticipates what will happen to all in the age to come.

Resurrection: See page 478

53 The series of things that happen at the death of Jesus culminates in some of the dead being raised; **and coming forth from their tombs after his resurrection, they entered the holy city and appeared to many.** The **holy city** is a term for Jerusalem (see 4:5). The Greek word for **appeared** is literally "were made visible": the dead who were raised by God were made visible by God to many in Jerusalem. In a prophecy of Ezekiel, God promised, "O my people, I will open your graves and have you rise from them, and bring you back to the land of Israel" (Ezek 37:12). Matthew provides no description of what those who had been raised looked like in their risen state, nor does he tell what became of them after their appearances in Jerusalem.

Matthew's account is a bit awkward. He wants to speak of some being raised from the dead at the death of Jesus, but he is apparently aware of the early tradition that Jesus was the first to be raised from the dead (Rom 8:29; 1 Cor 15:20-23; Col 1:18), and Jesus is not yet risen. Hence Matthew defers anyone seeing those who are raised until **after his resurrection.** We must not push Matthew's account further than its intended message, which is that Jesus' death is a turning point of cosmic significance. The darkness, earthquake, and splitting of rocks call to mind the "day of the Lord," when God will come in judgment; the raising of the dead calls to mind Daniel's prophecy of the dead rising to be rewarded or punished (Dan 12:2-3). By associating Jesus' death with what is expected to happen at the end of this age, Matthew conveys that Jesus' death marks the beginning of the end.

For reflection: How do I interpret the events that follow the death of Jesus?

54 The centurion and the men with him who were keeping watch over Jesus: the soldiers who crucified Jesus "sat down and kept watch over him" (27:36) as he hung on the cross. They are commanded by a **centurion,** an officer nominally in charge of one hundred soldiers. The centurion and those he commanded would have been Gentiles. They **feared greatly when they saw the earthquake and all that was happening.** They would have experienced the midday darkness and the earthquake; they may have seen tombs opened—there are a number of ancient tombs within sight of Golgotha. What they saw filled them with great fear and awe. **They said, "Truly, this was the Son of God!"** Jesus had been mocked for any pretensions he had to be **the Son of God:** how can he be God's Son if he dies on a cross (27:40, 42-43)? The upheavals triggered by his death demonstrate that he was indeed special to God: only God could so convulse the earth.

On the lips of Gentiles, the expression **the Son of God** might mean some sort of divine being. Matthew's readers, however, know that Jesus is **the Son of God** in a unique sense: he is the beloved Son (3:17; 17:5), who knows God as only the Son can know the Father (11:27). While Jesus is the fulfillment of God's plans for the Jewish people, Matthew signals that Gentiles will be incorporated into God's plans. After his birth, Gentile magi paid homage to Jesus (2:1-12); after his death, Gentile soldiers recognize him as the Son of God.

Son of God: See page 52

For reflection: What do I mean when I say that Jesus is the Son of God? What does it mean for me that the Son of God died on a cross?

The Women at Golgotha
⁵⁵ There were many women there, looking on from a distance, who had followed Jesus from Galilee, ministering to him. ⁵⁶ Among them were Mary Magdalene and Mary the mother of James and Joseph, and the mother of the sons of Zebedee.

Gospel parallels: Mark 15:40-41; Luke 23:49
NT: Matt 20:20-21; Luke 8:2-3

55 After recounting the crucifixion of Jesus and events that followed it (27:33-54), Matthew adds that **there were many women there** at Golgotha, looking on **from a distance**: Romans apparently kept family and friends some distance away from those being crucified. The women were **looking on**, observing Jesus' crucifixion; that is all they could do. They **had followed Jesus from Galilee, ministering to him.** Matthew has described Jesus calling men to follow him as disciples (see 4:18-22; 8:19-22; 9:9; 19:21); this is the first notice that there were women who **followed** Jesus. **Ministering to** can also be translated "served"; it can mean providing meals and waiting at table (see 8:15) but also a broader range of service (see 25:44). Jesus called his disciples to serve one another in imitation of his example of service (20:26-28). The women at Golgotha had followed Jesus and served him as he traveled **from Galilee** to Jerusalem; presumably they had also followed and served him during his ministry in Galilee. That there were **many women** present at Golgotha may indicate that he had a sizeable number of women disciples.

Galilee: See page 68

Matthew does not report that any of Jesus' men disciples were nearby when he died. They ran away when he was arrested (26:56) and are conspicuously absent. Ironically, it is those who are not mentioned during Jesus' public ministry who remain faithful to him and follow him to the cross, keeping watch with him as he dies.

For reflection: What can I learn from the example of the women who served Jesus and kept watch at Golgotha?

56 Matthew identifies three of the women at Golgotha. **Among them were Mary Magdalene,** the **Mary** who is from Magdala, a town on the western shore of the Sea of Galilee about four miles from Capernaum. A second woman present is **Mary the mother of James and Joseph.** The name **Mary** was common among first-century Palestinian Jewish women; this **Mary** is identified as the **mother of James and Joseph.** Matthew earlier listed a James and Joseph among the brothers of Jesus (13:55), but the James and Joseph who were among Jesus' male relatives were not necessarily the same as those mentioned here; James and Joseph also were common Jewish names. Matthew characteristically refers to Mary the mother of Jesus as "his mother" (1:18; 2:11, 13, 20-21; 13:55), and it would be very odd for him to identify her now in another way. Hence **Mary the mother of James and Joseph** is not the mother of Jesus. Matthew identifies a third woman among the many present as **the mother of the sons of Zebedee.** Her sons have fled (26:56); she has remained to be near Jesus. She is the only one of the three women to have appeared earlier in Matthew's gospel. While traveling with Jesus from Galilee to Jerusalem (see 19:1-2; 20:17), she asked that her two sons sit at the right and left of Jesus in his kingdom (20:20-21). Jesus said that would mean sharing his sufferings (20:22). This has now been graphically displayed for her, as she watched Jesus crucified with one man on his right and one on his left (27:38).

The women who ministered to Jesus looked on as he died, and it will turn out that this too will be of service to him—ultimately the most important thing they will do for him.

The Burial of Jesus

57 **When it was evening, there came a rich man from Arimathea named Joseph, who was himself a disciple of Jesus. 58 He went to Pilate and asked for the body of Jesus; then Pilate ordered it to be handed over. 59 Taking the body, Joseph wrapped it [in] clean linen 60 and laid it in his new tomb that he had hewn in the rock. Then he rolled a huge stone across the entrance to the tomb and departed. 61 But Mary Magdalene and the other Mary remained sitting there, facing the tomb.**

> Gospel parallels: Mark 15:42-47; Luke 23:50-56; John 19:38-42
> OT:Deut 21:22-23
> NT:Matt 27:55-56

57 **When it was evening, there came a rich man from Arimathea named Joseph.** For Jews, sundown marks the beginning of a new day, and it is now **evening,** before sunset. The following verses describe **Joseph** burying the body of Jesus. He does so before sunset because Deuteronomy prohibits the corpse of an executed man hanging on a tree overnight (Deut 21:22-23); first-century Jews interpreted this law to apply to those who had been crucified.

> *If a man guilty of a capital offense is put to death and his corpse hung on a tree, it shall not remain on the tree overnight. You shall bury it the same day.*
>
> *Deuteronomy 21:22-23*

Joseph is **a rich man from Arimathea, who was himself a disciple of Jesus.** He is **from Arimathea,** a town in Judea whose location is uncertain. While Arimathea is his hometown, Joseph may now live in Jerusalem. He is **a disciple of Jesus,** although this is the first time he is mentioned in Matthew's gospel. Matthew does not say how he knew of Jesus' death. Joseph is a **rich man** as well as a disciple of Jesus. Jesus apparently did not ask him to give up all his possessions, as he asked another rich man (19:21). Those with wealth can be disciples of Jesus, despite the dangers of wealth (see 6:19-20, 24; 19:23-24); Jesus can ask them to serve him with their wealth, as Joseph now does.

Disciple: See page 66

58 **He went to Pilate and asked for the body of Jesus.** Romans sometimes left bodies on crosses until they were eaten by scavenging birds and animals; crucifixion was meant to be a gruesome deterrent to crime, and the more gruesome the better. However, in light of the Jewish abhorrence of a corpse remaining on a cross overnight, Romans apparently allowed the bodies of Jews to be removed after death. The corpses of those crucified would normally be thrown into a pit or common grave for criminals and not given to their families or friends for proper burial. When Joseph **asked for the body of Jesus,** though, **Pilate ordered it to be handed over** to him. In Matthew's account, Pilate was not convinced that Jesus deserved crucifixion (27:18-19, 23-24); Joseph is a rich man and may have sufficient clout with Pilate to get the body of Jesus as a favor. Pilate **ordered** his soldiers to remove the body of Jesus from the cross and turn it over to Joseph.

Pilate: See page 619

59 **Taking the body** from the soldiers, **Joseph wrapped it [in] clean linen.** As a rich man, Joseph presumably had servants to help him with Jesus' burial. Corpses were usually washed (see Acts 9:37), anointed with oils or spices, and wrapped in burial cloths. Matthew does not say anything about Joseph washing or anointing Jesus' body, perhaps because Jesus already received an anointing in anticipation of his burial (26:6-12). Wrapping Jesus' body in **clean linen** expresses care and respect. Although Jesus has been executed as a criminal and must be buried rather quickly, Joseph nevertheless treats his body with dignity. It is the last loving act he can do as a disciple for his master.

60 Joseph took the body of Jesus **and laid it in his new tomb that he had hewn in the rock.** The tombs of the wealthy were **hewn** in the limestone hills around Jerusalem and intended for family burials generation after generation. Joseph, a rich man, had a **new tomb** hewn for himself and his family, and he **laid** the body of Jesus on one of the shelves in his tomb. Since it is a **new** tomb, Jesus is apparently the first to be buried in it. Joseph not only provides a decent burial place for Jesus but in effect adopts Jesus into his family by placing his body in his family tomb. We might expect someone of Joseph's social status to be wary of being identified with a man rejected by Jewish authorities and executed as a criminal, but Joseph indelibly associates himself with Jesus, heedless of the consequences for himself.

> For reflection: What lessons about discipleship can I learn from Joseph of Arimathea?

Then he rolled a huge stone across the entrance to the tomb and departed. Tombs had rather small entrances, forcing one to crouch down to enter them. Tomb entrances were closed up with a **stone,** either a boulder

---

BACKGROUND: BURIAL PRACTICES Jewish burials took place as soon as possible after death. The corpse was washed and anointed with ointments and perfumes and wrapped in cloth. Ordinary Jews were buried in simple graves dug in the ground; wealthy Jerusalem Jews were buried in cavelike tombs carved into the limestone hillsides surrounding the city. These tombs usually contained several chambers and served entire families for several generations. Such burials were usually a two-step process. First, the corpse lay on a shelf in the tomb for about a year. Then, after the flesh had decayed away, the bones were collected and placed in a pit containing the bones of the person's ancestors. Or, in Jerusalem at the time of Jesus, bones were often placed instead in an ossuary, a lidded box carved from limestone; typically such boxes were about twenty-four by eighteen by twelve inches. The box was then set in a recess in the tomb complex. Sometimes the bones of several members of a family were placed in the same box. In 1990, archaeologists excavated a tomb on the southern edge of Jerusalem and found a bone box with an Aramaic form of the name "Caiaphas" inscribed on it. Inside were bones identified as those of a man about sixty, an adult woman, a teenage boy, a young child, and two infants. Archaeologists believe that the bones of the man are those of the Caiaphas who was high priest from A.D. 18 to 36. *Related topic: Tomb of Jesus (page 659).*

or a wheel-shaped stone that could be rolled into place. Tombs were not permanently sealed, because they would be used for multiple burials; a stone rolled across the entrance kept out scavenging animals and deterred tomb robbers but could be removed for future burials. Joseph, presumably with the help of his servants, rolled a **huge stone** across the tomb entrance, securely barricading it. Then he **departed,** his burial of Jesus completed. Joseph departs as well from the pages of Matthew's gospel as abruptly as he appeared. He had one supreme service to perform for Jesus; everything he did earlier or later as a disciple of Jesus has been forgotten. In our own lives, even if we do nothing that will be remembered by future generations, all that we do in service of Jesus is remembered by him.

61 **But Mary Magdalene and the other Mary remained sitting there, facing the tomb.** The **other Mary** is Mary the mother of James and Joseph; she and **Mary Magdalene** were among the women who looked on from a distance as Jesus was crucified (27:55-56). They continue to look on as Jesus is buried. Matthew does not explain why they do not take part in the burial; perhaps Joseph's servants made their assistance unnecessary. They sat **facing the tomb,** able to see the body of Jesus being carried into the tomb. They **remained sitting there** for a while. Sitting can be a posture of mourning (Job 2:8, 13; Psalm 137:1; Jonah 3:6); perhaps they remained at the tomb to mourn Jesus' death. Their observing his burial continues what will turn out to be their most important service to him.

For reflection: What do I imagine went through the minds of the two Marys as they sat facing the tomb of Jesus?

ORIENTATION: *At the time Matthew wrote his gospel, some were charging that Jesus' disciples had taken his body from the tomb so that they could claim that he had been raised from the dead. Matthew counters such charges by telling how the tomb was secured (27:62-66; see also 28:4, 11-15).*

The Guard at the Tomb
62 **The next day, the one following the day of preparation, the chief priests and the Pharisees gathered before Pilate** 63 **and said, "Sir, we remember that this impostor while still alive said, 'After three days I will be raised up.'** 64 **Give orders, then, that the grave be secured until the**

third day, lest his disciples come and steal him and say to the people, 'He has been raised from the dead.' This last imposture would be worse than the first." **65** Pilate said to them, "The guard is yours; go secure it as best you can." **66** So they went and secured the tomb by fixing a seal to the stone and setting the guard.

NT: Matt 12:40; 16:21; 17:23; 20:19; 28:4, 11-15

62 It is now **the next day,** the day after Jesus was crucified. Matthew refers to this day as **the one following the day of preparation,** which is an awkward way of indicating that it is the Sabbath. **The day of preparation** is the day before the Sabbath, when one does work that cannot be done on the Sabbath, such as preparing meals to be eaten on the Sabbath. **The chief priests and the Pharisees gathered before Pilate.** The **Pharisees** have been absent from the scene since 22:41-46 and did not play a role in the events that led to Jesus' death. Now they reappear, linked with **the chief priests.** For Matthew's readers, the Pharisees of the time of Jesus are the forerunners of later Jewish leaders who reject Jesus as the Messiah. Chief priests and Pharisees go to **Pilate** with a request that they do not want to delay until after the Sabbath.

High priest, chief priests: See page 566

Pharisees: See page 231

Pilate: See page 619

63 They tell Pilate, **Sir, we remember that this impostor while still alive said, "After three days I will be raised up."** Jesus told his disciples that he would be raised on the third day (16:21; 17:23; 20:19). His only public statement about his being raised was cryptic: "Just as Jonah was in the belly of the whale three days and three nights, so will the Son of Man be in the heart of the earth three days and three nights" (12:40). Some Pharisees heard Jesus say this (see 12:38); perhaps it forms the basis of what they tell Pilate. They contemptuously refer to Jesus as **this impostor.** Jesus has been mocked as a so-called king of the Jews (27:27-31, 37), as claiming he could destroy and rebuild the Temple (27:40), as pretending to be the Son of God (27:40, 43). For those who mocked him, and for the chief priests and Pharisees, he was an **imposter.**

64 They request that Pilate **give orders, then, that the grave be secured until the third day.** They ask Pilate to **give orders** about Jesus' grave, even

though Pilate has tried to wash his hands of involvement with Jesus (27:24). Whether **the third day** is to be calculated from the day of Jesus' death or from when the chief priests and Pharisees are making their request of Pilate is unclear. Their intent, however, must be to have Jesus' grave **secured** until it is past the time when Jesus said he would be raised. They ask that the grave be secured **lest his disciples come and steal him and say to the people, "He has been raised from the dead."** Jesus' disciples hardly seem up to carrying off such a bold scheme: the men were last seen fleeing into the night or denying acquaintance with Jesus (26:56, 69-75). But the chief priests and Pharisees are taking no chances. They are concerned about what the disciples might **say to the people** after making off with Jesus' body. The chief priests have been uneasy about the crowds who revered Jesus (21:46; 26:5), and they do not want them to believe **he has been raised from the dead.** They tell Pilate, **This last imposture would be worse than the first.** By **the first** imposture they may refer to Jesus' claim that he is the Messiah and Son of God who will sit at the right hand of God and come in glory (26:63-64). The **last imposture** would be that **he has been raised from the dead,** which would vindicate his earlier claims.

He has been raised from the dead will indeed be the message that the disciples and the early church proclaim (some instances are Acts 2:24, 32; 3:15; 4:10; 5:30; 10:40; 13:30; Rom 6:4; 1 Cor 15:4, 20); that is the heart of the gospel. The raising of Jesus is a major point of contention between Matthew's church and Jewish leaders who do not accept Jesus as the Messiah. Matthew's church proclaims to the **people** of its time, **he has been raised from the dead.** Their opponents deny this, dismissing it as a hoax (see 28:11-15).

> For reflection: When I speak to others about Jesus, what do I single out as the most important things to say about him? How often do I proclaim, "He has been raised from the dead"?

65 **Pilate said to them, "The guard is yours; go secure it as best you can."** The Greek for **the guard is yours** is a bit ambiguous; it will become evident that Pilate places soldiers in the Roman army at the disposal of the chief priests and Pharisees (see 28:14). In Matthew's account, Pilate seems pliant, doing whatever is requested of him (see also 27:21-26, 58). Pilate tells the chief priests and Pharisees to **go secure it as best you can,** making the security of Jesus' tomb their responsibility, not his.

66 **So they went and secured the tomb by fixing a seal to the stone and setting the guard.** We should probably visualize **fixing a seal to the stone** as pouring molten wax between the stone blocking the entrance to Jesus' tomb and the tomb itself, and then imprinting the still-soft wax with a signet ring (see Dan 6:18). Anyone moving the stone would crack the wax and would not be able to reduplicate the seal. An unbroken seal would be evidence that no one had entered the tomb. And lest anyone try to enter it, soldiers are posted at the tomb as a **guard.** Ironically, the more efforts are made to prevent tampering with Jesus' body, the more implausible becomes claims that his disciples stole it. There is also an irony in trying to seal a tomb with wax when God can split asunder rock as he raises the dead from their tombs (27:51-52).

CHAPTER 28

He Has Been Raised!
[1] After the sabbath, as the first day of the week was dawning, Mary Magdalene and the other Mary came to see the tomb. [2] And behold, there was a great earthquake; for an angel of the Lord descended from heaven, approached, rolled back the stone, and sat upon it. [3] His appearance was like lightning and his clothing was white as snow. [4] The guards were shaken with fear of him and became like dead men. [5] Then the angel said to the women in reply, "Do not be afraid! I know that you are seeking Jesus the crucified. [6] He is not here, for he has been raised just as he said. Come and see the place where he lay. [7] Then go quickly and tell his disciples, 'He has been raised from the dead, and he is going before you to Galilee; there you will see him.' Behold, I have told you." [8] Then they went away quickly from the tomb, fearful yet overjoyed, and ran to announce this to his disciples.

Gospel parallels: Mark 16:1-8; Luke 24:1-10; John 20:1-2
NT: Matt 16:21; 17:9, 23; 20:19; 26:32; 27:55-56, 61, 65-66

1 **After the sabbath, as the first day of the week was dawning, Mary Magdalene and the other Mary came to see the tomb.** The other Mary is the Mary who has sons named James and Joseph (26:56). She and **Mary Magdalene** were among the women who kept watch at Golgotha during Jesus' crucifixion, "looking on from a distance" (26:55). These two Marys also watched, "facing the tomb," as Joseph of Arimathea buried the body of Jesus before the beginning of the Sabbath (27:61). Now the Sabbath is over, and early in the morning, **as the first day of the week was dawning,** the two Marys return to the tomb of Jesus. Matthew has recounted Jesus' tomb being blocked with a huge stone, sealed, and guarded (27:60, 65-66), so the women have no hope of being able to enter it. They come **to see the tomb:** the Greek word translated "see" is the same word used for their "looking on" as Jesus is crucified (27:55). The women may have come to mourn (see 27:61), but by being present and seeing what happens they continue to be witnesses to Jesus' death and the events that follow it.

2 **And behold, there was a great earthquake; for an angel of the Lord descended from heaven, approached, and rolled back the stone.** The women witness an **angel** from heaven rolling away the **stone** blocking the

entrance to the tomb of Jesus, accompanied by a **great earthquake.** Earthquakes were associated with God's coming down on Mount Sinai to make a covenant with Israel (Exod 19:18) and his coming in judgment on the "day of the LORD" (Isaiah 24:19-21; Joel 4:14-16; Nahum 1:5). The earthquakes after Jesus died (27:50-51) and at the opening of his tomb signal that God is doing something earthshaking. After rolling back the stone, the angel **sat upon it**—a posture of triumph.

Angels: See page 33

Matthew doesn't write that Jesus came forth from the tomb after the angel rolled the stone away, as if Jesus was trapped in the tomb until an angel freed him. The angel rolls the stone away so that it can be seen that Jesus is not in the tomb (verse 6).

3 While Scripture sometimes portrays angels looking like young men (Tobit 5:4-5; Dan 8:15-16), this angel has the appearance of a heavenly being: **his appearance was like lightning and his clothing was white as snow.** His looking like **lightning** echoes how an angel is described in the book of Daniel (Dan 10:6); **clothing** as **white as snow** echoes how God is gloriously clothed (Dan 7:9). Angels act on behalf of God and can radiate God's glory. Matthew's readers can recall that Jesus' "face shone like the sun and his clothes became white as light" during his transfiguration (17:2), a foretaste of his sharing in his Father's glory (16:27).

4 There are soldiers stationed at the tomb (27:66), and at the sight of the angel **the guards were shaken with fear of him and became like dead men**—they fainted dead away. There is an irony in their becoming **like dead men** in the aftermath of Jesus being raised from the dead.

5 **Then the angel said to the women in reply, "Do not be afraid!"**—literally, "*You* do not be afraid!" **In reply** has the sense of in response to the guards' reaction. The angel tells the two Marys that while the guards were so fearful they passed out, the women are to have no fear. Yet it is natural to be fearful when confronted with the awesome. The disciples "cried out in fear" when they saw Jesus walking on the Sea of Galilee (14:26); they "were very much afraid" when they heard the voice from heaven during Jesus' transfiguration (17:6). Each time, Jesus told them, "Do not be afraid" (14:27; 17:7), and that is the angel's message to the women.

For reflection: Have I ever had an intense experience of divine presence or power? What was my reaction?

The angel tells the two Marys, **I know that you are seeking Jesus the crucified.** Here **seeking** seems to have the sense of being concerned about: the women did not come to the tomb expecting to see Jesus, but they came because of Jesus. The angel speaks of **Jesus the crucified:** the Greek grammatical form used for **crucified** signifies a continuing condition resulting from a past action. Jesus' crucifixion is now part of his identity. Being raised from the dead does not erase his crucifixion as if it never happened; he remains **Jesus the crucified** in his risen glory (see also John 20:20, 25, 27; 1 Cor 1:23; 2:2).

For reflection: How does Jesus being "Jesus the crucified" shape my understanding of him?

6 The angel tells the women, **He is not here, for he has been raised just as he said.** Implied by **he has been raised** is that he has been raised by God. Jesus spoke of his being raised (16:21; 17:9, 23; 20:19; 26:32), and it has happened **just as he said.** Because he has been raised, **he is not here** in the tomb. The angel invites the women to **come and see the place where**

BACKGROUND: TOMB OF JESUS At the time of Jesus, an abandoned limestone quarry lay just outside the western wall of Jerusalem. Here Golgotha rose as a hump of unquarried rock. Tombs were dug in the old quarry, just as tombs were dug into virtually all the hills surrounding biblical Jerusalem. The tomb in which Jesus' corpse was buried, located less than two hundred feet from Golgotha, was cut into the side of the quarry. This tomb had at least two chambers: a small antechamber at its entrance and a second chamber with a shelf cut into its wall where a corpse could be laid. There were likely other chambers for other corpses or for their bones after the flesh had decayed away. After Jesus' body was taken down from the cross, it was placed on the shelf in the second chamber. In the fourth century, the Roman emperor Constantine ordered a church to be built at the site of Golgotha and the tomb of Jesus. Workers cut away the hillside surrounding the tomb of Jesus in order to isolate it as a freestanding chapel. This chapel was largely destroyed in the eleventh century and has been rebuilt several times since. Today Golgotha and the tomb of Jesus are within the Church of the Holy Sepulchre in Jerusalem. *Related topics: Burial practices (page 652), Golgotha (page 633).*

he lay. Whether they enter the tomb or just peer in through the doorway is unclear, but in either case they are able to **see** that Jesus is not there. They came that morning "to see the tomb" (verse 1), and now they **see** that it is an empty tomb. They continue to carry out their role as eyewitnesses.

Neither the angel nor Matthew provides a description of Jesus' being raised; the event itself is sheathed in the darkness of the sealed tomb. Nor are we told exactly when it happened. There are no witnesses to the resurrection of Jesus, only to its aftermath.

7 The angel charges the women to **go quickly and tell his disciples, "He has been raised from the dead, and he is going before you to Galilee; there you will see him."** They are to **go quickly** because of the urgency of the message they bear. The angel's words to the women, **He has been raised** (verse 6) are to be their proclamation to **his disciples.** An apostle is someone who is sent on a mission; Jesus sent out twelve as apostles bearing the message of the kingdom of heaven (10:1-8). Now Mary Magdalene and Mary the mother of James and Joseph are sent as apostles to the apostles, bearing the message that Jesus **has been raised from the dead.** They are to tell them that **he is going before you to Galilee; there you will see him.** On the night before he died, Jesus told his disciples, "after I have been raised up, I shall go before you to Galilee" (26:32). Jesus has been raised and is going to Galilee; **there** his disciples **will see him.** The angel adds, **Behold, I have told you** as an exclamation point to his message.

Galilee: See page 68

For reflection: What is the significance for me that "he has been raised from the dead"?

8 The two Marys set out to do what the angel asked them. **Then they went away quickly from the tomb, fearful yet overjoyed, and ran to announce this to his disciples.** Despite the angel's telling them, "Do not be afraid" (verse 5), they are still **fearful,** just as lightning striking nearby might leave someone's heart pounding. **Yet** they are also **overjoyed** that Jesus has been raised from the dead. Perhaps their encounter with a messenger from God has contributed to their joy. When God speaks to us, not only his message but also his very speaking to us can fill us with awe and joy. The women

went quickly and **ran** to make their announcement. They want to get word as soon as possible to the other disciples that Jesus has been raised—news more earthshaking than a great earthquake (verse 2).

For reflection: When have I experienced the greatest joy in my relation-ship with God? What was its source?

We should recall that the **disciples** fled when Jesus was arrested (26:56), save for Peter, who tagged along at a distance and then vehe-mently denied knowing Jesus (26:58, 69-75). These same disciples are to be told that Jesus has been raised and that they will see him in Galilee. The risen Jesus is God-with-us (see 1:23), inviting us to come to him (11:28) even though we may avoid and disavow him. We can turn away from Jesus; he does not turn away from us.

Jesus Appears to the Two Marys

⁹ And behold, Jesus met them on their way and greeted them. They ap-proached, embraced his feet, and did him homage. ¹⁰ Then Jesus said to them, "Do not be afraid. Go tell my brothers to go to Galilee, and there they will see me."

Gospel parallels: Mark 16:9; John 20:14-17
NT: Matt 12:49-50; 26:32; 27:55-56, 61; 28:1-8; 1 Cor 15:1-8

9 As the angel at the tomb instructed, Mary Magdalene and Mary the mother of James and Joseph run to tell the disciples that Jesus has been raised and will meet them in Galilee (28:1-8). **And behold, Jesus met them on their way.** Jesus' appearance is quite unexpected, since the an-gel had said that he was going to Galilee (28:7). But **behold,** Jesus makes himself present to the two Marys. Perhaps we can draw the lesson that Jesus cannot be boxed in by our expectations; he reserves the right to surprise us. Perhaps the lesson is also that Jesus is with those who carry out his work, just as he is present with those who gather together in his name (18:20).

Jesus **greeted** the two women, literally, said to them, "Rejoice." This is a standard Greek greeting, sometimes translated "Hail" (26:49; 27:29), but its literal sense has special meaning as Jesus' greeting to the women. They were "overjoyed" to hear that Jesus had been raised (28:8), and they should rejoice even more in his presence. They recognized that it is Jesus, for **they approached** him, drawing closer to him. They **embraced** or grasped **his feet,** perhaps to kiss them, a gesture of veneration. They prostrated themselves before Jesus as an act of **homage.**

While Matthew provides no description of what the risen Jesus looks like, his account conveys some important truths. The two Mary's immediately recognize Jesus: the risen Jesus is the Jesus they previously knew. The women embrace Jesus' feet: the risen Jesus has a body that is in some way tangible; he is not a ghost. The women pay homage to Jesus: the risen Jesus is due worship.

10 **Then Jesus said to them, "Do not be afraid."** While an angel has already told the women not to be afraid (28:5), Jesus' exhortation carries greater meaning. When Jesus came walking on the sea to his disciples, he told them, "Take courage, it is I; do not be afraid" (14:27). Jesus' presence should extinguish every fear, since he promises to be with his disciples forever (18:20; 28:20). His words to the two Marys are a message for every follower of Jesus in every situation: **do not be afraid,** for he has been raised and is with us.

For reflection: What do my fears reveal about my faith in Jesus?

Jesus reaffirms the mission given the women by the angel: **Go tell my brothers to go to Galilee, and there they will see me.** Jesus refers to his disciples as **my brothers** despite their having abandoned him (26:56). His disciples are his brothers and sisters, his family gathered around him (12:49-50). He taught his disciples to take the first step in being reconciled (5:23-24); he taught them that they must grant forgiveness (6:14-15; 18:21-35). Jesus practices what he requires. He shed his blood for the forgiveness of sins (26:28), and he forgives his **brothers** for abandoning and denying him.

Galilee: See page 68

This is the third time in Matthew's gospel that the disciples are summoned to **Galilee** to meet the risen Jesus (26:32; 28:7, 10), creating a sense of anticipation that something of great consequence will happen there.

Paul reminded the Christians of Corinth of the gospel that he had received and passed on: "Now I am reminding you, brothers, of the gospel I preached to you. . . . For I handed on to you as of first importance what I also received: that Christ died for our sins in accordance with the scriptures; that he was buried; that he was raised on the third day in accordance with the scriptures" (1 Cor 15:1, 3-4). No one could offer better eyewitness testimony to what Paul proclaimed than Mary Magdalene and Mary the mother of James and Joseph. They looked on as Jesus died and was buried (27:55-56, 61); they saw the empty tomb and the risen Jesus (28:6, 9-10). Their faithfulness to Jesus was of unique service to him and to the gospel.

For reflection: What service can I do for Jesus? What is the lesson of the two Marys for me?

The Report of the Guard
11 **While they were going, some of the guard went into the city and told the chief priests all that had happened.** **12** They assembled with the elders and took counsel; then they gave a large sum of money to the soldiers, **13** telling them, "You are to say, 'His disciples came by night and stole him while we were asleep.' **14** And if this gets to the ears of the governor, we will satisfy [him] and keep you out of trouble." **15** The soldiers took the money and did as they were instructed. And this story has circulated among the Jews to the present [day].
NT: Matt 27:62-66; 28:1-4

11 Mary Magdalene and Mary the mother of James and Joseph are on their way to tell the disciples that Jesus has been raised from the dead and that they will see him in Galilee (28:7-10). **While they were going, some of the guard went into the city and told the chief priests all that had happened.** The **guard** are soldiers whom Pilate had placed at the disposal of **the chief priests** to secure the tomb of Jesus and prevent his disciples from removing his body (27:64-66). Some of them now go **into the city:** Jesus' tomb lay outside the walls of Jerusalem. They tell **the chief priests all that had happened.** They could report that there was a great earthquake and that an angel of awesome appearance rolled back the stone and sat on it, and that they were so terrified that they passed out (28:2-4). They woke up to find the tomb empty.

High priest, chief priests: See page 566

12 **They assembled with the elders and took counsel.** What do the chief priests and elders do now that the tomb of Jesus is empty? One response would be to accept that Jesus has been raised from the dead as he said he would be (27:63). The guards' report of earthquake, angel, and empty tomb are certainly consistent with Jesus' being raised, even if no one witnessed the event itself. Just as the soldiers who crucified Jesus recognized him as the Son of God after his death (27:54), so the chief priests and elders could recognize him as the Messiah and Son of God (26:63) after he was raised. Tragically, they do not do so. They were so opposed to Jesus that they wanted him dead (26:3-4, 14-16, 66; 27:1, 20), and nothing seems able to change their minds or hearts about him.

Elders: See page 451

> For reflection: Do I have any wrong beliefs or attitudes that are so entrenched that nothing causes me to reexamine them?

These leaders want Jesus to remain dead in the eyes of the people (see 27:64). They cannot deny that Jesus' tomb is empty, but they can provide an explanation for the empty tomb that will counter claims that he has been raised from the dead. **They gave a large sum of money to the soldiers,** just as they had given money to Judas to accomplish their aims (26:14-16).

13 They bribe the guards to change their story: **You are to say, "His disciples came by night and stole him while we were asleep."** The guards had been posted so that Jesus' disciples' could not remove his body (27:64-66), but now they are to claim that they had! It is not a very convincing claim. How could they have slept through a huge stone (27:60) being rolled away? And if they were asleep, how did they know that it was Jesus' **disciples** who removed his body? But the chief priests cannot come up with a more plausible explanation for the empty tomb; this one will have to do. The guards are to circulate their story so that people will not believe the proclamation that Jesus has been raised from the dead (see 27:64).

14 They also tell the guard, **And if this gets to the ears of the governor, we will satisfy [him] and keep you out of trouble.** If the guards tell people that Jesus' body was stolen while they slept, it is likely that Pontius Pilate

the governor will hear about it. He will not be pleased that his soldiers fell asleep while on guard duty—a severe dereliction of duty in any army, and one that is severely punished. **If this gets to the ears of the governor** may refer not to casual overhearing but to formal charges. If the soldiers are brought before Pilate and charged with dereliction of duty, the chief priests and elders **will satisfy** Pilate **and keep** the soldiers **out of trouble.** The word translated **satisfy** might have the connotation of "bribing" Pilate, just as the soldiers were bribed. However, Pilate might not need bribing. Which account would Pilate prefer that people accept: that a man he had executed has been raised from the dead or that the corpse of an executed criminal was stolen by his friends? Pilate wanted to wash his hands of involvement with Jesus (27:24) and a stolen Jesus would be less bothersome than a risen Jesus.

15 **The soldiers took the money**—a large sum (verse 12)—**and did as they were instructed. And this story has circulated among the Jews to the present [day].** The **present** is when Matthew is writing his gospel, likely over fifty years after the soldiers were bribed. That this **story** is still being **circulated among the Jews** is why Matthew includes his accounts of the tomb of Jesus being guarded and the guards being bribed (27:62-66; 28:11-15). The church's proclamation that Jesus was raised from the dead is being challenged by some who claim that his disciples stole his body. A Christian writer named Justin (who lived from about A.D. 100 to 165) indicates that this story was still in circulation in the middle of the second century. Matthew wants his readers to know that the story is a fraud. Jesus truly was raised.

Even though the claim "They stole the body" is untrue, belief that Jesus has been raised from the dead is not easy to accept in all its implications. If Jesus has been raised to judge every woman and man at the end of this age, then becoming his disciple and living according to his teachings is a matter of eternal importance. We cannot accept the proclamation that "Jesus has been raised" and then ignore his invitation to come to him and take on his yoke (11:28-30). We do not truly accept him as risen unless we model our lives on his and obey his teachings.

For reflection: If the Sermon on the Mount (Matt 5–7) sets the standard, does the way I live proclaim that I believe that Jesus was raised from the dead?

665

The Charter of the Church

16 The eleven disciples went to Galilee, to the mountain to which Jesus had ordered them. **17** When they saw him, they worshiped, but they doubted. **18** Then Jesus approached and said to them, "All power in heaven and on earth has been given to me. **19** Go, therefore, and make disciples of all nations, baptizing them in the name of the Father, and of the Son, and of the holy Spirit, **20** teaching them to observe all that I have commanded you. And behold, I am with you always, until the end of the age."

OT:Dan 7:13-14

NT:Matt 1:23; 10:1-10; 18:20; 26:32; 28:7-10; Mark 16:14-16

16 **The eleven disciples went to Galilee, to the mountain to which Jesus had ordered them.** Since Judas hanged himself (27:5), the twelve whom Jesus had specially chosen (10:1-4) are reduced to **eleven.** Before his death, Jesus told his disciples that "after I have been raised up, I shall go before you to Galilee" (26:32). An angel at the empty tomb echoed Jesus' words (28:7), and the risen Jesus told Mary Magdalene and Mary the mother of James and Joseph, "Go tell my brothers to go to Galilee, and there they will see me" (28:10). The thrice-repeated summons signals that something of great importance will happen when the disciples encounter Jesus in **Galilee.** Jesus began his public ministry and called his first disciples in Galilee (4:12-23); there will be a new beginning where Jesus' mission began. The two Marys presumably delivered their message to the disciples, and the eleven **went to Galilee, to the mountain to which Jesus had ordered them.** There was no mention of a **mountain** in the three summons to Galilee (26:32; 28:7, 10). However, Matthew's gospel is a condensed account, omitting many things that Jesus did and said. Matthew's readers can recall mountains where Jesus taught (5:1-2), healed (15:29-31), and was transfigured (17:1-2). That Jesus will again be on a **mountain** with his disciples may signal that what happens will be the culmination of what happened on mountains in the past.

Galilee: See page 68

17 **When they saw him, they worshiped.** The eleven disciples **saw** the risen Jesus, as they had been promised (28:7, 10). His presence implies that he has been raised from the dead, as he foretold (16:21; 17:9, 23; 20:19; 26:32). **They worshiped** him. The Greek word translated **worshiped** means to prostrate oneself before another; it was translated "did . . . homage" to

describe the response of the two Marys when they met the risen Jesus (28:9). The sight of Jesus, crucified but raised from the dead, causes the eleven to fall down before Jesus in worship.

They worshiped **but they doubted.** Matthew does not explain what they **doubted,** but the Greek word he uses for **doubted** has connotations of being of being divided and wavering. It is found in only one other passage in the New Testament. When Peter walked on the water, became frightened, and began to sink, Jesus said to him, "O you of little faith, why did you doubt?" (14:31). Peter wavered in the waves; now the disciples waver at the sight of the risen Jesus. They worship him but are beset by doubts and hesitations. Matthew may leave the nature of their doubts vague so that they can stand for all the wavering and doubts that will assail later disciples of Jesus. The mixed condition of individual disciples will mirror the mixed condition of the church. The church will gather in good and bad (22:10); it will be like a field with weeds and wheat (13:24-30, 36-43) or a fishing net that hauls in all sorts of things (13:47-50). So too, disciples of Jesus will have faith and doubts, joy and fear (28:8), love and selfishness. They should not despair over their mixed condition; they are in the company of the eleven who worshiped but doubted.

For reflection: How do I understand the disciples' both worshiping and doubting? What message does their mixed reaction have for me?

18 **Then Jesus approached and said to them, "All power in heaven and on earth has been given to me."** Jesus draws near to them in their worshiping and doubting. He speaks of what **has been given** him by God: he has received **all power in heaven and on earth.** In its previous occurrences in Matthew's gospel, the Greek word translated **power** was translated as "authority": Jesus taught with authority (7:29), had authority to forgive sins and heal (9:6, 8), and acted with authority (21:23-24, 27). Now his authority, or **power,** is unlimited; God has given him **all power in heaven and on earth.** Here **heaven** and **earth** represent the entire universe. Jesus earlier said that "all things have been handed over to me by my Father" (11:27). Jesus had been given the authority to make his Father known and teach his ways, to forgive sins and expel demons, to heal the sick and raise the dead. Jesus' exercise of his authority was limited to the places he visited, but now it has no limitations. Raised from the dead he has **all power in heaven and on earth.**

Matthew's readers who are familiar with the book of Daniel can recall Daniel's vision of "one like a son of man" receiving "dominion, glory, and kingship" from God (Dan 7:13-14). Jesus echoed this passage when speaking of his exaltation and his coming in glory (24:30; 26:64); raised from the dead, he has been given **all power** and dominion.

19 Because Jesus has been given all power in heaven and on earth, he tells his disciples, **Go, therefore, and make disciples of all nations.** Jesus entrusts his disciples with a mission despite their doubts and wavering (verse 17). The first time Jesus sent them on a mission, he did not let them carry provisions; they were to depend on God to provide for them (10:9-10). Now Jesus has been given all power, and they are to depend on his power rather than their own as they **go** on mission. They are to go to **all nations.** When Jesus previously sent them out, he limited their mission to "the lost sheep of the house of Israel" (10:5-6), just as his own mission was then limited (15:24). Now he has all power on earth, and their mission is to all the earth—to **all nations.** This does not terminate the disciples' mission to Jews; it widens the scope of their mission to include Gentiles as well. Earlier events have foreshadowed the inclusion of Gentiles (2:1-12; 8:5-13, 28-34; 15:21-28; 27:54).

The disciples of Jesus are sent to **make disciples.** In the Greek of Matthew's gospel, the command to **make disciples** stands out as if it were in capital letters; the other instructions in this and the following verse (going . . . baptizing . . . teaching . . .) are subordinate to it. **Disciples** are those who accept Jesus' invitation to come to him (11:28-30), who leave behind impediments (4:20, 22; 8:21-22; 10:37; 19:21), who deny themselves (16:24), who model their lives on his (20:26-28), who do the will of his Father (7:21) and become the new family of Jesus (12:48-50). To **make** disciples means to form new followers of Jesus as Jesus formed his first disciples, teaching them how they are to believe and behave, love and forgive, pray and persevere (5:3–7:27; 10:16-42; 16:24-27; 17:20; 18:1-35; 20:25-28; 21:21-22; 23:3-12).

Disciple: See page 66

For reflection: If the central mission of disciples of Jesus is to make disciples, how well am I carrying out my mission?

Making disciples includes **baptizing them in the name of the Father, and of the Son, and of the holy Spirit.** There has been no indication in Matthew's gospel that Jesus or his disciples previously baptized anyone. There has been a baptism of repentance administered by John, which was a washing in water to symbolize a washing away of sins (3:6, 11). John's baptism foreshadowed Christian baptism. The early church will incorporate new members by baptism (Acts 2:38, 41; 8:12-13, 38; 9:18; 10:48; 16:15, 33; 19:5).

The disciples are to baptize **in the name of the Father, and of the Son, and of the holy Spirit.** This too is foreshadowed in connection with John's baptism. After Jesus was baptized by John, the heavens were opened, and Jesus "saw the Spirit of God descending like a dove [and] coming upon him. And a voice came from the heavens, saying, 'This is my beloved Son, with whom I am well pleased'" (3:16-17). The **Father** proclaims Jesus to be his **Son,** and the **holy Spirit** descends upon him. Those who are being made disciples are to be baptized **in the name of** the Father, Son, and Holy Spirit. The **name** of a person represents the person (see 6:9; 10:22). To be baptized **in the name of the Father, and of the Son, and of the holy Spirit** means to be immersed in the Father, Son, and Spirit, making one a son or daughter of the Father, a sister or brother of Jesus, and a bearer of the Holy Spirit (see Rom 8:14-17; Gal 4:4-7).

The Spirit: See page 21

For reflection: What difference does my having been baptized make in my life?

BACKGROUND: BAPTISM The Greek word *baptize* means to dip, plunge, immerse, drench, soak, or wash. Mark uses a variant of this word to describe the washing of dishes (Mark 7:4). There is some indication that John's baptism involved fully immersing a person in water: John 3:23 suggests that John needed ample water, and Mark 1:10 speaks of Jesus "coming up out of the water" after being baptized. In Matthew's gospel, after his resurrection Jesus directs his disciples to "make disciples of all nations, baptizing them in the name of the Father, and of the Son, and of the holy Spirit" (Matt 28:19). In Acts, Peter exhorts the crowd that gathered on Pentecost to "repent and be baptized, every one of you, in the name of Jesus Christ for the forgiveness of your sins; and you will receive the gift of the holy Spirit" (Acts 2:38). Baptism is "the bath of rebirth / and renewal by the holy Spirit" (Titus 3:5) that allows one to enter the kingdom of God (John 3:5).

20 Jesus tells his disciples to make disciples, **teaching them to observe all that I have commanded you.** Jesus is God's authorized teacher (see 11:27; 23:8); those who teach on his behalf pass on his teachings. **All that Jesus commanded** inlcudes all the teachings that Matthew has recounted in the course of his gospel, including the Sermon on the Mount (5:1–7:27), instructions about enduring persecution (10:16-42), parables about the kingdom of heaven (13:1-53), admonitions about care for little ones and forgiveness (18:1-35), warnings about what to do while awaiting Jesus' coming (24:3–25:46), and other teachings scattered throughout the gospel such as the two great commandments (22:36-40). Observing **all** of these teachings is **commanded,** for they reveal the will of God (see 11:27), and nothing can substitute for doing God's will (7:21-23).

> *For reflection: How completely do I obey the commands of Jesus presented in the Gospel of Matthew?*

Jesus concludes his words to his disciples with a promise: **And behold, I am with you always, until the end of the age.** In the Greek of Matthew's gospel, the I is emphatic: Jesus tells his disciples that **I** will be with you. Jesus is God-with-us (see 1:23), present when disciples gather in his name (18:20), present as they go to make disciples. Those who receive the disciples receive Jesus (10:40). Jesus does not explain the manner of his continuing presence but assures his disciples that he will be with them. Jesus will be present with his disciples **always:** the Greek expression translated **always** is literally "all the days," concluding a litany of "alls." Jesus has been given *all* power; he sends his disciples to *all* nations to teach *all* he has commanded; he will be with them *all* days. He will remain with them **until the end of the age,** when he will come in glory to judge all men and women (13:40-43; 16:27; 24:30-31; 25:31-45). Jesus' coming in glory at the end does not mean that he will be absent in the interim; Jesus remains present to his disciples, but with a different mode of presence than he will manifest at the end of the age.

The age to come: See page 250

> *For reflection: How do I experience Jesus being present to me?*

So Matthew's gospel ends. The last glimpse Matthew give us of Jesus is of him with his disciples, promising to be with them always. Matthew's final word to his readers is that Jesus, God-with-us, remains with us.

There is a wealth of meaning packed into the final verses of Matthew's gospel. They are the charter of the church, providing its mandate and message. They are an instruction for every later follower of Jesus, commanding us to obey all that Jesus teaches, sending us to share the call to discipleship, promising us that Jesus will be with us always.

For reflection: What is my reaction to the conclusion of Matthew's gospel?

THE WRITING AND INTERPRETATION OF THE GOSPEL OF MATTHEW

The Writing of the Gospels

Each of the four gospels is a product of a three-stage process.[1]

The *first stage* is what Jesus did and taught while on earth.[2] He called disciples who saw his works and heard his teachings and could serve as his witnesses after his resurrection and ascension. In his teachings, "Jesus accommodated himself to the mentality of his listeners,"[3] speaking as a Palestinian Jew of the first third of the first century to other Palestinian Jews.

In the *second stage*, the apostles and other witnesses handed on to their hearers what Jesus had said and done but "with that fuller understanding which they, instructed by the glorious events of Christ and enlightened by the Spirit of truth, now enjoyed."[4] The apostles in their preaching took into account the circumstances of their audiences and interpreted Jesus' words and deeds according to the needs of their listeners. They used modes of speaking that were suited to their purposes and to the mentality of their listeners.[5]

In the *third stage*, the authors of the four gospels "selected certain of the many elements which had been handed on, either orally or already in written form," and incorporated them in their gospels, sometimes synthesizing these elements or explaining them in light of the situation of those for whom they wrote, "but always in such a fashion that they have told us the honest truth about Jesus."[6]

> From what they had received, the sacred writers above all selected the things which were suited to the various situations of the faithful and to the purposes which they had in mind, and adapted their narration of them to the same situations and purpose. Since the meaning of a statement also depends on the sequence, the evangelists, in passing on the words and deeds of our savior, explained these now in one context, now in another, depending on (their) usefulness to the readers. . . . For the truth of a story is not at all affected by the fact that the evangelists relate the words and deeds of the Lord in a different order, and express his sayings not literally but differently, while preserving their sense.[7]

That the written gospels are the result of a three-stage process has implications:

- The gospel authors present incidents and teachings from Jesus' public ministry in an order suited to their purposes in writing, which is not necessarily the order in which they historically occurred. Accounts from the four gospels cannot be synthesized to produce an actual timeline of events from Jesus' baptism by John to the Last Supper. Each gospel narration must be read for the meaning that events have in the order in which they are recounted.

- In expressing the teachings of Jesus, the gospels do not necessarily transmit the exact words Jesus used. Jesus taught in Aramaic; the gospels were written in Greek. Just as Jesus accommodated his teachings to his listeners, so those who passed on his teachings also formulated them in light of the needs of their audiences, while preserving the sense of Jesus' words.

- Because the gospel authors were writing for different audiences and had different purposes in writing, each of the four gospels has its distinctive traits and emphases. The four gospels cannot be combined or harmonized into a single document that preserves the unique riches of each. Rather, each gospel must be read as an inspired presentation of the life and teachings of Jesus and relished for its particular perspective.

That the gospels came to be written by a three-stage process does not mean that they are not reliable witnesses to Jesus. The Second Vatican Council stated that "Holy Mother Church has firmly and with absolute constancy maintained and continues to maintain, that the four Gospels just named, whose historicity she unhesitatingly affirms, faithfully hand on what Jesus, the Son of God, while he lived among men, really did and taught for their eternal salvation, until the day when he was taken up."[8]

The Gospel of Matthew

Neither Matthew nor any of the gospel authors signed his name to his gospel. The heading, "According to Matthew" was added to this gospel sometime in the early part of the second century. A second-century tradition recounted by the fourth-century historian Bishop Eusebius claimed that "Matthew compiled the *Sayings* [of Jesus] in the Aramaic language and everyone translated them as well as he could."[9] The significance of this tradition has been debated at great length. Some have interpreted it to mean that the apostle Matthew wrote a gospel in Aramaic and that the Gospel of Matthew in the New Testament is a Greek translation of Matthew's work. Most scholars reject this, pointing out that the Gospel of Matthew shows signs of having been written in Greek and not being a translation. Further, most scholars believe that the Gospel of Matthew draws heavily on the Gospel of Mark, and if the author of the Gospel of Matthew was an eyewitness to the public ministry of Jesus it would be odd for him to be so dependent on an account written by someone like Mark who was not an eyewitness. Perhaps the author of this gospel drew on traditions going back to Matthew, but it is unlikely that the author was this apostle.

Most scholars believe that the Gospel of Matthew was written sometime around A.D. 85, possibly in the Syrian city of Antioch. Antioch was a Greek-speaking city with a large Jewish community. Matthew's gospel shows signs of having been written for a church community that was originally Jewish Christian in its composition, that is, made up of Jews who followed Jewish laws and practices even as they accepted Jesus as the Messiah. Increasingly, though, Gentile converts were entering the church. The extent to which Gentile converts were bound by Jewish laws and practices was debated in Antioch (see Gal 2:11-14). Matthew's gospel was written for a church in transition, showing how Jesus was the fulfillment of what God had begun with the people of Israel and was now extending to all peoples.

Just as Matthew's church was in transition, so was Judaism. There was considerable diversity within Judaism during the lifetime of Jesus, even though the law of Moses and the Temple were revered by all Jews. Various groups or movements espoused different interpretations of the law; the Pharisees were only one of the movements with an agenda for Judaism. The destruction of the Temple in A.D. 70 was a shattering event, forcing Jews to develop a religious way of life that was not dependent on the Temple, priesthood, and sacrifice. The successors of the Pharisees—those who became known as rabbis—proposed a program for the future of Judaism centered on living out the law of Moses in daily life. Matthew's church also had its program for the future of Judaism; it proclaimed that Jesus was the Messiah and the authentic interpreter of the law of Moses. Matthew's church was in competition with the early rabbis for the allegiance of Jews. The views of the rabbis began to prevail in synagogues, and Matthew's church found itself increasingly alienated from such synagogues. Matthew's church was on its way to becoming a body independent of Judaism.

Interpreting the Gospel of Matthew

Biblical scholars have developed various methods for analyzing the gospels; some of these methods address the process by which the gospels came to be written. Some methods try to reconstruct the first stage of gospel tradition—what Jesus did and said. Other methods address how the gospel message was handed on during the second stage of tradition, examining the modes of speech or literary forms employed. Still other methods examine how a gospel author edited the written and oral traditions he incorporated in his gospel or analyze the narrative techniques he employed in telling the good news of Jesus Christ.

Each of these methods can contribute to our understanding of the gospels, but each of them also has its limitations.[10] Reconstructions of what Jesus "really" did and said are speculative and inevitably shaped by the methods employed in making the reconstruction, as well as by the data provided by the gospels. While the modes of speaking that might have been used during the oral transmission of the gospel can be studied, it is each gospel as a written document that is inspired Scripture, not reconstructed earlier versions of individual stories and teachings.

If we know or can reconstruct the sources a gospel writer used in writing his gospel, then the way he edited his sources can be an indication of the message he wanted to convey in his gospel. Most scholars hold that the author of the Gospel of Matthew drew on the Gospel of Mark. Where there is material common to both Matthew and Mark, the way Matthew edited Mark provides clues to Matthew's interests and emphases. I made use of such clues in writing my exposition of Matthew's gospel, even though I do not make explicit comparisons of the two gospels in my exposition.

Matthew drew not only on the Gospel of Mark but also on various written and oral traditions in circulation in the early church. Luke in writing his gospel also used Mark and other sources. The material that is not found in Mark but that is found in both Matthew and Luke appears to be largely drawn from a common source. However, studying how Matthew and Luke made use of this common source is difficult because we can only reconstruct this source on the basis of what is found in Matthew and Luke.

The exposition of the Gospel According to Matthew contained in this book focuses on the Gospel of Matthew as it is found in the Bible—on the final product, not on the pieces that Matthew might have assembled in producing the final product.

The Second Vatican Council spoke of the inspired meaning of Scripture in terms of the meaning expressed by the authors of the biblical books: "Since, therefore, all that the inspired authors, or sacred writers, affirm should be regarded as affirmed by the Holy Spirit, we must acknowledge that the books of Scripture, firmly, faithfully and without error, teach that truth which God, for the sake of our salvation, wished to see confided to the sacred Scriptures."[11] The council also spoke of "the meaning which the sacred writers really had in mind, that meaning which God had thought well to manifest through the medium of their words."[12] The council linked the meaning an inspired author "intended to express" with what he "did in fact express" by his words.[13] The focus of this exposition of the Gospel of Matthew is on what Matthew expressed by his words, since they convey the inspired meaning of his gospel.

Understanding the meaning expressed by Matthew's words involves an interaction between his words and a reader. (By analogy, music is not simply notes on a piece of paper but exists in performance and listening.) Meaning comes alive in an encounter between a reader and a text. Each reader brings his or her perspective, knowledge, experiences, questions, and interests to a text, and these influence what a reader takes away from a text. This does not mean that a biblical text is a blank slate on which we can write whatever meaning we like; it does mean that there is a richness of meaning in Scripture that no single reading or reader can fully capture.

All of us in reading the Gospel of Matthew bring our knowledge of and experience of Jesus to the text: none of us is hearing about Jesus for the very first time. Our understanding of Jesus is shaped by many factors: by what we have read in the rest of the New Testament about Jesus, by centuries of theological reflection on Jesus, by church pronouncements on Jesus, and by our own experiences of Jesus in private prayer, public worship, and the Christian community. Even if we wanted to, we would not be able to set all this aside in reading the Gospel of Matthew. As we read Matthew's words about Jesus, we understand them in light of our previous understanding of Jesus, even as Matthew's words enrich, challenge, and modify our understanding of Jesus and his message.

My exposition of the Gospel of Matthew represents my understanding of this gospel. If my life experiences and education had been different, if I were part of a different culture or church body, I would have been alert to facets of meaning in Matthew that escape my notice. I hope that my reading of Matthew will aid others in arriving at their own reading of Matthew, and in encountering the Jesus he proclaims.

1. The Second Vatican Council in its decree on revelation summarizes the three stages that culminated in the written gospels (Second Vatican Council, *Dogmatic Constitution on Divine Revelation* [*Dei Verbum*] [1965], section 19; hereafter abbreviated as *Revelation*). The decree cites the Pontifical Biblical Commission's *Instruction on the Historical Truth of the Gospels* (Pontifical Biblical Commission, *Instruction on the Historical Truth of the Gospels* [*Sancta mater Ecclesia*] [1964]; hereafter abbreviated as *Truth*), which described "the three stages of tradition by which the teaching and the life of Jesus have come down to us" (*Truth*, section 6).

2. *Revelation*, 19.

3. *Truth*, 7.

4. *Revelation*, 19

5. *Truth*, 8.

6. *Revelation*, 19.

7. *Truth*, 9.

8. *Revelation*, 19.

9. Eusebius, *The History of the Church from Christ to Constantine*, trans. G. A. Williamson (Baltimore: Penguin Books, 1965), 152.

10. See Pontifical Biblical Commission, *The Interpretation of the Bible in the Church* (Rome: Libreria Editrice Vaticana, 1993), chap. 1.

11. *Revelation*, 11.

12. *Ibid.*, 12.

13. *Ibid.*

SELECTED BIBLIOGRAPHY

Commentaries on the Gospel of Matthew

Davies, W. D., and Dale C. Allison. *The Gospel According to Saint Matthew.* 3 vols. Edinburgh: T & T Clark: 1988–1997.

Hagner, Donald A. *Matthew.* 2 vols. Word Biblical Commentary. Vol. 33A–B. Dallas: Word Books, 1993–1995.

Harrington, Daniel J. *The Gospel of Matthew.* Sacra Pagina Series. Vol. 1. Collegeville, MN: Liturgical Press, 1991.

Hill, David. *The Gospel of Matthew.* The New Century Bible Commentary. Grand Rapids, MI: Eerdmans, 1972.

Luz, Ulrich. *Matthew 1–7.* A Continental Commentary. Minneapolis: Fortress, 1989.

———. *Matthew 8-20.* Hermenia. Minneapolis: Fortress, 2001.

———. *Matthew 21–28.* Hermenia. Minneapolis: Fortress, 2005.

Meier, John P. *Matthew.* New Testament Message. Wilmington, DE: Michael Glazier, 1979.

Montague, George T., SM. *Companion God: A Cross-Cultural Commentary on the Gospel of Matthew.* New York: Paulist, 1989.

Nolland, John. *The Gospel of Matthew.* The New International Greek Testament Commentary. Grand Rapids, MI: Eerdmans, 2005.

Schnackenburg, Rudolf. *The Gospel of Matthew.* Translated by Robert B. Barr. Grand Rapids, MI: Eerdmans, 2002.

Schweizer, Eduard. *The Good News According to Matthew.* Atlanta: John Knox, 1975.

Senior, Donald. *Matthew.* Abingdon New Testament Commentaries. Nashville, TN: Abingdon, 1998.

Studies and Resources

Binz, Stephen J. *The Passion and Resurrection Narratives of Jesus: A Commentary.* Collegeville, MN: Liturgical Press, 1989.

Bornkamm, Günther, Gerhard Barth, and Heinz Joachim Held. *Tradition and Interpretation in Matthew.* Philadelphia: Westminster Press, 1963.

Brown, Raymond E., SS. *An Adult Christ at Christmas.* Collegeville, MN: Liturgical Press, 1978.

————. *The Birth of the Messiah*. 2nd ed. New York: Doubleday, 1993.

————. *The Churches the Apostles Left Behind*. New York: Paulist, 1984.

————. *A Coming of Christ in Advent*. Collegeville, MN: Liturgical Press, 1988.

————. *The Death of the Messiah: From Gethsemane to the Grave: A Commentary on the Passion Narratives in the Four Gospels*. 2 vols. The Anchor Bible Reference Library. New York: Doubleday, 1994.

————. *An Introduction to New Testament Christology*. New York: Paulist Press, 1994.

————. *An Introduction to the New Testament*. The Anchor Bible Reference Library. New York: Doubleday, 1997.

Brown, Raymond E., SS, and John P. Meier. *Antioch and Rome: New Testament Cradles of Catholic Christianity*. New York: Paulist, 1983.

Brown, Raymond E., SS, Karl P. Donfried, and John Reumann, eds. *Peter in the New Testament*. Minneapolis, MN: Augsburg, 1973.

Brown, Raymond E., SS, Karl P. Donfried, Joseph A. Fitzmyer, SJ, and John Reumann, eds. *Mary in the New Testament*. Philadelphia: Fortress, 1978.

Brown, Raymond E., SS, Joseph A. Fitzmyer, SJ, and Roland E. Murphy, OCarm, eds. *The New Jerome Biblical Commentary*. Englewood Cliffs, NJ: Prentice-Hall, 1990.

Catechism of the Catholic Church. 2nd ed. Washington, DC: United States Catholic Conference, 1997.

Chancey, Mark A. *The Myth of a Gentile Galilee*. Society for New Testament Studies Monograph Series 118. Cambridge: Cambridge University Press, 2002.

Charlesworth, James H., ed. *The Old Testament Pseudepigrapha*. 2 vols. Garden City, NY: Doubleday, 1983–1985.

Chilton, Bruce. *A Galilean Rabbi and His Bible: Jesus' Use of the Interpreted Scripture of His Time*. Wilmington, DE: Michael Glazier, 1984.

Collins, John J. *The Apocalyptic Imagination: An Introduction to the Jewish Matrix of Christianity*. New York: Crossroad, 1987.

Davies, W. D. *The Sermon on the Mount*. London: Cambridge, 1966.

"The Didache." In *Early Christian Writings: The Apostolic Fathers*. Translated by Maxwell Staniforth. New York: Penguin Books, 1968.

Donahue, John R., SJ. *The Gospel in Parable*. Minneapolis: Fortress Press, 1990.

Dunn, James D. G. *Jesus Remembered*. Christianity in the Making, vol. 1.

Grand Rapids, MI: Eerdmans, 2003.

Efroymson, David P., Eugene J. Fisher, and Leon Klenicki, eds. *Within Context: Essays on Jews and Judaism in the New Testament*. Collegeville, MN: Liturgical Press, 1993.

Eusebius. *The History of the Church from Christ to Constantine*. Translated by G. A. Williamson. Baltimore: Penguin Books, 1965.

Evans, Craig A., and Stanley E. Porter, eds. *Dictionary of New Testament Background*. Downers Grove, IL: InterVarsity Press, 2000.

Fitzmyer, Joseph A., SJ. *The Biblical Commission's Document "The Interpretation of the Bible in the Church": Text and Commentary*. Rome: Pontificio Istituto Biblico, 1995.

————. *A Christological Catechism: New Testament Answers*. New York: Paulist Press, 1991.

————. *Responses to 101 Questions on the Dead Sea Scrolls*. New York: Paulist Press, 1992.

————. *To Advance the Gospel: New Testament Studies*. Grand Rapids: Eerdmans, 1998.

Flannery, Austin P., OP, ed. *Documents of Vatican II*. New York: Pillar Books, 1975.

Fredriksen, Paula. *Jesus of Nazareth, King of the Jews: A Jewish Life and the Emergence of Christianity*. New York: Vintage Books, 2000.

Freedman, David Noel, ed. *The Anchor Bible Dictionary*. 6 vols. New York: Doubleday, 1992.

Freyne, Seán. *Galilee, from Alexander the Great to Hadrian, 323 B.C.E. to 135 C.E.: A Study of Second Temple Judaism*. Wilmington, DE: Michael Glazier, 1980.

————. *Galilee, Jesus, and the Gospels: Literary Approaches and Historical Investigations*. Philadelphia: Fortress Press, 1988.

————. *The World of the New Testament*. Wilmington, DE: Michael Glazier, 1980.

García Martínez, Florentino, ed. *The Dead Sea Scrolls Translated: The Qumran Texts in English*. Translated by Wilfred G. E. Watson. 2nd ed. Grand Rapids, MI: Eerdmans, 1996.

Green, Joel B., and Scot McKnight, eds. *Dictionary of Jesus and the Gospels*. Downers Grove, IL: InterVarsity Press, 1992.

Hamm, Dennis, SJ. *The Beatitudes in Context*. Wilmington, DE: Michael Glazier, 1990.

Hendrickx, Herman. *Passion Narratives*. London: Geoffrey Chapman, 1984.

Hengel, Martin. *Crucifixion in the Ancient World and the Folly of the Message of the Cross*. Philadelphia: Fortress Press, 1977.

Horsley, Richard A. *Bandits, Prophets, and Messiahs: Popular Movements in the Time of Jesus*. With John S. Hanson. San Francisco: Harper & Row, 1988.

Hultgren, Arland J. *The Parables of Jesus: A Commentary*. Grand Rapids, MI: Eerdmans, 2000.

John of the Cross. *The Ascent of Mount Carmel*. In *The Collected Works of St. John of the Cross*. Translated by Kieran Kavanaugh, OCD and Otilio Rodriguez, OCD. Garden City, NY: Doubleday, 1964.

Jonge, Marinus de. *God's Final Envoy: Early Christology and Jesus' Own View of His Mission*. Grand Rapids, MI: Eerdmans, 1998.

Kingsbury, Jack Dean. *Matthew: Structure, Christology, Kingdom*. Minneapolis, MN: Fortress, 1975.

Kodell, Jerome, OSB. *The Eucharist in the New Testament*. Wilmington, DE: Michael Glazier, 1988.

Lambrecht, Jan. *The Sermon on The Mount*. Wilmington, DE: Michael Glazier, 1985.

Leaney, A. R. C. *The Jewish and Christian World, 200 B.C. to A.D. 200*. Cambridge: Cambridge University Press, 1984.

Léon-Dufour, Xavier, SJ. *Sharing the Eucharistic Bread: The Witness of the New Testament*. Translated by Matthew J. O'Connell. New York: Paulist Press, 1987.

Luz, Ulrich. *The Theology of the Gospel of Matthew*. Cambridge: Cambridge University Press, 1995.

McNamara, Martin, MSC. *Intertestamental Literature*. Wilmington, DE: Michael Glazier, 1983.

———. *Palestinian Judaism and the New Testament*. Wilmington, DE: Michael Glazier, 1983.

Meier, John P. *A Marginal Jew: Rethinking the Historical Jesus*. 3 vols. New York: Doubleday, 1991–2001.

———. *The Vision of Matthew: Christ, Church, and Morality in the First Gospel*. New York: Paulist, 1978.

Meyers, Eric M., and James F. Strange. *Archaeology, the Rabbis, and Early Christianity*. Nashville, TN: Abingdon, 1981.

Murphy-O'Connor, Jerome, OP. *The Holy Land: From Earliest Times to 1700*. 4th ed. Oxford Archaeological Guides. Oxford: Oxford University Press, 1998.

Pontifical Biblical Commission. "Instruction on the Historical Truth of the Gospels." 1964. Translation and commentary in Joseph A. Fitzmyer, *A Christological Catechism: New Tetsament Answers*. New York: Paulist, 1991.

Pontifical Biblical Commission. *The Interpretation of the Bible in the Church*. Rome: Libreria Editrice Vaticana, 1993.

Reed, Jonathan L. *Archaeology and the Galilean Jesus: A Re-examination of the Evidence*. Harrisburg, PA: Trinity Press, 2000.

Rossé, Gérard. *The Cry of Jesus on the Cross: A Biblical and Theological Study*. Translated by Stephen Wentworth Arndt. New York: Paulist Press, 1987.

Rousseau, John J., and Rami Arav. *Jesus and His World: An Archaeological and Cultural Dictionary*. Minneapolis, MN: Fortress Press, 1995.

Russell, D. S. *The Method and Message of Jewish Apocalyptic, 200 B.C.–A.D. 100*. Philadelphia: Westminster Press, 1964.

Saldarini, Anthony J. *Jesus and Passover*. New York: Paulist, 1984.

———. *Pharisees, Scribes and Sadducees in Palestinian Society: A Sociological Approach*. Wilmington, DE: Michael Glazier, 1988.

Sanders, E. P. *Jesus and Judaism*. Philadelphia: Fortress Press, 1985.

Schneiders, Sandra M. *The Revelatory Text: Interpreting the New Testament as Sacred Scripture*. 2nd ed. Collegeville, MN: Liturgical Press, 1999.

Senior, Donald, CP. *The Gospel of Matthew*. Nashville, TN: Abingdon, 1997.

———. *The Passion of Jesus in the Gospel of Matthew*. Wilmington, DE: Michael Glazier, 1985.

———. *What Are They Saying About Matthew?* New York: Paulist, 1996.

Stanley, David M., SJ. *Jesus in Gethsemane*. New York: Paulist Press, 1980.

Stein, Edith. *The Science of the Cross*. Translated by Josephine Koeppel, OCD. Washington, DC: ICS Publications, 2002.

Tanner, Norman P., SJ, ed. *Decrees of the Ecumenical Councils*. 2 vols. Washington, DC: Georgetown University Press, 1990.

Thompson, William G., SJ. *Matthew's Story: Good News for Uncertain Times*. New York: Paulist, 1989.

VanderKam, James C. *The Dead Sea Scrolls Today*. Grand Rapids, MI: Eerdmans, 1994.

Westerholm, Stephen. *Understanding Matthew: The Early Christian Worldview of the First Gospel*. Grand Rapids, MI: Baker Academic, 2006.

Williamson, Peter S. *Catholic Principles for Interpreting Scripture: A Study of the Pontifical Biblical Commission's "The Interpretation of the Bible in the Church."* Rome: Pontificio Istituto Biblico, 2001.

INDEX OF BACKGROUND MATERIAL AND COMMENTS

Note: *Italics* indicate comments.

Palestine

at the time of Jesus

Jerusalem

at the time of Jesus

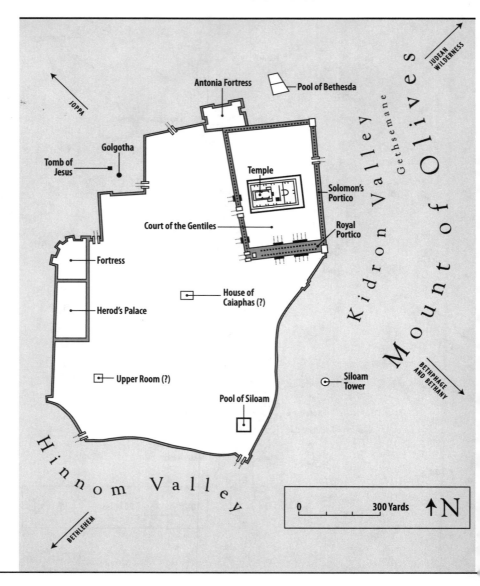